Descendants

of

Jacob Amidown

(1720-1790)
of
Woodstock, Connecticut
and Dudley, Massachusetts
(to 1930)

By
Commander Christopher D. Amaden
United States Navy
and
Nancy K. Ameden Mullen

HERITAGE BOOKS
2007

HERITAGE BOOKS

AN IMPRINT OF HERITAGE BOOKS, INC.

Books, CDs, and more—Worldwide

For our listing of thousands of titles see our website
at
www.HeritageBooks.com

Published 2007 by
HERITAGE BOOKS, INC.
Publishing Division
65 East Main Street
Westminster, Maryland 21157-5026

International Standard Book Number: 978-0-7884-4192-9

Dedicated to our spouses,

Sara Amaden

and

John A. Mullen

TABLE OF CONTENTS

List of Illustrations

List of Abbreviations

&	and	dept.	department
abt.	about	DHHS	Dept. of Health
aft.	after		and Human
Ala.	Alabama		Services
app.	application	dist.	district
Ark.	Arkansas	div.	divorced
Ariz.	Arizona	dw.	dwelling
Aug.	August	Ed(s).	editor(s)
b.	born	ED	enumeration
bap.	baptized		district
bef.	before	Epis.	Episcopal
bet.	between	fam.	family
bur.	buried	Feb.	February
c.	about	FHL	Family History
Calif.	California		Library
Cem.	Cemetery	Fla.	Florida
cens.	census	fr.	from
cert.	certificate	Ga.	Georgia
Ch.	Church	Gen.	Genealogical
Co.	Company,	hhd.	household
	County	Ia.	Iowa
col.	column	Ill.	Illinois
Col.	Colony	Inc.	Incorporated
Colo.	Colorado	Ind.	Indiana
comp.	compiler	Jan.	January
Conn.	Connecticut	Kans.	Kansas
d.	died	Ky.	Kentucky
D.A.R.	Daughters of	La.	Louisiana
	the American	ln.	line
	Revolution	m.	married
dau.	daughter	Mass.	Massachusetts
D.C.	District of	Md.	Maryland
	Columbia	Mich.	Michigan
Dec.	December	micropub	micro-

	publication	Terr.	Territory
Minn.	Minnesota	Tex.	Texas
Mo.	Missouri	U.S.	United States
Mt.	Mount,	Va.	Virginia
	Mountain	vol(s).	volume(s)
nat'l	national	V.R.	vital records
N.D.	North Dakota	Vt.	Vermont
Neb.	Nebraska	Wash.	Washington
N.H.	New Hampshire	Wisc.	Wisconsin
N.J.	New Jersey	WPA	Works Progress
no.	number		Administration
Nov.	November	W. Va.	West Virginia
N.Y.	New York	WWI	World War I
Oct.	October	WSGS	Wisconsin State
Oh.	Ohio		Genealogical
Ore.	Oregon		Society
O.V.I.	Ohio Volunteer	Y.M.C.A.	Young Men's
	Infantry		Christian
P.I.	Philippine		Association
	Islands		
pp.	pages		
Penna.	Pennsylvania		
P.O.	post office		
pop.	population		
prob.	probably		
reg.	registration		
R.I.	Rhode Island		
RR	railroad		
S.C.	South Carolina		
sched.	schedule		
SD	supervisor's		
	district		
S.D.	South Dakota		
sect.	section		
Sept.	September		
sh.	sheet		
Soc.	Society		
St.	Saint		
Tenn.	Tennessee		

Acknowledgements

We are most grateful for the help we have received from so many friends and genealogists. This book would not have been possible without their help. In the course of our research we have discovered cousins and genealogists who have made enormous contributions, and become friends.

In particular, the late Arnold Sinclair Foote, historian of the Amadon Family Association, deserves our undying thanks. His willingness to share and clarify confusing relationships has been freely offered without limit. And we are pleased to call him a personal friend.

Bev Luke is an Amaden descendent we met through the America Online Genealogy Forum, as she queried whether Amaden was a valid spelling for an unusual name. Her residence on the west coast has been an invaluable aid to searching out the sparse details of those Amadens who traveled to the western frontier in its early days. And she, too, we are pleased to call a friend.

John Austin, genealogist of Warren County, New York, has freely shared of his research and of his knowledge of the historical roots of the area. His deep knowledge has helped to make the history of the county come alive.

Stacy Niedzwiecki has shared her details on the family. In addition she has shared of her professional graphics expertise to provide us with portraits of family members that are real treasures.

Dozens of other genealogists have shared with us, and helped to make this book a reality. To all of them, we extend our deep gratitude. With some trepidation least we overlook someone, we express our appreciation to:
  o David Amidon

- o Les Amidon
- o Joe and Nancy (Amaden) Erwin
- o Betty Farr
- o Andrea Herman, Crandall Public Library, Glens Falls, New York
- o Doris S. Monterey
- o Bill Nyland
- o Eric Taylor, Museum of Snohomish County History, Everett, Washington

And finally, and most importantly, we express our appreciation to our spouses and children, Sara, Chloe, and Jonathan Amaden and John Mullen, for their toleration of our many hours spent in dusty archives, arcane Internet sites, and word processing to craft this book. This book could not have come to fruition without their support and assistance.

Preface

The genesis of this book was a discovery by the authors that each was passionate about genealogy, and each desired to publish the Amidown genealogy. The authors are sixth cousins. When they first became acquainted in about 1995, each had a vague thought to publish the family genealogy someday. They agreed it made sense to collaborate, and the book was born.

So long as Chris was actively employed as a submariner and Nancy was employed as a traveling consultant, research progressed steadily but slowly. In 2002 Nancy retired to make time for her genealogy passion, and Chris began to teach submariners, rather than being one, making it possible for the book to progress more rapidly. We have agreed it is time to temporarily abate the research and publish what we have learned.

In the twenty-first century, identity theft is a major concern. We have decided to protect the identity of our families by publishing this genealogy only to 1930, the last year that the U.S. census is publicly available.

The availability of the complete census online suddenly gave a great boost to our ability to track the more elusive members of the family. But the techniques used by Ancestry.com to index the census, while a great boon to researchers, created an index filled with errors. In the footnotes, we have used the spellings of household names from the Ancestry index. Hopefully future corrections will improve the indexes. Since the footnotes also contain all the information needed to find each specific entry regardless of the indexing of the primary householder, we trust the footnotes will still be useful once Ancestry improves its indexes, or other indexes become available.

Place names have evolved over the centuries. We have attempted to use the place names that were in effect at the historic time referenced. So we find Roger Amidown in "Plymouth Colony" in 1661, rather than "Massachusetts."

Calendars changed as well. In the time of our earliest American ancestors, March 25 was the beginning of the year. That made March the first month, with January the eleventh month of the year. So a child born in the January following April 1661 was born in 1661. European dating was gradually evolving to use January 1 as the start of a new year. That practice was adopted in the British colonies in 1752. For the prior 170 years, both calendars were used side-by-side. The year which started March 25 was called "Old Style;" the year which started on January 1 was called "New Style." Dates between January 1 and March 25 generally were written with both years, such as 1742/1743 or 1742/3. The system is not only confusing for us, it was confusing for the record keepers at the time. The practice was discontinued in 1752 when all recordkeeping adopted the New Style.

We have worked diligently to conform to the highest standards of scholarship now being promulgated by the professional genealogy community. Thus sources for every fact are cited. At the same time we are grateful to John Colletta for his advocacy of the incorporation of enough historical information in the individual biographies to give life and flesh to our ancestors. While we have not come close to delivering the richness of story provided by John in his recent family history, *Only a Few Bones*, we have tried to incorporate enough social history to provide a sense of who the Amidowns/Amadens/Amedens/Amidons were as individuals. By the necessity of available information (census, vital, church, court, and military records), these individual stories are only a small part of what their true lives were.

We hope you enjoy these *Descendants of Jacob Amidown.*

Christopher D. Amaden
Nancy K. Ameden Mullen

Chapter 1 Jacob and His Lineage

Generation 1: Roger Amadowne (ca. 1615–1673)

1. ROGER AMADOWNE[1] was born about 1615, died at Rehoboth, Plymouth Colony, about 11 November 1673 and was buried two days later at Rehoboth.[1] He married first between December 1637 and 1640, SARA ___. His marriage date is derived based on his receiving a single man's allotment of land in December 1637 and the birth of his first child in 1640. Sara died at Rehoboth on 20 June 1668.[2] He married second on 27 December 1668, JOANNA HARWOOD.[3] She was born at Boston, Massachusetts Bay Colony, on 10 December 1642, the daughter of GEORGE and JANE (___) HARWOOD.[4] She died at Rehoboth on 1 July 1711.[5] Holmes Ammidown, who wrote of the family in his 1877 book *The Ammidown Family* (which is rife with errors), said of the family name:

> It is of French origin, of that class known as Protestants, commonly called Huguenots. . . . So far as ascertained the name in western France, at Rochelle, Bordeaux, the departments of Gironde and Charente, is Amidon and Amadon, the latter is believed to be the correct French name . . . Many of the inhabitants, foreseeing the hopelessness of their cause, and fearing to fall into the hands of the Catholics, sought and obtained passage by the English ships

---

[1]   James N. Arnold, *Vital Record of Rehoboth, 1642–1896. Marriages, Intentions, Births, Deaths, with Supplement containing the Record of 1896, Colonial Returns, Lists of the Early Settlers, Purchasers, Freemen, Inhabitants, the Soldiers serving in Philip's War and the Revolution* (Providence: Narragansett Historical Publishing, 1897), 897-8.

[2]   Arnold, Vital Record of Rehoboth, 791.

[3]   Charles Henry Pope, *The Pioneers of Massachusetts, A Descriptive List* (Baltimore: Genealogy Publishing Co., 1965), 17.

[4]   William S. Appleton, ed., *Boston Births, Baptisms, Marriages, and Deaths 1630–1699* (Boston: Rockwell & Churchill, 1888), 13.

[5]   Arnold, *Vital Record of Rehoboth*, 791 [called Joan]. Note that Plymouth Colony became part of Massachusetts, a Royal Province, in 1691.

to that country; among this class who in 1627 and 28 escaped to England, was the ancestor of this family.[6]

Probably taking his lead from Ammidown, Frank Best wrote:

Tradition has it that Roger Amadowne was a French Huguenot, who, after the revocation of the Edict of Nantes, was compelled to flee from France; that he went to England, where he remained for several years and then emigrated [sic] to America. No information has been obtained concerning the date and place of his birth, or of his parentage.[7]

On the records of Plymouth Colony and at Rehoboth his name is generally spelled Amadowne.

A thorough search of the Protestant parish records in La Rochelle from 1600 to 1620 has yielded no family names similar to Amadowne. It is true that the French family name Amadon is noble, registered for the parish of St-Chamant in Bas-Limousin (central France). ALEXANDRE AMADON was granted nobility in March 1612 (there were seven ways to obtain French Nobility;[8] in this case it appears Alexandre acquired it though owning a fief). Alexandre married FRANÇOISE DE CHAUVAL. Their son JEAN AMADON married on 15 December 1630 MARGUERITE DE BARRAT (or BARRET). Roger or his father could very well be related to Alexander. If Roger is of French origin, it would make perfect sense that they originated in Bas-Limousin and left for England via La Rochelle, but no proof has been found to support this hypothesis.[9]

Roger was first explicitly listed in America during the second division of lands of Salem on 25 December 1637:

Att a meeting the 25th, of the 10th moneth, 1637 being present Mr. Endicott, Mr. Connant, John Woodbury, John Balch, Peeter Palfry, Jefry Massie, William Hathorne. It is agreed that the marsh & meadow Land that haue been formerly layed in comon to this Towne shall now be

---

[6]   Holmes Ammidown, *Genealogical Memorial, Family Record, The Ammidown Family, Southbridge, Mass.* (New York,N.Y.: Holmes Ammidown, 1877), 4.

[7]   Best, *Amidon Family*, 2. Note that the revocation of the Edict of Nantes actually occurred in 1685, but escalating persecution of Huguenots from 1610 onwards caused thousands to flee France before that date.

[8]   "French nobility," online <www.baronage.co.uk/2001/french-1.html>.

[9]   Abby Joseph Nadaud, *Nobiliaire du diocèse et de la généralité de Limoges*, 4 volumes. (Limoge, 1863-1882), 1:28.

appropriated to the Inhabitants of Salem, proportioned out vnto them according to heads of their families — To those that have the greatest number of acre thereof & to those that haue least not above an acre & to those that are betweene both 3 qrters of an acre, alwais provided & it is agreed that none shall sell away their proportions of meadow, more or lesse, nor lease them onto any above 3 yeares, vnless they sell or lease out their howses with their meadow.[10]

Roger Aimedowne was granted half an acre in the division of lands. The record also explicitly listed Roger as one person indicating that he was not married at this time. Roger is the 98th name of 224 names shown. The handwriting has also been read as Aimedoune, which emphasizes a French pronunciation over an Anglicized one.

The date appears in the record as 25th of the 10th "moneth" 1637, because seventeenth century Christians objected to the names of the months, which are based on the names of pagan gods. Under the Julian calendar, which was followed until 1752, the first month of the year was March.

Roger may have arrived in Salem in July of 1637. In the Salem town records we find:

A towne meeting ye 30th of the 5th moneth [July] ...

Wm Huson desireth a houslot in ye necke

Bryan Grange desireth ye same

Tho : Chadwell & Roger (blank) desire ye same.

A towne meeting ye 7th of 6th moneth [August] ...

Marmaduke Percie, James Moulton, John Gedney, are admitted for inhabitants.

John Harbert is likewise admitted & is to haue half an acre in ye neck, ...

It is granted to mr Stephens to haue 18 poole of ground by ye waters side in length & 12 poole in length & 12 poole in bredth in ye narrow ye neck for the building of Shipps, provided yt it shal be imployed for yt ende,

---

[10] Sidney Perley, *A History of Salem Massachusetts*, 3 volumes. (Salem: Sidney Perley, 1924), 1:463. This record was handwritten by Roger Connant and transcribed in Perley's *History of Salem*.

Wm Huson Tho : Chadwell & Roger (blank) shall haue
each of them halfe an acre of grounds at But pynte neere
where Hollinwood buil[ds.] [11]

The evidence that Roger (blank) who arrived in July of 1637 is
Roger Amadowne is circumstantial, but significant. The reason for
omitting his last name is unknown, but one could reason that it was
difficult to pronounce and subsequently Anglicized to Aimedowne
(obliquely supporting Holmes Ammidown's assertion that Roger is
French). We know that Roger was a shipwright from his time in the
1640s in Weymouth, Massachusetts Bay Colony.[12][13] His occupation
gives us some clues as to where he lived and with whom he
associated. The Neck of Salem was the location of shipbuilding and is
where Roger (blank) was given land. Near to Roger Amadowne's
name in the second division land list were Richard Hollingsworth
(seventeen names above), William Stephens (six above), James
Moulton (one below), Jo. Gidney (two below), and John Harbert
(twenty-five below), all people associated with shipbuilding or living
at the Neck, suggesting that the second division land list was
generated based on the individual's location. It is reasonable to
assume that Roger worked for Richard Hollingsworth in the summer
and fall of 1637 and received his land grant in December.

Another interesting aspect of Roger's arrival in America is that on
4 June 1661, the Plymouth court accepted a petition and stated,
"Libertie is granted unto some who were formerly servants who have
had due unto them by covenant, to nominate some persons to the
Court, or to some of the magestrates to bee deputed in their behalfe, to
purchase a p[ar]cell of land for their accomodations att Saconett."[14]
Roger Annadowne is eighth of twenty-seven on the list (he is crossed
off one such list along with three others with no reason given, but is
listed in all other such references). This implies that Roger was in
servitude, quite likely for passage to America.

---

[11]   Martha O. Howes and Sidney Perley, eds., *Town Records of Salem, 1634-1659 Essex Institute Historical Collections*, IX volumes, Second Series, (Salem: Essex Institute Press, 1869), 1:52-54.
[12]   Edward Everett Hale Jr., ed., *Notebook Kept by Thomas Lechford, Esquire: Lawyer in Boston, Massachusetts Bay 1638–1641* (Camden: Picton Press, 1988).
[13]   George Walter Chamberlain, *History of Weymouth, Massachusetts, Genealogy of Weymouth Families,* 4 volumes. (Weymouth: Weymouth Historical Society, 1923), 3:13.
[14]   Nathaniel B. Shurtleff and David Pulsifer, eds., *Records of the Colony of New Plymouth in New England*, 3 volumes. (New York: AMS Press, 1968), 3:216.

It appears that Roger left Salem in 1638 once spring came. The possible reasons for leaving are numerous. In fact, the majority of "original" settlers left within a year. For Roger, it could have been that Salem was a strict Puritan town; Hollingsworth's work wasn't steady, safe or profitable; or perhaps Roger was an indentured servant and his term had expired. With a new skill, Roger could have wanted to start his own business. The first Salem town grant for a shipyard was given on 7 August to William Stephens, who had come from Boston in 1636. Richard Hollingsworth bought Mr. Stephens's shipyard in 1637. Both shipwrights employed workmen. Perhaps Roger came to Salem with Stephens from Boston, and then left when Stephens sold out. Roger is not listed in any other surviving (and extensive) Salem records, which included church, deed (beginning in 1641), quarterly punishment records — (very thorough including witnesses and accusers) and probate records. Roger was never "Received for an Inhabitant," as would have been documented in the town and church records. This all leads to the conclusion that his stay in Salem was brief. Nearly all marriages in Salem were recorded, suggesting that Roger left Salem before his marriage.

By July 1640 Roger moved on to Weymouth. Salem lies about fifteen miles north of Boston on the Atlantic coast. Weymouth lies about equidistant to the southeast of Boston, off Hingham Bay. His daughter Sara was born in Weymouth on 10 December 1640. There Roger worked as a shipwright,[15] meaning that he worked in the construction or repair of ships. He is also mentioned in a record of the Colony of Connecticut in 1643, which alludes to a debt owed to Roger Anadowne — probably shipbuilding or repair services.[16] Clearly Roger had business in Boston, but could have still been living in Weymouth. In 1647, William Piggott wrote to Gov. John Winthrop, complaining of mistreatment of his son who had been apprenticed to Roger Ammidon, including attempts "to sell him underhand without the consent of the magistrate, once to a Scot bound to and now to one Mr. Gross, a brewer."[17] In Isaac Grosse's will of

---

15   Hale, *Notebook Kept by Thomas Lechford*.

16   Connecticut (Colony). *The Public Records of the Colony of Connecticut, from April 1636 to October 1776 ... transcribed and published*, [in accordance with a resolution of the General assembly], 15 volumes. (Hartford: Brown & Parsons. 1850–1890). 1:84.

17   *Winthrop Papers, 1498–1654*, 5 volumes. (Boston: The Massachusetts Historical Society, 1925–1947), 5:155.

1649, "Roger Amadowne of Waymoth" is listed as a debtor to the estate. But by that time, Roger had already left the Weymouth area and settled in Rehoboth.

The origins of Roger's wife, Sara, are yet another mystery. No record of their marriage survives, but clearly they married between his acceptance of land in Salem in December 1637 and the birth of their child Sara. Assuming he stayed in Salem through the winter of 1637/8, he probably didn't marry in Salem because there is no record of it. And if we assume that he and Sara were married before their daughter was conceived, then they married between April 1638 and March 1640. Given that Sara was still a member of the North Weymouth church in 1640 when they were in Boston, this indicates a close tie to Weymouth and hence a very good candidate town for marriage. But just like Salem, the Weymouth marriage records are complete and no mention is made of their marriage. One other mention of Sara's origins has been made. In a speech delivered on the centennial of Onondaga County, New York, in 1898, Fanny Amidon made some remarks about the origins of the Amidon family and the line that came to Onondaga County. This presentation followed an incorrect genealogy of the family as outlined in Holmes Ammidown's book. As part of this speech, she mentioned that Roger's wife was Sara Hutchings.[18] No further results have been found from this lead.

By 1643, Roger and Sara were in Boston, where their daughter Lida was born on 27 February 1643. The birth is recorded to Roger and Sara Amadowne, which is the first mention of Roger's wife. The baptismal record indicates that Roger and Sara were still members of the Church of North Weymouth.[19] It may be that they were in Boston on business, or it may be that Sara had returned to Boston to be with family for the birth of her first child. No record has been found to indicate that Roger and Sara were living in Boston at the time.

During this time Roger's former pastor in Weymouth left with part of the congregation and created a settlement at Rehoboth, forty miles south of Boston, close to the Rhode Island line. Roger and Sara joined the new settlement where, in 1648, Roger was listed forty-third on the list of proprietors.[20] He is mentioned in July of that year in the town record book:

---

18   "The   Amidon   Family,"   online   <www.rootsweb.com/~nyononda/ AMIDON.HTM>.

19   Appleton, *Boston Births*, 16.

20   Ammidown, *Ammidown Family*, 11; Best, *Amidon Family*, 4.

At a meeting of the townes men, being appointed by the towne in generall, to accomidate Roger Ammidowne, wee haue giuen him a house lott of six acres between Walter Palmores house lot and the mill, also three acres of salt marsh in Watchemoqit neck being in two plotes, the on[e] lying against the land in the river, and the other a round plot lying near the end of Mr Pecks lot in the neck, also two acres of fresh meadow be it more or less, wch was layed out to Mr Browne.[21]

Later Rehoboth divided and the older portion, with Roger's parcel, took the name Seekonk. Roger's home was located in present day East Providence, Rhode Island, bounded by Centre Street, North Broadway, State Road 114, and the Ten Mile River.

Roger's Lot in Modern East Providence

John G. Erhardt wrote several volumes on the history of Rehoboth and included a drawing of the homelots circa 1675 (see next page).

Roger continued to work as a shipwright, apparently working at a shipyard in neighboring Warwick, Rhode Island. According to Warwick court records:

---

21   Richard LeBaron Bowen, *Early Rehoboth, Documented Historical Studies of Families and Events in This Plymouth Colony Township*, 4 volumes. (Rehoboth: Privately printed, Concord, N.H., 1945–1950), 2:14.

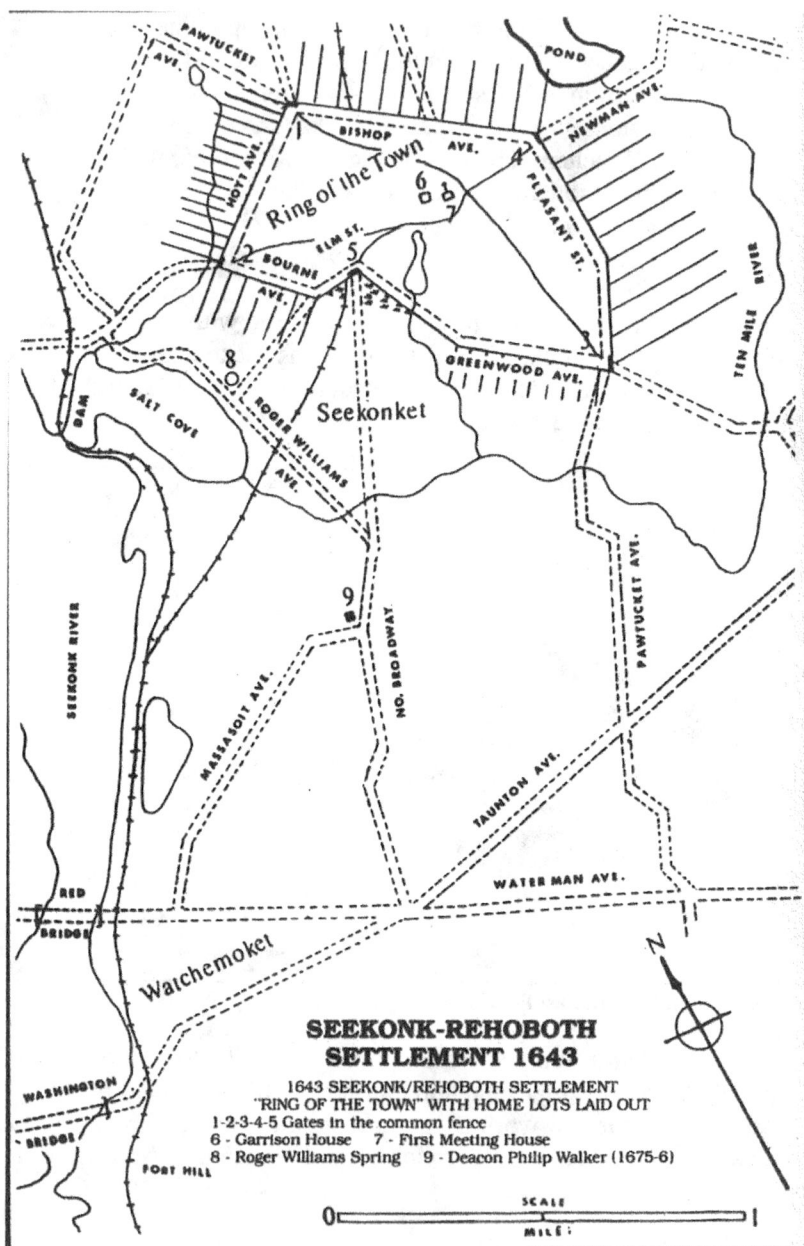

Seekonk-Rehoboth Settlement 1643, *courtesy Annawan Historical Society*

> Ane Action of a hundred pound upon neglect entered by Robert Hearngton mariner and master of the Barke Debora plaintive agst Roger Anadown ship Carpenter Defendant Warwicke the 3 of June 1657. [22]

This being the last reference we have to Roger's shipwright work, it appears that, based on the quantity of land he was awarded, Roger probably lived out most of his life in Rehoboth as a planter. Roger was an active member of the community. He took the Oath of Fidelity and became a freeman in 1658.[23] On 22 June 1658 Rehoboth divided meadow lands on the north side of the town into lots for residents according to their estate. Roger Amadowne was forty-third on the list.[24] On 1 Mar 1658/9, he served on his first Coroner's Jury when Nathaniell West from Rhode Island fell through the ice and drowned. In 1660 his standing in the community was recognized when he was called "Goodman" Amadowne in a town record entry that authorized William Sabine to build a mill bridge as far as the foot of the hill by Goodman Amadowne. He served on a coroner's jury again on 10 June 1661 when Robert Allin was found dead on his bed. Roger served on the Plymouth Court on 3 June 1662 to hear a dispute over land between local Indians. He served on another coroner's jury on 27 July 1664 when Rebeckah Sale hung herself in her house. We are again reminded of the difficulty of life in the colonies when we read that Elizabeth Walker, a two and a half year old child who had been sent alone to school, accidentally drowned in the river. Her body was found by two youths who showed the body to the wife of Nicholas Jyde and to Sara[h] Amadowne, and then to William Sabine, on 7 August 1664.[25]

On 7 June 1665, the Plymouth Court ruled:

> Fifty acres of land is graunted vnto Roger Annadowne, lying att a place called the Ten Mile River, being a pte of that land which Captaine Willett bought, lying on the bounds of Rehoboth (The North Purchase); the said fifty acres of land, with all and singulare the appurtenances belonging

---

22   Librarian of the Rhode Island Historical Society, ed., *The Early Records of the Town of Warwick.* (Providence: E. A. Johnson & Co. Publishers, 1926), 208.

23   Shurtleff, *Colony of New Plymouth,* 8:178. Arnold, *Vital Record of Rehoboth,* 918.

24   Arnold, *Vital Record of Rehoboth,* 914.

25   John G. Erhardt, *Rehoboth, Plymouth Colony, 1645–1692,* 3 volumes. (Greenwich, Rhode Island: Greenwich Public Library, 1983–1990), 2:98–166.

therunto, to appertaine to him, the said Roger Annadowne, to him and his heires and assignes for ever.[26]

The allocation of land was apparently related to the 1661 petition to the court described earlier that suggested Roger arrived as an indentured servant.

In Rehoboth on 20 June 1668, Roger's wife Sara died.[27] Roger quickly married Joanna Harwood on 27 December 1668,[28] and just over a year later they had a son Philip, the sole surviving son who carried on the family name.

In 1671, Roger Amydown was assessed two shillings to help pay Rehoboth town debts. This levy was one of the smaller levies, which ranged from nineteen shillings to four pence.[29]

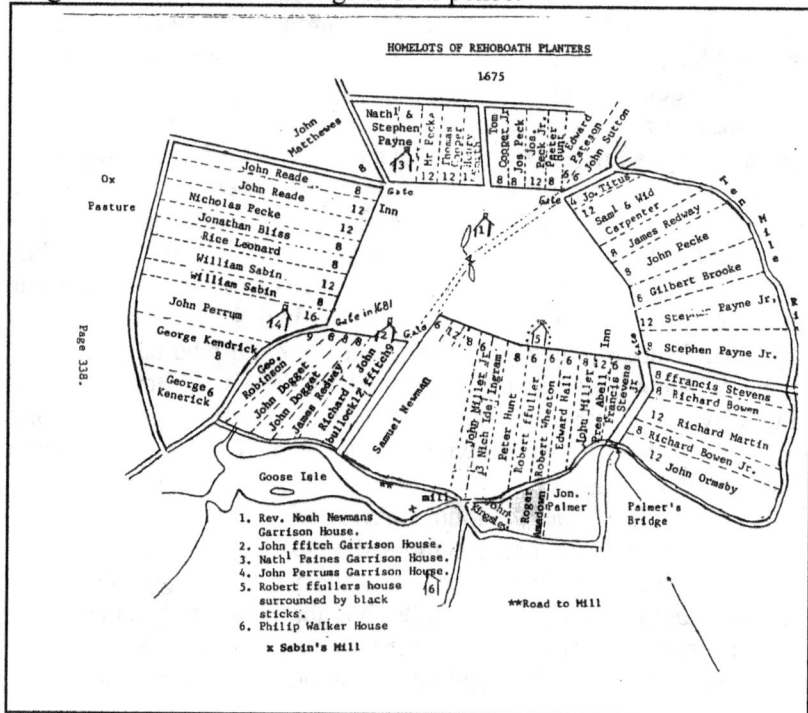

Homelots of Rehoboth Planters (*courtesy of John G. Erhardt*)

26   Erhardt, *Rehoboth*, 2:172.
27   Arnold, *Vital Record of Rehoboth*, 791.
28   Pope, *The Pioneers of Massachusetts*, 17.
29   Bowen, *Early Rehoboth*, 1:39.

Roger died November 1673. The exact date of death is not certain; however, the coroner's jury reported on 11 November 1673. So he most likely died either that day or one day earlier. This jury of twelve men reported:

> Wee, whose names are underwritten, being impannelled upon a corrowner's inquest by the honored Mr. James Browne, Assistant, to sitt upon the corpps of Roger Annadowne, deceased, occationed by some late striffe between his wife and him, hearing all evidences, ponderingt all cercumstances, and viewing the corpes, wee find noe wound nor bruise that might hasten his death.[30]

Roger was buried on 13 November 1673.[31] According to Robert S. Trim, area historian, "as the Newman churchyard was the only place of burial in Rehoboth from the first settlement until well after 1700, this definitely had to be the place of burial . . ., if they are listed as dying in Rehoboth."[32] This cemetery is located in present day East Providence, Rhode Island. At the time, many were buried with only wooden crosses — stone was reserved for the wealthier or perhaps a dearly beloved child.

The estate was inventoried by Philip Walker and Anthony Perry (a future in-law) on 20 November 1673.[33] The real estate included the "houssing and homlott" £45; "13 acres of upland and a peece of salt Marsh att the end of it" £14; "3 acres of land lying neare shapstree" £1 10 s; and "100 pound Comonage" £8.

The estate was indebted to: "Mr Stephen Paine senir, Thomas Olney of Providence, Leift peter hunt, George Kenricke, Abraham Peren, Thomas Wilmouth, Jeremiah Wheaton, Philip Walker, Anthony Perrey."

Debts owing to the estate were from: "John Cobley, Nathaniel Dickens." There were some troubles during the appraisal, to wit:

> the widdow of Roger Annadowne Did not bringe out to us
> . . . the Aprissors of the estate . . .. any of the Moveables that
> shee brought with her att her Marriage.

Also from the estate records we learn that,

---

[30]   Best, Amidon Family, 4.
[31]   Arnold, Vital Record of Rehoboth, 791, 897-8.
[32]   Letter from Robert S. Trim to Miss Buckland, 14 April 1979; Held by the Blanding Public Library, Rehoboth, Massachusetts.
[33]   George Ernest Bowman, "Plymouth Colony Wills and Inventories," Mayflower Descendant, volume 25 (1916):122.

there is an Iron pott prised att 14s . . . which is since that time Challenged by Jeremiah Wheaton as Given him by his father in law Roger Annadowne . . . there was 9 acres & an halfe of upland and an acree of Fresh meddow prised att 8 pounds which is not put into the sume; which since that time Testimony Doth shew it was Given to Ebenezer Annadowne by his father; of these prticulars our honered Majestrate mr James Browne Can further enforme the honored Court.

The inventory was exhibited to "the Court held att Plymouth the 29th of October [*sic*] 1673 on the oath of Joannah Annadowne widdow." The date was most probably in November. See Appendix I for the complete inventory.

His estate was settled on 4 March 1673/4, as presented to the Plymouth Colony Court:

Whereas Roger Annadowne, of Rehoboth, late deceased, died intestate, for the more equall desposing of his estate, it is mutually concluded by and between Joanna Annadowne and John Coblech, of Swansey, in the behalfe of Ebinezer, the eldest son of the said Annadowne, and with the advice and consent of John Harrod, of Patucksett, in the jurisdiction of Providence Plantations, brother unto the said widdow Annadowne, and with the consent and approbation of the Court, that what remaines of the said estate shall be disposed of and settled as followeth: —

Viz. Imp^r, that twenty four acres of upland and a peece of salt marsh belonging therunto, lying att Wachamaucutt Necke, and fifty pounds commonage within the township of Rehoboth, and one acre of fresh meddow lying att a place called the 40 acre meddow, shall be and is settled and confeirmed unto and upon the said Ebenezer, to him and his heires and assignes for ever.

Alsoe, it is agreed and concluded by and between the p[ties] above named, that one other acree of fresh meddow, lying att the aforesaid 40 acre meddow, be settled unto Jeremiah Wheaton, and likewise ten acres of upland, lying att Wachamaucutt Necke.

Furthermore, that John Johnson shall have a coate of the said Roger Annadowne, vallued att two and twenty shillings, and a horse, harnis and cart, vallued att eighteen shillings.

Finally, that the remainer of the whole estate, be it more or lesse, shall belonge and appertaine unto the said widdow Annadowne, provided, that att her decease, that the house, and land lying about the house, being twelve acres, more or lesse, and fifty pounds commonage, and three or four acrees of upland lying att Deare Hill, shall appertaine unto Phillip and Henery Annadowne, her children, in equall and like proportions, and provided, that shee pay all such due debts as are due and owing to any out of the said estate.[34]

Roger's second wife Joanna Harwood was quite a bit younger than he. They married in 1668; she was twenty-six, and Roger was about fifty-five. Perhaps because of this age difference, Holmes Ammidown thought that her marriage was to a son named Roger. Fortunately, Roger's estate clarifies this misconception by making reference to his children from both his marriages. Joanna's parents were George and Jane Harwood. According to the historian James Savage, George was a carpenter who had three children in Boston and perhaps removed to New London, Connecticut.[35] Nothing further has been found on George or Jane. The names Harrod and Harwood have both been used for this surname. After the record of her birth and baptism, the next record we find of Joanna is her being called before a Providence, Rhode Island, town meeting on 6 December 1661 by the Town Deputies to "...cause Johana Harrad to com before them And to See what Securetye may be put in, to cleare the Towne of what charges may arise concerning her, And if none will put in Sufficient Securety then to Send her back againe unto Boston and this to be don without delay."[36] Apparently a bond was signed for Joanna by Thomas Hopkins and Edward Inman. Two years later on 7 December 1663, this bond was ordered to be "delivered unto the Towne for theire Securitye from any charge that they might Expend for the releife of Johanna Harrud; (Tho: Hopkins having desired the saide Bond to be returned unto him,) it shall be returned unto the said Tho: Hopkins; by the Towne Clarke."[37] Joanna's connection to these two men is

---

[34]   Erhardt, *Rehoboth*, 2:264.

[35]   James Savage, *Genealogical Dictionary of The First Settlers of New England, Before 1692*, volume 2, (Baltimore, Md.: Genealogical Publishing Co, Inc., 1990).

[36]   Horatio Rogers, ed., *Early Records of the Town of Providence*, (Providence: Rhode Island Historical Society, 1892–1915), 15:878.

[37]   Rogers, *Town of Providence*, 3:36.

unknown. There is speculation that she was related to Edward Inman's first wife, whose name is unknown. They had a daughter named Joanna about 1640. Another possibility is that Joanna was a servant in their homes.[38] The exact charge against Joanna isn't mentioned. We know that her brother, John, had also moved from Boston to the Providence area. He was mentioned as providing counsel to Joanna during the settling of Roger's estate in 1643: "with the advise and consent of John Harrod of Patuckett, in the jurisdiction of Providence Plantations, brother vnto the said widdow Annadowne." As a woman, she may not have been allowed to represent herself.

When Roger died, Johanna was considered suspect due to a quarrel. She was subsequently cleared in the coroner jury's report. When it was time to inventory Roger's estate, she obstructed some aspects of it. It isn't certain as to her mindset or intentions. In 1674, "Wid. Amidown" is listed among the Rehoboth taxpayers. On 9 April 1684, "Wid. Amidowne" is number forty-two of eighty-six residents receiving a division of land in Rehoboth.[39] After her death in 1711, the town

> voted to Philip Amidown and John Thomson and his wife Mehettebele Thomson ten pounds of that part of Estate which was not Expended In the maintenance of their Mother Ammidown ...be it hereby understood ye the sd Philip Amidown and sd Thomson had yielded up their Right to the whole Estate to the Town for their maintaining of their Mother and Their being Twenty pounds left not expended — the sd Town saw cause to give Two pounds of it to the persons before named.[40]

Then in March 1712, "Likewise — Town give up their Right in what money left of Estate of Widow Ammidown not expended — to heirs of widow."[41]

On 15 December 1665 in Warwick, Rhode Island, Mary Amidowne married John Johnson (alias Worrell). A John Johnson was mentioned in Roger's estate as receiving a coat, horse, and

---

[38]   Dean Crawford Smith, *The Ancestry of Emily Jane Angell, 1844–1910*, (Boston: New England Historic Genealogical Society, 1992); online <inman.surnameweb.org/documents/angell.htm>.

[39]   Erhardt, *Rehoboth*, 2:43.

[40]   Erhardt, *Rehoboth*, 3:158–159.

[41]   Erhardt, *Rehoboth*, 3:161.

harness. Mary is likely one of Roger's children from his first marriage (based on her marriageable age), possibly a nickname or middle name for Sarah or Lydia. They raised a family in Rehoboth and moved to Westerly, Rhode Island, in the 1680s. They continued their family in Westerly, where he died in 1702 and she in 1703.

Children of ROGER and SARA (___) AMADOWNE:

i. EBENEZER[2] AMADOWNE, d. after 25 March 1676 when he donated one shilling six pence to support King Phillip's War.[42]

ii. MARY AMADOWNE, d. Westerly, R.I. Colony, 1703;[43] m. Warwick, R.I. Col., 15 Dec. 1665 John Johnson,[44][45] d. Westerly, R.I. Col., 1702.[46]

iii. SARAH AMADOWNE, b. Weymouth, Massachusetts Bay Colony, 10 Aug. 1640.[47]

iv. LYDIA AMADOWNE, b. Boston, Massachusetts Bay Colony, 27 April 1643.[48]

v. HANNAH AMADOWNE, b. Rehoboth, Plymouth Colony, 20 Sept. 1652;[49] d. Rehoboth, Mass., 13 Sept. 1719;[50] m. JEREMIAH

---

[42] Arnold, *Vital Record of Rehoboth*, 920.

[43] John Osborne Austin, *Genealogical Dictionary of Rhode Island Families Comprising three Generations of Settlers Who Came Before 1690*, (Baltimore, Genealogical Publishing Company, 1995), 114.

[44] Town Clerk, *Records of Warwick, Rhode Island*, no page number, [John Worroll Alias Johnson & Mary Anna
Downe both of Pawtuxet ye towne
ship of Warwicke were married out A
Tuesday being ye 15th of December 1668
Mr Benajamine Smith Court all asistant
ye Collony off Roadiland].

[45] James N. Arnold, *Vital Records of RI 1636-1850*, (Narragansett Historical Publishing Co., 1894), Volume 1 [Kent County, Warwick Marriages], Part 1, Section 2, pages 72, 136.

[46] *Westerly TC & Probate*, vol. 2(1) 1699-1719, p. 22, cited in Alden Gamaliel Beaman, comp., *Washington County, Rhode Island births from probate records, 1685-1860 : comprising the towns of North Kingstown, South Kingstown, Exeter, Westerly, Charleston, Richmond, Hopkinton* (Princeton, Mass.: Alden Gamaliel Beaman, 1978), p. 181.

[47] Chamberlain, *History of Weymouth*, 3:13.

[48] Appleton, *Boston Births*, 14.

[49] Arnold, *Vital Records of Rehoboth*, 523 [called Joanna].

[50] Arnold, *Vital Records of Rehoboth*, 886 [Anna Wheaton, widow].

WHEATON, son of ROBERT and ALICE (BOWEN) WHEATON, b. Salem, Mass. Bay Col., 1643,[51] d. between 1689–1719.[52]

Children of ROGER and JOANNA (HARWOOD) AMADOWNE:

2. vi. PHILIP AMIDOWN, b. Rehoboth, Plymouth Colony, 26 Jan. 1669/70.
   vii. HENRY AMIDOWN, b. Rehoboth, Plymouth Colony, 24 Jan. 1670/71;[53] d. 17 Dec. 1694.[54]
   viii. MEHITABLE AMIDOWN, b. Rehoboth, Plymouth Colony, 27 Aug. 1672;[55] d. aft. 1711; m. Rehoboth, Mass., 23 Dec. 1709 JOHN THOMPSON.[56]

Generation 2: Philip Amidown (1670–1747)

2. PHILIP AMIDOWN[2] *(Roger Amadowne[1])* was born at Rehoboth, Plymouth Colony, on 26 January 1669/70,[57] and died at Oxford, Massachusetts, on 15 March 1746/7.[58] He married first at Rehoboth on 27 May 1698, MEHITABLE PERRY.[59] She was born at Rehoboth on 30 April 1680,[60] daughter of SAMUEL and MARY (MILLARD) PERRY,[61] and died at Rehoboth on 4 July 1699.[62] Philip married second at Rehoboth on 16 August 1700, ITHAMAR WARFIELD.[63] She

51 William Richard Cutter, *New England Families Genealogical and Memorial: Third Series*, 4 volumes (Publication: 1913. Reprint Baltimore Genealogical Publishing Co., Inc., 1996), IV:1756.
52 Jeremiah was enumerated in a 1689 Rehoboth census (Bowen, *Early Rehoboth*, I:56) and his wife was listed as a widow when he died in 1719.
53 Arnold, *Vital Records of Rehoboth*, 523.
54 Henery Annadown inventory, Bristol County probate docket # 4217, Massachusetts Judicial Archives, Columbia Point, Massachusetts.
55 Arnold, *Vital Records of Rehoboth*, 524.
56 Arnold, *Vital Records of Rehoboth*, 11.
57 Arnold, *Vital Record of Rehoboth*, 523 [Amydowne Philip, of Roger].
58 [Anonymous], *Vital Records of Oxford, Massachusetts to the end of the year 1849*, (Worcester, Massachusetts: Franklin P. Rice, 1905), 267.
59 Arnold, *Vital Record of Rehoboth*, 10 [Intentions - Perry, Mehittabell and Philip Ammidowne. Marriage - Phillip Ammidowne and Mehittabell Peren].
60 Arnold, *Vital Record of Rehoboth*, 715.
61 Francis Davis McTeer and Frederick C. Warner, "The Millards of Rehoboth, Massachusetts," *The Detroit Society for Genealogical Research Magazine*, Volume 23, No 2 (Winter 1959):59.
62 Arnold, *Vital Record of Rehoboth*, 791 [record indicates 1697, which must be a typo for 1699 based on her marriage, child's birth and Philip's second marriage.]
63 Arnold, *Vital Record of Rehoboth*, 10.

was born at Medfield, Massachusetts, on 28 March 1676,[64] the daughter of JOHN and HANNAH (RANDALL) WARFIELD,[65] and died after May 1747.[66] Her father was a deacon and resident of Mendon.

Philip's father died when he was a young boy, a mere three years old. He grew up in Rehoboth, raised by his widowed mother, who did not remarry, but received assistance from the town. Philip and his brother Henry were listed as "orphants" in the town listing of inhabitants in 1689.[67] His twenty-three year old brother Henry died in 1694, and Philip was the administrator of his estate. At the age of twenty-eight, Philip married Mehitable Perry, also a lifelong Rehoboth resident. Sadly, this first marriage ended after only thirteen months when she died in 1699, at nineteen years of age, leaving him a five-month-old infant son (our ancestor Henry, their only child). Thirteen months later, Philip married Ithamar Warfield.

Thomas Jefferys, *A Map of the Most Inhabited Part of New England*, 1755 (cropped)(*Library of Congress*)

---

64 [Anonymous], *Vital Records of Medfield, Massachusetts to the Year 1850* (Boston: Stanhope Press, 1903), 100.
65 Their marriage record: *Vital Records of Medfield*, 180.
66 The last record of her is in her husband Philip's will.
67 Bowen, *Early Rehoboth*, 1:57. Arnold, *Vital Record of Rehoboth*, 917.

Philip and Ithamar lived in Rehoboth for a few years (buying a horse in 14 February 1700/1[68]). Then, based on the birth location of their son Ichabod in 1704, they relocated to her hometown of Mendon, Massachusetts, twenty-five miles northwest of Rehoboth. There he served as minister for one shilling and shared in the division of lands in 1713.[69] In Mendon, they had six or seven children (the birth location of their first child Roger in 6 February 1701/2 is unknown).

In 1717 the family moved fifteen miles west to Oxford, Massachusetts. Philip bought the homelot of Joseph Chamberlain Jr. on 24 April 1717,[70] [71] where Ithamar's last child Hannah was born. In this land transaction, Philip was listed as a cooper. According to the Oxford town records of 17 January 1718, Philip was appointed to a committee for the construction of the first meetinghouse. As expected, both Philip and Ithamar were active in the newly formed Oxford Church. They were among sixteen couples who signed the covenant in 1720.[72] On 26 April 1726, Philip gave to his eldest son, Henry, a thirty-two acre portion of the land bought in 1717:

> To all people to whom these presents shall come, greetings. Know ye that Phillip Amidown of Oxford in the County of Suffolk in ye province of Massachusetts Bay in New England, cooper, for and in consideration of love good will and affection which I have and do bear toward my loving son Henry Ammidown of Oxford aforesd...this twenty sixth day of April Anno Domini 1726 and in the twelfth year of the reign of our sovereign Lord George of Great Brittain our King [George I reigned from 1714–1727].[73]

In 1730, Philip was appointed Selectman, and in 1735, he was appointed Constable. Throughout the 1740s, Philip bought and sold

---

[68]   Rehoboth Town Meetings, 1636-1966, Book 15:226, Town Clerk's office, Rehoboth, Massachusetts.

[69]   Anonymous, *The Proprietor's Records of the Town of Mendon, Massachusetts* (Boston: Rockwell and Churchill Press, 1899), 854.

[70]   George F. Daniels, *History of the Town of Oxford, Massachusetts with Genealogies and notes on persons and estates*, (Oxford, Mass.: Published by the author, with the co-operation of the town, 1892), 304.

[71]   Worcester County Deeds, Book 19:352, Worcester County Register of Deeds, Worcester, Massachusetts. This deed was recorded late, in 1745.

[72]   Lucius E. Ammidown, *The Ammidown Family*, Quinabaug Historical Society Leaflets, delivered March 26, 1906, Volume 3, No. 8, page 97.

[73]   Worcester County Deeds, Book 16:105.

land with his sons and others in Mendon, Oxford, and Dudley, the town due south, and selling the remainder of his original homelot to his son Ephraim on 15 December 1743.[74] During his life he worked as a cooper and farmer in Oxford. As his health failed, he penned his Last Will and Testament (Appendix II), leaving the use and income from one quarter of the farm, along with the use of the house and half the barn, and all personal items to his wife for her lifetime. He allocated three pounds good money to his children: Henry, Roger, Ichabod, Philip, John, and son Ithamar's heirs: Mary Chamberlain and Hannah Wheelock. The first five named sons were to divide his carpentry tools. The two named daughters were to divide his household goods after his wife's death. His favorite son Ephraim was to receive all his real and personal property. Philip died on 15 March 1747.

Child of PHILIP and MEHITABLE (PERRY) AMIDOWN:

3. i. HENRY AMIDON[3], b. Rehoboth, Mass., 8 Feb. 1698/99.

Children of PHILIP and ITHAMAR (WARFIELD) AMIDOWN:

   ii. ROGER AMIDOWN, b. 6 Feb. 1701/2;[75] m. (1) Oxford, Mass., 27 Oct. 1731 ELIZABETH HAWKINS,[76] dau. of THOMAS HAWKINS;[77] m. (2) Dudley, Mass., 28 Feb. 1757 RACHEL (___) RICE, widow. [78] [79]

   iii. ICHABOD AMIDOWN, b. Mendon, Mass., 1 May 1704;[80] m. Mendon, Mass., 7 Mar. 1732 MARGERY ALDRICH,[81] b. Mendon, Mass., 14 March 1714, daughter of JACOB and MARGERY (HAYWARD) ALDRICH,[82] d. Mendon, Mass., 7 Oct. 1767. [83]

---

74   Daniels, *History of the Town of Oxford*, 305.

75   Best, *The Amidon Family*, 8.

76   *Vital Records of Oxford*, 127.

77   Best, *The Amidon Family*, 8.

78   Marriages, unpaginated, *Congregational Church, Dudley, Massachusetts.*

79   [Anonymous], *Vital Records of Dudley, Massachusetts to the end of the year 1849*, (Boston: Franklin P. Rice, 1908), 134.

80   Thomas W. Baldwin, compiler, *Vital Records of Mendon, Massachusetts, To The Year 1850*, (Boston:Wright & Potter Printing Company, 1920), 23.

81   Baldwin, *Vital Records of Mendon*, 238.

82   Baldwin, *Vital Records of Mendon*, 17. We have been unable to access the original record to determine whether this date should be presented as 1614/15, or, if the transcriber changed the date, perhaps it should be presented as 1613/14.

83   Baldwin, *Vital Records of Mendon*, 448.

iv. MARY AMIDOWN, b. Mendon, Mass., 30 March 1706;[84] m. Oxford, Mass., 8 July 1728 BENJAMIN CHAMBERLAIN.[85]

v. PHILIP AMMIDOWN, b. Mendon, Mass., prob. 1708;[86] bap. Dudley, Mass., 11 June 1749;[87] [88] d. 1779;[89] m. Uxbridge, Mass., 28 July 1731 SUBMIT BULLARD,[90] b. Medfield, Mass., 2 April 1711, dau. of JOSEPH and MARGARET (CHENEY) BULLARD,[91] d. 1780.

vi. EPHRAIM AMIDOWN, b. Mendon, Mass., 28 March 1710;[92] d. 1786 prob. Oxford;[93] m. (1) Dedham, Mass., 10 March 1735/6 HANNAH DEAN,[94] b. Dedham, Mass., 8 June 1705, dau. of JOHN and HANNAH (____) DEAN,[95] d. after 4 April 1739/40; [96] m. (2) Oxford, Mass., 24 Feb. 1742/3 HANNAH SMITH, [97] b. Needham, Mass., 1 Aug. 1715, dau. of JOHN and MARY (ACORRS) SMITH,[98] d. Oxford, Mass., 14 Sept. 1807.[99]

vii. ITHAMAR AMIDOWN, b. Mendon, Mass., 25 April 1712;[100] d. before 10 Feb. 1740/41;[101] m. 2 March 1735/6 RUTH

---

84   Baldwin, *Vital Records of Mendon*, 23.

85   *Vital Records of Oxford*, 127.

86   Baldwin, *Vital Records of Mendon*, 23.

87   Marriages, unpaginated, *Congregational Church, Dudley, Massachusetts,* [Philip Son of Philip Amidown].

88   *Vital Records of Dudley,* 11.

89   Best, *The Amidon Family*, 8.

90   Thomas W. Baldwin, compiler, *Vital Records of Uxbridge, Massachusetts, to the Year 1850*, (Boston: Wright & Potter Printing Company, 1916), 205.

91   *Vital Records of Medfield*, 26.

92   Baldwin, *Vital Records of Mendon*, 23.

93   Based on his will of 13 April 1786 being disapproved on 6 June 1786.

94   *Vital Records of Oxford*, 126. Robert Brand Hanson, Ed., *Vital Records of Dedham, Massachusetts 1635-1845* (Camden, Maine: Picton Press, 1997), 223.

95   Hanson, *Vital Records of Dedham*, 48.

96   Birth of daughter Keziah at Oxford: Rice, *Vital Records of Oxford*, 11.

97   *Vital Records of Oxford*, 126.

98   Robert Brand Hanson, ed., *Vital Records of Needham, Massachusetts, 1711-1845* (Camden, Maine: Picton Press, 1997), 90.

99   *Vital Records of Oxford*, 267.

100   Baldwin, *Vital Records of Mendon*, 23.

101   Based on baptism of his children. Ithamar and Ebenezer were baptized as "sons of the Widow Ruth Ammadown" in Sutton, Mass. [Anonymous], *Vital Records of Sutton, Massachusetts To the Year 1850* (Boston: Franklin P. Rice, 1907), 10.

CURTIS,[102] b. Plympton, Mass., 20 May 1710, dau. of JOHN and CHARITY (MAY) CURTIS.[103]

viii. JOHN AMIDOWN, b. Mendon, Mass., 19 March 1713/4;[104] d. Hardwick, Mass., bet. 15 March and 12 May 1755;[105] m. Oxford, Mass., 14 July 1737 SARAH HASTINGS,[106] bap. 9 May 1714 Christ Church, Cambridge, Mass., dau. of DANIEL and ABIGAIL (COOKSEY) HASTINGS.[107] John lived in Lamtown, Mass., at the time of his marriage.

ix. HANNAH AMIDOWN, b. Oxford, Mass., 2 Feb. 1717/8;[108] m. Mendon, Mass., 16 Feb. 1737/38 SAMUEL WHEELOCK,[109] b. Mendon, Mass., 6 Sept. 1714, son of OBADIAH and ELISABETH (DARLING) WHEELOCK,[110] d. Tyringham, Mass., about Dec. 1792. [111]

Generation 3: Henry Amidown (1699–1778)

3. HENRY AMIDOWN[3] *(Philip[2], Roger Amadowne[1])* was born at Rehoboth, Massachusetts, on 8 February 1698/99[112] and died at Ashford, Connecticut, on 5 March 1778.[113] He married at Oxford, Massachusetts, on 31 March 1718/9, MELTIAH CHENEY.[114] She was born at Medfield, Massachusetts, on 14 October 1690, the daughter of JOSEPH and HANNAH (THURSTON) CHENEY,[115] and died at Ashford on

---

102   Best, *The Amidon Family*, 99.
103   [Anonymous], *Vital Records of Plympton, Massachusetts To the Year 1850*, (Boston: Franklin P. Rice,, 1923), 79.
104   Baldwin, *Vital Records of Mendon*, 23.
105   Best, *The Amidon Family*, 11.
106   *Vital Records of Oxford*, 127.
107   Stephen Paschall Sharples, ed., *Records of the Church of Christ at Cambridge in New England 1632-1830*, (Boston: Eben Putnam, 1906), 68, 71.
108   *Vital Records of Oxford*, 10.
109   Baldwin, *Vital Records of Mendon*, 237.
110   Baldwin, *Vital Records of Mendon*, 209.
111   American Antiquarian Society, *Index of Obituaries in Massachusetts Centinel and Columbian Centinel, 1784 to 1840*, 5 volumes (Boston: G. K. Hall Co., 1961), 5:4832. Note – the death notice was originally published in 15 Dec. 1792 *Columbian Centinel*.
112   Arnold, *Vital Record of Rehoboth*, 523.
113   Ashford Town Clerk, Vital Records, Book 4:17 [Henry Amidown Departed this life March ye 5th 1778].
114   *Vital Records of Oxford*, 126.
115   *Vital Records of Medfield*, 29 [Chany, Melitiah].

17 May 1780.[116]

There is another marriage between these families. Meltiah's niece, Submit Bullard, (through Meltiah's older sister Margaret and Joseph Bullard - who married in Medfield on 25 June 1681[117]), married Henry's half-brother Philip (see page 20).

Henry grew up in Mendon, where all his younger siblings were born. He was mentioned in his grandfather Samuel Perry's will in 1706.[118] Relocating to Oxford with his father in 1717, he married there in 1718 at the age of nineteen. There, Meltiah bore their four children. As was the custom for young married men, Henry was selected to be the town's hog reeve in 1722.[119] The hog reeve was the equivalent of dogcatcher, but for the loose hogs. This experience did not seem to garner a sense of community for Henry because he was not selected for any future town positions. In 1726, his father gave him thirty-two acres of land in Oxford adjoining his own; Henry was identified as a husbandman. The title "Husbandman" was used to indicate someone who farmed for a living, while a "Yeoman" was someone who cultivated a small farm. In 1742, Henry sold this land to his son Jacob; both men were identified as husbandmen.[120]

Leaving Oxford in 1744, Henry established his homestead in Ashford, Connecticut, twenty-five miles southwest of Oxford, where he purchased "one hundred acres" from Stephen Chapman. The one hundred acres was merely an approximation, with few measurements involved. As this land was parceled out, a better amount would have been 140 acres. Over the next three years he sold forty-five acres to his son-in-law William Curtis and twenty-seven and one-half acres to his son Henry Jr., leaving him with about fifty acres for the family homestead, on which he lived out his life. Over time, his other sons, Joseph and Jacob, purchased portions of this land from Henry Jr. When Henry Sr. died in 1778 at the advanced age of seventy-nine, it appears that his son Joseph took over the old homestead. There is no

---

116   Ashford Town Clerk, Vital Records, Book 4:17 [Melatiah Amidown Departed this life May ye 17, 1780].

117   *Vital Records of Medfield*, 124 [Chany, Margrett].

118   Samuel Perry will, Bristol County probate book 2:159, Taunton, Massachusetts. The will is dated 2 November 1705, probated 3 July 1706 [grandson Henry Annedown twenty shillings].

119   Town Clerk, *Town Proceedings, births, deaths, and miscellaneous records, 1713-1752, Oxford, Massachusetts*, March 6, 1721/2, page 17.

120   Worcester County Deeds, Book 16:105.

extant probate record or will, but Joseph sold the lot in 1802 to Benjamin Chapman Jr.[121] Henry's wife Meltiah died two years after him in 1780 at the age of ninety!

According to his land transactions, Henry lived his life as a farmer. At the end of his long life, he was active as a recruiter during the Revolutionary War.[122] His son Henry was a Captain in the war, and Henry Sr. had at least seven grandchildren who also served. No burial location has been identified for his wife or him.

Children of HENRY and MELTIAH (CHENEY) AMIDOWN:[123]

4. i.   JACOB[4] AMIDOWN, b. Oxford, Mass., 28 Feb. 1720.

   ii.   MEHITABLE AMIDOWN, b. Oxford 15 Jan. 1722/3;[124] m. Dudley, Mass., 12 Dec. 1742, WILLIAM CURTIS, [125] b. Plympton, Mass., 9 July 1721, son of FRANCIS and SARAH (RANSOM) CURTIS.[126]

   iii. JOSEPH AMIDOWN, b. Oxford Feb. 1724/5; [127] d. Onondaga Co., N.Y., 27 Nov. 1810; [128] m. Ashford, Conn., 1762, PATIENCE CHAFFEE, [129] b. Attleboro, Mass., 16 Jan. 1742/3, dau. of DAVID and MARTHA (WALKER) CHAFFEE,[130] [131] bap.

---

121   Town Clerk, Ashford Deeds, Books A, D, H, 14, Ashford Register of Deeds, Ashford, Connecticut.

122   [Anonymous], *Town of Ashford, Conn.. Supplement to Commemorative Issue Two Hundred Fiftieth Anniversary*, inside cover page.

123   Clarence Winthrop Bowen, *The History of Woodstock, Conn.* (Norwood, Mass.: The Plimpton Press, 1930), 190.

124   Town Clerk, *Town proceedings, . . . Oxford, Massachusetts*, 13 [Mehitabel the daughter of henery Amidown and Meltiah his [wife] was [b]orn Jan' 15 1723]. The Oxford Town Clerk of this era, Richard Moore, often erred and used the historical year format instead of the double slash dates.

125   Town Clerk, *Dudley Town Records*, unpaginated [These may Certify that William Curtis of Dudley was married to Mehitable Amidown of sd town this day by me Perley Howe, Clerk].

126   *Vital Records of Plympton, 80.*

127   Town Clerk, *Town proceedings, . . . Oxford, Massachusetts*, 13 [Joseph ye son of henery Amidown born and Meltiah his wife on Feb 1725]. As above, we believe the historical year format was used for this record.

128   William H. Chaffee, *The Chaffee Genealogy (embracing the Chafe, Chafy, Chafie, Chafee, Chaphe, Chaffy, Chaffie, Chaffey, Chaffe, Chaffee Descendants of Thomas Chaffe, of Hingham, Hull, Rehoboth and Swansea, Massachusetts also certain Lineages from Families in the United States, Canada, England, not descended from Thomas Chaffe) 1635-1909*, (N.Y.: The Grafton Press, 1909), 98.

129   Chaffee, *The Chaffee Genealogy*, 98.

130   [Anonymous], *Vital Records of Attleborough, Massachusetts, to the End of the Year 1849, Births-Marriages-Deaths*, (Salem: The Essex Institute, 1934), 69.

First Congregational Church, Rehoboth, Mass., 27 Feb. 1742/3,[132] d. South Onondaga, N.Y., 1816, bur. Navarino, N.Y. [133]

iv.   CAPT. HENRY AMIDOWN, b. Oxford 3 May 1727;[134] d. Willington, Conn., 1798;[135] m. Pomfret, Conn., 25 Sept. 1751, SARAH DOUBLEDAY,[136] b. 21 July 1731, dau. of NATHANIEL and MARY (ATWELL) DOUBLEDAY,[137] d. Willington, Conn., 8 Jan 1794.[138]

Generation No. 4: Jacob Amidown (1720–ca. 1790)

4. JACOB[4] AMIDOWN *(Henry[3], Philip[2], Roger[1] Amadowne)* was born in Oxford, Massachusetts, on 28 February 1720[139] and died between 7 April 1788 and probably 1790[140] (but no later than 31 May 1794 when his widow's marriage intentions were published[141]). He married first at Dudley, Massachusetts, on 27 December 1744 ELIZABETH CURTIS.[142] She was born in Plymouth, Massachusetts, on 20 May 1704, the daughter of JOHN and CHARITY (MAY) CURTIS. [143]

---

131   Chaffee, *The Chaffee Genealogy*, 98.
132   Arnold, *Vital Record of Rehoboth*.
133   Chaffee, *The Chaffee Genealogy*, 98.
134   Town Clerk, *Town proceedings, . . . Oxford, Massachusetts*, 13 [henery the son of henery amidown and Meltiah was born may 3 - 1727].
135   Henry Amidon estate, Register of Probate Records, Town of Stafford, Stafford District, Connecticut: microfilm no. 5744, vol. 6, 12-15, Family History Library, Salt Lake City, Utah, [Capt. Henry Amidon, late of Willington]. Estate was distributed 18 June 1798.
136   Lorraine Cook White, *The Barbour Collection of Connecticut town vital records – Pomfret*, vol. 34 (Baltimore: Genealogical Publishing Co., 1994), 1:103.
137   Boston Registry Department. *Boston Births from A.D. 1700 to A.D. 1800*. (Boston: Rockwell & Churchill, 1894), 202.
138   Willington, Connecticut, Vital Records, B:14, Willington Registrar of Vital Statistics.
139   *Vital Records of Oxford*, 11.
140   Jacob was listed in the Dudley Town Records as having taxes abated on 4 April 1788. The 1790 U.S. Census lists his wife "Irena Ammedown," with their four daughters. She was probably a widow at that time.
141   Jay Mack Holbrook, *Massachusetts Vital Records: Sturbridge 1723–1891*, (Oxford, Mass., Holbrook Research Institute, 1986), no page number, fiche 4.
142   Ammedon-Curtis marriage, 27 December 1744, in Marriage Book (original volume), unpaginated, Congregational Church, Dudley, Massachusetts.
143   Lee D. VanAntwerp, compiler, *Vital Records of Plymouth, Massachusetts to the year 1850* (Camden, Maine: Picton Press, 1993), 33.

He married second at Woodstock, Connecticut, on 10 June 1773 IRENE JOHNSON.[144] She was born at Killingly, Connecticut, on 22 November 1748, the daughter of JOHN and ELIZABETH (WHITMORE) JOHNSON JR.,[145] and baptized at Killingly on 9 Aug 1752.[146] She died between 1 January and 28 April 1837 in Tinmouth, Vermont.[147]

It has long been believed that Jacob's second wife was named Joena Johnson. But a careful examination of the original handwritten marriage record revealed the truth. Eighteenth century handwriting did not distinguish between I and J. And the loopy form of the "r" allowed it to be interpreted as "o." This explains why there were no subsequent records for the Widow Joena Amidown as well as the mysterious presence of the Widow Irena Amidown. Furthermore, the name Joena or Joanna appears nowhere else in the lineage, but a daughter was named Irene, and son John also named a daughter Irene.

Jacob grew up in Oxford, Massachusetts. In the early 1740s, Jacob's father, Henry Amidown, decided to leave Oxford for nearby Ashford, Connecticut. In 1742 at the age of twenty-two, Jacob purchased from his father thirty-two acres in Oxford, which Henry had received from his father Philip. Three years later in neighboring Dudley, Massachusetts, Jacob married Elizabeth Curtis. They were both listed as "of Dudley."

Elizabeth was originally from the city of Plymouth. Her sister Ruth had married Jacob's uncle Ithamar in 1735 (see page 20). Also, Elizabeth's nephew William Curtis had married Jacob's sister Mehitable (see page 23). Jacob was younger than Elizabeth by sixteen years; he was twenty-four years old, and she was forty! There is no record of any children or of her death.

By 1752, Jacob sold his thirty-two acre parcel in Oxford and belatedly joined his parents and siblings in Ashford. Jacob bought from his brother ,Joseph, thirteen and one-half acres of land, part of Henry's original "hundred acre" purchase. Jacob is listed as a husbandman.

---

[144]   First Congregational Church of Woodstock, 167, City Hall, Woodstock, Connecticut.
[145]   Killingly, Connecticut, Vital Records, Book 1:38. Killingly town clerk. Marriage of her parents was also in Killingly on 17 May 1748, Book 1:77.
[146]   Marilyn Labbe, comp., *First Congregational Church Thompson, Conn., 1730-1930*, (Danielson, Conn.: Killingly Historical Society, 2000), 65.
[147]   [Anonymous], *Congregational Church of Christ (Tinmouth, Vermont), 1780-1868* (Salt Lake City, Utah: Genealogical Society of Utah, 1956), 210.

In 1755 war erupted between England and France. The battles of the French and Indian War were far removed from Massachusetts and Connecticut, but as colonies of England, they were required to provide soldiers. Colonial records do not show Henry Amidown or his sons participated in the war.

Jacob lived in Ashford for five years. In 1757, he sold the property to his other brother, Henry. By then, Jacob was listed as a *Cordwainer*. Cord'wain was a Medieval term for Spanish leather (goatskin tanned and dressed), and hence any leather handsomely finished, colored, gilded, or the like.[148] This is also the source of the term Cordovian leather. So a cordwainer was a leather worker and had a slightly higher connotation than a simple boot maker.

Jacob returned to Dudley, Massachusetts, where he bought two adjoining parcels of land in 1758. He sold these parcels in 1761, presumably leaving him without property. Moving southwest five miles across the state border, Jacob bought land in the northern part of Woodstock, Connecticut, in 1772. He was listed "of Woodstock," indicating that he may have been renting the land prior to its purchase.

Marrying Irene Johnson in June of 1774 at the First Congregational Church, located in present day North Woodstock, Jacob started a new family. In March and May of 1775, Jacob sold his land in Woodstock. Then, interestingly, Irene was accepted into the First Congregational Church, Dudley, with the following entry: "Irene the wife of Jacob Amidon made Confesion of ye sin of Fornication and was received into covenant July 9th 1775."[149] Two weeks later, their son Jacob and daughter Ursula (spelled Irsula in the record) were baptized at the Dudley church. From later records, we know that Ursula was born between October 1771 and August 1772. Ursula's birth prior to Jacob and Irene's marriage in June 1773 would explain the "Fornication" charge. Why the children were not baptized at the Woodstock church (was the church without a pastor at the time?) and why Jacob sold his land in Woodstock are not clear. Once she had admitted her sins, the Dudley congregation accepted Irene into the church and then baptized the children. Over the next ten years, their subsequent five children were baptized at either the Dudley or Woodstock church.

When the Revolutionary War broke out in 1775, Jacob was fifty-

---

[148] *Merriam-Webster Online*, "cordwainer," online <www.m-w.com/dictionary/cordwainer>.

[149] Irena Amidon admitted as member, 9 July 1775, Marriages Book, unpaginated, First Congregational Church, Dudley, Massachusetts.

five years old. He did not serve in the war, but he could have been a worker at one of the war camps – such as a boot maker or repairman. At the very least, we know that he was an American patriot because he named his third son after General Horatio Gates, a hero in New England for his actions at the Battle of Saratoga.

The last known record of Jacob is from the Dudley Town Records. In 7 April 1788, the town voted to abate (i.e., reduce) his taxes, along with a list of five others.[150] The first federal census taken in 1790 listed Irena Ammedown in Dudley along with four other females – likely her four daughters.[151] Jacob, who would have been seventy years old, had probably died. Four years later on 9 July 1794, the "widow Irene Ammidown of Sturbridge" married David Aldrich in Sturbridge, Massachusetts[152] — about ten miles west of Dudley and due north of Woodstock.

Where were Jacob and Irene's sons in 1790? According to an early family history of Jacob (Sr.)'s son John, there was a falling out between Jacob and his sons.[153] The three boys, aged ten, fourteen, and sixteen years old, had likely joined Irene's family who had relocated to Tinmouth, Vermont. The most identifiable member of this family was Irene's brother Elihu Johnson.

Elihu Johnson served in the Revolutionary War from a unit out of Woodstock, Connecticut. He was a private serving in Connecticut's Third Regiment, 7th Company under Capt. Ephraim Manning from 10 May to 15 December 1775.[154] He subsequently joined the ill fated Québec Expedition led by Colonel Benedict Arnold, during which Elihu was captured and returned in early 1776. Elihu next appears in Tinmouth, Vermont, in 1780. He served several times in the Vermont

---

[150]   Town Clerk, *Town Records of Dudley, Masachusetts, 1754–1794* (Pawtucket, RI: The Adam Sutliffe Co., 1894), 300.

[151]   Irena Ammedown household, 1790 U.S. census, Worcester County, Massachusetts, Town of Dudley, page 175, line 4; National Archives micropublication M637, roll 4.

[152]   [Anonymous], *Vital Records of Sturbridge, Massachusetts, to the year 1850* (Boston: New England Historic Genealogical Society, 1906), 155.

[153]   Family tree notes by Walter Edward Delano (born Walter Edward Ameden), grandson of John Ameden, as described in email from Bill Nyland to Nancy K. Mullen, 10 June 2000.

[154]   *Connecticut Men in the Revolutionary War, 1775–1783*, online (Provo, Utah: MyFamily.com, Inc., 2003). Original data: Henry P. Johnston, ed. *The Record of Connecticut Men in the Military and Naval Service During the War of the Revolution 1775–1783*. Volumes 1–2. (Hartford, Conn.: 1889). 2:56, 57, 92.

militia, serving under officers of Vermont's 3rd Regiment, 4th Company (Captains John Spafford and Orange Train). One of the other brothers, Jacob Johnson, also served in the same unit.[155] In the 1791 federal census of Vermont (delayed a year due to its belated admission to the Union), Irene's brothers Elihu, Jacob, and John Johnson were all living in Tinmouth.[156] Jacob Johnson is a good candidate for housing Irene's boys. Beside himself, his enumeration included two men over sixteen years old and four boys under sixteen.

Three years later, Elihu sold land in Tinmouth[157] and bought land in neighboring Wallingford, Vermont. From 1795 to 1798, Elihu bought and sold land in Wallingford, including a grist mill.[158] Of particular interest is a half-acre lot and dwelling house adjacent to Nathaniel Ives, Lent Ives, and Nathan Gould.

As they reached adulthood, Irene's sons began to appear in the records of Wallingford. First her eldest son Jacob was selected as a Surveyor of Highways in a town meeting at Wallingford in 1797.[159] Two months later, he married there Chloe Ives, daughter of Nathaniel Ives. In 1800, Jacob bought the same half-acre lot and dwelling house his uncle had sold (one likely scenario is that the boys had lived in the house, Elihu had to sell it, they did not have the money to buy it until later).[160] The 1800 federal census from Wallingford includes Irene's sons Jacob Amaden and Horatio Gates Ameden. And finally in 1801, her middle son John Ameden appeared as a witness to a land sale in Wallingford.[161]

The Johnson and later Amidown families' move to Vermont before 1800 was part of a population explosion experienced after Vermont

---

155 *Connecticut Men in the Revolutionary War, 1775-1783*, II:188, 241, 379.

156 Elihu, John and Jacob Johnson households, 1790 U.S. census, Rutland County, Vermont, Town of Tinmouth, page 45, column 2, line 18, 22, 23; National Archives micropublication M637, roll 12.

157 Town Clerk, Tinmouth Deeds, Tinmouth Register of Deeds, Tinmouth, Vermont, Book 2:325.

158 Town Clerk, Wallingford Deeds, Wallingford Register of Deeds, Wallingford, Vermont, Book 2:329-331, 405, 476.

159 Town Clerk, *Town Records of Wallingford, Vermont*, no page #, dated 7 March 1797.

160 Wallingford Deeds, Book 3:39.

161 Wallingford Deeds, Book 3:184-185.

Year	Population
1791	536
1800	912
1810	1386
1820	1570

Walter Thorpe, *History of Wallingford, Vermont*
(Rutland, Vt.: The Tuttle Co., 1911), 170.

Table 1 - Growth of Wallingford, Vermont

ceased to be an independent republic in 1791 and joined the United States as the fourteenth state.

Irene's history before Jacob is quite interesting. At age four, Irene was baptized at the Thompson Congregational Church in Killingly, Connecticut. Her baptismal record reveals that she, too, was born out of wedlock: "John Johnson Jr. and wife after a confession of ye sin of fornication &c: had their children baptized Irene & Rhoda." John Johnson Jr. was a farmer and lived in that northern part of Killingly known today as Thompson – six miles due east of Woodstock. He sold the last of his land in Killingly in 1750.[162] In 1756, John was still "of Thompson" when his son Elihu was baptized at Killingly (though recorded at the Dudley Church). Irene's other siblings (Silence, Lydia, Jacob, and John Ayer Johnson) were baptized at the Thompson Congregational Church (Thompson was a parish of Killingly until 1785) in the years before 1769. Irene married Jacob in 1773 in Woodstock, and it was out of Woodstock that her brother Elihu served in the Revolutionary War in 1775. No marriage records for her siblings have been found in the Killingly or Woodstock area.

Widowed in her early forties, Irene was living in Dudley, Massachusetts, in 1790 and remarried at Sturbridge, Massachusetts, on 9 July 1794 to DAVID ALDRICH.[163] David is most likely the son of DAVID and SARAH (BENSON) ALDRICH, born at Douglas, Massachusetts, on 15 February 1743/44.[164] He married first PHEBE TRASK, daughter of ROBERT and ABIGAIL (CARRILL) TRASK. They had nine children, the last born in 1790. According to A. James

---

[162] Town Clerk, Killingly Deeds, Book 3:203, Killingly Register of Deeds, Killingly, Connecticut.

[163] Holbrook, *Vital Records: Sturbridge*, fiche 4.

[164] [Anonymous], *Vital Records of Douglas, Massachusetts, to the End of the Year 1849* (Worcester, Massachusetts: Franklin P. Rice, 1906), 9.

Aldrich's book, *George Aldrich Genealogy*,[165] David left Phebe about 1790 and was never heard from again. There are no other known candidates who could have been Irene's second husband.

By 1800, Irene and David had moved up to Hinsdale (present day Vernon), Vermont.[166] In the census record, David is listed as greater than forty-five years old with a woman also greater than forty-five years old (Irene), with no one else in the household. Irene's sons were living in Wallingford, Vermont (seventy miles away). The whereabouts of her daughters at this time is uncertain. They may have gone to Vermont or stayed in Woodstock. The first appearance of one of the daughters is Ursula in 1809 in Woodstock.

Soon after the 1800 census, Irene and David joined her sons in Wallingford. David was mentioned in the Wallingford town records, first on 6 April 1802 (with wife and family), again on 14 July 1802 (alone), and finally on 5 November 1807 (with Rhody Johnson who lived with him), as a person being "warned out" of town.[167] "Rhody" Johnson was Irene's sister Rhoda. A family was "warned out" if the town considered the family likely to become a financial burden to the town (widows with children, widowers, injured, etc.). By 1810, David was living in nearby Tinmouth, Vermont, with two females under ten years old and one female between sixteen and twenty-five years old – clearly Irene at about sixty-two years of age was not with him.[168] Then we discover that on 14 September 1814, "Irena the wife of David Aldrich was admitted on letter of recommendation from the church at Wallingford" into the Tinmouth Congregational Church.[169] It appears that David and Irene were living separately in 1810, and that Irene later joined David in Tinmouth. The 1820 federal census shows David in Tinmouth living with three females over forty-five years old (Irene, Rhoda, and someone else – Rhoda died in Tinmouth

165   Alvin James Aldrich, *George Aldrich Genealogy* (Decorah, Iowa: Anundsen Publishing Company, 1971-88).
166   David Aldrich household, 1800 U.S. census, Windham County, Vermont, Hinsdale town, page 558, line 3; National Archives micropublication M32, roll 52.
167   Alden M. Rollins, *Vermont Warnings Out*, vol. 2 (Camden Maine: Picton Press, 1997), 128, 130, 131.
168   David Aldrich household, 1810 U.S. census, Rutland County, Vermont, Town of Tinmouth, page 187, line 11; National Archives micropublication M252, roll 65.
169   *Congregational Church (Tinmouth)*, 10.

in 1821).[170] That raises some questions. Who were the two girls and one young woman living with David in 1810 (her daughter Irene was about twenty-four in 1810)? Who was the third older woman living with David and Irene in 1820 (another of Irene's sisters)? David was never admitted into the Tinmouth church and never held land in Hinsdale, Wallingford, or Tinmouth.

Irene died in Tinmouth in early 1837. The entry in the church records simply states under deaths, "1837 Mrs. Irena Aldrich (Mr. Avery preached)," with no specific date or age. The subsequent, and chronological, entry is dated April 28th. Neither David nor Irene is listed in the 1830 federal census of Tinmouth. David likely died in the 1820s, and Irene moved in with friends or perhaps one of her daughters' families.

Children of JACOB and IRENE (JOHNSON) AMIDOWN:

5. i. URSULA[5] AMIDON, b. Conn. bet. 17 Oct. 1771 and 30 Aug. 1772, bap. Dudley, Mass., 23 July 1775.
6. ii. JACOB AMADEN JR., b. bet. 21 Feb. 1773 and 22 Feb. 1774, bap. Dudley, Mass., 23 July 1775.
7. iii. JOHN AMEDEN, bap. N. Woodstock, Conn., 14 April 1776.
8. iv. ELIZABETH AMIDON, b. bet. 31 Aug. 1777 and 15 Feb. 1778, bap. Woodstock 15 Feb. 1778.
9. v. HORATIO AMEDEN, bap. Dudley 4 June 1780.
10. vi. SILENCE AMIDOWN, bap. Dudley 22 June 1783.
11. vii. IRENE AMIDOWN, bap. Woodstock 11 April 1786.

---

[170] David Aldridge household, 1820 U.S. census, Rutland County, Vermont, Town of Tinmouth, page 519, line 23; National Archives micropublication M33, roll 126.

Chapter 2 Fifth Generation

Ursula (Amidon) Cole (1772-1855)

5. URSULA[5] AMIDON *(Jacob[4] Amidown, Henry[3], Philip[2], Roger[1] Amadowne)* was born in Connecticut between 17 October 1771 and 30 August 1772,[1] baptized at Dudley, Massachusetts, on 23 July 1775,[2] and died at Springfield, Massachusetts, on 17 December 1855.[3] She married before 22 March 1809 ____ COLE. [4]

Ursula was probably born and raised in Woodstock, Connecticut, the eldest in the family of seven children. Her father probably died while she was still a teenager, forcing her to help her mother raise the younger children. Her brothers seem to have been sent to Vermont to live with Ursula's uncles, leaving Ursula and her mother with the three younger girls. Being about eighteen years of age, she is likely one of the women living in her mother's household in Dudley, Massachusetts, in the 1790 Federal census. Four years later, her mother married David Aldrich. Ursula could have married Mr. Cole at about the same time. The 1800 federal census showed that, by 1800, her mother and stepfather David Aldrich had relocated to Vernon, Vermont, but Ursula and the other girls were not with them; their household included only David and his wife. Ursula may have been living near Wallingford, Vermont, with her brothers.

She was already called Ursula Cole on 22 March 1809 when she and Hannah Ledoyt purchased land in Woodstock, Connecticut. Less than four months later, Ursula delivered Mr. Whitmore's daughter, Aurelia.[5] Although the child was born in Woodstock, there were no

---

[1]   Elizabeth Amidon household, 1850 census, Windham County, Connecticut, population schedule, town of Woodstock, page 252, dwelling 109, family 126; National Archives micropublication M432, roll 51. Her age was given as 78 and birth location as Connecticut. Her death record of 17 October 1855 gives her age as 83 and birth location as Vermont.

[2]   Irsula Amidon baptism, Baptism book, unpaginated, Dudley Congregational Church, Dudley, Massachusetts. [1775 July 23[d] Irsula, Jacob Children of the Wife of Jacob Amidon].

[3]   Ursula Cole death, *Vital Records of Springfield. Massachusetts, 1638-1887*, Deaths, vol. 4, page 34, number 42 (Salt Lake City: Genealogical Society of Utah, 1958), microfilm 185417, Family History Library, Salt Lake City, Utah.

[4]   Woodstock [Conn.] Land Records, Book 12:291 (Abram Paine & Henry Work to Ursula Cole & Hannah Ledoyt), Woodstock town clerk, Woodstock, Connecticut.

[5]   *Woodstock Vital Records*, 234.

men named Whitmore living in Woodstock at the time. There were, however, several Whitmores living in nearby Thompson and Killingly, Connecticut. The identity of both men in Ursula's life remains a mystery.

Ursula and Hannah's property lay just west of the Woodstock town hall, an area at the time known as the *Society of New Roxbury*. The property included a shoemaker's shop. When Hannah died on 18 October 1819 at the age of sixty,[6] she left her share of the property to both Ursula and Ursula's young daughter Aurelia Whitmore along with several personal possessions accounting for more than a third of her estate.[7] Hannah had never married and no family connection has been made to Ursula; perhaps, the elderly Hannah had taken in the pregnant Ursula, whereby they took care of each other. The 1820 census, taken after Hannah's death, shows Ursula living alone with a female child age ten to sixteen (Aurelia).[8]

In 1827, Ursula bought another lot of land in Woodstock and sold her share of the lot containing the shoemaker's shop, contingent on Aurelia selling her share at age twenty-one. Ursula lived on the new parcel until the 1850s, first with her daughter Aurelia (who married in 1830) and with her sister Elizabeth (based on the fact that Elizabeth was with her in the 1850 census and a woman of her age was listed with Ursula in the 1830 and 1840 censuses).

Ursula and the elderly unmarried Elizabeth are found in the census in Woodstock in 1830,[9] 1840,[10] and 1850.[11] In 1850, Elizabeth was listed as head of household, but it was Ursula who owned $400 of real estate – the parcel purchased in 1827.

Quite aged in 1855, Ursula sold her Woodstock lot from Springfield, Massachusetts. She must have just recently relocated there since she was not listed in the *1854 Springfield City Directory*. Her daughter Aurelia and son-in-law Rufus Elmer had relocated to

---

[6] *Woodstock Vital Records*, 356.

[7] Hannah Ledoyt will, Pomfret Probate Books, 13:47-49, 16:141, Pomfret District Probate Court, Pomfret, Connecticut; microfilm no. 5419, FHL.

[8] Ursula Coles household, 1820 U.S. census, Windham County, Connecticut, Woodstock, p. 381:6; National Archives micropublication M33, roll 3.

[9] Lula Cole household, 1830 U.S. census, Windham County, Connecticut, Woodstock, page 390, line 13; National Archives micropublication M19, roll 11.

[10] Ursula Cole household, 1840 U.S. census, Windham County, Connecticut, Woodstock, page 235, line127; National Archives micropublication M704, roll 329.

[11] Elizabeth Amidon household, 1850 U.S. cens., Windham Co., Conn., pop. sched., Woodstock, p. 252, dw. 109, fam. 126.

Springfield in the 1830s.

Ursula's death certificate indicated that she was born in Vermont and had parents John (sic) and Irene Amidon. The fact that her family believed she came from Vermont supports the premise that she had spent some time with her mother and brothers in Vermont. Her father's death well before the birth of her daughter Aurelia (the likely informant) may have contributed to the misidentification of her father provided on the death certificate.

Child of ___ WHITMORE and URSULA (AMIDON) COLE:

12. i. AURELIA[6] WHITMORE, b. Woodstock, Conn., 9 July 1809.

Jacob Amaden Jr. (1774–1819)

6. JACOB[5] AMADEN JR. *(Jacob*[4] *Amidown, Henry*[3]*, Philip*[2]*, Roger*[1] *Amadowne)* was born between 22 February 1773 and 21 February 1774,[12][13] baptized at Dudley, Massachusetts, on 23 July 1775,[14] and died at Tinmouth, Vermont, 21 February 1819 from "a fit in bed."[15] He married at Wallingford, Vermont, on 30 March 1797, CHLOE IVES.[16] Chloe was born at Connecticut between 21 July and 20 September 1778[17] and baptized at Cheshire, Connecticut, on 20 September 1778,[18] the daughter of NATHANIEL and REPENTENCE (WISE) IVES.[19] She died after 29 July 1860.[20]

---

[12] Hance, *Extracts from the Rutland Weekly Herald 1816 – 1820*, typed & indexed by Joann H. Nichols, Brattleboro, Vt. (Rutland, Vt.: D. D. Hance, 2001?). [9 Mar. 1819--Died Tinmouth, eve of Feb. 21st, Jacob Amedown, 44th year.]

[13] *Congregational Church (Tinmouth)*, 257. [A.D 1819 Feb'y 21 - Mr. Amadon aged 45 years in a fit in bed - I preached-]

[14] Jacob Amidon baptism, Dudley Congregational Church Baptisms. *Vital Records of Dudley*, 11.

[15] *Congregational Church (Tinmouth)*, 257.

[16] Marriage Records, 1:124, City Clerk, Wallingford, Vermont.

[17] Ephraim H. Rere (sic) household, 1850 census, Jefferson County, New York, population schedule, Watertown, page 266, dwelling 67, family 76; National Archives micropublication M432, roll 514. Chloe Crossman's age was given as 71 and birth location as Connecticut. Her baptismal record is dated 20 September 1778.

[18] Rev. John Foot, *Congregational Church of Cheshire, Connecticut (1724-1917)*, 12 volumes (Hartford, Connecticut State Library, 1939), entry #590, 2: 26.

[19] Chloe's parents were identified by several factors: (1) Chloe Ives was a witness to a land sale by Nathaniel Ives to Nathan Goshen on 23 May 1796, (2) Chloe named a son Nathaniel Ives, and (3) all of the other Ives men in Wallingford had already come from Cheshire several years prior to Chloe's birth, and only Nathaniel and his brother Lent were left by 1797. Lent's 1790 Federal census already accounts for his daughters, and there was no mention of her in his pension record. Nathaniel Ives married Repentance Wise on 20 August 1771 in *Cheshire -*

After the record of his baptism in 1775, the first record of Jacob was twenty-two years later at a Wallingford, Vermont, town meeting on 7 March 1797, when he was selected Surveyor of Highways.[21]

What happened during the years in between? Jacob and his brothers spent most of their formative years living with their parents in Dudley, Massachusetts, and Woodstock, Connecticut. Near their father's death in the late 1780s, the teenage boys likely joined their uncles Elihu, Jacob, and John Johnson in Rutland County, Vermont. Like their uncles, Jacob and his brothers owned very little land and were likely tradesmen.

Three weeks after being appointed as Highway Surveyor in March 1797, the twenty-four year old Jacob married eighteen-year-old Chloe, the daughter of Nathaniel Ives. William Fox, a Justice of the Peace and town clerk, presided. Their first child, Aurelia, was born the next year. Jacob first bought land in Wallingford in 1800,[22] but sold it the following year.[23] Jacob was listed in the 1800 federal census in Wallingford along with one female aged twenty-six to forty-four (wife Chloe) and one female under ten (daughter Aurelia).[24] He was listed in nearby Clarendon, Vermont, in 1803,[25] on a list of Wallingford residents in 1803,[26] and in Wallingford for the 1810

Connecticut: Town History, 1694-1840. [database online] (Provo, Utah: Ancestry.com, 2001). Original data: Joseph P. Beach. *History of Cheshire, Connecticut from 1694 to 1840,* Including Prospect which, as Columbia Parish, was a part of Cheshire until 1829. (Cheshire, Conn.: Lady Fenwick Chapter, D.A.R., 1877), record 11,052.

[20] Ephraim Bore (sic) household, 1860 U.S. census, Williams County, Ohio, population schedule, town of St. Joseph, page 119, dwelling 383, family 367; National Archives micropublication M653, roll 1052.

[21] *Wallingford Town miscellaneous records 1772-1890,* Wallingford, Vermont, 7 March 1797, undated; microfilm no. 29216, item 1, FHL.

[22] Wallingford Deeds, 3:39 [17 February 1800, Yerra Willaby grantor, Jacob Amidon of Wallingford, Vt. grantee, neighbors included Nathaniel and Lent Ives].

[23] Wallingford Deeds, 3:163 [2 October, 1801, Jacob Amidon of Wallingford, Vt., grantor, Eliakem Johnson grantee].

[24] Jacob Amidon household, 1800 U.S. census, Wallingford, Rutland Co., Vt., page 120/248/254, line 5.

[25] Ronald V. Jackson, Accelerated Indexing Systems, comp., *Vermont Census, 1790-1860* (Provo: Utah: Ancestry.com, 1999). Compiled and digitized by Mr. Jackson and AIS from microfilmed schedules of the U.S. Federal Decennial Census, territorial/state censuses, and/or census substitutes. [Amedwn, Jacob, in 1803 Clarendon, Vt. listing].

[26] Wallingford Deeds, 3:289 – Jacob Ameden was one of forty-four residents supporting the erection of a public house of worship.

federal census.[27] The census shows Jacob living with his family of one female twenty-six to forty-four (Chloe), one female ten to sixteen (daughter Aurelia), and three males under age ten (sons Horatio Gates, John, and Nathaniel Ives). The family was complete three years later in 1813 when Elizabeth was born.

Jacob sold sixteen acres and a house in Wallingford in 1816.[28] Curiously, there is no record of him purchasing this land. It was likely an unrecorded gift from his father-in-law Nathaniel Ives. Nathaniel himself left Wallingford in 1815 to move to Rutland, the county seat. Based on daughter Aurelia's marriage in West Rutland in 1818, Jacob's family may have also removed to the Rutland area for a few years before moving to Tinmouth.

Never owning much land, Jacob was likely a carpenter, as were two of his sons, Horatio and Nathaniel. There is no indication that Jacob served in the War of 1812 or had any other military service. But records for the War of 1812 are extremely weak, and Vermont was so intimately involved that it is hard to imagine how Jacob could have been unaffected by the war.

Jacob's early death in 1819 in Tinmouth at age forty-four caused some disarray in the family. In early 1820, his son Horatio Gates Amaden requested and was placed under the guardianship of Chauncey Thrall of Rutland, Vermont. (This court decree is the first time the family name was spelled Amaden. From then on, all of Jacob's children used this spelling.) Jacob's daughter Aurelia had already married Ephraim Rose. They were married by Chauncey Thrall, a neighbor to Aurelia's grandfather Nathaniel Ives in Rutland, before Thrall became guardian of Horatio Gates Amaden. In the 1820 federal census Ephraim and most of the family were living in Tinmouth. Ephraim Rose's census record accounted for them as follows: one male under ten years old (Nathaniel—ten), one male sixteen to eighteen (Horatio—seventeen), one male sixteen to twenty-six (Ephraim—twenty-two), one female under ten (Elizabeth—seven), and one female sixteen to twenty-six (Aurelia—twenty-two). Horatio apparently had rejoined the family and John may have been

---

[27] Jacob Ameden, 1810 U.S. census, Rutland Co., Vt., Wallingford, page 223/403/115, line 20.

[28] Wallingford Deeds, 4:907 [12 April 1816, Jacob Amedan of Wallingford, Vt. grantor, Seth E. Leonard, grantee].

with his mother.[29]

But where was mother Chloe, and why had the oldest son Horatio requested a guardianship? No answer has been found.

It appears that the Amaden family stayed together over the next twenty-five years. They left Tinmouth around 1822 and returned to Ephraim Rose's home in Granville, Massachusetts, where Ephraim and Aurelia's son Justus Rose was born. After six years, they briefly removed to Troy, New York, where John Amaden married, and then continued on to St. Lawrence County, New York, by about 1828. The whole family resided in St. Lawrence County until 1844 when Horatio Gates Amaden and his family left for Ohio.[30]

Jacob's wife Chloe Ives was likely born in Cheshire, Connecticut, where her family resided. The Ives family moved to Wallingford, Vermont, as some of the earliest settlers in 1779. After Jacob's death, most of Chloe's children were accounted for, but Chloe and her son John's location in the 1820 federal census has not been found. Perhaps Chloe was living with one of her siblings or her new husband. The 1850 Federal census shows that she had remarried to a Mr. Crossman. When her sister Lucinda Ives died in 1841, her will included her niece, the former Charlotte Crossman of Williston, Vermont. Chloe may have traveled with (or later joined) her children to St. Lawrence County, New York, in the 1820s. She may have been the fifty-to-sixty year old woman in son John's household in the 1830 federal census,[31] and again the sixty-to-seventy year old woman in son Horatio's household in the 1840 federal census.[32] Moving on to her daughter and son-in-law Aurelia and Ephraim Rose in Watertown, New York, she appears in the 1850 federal census as Chloe

---

[29] Ephraim Rose household, 1820 U.S. census, Rutland Co., Vt., Tinmouth, page 523, line 13.

[30] Ephraim Rose and Aurelia Rose, widow, Civil War Pension Application File SO 3245, SC 11607, WC 17677; Records of the Veterans Administration, Record Group 15; National Archives, Washington, D.C. Timeline and events provided by the Widow Pension of Aurelia (Amaden) Rose, filed 13 April 1878.

[31] John Amaden household, 1830 U.S. census, St. Lawrence County, New York, town of Morristown, page 191, line 19; National Archives micropublication M19, roll 107.

[32] Horatio G. Ameden household, 1840 U.S. census, St. Lawrence County, New York, town of Parishville, page 266, line 8; National Archives micropublication M704, roll 335.

Crossman.[33]

In 1857, Chloe's daughter Aurelia and husband Ephraim Rose followed Horatio Gates Amaden to Ohio. They were listed in the 1860 federal census as "Ephraim Rose" and "Arvilla Rose", along with "Nancy Rose" — age eighty, all born in New York.[34] The "Nancy Rose" of this very poor census entry is the last record we have of Chloe.

Jacob and Chloe's children were likely born in Wallingford, Vermont. The Wallingford church records, however, are missing. Furthermore, Jacob's land transactions in Wallingford are incomplete (along with a listing in Clarendon in 1803). Hence, it is not certain that they were all born there.

Children of JACOB and CHLOE (IVES) AMADEN:

13. i.   AURELIA[6] AMADEN, b. Vt. 1798.

14. ii.   HORATIO AMADEN, b. Wallingford, Vt., 25 April 1803.

15. iii. JOHN AMADEN, b. Rutland Co., Vt., abt. 1807.

16. iv.   NATHANIEL AMADEN, b. Vt. 1810.

17. v.   ELIZABETH AMADEN, b. abt. 1813.

John Ameden (1776–1839)

7. JOHN[5] AMEDEN (*Jacob[4] Amidown, Henry[3], Philip[2], Roger[1] Amadowne*) was baptized at North Woodstock, Connecticut, on 14 April 1776,[35] and died 28 August 1839.[36] He married at Queensbury, New York, on 16 November 1802 Rachel Sumner.[37] She was born at Vermont in about 1784,[38] and died 23 December 1851.[39] John Austin, a genealogist who studies the old families of

---

[33] Ephraim H. Rere hhd, 1850 U.S. cens., Jefferson Co., N.Y., pop. sched., Watertown, pages 531-2, dwelling 67, family 76.

[34] Ephraim Bore household, 1860 U.S. cens., Williams Co., Oh., St. Joseph, page 119, dwelling 383, family 367.

[35] Baptism book, 1776 April 14th , North Woodstock Congregational Church.

[36] John Ameden tombstone, Lake George Cemetery, Lake George, New York; photographed by Nancy K. Mullen, 1995.

[37] H. P. Smith, ed., *History of Warren County* (Syracuse: D. Mason & Co., 1885), 409.

[38] Alva Nichol's household, 1850 U.S. census, Warren County, New York, population schedule, Caldwell, page 6, dwelling 71, family 74; National Archives micropublication M432, roll 609.

[39] Rachel Ameden tombstone, Lake George Cem., Lake George, N.Y.

Warren county, New York, suggests that she may be the daughter of

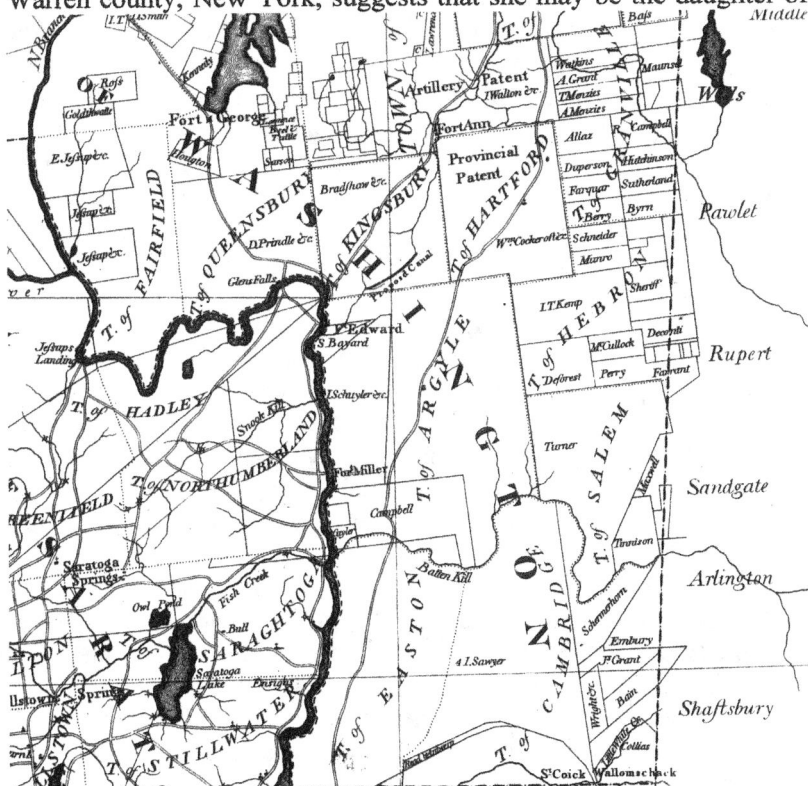

Northeast New York, 1801. Courtesy: Jonathan Sheppard Books

CALEB SUMNER of Fort Ann, or otherwise related to him in some way.[40] Author Chris Amaden suggests that she may be the daughter of DANIEL SUMNER of Wells, Vermont. Family tradition says that Rachel is related to The Honorable Charles Sumner, the anti-slavery senator from Boston who was beaten unconscious by South Carolina congressman Preston Brooks in the Senate cloakroom in 1856. Until Rachel's parents can be determined, any possible connection to Charles Sumner is speculation.

---

[40] Letter from John Austin to Nancy K. Mullen, 19 May 1996; held in 2006 by Mullen.

Caleb Sumner household, 1790 U.S. census, Washington County, New York, Westfield, page 203, line 2; National Archives micropublication M637, roll 6.

John grew up in Woodstock, Connecticut, where he was "orphaned" by the death of his father before he was fourteen. By the 1790 census, his mother was a widow, raising his four sisters by herself. John was not living with them, but where he was in 1790 and 1800 has not been found. It is likely that he was living with his mother's brothers in Vermont. He was definitely in Wallingford, Vermont, on 26 February 1801 when he witnessed two deeds executed by Eliphalet and Sally Jackson.[41]

By 1802 John had moved fifty miles west to New York where he lived out his life. John's descendants believed that the Amedens were descended from three immigrant brothers, one of whom settled in New York, one of whom settled in Vermont, and one of whom disappeared. This tradition may be a corruption of the fact that John and his two brothers left Connecticut, with John settling in New York, Jacob settling in Vermont, and Horatio moving around.

John and Rachel were married in 1802 by Judge William Robards, when John was twenty-six and Rachel was barely eighteen. John's occupation has not been identified but he came from a family tradition of craftsmen rather than farmers. The portion of Washington County that became Warren County is primarily mountainous. Today much of the county lies within the mountain preserve that was established as the Adirondack State Park. Most residents made their living from farming the timber that grew on the mountain slopes. Where mountain valleys were wide enough for farming, the farms focused on cattle and dairy.[42] It is likely that John worked as a millwright or other skilled laborer in the timber industry. In the next ten years, Rachel delivered two girls and three boys. John appears in the 1810 census in Queensbury with two males under age ten (Samuel and Johnson) and two females under ten (Irena and an unidentified girl).[43] Examination

---

[41] Wallingford Land Records, 3:184 & 185, Town Clerk, Wallingford, Vermont.

[42] J.H. French, *Gazetteer of New York State, Embracing a Comprehensive View of the Geography, Geology, and General History of the State, and a Complete History and Description of Every County, City, Town, Village and Locality, with Full Tables of Statistics*, online <www.rootsweb.com/~nywarren/ history/1860french2.html#Top>, printout dated 8 September 2004. Previously published in hard copy (Syracuse: R.P. Smith, 1860).

[43] John Amedon household, 1810 U.S. census, Queensbury, Washington County, New York, page 297, line 22; National Archives micropublication M252, roll 30.

of his neighbors suggests that he lived in the area called *The Oneida* in east central Queensbury. [44]

In 1813, the residents of the northwestern portion of Washington County formed a new county: Warren County. The county took the name of a Revolutionary War hero, General Joseph Warren.[45] When Rachel delivered another boy the following year, he, too, was named Warren.

The year 1814 was a difficult year for the tiny settlements of Warren County. The War of 1812 came to Plattsburgh, New York, on 11 September 1814 with the British invasion of Lake Champlain. The defeat of Napoleon in April 1814 allowed Britain to turn her attention to ending the little war in America. Until 1814, Britain had fought a defensive war with minimal resources. Now the full strength of the experienced army and navy could be moved to North America. The British strategy was to invade New York at Lake Champlain, forcing the northern states to demand peace. Meanwhile the army and navy would bring the war home to the coastal cities, culminating in the seizure of New Orleans to gain control of the Mississippi River.[46]

Plattsburgh lies on the west shore of Lake Champlain, only ninety miles north of Caldwell, then county seat for Warren County. Fifteen hundred healthy soldiers were based at Plattsburgh to combat a British force of ten thousand. Three thousand militiamen from New York and Vermont rushed to Plattsburgh to bolster her defenses. Most of the male citizens of Warren and Washington counties joined the militia.[47] The Battle of Plattsburgh was primarily a naval battle, won by the Americans through the wise strategies of Commodore Thomas McDonough. The land battle fizzled when the British forces got lost trying to find a ford to cross the Saranac River. Coupled with the loss of the naval battle, British General Sir George Prevost decided Plattsburgh was not worth the sacrifices his army would have to make. He retreated to Canada, and the Canadian offensive came to an end.[48] There are no available records that name the men from

---

[44] Letter from John Austin to Nancy Mullen, 10 November 2004; held by Nancy Mullen.

[45] French, *Gazetteer of New York State.*

[46] Harry L. Coles, *The War of 1812* (Chicago: University of Chicago Press, 1965), 151.

[47] [Anonymous], *History of Washington Co., New York* (Philadelphia: Everts & Ensign, 1878), 191.

[48] Coles, *War of 1812,* 170.

Queensbury who fought, so we can't confirm that John was one of them. Since it is reported that most of the men of the county enlisted to defend Plattsburgh, we can assume John did as well. In any event with six small children in the house and fears of Indian depredations in support of the British cause, it would certainly have been an anxious time!

John and Rachel mortgaged part of the north half of lot eleven in Moses Harris Jr's patent to Thomas Jenkins in 1815.[49] This is in an area called *Harrisena* in the northeast part of Queensbury town. No record has been found for John's acquisition of this land; perhaps Rachel inherited it from her father. A depression gripped the local economy in 1815, which may have triggered John's need to mortgage the land. The depression was aggravated by the 1816 weather, which saw ice in every month of the year, including snow in June, thanks to the cataclysmic eruption of the Tambora volcano in Indonesia. While John was not a farmer, the extreme pressure created by the crop failures would certainly have stressed all residents trying to get work in the trades.

John was still in Queensbury in 1820 with two boys under age ten (Warren and Hamilton), two boys under age sixteen (Samuel and Johnson), two girls under age ten (Eliza and an unidentified girl), one girl under age sixteen (the unidentified girl from 1810) and one girl under age eighteen (Irena). John's industry was identified as "Manufactures," confirming that John was a tradesman.[50] In 1824, John and Rachel buried their toddler Almond in Lake George Cemetery in the center of Lake George. At the time, the village was called Caldwell and was the county seat for Warren County. Since there is a cemetery close to Harrisena and French Mountain creates a formidable barrier between Harrisena and Lake George, it is unlikely that John and Rachel were still living in Harrisena by 1824. Transportation was still a major challenge in the region. It was only in about 1820 that the first turnpike was built from Glens Falls to Lake George. It is likely that John and Rachel were living close to the southern shores of Lake George in 1824, by the road that followed the shoreline into Caldwell, or near the hamlet of French Mountain, which lay on the turnpike to Caldwell. An analysis of their neighbors

---

[49] Warren County Mortgages, Book A:524-6, County Clerk's Office, Municipal Center, Lake George, New York.

[50] John Ammoden household, 1820 U.S. census, Queensbury, Warren County, New York, page 205, line 25; National Archives micropublication M33, roll 76.

in the 1820 census suggests they had moved to the north end of what is now called Ridge Road, quite near Lake George.[51]

In 1830 John was still in the town of Queensbury, with a boy who was age five to ten (William), a boy age fifteen to twenty (Warren), a man age twenty to thirty (Johnson), two girls age ten to fifteen (Eliza and the unidentified girl from 1820).[52]

John seems to have adopted the unique "Ameden" spelling before 1802. Judge Robards's marriage record has been transcribed as Amiden, showing the early use of the second "e." The 1810 census calls him Amedon; in 1820 it's Ammoden; in 1830 it's Amidon. The family tombstones say Ameden.

On 8 April 1834, the Court of Common Pleas at the county courthouse in Caldwell found for John Amiden. He was appealing a judgment that had earlier been rendered in favor of Henry Harris.[53] Unfortunately for the family historian, there are no records that describe the dispute.

In 1837-8 another financial crisis gripped the county. Money was extremely scarce, making it difficult to sell goods or services for cash. Business failures were endemic. Many in the county lost everything.[54] Specific records relating to John have not been found, but we can imagine the degree of concern that must have burdened him in the last years of his life.

John died in 1839 at age sixty-three. Rachel survived him by twelve years, living out the rest of her life in the homes of her son Warren[55] and her daughter Irena Nichols.[56] She died in 1851 at age sixty-seven. John and Rachel are both buried in Lake George Cemetery in the center of the village of Lake George, on a hill overlooking the lake.[57]

Children of JOHN and RACHEL (SUMNER) AMEDEN:

18.   i.   IRENA[6] AMEDEN, b. Washington Co., N.Y., 23 Sept. 1803.

---

[51] Letter, John Austin to Nancy K. Mullen, 10 November 2004.

[52] John Amidon household, 1830 U.S. census, Queensbury, Warren County, New York, page 67, line 19; National Archives micropublication M19, roll 111.

[53] *John Amiden v. Henry Harris*, Minutes of Common Pleas, 1813-1854, box 537:329, Warren County, New York.

[54] *History of Washington County*, 198.

[55] Warren Ameden household, 1840 U.S. census, Queensbury, Warren County, New York, page 296, line 13; National Archives micropublication M704, roll 349.

[56] Alva Nichols household, 1850 U.S. cens., Warren Co., N.Y., pop. sched., Caldwell, p. 6, dwelling 71, family 74.

[57] John Ameden tombstone, Lake George Cemetery, Lake George, New York.

19. ii.   SAMUEL AMIDON, b. Washington Co., N.Y., 27 Feb. 1805.
20. iii. JOHNSON AMEDEN, b. Queensbury, N.Y., Feb. 1809.
21. iv.   HAMILTON AMEDEN, b. Queensbury 15 March 1811.
22. v.   WARREN AMEDEN, b. Queensbury abt. 1814.
23. vi.   ELIZA AMEDEN, b. Queensbury 8 March 1816.
        vii. ALMOND AMEDEN, b. 1822; d. 23 March 1824; bur. Lake
              George Cemetery, Lake George, N.Y.[58]
24. viii. WILLIAM AMEDEN, b. Queensbury, N.Y., 28 May 1824.

Elizabeth Amidon (1778– aft 1850)

8. ELIZABETH[5] AMIDON (*Jacob[4] Amidown, Henry[3], Philip[2], Roger[1] Amadowne*) was born between 31 August 1777 and her baptism at Woodstock, Connecticut, on 15 April 1778.[59] She is probably one of the women found in her mother's household in Worcester County, Massachusetts, in the 1790 census, when she would have been twelve years old.

Elizabeth is probably the second woman in her sister Ursula's household in Woodstock, Connecticut, in 1830[60] and 1840.[61]

In 1835, Elizabeth sold land, a house, a barn, and other buildings in Woodstock. This land was formerly owned by the "Widow Jane Weaver, late of Woodstock." [62] This land had been sold to Jane from her son William in 1827. Jane died in 1833 at the age of seventy-two. As with Elizabeth's sister Ursula and her benefactor Hannah LeDoyt, the relationship between Elizabeth and Jane Weaver is unknown. Elizabeth was possibly a nanny and received the land in compensation.

In 1850 Elizabeth, then seventy-two years old, and Ursula, then seventy-eight, were still living together in Woodstock. Although Elizabeth was listed first, it was the older, widowed Ursula who owned real estate. Since Elizabeth was not found in the 1860 census,

---

58 Almond Ameden tombstone, Lake George Cemetery, Lake George, New York; transcribed by Nancy Mullen in July 1994.

59 Baptism book, 1778 Feb 15th Elisabeth Daughter of Jacob Ammedon, unpaginated, Congregational Church, North Woodstock, Connecticut. Birth based on age during 1850 Federal census and baptism date.

60 Lula Cole household, 1830 U.S. cens., Woodstock, Windham Co., Conn., p. 390, line 13.

61 Ursula Cole household, 1840 U.S. cens., Woodstock, Windham Co., Conn., p. 235, line 27.

62 Town Clerk, Woodstock Land Records, Book 20:420, 21:89, Elizabeth Ammidon to Caleb Healey.

she probably died during the decade. Her sister Ursula had relocated near her daughter in Springfield, Massachusetts, by 1855, which suggests that Elizabeth died before 1855. She never married.

Horatio Gates Ameden (1780–1849)

9. HORATIO GATES[5] AMEDEN (*Jacob[4] Amidown, Henry[3], Philip[2], Roger[1] Amadowne*) was baptized at Dudley, Massachusetts, on 4 June 1780,[63] died at Dorset, Vermont, on 30 March 1849,[64] and is buried in Maple Hill Cemetery, Dorset, Vermont. He married first about 1803[65] SALLY BRADLEY. She was born at Vermont in 1784,[66] the daughter of BENJAMIN and HANNAH (MILES) BRADLEY,[67] died at Dorset, Vermont, 9 August 1852,[68] and is buried beside Horatio in Maple Hill Cemetery. He married second between 1816 and 1820 EUNICE (SOUTHWICK) SPOOR. She was born at Williamstown, Massachusetts, on 18 February 1794, the daughter of SAMUEL SOUTHWICK.[69] She died at Dorset on 11 October 1857 from dropsy,[70] and is buried with several of her children in Hebron Cemetery, Hebron, New York.[71]

It is uncertain where Horatio grew up. He is missing from his mother's household in Dudley, Massachusetts, in 1790, when she appears in the federal census with only her four daughters. Horatio was about ten years old at the time. It is likely that Irena sent her sons to Vermont to live with her brothers after their father died.

---

[63] Baptism book, 1780 June 4th Horatio Son of the Wife of Jacob Ammidon, unpaginated, Congregational Church, Dudley, Massachusetts. *Vital Records of Dudley*, 11.

[64] Horatio G. Ameden death record, *General index to vital records of Vermont, early to 1870*, (Salt Lake City: Genealogical Society of Utah, 1951).

[65] Based on the birth of their first child.

[66] Sally Ameden death record, *General index to vital records of Vt., to 1870*. States her age at death as 68.

[67] Letter from Sally Bailey (Wallingford Town Historian, P.O. Box 176, Wallingford, VT 05773) to Grace Ameden, undated; copy held in 2004 by Nancy K. Mullen.

[68] Sally Ameden death record, *General index to vital records of Vt., to 1870*.

[69] Hebron Cemetery Burial Book, in possession of Stacy Niedzwiecki, great-granddaughter of Eunice Ameden.

[70] Eunice Amidon death record, *General index to vital records of Vt., to 1870*.

[71] Eunice S. Spoor Ameden tombstone, Hebron Cemetery, Washington County, New York; transcribed by Nancy K. Mullen, July 1994.

Horatio first appears as a head of household in Wallingford, Vermont, in the 1800 census. He was a male, age sixteen to twenty-six, living alone.[72]

Spirituality must have been an important component of the young man's life. On 21 July 1802, while he was probably still single, he was among those who gathered to form a Congregational Society "for the Support of the Gospel."[73] In 1803 he was appointed one of the "hawards" for Wallingford.[74] Hawards or haywards were responsible for rounding up stray hogs or cattle and fining their owners for allowing them to run free.[75] The role was usually assigned to newly married young men. It was at about this time, 1803, that Horatio married Sally Bradley. The Bradleys were some of the earliest settlers of Wallingford, arriving at the time of the Revolution, and Sally's father Benjamin was active as a community leader. We can hope that he took the young man under his wing and showed him the ropes in the young settlement. The first child, Eliakim, was born in 1804. On 27 May 1808, Horatio stood as a witness to a land sale by Barnabus Swift to Eliakim Johnson.[76]

By 1810 Horatio and Sally had a boy under age ten (Eliakim), and were living next door to her father, Benjamin Bradley.[77] The next year Sally delivered little Eliza who only lived one year. On 10 November 1812 Horatio made his first land purchase, buying five acres from Rufus Richards for forty dollars.[78] In 1813 Horatio was appointed a tythingman in Wallingford.[79] A tythingman kept the drowsy awake in church and ensured no tavern loafers skipped church.[80] At the same time, the town voted to discontinue the road that runs south past William York's land to the land owned by

---

[72] Horatio Amidon household, 1800 U.S. cens., Rutland Co., Vt., Wallingford, page 248, line 12.

[73] Walter Thorpe, *History of Wallingford, Vermont* (Rutland, Vermont: The Tuttle Co., 1911), 86.

[74] *Wallingford Town miscellaneous records 1772-1890*, 8 March 1803, page 44.

[75] Barbara Jean Evans, *A to Zax, A Comprehensive Dictionary for Genealogists & Historians*, 3rd edition (Alexandria, Va.: Hearthside Press, 1995), 136.

[76] Wallingford Land Records, 1762-1854, Book 4:265.

[77] Horatio Ameden household, 1810 U.S. census, Wallingford, Rutland Co., Vt., page 141, line 14.

[78] Wallingford Land Records, 1762-1854, Book 4:646.

[79] *Wallingford Town miscellaneous records 1772-1890*, 2 March 1813, page 69.

[80] Evans, *A to Zax*, 264.

Horatio G. Ameden.[81]

In 1814 Horatio and Sally tried again and had another child, naming her also Eliza.[82]

Two months later on 16 March 1814, seventeen months after buying the land from Rufus Richards, Horatio sold it to Eliakim H. Johnson for forty dollars. But six months later, on 19 September 1814, he bought thirty-three and a third acres from Joel Hall and William Fox Jr. for $250. He mortgaged the land to the men from whom he had just bought it, to cover loans from them of $165. A month later, on 22 October 1814, Horatio bought another twenty acres from Calvin Millins for $130. But four months later, on 22 February 1815, Horatio sold fifty of the fifty-three-and-a-third acres to Benjamin Stephens for $370. Three months later, on 30 May 1815, Horatio bought nine acres from Ebenezer Towner for twenty-four dollars, but sold that land to Jedediah Johnson on 4 July 1815. So after all those transactions, Horatio was left with three and a third acres.[83]

On 19 April 1817, the *Rutland Weekly Herald* reported that Horatio's land in Wallingford was to be sold at auction to pay delinquent 1816 taxes.[84] Was Horatio's inability to pay his taxes a function of "The Year Without a Summer", thanks to the cataclysmic eruption of the Tampora Volcano in Indonesia in 1815?

Sometime between 1816 and 1820, Horatio left Sally, moved across the state line to Hebron, New York, and married Mrs. Eunice (Southwick) Spoor. Eunice had married Elijah Spoor prior to 1812, when their son Sylvester was born. No record has been found of Elijah after 1814.[85] Horatio is seen living in Hebron in 1820 with Eunice, a young woman aged sixteen to twenty-six, and two boys under age ten (Sylvester Spoor and John Ameden).[86] At this time Sally was reported as head of household in Wallingford, living with

---

81 *Wallingford Town miscellaneous records 1772-1890,* 2 March 1813, page 77.

82 Eliza Baldwin death record, *General index to vital records of Vermont, early to 1870.*

83 Wallingford Land Records, 1762-1854, Book 4.

84 Hance, *Extracts from the Rutland Weekly Herald 1816-1820,* 15-6.

85 "My 3rd Great-Grandmother, Eunice Southwick Spoor Amedon," <artistic designs.home.att.net/genealogy/peoplefiles/EuniceSouthwickSpoorAmedon.html>, downloaded 21 September 2004.

86 Horatio Ameden household, 1820 U.S. census, Hebron, Washington County, New York, page 353, line 12; National Archives micropublication M33, roll 76.

an older woman over age forty-five (her mother), a girl under age ten (Eliza), a man aged sixteen to twenty-six (Eliakim) and a boy sixteen to eighteen (Eliakim).[87] Eliakim, sixteen, would have appeared in both counts. The very next year Horatio and Eunice's first child, the boy John, died.

Horatio was a bigamist or was living with Eunice without benefit of marriage, because on 7 March 1825 he executed his right as Sally's husband to control her property, and sold her inheritance from her father's estate, consisting of thirty acres with a dwelling house and five acres with a barn.[88] Two weeks later Sally

Eunice (Southwick) (Spoor) Ameden
(Courtesy: Stacy Niedzwiecki)

bought fifty acres in Dorset from Amos Lewis for $700.[89] The 1830 census shows her living in Dorset with her children, Eliakim and Eliza, and an unidentified child.[90] Her mother had died in 1824.

The year 1830 found Horatio still in Hebron with Eunice and a much larger family: two boys age five to ten (Larnard and Nathaniel) and two girls under five (Jane and Hannah).[91] Sylvester Spoor was not in the household; he may have been working on a neighboring farm. Frances Ann was born that year, and a year later little Hannah died.

On 23 September 1836 Sally bought two more small parcels. One

---

[87] Sally Amadon household, 1820 U.S. census, Wallingford, Rutland Co., Vt., page 246, line 27.

[88] Wallingford Land Records, Book 5:474, 475.

[89] Dorset Land Records, Book 7:177.

[90] Eliakim Amydon household, 1830 U.S. census, Bennington County, Vermont, town of Dorset, page 130, line 13; National Archives micropublication M19, roll 184.

[91] Horatio G. Amadon household, 1830 U.S. census, Washington County, New York, town of Hebron, page 244, line 1; National Archives micropublication M19, roll 111.

was a couple of acres adjacent to her existing property from Henry W. Bell, which was part of the estate of her neighbor Asa Lanfear, for seventy dollars. She also bought another six acres from Henry Bell for $230.[92]

By 1839, the wandering Horatio returned to Sally. On 17 January 1839, Horatio gave his son Eliakim and his daughter Eliza "a certain messuage room in the possession of Sally Amidon ... being all the probate estate belonging to her lying in said town of Dorset."[93] This seems to coincide with Horatio's return to Sally after living with Eunice Spoor Southwick for twenty years. What is a messuage? Not to be confused with our modern concept of massage. A messuage is "a tract of land with the buildings thereon."[94] How Sally acquired this land has not been determined – perhaps it was an inheritance from her mother.

On 4 July 1839, Sylvester Spoor gave a one-acre triangular lot to his mother Eunice, probably as a way to care for her after being abandoned by Horatio. The property was part of lot seven in Campbell's Patent, "lying along the road from the turnpike to Chamberlin Mills." In addition, he gave her a small lot of about one hundred feet by two hundred feet lying along the same road.[95] Perhaps the small lot was the dwelling, and the larger parcel was for farming.

In 1840, the census taker found Horatio and Sally in Dorset. Their daughter Eliza appears to be living with them.[96] Later that year, on 4 November, Sally bought a twelve-acre parcel adjacent to the northeast corner of her existing property from David C. Baldwin. Horatio's return didn't seem to have stopped all of her business ventures. However, it was Horatio who rented that same parcel to their new son-in-law, George Baldwin, on 2 April 1842 for a span of three years. [97]

Eunice appears as head of household in Hebron in 1840, twenty

[92]   Dorset Land Records, 11:548 & 126.

[93]   Dorset Land Records, 11:319.

[94]   *Merriam-Webster Online*, "messuage," see "premises" definition 3, online <www.m-w.com/dictionary/messuage>.

[95]   Washington County Deeds, Book YY:21-3, Washington County Clerk's Office, Fort Edward, N.Y.

[96]   Horatio Amedon household, 1840 U.S. census, Dorset, Bennington County, Vermont, page 221, line 30; National Archives micropublication M704, roll 539.

[97]   Washington County Deeds, Book 12:169, 191.

miles west of Dorset, with all five of her surviving children: a female age five to ten (Frances Ann), another female age ten to fifteen (Jane), two males age fifteen to twenty (Larnard and Nathaniel), one male age twenty to thirty (Sylvester), and one very elderly man age ninety to one hundred![98] Eunice may have needed to convert part of her property to cash when on 15 April 1848 she sold the small lot along the side of the turnpike where her property adjoined the East Presbyterian Society to Thomas S. McFarland for two hundred dollars.[99] The fact that the 1850 census found her living with her daughter Frances lends credence to the thought that what she sold was a dwelling lot.

Horatio did not survive the next decade, dying in 1849 at age sixty-eight. In 1850, Eunice was living with her daughter Frances Ann Parkerson in Hebron.[100] Sally was living with her daughter Eliza Baldwin in Dorset.[101] The 1850 census is the only extant record which calls her Sarah; while Sally was commonly a nickname for Sarah, there is no authoritative record that actually names Sally as Sarah. Sally died three years later and is buried beside Horatio in Maple Hill Cemetery in Dorset. Eunice lived another five years after Sally. She died in Dorset from heart disease and dropsy.[102] We have to wonder what took her to Dorset, the city where her husband's and his first wife's lives ended. Eunice is buried among most of her children in Hebron Cemetery.

Children of HORATIO and SARAH (BRADLEY) AMEDEN:

25. i.   ELIAKIM⁶ AMEDEN, b. Wallingford, Vt., 22 April 1804.

      ii. ELIZA AMEDEN, b. Wallingford 23 Oct. 1811;[103] d. Wallingford 13 Nov. 1812;[104] bur. Green Hill Cem.,

---

⁹⁸ Eunice Amidon household, 1840 U.S. census, Hebron, Washington County, New York, page 171, line 25; National Archives micropublication M704, roll 348.

⁹⁹ Washington County Deeds, Book 18:594-5.

¹⁰⁰ Hiram Parkson household, 1850 U.S. census, Washington County, New York, population schedule, Town of Hebron, page 298, dwelling 1319, family 1416; National Archives micropublication M432, roll 610.

¹⁰¹ George Baldwin household, 1850 U.S. census, Bennington County, Vermont, population schedule, Town of Dorset, page 77, dwelling 153, family 267; National Archives micropublication M432, roll 921.

¹⁰² Eunice Amidon death record, *General index to vital records of Vt., to 1870.*

¹⁰³ Eliza Ameden death record, *General index to vital records of Vt., to 1870.* The death record gives her age as "1 year, 21 days."

¹⁰⁴ Eliza Ameden death record, *General index to vital records of Vt., to 1870.*

Wallingford.[105]

26. iii.   ELIZA AMEDEN, b. Vt., 1 Jan. 1814.

Children of HORATIO and EUNICE (SOUTHWICK) AMEDEN:

iv.   JOHN AMEDEN, b. 2 May 1820; d. 17 April 1821; bur. Hebron Cemetery, Hebron, N.Y.[106]

27. v.   LARNARD AMEDEN, b. Hebron, N.Y., 1824.

28. vi.   NATHANIEL AMEDEN, b. Hebron 1825.

29. vii.   JANE AMEDEN, b. prob. Hebron, N.Y., Nov. 1826.

viii.   HANNAH AMEDEN, b. 30 August 1828; d. 26 July 1831; bur. Hebron Cemetery, Hebron.[107]

30. ix.   FRANCES AMEDEN, b. Hebron 7 Sept. 1830.

Silence Amidown (1783–)

10. SILENCE[5] AMIDOWN (*Jacob[4] Amidown, Henry[3], Philip[2], Roger[1] Amadowne*) was baptized at Dudley, Massachusetts, on 22 June 1783.[108] She was certainly one of the girls in her mother's household in 1790. She may have gone to Vernon, Vermont, with her mother and stepfather, but left her mother's household before 1800. No further record has been found for her.

Irene Amidown (1786–)

11. IRENE[5] AMIDOWN (*JACOB[4] AMIDOWN,, HENRY[3], PHILIP[2], ROGER[1] AMADOWNE)* was baptized at Woodstock, Connecticut, on 11 April 1786.[109] She was certainly one of the girls in her mother's household in 1790. She may have gone to Vernon, Vermont, with her mother and stepfather, but left her mother's household before 1800. No further record has been found for her.

---

[105] Eliza Ameden death record, *General index to vital records of Vt., to 1870.*

[106] John D. Ameden tombstone, Hebron Cemetery, Washington County, New York; transcribed by Nancy Mullen, July 1994.

[107] Hannah M. Ameden tombstone, Hebron Cemetery, Washington County, New York; transcribed by Nancy Mullen, July 1994.

[108] Baptism book, 1783 June 22nd Silence Daughter of Jacob Ammidon, unpaginated, Congregational Church, Dudley, Massachusetts. *Vital Records of Dudley,* 11.

[109] Baptism book, 1786 April 11th Irene, Daughter of Jacob Ammedon, 103, Congregational Church, North Woodstock, Connecticut.

Chapter 3 Sixth Generation

Aurelia (Whitmore) Elmer (1809–1892)

12. AURELIA[6] WHITMORE *(Ursula[5] Amidon, Jacob[4] Amidown, Henry[3], Philip[2], Roger[1] Amadowne)* was born at Woodstock, Connecticut, on 9 July 1809,[1] and died at Chicago, Illinois, on 15 November 1892.[2] She married at Woodstock on 28 February 1830[3] RUFUS ELMER, son of RUFUS and ROXANNA (LEE) ELMER. He was born at Vernon, Vermont, on 29 April 1807,[4] and died at San Francisco, California, on 8 January 1870.[5]

Aurelia was the daughter of Ursula (Amidon) Cole and an unnamed Mr. Whitmore. Prior to her pregnancy, Ursula had probably been living in Vernon, Vermont, with her mother or with her uncles in Wallingford, Vermont. It may have been her pregnancy that sent her to Connecticut, where Aurelia was born. Jointly with Hannah Ledoyt, Ursula bought a home, land, and a boot maker's shop in Woodstock just before Aurelia's birth. Aurelia grew up in Woodstock. She is counted in Hannah Ledoyt's Woodstock residence in the 1810 census. When Hannah died in 1819, she left her home to Ursula and Aurelia, still a minor. Ursula appears in the 1820 census for Woodstock, living alone with a female child age ten to sixteen (Aurelia).

Rufus Elmer's family also lived in Vernon. The family appeared in the 1810 and 1820 censuses.[6] At some point shortly before 1830 Rufus and at least three siblings, Willard, Nelson, and Electa, left their parents in Vernon and established a shoe manufacturing business in Woodstock,[7] likely using Ursula's shop. There Rufus married

---

¹   [Anonymous], *Vital Records of Woodstock 1686-1854* (Hartford: The Case, Lockwood and Brainard Co., 1914), 241, 518.

²   Aurelia Elmer, death certificate no. 00004416 (1892), Cook County Clerk, Chicago, Illinois.

³   Bowen, *History of Woodstock*, 8:481.

⁴   Rufus Elmer entry, Vernon, Vermont, *Records 1763-1901*, Book 1: 503, microfilm 29030, Family History Library, Salt Lake City, Utah.

⁵   Rufus Elmer obituary, *San Francisco [California] Call*, 12 January 1870.

⁶   Rufus Elmer household, 1810 U.S. census, Windham County, Vermont, Vernon, page 384, line 3; National Archives micropublication M252, roll 65.

     Rufus Elmer household, 1820 U.S. census, Windham County, Vermont, Vernon town, page 136, line 1; National Archives micropublication M33, roll 128.

⁷   Rufus Elmore household, 1830 U.S. cens., Windham Co., Conn., Woodstock, p. 388, line 27.

Aurelia. Their first two children, Marshall and Mary, were born in Woodstock. Rufus sold land in Woodstock in April 1836. At about this time a third child, Henry, was born. By the time little Henry died in 1839, Rufus had left the Woodstock shoe business to his brother Nelson. He and Aurelia had relocated to Springfield, Massachusetts, where Rufus was a shoe dealer for the next few decades.

Springfield was developing as an industrial city. Paper was the largest industry, but boots and shoes was the fourth largest industry of the eighteen in Springfield in 1837.[8] Rufus quickly joined The Old Mechanics' Association. The association of master mechanics had been founded in 1824 to develop apprentices by establishing courses and a library for candidates. The annual meetings featured an address by one of the members: Rufus presented the address in 1841.[9]

The 1840 census shows Rufus Elmer living in Springfield with a woman in her thirties (Aurelia), a boy aged five to ten (Marshall) and a girl aged five to ten (Mary). There is also a male in his twenties, probably Rufus's brother Willard. In addition, there are two females in their teens, who could be family members (Rufus's sister Clarissa "Clara" was eighteen and probably living with Rufus.[10]) Mary died in 1842, not yet nine years old. Another son, Francis, was born in 1844 but lived only nineteen months, dying of typhus fever.

The 1850 census shows Rufus working as a boot and shoe dealer in Springfield. With him are Aurelia and son, Marshall, their only surviving child. Also with them were Rufus's sister Clara and her husband Libbeus C. Smith, who was a shoe dealer – probably an employee in Rufus's business.[11] By 1850 Nelson and Willard had followed Rufus to Springfield. Willard boarded with Rufus on Bliss Street in 1855, while Nelson had his own home on Pynchon Street. Marshall was still living at home with Rufus and Aurelia, and clerking in his father's store. Nelson and Rufus were again in business together.[12]

---

[8]   Michael F. Konig and Martin Kaufman, *Springfield 1636-1986* (?: Springfield Library and Museums Association, 1987), 82.

[9]   Mason A. Green, *Springfield Memories* (Springfield, Massachusetts: Whitney and Adams, 1876), 51-8.

[10]   Rufus Elmer household, 1840 U.S. census, Hampden Co., Massachusetts, Springfield, page 30, line 5; National Archives micropublication M704, roll 185.

[11]   Rufus Elmer household, 1850 U.S. census, Hampden County, Massachusetts, population schedule, Springfield town, page 78, dwelling 553, family 635; National Archives micropublication M432, roll 319.

[12]   *Bessey's Springfield Directory 1855-6* (Springfield: M. Bessey, 1855), 75.

By 1852 Rufus was active in Spiritualism. He and a reluctant Aurelia went to a meeting at the home of a local medium, Henry Gordon, and were introduced to Daniel Douglass Home, a medium who was visiting Springfield. After the session, their host left to escort some of the attendees home, leaving the Elmers and a few others with Daniel Home. Aurelia made it clear that she was deeply opposed to Spiritualism. Daniel went into a trance and told her the names of her mother, father, brothers, and sisters, then of her children who had died. He repeated the last words of two of her children. He did the same for other guests still remaining, and Aurelia became a believer. Daniel became a good friend, and stayed with them for some time. He performed six or seven séances a day for large crowds in the Elmer's home. A Harvard University professor came to the home to investigate. His report described movement of a table and other sensations that caused him to state, "We were constrained to admit that there was an almost constant manifestation of some intelligence which seemed, at least, to be independent of the circle."[13]

In 1853, Hampden Hall in Springfield was host to a convention of about three hundred believers. *The Springfield Republican* reported that Rufus Elmer offered a motion to permit the expression of views opposed to Spiritualism, but the convention compromised on a resolution that simply admitted "of a wide private construction."[14]

When the Massachusetts Spiritualism Convention met in Boston in June 1855, Rufus served on the business committee. Elected to serve on the State Central Committee, he was tasked with helping spiritualists in other parts of the country organize a national convention of spiritualists.[15]

Spiritualism was a national obsession between 1848 and 1870. It was a religious movement using mediums, psychics, and clairvoyants to contact the spirit world. It declined after 1870 as charlatans took advantage of the craze, and it became more entertainment than

---

[13]   Daniel Douglass Home, *Incidents in My Life* (N.Y.: Carleton, 1863), 43-51, online <www.harvestfields.ca/ebook/01/068/ 02.htm>.

[14]   "Spiritualist Convention in Springfield, Massachusetts, including notes of a trance anti-slavery skit" *Springfield (Massachusetts) Republican*, Springfield, Massachusetts, 7-9 April 1853, online <www.spirithistory.com /53spring.html>, downloaded June 2006.

[15]   "The Convention in Boston," *Spiritual Telegraph*, New York, New York, 24 June 1854, online <www.spirithistory.com/54mass.html>, downloaded 27 October 2004.

religion. During the height of Spiritualism, women found their first opportunity to speak out on political and social issues, such as slavery and women's rights, from a trance state for which they could not be held personally responsible. As Spiritualism declined after 1870, women began to speak publicly without the cover of spirits.[16]

Rufus was clearly a man of energy, sociable, and likable. In 1855, not content with his business and his activities in the Spiritualist movement, he served on the common council for Springfield.[17]

By 1859 brother Willard had moved out of Rufus's household and was a farmer, living on Mill Street.[18]

The 1860 census shows Rufus working as a wholesale shoe dealer, living with Aurelia, Marshall, and Marshall's wife, Mary, in Wilbraham, a village within the town of Springfield. Rufus must have been doing very well financially, as he claimed forty thousand dollars in personal property, whereas most of his neighbors claimed about one thousand. The valuation probably includes the valuation of inventory in his wholesale business.[19]

Rufus wrote his will in Springfield on 1 September 1869. Soon thereafter, the family moved to San Francisco, where Rufus's death on 8 January 1870 was reported in the *San Francisco Call*. The obituary refers to him as "late of Springfield, Mass.," which implies that he was no longer of Springfield. The probate file refers to Aurelia as both "of Springfield" and "temporarily of San Francisco." The family does not appear in the 1869 San Francisco directory.[20] The 1870 census shows the widowed Aurelia living in San Francisco with Marshall, Mary, and their children.[21]

---

[16] Dwight A. Radford, "From Seances to Ouija Boards," *NGS NewsMagazine*, volume 30, number 2 (June/July 2004): 24-31.

[17] Alfred Minot Copeland, *A History of Hampden County, Massachusetts* (?: The Century Publishing Company, 1902); online <www.rootsweb.com/~mahampde/sp_offic .htm>.

[18] *Springfield, Massachusetts City Directory Listing 1859* (Springfield: Samuel Bowles and Company, 1859).

[19] Rufus Elmer household, 1860 U.S. census, Hampden County, Massachusetts, population schedule, Springfield town, page 297, dwelling 2347, family 2543; micropublication M653, roll 503.

[20] Henry G. Langley, compiler, *Langley's San Francisco Directory, 1868-9*, (San Francisco: Henry G. Langley, 1868).

[21] Marshall Elmer household, 1870 U.S. census, San Francisco County, California, population schedule, 9th ward, page 193, dwelling 1468, family 1679; National Archives micropublication M593, roll 83.

Rufus's will was probated in Springfield, where his will was proved on 21 January 1870. He named Aurelia as his executrix, and left everything to her, explicitly leaving nothing to Marshall, his only other heir. His estate was valued at less than six thousand dollars, a very substantial decline from the forty thousand claimed on the 1860 census.[22] His brother Nelson was still running the shoe business in 1870.[23] It seems likely that Rufus sold his interest in the business to his brother in order to bestow substantial wealth on his son Marshall so Marshall could set up business for himself in San Francisco without waiting for his inheritance.

Rufus was buried in the Masonic Cemetery in San Francisco. With the thousands of deaths from the San Francisco earthquake of 1906 and its subsequent population boom, San Francisco urgently needed space. San Francisco ordered the vast number of cemeteries removed, starting in 1910. On 19 June 1911 Rufus's remains were sent to the Independent Order of Odd Fellows Crematory for cremation, and were re-interred at Woodlawn Memorial Park - Masonic, in Colma, California, on 28 June 1911.[24] The gravestones of the San Francisco Masonic Cemetery were pushed into the bay as part of the foundation of the Golden Gate Bridge.

Rufus was held in proud esteem by his birthplace. The 1891 history of Vernon, Vermont, had this to say about Rufus:

> RUFUS ELMER, son of Rufus, grandson of Reuben and great-grandson of Jacob Elmer, one of the early settlers of Vernon, died at San Francisco, Jan. 8, 1870, of heart disease. A letter states that he was conscious to the last; said he was prepared to die. No man has lived in this city for the last generation who was more widely known, or that had the confidence of the community to a greater degree than Rufus Elmer. He was emphatically a radical on all subjects, generally living ahead of his age and always ready to defend his cause. Those who did not agree with him, could but respect his earnestness and integrity to what he believed right. He was born in

---

[22]   Rufus Elmer, Hampden County probate file no. 3949, will book 43, page 15, Probate Court, Springfield, Massachusetts.

[23]   *Springfield, Massachusetts City Directory 1870-71* (Springfield: Samuel Bowles and Co., 1870).

[24]   Ron S. Filion, *San Francisco History: Masonic Cemetery*, online <www.sfgenealogy.com/sf/history/hcmmas.htm>.

Vernon, moved in early life to Woodstock, Conn., where he engaged in shoe manufacturing.[25]

Aurelia did not stay on the west coast very long. The 1880 census shows her living with Rufus's sister Clara and her husband Libbeus Smith back in Springfield.[26] Her son Marshall left San Francisco in the 1870s and moved to Chicago alone. Aurelia joined him there in about 1884,[27] where she died from influenza on 15 November 1892 at the ripe old age of eighty-three. Her body was sent back to Springfield for burial at Springfield Cemetery.

Children of RUFUS and AURELIA (WETMORE) ELMER:

31. i. MARSHALL ELMER, b. Woodstock, Conn., 5 April 1831.[28]

  ii. MARY ELMER, b. Woodstock, Conn., 17 Oct. 1833;[29] d. Springfield, Mass., 8 Oct. 1842.[30]

  iii. HENRY ELMER, b. abt. 1836; d. Springfield, Mass., 24 May 1839.[31]

  iv. FRANCIS ELMER, b. Springfield, Mass., 11 March 1844; d. Springfield, Mass., 13 Oct. 1845 from typhus fever,[32] bur. Springfield Cemetery.

Aurelia (Amaden) Rose (1798–1883)

13. AURELIA   AMADEN *(Jacob Amaden⁵, Jacob⁴ Amidown, Henry³, Philip², Roger¹ Amadowne)* was born at Vermont in 1798[33]

---

²⁵ Abby Maria Hemenway, *Vermont Historical Gazetteer, A Local History of All the Towns in the State*, volume 5 (Brandon, Vermont: Mrs. Carrie H. Page, 1891), II:302.

²⁶ Libbeus Smith household, 1880 U.S. census, Hampden County, Massachusetts, population schedule, Springfield town, ED 315, SD 60, sheet 2, dwelling 13, family 15; National Archives micropublication T9, roll 536.

²⁷ *The Lakeside Annual Directory of the City of Chicago, 1884* (Chicago: The Chicago Directory Company, 1884), 439.

²⁸ Bowen, *History of Woodstock*, 4: 680-1.

²⁹ Ibid.

³⁰ Clifford L. Slott, *Vital Records of Springfield, Massachusetts to 1850*, (U.S.A.: New England Historic and Genealogical Society, 2002), Newspaper Vital Records, Springfield Republican 1824-1847, Saturday, 15 October 1842.

³¹ Slott, *VR of Springfield*, Book 2 Deaths 1728-1844. The death record says he was three years old.

³² Slott, *VR of Springfield*, Book 4, Births, Marriages and Deaths 1843-1849. The death record gives his birthplace and his age as one year, seven months, two days, from which his birth date was derived.

³³ Ephraim Rose obituary, *Bryan Press*, Bryan, Ohio, 18 March 1875, page 3. Called her one year his junior. See also census records, 1850, 1860, 1870, 1880, cited in subsequent pages.

and died at Hicksville, Ohio, on 9 May 1883.[34] She married at West Rutland, Vermont, on 23 August 1818,[35] EPHRAIM HOWE ROSE. He was born at Granville, Massachusetts, on 21 October 1797, the son of JUSTUS and ADA (HOWE) ROSE[36] and died at Edgerton, Ohio, on 11 March 1875.[37]

Aurelia was likely born and raised in Wallingford, Vermont, where she was counted in her father's household in 1800 and 1810. The family sold their home in Wallingford in 1815, perhaps moving north towards Rutland. Aurelia married in West Rutland in 1818 to Ephraim Rose, a veteran of the War of 1812.

Ephraim had been a farmer before the war, likely on his father's farm. His wife later described him as being five feet four inches tall, having dark hair and blue eyes, with a light complexion.

Ephraim had enlisted from his hometown of Granville, Massachusetts, in June 1813, a few months shy of his sixteenth birthday, as the war was moving from the holding action of 1812 into a fierce battle with the world's super-power. Ephraim served for a year and a half in Captain Chauncey Ives's Company in the Thirty-Seventh Regiment of Massachusetts Infantry, commanded by Colonel Benjamin. This regiment served out of Fort Griswold in Groton, Connecticut. He was discharged at New London, Connecticut, and moved up to Rutland.

When Aurelia's father, Jacob Amaden, died in Tinmouth in 1819, she and Ephraim relocated there and made a home for her young siblings.[38] They lived in Tinmouth for several years. Ephraim served in the militia of Tinmouth, listed in 1821 as the company's fife player. In the same year, Ephraim Rose was a witness to a Rutland land sale by Aurelia's grandfather, Nathaniel Ives. Also witnessing the land

---

[34] Justus Rose letter, Ephraim Rose and Aurelia Rose, widow, Civil War Pension Application File SO 3245, SC 11607, WC 17677; Records of the Veterans Administration, Record Group 15; National Archives, Washington, D.C.

[35] Hance, *Extracts from the Rutland Weekly Herald 1816-1820*, 28.

[36] Christine Rose, *Ancestors and Descendants of Robert Rose of Wethersfield and Branford, Connecticut, Who Came on the Ship "Francis" in 1634 from Ipswich, England* (San Jose, California: Rose Family Association, 1983), 227.

[37] Ephraim Rose and Aurelia Rose, widow, Civil War Pension Application File SO 3245, SC 11607, WC 17677; Records of the Veterans Administration, Record Group 15; National Archives.

[38] Ephraim H. Rose household, 1820 U.S. cens., Rutland Co, Vt, Tinmouth, p. 523: 13.

sale was Chauncey Thrall – Nathaniel's neighbor and justice of the peace who married Aurelia and Ephraim.

The family left the following year for Massachusetts. They went back to Ephraim's hometown of Granville in south central Massachusetts, twenty miles from present-day Springfield. Their son Justus O. Rose was born in 1825 in neighboring Westfield. Ephraim came from a large family, and apparently bonded with two of his siblings. One was his sister Damaris Rose. Damaris married Nathan Knox in 1825 in Granville. Nathan was also a War of 1812 veteran and had recently lost his wife after the birth of their fifth child; he had been an original settler of Russell, New York, in 1806. The other sibling was Ephraim's younger brother Freeman Rose.

From Massachusetts, Ephraim, Aurelia, and family moved to Troy, New York, around 1826 and then up to St. Lawrence County, New York, on the St. Lawrence River bordering Canada by 1827. Why all the way up to St. Lawrence County? Because, that is where Nathan Knox, Ephraim's brother-in-law, had returned after marrying Damaris. The 1830 federal census enumerated them all as living in Morristown;[39] however, they were likely living in Russell which, in 1830, was not enumerated separately. Nathan Knox was an early settler of Russell and owned land only in Russell. Enumerated in the same area was Aurelia's brother John Amaden, housing enough family members to account for the other siblings and their mother. Ephraim and Nathan must have struck up a close friendship because he and Aurelia named one child after Nathan and another after Ephraim's sister (and mother): Nathan and Ada Damaris Rose.

Nathan Rose likely died young since the census records for the family never indicated a second son. Their daughter, Ada Damaris Rose, was represented in the 1840 federal census as a girl five to ten years old. She died suddenly in 1848 at the age of fifteen, in Russell, cause unknown. Their only remaining son Justus Rose lived a long life and looked after his mother in her widowhood.

The family was enumerated in Russell in 1840[40] along with the families of Freeman Rose, Nathan Knox, and John Amaden. Ephraim and Justus were in agriculture and probably worked on Nathan's farm.

---

[39] Ephraim H. Rose household, 1830 U.S. cens., St Lawrence Co., N.Y., Morristown, p. 192, line 9.
[40] Ephraim H. Rose household, 1840 U.S. cens., St. Lawrence Co., N.Y., Russell, p. 262, line 29.

On 25 September 1844, Justus was emancipated from his father in Russell.[41] Since Justus was only nineteen, shy of twenty-one — the age of majority — the emancipation legally meant that Ephraim was giving up authority over Justus. Justus may have wanted to get married, he may have completed a certain amount of work under his father's supervision, or he may just have wanted to start his own business.

In 1846, Aurelia and Ephraim joined the Stone Street Presbyterian Church in Watertown, New York. They lived there for the next ten years.[42] Ephraim was a peddler in the 1850 federal census,[43] and a clothier in the 1855 Watertown directory.[44]

While in Watertown in 1850, Ephraim applied for a Warrant Land Bounty due to his service in the War of 1812.[45] It appears that he was issued Warrant #16898 for 160 acres but never redeemed it. It could be that the land available did not interest him.

The church records stated that Aurelia and Ephraim left on 8 June 1857 for Milford, Ohio, where her brother Horatio Amaden was living. They settled just north of Horatio's home in Edgerton village, St. Joseph Township, Ohio.[46] Their son Justus had been in Edgerton since 1854 and in 1860 was living next door to his cousin Morton Amaden. Both were painters and likely working together.

Ephraim and his wife were well received in their new home.[47] When Ephraim filed for a pension in 1871, two of his neighbors

---

[41] James M. Austin, no article title provided, transcription of *St. Lawrence Republican and General Advertiser*, Ogdensburg, New York, 1 Oct 1844. Online <www.rootsweb.com/~nystlawr/1850_VR_NewsItems.htm>.

[42] *Stone St. Presbyterian Church, Watertown, Jefferson Co., N.Y., 1831-1885* (typescript, Flower Memorial Library, Genealogy Dept., Watertown, N.Y.).

[43] Ephraim H. Rere (sic) household, 1850 U.S. cens., Jefferson Co., N.Y., pop. sched., Watertown, pp. 531-2, dwelling 67, family 76.

[44] *Watertown, North Watertown and Juhelvville Business and Residence Directory for 1855* as transcribed by GenWeb Volunteers; online <www.rootsweb.com/~nyjeffer/1855wcd.htm>.

[45] Ephraim Rose land bounty file #50-160, WT 16898, National Archives, Washington, D.C.

[46] Ephraim Rose household, 1860 U.S. census, Williams County, Ohio, population schedule, St. Joseph township, page 119, dwelling 383, family 367; National Archives micropublication, roll M653 roll 1052.

[47] Justice O. Rase household, 1870 U.S. census, Williams County, Ohio, population schedule, St. Joseph township, page 246, dwelling 229, family 229; National Archives micropublication, roll M593, roll 1282.

testified of his residency and loyalty to the country. When he died four years later, the *Bryan Press* wrote:

> The funeral of Ephraim H. Rose took place here Friday. Mr. Rose has been a resident of this County upwards of twenty years. He was a soldier of the War of 1812, and was the oldest inhabitant of St. Joseph Township, having attained the ripe old age of seventy-seven years. He has been a member of the Presbyterian Church upwards of fifty years. Mrs. Rose is one year his junior, and bids fair for many a year of active duty.[48]

Aurelia filed for and received a widow's pension in 1878. She moved soon thereafter with her son Justus to Hicksville, Ohio,[49] where she died in 1883.

Ephraim and Aurelia are both buried at Maple Grove Cemetery, Edgerton, Ohio.[50] Ephraim lived to age seventy-seven; Aurelia outlived him by nine years and died at age eighty-five.

Children of EPHRAIM and AURELIA (AMADEN) ROSE:

32.   i.   JUSTUS ROSE, b. Westfield, Mass., 6 May 1825.

    ii. NATHAN ROSE.[51]

    iii. ADA DAMARIS ROSE, b. abt. 1833; d. Russell, N.Y., 11 Feb. 1848.[52]

Horatio Gates Amaden (1803–1884)

14. HORATIO GATES AMADEN (*Jacob Amaden[5], Jacob[4] Amidown, Henry[3], Philip[2], Roger[1] Amadowne*) was born at Wallingford, Vermont, on 25 April 1803 and died at Milford, Ohio, on 9 July 1884. He married first CHARLOTTE JOHNSON in 1833.[53] She was born about

---

48   *Bryan [Ohio] Press,* 18 March 1875.

49   J. O. Rose household, 1880 U.S. census, Defiance County, Ohio, population schedule, Hicksville township, page 181C-D, dwelling 229, family 229; National Archives micropublication, roll M593 roll 1282.

50   ?, *St. Joseph Township, Ohio Cemetery Records* (Bryan, Ohio: Williams County Genealogical Society, 1993) 56.

51   Rose, *Ancestors and Descendants of Robert Rose,* 227.

52   Rose, *Ancestors and Descendants of Robert Rose,* 227 provides a daughter named Damaris. 1830 federal census entry for Ephraim Rose gives a girl aged 5-10 years old. *Death Records for Russell, NY,* online <freepages.genealogy. rootsweb.com/stlawgen/MISC/Vital%20Records/1848_russell_death.HTM> provides the death of Ada D. Rose (?), age 15 on 11 Feb. 1848.

53   Best, *Amidon Family,* 136.

1818 in New York[54] and died on 25 September 1846.[55] Horatio married second between 1846 and 1850 ESTHER A. ___.[56] She was born in Pennsylvania in 1812[57] and died about 1880.

Horatio Gates Amaden, known often as "Gates", was named for his uncle who had been named for the Revolutionary War hero of New Englanders for his victory at Saratoga. Horatio Gates Amaden grew up in Wallingford and learned the trade of carpentry. He was counted in his father's household in Wallingford in 1810.

In 1819 when Horatio was sixteen years old, his father Jacob died. The following year Horatio appeared before the Rutland County Court where he requested, and was granted, that Chauncey Thrall be assigned as his guardian.[58] An esteemed member of the community, a lawyer, a justice of the peace, and a member of the Legislature, Chauncey had several connections to the Amaden family. Chauncey was born in Granville, Massachusetts – the same town in which Horatio's brother-in-law Ephraim Rose was born – and came to Rutland County, Vermont, as a young man in 1790. He was the justice of the peace who married Ephraim to Horatio's sister Aurelia Amaden. And he was a neighbor of Horatio's grandfather Nathaniel Ives. Yet Horatio was not enumerated with him in 1820. In the 1820 federal census, Chauncey's household accounted for his sons and no other boys.[59]

Horatio's mother Chloe does not appear in the 1820 federal census as a head of household. It is likely that she had remarried.

---

54   Birth date based on age from cemetery stone – see death citation. Birth location based on her son: John Amaden, Lucas County death certificate #49365, Ohio Department of Health, Columbus.

55   ?, *Center Township Williams County, Ohio Cemetery Records (Inclusive to January 1992)* (?: Williams County Genealogical Society, 1992), 79, "Amadon (last 2 letters uncertain), Charlotte, w/o J. G., aged 28 (broken stone in name and dates) now gone." Row 7 from the road, 1st lot, south to north.

56   Marriage date based on death of first spouse and appearance in 1850 census: Horatio G Ameden household, 1850 U.S. census, Putnam County, Ohio, population schedule, town of Union, page 14, dwelling 24, family 24; National Archives micropublication M432, roll 723.

57   Ibid.

58   Rutland County Probate Book 10:483, Rutland County Probate Office, Rutland, Vermont. Additional data provided in separate folder labeled "Horatio Gates Amaden" dated 10 Apr 1820 located at the Rutland County Probate Office.

59   Chauncey Thrall household, 1820 U.S. census, Rutland Co., Vt., Rutland, page 502, line 1. Sons were Jonathan b. 1794, Chauncey b. 1801, Samuel b. abt. 1808 (died young), Samuel Rowley b. abt 1811.

Instead it is Ephraim Rose's household that seems to include his wife Aurelia and her siblings Horatio, Nathaniel, and Elizabeth Amaden.[60] Horatio, now seventeen, may have been helping with the family, or had simply ended his relationship with Chauncey Thrall.

By 1824, Horatio journeyed with his siblings as they traveled south to Ephraim's hometown, Granville, Massachusetts. Staying for just a few years, they moved west to the Troy-Schenectady, New York, region before arriving in St. Lawrence County on the Canadian border in 1827. The family settled in Russell, New York, where Horatio's brother-in-law Ephraim had family.

In the 1830 federal census, Horatio was probably enumerated in his younger brother John's household. They were listed as living in Morristown, New York; however, they were probably at Russell, which was not enumerated separately. Of the Amaden siblings, John was the only male who was married (when the family was living in Schenectady), which is likely why he was listed as the head of household.[61] The other married Amaden sibling, Aurelia, was enumerated in the same town with her husband Ephraim Rose.

Two years later on 13 September 1832 Horatio enlisted in the United States Army, Second Infantry, Company D, at Sackets Harbor, New York. He was twenty-eight years old and a house joiner by occupation. We learn through his inspection by the Recruiting Officer that he stood five feet eight-and-a-half inches tall, had blue eyes and "ligte" hair, with a fair complexion. His enlistment was for five years, and for that he received a bounty of six dollars. Horatio gave his full name with a birth location of Rutland, Vermont. Although he signed the document twice, his penmanship indicated that he was not in the habit of writing. Military service must not have sat well with Horatio. That December he deserted. The following July he was apprehended. When those cold days of December returned in 1833, he deserted again – no subsequent apprehension was recorded.[62]

---

[60] Ephraim Rose household, 1820 U.S. cens., Rutland Co., Vt., Tinmouth, p. 523, line 13.

[61] John Amaden household, 1830 U.S. cens., St. Lawrence Co., N.Y., Morristown, p. 191, line 19.

[62] "Descriptive and Historical Register of Enlisted Soldiers in the United States Army", surname "A", *New York Army Register Book*, 1832, no page #. *Recruiting Book of Lt K. Bradley, 2nd Regt, Infr, Recruiting Officer*, duplicate #41, entries #4 & 6 - enlistment papers of Horatio Gates Amaden, no page #. Both documents obtained from National Archives. Best reported his enlistment as 1830.

Somewhere and sometime in all this desertion and apprehension, Horatio found time to marry Charlotte Johnson in 1833. This date suggests that Charlotte was only fifteen at marriage, so it is more likely that the marriage was later or Charlotte was born earlier.

There are very few records about Charlotte Johnson. Of her four children, only two had death certificates. Both identified their mother as Charlotte Johnson, with only one providing a birth location for her, of New York. The 1880 census records and later for her children identify her birth state mostly as New York, but a few show her born in Vermont. Her grave marker, now destroyed, had her age as twenty-eight in 1846, implying a birth in 1817 or 1818. Ebenezer Johnson is a likely candidate to be her father.

Ebenezer Johnson's travels mirrored those of the Amaden family. He was born in Rutland County, Vermont, in 1795.[63] His father had moved to Essex County, New York, in the Adirondack Mountains by 1810[64] and settled in St. Lawrence County, New York, by 1820.[65] It is known that Ebenezer married in 1819 to Elizabeth Ryan. But he may have had a first wife who died young. In 1830, Charlotte would have been twelve or thirteen years old. The 1830 federal census has a fifteen to twenty year old girl in Ebenezer's household, perhaps a mistaken age for Charlotte.[66] The link that connects them is that Ebenezer also left St. Lawrence County in 1842 and settled in Defiance County, Ohio. When Charlotte died in 1846, her son Henry lived with Betsey (Johnson) Babbage, the oldest daughter of Ebenezer and Elizabeth (Ryan) Johnson.[67] Regrettably, no other leads on Charlotte's parents have been found.

---

[63] Paul Franklin Johnson, ed., *Captain John Johnson of Roxbury, Massachusetts, Generations I to XIV including the Generations I to IX from the 1932 and 1935 Manuscript of Frank Leonard Johnson, Completed with Additions and Corrections by Ada Johnson Modern, 1948* (Los Angeles: privately printed, 1951), 96.

[64] Comfort Johnson household, 1810 U.S. census., Essex County, New York, Keene, page 28, line 21; National Archives micropublication M252, roll 27.

[65] Comfort Johnson household, 1820 U.S. census, Saint Lawrence Co., New York, Fowler, page 11, line 27; National Archives micropublication M33, roll 79.

[66] Ebenezer Johnson household, 1830 U.S. cens., St. Lawrence Co., N.Y., Pierpont (sic), p. 5, line 4.

[67] William Babbage household, 1850 U.S. census, Defiance County, Ohio, population schedule, town of Hicksville, page 90, dwelling 1206, family 1206; National Archives micropublication M432, roll 674.

Horatio and Charlotte may have had a son born to them soon after they married because a boy of five to ten years old was enumerated with the family in 1840. The 1840 census shows Horatio living in Parishville in St. Lawrence County, New York, with the boy already mentioned and two younger boys (sons Morton A. born in 1836 and Henry born in 1840), a woman twenty to thirty years old (his wife Charlotte), and another woman sixty to seventy years old, who could have been his mother, Chloe. Listing three engaged in agriculture and one in manufacture and trade, the whole family was actively employed.[68] Their last son John was born in New York in 1842. Family notes incorrectly indicate that he came from Watertown, New York, located eighty miles southeast of Parishville, near the east end of Lake Ontario. This may be a merging of facts because Horatio's sister Aurelia and brother John both lived in Watertown for several years after Horatio left New York.

In the 1830s, several trailblazers from St. Lawrence County, New York, explored the wilderness of Ohio and took advantage of government land offers. Word made its way back, and more settlers followed. Among them were the families of Nathaniel Crary, whose daughter married Horatio's son John Amaden, and Ebenezer Johnson, who may have been the father of Horatio's first wife, Charlotte. Horatio and family packed up and moved to Williams County, Ohio, in 1844. They very likely took a steamboat across Lake Ontario, through the Welland Canal, bypassing the impassable Niagara Falls, and through Lake Erie to Toledo, Ohio. From Toledo, settlers would continue their travels by the barely completed Wabash & Erie Canal to Williams County. Williams County was "a swampy wilderness owned by the American Land Company of New York."[69] Although a wilderness, it was expanding. The Wabash & Erie Canal, completed in 1843, connected Toledo and the south of Williams County, which in 1845 split off to become Defiance County. By 1860 railroads had replaced canals as the major transportation means in northwest Ohio.

Soon after arriving in Williams County, Horatio and Charlotte had their last child, Aurelia Nancy Amaden. Charlotte died in 1846 and was buried in Williams Center Cemetery in Center, Ohio. Horatio apparently found foster homes for his children. In the 1850 federal

---

68 Horatio G. Ameden household, 1840 U.S. cens., St. Lawrence Co., N.Y., Parishville, p. 267, line 9.

69 Williams County, Ohio USGenWeb site, online <www.rootsweb. com/~ohwillia/>.

census, Morton was living with RUBEN CISCO and his family in Farmer, Ohio. Henry was with WILLIAM and BETSEY TRIPHENA (JOHNSON) BABBAGE in Hicksville, Ohio. The last son, John, has not been found in the 1850 federal census. Aurelia, often called Nancy, was living with JACOB and ANNA (MILLER) TEEMS. Jacob was a carpenter in Centre, Ohio, where Charlotte (Johnson) Amaden was buried. Probably the family was living there at the time of her death. Aurelia was raised by Jacob and Anna Teems, who had no children of their own. In the meantime, Horatio found a second wife, Esther, and was living with her further south in Putnam County, Ohio.[70]

Returning to the area, Horatio bought two acres of land in Milford, Ohio, and reunited with at least two of his sons. In 1860 the family consisted of Horatio, his wife Esther, and sons Henry and John.[71] The oldest son, Morton, had just married and was living further north in Williams County, Ohio (next door to his cousin, Justus O. Rose). Horatio and sons were all carpenters. They likely built homes throughout the region. That is until the Civil War began.

Undaunted by his own military experience, Horatio permitted his son, Henry, to enlist, at age nineteen, on 29 August 1861 in Milford. He served in Company E, 21st Ohio Infantry, until discharged on 15 November 1864. Eldest son Morton enlisted next on 25 September 1861 and served in Company C, 38th Ohio Infantry, mustering out in July 1865. Horatio's youngest son John did not serve.

As Horatio aged, his occupation shifted. As a young man he called himself a house joiner. Later census records listed him as a carpenter and finally as a cabinet maker.[72] Mrs. Kathleen Walter of Hicksville, Ohio, a great-great-granddaughter of Horatio, has in her possession a hutch made by him inscribed with the name "Gates."

Horatio and his son John had a parting of ways at some point. This break in the family was evident in that John's son Walter Amaden, born the same year Horatio died, did not know his

---

[70] Horatio G Ameden household, 1850 U.S. cens., Putnam Co., Oh., pop. sched., Union, p. 14, dwelling 24, family 24.

[71] H. Amadown household, 1860 U.S. census, Defiance County, Ohio, population schedule, town of Milford, page 391, dwelling 656, family 652; National Archives micropublication M653, roll 947.

[72] Gates Amidon household, 1870 U.S. census, Defiance County, Ohio, population schedule, town of Milford, page 145, dwelling 217, family 218; National Archives micropublication M593, roll 1195.

H. G. Amaden household, 1880 U.S. cens., Defiance Co., Oh., pop. sched., Milford, SD 1, ED 237, p. 7, dwelling 74, family 77.

grandfather's name (but did know his grandmother's name even though she had died forty years prior). Walter wrote in a letter once to one of his cousins, "[t]he father of John and Henry Amaden, I believe, was named John... I never saw him, but have heard my father speak of him. I am told that he had a habit of imbibing quite heavily..." There are no records to indicate that son Morton nor daughter Nancy ever interacted with Horatio after their mother died.

Esther, Horatio's second wife, died soon after the 1880 census. Nothing much is known of her. She was buried in Six Corners Cemetery, Hicksville, Ohio. Her tombstone gives a date of death as 1879. Her presence in the 1880 census suggests that the tombstone was erected sometime later, when memories were getting fuzzy. Horatio sold his two-acre lot in 1883. He likely moved in with his son Henry, who was still in Milford, and died the following year.

Children of HORATIO GATES and CHARLOTTE (JOHNSON) AMADEN:

33. i. MORTON AMADEN, b. St. Lawrence Co., N.Y., 1836.
34. ii. HENRY AMADEN, b. Hermon, N.Y., 8 May 1840.
35. iii. JOHN AMADEN, b. Watertown, N.Y., 20 Jan. 1842.
36. vi. AURELIA AMADEN, b. Ohio, abt. 1844.

John Amaden (1807–1891)

15. JOHN AMADEN *(Jacob Amaden[5], Jacob[4] Amidown, Henry[3], Philip[2], Roger[1] Amadowne)* was born at Rutland County, Vermont,[73] in about 1807[74] and died at Watertown, New York, on 4 May 1891.[75] He married at Schenectady, New York, on 19 November 1826, NANCY FODDER.[76] She was born at Rotterdam, New York, on 2 November 1808, the daughter of ISAAC and EVE (BUCHANAN) FODDER[77] and died at Watertown, New York, on 17 March 1872.[78]

---

[73] Jonathan Pearson IV, transcriber, *Marriages at St. George's Church (Episcopal), Schenectady, NY - 1771-1850*, Cliff Lamere website, online <freepages.genealogy.rootsweb.com/~clifflamere/Mg/MG-StGeorge-Schen-Br .htm>.

[74] John Amilton household, 1850 U.S. cens., Jefferson Co., N.Y., pop. sched., Watertown, p. 280, dwelling 214, family 237.

[75] John Amaden, death certificate no. 1736, Vital Records Section, State Department of Health, Albany, New York .

[73] Pearson, *Marriages at St. George's Church.*

[77] Ancestry.com. *New York Births and Baptisms, Schoharie and Mohawk Valleys, 1694-1906*, online (Provo, Utah: Ancestry.com, 2002). Original data

John was likely born in Wallingford, Vermont, where he was counted with his family in the 1810 census. The family probably relocated to Rutland, the county seat, about 1817, and then to Tinmouth by 1819, where John's father died. John does not appear to have been with his sister and brother-in-law Aurelia and Ephraim Rose, as were his other siblings, in the 1820 census. He may have been with his mother, who likely had remarried. John's marriage in Schenectady corresponds with the travels of his siblings Aurelia (Amaden) Rose and Horatio Amaden. The notes column of John's marriage record listed Rutland, Vermont, for him and Rotterdam, New York, for his wife. Rotterdam is where she was born, but it could have referred to her residence. Likewise, John could have been residing in Rutland.

From Schenectady, John and Nancy moved north to St. Lawrence County, New York, with his siblings. In the 1830 federal census, John was listed as living in Morristown, New York; however, the family was more likely living in nearby Russell, which had not been separately enumerated. In John's household, we find three men whose ages match John and his brothers, Horatio and Nathaniel, and three women whose ages match Nancy, his sister Elizabeth, and his mother Chloe.[79] That would leave only John's sister Aurelia, who was living nearby in her husband's household.

Over the next twelve years, Nancy gave birth to six children. Their birth locations indicate that the family, or at a minimum Nancy, moved around New York a bit. The first child was Aurelia, who was born in St. Lawrence County in 1830. In 1832, their daughter Ellen Louisa was born in Pierrepont in St. Lawrence County. Two years later, son George was born in Oneida County. Back again to St. Lawrence County in 1836 for Mary's birth, the family was residing in Russell for the 1840 federal census.[80] Edwin was born in Pierrepont in 1841. In 1842, their last child Elenor was born in New York.

---

extracted by Arthur and Nancy Kelly of Kinship Publishers from Schenectady Reformed Church, Baptisms, 1694-1811 (Schenectady city, Schenectady).

[78]   *Stone St. Presbyterian Church,* liber G:195.

[79]   John Amaden household, 1830 U.S. cens., St. Lawrence Co., N.Y., Morristown, p. 191, line 19.

[80]   John Amaden household, 1840 U.S. cens., St. Lawrence Co., N.Y., Russell, p. 254, line 20.

Finally settling in Watertown by 1850, the entire family was together.[81] John's occupation was a Dyer (one who imparts a color by dying[82]), something he returned to over the years. In 1855, John became a hostler at the Jefferson County Hotel.[83] As a hostler, he attended to the guests' horses. Soon thereafter he and Nancy ran a boarding house at 24 Public Square, in downtown Watertown.[84] They lived there over the next several years, until her death in 1872.

After his wife's death, John moved in with his eldest daughter, Aurelia, and her husband Edwin Rounds. He took up the trade of soap maker and briefly moved out in 1880. John died at Aurelia's house in 1891 at the age of eighty-four. He is buried alongside Nancy at Brookside Cemetery in Watertown.[85]

Children of JOHN and NANCY (FODDER) AMADEN:

37. i. AURELIA AMADEN, b. St. Lawrence Co., N.Y., Aug. 1830.
38. ii. ELLEN AMADEN, b. Pierrepont, N.Y., 11 May 1832.
39. iii. GEORGE AMADEN, b. Oneida Co., N.Y., 1834.
40. iv. MARY AMADEN, b. St. Lawrence Co., N.Y., Nov. 1836.
41. v. EDWIN AMADEN, b. Pierrepont, N.Y., 10 Sept. 1841.
42. vi. ELENOR AMADEN, b. St. Lawrence Co., N.Y., 1842.

Nathaniel Ives "Amos" Amaden (1810–1872)

16. NATHANIEL IVES "AMOS" AMADEN *(Jacob Amaden⁵, Jacob⁴ Amidown, Henry³, Philip², Roger¹ Amadowne)* was born at Vermont in 1810[86] and died at Grand Island, California, 28 February 1872.[87] He married first LUCIA A. FOX.[88] She was born at New Hampshire in

---

⁸¹ John Amilton household, 1850 U.S. cens., Jefferson Co., N.Y., pop. sched., Watertown, p. 280, dwelling 214, family 237.

⁸² *Merriam-Webster Online*, "dyer" online <www.m-w.com/dictionary/dyer>.

⁸³ *Watertown Business and Residence Directory for 1855.*

⁸⁴ Nancy Amidon household, 1860 U.S. census, Jefferson County, New York, population schedule, Watertown, page 28, dwelling 198, family 195; National Archives micropublication M653, roll 762.

⁸⁵ John Amaden, New York death certificate no. 1736.

⁸⁶ Nathan G. Amadan household, 1850 U.S. census, Saint Lawrence County, New York, population schedule, town of Pierepont (sic), page 389, dwelling 125, family 125; National Archives micropublication M432, roll 590.

⁸⁷ "Three Men Drowned," *Weekly Sutter (Yuba City, California) Banner*, 16 March 1872.

⁸⁸ Martin Amaden, death certificate no. 53955, Sutter County Recorder, Yuba City, California. Cites his mother's name as Lucia Fox.

about 1815,[89] the daughter of JACOB and SUSAN (PARKER) FOX.[90] She died after 1860,[91] and likely before 1865 when Nathaniel married again. He married second at Colusa, California, on 6 July 1865, ELIZABETH PAINTER.[92]

Like his siblings, Nathaniel was probably born in Wallingford, Vermont. There in 1810 his father, Jacob Amaden, was resident with three boys in his household, sons Horatio, John, and Nathaniel. Nathaniel was named after his maternal grandfather, Nathaniel Ives, and was sometimes referred to as Ives. Later in life he was called Amos.

After his father's death in 1819, Nathaniel likely lived with his older sister Aurelia and her husband Ephraim H. Rose. Ephraim's household in 1820 in Tinmouth included a young man Nathaniel's age.[93] Continuing to follow Aurelia, he moved to the Springfield, Massachusetts, area in the early 1820s, up to Troy, New York, for a few years, finally settling in St. Lawrence County, New York, by 1827. In 1830, he was likely living in his brother John Amaden's large household of six people, all enumerated as living in Morristown,[94] but more likely living in nearby Russell (see a more detailed discussion of Russell in Aurelia Amaden's biography number 13 above).

Lucia Fox's family lived in Parishville, New York – only twenty-four miles from Russell on the historic St. Lawrence Turnpike, a road built in response to the War of 1812 to transport ordnance parallel to the St. Lawrence River. This turnpike connected several key towns where Amaden families lived: Parishville, Pierrepont, Russell, Hermon, and Watertown.

---

    89   Nathan G. Amadan household, 1850 U.S. cens., St. Lawrence Co., N.Y., pop. sched., Pierepont (sic), p. 389, dwelling 125.
    90   George Henry and Clarrisa (Grang) Fox, *Fox Family Records*, Fayette County Iowa Genalogical Society.
    91   N. I. Anderson household, 1860 U.S. census, Fayette County, Iowa, population schedule, town of Westfield, page 188, dwelling 1451, family 1244; National Archives micropublication M653, roll 322.
    92   Amaden-Painter marriage record, Colusa County Marriage Records Book A:77, Recorder's Office, Colusa, California.
    93   Ephraim Rose household, 1820 U.S. cens., Rutland Co., Vt., Tinmouth, p. 523, line 13.
    94   John Amaden household, 1830 U.S. cens., St. Lawrence Co., N.Y., Morristown, p. 191, line 19.

Nathaniel and Lucia married when Lucia was about seventeen. They welcomed their first daughter, Beulah E. Amaden, to the family in about 1833. Nathaniel and Lucia lived in Parishville for the next several years where he rented land.[95] The 1840 census shows the family in Parishville with Beulah and a young boy, likely a son who died young.[96] Four houses away lived Lucia's brother, Stephen Fox and his young wife.

Their next child, Almira, came in April of 1841, followed by Albert Allen in 1844, and Stephen in 1848. Stephen was born in Pierrepont. His birth was recorded during a two-year experiment in New York State for recording vital records in 1847 and 1848. The growing family was seen in Pierrepont in the 1850 census with Nathaniel listed as a carpenter and the older children, Beulah, Almira, and Albert, attending school.[97]

Lucia's brothers Daniel, Stephen, and Lyman Fox left St. Lawrence County in 1849 and settled in Franklin, Illinois. Nathaniel and his family soon followed; their son Martin Eugene was born in Illinois on 13 September 1851. The following year, Lucia's parents and remaining siblings joined the growing throng in Illinois.

All of these families removed from Franklin to Westfield Township, Iowa, in 1855 and 1856. The Iowa 1856 state census shows the Amaden family having just arrived in Westfield. Nathaniel's young son Stephen, who was not listed, had likely died.[98] Nathaniel was still carrying on the carpentry trade.

Still in Westfield in 1860, their daughter Almira had married and was living next door with her husband, George Walker, and children from his first marriage. Nathaniel was now employed as a farmer. Their oldest daughter, Beulah, age twenty-five, was still with them. The census taker recorded Nathaniel's surname as Anderson, but his census data, recording the presence of wife Lucia "Lucy," daughter Beulah, and sons Albert "N. A.," and Martin in the household, and the

---

[95] Mary Smallman, transcriber, *Parishville Land Office Book*, File #25, St. Lawrence County Historian, St. Lawrence County Historical Society, Canton, N.Y.

[96] Nathaniel I. Amaden household, 1840 U.S. cens., St. Lawrence Co., N.Y., Parishville, page 268, line 11.

[97] Nathan G. Amandan household, 1850 U.S. cens., St. Lawrence Co., N.Y., pop. sched., Pierepont (sic), page 389, dwelling 125, family 125.

[98] N. J. Amadan household, 1856 Iowa state census, Fayette County, town of Westfield, item #137; transcribed in letter from Fayette County Genealogical Society, West Union, Ia.

proximity of Almira next door make it clear that this is our Nathaniel.[99]

Soon after the Civil War unleashed its fury in 1861, Nathaniel's daughter, Almira, and her husband, George Walker, left Iowa behind for the lure of Sutter County, California. Nathaniel and his family followed within two years. Sometime in the early 1860s, Nathaniel's wife Lucia died.

Not much is known of Nathaniel's second wife Elizabeth Painter, except for their marriage record from 1865. Nathaniel was without a wife in the 1870 census, when he was living alone with J. W. Welch, probably the farmer who employed him.[100] Living in nearby Butte County, there was an apparently unmarried head-of-household named Eliza Painter from Kentucky, who was Nathaniel's age.[101] Had they tried marriage, and given it up within five years? When Nathaniel died in 1872, he was identified as a widower.

When George and Almira Walker moved to Grand Island, west of Yuba City on the Sacramento River, Nathaniel moved in with them. The events surrounding his death in 1872 are captured in this article from the *Weekly Sutter Banner*:

> Three Men Drowned. - Three men, formerly residents of this county, named Amos Amaden, William C. Smith, and Charles Roff, were drowned in the Sacramento at Grand Island on February 28th. It appears they had constructed a raft to cross the river and obtain provisions, of which they were out. The river being high and the current very strong, the raft, in some manner broke in pieces, leaving the unfortunate men devoid of any possible means to escape the death which so evidently stared them in the face. Mr. Roff was a painter by occupation, and while in this place was married to

---

[99] N. J. Anderson household, 1860 U.S. census, Fayette County, Iowa, population schedule, town of Westfield, page 188, dwelling 1451, family 1244; National Archives micropublication M653, roll 322.

[100] J. W. Welch household, 1870 U.S. census, Sutter County, California, population schedule, town of Butte, page 90, dwelling 39, family 32; National Archives micropublication M593, roll 92.

[101] Eliza Painter household, 1870 U.S. cens., Sutter Co., Calif., pop. sched., Butte, page 13, dwelling 169, family 150.

Mrs. Walker, a widow with two children, who have since resided at Grand Island. Mr. Amaden, a widower, and father-in-law of Roff, made his home at the residence of his daughter. He has two sons, one living in this county. Mr. Smith leaves a wife and seven or eight children. Some years ago he kept Tule House on Butte Slough, but for a long time has resided in Bear Valley. Both families are left in poor circumstances. It is hoped the warm hand of Charity will be extended to them.[102]

Children of NATHANIEL IVES and LUCIA (FOX) AMADEN:
  i.   BEULAH E. AMADEN, b. N.Y., abt. 1833;[103] d. 1860-72.[104]
43. ii. ALMIRA AMADEN, b. prob. Parishville, N.Y., April 1841.
44. iii. ALBERT AMADEN, b. N.Y., 7 April 1844.
  iv. STEPHEN A. AMADEN, b. Pierrepont, N.Y., 6 May 1848;[105] d. bet. 1850-1856.[106]
45. v. MARTIN AMADEN, b. prob. Franklin, Ill., 13 Sept. 1851.

Elizabeth C. "Eliza" (Amaden) Axtell (abt 1813 - 1856)

17. ELIZABETH C. "ELIZA" AMADEN *(Jacob Amaden[5], Jacob[4] Amidown, Henry[3], Philip[2], Roger[1] Amadowne)* was born about 1813, and died at Lisbon, New York, on 22 February 1856.[107] She married HENRY EDWIN AXTELL on 5 October 1836.[108] He was born at Pierrepont, New York, on 5 August 1814, son of HENRY and SARAH T. (WOODRUFF) AXTELL,[109] and died at Lisbon on 24 May 1890.[110]

---

¹⁰² *Weekly Sutter (Yuba City, Calif.) Banner,* 16 March 1872.
¹⁰³ Nathan G. Amadan household, 1850 U.S. cens., St. Lawrence Co., N.Y., pop. sched., Pierepont (sic), page 389, dwelling 125, family 125.
¹⁰⁴ N. J. Anderson household, 1860 U.S. cens., Fayette Co., Ia., pop. sched., Westfield, page 188, dwelling 1451, family 1244.
   Weekly Sutter (Yuba City, Calif.) Banner. Death range provided by 1860 census and 1872 obituary of father.
¹⁰⁵ Mary Smallman, St. Lawrence County Historian.
¹⁰⁶ Death range provided by presence in 1850 federal census (cited above), but not in 1856 Iowa State census or subsequent federal censuses.
¹⁰⁷ James M. Austin, transcription of vital records from *St. Lawrence Republican and General Advertiser,* Ogdensburg, New York, 26 February 1856. Online <www.rootsweb.com/~nystlawr/1860_VR_ViTALS.htm>.
¹⁰⁸ Carson A. Axtell, compiler, *Axtell Genealogy* (Fairhaven, Mass.: The Darwin Press, 1945), 78-79.
¹⁰⁹ Ibid.

Eliza's birth location is uncertain. All records indicate that her parents were residing in Wallingford, Vermont, at the time of her birth, but her 1850 census entry and her children's 1880 census entry placed her birth in New York.

Eliza's early life must have been spent moving from town to town. Her father Jacob died in Tinmouth, Vermont, when she was but six years old. Her older sister Aurelia had already married Ephraim Rose, and they apparently took in most of the family after Jacob's death. The 1820 census shows this large family living in Tinmouth, including a young girl under ten years old, likely Eliza.[111] Over the next several years, the Rose family moved south to the Springfield, Massachusetts, area, then up to Troy, New York, finally settling in St. Lawrence County, New York, by 1827.

By 1830, Eliza's brother John had married. Eliza was likely enumerated in his large household, which was listed in Morristown, but was quite likely the town of Russell (see Aurelia Amaden's entry number thirteen, page 59, for further discussion on Russell).[112]

Eliza's future husband, Henry Axtell, was living in nearby Pierrepont, New York. Early in life, he went by his middle name Edwin, probably to prevent confusion with his father Henry. The Axtell family came to Pierrepont in 1813 in an ox-drawn carriage from Pittsford, Vermont. According to the *Axtell Genealogy*, Henry and Eliza married on 5 October 1836.[113] This book contains several errors in the years for Henry's family's vital records (although month and day were often correct), and it is suspected that this is the case with this marriage because their daughter Frances was born 30 August 1836 in Lisbon, New York. Over the next ten years, Henry and Eliza had four additional children.

By 1840, the family had removed to Antwerp, New York, where their daughter Addie was born. The family owned land in Lisbon, but spent much of their time in Moriah, near the Vermont border. They

---

[110] Henry Axtell entry, Lisbon Vermont Town Clerk, *Register of Births, Deaths and Marriages in the town of Lisbon, St. Lawrence County, New York* (Lisbon, N.Y.: Registrar of Vital Statistics, 1981); microfilm 1311926, FHL, Salt Lake City, Utah.

[111] Ephraim Rose household, 1820 U.S. cens., Rutland Co., Vt., Tinmouth, p. 523, line 13.

[112] John Amaden household, 1830 U.S. cens., St. Lawrence Co., N.Y., Morristown, p. 191, line 19.

[113] Axtell, *Axtell Genealogy*, 78-79.

were living there in the 1850 federal census; Henry was employed as a teamster.[114] No record of the purchase of the Moriah property has been found, but the three-quarter acre lot was sold in 1851.[115] The family removed to Lisbon.

The family faced several tragedies in the 1850s. Their son, Harlon, died in 1852, followed by the death of another son, John. Then, Elizabeth died in 1856 as explained in this excerpt from the *St. Lawrence Republican* newspaper,

> Upon sitting at the breakfast table, [she] grasped her head and said "It seems as if my head would burst" and died of apoplexy 2 hours later.[116]

Apoplexy is an old medical term, often meaning stroke.[117] Her death was soon followed by that of their youngest son, Henry, in 1857.

Henry remarried to ABIGAIL H. (RAYMOND) ALDRICH,[118] widow of DANFORTH ALDRICH.[119] Abigail was born in New York on 9 August 1819, the daughter of JOHN RAYMOND.[120] Their marriage date of 5 September 1854 from *Axtell Family* is likely early by two years (neither first spouse had died); and, Henry, alone, bought a farm, mill, and farm house in Moriah in June 1856. He, along with his wife Abigail, sold the lot two years later, with a two-year lease clause for his son-in-law Hubbard Chapman.[121]

Henry and Abigail returned to Lisbon and lived out the rest of their years there. They adopted several children and always kept a very full house. Henry died in 1890. By this time his only biological child still living was his eldest daughter Frances. The burial place for Elizabeth and her young sons has not been located, but Henry and

---

114 Edwin Axtell household, 1850 U.S. census, Essex County, New York, population schedule, town of Moriah, page 32, dwelling 450, family 497; National Archives micropublication M432, roll 503.

115 Essex County Deeds, Book KK:44, County Clerk, Elizabethtown, N.Y.

116 Elizabeth Axtell obituary, *St. Lawrence Republican*, Ogdensburg, N.Y., 26 February 1856.

117 *Merriam-Webster Online*, "apoplexy."

118 Axtell, *Axtell Genealogy, 78-79.*

119 Aldrich, *George Aldrich Genealogy.*

120 Elizabeth Axtell death cert. #1081, Lisbon Vt, *Births Deaths & Marriages.*

121 Essex County, New York Deeds, Book RR: 233-234.

Abigail are buried at White Church Cemetery in Lisbon.[122]
Children of HENRY and ELIZA (AMADEN) AXTELL:

46. i. FRANCES AXTELL, b. Lisbon, N.Y., 30 Aug. 1836.

ii. HENRY EDWIN AXTELL, b. N.Y, 30 Aug. 1838, d. 25 Dec. 1857.[123]

47. iii. ADDIE AXTELL, b. Antwerp, N.Y., 12 July 1840.

iv. HARLON W. AXTELL, b. N.Y., 10 Jan. 1843, d. Aug. 1852.[124]

v. JOHN H. AXTELL, b. N.Y., abt. 1846,[125] d. abt. 1850-56.[126]

Irena (Ameden) Nichols (1803–1884)

18. IRENA AMEDEN (John[5], Jacob[4] Amidown, Henry[3], Philip[2], Roger[1] Amadowne) was born at Washington County, New York, on 23 September 1803, and died on 19 February 1884.[127] She married ALVA NICHOLS, who was born in New York in 1801 or 1802[128] and died on 24 February 1853.[129]

Irena grew up in the town of Queensbury, New York. She is surely one of the girls shown in her father's household in 1810 and again in 1820.

Alva's birthplace has not been identified. But he was in Caldwell by 1822 when he was convicted of grand larceny on the oath of John Elliot, dated 26 February. He was fined three dollars.[130]

Irena and Alva probably married before 1829. In January 1829 Martha Jane was born. In 1830 Alva and Irena appear in the census with two girls under age five, living in Caldwell,[131] which is a town

---

122 St. Lawrence County Historical Association, *Lisbon, New York Cemeteries* (typescript by St. Lawrence County Historical Association); microfilm 1451080, FHL, Salt Lake City, Utah.

123 Axtell, *Axtell Genealogy*, 78-79.

124 Ibid.

125 Edwin Axtell household, 1850 U.S. cens., Essex Co., N.Y., pop. sched., Moriah, page 32, dwelling 450, family 497.

126 *St. Lawrence Republican*, 26 Feb. 1856. John's mother's obituary indicates that only three children survived her, and John does not appear in the 1860 census with his father.

127 Irena Nichols tombstone, Lake George Cem., Lake George, N.Y.

128 Alva Nichols household, 1850 U.S. cens., Warren Co., N.Y., pop. sched., Caldwell, page 6, dwelling 71, family 74.

129 Alva Nichols tombstone, Lake George Cem., Lake George, N.Y.

130 *John Elliott v. Alva Nichols*, Minutes of Common Pleas, 1813-1854, Warren County, New York; John Austin's letter to Nancy Mullen, 19 May 1996.

131 Alva Nichols hhd, 1830 U.S. cens., Warren Co., N.Y., Caldwell, p. 24, ln 3.

adjacent to Queensbury where Irena had grown up. The second girl has not been identified. She could have been born as early as 1825, or as late as 1830. She is probably a daughter, but not necessarily so. This 1830 census may have been about the time that Alva leased a small lot on the Plank Road just south of the village of Caldwell from William Caldwell. The village was named for William's father, General James Caldwell, who was the patentee for almost sixteen hundred acres in the area.[132] It was he who led the first band of settlers into the area and established lumbering, tanning and farming as the early industries.[133]

Alva's lot measured just one hundred feet on a side. The lease is not recorded, but is only referenced in a later deed, which will be discussed later. As the Plank Road moved north into the village, it was called Canada Street. Irena's sister Eliza Ann and her husband Horace Welch bought a lot diagonally opposite from Irena on Canada Street in 1867.

Irena and Alva remained on their small lot in Caldwell. In about 1832 Irena bore a third daughter, Ann. In about 1835 Oscar was born. On 25 November 1838 little Martha Jane died. In that same year Alva was assessed for two and one-half days' work by highway district fifteen of Caldwell.[134]

The 1840 census shows the family with a boy aged five-ten (Oscar), a girl aged five-ten (Ann) and a girl ten-fifteen (the unnamed older daughter).[135] The family was complete in about 1843 with the birth of another daughter, Adelia.

By 1850, Alva had still not acquired a trade and appears as a "laborer." Irena's father had died, and her widowed mother, Rachel Ameden, was living with them in Caldwell. The oldest girl was gone from the household, probably by death or marriage, since there is no subsequent record of her. Ann had married and left home. The two younger children, Oscar and Adelia, were still living with their

---

[132] Smith, *History of Warren County*, 565-6.

[133] ?, *Warren County, A History and Guide* (Glens Falls, N.Y.: Warren County Board of Supervisors, 1942), 166.

[134] John Austin, "Re: Ameden genealogy," email message to Nancy K. Mullen, 16 July 2005.

[135] Alva Nichols household, 1840 U.S. cens., Warren Co., N.Y., Caldwell, p. 361, ln. 1.

parents.[136] One year later, Rachel Ameden died. Two years later, when Adelia was only nine or ten years old, and Oscar was only seventeen, Alva died. He is buried in Lake George Cemetery, in Caldwell village, now Lake George, New York.[137] We can only imagine Irena Nichol's grief at losing first her mother, then her husband in such a short span of time.

Somehow Irena acquired one hundred fifty dollars over the year following Alva's death. On 9 June 1854 she bought from Catherine E. Van Cartland and Hildur Louisa Parmalee the small lot where they had lived since Alva had leased it from William Caldwell.[138] The 1855 state census shows the widowed Irena living there with her two younger children, working as a washer-woman.[139]

Irena continued to live with her children, Oscar and Adelia, for the next decade. Hers was one of the poorest families in the neighborhood, with only five hundred dollars in real estate and one hundred dollars in personal property on the 1860 census.[140] Irena's real estate was her lot on the Plank Road.

By 1870, both children had married. Irena divided her small lot on 3 August 1870, giving the north half to Oscar at the future time of Irena's death.[141] The south half, with the house, she gave to Adelia, with the stipulation that "Irena shall be given a home by said Adelia, that Adelia provide food, raiment, care and medical assistance to Irena suitable to her station in life for her natural life."[142] Oscar had become a carpenter and built a home on his new property. Adelia provided her mother with two grandchildren very close at hand.[143] Three years later, on 26 May 1873, Oscar decided to transfer title of

---

136 Alva Nichols household, 1850 U.S. cens., Warren Co., N.Y., pop. sched., Caldwell, p. 6, dwelling 71, family 74.

137 Alva Nichols tombstone, Lake George Cem., Lake George, N.Y.

138 Warren County Deeds, Book V:379.

139 Irena Nichols household, 1855 New York state census, Warren County, Caldwell township, household 35; reported by John Austin, "Re: Ameden genealogy," email message to Nancy K. Mullen, 16 July 2005.

140 Irena Nichols household, 1860 U.S. census, Warren County, New York, population schedule, Caldwell town, page 14, dwelling 106, family [blank]; National Archives micropublication M653, roll 873.

141 Warren County Deeds, Book 22:239-40.

142 Warren County Deeds, Book 22:235-6.

143 Irena Nichols household, 1870 U.S. census, Warren County, New York, population schedule, Caldwell town, page 4, dwelling 24, family 21; National Archives micropublication M593, roll 1109.

his property to his wife. This was accomplished by selling the land to his mother for one hundred dollars.[144] She immediately sold it to Oscar's wife, Emma, on the same day for the same amount.[145]

Something persuaded Irena to remove the contingency on her gift of the land and house to Adelia. On 20 September 1875 Irena executed a new deed, giving the house and land to Adelia without the conditions earlier associated with the gift.[146]

By 1880 Irena was seventy-six years old and was still being cared for by Adelia, who now had three children.[147] Oscar continued to live next door, and now had one child. Irena lived to be eighty years old. She is buried in Lake George Cemetery.[148]

Children of ALVA and IRENA (AMEDEN) NICHOLS:

    i.   Prob. FEMALE NICHOLS, b. 1825-30.[149]

    ii. MARTHA JANE NICHOLS, b. abt. Jan. 1829, d. 25 Nov. 1838, bur. Lake George Cem.[150]

48. iii. ANN NICHOLS, b. prob. Lake George, N.Y., 21 Oct. 1831.

49. iv. OSCAR NICHOLS, b. N.Y., March 1836.

50. v. ADELIA NICHOLS, b. Caldwell, N.Y., July 1843.

Samuel Amidon (1805–1876)

19. SAMUEL AMIDON (John Ameden[5], Jacob[4] Amidown, Henry[3], Philip[2], Roger[1] Amadowne) was born in Washington County, New York, on 27 February 1805.[151] He died at New Lisbon, Wisconsin, on 12 June 1876.[152] He married first HANNAH _____. She was born at Fort Ann, New York, on 9 March 1808.[153] She died on 17 May

---

144 Warren County Deeds, Book 27:99-100.

145 Warren County Deeds, Book 27:113-4.

146 Warren County Deeds, Book 31:106.

147 Orville Lockwood household, 1880 U.S. census, Warren County, New York, population schedule, Caldwell town, ED 112, SD 6, page 18, dwelling 213, family 213; National Archives micropublication T9, roll 941.

148 Irena Nichols tombstone, Lake George Cem., Lake George, N.Y.

149 Alva Nichols hhd, 1830 U.S. cens, Warren Co., N.Y., Caldwell, p. 24.
    Alva Nichols hhd, 1840 U.S. cens, Warren Co, N.Y., Caldwell, p. 361.

150 Martha Jane Nichols tombstone, Lake George Cem., Lake George, N.Y.

151 Samuel Amidon tombstone, New Lisbon City Cemetery, New Lisbon, Wisconsin, transcribed by Nancy Mullen, December 2001. "Age seventy-one years, three months, sixteen days."

152 Samuel Amidon death notice, *The Mauston Star*, Mauston, Wisconsin, 22 June 1876, page 1, column 6.

153 Hannah Amidon tombstone, New Lisbon City Cemetery, New Lisbon, Wisconsin. "Age sixty-one years, two months, eight days."

1869,[154] probably in New Lisbon. Samuel married second at Jefferson County, Wisconsin, on 14 April 1870, MARIETTE (SHELDON) SLOCUM. She was born probably at Queensbury, New York in about 1816, the daughter of SENECA and ABIGAIL (__) SHELDON.[155] She died at Hood River, Oregon, in 1879.[156]

Samuel grew up in the town of Queensbury, New York. At his birth Queensbury was in the western part of Washington County. In 1813 the western part of the county split off and became Warren County. Samuel appears in his father's household in 1810 and again in 1820. In 1824 when he was nineteen years old Samuel left home and settled in the town of Fort Ann in Washington County.[157] On 11 May 1829 he and Isaac Finch bought from Asahel Potter interests in two leases held by Ephraim Griscel for eight hundred dollars each: a one-half acre lot in Fort Ann, Washington County, renting for six dollars annually for 999 years;[158] and a one-fourth acre lot in Fort Ann renting for $10.50 annually for 999 years.[159] He does not appear in the 1830 census in Fort Ann; he was probably boarding with a Fort Ann family.

He and Isaac Finch were successfully sued by Eliphalet D. Mattison in 1832. They appealed the decision, but the extant minutes of the Court of Common Pleas record that the decision for Mattison was upheld on 7 December 1832. Unfortunately, the minutes do not record the nature of the dispute.[160]

A year later, on 1 June 1833, Samuel and Isaac sold interest in two different leases to Asahel Potter and Morris Grant: one for land in the village of Salem, New York, for four hundred twenty-five dollars, and

----

154 Ibid.
155 Samuel Amidon household, 1870 U.S. census, Juneau County, Wisconsin, population schedule, New Lisbon village, page 84, dwelling 112, family 119; National Archives micropublication M593, roll 1720.
156 Donna Wilson, "Re: Marietta Sheldon," email to Christopher D. Amaden, 12 September 2005.
157 Samuel Ammidon household, 1855 New York state census, Washington County, Fort Ann township, microfilm roll 1, page 64. States Samuel had lived in town of Fort Ann for thirty-one years.
158 Washington County Deeds, Book AA:440-2.
159 Washington County Deeds, Book AA:442-4.
160 *Isaac Finch and Samuel Amedon ads Eliphalet D. Mattison*, Minutes of Common Pleas, 1831-44, Book 13223-5:153, Washington County Archives, Roll 911, blip M-000.

the second for two hundred seventy-five dollars.[161] The acquisition of these leases is not recorded. But clearly Samuel and Isaac were doing a lot of business together.

He must have married Hannah at about this time. Their first child, Sylvia, was born in Fort Ann in 1832. A son Orlen arrived in 1834, and another, Llewellyn, in 1836 or 1837. Perhaps Samuel decided to move his growing family out of the village to a farm. On 27 June 1837 he purchased two hundred ninety-four acres in the town of Fort Ann, mortgaged by Darius Grout, his next-door neighbor.[162] Little Orlen died in 1839 and is buried in Brown Cemetery in Fort Ann.[163] Samuel and Hannah sold the farm two years later, on 10 December 1841.[164]

Samuel appears as head of household in Fort Ann in 1840, with a woman age thirty to forty (Hannah), a boy ten to fifteen (probably his younger brother William), a boy under age five (Llewellyn), and a girl age five to ten (Sylvia).[165]

At some time in this decade, Samuel changed the spelling of the family name, as his father had done before him. Perhaps, like his father, there was a family dispute and Samuel wanted to distance himself from the family. He was still using his father's spelling in 1839 when Orlen died and "Ameden" was inscribed on his tombstone. By 1850, all documents for Samuel used the "Amidon" spelling.

In 1850, Samuel was again working as a blacksmith in Fort Ann. He was also acquiring more real estate than his neighbors: his real estate was valued at fourteen hundred dollars. This was a trend that was to continue for the rest of his life. Living with him in 1850 were Hannah, Sylvia and Llewellyn.[166] Sylvia moved out when she married William Baker in March 1855; they moved almost immediately to Wisconsin. In June of that year the New York state

---

161 Washington County Deeds, Book II:82-4.

162 Washington County Deeds, Book SS:587-90.

163 Historical Data Services, *Cemetery Records of the Township of Fort Ann, Washington County, New York* (Queensbury, N.Y.: Historical Data Services, 1995), 6. Age five years nine days.

164 Washington County Deeds, Book 3:459.

165 Samuel Amidon household, 1840 U.S. cens., Washington Co., N.Y., Fort Ann town, page 241, line 13.

166 Samuel Amidon household, 1850 U.S. cens., Washington Co., N.Y., pop. sched., Fort Ann town, page 91, dwelling 368, family 368.

census lists Samuel as a merchant, living in a house made of boards, valued at five hundred dollars.[167]

The federal land grant system made land available at bargain prices for those willing to head West and tame the frontier. Hannah led the way on 28 November 1853 when she bought forty acres in the northeast corner of the village of Leroy, now called Oakdale, in Monroe County, Wisconsin, for fifty dollars. Was she taking advantage of an inheritance that provided some extra cash?[168] Sylvia and William Baker arrived in Leroy in September 1855. Perhaps they scouted out the opportunities and identified good land for Samuel to buy. One month later Samuel followed Hannah's lead. On 25 October 1855, he paid one hundred dollars for eighty acres in the northeast corner of Monroe County. He was still "of Washington County, New York" when he executed the sale.[169]

A year later, Samuel, Hannah, and Llewellyn joined William and Sylvia in Leroy. They would have followed Sylvia's path down the St. Lawrence River to Buffalo, then through Lakes Erie, Huron and Michigan, along the new military road to Portage and up the rough La Crosse road to Leroy.[170] The land around Leroy was oak savanna, a mixture of oak trees and prairie. Clearing the land of oak trees would have been hard going, but survival depended on getting a cash crop planted. In Wisconsin in the 1850s, that meant wheat. By the 1860s Wisconsin led the nation in wheat production.[171]

On 21 October 1859 Samuel sold the land he had bought from the federal government.[172] Hannah's land seemed to provide a more desirable residence and farm.

The 1860 census shows Samuel's family settled in Leroy, Wisconsin, on Hannah's land. William and Sylvia Baker lived next door. Both were farmers, both owning land worth twenty-five

---

[167] Samuel Ammidon household, 1855 N.Y. state census, Washington Co., pop. schedule, Fort Ann, roll 1, page 64.

[168] Hannah Amidon land entry file#10657, National Archives, Washington, D.C. Northwest quarter of the northwest quarter of section 10, township 17N of range 1E.

[169] Samuel Amidon land entry file#9685, National Archives, Washington, D.C. West half of the southwest quarter of section 20 in township 19N of range 1E.

[170] The Wisconsin Cartographers' Guild, *Wisconsin's Past and Present: A Historical Atlas* (Madison, Wisc.: The University of Wisconsin Press, 1998), 50-1.

[171] The Wisc. Cartographers', *Wisconsin's Past and Present*, 40-3.

[172] Monroe County Deeds, Book 9:350, Monroe County Clerk's Office, Sparta, Wisconsin.

hundred dollars, larger than most of the neighbors.[173] But Samuel wasn't content with his land holdings and he continued to acquire land. In 1862 he bought two parcels southeast of Leroy totaling forty-six acres. In 1864 Hannah sold a forty acre parcel adjacent to her federal land: no deed identifies how she acquired the land. At the same time Samuel bought another thirty acres just north of Oakdale, adjacent to Hannah's land, from his son-in-law William Baker. A month later, Samuel sold another eleven acres. At the same time, he sold to William 480 acres in various townships north of Oakdale. He also sold 218 acres in the town of Oakdale to Thomas Youngs.[174]

Farming must not have gone well for Samuel. He moved into the village of New Lisbon, just over the line into the adjoining county of Juneau and resumed his trade as a blacksmith in 1867. He bought two adjoining lots on the north side of Park Street, just west of Monroe Street.[175] The two lots probably provided both a blacksmith shop and a residence for Samuel and Hannah. He was "of Juneau County" on 27 April 1867 when he bought eighty acres south of Oakdale. In 1868 he sold eighty acres in Oakdale to George Grover.[176]

Hannah died on 17 May 1869 and is buried in New Lisbon City Cemetery. Samuel wasted no time finding a new wife. He married Mariette (Sheldon) Slocum the following April. Samuel and Mariette probably knew each other as children in Queensbury. She had married Ira Slocum and raised eight children with him in Woodstock, Illinois.[177] After Ira's death in 1867 she probably joined her brother, Talmadge Sheldon, who was living in Mauston, just east of Samuel's home in New Lisbon. The 1870 census shows Samuel and Mariette

---

[173] Samuel Amidon household, 1860 U.S. census, Monroe County, Wisconsin, population schedule, Leroy town, page 148, dwelling 1214, family 1200; National Archives micropublication M653, roll 1424.

[174] Monroe Co. Deeds, Books 11, 15, 18, 19.

[175] Juneau County Deeds, Book 13:169, Juneau County Clerk's Office, Mauston, Wisconsin.

[176] Monroe Co. Deeds, Book 19:414, 24:130.

[177] Ira Slocumb household, 1850 U.S. census, McHenry County, Illinois, population schedule, Greenwood, page 475, dwelling 91, family 91; National Archives micropublication M432, roll 117.

Ira Slocumb household, 1860 U.S. census, McHenry County, Illinois, population schedule, Dorr, page 525, dwelling 3478, family 3837; National Archives micropublication M653, roll 202.

living in New Lisbon with her son, Charles Slocum. Samuel's real estate was then valued at four thousand dollars.[178]

Samuel seemed to be more interested in city lots than farmland. In 1873 he sold 120 acres in Oakdale for $150.[179] At the same time he paid $150 for five lots in the Wilson and Dunn's Addition to the village of New Lisbon, in the block south of Lemonweir Street and west of Adams Street.[180] He also bought from James Slocum of Milwaukee (Marietta's son) an undivided one-eighth share in more than 720 acres in the town of Arpin in Wood County, north of New Lisbon.[181] Arpin was wild woodland in 1873. It was 1901 before there were enough settlers to create a town government.[182] Wood County was covered with pine savanna, which was easier lumbering than the oak of Monroe County. Pine could be floated down the Yellow River to the Wisconsin River, then out to the Mississippi. But floating logs down rivers was treacherous work. In 1873 the young Wisconsin Valley Railway built a rail line to Grand Rapids (now called Wisconsin Rapids) for the purpose of hauling out the timber that was being cut. The rail line was further extended over the next ten years to support the timber industry. It was probably this new rail line that caught Samuel's interest and led him to buy timber land in Wood County. Samuel was getting too old to log the land himself, and Arpin was about thirty miles from New Lisbon, as the crow flies. Most likely Samuel hired loggers to harvest his timber.

Samuel and his wife appear in New Lisbon in the 1875 Wisconsin census.[183] Samuel died there the next year on 12 June 1876. He is buried beside Hannah in New Lisbon City Cemetery.[184] When Sylvia and Llewellyn sold off their father's land after his death, they sold

---

178 Samuel Amidon household, 1870 U.S. cens., Juneau Co., Wisc., pop. sched., New Lisbon village, p. 84, dwelling 112, family 119.

179 Monroe Co. Deeds, Book 37:100.

180 Juneau Co. Deeds, Book 21:373.

181 Wood Co. Deeds, Book K: 364, Wood County Register of Deeds, Wisconsin Rapids, Wisconsin.

182 ?, *Histories of Wood County, WI Communities* (Wisconsin Rapids, Wisc.: Heart O' Wisconsin Genealogical Society, 1993), 5.

183 Samuel Amidon household, 1875 Wisconsin state census, Juneau County, village of New Lisbon, page 1, line 2;microfilm, Wisconsin Historical Society, Madison, Wisconsin.

184 Samuel Amidon and Hannah Amidon tombstones, New Lisbon City Cemetery, New Lisbon, Wisconsin.

eight hundred eighty acres, located in three counties, plus seven lots in the village of New Lisbon.[185]

Mariette is named in deeds in 1877 as part of the settlement of the estate.[186] She sold her interest in Samuel's lands to Llewellyn and Sylvia. Then she bought back two hundred acres of the land in Wood County, while selling to Llewellyn and Sylvia her undivided one-eighth interest in the remaining Wood County land. She had held this interest before she married Samuel. Since James Slocum also held a one-eighth interest, that he had sold to Samuel, it is quite likely that James and Mariette shared an inheritance of those lands from Ira Slocum.

After settling Samuel's estate, Marietta followed many other Wisconsinites to the lumber towns of Oregon, where she died in 1879.

Children of SAMUEL and HANNAH (___) AMIDON:

51. i. SYLVIA AMIDON, b. Fort Ann, N.Y., 2 Feb. 1832.

ii. ORLEN B. AMEDEN, b. 4 April 1834; d. 13 April 1839; bur. Brown Cem., Fort Ann, N.Y.[187]

52. iii. LLEWELLYN AMIDON, b. Fort Ann, N.Y., 14 Aug. 1835.

There were no children by Samuel's second wife.

Johnson Ameden (1809–1880)

20. JOHNSON AMEDEN *(John[5], Jacob[4] Amidown, Henry[3], Philip[2], Roger[1] Amadowne)* was born February 1809[188] probably in the town of Queensbury, New York, and died at Johnsburg town, New York, on 7 June 1880.[189] He married first in August 1834 MARY ANN GRIFFIN.[190] She was born on 31 December 1815[191] probably in Queensbury, New York, daughter of JONATHAN and SIBIL (SEELYE)

---

185 Monroe Co. Deeds, Book 38:49-50.

186 Juneau Co. Deeds, Book 30:22.

187 Historical Data Services, *Cemetery Records of Fort Ann.*

188 Johnson Ameden tombstone, section 1, plot #116, Union Cemetery, Fort Edward, New York; transcribed by Nancy K. Mullen, July 1994.

189 "Ameden dies," *Sandy Hill* [N.Y.] *Herald*, 10 June 1880, p. 3.

190 Lineage application of Antoinette Hammond Hitt, national no. 94146, National Society, Daughters of the American Revolution, (Dr. Corbin Griffin), approved 3 June 1912. No proof of the marriage is cited in the application. Antoinette was the granddaughter of Johnson and Mary Ann (Griffin) Ameden. No corroborating source has been found.

191 Mary Ann Ameden tombstone, section 1, plot #116, Union Cemetery, Fort Edward, New York; photographed by Nancy K. Mullen, 1995.

GRIFFIN,[192] and died at Sandy Hill, New York, on 17 October 1850.[193] He married second before 1855 CYNTHIA B. _____. She was born in Warren County, New York, in about 1810,[194] and died on 11 March 1877.[195] He married third before 1880 NANCY S. (SHAW) HARRIS, the widow of Charles Harris.[196] She was born in New York in about 1817,[197] the daughter of MARY (___) (SHAW) HARRIS, and died 28 May 1895.[198]

Johnson's birthplace has been unclear. The death record of son Alembert says his father was born in Chestertown, town of Chester, New York.[199] But Johnson's parents married in Queensbury in 1802, and were still there in the 1810 census. They remained there through the 1820 and 1830 censuses. So it seems unlikely that Johnson was born in Chestertown, despite the statement by Alembert's wife after Alembert's death. It is most likely that he was born in Queensbury.

Johnson first appears implicitly in the 1810 census, which shows his father's household in the town of Queensbury in Washington County. By 1820 the family was still in the town of Queensbury, but now in Warren County, which had been created out of Washington County in 1813. By 1830 the family was beginning to disperse. Of the five boys, only the youngest two were still living at home. It is likely that the other three were serving apprenticeships in other households. Since Johnson became a millwright, it is quite possible that he was away from home in 1830, learning his trade.

Mary Ann Griffin's birthplace suffers the same uncertainty as Johnson's. Alembert's death certificate says his mother was born in

---

[192] Lineage application of Antoinette Hammond Hitt, national no. 94146, National Society, Daughters of the American Revolution, (Dr. Corbin Griffin), approved 3 June 1912.

[193] Mary S. Jackson and Edward F. Jackson, *Death Notices from Washington County, New York Newspapers, 1799-1880*, (Bowie, Maryland: Heritage Books, Inc, 1995), 15.

[194] Johnson Ameden household, 1855 N.Y. state cens., Washington Co., population schedule, Kingsbury, second district, family 241.

[195] Cynthia Ameden tombstone, section 1, plot #116, Union Cemetery, Fort Edward, New York.

[196] Letter, John Austin to Nancy K. Mullen, 19 July 1996.

[197] Johnson Ameden household, 1880 U.S. census, Washington County, New York, population schedule, Kingsbury town, third election district, SD 6, ED 151, page 17, dwelling 136, family 168; National Archives micropub. T9, roll 942.

[198] Letter, John Austin to Nancy K. Mullen, 19 July 1996.

[199] Alembert Ameden entry, Town of Johnsburg Deaths, Liber 394: Oct. 24, 1900, Town Clerk's Office, North Creek, New York.

Chestertown. But the census shows her family resident in Queensbury in 1810 and again in 1820.[200] So it is most likely that she was born in Queensbury.

Johnson and Mary Ann lived in the town of Chester in Warren County from the time of their marriage in 1835 until after the 1840 census, taken on 1 June 1840.[201] It was a remote mountain district at the time. It wasn't until 1850 or 1851 that a plank road was built between Warrensburgh and Chester, finally providing ready access to Chester from Caldwell.[202] Two sons, Sidney and Alembert, were born there. They may have planned to move to the town of Horicon, north of Chester. Johnson bought a fifty-acre parcel in the Brant Lake Tract from Charles L. Green and his wife Mary on 27 February 1840 for $375.[203] Instead, the family moved to the village of Sandy Hill, now called Hudson Falls, before the birth of their daughter Ellen on 5 July 1841. According to the 1855 New York State census, taken after Mary Ann died, Johnson and Sidney moved to the town of Kingsbury (which probably means the village of Sandy Hill) in 1840, but young Alembert didn't move there until 1841.[204] Perhaps Mary Ann was already pregnant with Ellen and left the baby home with Grandma until after the new baby was born.

The land in the Brant Lake Tract was not a good investment. Johnson and Mary sold it on 1 April 1847 to Moses Stickney for $200, about half of what they had paid for it seven years earlier. On this deed, Johnson and Mary are listed as being of Town of Kingsbury, the town which contained the village of Sandy Hill.[205]

The 1850 census shows Johnson and Mary still living in Kingsbury. Johnson was working as a millwright and owned real estate worth $1700. This was typical of the values of Johnson's neighbors, which ranged from $600 to $3000. A couple of neighbors had more wealth, at $7000 and $9000, but Johnson's wealth was

---

[200] Jonathan Griffin hhd, 1810 U.S. cens., Wash. Co., N.Y., Queensbury, p. 56.

Jonathan Griffin hhd, 1820 U.S. cens., Warren Co., N.Y., Queensbury, p. 204.

[201] Jonsan Ameden hhd, 1840 U.S. cens., Warren Co., N.Y., pop. sched., Chester town, page 338, line 31.

[202] J. W. Adams, *Supplement to the Warrensburgh News: Souvenir Edition* (Warrensburgh, N.Y.: Warrensburgh News, 1898), unpaginated.

[203] Washington County Deeds, 1840:20-1.

[204] Johnson Ameden household, 1855 New York state cens., Washington Co., Kingsbury, 2nd district, family 241.

[205] Washington County Deeds, 1847:172-3.

typical for a skilled laborer of the time.[206] What is a millwright? Millwrights install, repair, replace and dismantle machinery and heavy equipment.[207]

Johnson may have been drawn to Sandy Hill by improvements to the Champlain Canal. The canal had been completed in 1823, connecting Lake Champlain to Fort Edward, passing less than a mile east of Sandy Hill. To ensure adequate water in the canal, a feeder stream ran through Sandy Hill from west to east, drawing water from the higher elevations of the Hudson River west of Sandy Hill. The feeder was enlarged to make it navigable by 1829. In the 1830s work started to enlarge the locks of the canal. The canal feeder through Sandy Hill was enlarged between 1836 and 1839. The feeder was improved again in 1842. By 1850 most of the locks on the Lake Champaign end of the canal had been enlarged. Various projects to improve the canal continued through 1890.[208] There would have been plenty of work for Johnson.

Or perhaps Johnson was drawn by the expanding mills, factories and other industries that fueled Sandy Hill's growth, following the panic of 1837. Sandy Hill's population boomed from 1360 souls in 1855, to 1939 in 1865, and to 2350 in 1875.[209] Expanding mills and factories would have needed the skills of a millwright.

When Mary Ann died in 1850, Johnson buried her in Union Cemetery in Fort Edward.[210] Johnson was left with three children between the ages of nine and fourteen. They needed a mother, and Johnson didn't waste any time solving the problem. No marriage record has been found. But the 1855 state census shows Johnson living with his second wife, Cynthia, and his three children in Kingsbury town, Washington County. The census also shows that Cynthia had only lived in the township for four years.[211] This

---

[206] J. Amidan household, 1850 U.S. cens., Washington Co., N.Y., pop. sched., Kingsbury town, page 214, dwelling 77, family 82.

[207] Bureau of Labor Statistics, U.S. Department of Labor, *Occupational Outlook Handbook, 2004-05 Ed.* Millwrights, online < www.bls.gov/oco/ ocos190.htm>.

[208] Canal Society of New York State, *Champlain Canal: Watervliet to Whitehall* (?: Canal Society of New York State, 1985), 3-4.

[209] *History and Biography of Washington County and the Town of Queensbury, New York* (New York: Gresham Publishing Company, 1894), 86-87.

[210] Mary Ann Ameden tombstone, Union Cemetery, Fort Edward, N.Y.

[211] Johnson Ameden household, 1855 N.Y. state cens., Washington Co., pop. sched., Kingsbury, second dist., fam. 241.

suggests that Johnson married a girl from back home in Warren County, and would place their marriage in about 1851.

Johnson's work as a millwright must have required him to travel to various project sites and to find a room to board while on the project. In 1855, he was found guilty of failing to pay his board of three dollars per week for seven weeks. He was back in court on 2 February 1856, appealing the judgment against him.[212]

At some point, Johnson acquired a lot on Main Street in Sandy Hill. There is no deed recording the purchase. Both his parents and Mary Ann's parents were long-time residents of Warren County, not Washington County, so it is unlikely that either of them inherited the property. We know that the 1850 census said Johnson owned land valued at $1700, which did not include the Brant Lake lot, it having already been sold. We know Johnson owned a lot on the west side of Main Street because he bought adjacent land from Ralph Freeman and his wife Susan on 1 October 1859. He paid $150 for 12/43 of an acre. That deed specified that the purchased land was adjacent to land he already owned.[213]

A month later, Johnson again expanded his property in Sandy Hill by buying an adjoining six-tenths of an acre from Roswell Weston for $300.[214] Three years later, Johnson expanded again when he bought an unspecified amount of land on the north side of Williams Street adjacent to his existing property, paying $425 on 9 December 1862.[215] If land prices were stable in those three years, then the new purchase was probably about an acre.

By 1860, Johnson's family had started to disperse. Sidney had married and had his own home a few blocks away in Sandy Hill.[216] Alembert was a machinist, still living at home. Ellen, now eighteen, was also living at home. Johnson's real estate had depreciated slightly to $1500,[217] despite his two small purchases in 1859.

---

[212] Johnson Ameden v. ?, Washington County Court Records, 2 February 1856, Washington County Municipal Center, Fort Edward, New York.

[213] Washington County Deeds, 1859.

[214] Ibid.

[215] Washington County Deeds, 1862.

[216] Sidney Amiden household, 1860 U. S. census, Washington County, New York, population schedule, Kingsbury town, page 580, dwelling 52, family 58; National Archives micropublication M653, roll 875.

[217] J. Amidown household, 1860 U.S. cens., Washington Co., N.Y., pop. sched., Kingsbury town, page 565, dwelling 144, family 144.

Alembert married in 1862. His wife, Elsie King, dealt actively in real estate. She and Alembert sold a property in the village of Glens Falls in Warren County to Johnson on 16 March 1868 for $500.[218] On the same day, Johnson and Cynthia sold the same property to youngest child, Ellen, for the same price, $500.[219] Ellen and Fernando Hammond had been married just thirteen months, so this may have represented their purchase of a business for Fernando. It must not have been a home for them because the 1870 census shows Ellen and Fernando living with Johnson and Cynthia.

By 1870, Johnson and Cynthia had an empty nest – well, almost. Ellen had married and had a daughter, but was living with Johnson and Cynthia. Alembert had married and moved back to Warren County. Sidney had died young in 1862 at age twenty-six, leaving a daughter Mary Ann, no doubt named for Sidney's mother who had died when Sidney was just a boy. Sidney's wife, Susan, had re-married in 1867, leaving Mary Ann in the care of her grandparents. Perhaps the girl was unable to accept her mother's re-marriage, or perhaps her new stepfather didn't want any children in the house. Johnson's wealth had almost doubled in the last decade, with real estate now worth $2500.[220] The growth was primarily from a lot in Sandy Hill on Canal Street that Johnson bought on 14 March 1870. No deed was recorded, but the purchase is mentioned in a deed dated 13 January 1877 when Johnson and Cynthia sold the lot to Ellen for $1000.[221] Perhaps this was finally a home for Fernando and Ellen, so they didn't need to live with her parents anymore.

Cynthia died later that same year and is buried on the other side of Johnson from his first wife, in Union Cemetery.[222] Yet again, Johnson married. His third wife was also widowed. Johnson's new mother-in-law, the twice widowed Mary Harris, was now eighty-six, and probably frail. 1880 found her living with Johnson and Nancy. Sidney's daughter, Mary Ann, was still living with them. Life was getting more difficult than ten years earlier. The census shows that Johnson was unemployed for six months of the last twelve

---

218　Warren County Deeds, 1868.
219　Ibid.
220　Johnson Ameden household, 1870 U.S. census, Washington County, New York, population schedule, Kingsbury town, Sandy Hill post office, page 423C, dwelling 59, family 64; National Archives micropublication M593, roll 1111.
221　Washington County Deeds.
222　Ibid.

months.[223] With Johnson now seventy-one years old, he and Nancy probably needed the help of a young woman around the house.

We have to wonder whom the census taker talked to when he visited the Ameden house in Sandy Hill on that 7 June 1880. For that was the very same day that Johnson died. But he died in Johnsburg, Warren County, according to the death notice in the paper.[224] Johnsburg is a mountain township, a small chunk of the Adirondack State Park and home to garnet mining. Perhaps Johnson was working on a project at the mines. He was boarding at the home of Charles Pettys, a carpenter who provided board for several other tradesmen.[225] When Johnson didn't make an appearance by 5:45 A.M., Charles went into his room and found him dead. Charles Shaw was also boarding with Charles Pettys. He was the overseer for Johnson's project and testified at the coroner's inquest:

> I reside here. Have known Mr. Ameden about one month. Have been with him about considerably. He always appeared nervous, not physically strong. The shaking of his hand was as bad a month ago as during the last few days. He claimed to me he was not able to do hard work, yet did considerable hard work and was busy all the time. He appeared as well yesterday as usual. Do not know his age. He was highly respected by myself and all in my employ.[226]

Dr. Martin, the local physician, testified that he had never treated Johnson, but he concluded that death was caused by "paralysis of the heart."[227] He was buried in Union Cemetery between his first two wives.[228]

Johnson died without leaving a will. His widow, Nancy, was appointed executrix of his estate. Nancy stated that his personal property was less than one thousand dollars. Alembert, Ellen, and the

---

223 Johnson Ameden household, 1880 U.S. cens., Washington Co., N.Y., pop. sched., Kingsbury, SD 6, ED 151, sheet 17, dwelling 136, family 168.
224 Johnson Ameden obituary, *Sandy Hill* [N.Y.] *Herald*, 10 June 1880.
225 Charles Pettys household, 1880 U.S. cens., Warren Co., N.Y., pop. sched., Johnsburg, SD 6, ED 117, sheet 26, dwelling 249, family 255.
226 Stephen Amadon inquest, 8 June 1880, Records Storage Center, Municipal Center, Lake George, New York.
227 Ibid.
228 Johnson Ameden tombstone, Union Cemetery, Fort Edward, New York.

granddaughter Mary were listed as heirs.[229]

After Johnson's death and the settlement of his estate, Nancy relocated to Washington D.C. where she was listed in the city directory in 1890.[230] She died on 28 May 1895 and is buried in Union Cemetery, Fort Edward, beside her first husband, Charles Harris.

Children of JOHNSON and MARY ANN (GRIFFIN) AMEDEN:

i. SIDNEY AMEDEN, b. Warren Co., N.Y., 1836;[231] d. 9 Dec. 1862;[232] bur. Union Cem., Ft. Edward, N.Y.;[233] m. Sandy Hill, N.Y., 18 Nov. 1858, SUSAN M. KNAPP,[234] b. N.Y., abt. 1842,[235] prob. dau. of JOHN and MARGARET (___) KNAPP.[236] She married second at the Methodist Church, Sandy Hill, N.Y., 26 June 1867, FRANKLIN S. LITTLE of Fort Edward.[237] Sidney's parents raised Sidney's daughter.

Child of SIDNEY and SUSAN M. (KNAPP) AMEDEN:

a. *Mary Ann Ameden,* b. N.Y., April 1860.[238]

53. ii. ALEMBERT AMEDEN, b. Chester, N.Y., Nov. 1839.

54. iii. ELLEN AMEDEN, b. Sandy Hill, N.Y., 5 July 1841.

There were no children by Johnson's other wives.

---

[229] Johnson Ameden probate file no. 430, Washington County center, Fort Edward, New York.

[230] *Washington D.C. City Directory, 1890* (?: Boyd, 1890).

[231] Johnson Ameden hhd, 1855 N.Y. state cens., Washington Co., Kingsbury, second district, family 241.

[232] Sidney Ameden tombstone, sect. 1, plot #116, Union Cem, Ft Edward, NY.

[233] Ibid.

[234] Jackson and Jackson, *Marriage Notices from Washington County,* 66.

[235] Sidney Amiden hhd, 1860 U.S. census, Washington Co., N.Y., pop. sched., Kingsbury, Sandy Hill post office, page 580, dwelling 52, family 58.

[236] John Knapp household, 1850 U.S. cens., Washington Co., N.Y., pop. sched., Kingsbury, p. 231, dw. 317, fam. 348. The 1850 census does not show relationship, so the notion that Susan is the daughter of John and Margaret Knapp needs verification.

[237] Little-Amedon marriage, 26 June 1867, Hudson Falls Methodist Church, Sandy Hill (now Hudson Falls), N.Y.; transcribed in *New York DAR Cemetery Church & Town Records,* vol. 55 (Washington, D.C.: National Society of the Daughters of the American Revolution, ?), 255.

[238] Johnson Ameden household, 1860 U.S cens., Washington Co., N.Y., pop. sched., Kingsbury, page 580, dwelling 52, family 58.

Hamilton Ameden (1811–1885)

21. HAMILTON AMEDEN *(John[5], Jacob[4] Amidown, Henry[3], Philip[2], Roger[1] Amadowne)* was born at Queensbury, New York,[239] on 13 March 1811, and died at Queensbury, New York, on 9 June 1885.[240] He married on 29 July 1835, EMILY JANE OGDEN. She was born at Queensbury in March 1816,[241] the daughter of REUBEN and BETSEY (___) OGDEN. She died at Butternut Flats in Queensbury on 17 January 1903.[242]

Hamilton is undoubtedly one of the boys in his father's household in 1820, but not in 1830. By 1830 he was nineteen, and may have been apprenticed to a local carpenter.

Hamilton and Emily Jane married in 1835. At about the same time he bought nine acres in the Butternut Flats section of Queensbury near Glen Lake from his cousin Johnson Ameden. On 28 October 1839 he bought two more parcels at one acre each in Queensbury from Johnson. By 1840 they had one son, Archibald Ogden "A.O."[243] Two years later Hamilton bought five acres from Phineas G. Austin for $125. Three months later Hamilton and Emily Jane sold the nine-acre parcel for $600 to Henry Ray. Four months later, on 2 October 1842, Hamilton paid $1200 to Dudley and Julia Hubbel for a forty-acre parcel between Long Pond and Round Pond. Round Pond is just south of Glen Lake. This was probably the farm on Walkup Road where they lived out their lives.[244] Emily joined the Episcopal Church of the Messiah, where she was a longtime member.

By 1845, two more children had joined the family: Helen and Eugene.[245] On 4 April 1849 Hamilton expanded the family homestead when he paid fifty dollars to Reuben Seelye for land

---

[239] Hamilton Ameden household, 1855 New York state census, Warren County, population schedule, Queensbury, family 170.

[240] Hamilton Ameden probate file 1623, Warren County Municipal Center, Lake George, New York.

[241] Jane Amidon household, 1900 U.S. census, Warren County, New York, population schedule, town of Queensbury, SD 5, ED 101, sheet 1B, dwelling 23, family 23; National Archives micropublication T623, roll 1171.

[242] Emily J. Ameden, death certificate no. 2395, Town Clerk, Queensbury, New York.

[243] Hamilton Amadan household, 1840 U.S. cens., Warren Co., N.Y., Queensbury town, page 290, line 16.

[244] Warren Co. Deeds, L:86, 191, & 353, Lake George, N. Y.

[245] Hamilton Ameden household, 1845 New York state census, Warren County, Queensbury, district 1, line 74.

adjacent to the five acre plot on which his house stood.[246] By 1850 little Emma had joined the family and Hamilton was established as a carpenter. His real estate of $1500 was typical of his neighbors.[247] The house was a frame house worth $500.[248]

On 28 March 1854 Hamilton bought twenty-nine acres in the French Mountain Tract from Frederick Hubbell.[249] French Mountain lies in the northwest part of the town, north of Butternut Flats.

In 1856 and 1858 the last two children, Ida and Libbie, completed the family. The 1860 census shows the family in Glens Falls. Hamilton was listed as a mechanic, owning property worth $1800.[250] By 1870, Eugene had joined his father's occupation as a carpenter. Only "A.O." had left home, pursuing medical studies. Hamilton's property had increased in value to $2500.[251]

By 1880, Emma had also left home and was teaching school in Bolton, in the north part of the county, boarding with George Fish.[252] Ida was gone, perhaps teaching as well. Helen and Libbie were also teachers but, like Eugene, were still living at home.[253]

Hamilton must have taken ill in May 1885, because he wrote his will, leaving everything to his wife Emily Jane and naming her executrix. John B. Coffin and George Coffin were witnesses.[254] He died the following September and is buried in Jenkins Cemetery.[255] His obituary in the *Morning Star* said: "Although he had raised six children, this is the first death that has occurred in the family. He never used liquor or tobacco in any form and was remarkably healthy up to a few weeks before his death."[256]

---

246   Warren Co. Deeds, recorded 23 July 1889.

247   Hamilton Amedon household, 1850 U.S. cens., Warren Co., N.Y., pop. sched., Queensbury town, page 76, dwelling 290, family 302.

248   Hamilton Ameden household, 1855 N.Y. census, Warren Co., N.Y.

249   Warren Co. Deeds, recorded 18 Mar 1889.

250   Hamilton Amedon household, 1860 U.S. cens., Warren Co., N.Y., pop. sched, Queensbury, page 163, dwelling 1285, family [blank].

251   Hamilton Amedon household, 1870 U.S. cens., Warren Co., N.Y., pop. sched., Queensbury, Luzerne post office, page 13, dwelling 107, family 105.

252   George Fish household, 1880 U.S. census, Warren Co., N.Y., pop. sched., Bolton, SD 6, ED 111, sheet 14, dwelling 160, family 162.

253   Hamilton Ameden household, 1880 U.S. cens., Warren Co., N.Y., pop. sched., Queensbury, SD 6, ED 120, sheet 5, dwelling 46, family 49.

254   Hamilton Ameden will (1885), Warren County Deed Book 50:129-30,.

255   Hamilton Ameden tombstone, Jenkins Cemetery, Queensbury, New York. Transcribed by Nancy K. Mullen, 1995.

256   "Hamilton Ameden," *Morning Star*, Glens Falls, N.Y., 11 June 1885.

Hamilton's death started a grief-stricken decade for Emily Jane. Three years after Hamilton's death her daughter Ida died at age thirty-two, leaving her husband ALLEN WORDEN, but no children. Allen was a farmer who lived the rest of his life with various family members. He never remarried. Two years after Ida's death, Emily Jane's eldest child, A.O., a physician in Glens Falls, died at age sixty-two. And two more years saw the death of daughter Emma at age forty-four. Emma's will left everything to her sisters Helen and Libbie, and named brother Eugene as executor. The witnesses were George and Mary Fish, suggesting that she was still boarding with them on 9 July 1891 when she took ill and wrote her will.[257]

Emily Jane survived Hamilton by seventeen years. She may have needed cash when she sold the French Mountain Tract to Warren J. Smith on 17 January 1889 for $175.[258] In 1900 she was still running her household with the help of daughters Helen and Libbie.[259] Helen died on 3 October 1902. She had written her will on 24 January 1894, leaving everything to her sister Libbie and naming her brother Eugene as executor.[260]

Libbie married William Clements six days after Helen's death, on 9 October 1902. We can imagine that the wedding was not the joyous occasion one normally associates with weddings. Libbie and William must have cared for the widowed and ailing Emily Jane. She died at home the following January. Her obituary described her thus:

> Where the deceased was best known she was highly esteemed. Though feeble for many months she still retained that careful solicitude for those dear to her that characterized her whole life, and when death so frequently visited her home in taking her loved ones from her, one by one, she still kept the One True faith, often saying, "God is good." Her whole life might well be compared to the proverb relating to a virtuous woman: "Her price is far above rubies; her children arise up and call her blessed; her husband also, and He praiseth her." The empty chair at the fireside tells its own story. During

---

[257] Emma J. Ameden will (1891), Warren County Will Book F:218, Municipal Center, Lake George, New York.

[258] Warren Co. Deeds, 17 January 1889, Lake George, N.Y.

[259] Jane Amidon household, 1900 U.S. cens., Warren Co., N.Y., pop. sched., Queensbury, SD 5, ED 101, sheet 1B, dwelling 23, family 23.

[260] Helen M. Ameden will (1894), Warren County Will Book H:47.

the last few weeks of her life she daily repeated the words; "Come unto me all ye that are weary and heavy laden and I will give you rest;" and quietly sleeping, she passed away without a struggle; and so "He giveth His beloved sleep; He giveth His beloved rest."[261]

In her will, written before Helen's death and proved on 11 May 1903, she left everything to her daughters, Helen and Libbie. She named Helen and her son Eugene as executors.[262] Since Helen had died without issue, all of the land that Hamilton had left to Emily Jane went to Libbie.[263] Libbie waited until 28 November 1916 to sell the forty acre tract that Hamilton had bought in 1842.

Emily Jane was buried beside Hamilton in Jenkins Cemetery.[264] Four children are buried near them: A.O., Helen, Emma and Ida.

Children of HAMILTON and EMILY JANE (OGDEN) AMEDEN:

55. i. ARCHIBALD AMEDEN, b. Queensbury, N.Y., 21 Oct. 1838.

    ii. HELEN M. AMEDEN, b. Queensbury[265] 4 Sept. 1841; d. Queensbury, 3 Oct. 1902;[266] bur. Jenkins Cem., Queensbury.[267] Never married.

56. iii. EUGENE AMEDEN, b. Warren County, N.Y., Oct. 1845.

    iv. EMMA JANE AMEDEN, b. Queensbury[268] 13 Sept. 1848; d. Queensbury, 19 April 1892;[269] bur. Jenkins Cem., Queensbury.[270] Never married.

57. v. ALIDA AMEDEN, b. prob. Queensbury, N.Y., 19 Sept. 1855.

    vi. GERTRUDE ELIZABETH "LIBBIE" AMEDEN, b. Queensbury[271] Sept. 1858; m. Queensbury 9 Oct. 1902, WILLIAM "WILL" M. CLEMENTS,[272] b. Sept. 1858, son of ALLEN and HARRIET

---

[261] "Mrs. Emily J. Ameden," *Morning Star*, Glens Falls, N.Y., 21 January 1903.

[262] Emily J. Ameden will (1903), Warren County Will Book H:136.

[263] Helen M. Ameden will (1894), Warren County Will Book H:47.

[264] Emily J. Ameden tombstone, Jenkins Cemetery, Queensbury, New York.

[265] Hamilton Ameden household, 1855 New York state cens., Warren Co., Queensbury, family 170.

[266] Helen M. Ameden, Queensbury, New York, death certificate no. 37074.

[267] Helen Ameden tombstone, Jenkins Cemetery, Queensbury, New York.

[268] Hamilton Ameden household, 1855 New York state cens., Warren Co., Queensbury, family 170.

[269] Emma J. Amedon, Queensbury, New York, death certificate no. 17764.

[270] Emma Ameden tombstone, Jenkins Cemetery, Queensbury, New York.

[271] Clements-Ameden marriage certificate, 9 October 1902, Queensbury, Warren County, New York.

[272] Ibid.

MATILDA (MILTON) CLEMENTS,[273] d. Queensbury 29 Aug. 1929, bur. Friends Cemetery, Queensbury.[274] Libbie was a music teacher in the town of Queensbury before her marriage,[275] but stayed home and kept house afterwards. Will was a farmer in Queensbury, a widower when he married Libbie.[276] After his death she still resided on the small farm on Ridge Road in 1930.[277] No children.

Warren Ameden (1814–1872)

22. WARREN AMEDEN *(John⁵, Jacob⁴ Amidown, Henry³, Philip²,
Roger¹ Amadowne)* was born at Queensbury, New York,[278] in about 1814, and died at Queensbury on 23 May 1872.[279] He married before 1838 ELIZABETH B. _____. She was born in Queensbury[280] in about 1812, and died 24 May 1880.[281]

Warren was born the year after the western part of Washington County split off, taking the name of a Revolutionary hero, General Joseph Warren. The enthusiasm carried to the new baby. He is certainly one of the sons in his father's household in 1820 and 1830.

Warren and Elizabeth must have married before 1838 when Elizabeth delivered their first child, Adela. But the little girl lived less than five months, and is buried in Sunnyside Cemetery.

Shortly after Adela's death, Warren purchased a couple of acres in the first general allotment of the town of Queensbury from Phineas G.

---

273 Ibid..

274 William Clements tombstone, Friends Cemetery, Queensbury, New York. Transcribed by Nancy Mullen, 1995.

275 Jane Amidon household, 1900 U.S. cens., Warren Co., N.Y., pop. sched., Queensbury, SD 5, ED 101, sheet 1B.

276 William Clements household, 1910 U.S. census, Warren County, New York, population schedule, town of Queensbury, SD 9, ED 172, sheet 10, dwelling 123, family 123; National Archives micropublication T624, roll 1086.

Will Clements household, 1920 U.S. census, Warren County, New York, population schedule, town of Queensbury, SD 10, ED 187, sheet 12B, dwelling 100, family 100; National Archives micropublication T625, roll 1272.

277 Elizabeth Clements household, 1930 U.S. census, Warren County, New York, population schedule, town of Queensbury, SD 5, ED 57-282, sheet 14B, dwelling 318, family 323; National Archives micropublication T626, roll 1656.

278 Warren Ameden hhd, 1855 N.Y. state cens., Warren Co., Queensbury.

279 Warren Ameden tombstone, Sunnyside Cemetery, Queensbury, New York. Transcribed by Nancy Mullen, 1995.

280 Warren Ameden household, 1855 N.Y. cens., Warren Co., Queensbury.

281 Elizabeth Ameden tombstone, Sunnyside Cemetery, Queensbury, N.Y.

and Ethelinda Austin on 16 March 1839. A year later, on 1 April 1840, they sold the property to Elijah Cole, making a sixty-seven percent profit in one year.[282]

By 1840 Warren had another child, Margaret, was established as a shoemaker, and was caring for his widowed mother, Rachel.[283] On 24 June 1842, Warren bought a quarter acre in the first division of Queensbury for one hundred dollars from Hiram and Huldah Barber. They sold the lot three years later on 17 Feb 1845 to Cornelius Benetry for two hundred sixty dollars, another nice profit![284] By 1845 Rachel had moved on to Warren's sister Irena, but another daughter, Irena Adelaide, had arrived in Warren's household.[285] In 1846 Elizabeth produced her only known son, Jacob, but the boy lived only fifteen months.

The 1850 census shows Warren and Elizabeth living with their daughters, Margaret and Adelaide. Warren was established as a shoemaker, holding real estate valued at four hundred dollars, one of the smaller holdings in the area. This census lists his wife as Elizabeth B. It might be that her maiden name started with B, but her maiden name has not been determined.[286]

The family was complete in 1851 with the birth of Elizabeth's last daughter, Zorada. In 1859 the family started to break up when Margaret married Adolphus Hawkes. The 1860 census shows Adelaide and Zorada still living at home.[287]

Warren may have been in failing health in 1867. On 19 June, Elizabeth bought a quarter acre in the part of Queensbury called Harrisena from daughter Margaret and her husband, Adolphus Hawkes, for three hundred dollars.[288] This property became their new residence. The next year, on 1 June 1868, Elizabeth bought another quarter acre adjoining their residence from Lyman and Ann Jenkins for fifty dollars.[289] Lyman Jenkins had witnessed Elizabeth's purchase from Margaret and Adolphus Hawkes. The low price of the

---

282 Warren County Deeds, J:400, K:450.

283 Warren Ameden hhd, 1840 U.S. cens., Warren Co., N.Y., p. 296, line 13.

284 Warren County Deeds, M:420-1, M:422.

285 Warren Ameden hhd, 1845 N.Y. state cens., Warren Co., Queensbury.

286 Warren Amidon hhd, 1850 U.S. cens, Warren Co, NY, pop sched, Queensbury town, page 138, dwelling 196, family 206.

287 Warren Amidon household, 1860 U.S. cens., Warren Co., N.Y., pop. sched., Queensbury, page 146, dwelling 1161, family [missing].

288 Warren County Deeds, 25:359.

289 Warren County Deeds, 25:358.

second purchase suggests that it was a gift. Perhaps Elizabeth was a Jenkins.

In 1868 Adelaide married George Allen. By the 1870 census, only Zorada was left living at home. The family real estate was now worth seven hundred dollars.[290]

Zorada married Harvey Smith, a Civil War veteran, in 1871. But their marriage bliss was short-lived. Zorada died nine months later. Warren had died five weeks earlier: was there a common disease that took both of them? There was a major diphtheria epidemic in neighboring Washington County in 1874-5; perhaps there was a similar epidemic in Warren County in 1872. Warren and Zorada were buried together in Sunnyside Cemetery. Elizabeth remained in the family home until her own death in 1880. She sold the combined half-acre to her daughter Irena and her husband George Allen for one thousand dollars, with the proviso that they would fence the premises, and that Elizabeth could occupy the premises.[291] When she died, she was buried beside Warren and Zorada and her other deceased children, Adela and Jacob, in Sunnyside Cemetery.

Children of WARREN and ELIZABETH B. (___) AMEDEN:

- i. ADELA AMEDEN, b. Queensbury, N.Y., 29 March 1838; d. 26 Aug. 1838; bur. Sunnyside Cemetery, Queensbury.[292]
- **58.** ii. MARGARET AMEDEN, b. Queensbury 14 Aug. 1838 or 1839.
- **59.** iii. IRENA "ADELAIDE" AMEDEN, b. Queensbury abt. Aug. 1842.
- iv. JACOB AMEDEN, b. Queensbury 5 Dec. 1846; d. 12 March 1848; bur. Sunnyside Cemetery, Queensbury ("He's gone our loved & favorite son / And let him sweetly rest).[293]
- v. ZORADA AMEDEN, b. Queensbury 20 March 1851; d. Queensbury 30 June 1872; bur. Sunnyside Cem., Queensbury; m. 3 Sept. 1871 HARVEY SMITH, b. 8 July 1845, d. 18 Jan. 1926. Harvey m. 2) 9 March 1873 ALICE M. LOWALL (three children); m. 3) Whitehall, N.Y., 15 May 1913 MYRA WOOD. Harvey served as a private in Company I, 96th Regiment, New York Volunteers, during the Civil War. Afterwards he was a mason in Fort Ann, N.Y.[294] He is

---

290 Warren Ammidon household, 1870 U.S. cens., Warren Co., N.Y., pop. sched., Queensbury – 1st election district, Luzerne P.O., p. 9, dw. 72, family 72.

291 Warren County Deeds, 27:225-6.

292 Delia A. tombstone, Sunnyside Cemetery, Queensbury, New York.

293 Jacob Ameden tombstone, Sunnyside Cemetery, Queensbury, New York.

294 Harvey Smith file, Civil War Pension Application File SC 717953.

buried in Elmwood Cemetery, Middle Granville, N.Y., in a circle of soldiers.[295]

Eliza Ann (Ameden) Welch (1816–1900)

23. ELIZA ANN AMEDEN *(John⁵, Jacob⁴ Amidown, Henry³, Philip², Roger¹ Amadowne)* was born at Queensbury, New York,[296] on 8 March 1816.[297] She died at Caldwell, New York, on 25 February 1900.[298] She married probably before 1837 HORACE WELCH.[299] Horace was born in Saratoga County, New York,[300] on 18 September 1811,[301] the son of STEPHEN and SARAH (BOWEN?) WELCH.[302] He died on 28 February 1875.[303]

Eliza Ann grew up in Queensbury. She appears there in her father's household in the 1820 and 1830 censuses.

Horace grew up in Saratoga, where he was enumerated in his father's household in 1820.[304] On 23 September 1837 he bought one-fifth acre on Canada Street in Caldwell, now called Lake George, from William Caldwell, son of the original patentee General James Caldwell, for 150 dollars.[305] Perhaps this purchase was made in preparation for his marriage. The 1855 census shows that he and Eliza Ann had moved to Caldwell in 1837. Horace worked as a boatman on Lake George, which lies only one block east of his residence on Canada Street.

As a boatman, Horace probably worked for the Lake George Steamboat Company. The Lake George steamboats served tourism from their start. In the nineteenth century there were not enough

---

[295] Margaret R. Jenks, *Granville Cemetery Inscriptions, Washington County, New York* (?: Privately published, 1993), Washington County Historian's Office, Fort Edward, N.Y.

[296] Eliza Ann Welch death certificate, Town of Lake George, New York.

[297] "Lake George Cemetery," *Patents*, South Glens Falls, N.Y., volume 9, number 5, September 1990.

[298] Eliza Ann Welch death certificate, Town of Lake George, New York.

[299] "Lake George Cemetery," *Patents*.

[300] Horace Welch household, 1855 N.Y. state cens., Washington Co., Caldwell, dwelling 24, family 24.

[301] "Lake George Cemetery," *Patents*.

[302] Alexander McMillan Welch, *Philip Welch of Ipswich, Mass., 1654 and His Descendants*, (Richmond, Va.: W. Byrd Press, 1947).

[303] Ibid.

[304] Stephen Welsh household, 1820 U.S. census, Saratoga County, New York, Saratoga, page 321, line 3; National Archives micropublication M733, roll 79.

[305] Warren County Deeds, I:415.

settlements along the lake to support a freight business, but Caldwell was an important tourist destination as early as 1820. The opening of the Glens Falls feeder canal in 1830 led to the commercial decline of Caldwell and substantive growth for Glens Falls and Fort Edward.[306] There was only one steamboat in operation on Lake George until 1869. From 1838 until 1848 it was a side-paddlewheeler named the *William Caldwell*, named for the man who sold Horace his residential lot. It was condemned in 1848, leaving no steamboat on Lake George for 1849. In 1850 the *John Jay* started serving tourists who sailed lovely Lake George. It burned in 1856. It was replaced by the *Minne-Ha-Ha*, which served on the lake for the rest of Horace's life. In 1869 a second ship, the *Ganouskie*, supplemented the *Minne-Ha-Ha*.[307]

Eliza Ann's first son William was born in March 1839. Why was he named William? Tradition says he should have been named for his father or his grandfathers. Perhaps he was named for William Caldwell, in grateful appreciation of the sale of their home. Eliza Ann's second son Horace Jr. was born fourteen months later. The 1840 census shows Horace living in Caldwell with his wife and two infant sons.[308] Over the next decade three more sons, Theodore, Eugene, and Walter, and a daughter Hortense were born. Little Eugene died before his second birthday.

Work in tourism may have been unreliable. On 22 August 1845 Horace and Eliza Ann sold their lot to Timothy Bowen for $200.[309] It is not clear where they lived after selling the lot.

A year later they sold one hundred acres in the first division of Queensbury to L.C.P. Seelye on 19 September 1840 for $900.[310] Further study of Warren County deeds is required to determine how they acquired this land. Perhaps it was an inheritance from Eliza Ann's father, although no deed was recorded for the purchase.

In the early fifties, Eliza Ann delivered two more daughters, Libbie and Tillie. In 1853 at age fourteen William left home to attend the U.S. Naval Academy, where he trained for four years. The 1855 state census shows that William had left the family fold, but all the

---

306   Smith, *History of Warren County*, 568.

307   Ogden J. Ross, *The Steamboats of Lake George, 1817 to 1932* (Albany: The Lake George Steamboat Company, c1932), 55-79.

308   Horace Welch household, 1840 U.S. cens., Warren Co., N.Y., Caldwell, page 361, line 13.

309   Warren County Deeds, N:89-90.

310   Warren County Deeds, N:428-9.

other children were still living with Horace and Eliza Ann in Caldwell. They owned their wood residence, valued at $450.[311]

In the early sixties, Horace Jr. seems to have had a religious conversion. He was baptized at St. James Episcopal Church in Caldwell on 24 May 1863, one day before his twenty-third birthday. Four months later on 27 September his three youngest siblings, Walter, Libbie, and Tillie, were also baptized at St. James.[312]

On 13 November 1867 Horace bought another lot on Canada Street from Julia Tucker for $1300. The property lay between Canada Street and the lake, diagonally across the street from Eliza Ann's sister Irena Nichols. It had 240 feet on Canada Street, 200 feet on the north side and 100 feet on the south side. It contained the Stone Store on the northwest corner and a red house on the southwest corner.[313] The property was adjacent to the extensive grounds of the Fort William Henry Hotel, which lay south of Horace's lot. Apparently there was some dispute about the exact location of the shared boundary. A deed with Theophilus and Harriet Roessle, owners of the hotel, on 4 October 1870 settled the boundary line.[314] This was the family home for the remainder of Horace's and Eliza Ann's lives. The 1870 census shows them living in Caldwell with William, Hortense, Walter, Libbie, and Tillie. Horace and Walter were listed as boatmen. William was a lieutenant in the Navy.[315] Horace Jr. was a pilot on the steamboat *Minne-Ha-Ha*, living in Caldwell with Elias S. Harris,[316] the captain of the *Minne-Ha-Ha*.[317] Theodore was married and living in Queensbury.

On 30 September 1871 Horace and Eliza Ann sold to Richard W. Hughes of Trenton, New Jersey, 8.75 acres in the southern part of Caldwell on the highway from the head of Lake George (that is, the south end) to the Glens Falls and Caldwell Plank Road for $2600.[318]

---

[311]   Horace Welch household, 1855 N.Y. state cens., Washington Co., Caldwell township, dwelling 24, family 24.

[312]   St. James Episcopal Church, Lake George, New York, baptism records, reported in letter from John Austin to Nancy K. Mullen, 19 May 1996.

[313]   Warren County Deeds, 17:268-9.

[314]   Warren County Deeds, 32:396.

[315]   Horace Welch household, 1870 U.S. cens., Warren Co., N.Y., Caldwell, page 541, dwelling 57, family 54.

[316]   Elias S. Harris household, 1870 U.S. cens., Warren Co., N.Y., Caldwell, page 539, dwelling 29, family 26.

[317]   Ross, *Steamboats*, 69.

[318]   Warren County Deeds, 24:198-200.

As with the sale described earlier, more work is needed with Warren County deeds to understand how they acquired this land.

The family seems to have continued with its religious fervor. Hortense was baptized at St. James on 26 May 1872. Both Horace Sr. and Eliza Ann were baptized on 24 August 1873.[319]

Sixteen months later Horace Sr. died at age sixty-three. He was remembered in his son William's obituary as "a plain man, who will be pleasantly recalled by many visitors to that summer resort, and whom we well remember as a man of most sterling character."[320] He was buried in Lake George Cemetery in the center of the village of Caldwell.[321] Eleven months after his death, Libbie married Albert Cheney.[322] She died eleven months later, probably from childbirth.[323] And eight months later Hortense died.[324] How Eliza Ann must have grieved! But now there was an infant to raise. The 1880 census shows Eliza Ann running her household in Caldwell. Horace Jr. had moved back home to care for his mother. Walter and Tillie were still living at home. Horace Jr. and Walter were selling hardware and groceries from the Welch Brothers Stone Store beside the house. And together they were raising four-year-old Elizabeth Cheney.[325] But the child died when she was only eight years old.[326]

Horace Jr. must have continued proselytizing his family. William was baptized at St. James on 5 December 1886. His commitment may have been a reflection of his poor health. He had retired from the Navy on 13 December 1886[327] because he had contracted consumption "from exposure incident to long service and recently to the damp and unwholesome winter climate of Callao."[328] He died a month later on 12 January 1887 at age forty-seven, and was buried in Lake George Cemetery. Horace Jr. survived him by only three years and died on 29 September 1890 at age fifty. He, too, is buried in Lake

---

[319] St. James Episcopal Church baptisms.

[320] *The U.S. Army and Navy Journal*, 15 January 1887, p. 488.

[321] "Lake George Cemetery," *Patents*.

[322] Letter from John Austin (Queensbury, NY, 12804) to Nancy K. Mullen, 19 July 1996.

[323] "Lake George Cemetery," *Patents*.

[324] Ibid.

[325] Eliza A. Welch household, 1880 U.S. cens., Warren Co., N.Y., Caldwell, SD 6, ED 112, page 20, dwelling 303, family 303.

[326] "Lake George Cemetery," *Patents*.

[327] "Retired," *Army and Navy Journal*, 18 December 1886, page 413.

[328] Letter from John Austin to Nancy K. Mullen, 19 July 1996.

George Cemetery. Theodore had moved to Montgomery, Alabama, where he died on 3 January 1895 at about age fifty-two. He was buried in Montgomery, and a memorial stone was placed in Lake George Cemetery with his family. At some time after 1880 Walter moved to Ohio, where he married in about 1898.

When Eliza Ann died of heart failure on 25 February 1900 at age eighty-three, only Tillie remained with her. Her husband, six of her eight children, and her granddaughter had died. Her final fifteen years had known grief upon grief. She, too, is buried in Lake George Cemetery with her husband and six of her children.[329]

Children of HORACE and ELIZA ANN (AMEDEN) WELCH:

    i.   WILLIAM WELCH, b. Caldwell, N.Y., 6 March 1839;[330] bap. St. James Epis. Ch., Caldwell, 5 Dec. 1886; d. Caldwell, N.Y., 12 Jan. 1887; bur. Lake George Cem.[331] Enlisted in U.S. Navy 18 Aug. 1862, served centel after the war, appointed ensign 12 March 1868, commissioned lieutenant 21 March 1870, lieutenant commander 23 April 1883.[332] His will left everything to his mother and siblings Horace, Walter and Tillie, disinheriting Theodore.[333]

    ii. HORACE WELCH, b. Caldwell 25 May 1840;[334] bap. St. James. Epis. Ch., Caldwell 5 Dec. 1863; d. 29 Sept. 1890; bur. Lake George Cem.[335] Steamboat pilot; merchant.

60. iii. THEODORE WELCH, b. Caldwell 4 Aug. 1842.

    iv. HORTENSE WELCH, b. Caldwell 11 Sept. 1844; bap. St. James Epis. Ch., Caldwell 26 May 1872; d. 13 Aug. 1877; bur. Lake George Cem.[336]

    v. EUGENE WELCH, b. Caldwell 26 Sept. 1846; d. 12 July 1848; bur. Lake George Cem.[337]

61. vi. WALTER WELCH, b. Caldwell 9 Aug. 1849.

62. vii. ELIZABETH "LIBBIE" WELCH, b. Caldwell 16 Dec. 1851.

63. viii. ELIZA "TILLIE" WELCH, b. Caldwell Jan. 1855.

---

[329] "Lake George Cemetery," *Patents*.

[330] Ibid.

[331] Ibid.

[332] William Welch obituary, *Army and Navy Journal*, 15 Jan. 1887, page 488.

[333] Warren County Deeds, 53:313.

[334] "Lake George Cemetery," *Patents*.

[335] Letter from John Austin to Nancy K. Mullen, 19 July 1996.

[336] "Lake George Cemetery," *Patents*.

[337] Ibid.

William A. Ameden (1824–1891)

24. WILLIAM A. AMEDEN *(John[5] Ameden, Jacob[4] Amidown, Henry[3], Philip[2], Roger[1] Amadowne)* was born probably at Queensbury, New York, on 28 May 1824, and died at Columbia County, Wisconsin, on 1 December 1891.[338] He married probably at Washington County, New York, before 1860, ESTHER AMELIA GILLETT. She was born at Washington County, New York, on 3 March 1831, the daughter of ADONIJAH and THEODOSIA (UTTER) GILLETT, and died at Pardeeville, Wisconsin, 20 February 1903.[339]

William grew up in Queensbury, the youngest child in the household. He appears in his father's household in the 1830 census. By 1840 his father had died. His mother was living with William's brother Warren, but William appears to be living with his oldest brother Samuel, who had married and was living in Fort Ann, in Washington County.[340] William remained in Washington County for the next several decades before following Samuel west to Wisconsin.

In 1850 William was living in Dresden, twenty miles north of Fort Ann, boarding with Horace Coats.[341] The census taker reported a sixteen year old female, Unity Amidon, also boarding with Coats. There is no other record of this girl. The census taker may have recorded her surname incorrectly. Seven doors from Coats was William's future father-in-law, Adonijah Gillett. William was the first in the family to work at farming. Ironically, unlike his tradesmen brothers, he never seems to have owned land. He seems to have been a farm laborer all his life.

Late in the decade, William married the young divorced daughter of his neighbor, Esther Amelia (Gillett) Holcomb. She had married Linus Holcomb Jr. in about 1850. Their first child, Theodosia, was born in Washington County in 1851. She was followed by two more children: Adonijah in 1854 and Esther in 1859. Linus and Esther apparently separated between the start of Esther's pregnancy in 1858 and 1860, since the 1860 census, taken on 1 August 1860, shows

---

[338] William Ameden tombstone, Pardeeville Cemetery, Pardeeville, Wisconsin. Transcribed by Nancy Mullen, December 2001.

[339] Esther Ameden tombstone, Pardeeville Cemetery, Pardeeville, Wisconsin.

[340] Samuel Amidon household, 1840 U.S. cens., Washington Co., N.Y., pop. sched., Fort Ann town, page 241, line 13.

[341] Horace Coats household, 1850 U.S. cens., Washington Co., N.Y., pop. sched., Dresden town, page 125, dwelling 21, family 21.

Esther married to William Ameden.[342] Esther's children were made wards of the state and placed in the custody of Linus's parents, Linus and Lucinda Holcomb, where the children were recorded in the 1860 census.[343] By 1865 Linus Jr. had married Julia ___ who was twenty years younger than he.[344]

William and Esther moved to Whitehall by 1866 and to Fort Ann by 1869. By 1870, Esther had borne three Ameden girls and a boy, named for his grandfather, Adonijah Gillette, who was also living with them. Esther's oldest child, Theodosia Holcomb, had come to live with them, no doubt helping with the young children.[345] But Theodosia left on Christmas Day the next year, when she married Simon Cobb. Esther's last child was another boy, William H. Ameden, born in August 1872.

At some time after William's birth, the family moved east to Wells, Vermont, where they are found in the 1880 census with all five children.[346] Perhaps they fled the financial panic of 1873. Or perhaps they fled the Whitehall diphtheria epidemic of 1874-5. In 1881 eldest child, Annis, married Isaac Mitchell in Wells.[347] Her marriage record says she was resident in Poultney, Vermont, at the time. Perhaps she was living and working there, or perhaps the whole family had moved there. In 1882 William decided to follow the example of his older brother Samuel. He moved his family to Bangor, Wisconsin, fifty miles west of Samuel's home in New Lisbon, despite the fact that Samuel had died six years earlier. Farming seems to have been unsuccessful in Bangor. In 1887 William moved the family to Huron, in eastern South Dakota, where they stayed for several years. There daughter Melissa married Fred Archer in 1887. And so the family began to break up.

---

[342] Wm. Amidon household, 1860 U.S. cens., Washington Co., N.Y., pop. sched., Dresden, page 148, dwelling 39, family 53.

[343] Linus Holcomb household, 1860 U.S. cens., Washington Co., N.Y., pop. sched., Whitehall, page 24, dwelling 1919, family 90.

[344] Linus Holcomb household, 1865 New York census, Washington County.

[345] Wm. Amidon household, 1870 U.S. cens., Washington Co., N.Y., pop. sched., Fort Ann, Fort Ann post office, page 9, dwelling 78, family 77.

[346] William Amidon household, 1880 U.S. census, Rutland County, Vermont, population schedule, Wells, SD Vt, ED 198, sheet 8, dwelling 64, family 69; National Archives micropublication T9, roll 1348.

[347] Mitchell-Ameden marriage, 3 July 1881, Records of marriages, births, and deaths, Book 1:14, Wells, Vermont; microfilm 2025060, FHL, Salt Lake City, Utah.

A land that had looked extremely promising in 1880 was losing its luster. Prairie fires and drought turned promising Dakota harvests into dust. Prices for corn and wheat fell. Many homesteaders gave up and moved back East. William and Esther seem to have joined the disillusioned throng. By 1891 William and Esther had returned to Wisconsin with their last daughter Hannah, and settled in Pardeeville in the south central part of the state. William died there in 1891 at age sixty-seven and is buried in the Pardeeville Cemetery. Esther survived him by twelve years, living with her son Adonijah, who had followed his parents to Pardeeville in 1892.[348] Esther died in 1903 at age seventy-one of pulmonary tuberculosis and cardiac disease.[349] She was buried beside William in Pardeeville Cemetery.

Children of WILLIAM A. and ESTHER (GILLETT) AMEDEN:

64. i. ANNIS AMEDEN, b. Dresden, N.Y., April 1861.

65. ii. MARY "MELISSA" AMEDEN, b. Dresden 30 Oct. 1863.

66. iii. HANNAH AMEDEN, b. Whitehall, N.Y., Nov. 1866.

67. iv. ADONIJAH AMEDEN, b. Fort Ann, N.Y., 14 Aug. 1869.

68. v. WILLIAM AMEDEN, b. prob. Fort Ann, N.Y., Aug. 1872.

Eliakim Ameden (1804–1876)

25. ELIAKIM AMEDEN *(Horatio[5] Gates Ameden, Jacob[4] Amidown, Henry[3], Philip[2], Roger[1] Amadowne)* was born at Wallingford, Vermont, on 22 April 1804.[350] He died at Winhall, Vermont, on 17 November 1876.[351] He married in 1830 PERMELIA HUBBARD. She was born at Putney, Vermont, on 17 March 1805, the daughter of

---

[348] Adonijah Ameden household, 1900 U.S. census, Columbia County, Wisconsin, population schedule, town of Pardeeville, ED 20, SD 9, sheet 3A, dwelling 63, family 64; National Archives micropublication T623, roll 1781.

[349] Esther Ameden death record, Columbia County, Wisconsin Deaths, Volume 2, Record 2014, microfilm, Wisconsin Historical Society.

[350] Eliakim Ameden birth record, Wallingford Vermont Town Clerk, *Town Miscellaneous Records*, volumes 1-2, 1772-1890 (Salt Lake City: Genealogical Society of Utah, 1952); microfilm 29216, FHL, Salt Lake City, Utah.

[351] Eliakim Ameden death record, Winhall Vermont Town Clerk, *Records of births, marriages, and deaths, v. 1-2, 1857-1896* (Montpelier, Vt.: Public Records Division, 197?), 2:172; microfilm 1844447, FHL, Salt Lake City, Utah.

SILAS and POLLY (___) HUBBARD.[352] She died at Winhall on 22 October 1889.[353]

Eliakim grew up in Wallingford, Vermont. He was enumerated in his father's household there in 1810. He served as witness to a deed from Samuel Long to Benjamin Stephens on 18 October 1819, though he was only fifteen years old.[354] He was there in his mother's household in 1820, having been abandoned by his father.

Permelia's childhood was spent in several Vermont towns. She was born in Putney, where the family lived for the births of five children. By 1810 they were in Winhall.[355] By 1820 they were in Middletown.[356] By 1830 they were back in Winhall.

Eliakim must have settled in Dorset before 1825 when he first bought land there. On 17 October 1825 he was described as being "of Dorset" when he paid twenty-five dollars for an undivided half of sixty acres in Dorset from Isaac Gray, who owned the land jointly with Amos Thompson.[357] On 10 April 1826 Eliakim bought out Amos Thompson's interest for another twenty-five dollars. Later that year, on 13 December 1826, he bought twelve and a half acres from Edmond Manly for five dollars. A year later on 25 September 1827 he bought fifty-six acres from Nathan Underhill of Rupert for $300. The following spring on 2 April 1828 he bought fourteen and three-quarter acres from Asa Lanfear for $230. This may have had a house or barn to command such a high price! In the fall he bought twenty-five acres from C. M. Fuller of Onondago County, New York, for $125.

In 1830 he was still living with his mother and his sister Eliza, who had moved to Dorset with him; with them in 1830 was also an unidentified boy aged five to ten.[358] The 1830 census suggests that

---

[352] Ken Stevens, *Vital Records of Putney, Vermont* (Pittsford, Vt.: The Genealogical Society of Vermont, 1992), 55. (HUBBARD, Parmely, son [sic] Silas and Polly, Mar. 17, 1805.)

[353] Permelia Amiden death record, Winhall Vermont Town Clerk, *Records of births, marriages, and deaths*, 2:182.

[354] Wallingford Land Records, 5:138.

[355] Silas Hubbard household, 1810 U.S. census, Bennington County, Vermont, Winhall, page 232, line 2; National Archives micropublication M252, roll 64.

[356] Silas Hubbard household, 1820 U.S. cens., Rutland Co., Vt., Middletown, p. 141, ln. 4.

[357] Dorset Land Records, volumes 7-11, Town Clerk, Dorset, Vermont; microfilm 28142, 28143, and 28144, FHL, Salt Lake City, Utah.

[358] Eliakim Amydon household, 1830 U.S. census, Bennington County, Vermont, town of Dorset, page 130, line 13.

he had not yet married Permelia on 1 June 1830, the official date of the census. She is probably one of the women her age in her father's household in Winhall.[359] Their son Crawford was born in Dorset in August 1830, so Eliakim and Permelia probably married in June or July. His marriage may have prompted him to prepare to leave Dorset. Having aggressively acquired land before his marriage, he now started selling it off at substantial profits. On 7 September 1831 Eliakim sold the twenty-five acres he had purchased from C. M. Fuller to Harvey Hawley for $150, making a twenty percent profit in three years. Two months later, on 1 November 1831, he sold the fourteen and three-quarter acres he had acquired from Asa Lanfear to Barsillai Hudson for $300, a thirty percent profit in thirty months. A year later, on 27 December 1832, he sold fifty of the fifty-six conveyed to him by Nathan Underhill to Edmund Manly for $280. Eliakim had now sold off all but seventy-two and a half acres of his original holding of 162.25 acres. By this time, according to the last Dorset deed, the family was living in Hebron, New York. Eliakim's father was living in Hebron, so the move must have reflected a desire to be closer to his father.

By 1837 the family was living in Sandgate, Vermont, according to the deed recording Eliakim's sale on 12 June 1837 to Elijah Corbett of Whitehall, New York, of all his remaining lands in Dorset. Clearly, living close to Horatio had not worked out for the young family and they had returned to Vermont.

On 12 February 1838 Eliakim paid $1300 to purchase the 200-acre Hazelton Farm in Sandgate from Gerrit and Rebeckah Wendell of Cambridge, New York, where he was already living, subject to a mortgage of $982.96.[360] The 1840 census shows Eliakim and Permelia living in Sandgate with Crawford.[361] On 22 May 1841 Eliakim paid five dollars to John Haseltine for a small piece of land with a house and adjoining sheds in Sandgate. On 7 June 1845, Eliakim sold most of Hazelton Farm to Major Hawley of Manchester, Vermont, for $825, excepting the portion northwest of the stream and dam used for his sawmill. Apparently it was a small sawmill and not

---

[359] Silas Hubbard household, 1830 U.S. census, Bennington County, Vermont, town of Winhall, page 143, line 7.

[360] Sandgate Land Records, volumes 10-13, Town Hall, Sandgate, Vermont; microfilm 28813 and 2131806, FHL, Salt Lake City, Utah.

[361] Eliakim Amadon household, 1840 U.S. census, Bennington County, Vermont, town of Sandgate, page 5, line 20.

Eliakim's primary business. On 6 August 1849 Eliakim purchased 205 acres from Cyrus J. Hurd of Sandgate for $150. He turned around and sold it to Major Hawley in June 1850 for $150. But he bought what must have been far more desirable land from Major Hawley on 12 March 1850 for $1000, under a mortgage payable at the rate of $150 per year.

The 1850 census found the family living in Sandgate and reports that Eliakim was a farmer. In addition to Crawford, there were two other children in the household: Henry, age thirteen, and Fidelia, age eight. Since Henry was not in the household in 1840, he probably was not a son. Fidelia may have been a daughter who died shortly thereafter, or may have been unrelated.[362] There are no further records for these two children after the 1850 census.

On 10 December 1853 Eliakim sold two acres to John Provan for four dollars. The land was adjacent to Provan's existing land. This may have been part of Hazelton Farm that Eliakim had retained or part of the land he had bought from Major Hawley in 1850. On 13 January 1854 Eliakim and Permelia sold all their land in Sandgate, consisting of five parcels together totaling more than 600 acres.

On 27 March 1856, Eliakim was recorded as being "of Manchester" when he bought five parcels of land in Winhall totaling well over 150 acres with a sawmill from James M. Cushing for $2500.[363] By 29 August, when Eliakim and Crawford together bought three parcels totaling seventy-one acres from Joshua and Eunice Wilder and Reuben Blood for $600, they were both recorded as being "of Winhall." So the family must have relocated to Winhall in the early summer of 1856. On 26 August 1858 Eliakim and Crawford bought another ten acres for $200 from John B. Messenger. On 30 March 1860 they bought sixty acres for $1200 from Beriah and Relief Wheeler.

In 1860 Eliakim was recorded in the town of Winhall, Vermont, Bondville post office, and reported as a hotelkeeper. He owned real

---

[362] Eliakim Ameden household, 1850 U.S. cens., Bennington Co., Vt., pop. sched., town of Sandgate, page 111B, dwelling 766, family 781.

[363] Winhall Land Records, volumes 6-10, Town Clerk, Winhall, Vermont; microfilm 2131821 & 2131822, FHL, Salt Lake City, Utah.

estate worth $2000, and personal property of $300. Crawford was still living with his parents and working the farm and sawmill.[364]

On 6 November 1866 Eliakim deeded over to Crawford much of the Winhall lands he had purchased in the previous eleven years, as well as land in Peru, Vermont. The sale price was $500, well below what Eliakim had paid, so this must have been Eliakim turning over his estate to Crawford. The deed provides additional insight into the sawmill operation. It assigns "the right and privilege of ponding and overflowing the Tollman Meadow by the present dam for the benefit of the mill and also the privilege of a two-acre mill yard in front of the mill and across the turnpike for piling logs and lumber."

In 1870 Eliakim and Permelia were living with two elderly women, Laura Davis and Lucinda Tyrell, next door to Crawford and his family. Eliakim's property had appreciated to $2500, and his personal property had grown to $1000.[365] Eliakim had retained ownership of the residences where he lived and where Crawford lived. On 25 September 1872 he transferred title of Crawford's house to his wife Permelia. Eliakim established himself as a man of stature in Winhall. He was elected a justice of the peace for the town. As justice of the peace, he validated the signature of his son Crawford on deeds dated 16 December 1872 and 23 April 1873. Eliakim was also elected Collector of Taxes for the town. He auctioned off 170 acres belonging to absent Phipp Richmond & Co. ("formerly of New York, now residence unknown") to pay back taxes of eleven dollars on 25 February 1875. On 1 March he bought three parcels of land from his son Crawford for $500. Crawford had paid fifty dollars for the parcels only two years later, making this look more like a cash gift to Crawford than an arm's length land deal. On 5 March Eliakim was again serving as Collector of Taxes when he auctioned off fifteen acres belonging to Elmira Dean to cover back taxes of $7.24.

In 1876 diabetes was a fatal disease. Suffering this incurable disease, Eliakim wrote his will on 27 February, leaving the use of everything to Permelia for her natural life. After her death, the estate was to be divided equally between his only surviving child, Crawford,

---

[364] Eliakim Amedon household, 1860 U.S. census, Bennington County, Vermont, population schedule, town of Winhall, page 230, dwelling 1824, family 1859; National Archives micropublication M653, roll 1316.

[365] Eleakim Amedon household, 1870 U.S. census, Bennington County, Vermont, population schedule, town of Winhall, page 10, dwelling 84, family 89; National Archives micropublication M593, roll 1615.

and his eldest grandchild, Mary.[366] Six months later, on 10 August, he sold one of the three lots he had acquired from Crawford to Vespation Benson for eighty-eight dollars. The next month, despite being terminally ill, he did his duty again as Collector of Taxes and auctioned off twenty-five acres belonging to Nathaniel Brown for back taxes of $5.39. Eliakim died at Winhall on 17 November 1876 from diabetes.

Sixteen months later on 27 March 1878, Allison O. Coleman, administrator for Eliakim's estate, petitioned Probate Court in Manchester for authorization to sell all Eliakim's real estate in order to pay debts and administrative charges. It took another eighteen months, until 5 November 1880, for Allison Coleman to sell to Permelia for $128 the barn and land surrounding the house that Eliakim had transferred to Permelia in 1872. On the same day, Permelia sold the house and barn and surrounding land to Crawford for $500, along with all the real and personal property given to her for her use by Eliakim's will. In return, Crawford gave her a mortgage on the property, payable by supporting and maintaining her during her natural life in a manner suitable to her social position in life and society, paying her bills, giving her a Christian burial and providing a monument similar to that at Eliakim's grave. However, the mortgage was released five days later when Crawford paid his mother $400. At the same time he deeded back to her the land and personal property she had deeded to him.

Permelia remained in Bondville running the farm. In 1880 she was head of household, living with Lorenzo Burbank, her granddaughter's widower, and their two small children.[367] Permelia was listed as a farmer in the Bennington directory for 1880-1.[368] By 1887, Permelia's health was probably failing. She sold the lands she had received from Eliakim and from Eliakim's executor to her grandson Silas Amidon for $400 on 16 June 1887, accepting a mortgage for $120.[369] She died in 1889 at age eighty-four.

Children of ELIAKIM and PERMELIA (HUBBARD) AMEDEN:

---

366   Winhall Land Records, 10:166.

367   Pamelia Ameden household, 1880 U.S. census, Bennington County, Vermont, population schedule, town of Winhall, SD 151, ED 41, page 14, dwelling 138, family 143; National Archives micropublication T9, roll 1341.

368   Hamilton Child, *Gazetteer and Business Directory of Bennington County, Vermont 1880-1* (Syracuse, N.Y.: Journal Office, 1880), 426.

369   Winhall Land Records, 10:525 & 526.

69.   i.   CRAWFORD AMEDEN, b. Dorset, Vt., 26 Aug. 1830.

  ii. **FIDELIA AMEDEN**, b. prob. Sandgate, Vt., 1842; d. aft. 1850. Might not be Eliakim's child.[370]

Eliza Ann (Ameden) Baldwin (1814 – 1857)

26.   ELIZA ANN AMEDEN *(Horatio Gates[5], Jacob[4] Amidown, Henry[3], Philip[2], Roger[1] Amadowne)* was born at Vermont on 1 January 1814.[371] She died at Winhall, Vermont, on 26 November 1857.[372] She married about 1841[373] GEORGE BALDWIN. He was born in Connecticut on 31 January 1812, the son of THOMAS and POLLY (___) BALDWIN,[374] and died at Dorset on 27 November 1884.[375]

Eliza grew up in Wallingford, Vermont, where she was enumerated with her mother in 1820. Before 1830 her mother moved to Dorset, Vermont, taking her children, Eliza and Eliakim. Eliza probably married in 1841. Her husband, George Baldwin, was a farmer in Dorset. Although George was born in Connecticut, the Baldwin family had been in Dorset since Benjamin Baldwin had been one of the original six Dorset settlers in 1769. He was soon joined by three brothers and two other male relatives. They established themselves in the fertile mountain valley called Dorset Hollow, where George Baldwin lived in 1841.[376]

It may have been their marriage that prompted George to buy eighty-eight acres adjacent to Eliza's mother, Sally Ameden, from Hiram Thompson on 1 April 1841. A year later, on 2 April 1842, he rented another twelve acres of adjacent land from Eliza's father, Horatio Ameden. The deed specifies that George would have the "use

---

370   Eliakim Ameden household, 1850 U.S. cens., Bennington Co., Vt., pop. sched., Sandgate, page 111B, dwelling 766, family 781.
371   George Baldwin household, 1850 U.S. cens., Bennington Co., Vt., pop. sched., Dorset, page 77, dwelling 254, family 267.
372   Eliza Baldwin death record, *Dorset Vermont Indexes to births, marriages, deaths, 1734-1994* (Salt Lake City: Genealogical Society of Utah, 1995). Microfilm 1985937, FHL, Salt Lake city, Utah.
373   Marriage date based on birth of first child in 1842, per 1850 census.
374   George Baldwin death record, Dorset Town Clerk, Dorset, Vermont.
375   Ibid.
376   Zephine Humphrey, *The Story of Dorset, Vermont* (Rutland, Vt.: Charles E. Tuttle Company, 1971), 169.

and occupancy" of the parcel for three years. Probably George needed better living quarters for the pending arrival of their first-born[377].

Eliza delivered Mary in 1842, Sarah the next year, Augusta two years later, Daniel two years after that, Pamelia the next year, and Joseph a year later. The 1850 census shows George and Eliza with their six young children living on a farm in Dorset worth $2000. Eliza's mother Sally was living with them, her father having just died a year earlier. Minuvia Hathaway, age eighteen, was also living with them, perhaps to help with the children.[378] On 15 January 1853 Eliza bought up all her brother's interest in their father's estate, probably because Eliakim was no longer living in Dorset.[379] In that same year George made several purchases to acquire sixty acres on the highway leading to Dorset Hollow, parts of which were known as the Lanfear place, the house lots of Thomas Baldwin, and the Barn lot.[380]

The decade of the 50's saw radical changes in the Baldwin household. Benjamin and Marsha were added to the family. Then Eliza died in 1857. At least eight pregnancies probably weakened her health. The timing of her death in 1857 suggests the cause may have been another, fatal, pregnancy. With a house full of young children, George had no time to waste. He married another Dorset resident, thirty-eight-year-old MARIETTA GRAY, on 6 May 1860.[381] Marietta moved to his farm in Dorset with his eight children. By 1860 the farm had appreciated to $3000. The eldest daughter Mary had found work as a teacher.[382]

Marietta delivered a girl on 2 August 1861, whom they named Bertha. Three years later, in 1864 at age forty-two, Marietta delivered a son, George W. In 1866 little Bertha died. And at some time during the decade Eliza's youngest boy Benjamin died. By 1870 Marietta's father had died and her widowed mother, LYDIA GRAY, was living with them. Of the children, only Eliza's youngest three, Pamelia,

---

377 Washington County Deeds, Book 12:57-59, 191.
378 George Baldwin household, 1850 U.S. cens., Bennington Co., Vt., Dorset, page 77, dwelling 254, family 267.
379 Washington County Deeds, Book 15:213.
380 Washington County Deeds, Book 15:315, 316, 345, and 346.
381 *Dorset Vermont Indexes to births, marriages, deaths, 1734-1994.*
382 George Baldwin household, 1860 U.S. cens., Bennington Co., Vt., Dorset, page 46, dwelling 343, family 359.

Joseph, and Marsha, were still living at home with their step-brother George W.[383]

Ten years later, George was sixty-nine and still farming, living with Marietta and his youngest son, George W. Pamelia was still living at home, working as a schoolteacher.[384] The other children were all gone.

George died in 1884 at age seventy-two from consumption. George W., Marietta's younger child, took over the farm and continued to care for his elderly mother.[385] Marietta was alive in 1910,[386] but was no longer with her son by 1920. She had probably died.[387]

Children of GEORGE and ELIZA (AMEDEN) BALDWIN:

70.   i.   MARY BALDWIN, b. prob. Dorset, Vt., abt. 1842.

    ii.   SARAH "SARAH" BALDWIN, b. prob. Dorset abt. 1843.[388] Not found after 1860.

    iii   SARAH "AUGUSTA" BALDWIN, b. prob. Dorset 22 May 1845; d. Dorset 15 May 1865.[389]

71.   iv   DANIEL BALDWIN, b. prob. Dorset abt. 1847.

72.   v.   PAMELIA BALDWIN, b. prob. Dorset March 1849.

73.   vi.   JOSEPH BALDWIN, b. prob. Dorset abt. Jan. 1850.

    vii. BENJAMIN BALDWIN, b. prob. Dorset abt. 1853;[390] d. bef. 1870.[391]

---

[383] Geo. Baldwin household, 1870 U.S. cens., Bennington Co., Vt., Dorset, page 11, dwelling 91, family 90.

[384] George Baldwin household, 1880 U.S. cens., Bennington Co., Vt., Dorset, SD 151, ED 27, page 3, dwelling 29, family 301.

[385] George W. Baldwin household, 1900 U.S. census, Bennington County, Vermont, population schedule, town of Dorset, SD 274, ED 29, sheet 9, dwelling 211, family 222; National Archives micropublication T623, roll 1689.

[386] George W. Baldwin household, 1910 U.S. census, Bennington County, Vermont, population schedule, town of Dorset, SD 120, ED 27, sheet 8A, dwelling 196, family 200; National Archives micropublication T624, roll 1612.

[387] Harry J. Bragle household, 1920 U.S. census, Bennington County, Vermont, population schedule, town of Dorset, SD 1, ED 37, sheet 4B, dwelling 18, family 19; National Archives micropublication T625, roll 1870.

[388] George Baldwin household, 1850 U.S. cens., Bennington Co., Vt., Dorset, page 77, dwelling 254, family 267.

[389] *Dorset Vermont Indexes to births, marriages, deaths.*

[390] George Baldwin household, 1860 U.S. cens., Bennington Co., Vt., Dorset, page 46, dwelling 343, family 359.

[391] Geo. Baldwin household, 1870 U.S. cens., Bennington Co., Vt., Dorset, page 11, dwelling 91, family 90.

viii. MARSHA BALDWIN, b. Dorset abt. 1855.[392]

Larnard S. Ameden (1824–1895)

27. LARNARD S. AMEDEN *(Horatio⁵ Gates Ameden, Jacob⁴ Amidown, Henry³, Philip², Roger¹ Amadowne)* was born at Hebron, New York, in 1824.[393] He died at Manchester, Vermont, on 22 March 1895.[394] He married at Washington County, New York, on 15 February 1849, ELISABETH B. CHASE.[395] She was born at Pittstown, New York, in 1827,[396] the daughter of ADAM CHASE.[397] She died at Manchester, Vermont, on 15 October 1874.[398]

Larnard S. Ameden (Courtesy: Stacy Niedzwicki)

Larnard grew up in Hebron, where he was enumerated in his father's household in 1840. He became a mason as did his brother Nathaniel. Probably both boys were taking up the vocation of their father. According to his military pension file, Larnard was of an average build, five feet ten inches, with a dark complexion, grey eyes, and black hair.[399]

---

392   George Baldwin household, 1860 U.S. cens., Bennington Co., Vt., Dorset, page 46, dwelling 343, family 359.

393   Larnard Ameden household, 1855 New York census, Washington County, New York, town of Hebron.

394   *General index to vital records of Vermont, 1871-1908* (Salt Lake City: Genealogical Society of Utah, 1967); microfilm 540053, FHL, Salt Lake City, Utah.

395   Washington County Vital Records, roll #1289, page 663, Blip X-0073, County Clerk's Office, Fort Edward, N.Y.

396   Ibid.

397   Larnard Ameden household, 1865 New York census, Washington County, New York, town of Hebron 1ˢᵗ district, family 71.

398   *General index to vital records of Vermont, 1871-1908.*

Elisabeth grew up in Pawlet, Vermont, about ten miles east of Larnard's home in Hebron.[400] Elisabeth and Larnard were married in 1849 by Reverend J. B. Hubbard of Granville, New York. They settled in Larnard's hometown of Hebron.

Their first child, Elizabeth, was born eleven months later. They may have thought the birth an auspicious omen for a large and prolific family. But to the contrary, the little girl lived only twenty days. And the subsequent children were destined to provide only a total of four grandchildren who lived to adulthood. Mary Frances came along in 1851, Leonard in 1853, and James Edwin in 1854. Little Leonard lived only seventeen days. The 1855 census found Larnard and Elizabeth in Hebron with Mary Frances and James Edwin.[401] In 1859 Elizabeth bore an unnamed son who died after five days. All three infants were buried with permanent stone markers in a family cemetery on Tipladys Road in Hebron right on the Vermont line. The family farm probably included the cemetery. The stone markers on the infants probably reflect the fact that Larnard was a stone mason, and could make the markers by his own hand.

The 1860 census found Larnard and Elisabeth still living in Hebron with Elisabeth's father Adam Chase living in their household, as well as their children, Mary Frances and James Edwin.[402] Although Adam is listed as head of household, neither he nor Larnard owned any land. In 1861 the family was complete with the arrival of Hattie Elizabeth.

The Civil War was ravaging the nation. Larnard enlisted as a private in Captain Josiah W. Culver's new Company H, 123rd Regiment, New York Volunteers, in Salem, New York, on 22 August 1862. They left New York on 5 September to bolster the defenses of Washington, D.C. They were at Washington for only a couple of weeks before being sent to Frederick, Maryland, where they stayed for ten weeks. They supported Burnside's campaign at Fredericksburg

---

[399] Larned Ammidon Certificate of Disability for Discharge, Civil War Pension Application File SC 85709 (Larnard S. Ameden); Records of the Veterans Administration, Record Group 15; National Archives, Washington, D.C.

[400] Adam Chase household, 1830 U.S. census, Rutland County, Vermont, population schedule, town of Pawlet, page 87, line 23; National Archives micropublication M19, roll 188.

[401] Larnard Ameden household, 1855 New York cens., Washington Co., N.Y.

[402] Adam Chase household, 1860 U.S. cens., Washington Co., N.Y., pop. sched., Hebron, page 50, dwelling 416, family 440.

in December and wintered at Stafford Court House until April 1863. They fought at Chancellorsville 1-5 May and fought at Gettysburg: on 2 July 1863 Larnard was observed to fall in the charge, to rise and fall again from an injury to his hip. On the march back to Williamsport, he was so lame that his compatriots had to carry his accouterments. He never recovered from the lameness incurred at Gettysburg. The

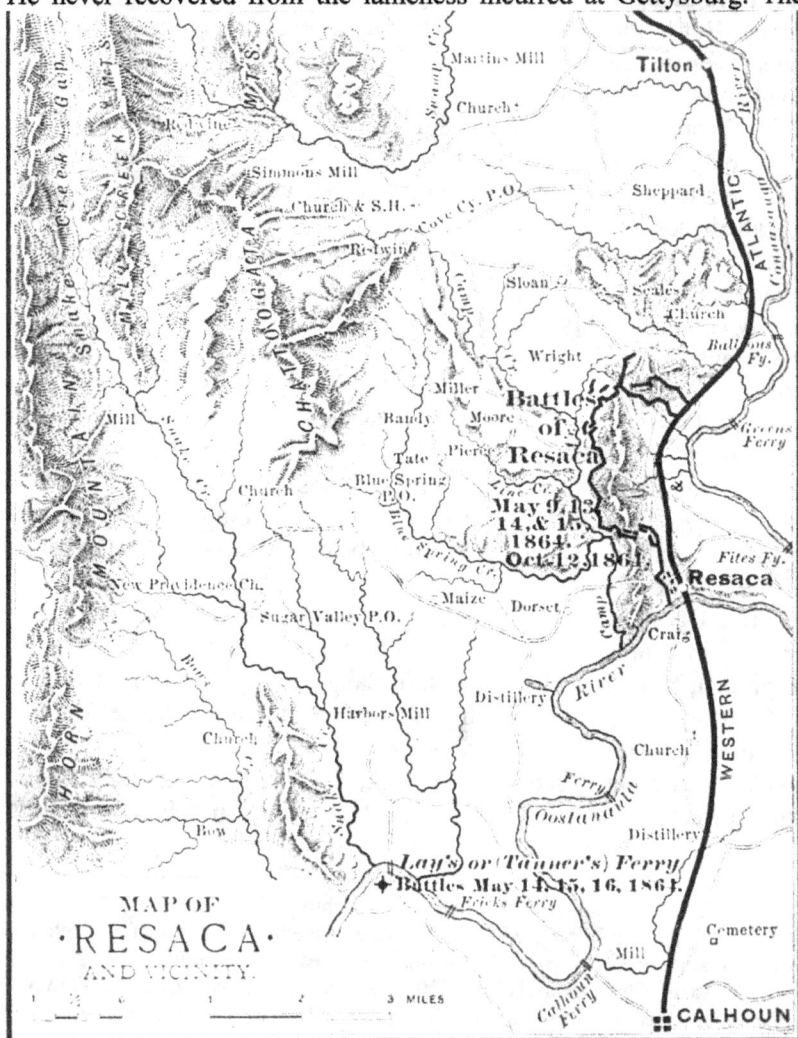

Resaca Battlefield (Courtesy: U.S. Historic Print and Map Company)

unit pursued Lee to Manassas Gap, Virginia, after Gettysburg.[403] The unit spent the winter guarding the Nashville & Chattanooga Railroad.

In the spring and summer of 1864 Larnard's unit participated in the Atlanta Campaign. Resaca, Georgia, was the site of the first major battle of the campaign. The Confederate Army was in place on the heights above Resaca, defending their Western & Atlantic Railroad supply line. On 15 May 1864, as part of Hooker's XX Corps, Larnard's Company H overran the Confederate right. Larnard's left eye was injured by a bursting shell that exploded on his left, scorching the hair on his head. But he carried on and fought with his unit at New Hope Church near Dallas, Georgia, where, on 29 May 1864, a musket ball passed through Larnard's right arm. He was admitted to Chattanooga Hospital in Tennessee for treatment, but was later transferred to Totten Hospital in Louisville, Kentucky, where he contracted lung fever. Thereafter his eyesight became progressively worse until he was completely blind in his left eye. After a month Larnard was transferred to Camp Dennison, Ohio. Larnard returned home on furlough in September to seek medical treatment. William Maynard was the local physician who treated him. He diagnosed disease of the heart because he was suffering from pain in his side, shortness of breath, irregular pulse, and general weakness. Dr. Maynard was a patriotic man, who didn't charge Larnard for treatment because he was a soldier. Larnard was discharged from the Army on 19 May 1865 for disability because the wound he received at New Hope Church prevented extension of the elbow joint.[404]

While Larnard was away fighting in the war, Elisabeth was overcoming their lack of land. On 1 October 1862 she purchased two lots in Campbell's Patent in Hebron from Larnard's mother for $300.[405] The 1865 New York census found Larnard and Elisabeth on their land with their three children and Elisabeth's father. They owned three and a half acres valued at $300. Two acres were plowed; the rest was meadow. They produced hay, apples (from six trees), butter and pork.[406] Clearly Elisabeth and the children had plowed and planted those two acres while Larnard was recovering in Army hospitals.

---

[403] "123rd Regiment, New York Infantry," *Civil War Soldiers and Sailors System,* online <"www.itd.nps.gov/cwss/">, downloaded 7 March 2005.

[404] Larned S. Ameden Civil War Pension SC 85709.

[405] Washington County Deeds, 1866.

[406] Larnard Ameden household, 1865 New York census, Washington County, New York, Hebron 1st district, family 71.

As soon as Larnard returned to Hebron, he was appointed a Collector for the town.[407] As the Collector, he was responsible for collecting taxes levied on every male citizen and upon land. He also would have been responsible for collecting special taxes for the repair and maintenance of public buildings.[408]

Two years later Elisabeth sold the lots she had purchased in 1862 to her brother-in-law Nathaniel Ameden for $500 on 1 April 1867.[409]

The family was still intact in Hebron in 1870. Larnard was still listed as a brick mason. The family homestead was valued at $400.[410] In March 1870 he requested a pension for his Civil War service. The pension must have been approved but at a nominal amount. In January 1871 he requested an increase in his pension. He again applied for increases to his pension in 1886, 1888, and 1892. At the time of his death, his pension was seventeen dollars a month.[411]

The family moved across the state line to Manchester, Vermont, after February 1873. It was probably in preparation for the move that they sold ten acres in lot number eight in Kemp's Patent, Hebron, to Larnard's half-brother Sylvester E. Spoor for $300 on 6 February 1873. By the time of the dower release the following August, they were settled in Manchester.[412]

On 1 August Larnard bought a lot of thirty-four rods – a bit less than one-quarter acre – in Barnumville on the northwest corner of Manchester from J. E. McNaughton for $175; the lot contained the house where Larnard and the family were living. A month later Charles H. Pond placed a lien on the property to secure payment for labor he had performed on the house earlier in June. A week later Larnard mortgaged the property, probably to pay Charles Pond.[413]

It was in Manchester that Mary Frances married Dexter Taylor in August 1874. There Elisabeth died of rheumatic fever in October 1874, at age forty-seven. And there James Edwin married in November 1874. In the space of four months Larnard's household had gone from a family of five to only Larnard and his youngest daughter

---

[407] *History of Washington County*, 390.

[408] Evans, *A to Zax: A Comprehensive Dictionary*, 66.

[409] Washington County deeds, 1867.

[410] Leornard Ameden household, 1870 U.S. cens., Washington Co., N.Y., pop. sched., Hebron, page 49, dwelling 414, family 422.

[411] Larned S. Ameden Civil War Pension SC 85709.

[412] Washington County Deeds, Book 74, page 386.

[413] Manchester deeds, 18:563, 565, 570, 608.

Hattie, who was still caring for her father in 1880.[414] His wartime injuries had left him a semi-invalid, although he was still working as a mason. One wonders who was caring for him in his final years after Hattie married her first cousin William Franklin Ameden in 1891.

Larnard died of pneumonia in 1895 at age seventy-one. He is buried with Elisabeth and his father-in-law in Hebron Cemetery.[415] He died without leaving a will. J. H. Hicks of Manchester was appointed administrator.[416]

Children of LARNARD and ELISABETH (CHASE) AMEDEN:

    i. ELIZABETH AMEDEN, b. 14 Jan. 1850; d. 3 Feb. 1850; bur. Tipladys Rd. Cem., Hebron, N.Y.[417]

74. ii. MARY "FRANCES" AMEDEN, b. prob. Hebron, N.Y. April 1851.

   iii. LEONARD J. AMEDEN, b. 8 Feb. 1853; d. 25 Feb. 1853; bur. Tipladys Rd. Cem., Hebron.[418]

75. iv. JAMES E. AMEDON, b. Hebron Aug. 1854.

   v. INFANT AMEDEN, b. 8 March 1859; d. 13 March 1859; bur. Tipladys Rd. Cem., Hebron.[419]

76. vi. HATTIE AMEDEN, b. Hebron 30 Sept. 1861.

Nathaniel William Ameden (1825–1890)

28. NATHANIEL WILLIAM AMEDEN *(Horatio[5] Gates Ameden, Jacob[4] Amidown, Henry[3], Philip[2], Roger[1] Amadowne)* was born at Hebron, New York, on 18 April 1825 and died on 20 August 1890.[420] He married about 1845 PHEBE MUNSON. She was born at Hebron in 1826,[421] the daughter of WILLIAM and RUTH (GETTY) MUNSON.[422] She died at Hebron on 18 November 1906.[423]

---

[414] L. S. Amidon household, 1880 U.S. cens., Bennington Co., Vt., pop. sched., Manchester, page 39, dwelling 410, family 428.

[415] Ameden/Chase monument, Hebron Cemetery, Hebron, N.Y.

[416] Larned S. Ameden Letter of Administration, Manchester [Vermont] Probate Court probate files volume 33, page 159.

[417] Elizabeth Ameden tombstone, Tipladys Rd. Cemetery, Hebron, N.Y., transcribed by Nancy K. Mullen in July 1995.

[418] Leonard J. Ameden tombstone, Tipladys Rd. Cem., Hebron, N.Y.

[419] Infant Ameden tombstone, Tipladys Rd. Cem., Hebron, N.Y.

[420] Nathaniel W. Ameden tombstone, East Hebron Cemetery, Hebron, New York; transcribed by Nancy K. Mullen, July 1995.

[421] N. Amidon household, 1850 U.S. cens., Washington Co., N.Y., pop. sched., Hebron, page 298, dwelling 1319, family 1414.

[422] Myron A. Munson, *The Munson Record*, volume 1 (New Haven, Conn.: The Munson Association, 1895), 598.

Nathaniel grew up in Hebron where he was enumerated with his father in 1830 and his mother in 1840. Phebe also grew up on a farm in Hebron as had both her parents. She was the sixth of thirteen children. She was enumerated in Hebron with her father in 1830[424] and in 1840.[425]

Nathaniel and Phebe married by 1845 and set up housekeeping in Queensbury.[426] Juliaette, their first child, was born in 1846 and William Franklin in 1848. Nathaniel's mother Eunice was aging, and Nathaniel took her into his household before 1850. Perhaps it was his aging mother that took Nathaniel and Phebe back to Hebron by 1850. The 1850 census shows Nathaniel and Phebe living in Hebron with Juliaette, William Franklin, and Nathaniel's mother.[427]

Like his father as a young man Nathaniel was apparently religious, and concerned for a suitable church in Hebron. With four others, he signed a covenant to organize the Second Advent Church on 1 January 1851. He served on the building committee, which erected a building for 200 people in the summer of 1851 at a cost of $900. The building was dedicated the following October.[428]

Hannah Maria was born late in 1850, Caroline in 1852 and Ashell Sheldon on Christmas Day 1854. Nathaniel bought thirty acres of farmland in Hebron from William and Mary Cain for $1000 on 1 April 1854.[429] The 1855 census shows Nathaniel and Phebe in Hebron with their five children.[430] Nathaniel bought another twenty-eight acres of farmland in an estate sale from John Munson for $500 on 11 October 1857.[431] John Munson was Phebe's first cousin, the son of her uncle John Munson; the estate sale was probably settling Uncle John's estate. John Nathaniel was born in 1857 and George in

---

423 Phebe Ameden, death certificate, Hebron Town Clerk, Hebron, New York.

424 William Munson household, 1830 U.S. cens., Washington Co., N.Y., Hebron, page 245, line 5.

425 William Munson household, 1840 U.S. cens., Washington Co., N.Y., Hebron, page 171, line 21.

426 Nathaniel Ameden household, 1845 N.Y. cens., Warren Co., N.Y., Queensbury, line 434.

427 N. Amidon household, 1850 U.S. cens., Washington Co., N.Y., pop. sched., Hebron, p. 298, dwelling 1319, family 1414.

428 *History of Washington County,* 397.

429 Washington County Deeds, 1854.

430 Nathaniel Ameden household, 1855 N.Y. cens., Washington Co., N.Y., Hebron.

431 Washington County deeds, 1857.

early 1860. The 1860 census shows the couple with their seven children. Nathaniel was working as a stone mason, like his brother Larnard. His farm was worth $1100.[432]

Nathaniel and Phebe sold to John S. Wheden on 18 March 1861 the twenty-eight acres they had purchased from John Munson's estate for $1025.

Phebe continued to deliver children. Lora was born in 1862, but John Nathaniel died in 1863 at age five, Hannah died on Christmas Eve 1864 at age fourteen, and Juliaette in 1865 at age eighteen. Nathaniel John was born in 1865, memorializing his dead brother. The 1865 census shows Nathaniel and Phebe still living in Hebron with their six surviving children: William, Caroline, Ashell, George, Lora and Nathaniel John. Nathaniel was a farmer, owning his own farm, living in a frame house worth $500. His farm was valued at $4800, his stock at $1000. He had seventy acres of improved land and fifty acres of unimproved. Twenty acres were plowed, twenty pasture, fifteen meadow, three in oats, and four in winter rye. He produced potatoes, apples, cider, maple syrup, honey, butter, pork, and wool.[433]

Little Nathaniel John died seven days before his first birthday in 1866. Phebe bore eleven children in all, but the remaining two have not been identified. They were probably also infant deaths. By the end of 1866 only five of Phebe's eleven children were still alive.

Nathaniel bought part of lot number seven in Campbell's Patent in Hebron from his sister-in-law, Elizabeth Ameden, for $500 on 1 April 1867.[434] The 1870 census shows the family diminished by Nathaniel John's death and economic reverses. Nathaniel and William were working as farm laborers. Nathaniel's real estate was now worth only one thousand dollars.[435]

In 1871 the family began to break up with William's marriage to Gusta Robbins. In 1872 Caroline married William Robin. In 1879 Ashell married Emily Taylor. The 1880 census for Hebron shows

---

[432] Nathaniel Ameden household, 1860 U.S. cens., Washington Co., N.Y., pop. sched., Hebron, page 50, dwelling 400, family 425.

[433] Nathaniel Ameden household, 1865 New York cens., Washington Co., N.Y, Hebron 1st district, family 55.

[434] Washington County deeds, 1867.

[435] Nathaniel W. Ameden household, 1870 U.S. cens., Washington Co., N.Y., pop. sched., Hebron, page 41, dwelling 344, family 352.

Nathaniel and Phebe with their remaining children: George and Lora. Nathaniel was again recognized as a farmer.[436]

Shortly before Ashell's marriage, Nathaniel and Phebe sold the land in Campbell's Patent to Newlon Parrish for $700 on 4 December 1878.[437] That land seems to have been a good investment, turning a nice profit in eleven years. A year later Phebe bought a 117-acre farm in Hebron on the Vermont line from her husband's half-brother, Sylvester Spoor, for $500 on 7 November 1879.[438] On 10 February 1883 she paid $700 to Newlon and Maria Parrish to re-acquire the land in Campbell's Patent they had sold to Newlon in 1878.[439]

George died of inflammation of the bowel in 1882 at age twenty-two, and Lora married H. William Lee in 1885. And so Nathaniel and Phebe found themselves with an empty nest. But they were not to enjoy their solitude for long. Nathaniel died in 1890 and was buried with five of his deceased children in East Hebron Cemetery.[440]

Phebe was living alone on the farm in 1900.[441] By then Ashell was her only child still living. Of her eleven offspring, only William Franklin and Ashell had produced grandchildren. Phebe died in 1906 and is buried beside her husband and five children in East Hebron Cemetery.[442]

Children of NATHANIEL and PHEBE (MUNSON) AMEDEN, all prob. born Hebron:

    i. JULIAETT AMEDEN, b. 1 Oct. 1846; d. 28 May 1865; bur. East Hebron Cemetery.[443]

77. ii. WILLIAM "FRANK" AMEDEN, b. Hebron, N.Y., 12 Sept. 1848.

   iii. HANNAH MARIA AMEDEN, b. Hebron 7 Oct. 1850; d. 24 Dec. 1864; bur. East Hebron Cemetery.[444]

---

[436] Nat Amadon household, 1880 U.S. cens., Washington Co., N.Y., pop. sched., Hebron, page 10, dwelling 81, family 83.

[437] Washington County deeds, 1878.

[438] Washington County deeds, book 90, page 231.

[439] Washington County deeds, book 93, page 472.

[440] Nathaniel W. Ameden tombstone, East Hebron Cemetery, Hebron, N.Y.

[441] Phoebe Ameden household, 1900 U.S. census, Washington County, New York, population schedule, town of Hebron, SD 5, ED 133, sheet 2A, dwelling 461, family 46; National Archives micropublication T623, roll 1172.

[442] Phebe Ameden tombstone, East Hebron Cemetery, Hebron, New York.

[443] Juliaett Ameden tombstone, East Hebron Cemetery, Hebron, New York.

[444] Hannah Ameden tombstone, East Hebron Cemetery, Hebron, New York.

    iv.   CAROLINE CLARIMON AMEDEN, b. Hebron 25 Oct. 1852; d. 1 Oct. 1878; bur. East Hebron Cemetery; m. at Hebron before 23 May 1872 WILLIAM H. ROBIN.[445]

78. v.   ASHELL AMEDEN, b. Hebron 25 Dec. 1854.

    vi.   JOHN NATHANIEL AMEDEN, b. Hebron 30 Aug. 1857; d. 22 May 1863; bur. East Hebron Cemetery.[446]

   vii.   GEORGE HERMAN AMEDEN, b. Hebron 4 March 1860; d. Hebron 5 Aug. 1882;[447] bur. East Hebron Cemetery.[448]

  viii.   LORA ALVIRA AMEDEN, b. Hebron 28 Feb. 1862; d. 30 June 1890; m. July 1885 H. WILLIAM LEE.[449]

    ix.   NATHANIEL JOHN AMEDEN, b. Hebron 20 Feb. 1865; d. 13 Feb. 1866; bur. East Hebron Cemetery.[450]

Jane E. (Ameden) Burke (1826–)

29. JANE E. AMEDEN *(Horatio⁵ Gates Ameden, Jacob⁴ Amidown, Henry³, Philip², Roger¹ Amadowne)* was born in November 1826 probably at Hebron, New York.[451] She married at Greenwich, New York, on 11 March 1847 JOSEPH ANDREW "ANDREW" BURKE.[452] He was born at Pennsylvania in November 1821.[453]

Jane grew up in Hebron, where she was recorded with the family in 1830 and with her mother in 1840. She and Andrew married in 1847. Where they initially set up housekeeping has not been found. Jane had two children, but only one survived to the 1900 census, which reported the fact. That child was a daughter, Jennie, who married in Oswego County, New York, in 1870, JOHN DANIELS, a teamster. The Daniels relocated immediately to Dubuque, Iowa.[454]

---

445   Jackson and Jackson, *Marriage Notices from Washington County*, 87.

446   John Ameden tombstone, East Hebron Cemetery, Hebron, New York.

447   George H. Amedon, death certificate, Hebron Town Clerk, Hebron, N.Y.

448   George Ameden tombstone, East Hebron Cemetery, Hebron, New York.

449   Best, *The Amidon Family*, 100.

450   Nathaniel J. Ameden tombstone, East Hebron Cemetery, Hebron, N.Y.

451   John Daniels household, 1900 U.S. census, Dubuque County, Iowa, population schedule, Julian, SD 3, ED 118, sheet 9B, dwelling 180, family 188; National Archives micropublication T623, roll 430.

452   Jackson and Jackson, *Marriages from Washington Co. Newspapers*, 154.

453   John Daniels household, 1900 U.S. census, Dubuque Co., Ia., pop. sched., Dubuque 5th ward, SD 3, ED 118, sheet 9B, dwelling 180, family 188.

454   John Daniels household, 1870 U.S. census, Dubuque County, Iowa, population schedule, Dubuque 3rd ward, page 54, dwelling 455, family 430; National Archives micropublication M593, roll 389.

Jane and Andrew followed by 1873,[455] and lived in Dubuque with the Daniels from at least 1880[456] through 1900, at 1664 Washington Street.[457]

Child of JOSEPH ANDREW and JANE (AMEDEN) BURKE:

79. i. JENNIE BURKE, b. N.Y. 5 Sept. 1849.

Frances Ann (Ameden) Parkerson (1830–1883)

30. FRANCES ANN AMEDEN *(Horatio[5] Gates Ameden, Jacob[4] Amidown, Henry[3], Philip[2], Roger[1] Amadowne)* was born at Hebron, New York, on 7 September 1830 and died at Greenwich, New York, on 16 June 1883.[458] She married before 1850 HIRAM F. PARKERSON. He was born in New York on 5 February 1826, a son of JOHN and POLLY ANN (TOMPKINS) PARKERSON.[459]

Frances Ann was born shortly after the census taker came by in 1830. She appears in the family census in Hebron in 1840.

Hiram was likely from Onondaga County, though his family has not been found in 1830 or 1840. Hiram and Frances Ann set up housekeeping in Hebron. In 1850 they were providing a home for Frances's older brother Nathaniel, his wife and their two children. They already had two-year-old Jane. And Frances's widowed mother was living with them. Hiram and Nathaniel were both masons, probably working together.[460]

By 1860, Hiram and Nathaniel were in their own homes in Hebron, just a few doors away from each other. Hiram and Frances Ann had two more daughters, Ella and Ida.[461]

By 1870, Hiram and Frances had moved southwest a few miles to Greenwich and had added a fourth daughter, Lena. The census records the value of their real estate at $1800 and assigns it to

---

[455] *Dubuque City Directory, 1873-4*; Wisc. Historical Soc., Madison, Wisc.

[456] Andrew Burke household, 1880 U.S. census, Dubuque County, Iowa, population schedule, Dubuque, page 182D, dwelling 234, family 250; National Archives micropublication T9, roll 338.

[457] John Daniels household, 1900 U.S. cens., Dubuque Co., Ia., pop. sched., Dubuque 5th ward, SD 3, ED 118, sheet 9B, dwelling 180, family 188.

[458] *Hebron Burial Book*, owned by Stacy Niedzwiecki, Rockford, Michigan.

[459] Hiram Parkson household, 1850 U.S. cens., Washington Co., N.Y., pop. sched., Hebron, page 298, dwelling 1319, family 1416.

[460] Hiram Parkson household, 1850 U.S. cens., Washington Co., N.Y., pop. sched., Hebron, page 298, dwelling 1319, family 1416.

[461] Hiram Parkson household, 1860 U.S. cens., Washington Co., N.Y., pop. sched., Hebron, page 50, dwelling 395, family 419.

Frances, not Hiram. Is this an error by the census taker? Washington County deeds need to be examined to learn the answer.[462]

By 1880, the three older girls had left home. Only thirteen-year-old Lena remained at home in Greenwich with her parents. Hiram was now age fifty-six, working as a brick mason.[463] Frances died in 1883 at age fifty-two and is buried near her parents and siblings in Hebron Cemetery.[464]

In 1900 the elderly Hiram Parkerson was living with his widowed daughter Jennie and his married grand-daughter Ada Morris in Greenwich, New York. He died on 24 November 1903 and is buried beside Frances Ann in Hebron Cemetery.

Children of HIRAM and FRANCES ANN (AMEDEN) PARKERSON:

80. i. JANE "JENNIE" PARKERSON, b. N.Y. April 1848.
    ii. ELLA PARKERSON, b. N.Y. abt. 1853.[465] Last record: parents' 1870 census.
    iii. IDA PARKERSON, b. N.Y. abt. 1859;[466] m. North Argyle, N.Y., 17 Jan. 1878 WILLARD BURTON, son of LEWIS and LENORA (___) (KING) BURTON;[467] Willard was half-brother of Andrew King, husband of Ida's sister Jane. Resided Hartford, N.Y., in 1880.
    iv. LENA M. PARKERSON, b. abt. N.Y. 1867.[468]

---

462 Hiram Parkerson household, 1870 U.S. cens., Washington Co., N.Y., pop. sched., Greenwich, page 52, dwelling 430, family 475.

463 Hiram Parkerson household, 1880 U.S. cens., Washington Co., N.Y., pop. sched., Greenwich, SD 6, ED 142, page 16, dwelling 116, family 140.

464 *Hebron Burial Book*, owned by Stacy Niedzwiecki, Rockford, Michigan.

465 Hiram Parkson household, 1860 U.S. cens., Washington Co., N.Y., pop. sched Hebron, page 50, dwelling 395, family 419.

466 Hiram Parkson household, 1860 U.S. cens., Washington Co., N.Y., pop. sched Hebron, page 50, dwelling 395, family 419.

467 Jackson and Jackson, *Marriages from Washington Co. Newspapers*, 33.

468 Hiram Parkerson household, 1880 U.S. cens., Washington Co., N.Y., pop. sched., Greenwich, SD 6, ED 142, page 16, dwelling 116, family 140.

Chapter 4 -- Seventh Generation
Grandchildren of Ursula Amidon

Marshall Elmer (1831—1894)

31. MARSHALL[7] ELMER *(AURELIA[6] WHITMORE, URSULA[5] AMIDON, JACOB[4] AMIDOWN, HENRY[3], PHILIP[2], ROGER[1] AMADOWNE)* was born at Woodstock, Connecticut, on 5 April 1831.[1] He died at Chicago, Illinois, on 19 December 1894.[2] He married before 1860[3] MARY ELIZABETH HARRISON. She was born at Springfield, Massachusetts,[4] in October 1834,[5] the daughter of GERSHON and BETSY ( ) HARRISON.[6] Mary died at San Francisco on 23 October 1927.[7] She married second in San Francisco in 1888 DANIEL WILBUR GUPTILL. Daniel was born in Illinois in about 1838, the son of DANIEL and ROSANNA MATILDA ( ) GUPTAIL, and died in San Francisco in 1919.

Marshall grew up in Springfield, where he was enumerated with his parents in 1840 and 1850. Two of his three siblings died as toddlers. His younger sister Mary lived only to age nine, dying when Marshall was eleven. So his teen years were those of an only child. He was listed with his parents in 1855–6 in the Springfield city directory, which showed him clerking in his father's store,[8] and in 1859.[9]

---

1   *Vital Records of Woodstock, 1686-1854*, 501.

2   Marshall Elmer death entry, number 00004589, Cook Co. Clerk, Chicago, Ill.

3   Rufus Elmer household, 1860 U.S. cens., Hampden Co., Mass., pop. sched., Springfield, page 297, dwelling 2347, family 2543.

4   Birthplace per birth records for her children in Springfield: Jay Mack Holbrook, *Massachusetts Vital Records: Springfield, 1640-1894* (Oxford, Mass.: Holbrook Research Institute, 1987), Births: 5:141, 165; 6:73.

5   Daniel D. Guptill household, 1900 U.S. census, San Francisco county, California, population schedule, San Francisco, SD 1, ED 155, sheet 3B, dwelling 45, family 66; National Archives micropublication T623, roll 104.

6   Gershom Harrisson household, 1850 U.S. cens., Hampden Co., Mass., pop. sched., Springfield, p. 172, dw. 1455, fam. 1594.

7   Mary Guptill entry, *California Death Index, 1905-1997*; California Genealogical Society, Oakland, California.

8   *Bessey's Springfield Directory 1855-6* (Springfield: M. Bessey, 1855), 75.

9   *Springfield, Massachusetts City Directory Listing.*

The daughter of a grocer, Mary Harrison also grew up in Springfield, where she was enumerated with her parents in 1840[10] and 1850.[11]

Marshall remained very close to his parents all their lives. He and his wife Mary lived with them until Marshall's father died in 1870. In the 1860 census, the household consisted only of his parents and the young newlyweds. But Mary's first child, William, was born a year later. Harrison was born in 1863. And Philip was born in 1868. The gap between Harrison and Philip probably reflects the uncertainties of the continuing Civil War.

Once Marshall married, he went into business with his father-in-law, Gershon Harrison, forming Harrison & Elmer, located at 112 East State Street in Springfield.[12]

At the end of 1869, Marshall's father, Rufus, turned the shoe business over to his brother Nelson. Marshall moved the family to San Francisco, capitalizing on the new rail link that opened in May 1869, with the famous ceremony at Promontory Point, Utah. Rufus died in San Francisco in January 1870. Marshall established a wholesale grocery business with Marcus E. Austin, which operated under the name Elmer & Co. at 421 Clay Street.[13] Marshall's father's will explicitly left nothing to Marshall,[14] so it may be that his father had financed the business before his death, instead of making Marshall wait for an inheritance.

The household at 140 Polk, on the fringe of downtown, was a large one. In addition to Marshall's wife, three children, and widowed mother, the household included Marshall's brother-in-law William P. Harrison, his wife Fanny Harrison, and a young male domestic from China, Long Ab.[15]

Apparently the house wasn't big enough. At some time between 1871 and 1873 the family moved to 314 Bush Street and operated a

---

[10] G. W. Harrison household, 1840 U.S. cens., Hampden Co., Mass., pop. sched., Springfield, p. 34, ln. 25.

[11] Gershom Harrisson household, 1850 U.S. cens., Hampden Co., Mass., pop. sched., Springfield, p. 172, dw. 1455, fam. 1594.

[12] *Springfield Massachusetts City Directory, 1864-65.*

[13] *Langley's San Francisco Directory, 1873,* page 233.

[14] Rufus Elmer, Hampden County probate file no. 3949, will book 43, page 15, Probate Court, Springfield, Massachusetts.

[15] Marshall Elmer household, 1870 U.S. cens., San Francisco Co., Cal., pop. sched., 9th ward, p. 193, dw. 1468, fam. 1679.

boarding house, which they called Elmer House.[16] Bush Street was one of the highly fashionable streets, where affluent women walked to show off their finery. The boarding house was at the southwest corner of Bush and Powell, two blocks north of Union Square.

Marshall seems to have found running his own business more than he could handle. He may have been unprepared for the volatile economic cycles and cutthroat competition of the West. Or he may have speculated in the Comstock silver mines that pauperized so many San Francisco residents. The year 1871 was a time of feverish speculation in the Comstock. In any event, Elmer & Co. was gone by 1873. At about that time Marshall left Mary to run the boarding house and raise their young sons alone.[17] He went to Chicago, where he boarded in a variety of hotels in the heart of the city. He worked initially as a clerk for the Star Union Railroad Company, which ran from Chicago to Jersey City, New Jersey.[18] By 1879 he was a foreman.[19]

By 1880 Mary had forty-six boarders in Elmer House, in addition to her three sons. Her mother-in-law had returned to Massachusetts and her brother had moved across the bay to East Oakland.[20] Mary's boarders reflected the great diversity of San Francisco, with boarders from the East Coast and the Midwest, from Europe and Asia, merchants and servants, skilled tradesmen and farmers, a railroad conductor and a sea captain. Mary recorded herself as a widow, although her absent husband was actually living in Chicago.[21]

Late in 1880 tragedy struck when twelve-year-old Philip died. It was compounded three years later when twenty-two-year-old William died, leaving Mary alone with her middle son Harrison. The boys were buried in the Masonic Cemetery in San Francisco. But the

---

[16] *Langley's San Francisco Directory, 1873,* page 218.

[17] Ancestry.com, *Chicago Voter Registration, 1888* [database online] (Provo, Utah: Ancestry.com, 2001), 208, 460. Original data: Ill. State Archives microfilm.

[18] *The Lakeside Annual Directory of the City of Chicago, 1874-5* (Chicago: The Chicago Directory Company, 1874), 376.

[19] *The Lakeside Annual Directory of the City of Chicago, 1879* (Chicago: The Chicago Directory Company, 1879), 376.

[20] Wm. P. Harrison household, 1880 U.S. census, Alameda County, California, population schedule, East Oakland, page 4, SD 21, ED 18, dwelling 6, family 6; National Archives micropublication T9, roll 62.

[21] Mary Elmer household, 1880 U.S. census, San Francisco County, California, population schedule, San Francisco, page 1, SD 1, ED 45, dwelling 20, family 21; National Archives micropublication T9, roll 74.

Masonic Cemetery was later slated to be razed. On 19 June 1911 their remains were sent to the Independent Order of Odd Fellows Crematory for cremation, and were re-interred at Woodlawn Memorial Park - Masonic, in Colma, California, on 28 June 1911.[22]

By 1888 Mary was fifty-five. Perhaps the boarding house was getting to be more than she could handle. On 12 June she sold the house to Charles Carr.[23] It continued to be known as the Elmer House, despite having different proprietors.[24] Mary and Harrison briefly moved to 26 Haight Street,[25] two miles from the city center. But later that year Mary married Daniel Wilbur Guptill, a stock broker from Illinois, living at 760 Oak Street in San Francisco. Mary and Daniel lived there for the rest of their lives.[26]

Mary's brother, William Pitt Harrison, died in 1916, naming his sister as Mrs. D. W. Guptill, thus unlocking the secret of what became of Mary.[27] Daniel died in 1919, after thirty-one years of marriage to Mary. Mary lived on alone in the Oak Street house, accompanied only by her Swedish maid, Augusta Anderson.[28] She died at San Francisco in 1927 at age ninety-three.

Marshall, alone in Chicago, must have been grateful to have his mother join him in about 1883. They settled into a house at 101 S. Halsted, fourteen blocks west of Grant Park (called Lake Park on the 1873 map) at the intersection with Monroe Street. Marshall's office was at 38 W. Van Buren, three blocks west of today's Grant Park and three blocks south of Monroe – a very reasonable walk.[29] Aurelia died in Chicago in 1892. Marshall moved to 310 West Van Buren,[30] but survived his mother by only two years, dying in 1894 at age

---

[22] Filion, *San Francisco History: Masonic Cemetery.*

[23] San Francisco deed book 1298, page 393.

[24] *Langley's San Francisco Directory 1889 (San Francisco: Henry G. Langley, 1889)*, 484.

[25] *Langley's San Francisco Directory 1888*, 442-3.

[26] Daniel W. Guptill household, 1910 U.S. census, San Francisco county, California, population schedule, San Francisco, SD 4, ED 161, sheet 7A, dwelling 106, family 163; National Archives micropublication T624, roll 98.

[27] Death Notice, *San Francisco Chronicle*, 5 February 1916, page 6, column 8.

[28] Mary E. Guptill household, 1920 U.S. census, San Francisco county, California, population schedule, San Francisco, SD 4, ED 87, sheet 8A, dwelling 55, family 225; National Archives micropublication T625, roll 134.

[29] *The Lakeside Annual Directory of the City of Chicago, 1884*, 439.

[30] *The Lakeside Annual Directory of the City of Chicago, 1892* (Chicago: The Chicago Directory Company, 1892), 471.

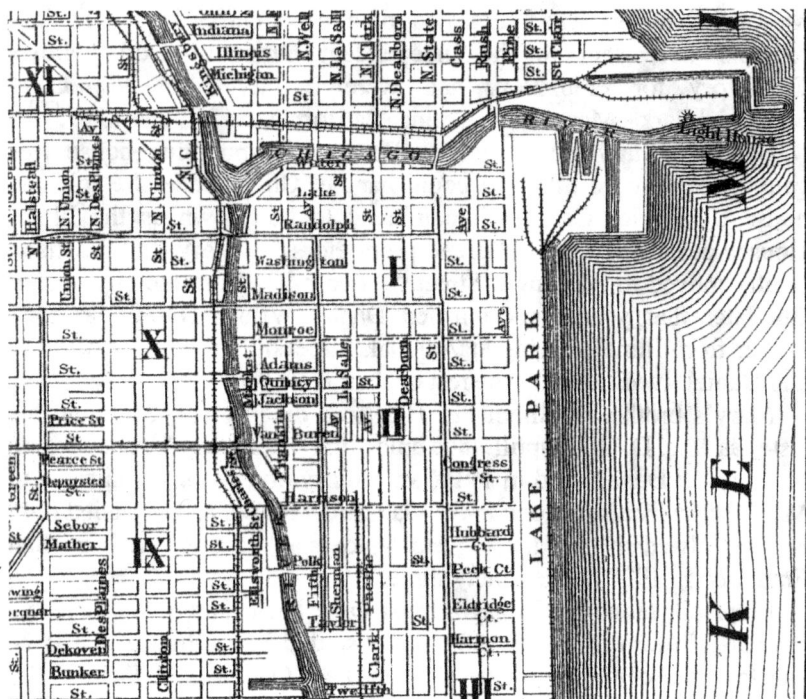

Chicago 1873 (Courtesy: Jonathan Sheppard Books)

sixty-three. He was buried with his mother in Springfield Cemetery, Springfield, Massachusetts on 24 December 1894.

Children of MARSHALL and MARY (HARRISON) ELMER:

i.   WILLIAM[8] R. ELMER, b. Springfield, Mass., 2 May 1861;[31] d. San Francisco, Calif., 9 July 1883;[32] bur. Masonic Cem., San Francisco, 11 July 1883.

ii. HARRISON ELMER, b. Springfield 6 Sept. 1863;[33] m. abt. 1893 MARY E. "STELLA" REES, b. abt. April 1866,[34] dau. ROBERT and

31 Holbrook, *Mass. VR: Springfield,* Births, 5:141.
32 Elmer, *San Francisco Call,* 10 July 1883.
33 Holbrook, *Mass. VR: Springfield,* Births, 5:165.
34 Stella Elmer household, U.S. 1900 census, New York County, New York, population schedule, Manhattan, SD 1, ED 255, sheet 6B, dwelling 48, family 90; National Archives micropublication T623, roll 1092. Stella was living in Manhattan with her mother. Harrison has not been found in 1900 – perhaps he was performing in France.

LUCY CARRIE (SHIPP) REESE.[35] Resident San Francisco 1910.[36] Harrison and Stella were active in theater and lived much of their adult lives in France (and perhaps England). Resident Home for Incurables, Bronx, N.Y., 1930.[37]

    Child of HARRISON and STELLA (REES) ELMER:

a. *Philip Rees Elmer*, b. Indianapolis, Ind., 5 Jan. 1896;[38] m. abt. 1919[39] *Emily* ___, b. N.Y. 3 April 1897.[40] Insurance broker. Resident Westfield, N.J., 1930.[41]

    Children of *Philip* and *Emily (___) Elmer:*

    1. Edward Philip Elmer, b. New York, N.Y.,[42] 17 May 1920.[43]

    2. Emily Adele "Emy Del" Elmer, b. New York, N.Y., 27 Dec. 1923.[44]

iii. PHILIP M. ELMER, b. Springfield 4 July 1868;[45] d. San Francisco, 15 Nov. 1880;[46] bur. Masonic Cem.

---

[35] Robert H. Reese household, U.S. 1870 census, Boone County, Indiana, population schedule, Sugar Creek, page 79/242, dwelling 648, family 637; National Archives micropublication M593, roll 300.
    Reese__Shipp marriage, *Indiana Marriage Collection 1800-1941*, ancestry.com.

[36] Daniel W. Guptill household, 1910 U.S. cens., San Francisco, Calif., pop. sched., San Francisco, SD 4, ED 161, sheet 7A, dwelling 106, family 163. This record says that one of Mary Guptill's children was still alive, which must refer to Harrison.

[37] Home for Incurables, 1930 U.S. census, Bronx, New York, population schedule, New York City, SD 26, ED 3-568, sheet 3A; National Archives micropublication T626, roll 1143.

[38] Philip Rees Elmer WWI registration card, Ancestry.com.

[39] Chula Rees Elmer household, 1920 U.S. census, Bronx, New York, population schedule, Westfield, SD 8, ED 20-168, sheet 6A, dwelling 132, family 132; National Archives micropublication T626, roll 1390.

[40] Emily Elmer entry, *Social Security Death Index*, Ancestry.com.

[41] Philip R. Elmer household, 1930 U.S. census, Union County, New Jersey, population schedule, Westfield, SD 2, ED 450, sheet 12A, family 275; National Archives micropublication T626, roll 1143.

[42] Edward Elmer obituary, *Daily News Sun*, Sun City, Arizona, 13 September 1993.

[43] Edward P. Elmer entry, *Social Security Death Index*, Ancestry.com.

[44] Emily E. Odell entry, *Social Security Death Index*, Ancestry.com.

[45] Holbrook, *Mass. VR: Springfield*, Births, 6:73.

[46] Elmer, *San Francisco Call*, 17 November 1880.

Chapter 5 -- Seventh Generation
Grandchildren of Jacob Amaden

Justus O. Rose (1825–1905)

32. JUSTUS O. ROSE[7] *(AURELIA[6], JACOB AMADEN[5], JACOB[4] AMIDOWN, HENRY[3], PHILIP[2], ROGER[1] AMADOWNE)* was born at Westfield, Massachusetts, on 6 May 1825, and died at Sandusky, Ohio, on 29 March 1905.[1] He married in 1846 MARY JANE SMITH.[2] Mary was born probably in New York about 1826[3] and died at Hicksville, Ohio, on 1 February 1890.[4]

Justus's parents left Westfield soon after his birth. They went up to Troy, New York, for a few years and finally settled in Russell, New York, where Justus's uncle Nathan Knox was an original settler. The 1830 federal census found the Rose family in Morristown; however, they were likely living in Russell since in 1830 it was not enumerated separately. The family likely was working on the Russell farm of Justus's uncle Nathan Knox.

The family was enumerated in Russell in 1840 as were the families of more of Justus's uncles: Freeman Rose, Nathan Knox, and John Amaden. Justus and his father Ephraim were in agriculture.

On 25 September 1844, Justus was emancipated from his father in Russell.[5] Since Justus was only nineteen, shy of twenty-one — the age of majority, it legally meant that Ephraim was giving up authority over him. Justus may have wanted to get married, may have completed a certain amount of work under his father's supervision, or may have wanted to start his own business.

---

[1]   Justus Rose obituary, *Defiance County, Ohio, Newspaper Obituaries*, undated collection, page 312/448, Defiance Public Library, Defiance, Ohio.

[2]   Ibid.

[3]   Justice O. Rass household, 1870 U.S. census, Williams County, Ohio, population schedule, St. Joseph, page 31, dwelling 229, family 229; National Archives micropublication M593, roll 1282.

[4]   Justus O. Rose, Civil War Pension Application File SO 571498, SC 803967; Records of the Veterans Administration, Record Group 15; National Archives, Washington, D.C. His obituary indicated her death date as 9 August 1890.

[5]   *St. Lawrence Republican and General Advertiser*, 1 October 1844. J. M. Austin, transcriber, online <www.rootsweb.com/~nystlawr/1850_VR_NewsItems. htm>.

No primary record of Justus's marriage to Mary Smith has been found. Justus's parents had relocated to Watertown and by 1846 had joined the Stone Street Presbyterian Church. His sister Ada stayed in Russell, dying there in 1848. So it is likely that Mary was from Russell, but she could have been from Watertown. According to the 1880 census,[6] her father was born in Vermont and mother in New Hampshire. The 1860 census gives her birthplace as Vermont; both the 1870 and 1880 censuses cite New York.

Justus and Mary's first child was George W. Rose. He was born in 1848. Justus had bought lots in Watertown in 1849 and 1850 from Hiram Townsend and his wife Luna,[7] so they likely lived in Watertown but they have not been located in the 1850 census. Justus and his wife Mary sold one of the lots on 3 November 1851 to James F. Starbuck.[8] That same year, their daughter Mary was born in New York, almost certainly in Watertown. On 8 April 1854 they sold a lot with a mortgaged home on the corner of High Street (present day Route 12) and Rutland Street in Watertown to his mother Aurelia.[9] This sale might represent the departure of Justus and Mary for Ohio.

Justus's uncle, Horatio Amaden, migrated to Williams County, Ohio, in 1842. Horatio was a carpenter and house builder. Justus followed him there, perhaps in search of work with his uncle. The 1860 census shows that Justus and his cousin Morton (Horatio's son) were living next to each other in St. Joseph Township, both of them painters.[10] Another person in Justus's household was Henry J. Rose. Henry was twenty-one years old and from New York. Likely he was Justus's cousin, perhaps a son of Freeman Rose.

In 1857 Justus's parents and maternal grandmother Chloe joined them in Saint Joseph, Ohio.

Once settled in Ohio, Justus and Mary had at least three additional children. In fact, according to Justus's obituary, he had a total of ten children – seven sons and three daughters, seven of whom died young. Only three of his children survived to adulthood.

---

6   J. O. Rose household, 1880 U.S. cens., Defiance Co., Oh., pop. sched., Hicksville, SD 1, ED 237, sheet 181C, dwelling 360, family 371.
7   Watertown Deeds, Book 92:35-36; Book 95:112-113, Jefferson County Clerk, Watertown, New York.
8   Watertown Deeds, Book 103:502.
9   Watertown Deeds, Book 116:446-447.
10 J. O. Rose household, 1860 U.S. cens., Williams Co., Oh., pop. sched., St. Joseph, page 115, dwelling 323, family 312.

The Civil War was a defining moment for Justus. Not only was he active as a recruiter for the cause (including recruiting his son), but he served two separate times, as detailed in his obituary:

[He] enlisted as private in Company C., 14th Regt., O. V. I. [Ohio Volunteer Infantry]; was enrolled on the 22nd of April, 1861, being the first to be enrolled in his company; was honorably discharged on the 13th of Aug., 1861. He then became recruiting officer in Williams County and on June 16, 1863, re-enlisted and was appointed Second Lieutenant in Company E, 86th Regt. O. V. I.; was mustered into the service July 14, 1863.[11]

Later in life, as was the tradition in the late nineteenth century, Justus was often called by his terminal military rank, Captain Rose. Returning to his life after the war, Justus continued his work as a painter – perhaps again with his cousin, Morton Amaden. Over the years, he served as a postmaster, ran for the coroner's office (and lost), and remained active in veteran's organizations. Justus remained in St. Joseph only a few years after his father's death. In 1879 he relocated to Hicksville with his wife, mother, and youngest son, and worked as a painter. Late in life after his wife had died, he moved to the Ohio State Soldiers and Sailors Home in Sandusky, where he died in 1905. He was buried at Maple Grove Cemetery in St. Joseph alongside his wife, parents, and son George.[12]

Children of JUSTUS and MARY (SMITH) ROSE:

i.   GEORGE W. ROSE, b. N.Y.[13] 26 June 1848;[14] d. Minneapolis, Minn., 12 March 1900;[15] bur. Maple Grove Cem., St. Joseph, Oh.[16] George served in Co. F, 182nd and Co. E, 86th Ohio Infantry, private, as a musician.[17] Was a railroad worker, bartender, and clerk. Never married.

---

¹¹   Justus Rose obituary, *Defiance County Newspaper Obituaries*, pp. 312/448.

¹²   Photos of grave marker held by Chris Amaden, taken 25 September 2004.

¹³   Justice O. Rass hhd, 1870 U.S. cens., Williams Co., Oh., pop. sched., St. Joseph, p. 31, dw. 229, fam. 229.

¹⁴   Justus O. Rose, Civil War pension file, SO 571498, SC 803967.

¹⁵   Geo W. Rose Death Certificate, Minnesota Department of Health, Section of Vital Statistics, Minneapolis, Minnesota.

¹⁶   Photos of grave marker held by Chris Amaden, taken 25 September 2004.

¹⁷   George W. Rose, Civil War Pension Application File SO 1132010, SC 843677.

ii.   MARY ELIZABETH ROSE, b. prob. Watertown, N.Y.,[18] 18 March 1851;[19] d. Spokane, Wash., 6 July 1926; bur. Greenwood Memorial Terrace, Spokane;[20] m. 1) Edgerton, Oh., 17 Oct. 1872 HORACE TITUS BROWN,[21] b. Hudson, Oh., 16 July 1844, son of HORACE R. and MARY ANN D. (PECK) BROWN,[22] d. Spokane, Wash., 1 June 1900,[23] bur. Greenwood Memorial Terrace, Spokane;[24] m. 2) Spokane, Wash., 29 March 1910 JAMES JONES HUNTINGTON,[25] b. Louisiana, Mo., 10 Aug. 1844, son of CHARLES RALPH and MARY E. (JONES) HUNTINGTON, d. Kansas City, Mo., 19 Oct. 1915, bur. Mt. Washington Cem., Kansas City.[26] Civil War service: Co. A., 10th Michigan Cavalry. Well established newspaper man, part owner of the *Spokane Falls Review.*

Children of HORACE and MARY (ROSE) BROWN:

a.   *Horace Oscar Brown*, b. Deer Lodge Co., Mt., 10 April 1873;[27] m. Montecello, Ind., 3 Oct. 1899 *Margaret Waddell Mack*,[28] b. Huntingdon, Quebec, Canada, 10 April 1873, dau. of *James Waddell* and *Agnes (Ross) Mack*.[29] Printer.

Child of *Horace* and *Margaret (Mack) Brown*:

1.   Helen E. Brown, b. Spokane 7 May 1900; m. Spokane 26

---

¹⁸   Justice O. Rass hhd, 1870 U.S. cens., Williams Co., Oh., pop. sched., St. Joseph, p. 31, dw. 229, fam. 229.

¹⁹   Justus O. Rose, Civil War pension file SO 571498, SC 803967.

²⁰   Mary E. Brown, death certificate record # 810, Registration # 848, State Department of Health, Olympia, Washington.

²¹   Horace T. Brown and Mary Brown, widow, Civil War Pension Application File SO 1038031, SC 830151, WC 526734; Records of the Veterans Administration, Record Group 15; National Archives, Washington, D.C.

²²   Brown family records maintained by Gil Murray, Cheney, Washington.

²³   Horace T. Brown and Mary Brown, widow, Civil War Pension File SO 1038031, WC 526734.

²⁴   Brown family records maintained by Gil Murray, Cheney, Washington.

²⁵   Rose-Huntington marriage, Spokane County, Washington, Marriage Certificate #A9565.

²⁶   James J. Huntington death certificate #30706, Missouri State Archives, Jefferson City, Missouri.

²⁷   Horace T. Brown and Mary Brown, widow, Civil War Pension File SO 1038031, WC 526734.

²⁸   Indiana Works Progress Administration, compiler, *Index to Marriage Record 1850 - 1920 Volume I Letters A – L* (White County, Indiana: WPA, 1938). Original Record Located: County Clerk's Office Monticello, Book C-7:82 and Book H-3R:21.

²⁹   Brown family records maintained by Gil Murray, Cheney, Washington.

June 1919 *Claudius Cornelius Murray*, b. Spokane 22
Feb. 1895, son of *Edward William* and *Genevieve (Low)
Murray*. Three children.[30]

b. *Mary Bell Brown*, b. Oh. 24 May 1876;[31] m. 1899
    Alexander Howie, b. Scotland Dec. 1871.[32] No children.[33]
c. *Waldo Washington Brown*, b. Spokane, Wash., 15 Feb.
    1890;[34] d. 14 Dec. 1918 in Spanish Flu Pandemic; bur.
    Greenwood Memorial Terrace;[35] m. *Elma Davis
    Stephens*,[36] b. Wash. Nov. 1896,[37] daughter of *Elmer M.
    Stephens*.[38]

    Children of *Waldo* and *Elma (Stephens) Brown*:
    1. Ramona Marie Brown, b. Arlington, Wash., 29 May
        1915.[39]
    2. Elma Liotta Brown, b. Wash. abt. Feb. 1916.[40]

iii. FRANK E. ROSE, b. Oh. abt. 1857; d. bet. 1860-1870.[41]
iv.   ADDIE D. ROSE, b. Oh. abt. 1859; d. bet 1870-1897.[42]

---

30   Ibid.
31   Horace T. Brown and Mary Brown, widow, Civil War Pension File SO
1038031, WC 526734.
32   Alexander Howie household, 1900 U.S. census, Spokane County,
Washington, population schedule, town of Spokane, Ward 4, SD 2, ED 69, sheet
198A, dwelling 210, family 227; National Archives micropublication T623, roll
1751.
33   Brown family records maintained by Gil Murray, Cheney, Washington.
34   Waldo Washington Brown record. Ancestry.com, *World War I Draft
Registration Cards, 1917-1918*.
35   Brown family records maintained by Gil Murray, Cheney, Washington.
36   Ramona Maria Brown, *Washington State Birth Index, Prior to 1910 –
1919*, online <www.ancestry.com>. Names her mother as Elma Davis Stephens.
37   William Stevens household, 1900 U.S. census, Snohomish County,
Washington, population schedule, town of Tulalip, SD 285, ED 216, sheet 8B,
dwelling 156, family 164; National Archives micropublication T623, roll 1750.
38   Elmer Stephens household, 1910 U.S. census, Snohomish County,
Washington, population schedule, town of Tualco, SD 1, ED 313, sheet 5B,
dwelling 88, family 89; National Archives micropublication T624, roll 1669.
39   Brown, *Washington State Birth Index, Prior to 1910 – 1919*.
40   Rosana J. Stephens household, 1930 U.S. census, Snohomish County,
Washington, population schedule, town of Monroe, SD 3, ED 96, sheet 14B,
dwelling 386, family 414; National Archives micropublication T626, roll 2520.
41   J. O. Rose household, 1860 U.S. cens., Williams Co., Oh., pop. sched., St.
Joseph, p. 115, dwelling 323, family 312. Not present in family's 1870 census.
42   Justice O. Rass household, 1870 U.S. cens., Williams Co., Oh., pop.
sched., St. Joseph, p. 31, 229, 229. Not mentioned in Justus Rose's pension
application of 1897 of living children.

v. SHERIDAN GRANT ROSE, b. Edgerton, Oh.,[43] 28 Dec. 1865;[44] m. Toledo, Oh., 18 June 1889, MARY MAGDALENE SULLIVAN,[45] b. Toledo 7 Nov. 1867, daughter of TIMOTHY and CATHERINE (O'NEILL) SULLIVAN.[46] Sheridan was a salesman.

Children of SHERIDAN and MARY (SULLIVAN) ROSE:

a. *John Harry "Harry" Rose,* b. Toledo 1 Feb. 1892;[47] d. Toledo 20 Sept. 1928;[48] bur. Calvary Cem., Toledo;[49] m. 1) Lucas Co., Oh., 24 June 1914 *Florence A. Wenzel,*[50] b. Toledo 17 April 1892, dau. of *Jacob F.* and *Bertha (Erne) Wenzel,*[51] d. Toledo 17 April 1918,[52] bur. Calvary Cemetery;[53] m. 2) *Clara J. Fahlbusch,*[54] b. Oh. 26 June 1892.[55] Shoe salesman.

    Child of *John* and *Florence (Wenzel) Rose*:
1. Harry A. Rose, b. Toledo 20 March 1915.[56]

    Child of *John* and *Clara (Fahlbusch) Rose*:
2. Thomas J. Rose, b. bet. 1920-1928.[57]

b. *Beatrice Mary Rose,* b. Toledo 15 April 1894;[58] m. Lucas Co., Oh., 5 Aug. 1925 *Adam Gideon Spieker,* b. Toledo 6 April 1891, son of *Henry John* and *Sophia D. (Kuhlman) Spieker.*[59] A. Gideon was a civic leader and CEO of Spieker Construction of Toledo.

---

[43]   John Harry Rose death certificate #56132, Ohio Dept. of Health. States his father was born in Edgerton.

[44]   Sheridan G. Rose death certificate #21525, Minn. Department of Health.

[45]   Rose-Sullivan marriage record, St. Francis de Sales Catholic Church, Toledo, Ohio, Volume 3 ½, page 592.

[46]   Mary M. Rose death certificate #04312, Ohio Department of Health.

[47]   John Harry Rose death certificate #56132, Ohio Department of Health.

[48]   J. Harry Rose obituary, *Toledo[Ohio] Blade,* 20 September 1928, page 36.

[49]   John Harrison Rose burial record #29700, Calvary Cem., Toledo, Ohio.

[50]   Rose-Wenzel marriage, Lucas County marriage records, page 609, Probate Judge, Toledo, Ohio.

[51]   Florence Wenzel birth record, *Toledo, Ohio, Birth Records,* page 34, Bowling Green State University.

[52]   Florence Rose obituary, *Toledo [Ohio] Blade,* 17 April 1918.

[53]   Florence Rose tombstone, Calvary Cemetery, Toledo, Oh., Sect. 8, Lot 52.

[54]   Fahlbusch family records maintained by John J. McGowan, Toledo, Oh.

[55]   Clara J. Clark, death certificate # 030155, Ohio Dept. of Health.

[56]   Harry A. Rose, death certificate # 19307, Ohio Dept. of Health.

[57]   Clara (Fahlbusch) Clark obituary, *Toledo [Ohio] Blade,* 11 April 1986. Names son Thomas.

[58]   Rose-Spieker marriage, Lucas County, Ohio, Marriage Record #48890.

[59]   Ibid.

Children of A. *Gideon* and *Beatrice (Rose) Spieker*:
1. Adam Gideon Spieker Jr., b. Toledo, Oh., 6 Nov. 1926.[60]
2. Mary Beatrice Spieker, b. Toledo 8 July 1928.[61]
3. Natalie Spieker, b. Toledo 26 June 1930.[62]

c. *Catherine Deborah Rose*, b. Toledo 18 June 1898;[63] m. *Henry Alfred Johnson*, b. N.Y.,[64] d. abt. 1928.[65]

Children of *Henry* and *Catharine (Rose) Johnson*:
1. Paul Alfred Johnson, b. Toledo 10 Jan. 1925.[66]
2. Mary R. Johnson, b. Toledo 28 Feb. 1928; d. Toledo 5 Sept. 1930; bur. Calvary Cem., Toledo.[67]

d. *Veronica Elizabeth Rose*, b. Toledo 20 Oct. 1902;[68] m. abt. 1925 *James Harry McGowan*,[69] b. Toledo 26 July 1896,[70] son of *John J.* and *Julia (Tobin) McGowan*. [71] James served in WWI in American Army Expeditionary Forces and was a Toledo police officer.

Children of *James* and *Veronica (Rose) McGowan*:
1. James Harry McGowan, b. Toledo, Oh., 12 Nov. 1926.[72]
2. John J. McGowan, b. Toledo 26 Aug. 1928.[73]

---

[60] Adam Gideon Spieker birth record, *Toledo Birth Records Index* (Toledo, Ohio: Board of Health, 1868-1910), 5105; Toledo-Lucas County Public Library, Toledo, Ohio.

[61] Mary (Spieker) Smith obituary, *Toledo [Ohio] Blade*, 28 August 2005.

[62] Natalie Spieker Cavalear obituary, *Toledo [Ohio] Blade*, 21 January 1993.

[63] Catherine Deborah Rose entry, Lucas County Births, Volume 6:211, Lucas County Courthouse, Toledo, Ohio.

[64] Mary R. Johnson, death certificate # 094701, Vital Statistics, Ohio Dept. of Health, Columbus, Ohio. Says her father was born in N.Y.

[65] Fahlbusch family records maintained by John J. McGowan, Toledo, Oh.

[66] Paul Alfred Johnson birth record, *Toledo Birth Records Index*.

[67] Mary R. Johnson, death certificate # 094701, Ohio Dept. of Health.

[68] Veronica Elizabeth Rose entry, *Lucas County, Ohio Birth Records*, 6:211.

[69] Fahlbusch family records maintained by John J. McGowan, Toledo, Oh.

[70] James Harry McGowan, Ancestry.com, WWI Draft Reg. Card #304.

[71] James Harry McGowan death certificate # 77594, Ohio Dept. of Health. Fahlbusch family records maintained by John J. McGowan, Toledo, Oh.

[72] James Harry McGowan birth record, *Toledo Birth Records Index*, p. 5236.

[73] John J. McGowan birth record, *Toledo Birth Records Index*, page 4081.

Morton Amaden (1836–1885)

33. MORTON A. AMADEN (*HORATIO[6], JACOB AMADEN[5], JACOB[4] AMIDOWN, HENRY[3], PHILIP[2], ROGER[1] AMADOWNE*) was born at St. Lawrence County, New York,[74] in 1836,[75] and died at Holton, Kansas, on 20 May 1885.[76] He married first at Williams County, Ohio, on 1 July 1860, NANCY M. LUCE.[77] Nancy was born about 1841 in Ohio[78] and died about 1869.[79] He married second at Bryan, Ohio, on 25 September 1873, FLORA MOORE (CRALL) MCQUILKIN, widow of ROBERT MCQUILKIN.[80] Flora was born at Wooster, Ohio,[81] on 22 March 1842, the daughter of DAVID M. and CATHERINE (__) CRALL. She died at Superior, Wisconsin, on 6 June 1919 and is buried at Mott Cemetery, Union, Indiana.[82]

Morton was the first child of Horatio and Charlotte Amaden. The family was living in Parishville, New York, a possible birth location for Morton, in 1840. When Morton was six years old, he and his family left St. Lawrence County for a "cross country" move to Williams County, Ohio. The reason for leaving New York is unknown. Perhaps his father, a carpenter, was following the expanse of the country in search of steady work. Regrettably, soon after their arrival in Ohio, Morton's mother Charlotte died in 1846. His father Horatio found foster homes for his children, where we find Morton in

---

[74] Notrum Amaden, Kane County Births, 1877-1900, Kane County Clerk, Geneva, Illinois; Microfilm 1481152, FHL, Salt Lake City, Utah.

[75] Reuben Cisco household, 1850 U.S. cens., Defiance Co., Oh., pop. sched., Farmer, p 75, dwelling 1014, family 1014.

[76] "Death of M. A. Amaden," *Holton Weekly Recorder*, Holton, Kansas, 21 May 1885, Thursday, page 8, column 6.

[77] Williams County Chapter: Ohio Genealogical Society, *Williams County, Ohio Marriage Records, December 2, 1824 - May 12, 1868*, 3 Volumes, (Bryan, Ohio: Williams County Chapter of the Ohio Genealogical Society, 1984), III-119.

[78] M. Amidon household, 1860 U.S. cens., Williams Co., Oh., pop. sched., St. Joseph, p. 115, dwelling 324, family 313.

[79] Year of death derived from birth of son Horace in 1858; Nancy wasn't listed with husband in census on 1 June 1870; listed as dead in son's guardianship file #1382, 2 August 1870, Williams County Courthouse, Bryan, Ohio.

[80] Flora McQuilkin Widow, Civil War Pension Application File SO -, SC 302395, WC 400376.

[81] Notrum Amaden, Kane County Births, 1877-1900. States her mother was born at Wooster, Ohio.

[82] Flora M. MacQuilkin death record, certificate #225, 7:32, Douglas County Recorder, Superior, Wisconsin.

1850 living with Reuben Cisco in Farmer Township, Ohio.[83] Unlike the other fourteen- to fifteen-year-olds in the neighborhood, Morton had not attended school that year. He likely worked as a farm hand.

Morton's brothers, Henry and John, reunited with their father by the 1860 census. It is uncertain if Morton ever rejoined his father, but he did take up house painting as a trade and maintained close ties to his siblings. Morton purchased land in Williams County on 10 July 1859[84] and married the next year to Nancy Luce. They were living in St. Joseph Township in 1860[85] next door to his cousin Justus Rose. Both men were painters.

But they were not painters for long. The Civil War broke out and Justus Rose was an early volunteer. He came back in August of 1861 after serving in Company C, 14th Regiment of the Ohio Infantry. Justus became a recruiter and perhaps recruited his cousin. Morton enlisted the next month, on 25 September 1861 in Company C, 38th Ohio Infantry Regiment.[86] Morton's unit was active throughout the war. He served the entire war, mustering out on 12 July 1865, having risen to the rank of Sergeant. During the war, he and Nancy had financial difficulties, being sued twice over promissory notes.[87]

Nine months after enlisting, his son Edwin was born in Edgerton, the largest village in St. Joseph Township. Edwin was likely named after Morton's uncle, Henry "Edwin" Axtell. Morton must have had furlough, because their next child, Franka, was born in 1864, but died the following year in Edgerton. Their last child, Horace, was born on 2 January 1868 in Edgerton.

Nancy's history is unknown. Unfortunately, like Morton's mother, Nancy died when her children were young – perhaps during or soon after Horace's birth. Horace was adopted in 1870 by ELIAS S. and MARIA CATHARINE (SPRANGLER) FRAGER. Nancy's properties were placed in probate with Morton's brother John Amaden, who

---

[83]   Reuben Cisco household, 1850 U.S. cens., Defiance Co., Oh., pop. sched., Farmer, p. 75, dw. 1014, fam. 1014.

[84]   Williams County Land Records, vol. 20: 450, Recorder, Bryan, Ohio.

[85]   M. Amedow household, 1860 U.S. cens., Williams Co., Oh., pop. sched., St. Joseph, p. 115, dw. 324, fam. 313.

[86]   Historical Data Systems, comp., *Military Records of Individual Civil War Soldiers* [database on-line] (Provo, Utah: Ancestry.com, 1999-).

[87]   Williams County, Ohio, court case, Roll 15, #153, Roll 16, #82.

applied for and was assigned administrator in 1873, just two days before Morton's second marriage.[88]

"M. A. Ammaden" was listed as a House and Sign Painter in the 1864 Patron's Guide of the *Williams County Atlas*. He was seen in the 1870 census living in St. Joseph with his remaining son Edwin.[89] In 1873, he married for a second time the widow Flora (Crall) McQuilkin. Their marriage was very rocky. Perhaps, like so many battle veterans, he suffered from post-traumatic stress disorder after serving four years in America's most brutal war. In 1875 Flora had him jailed for abuse and threatening to burn her house down![90] Morton's brother John bailed him out and bought land from him to defray the court costs. Soon thereafter, Morton, Flora, Edwin, and Flora's two daughters

Figure 1 Morton Amaden advertisement, *Holton Signal*, Holton, Kansas – courtesy Holton Genealogical Society

from her first marriage left for Batavia, Illinois, where their only child Notrum was born in 1878. Two years later Morton and Flora divorced.

Morton took his son Edwin and left for Holton, Kansas, where they boarded in the hotel of Fred Hust.[91] They may have been following the path of Elias Frager, the man who adopted Nancy's infant son Horace. Elias had moved to Wetmore, Kansas — only thirteen miles from Holton — in the early 1870s. Morton set up a paint store in Holton, where he lived out the rest of his life. Horace had taken the Frager name. He lived most of his life in Kansas, with a

---

[88]   Nancy Amaden Probate Record, Williams County estate case #1623, Williams County Courthouse, Bryan, Ohio.

[89]   Martin Amedon household, 1870 U.S. cens., Williams Co., Oh., pop. sched., St. Joseph, p. 253, dw. 352, fam. 352.

[90]   Morton A. Amaden probate record, Williams Co. estate case #1713.

[91]   Fred Hust household, 1880 U.S. census, Jackson County, Kansas, population schedule, Holton, SD 2, ED 108, page 128C, dwelling -, family -; National Archives micropublication T9, roll 383.

few years in Texas. When Morton died, Horace received land from Morton's estate and Elias testified to Horace's adoption.[92]

Morton's troubles continued to his death. Did his experiences during the Civil War shape him, or were his troubles his own making? In any event, his death was tragic. His obituary, with a temperance editorial, details the event:

> Our community was shocked yesterday morning [20 May 1885] to learn of the sudden death about nine o'clock of M. A. Amaden. The facts, as nearly as we could learn them, are as follows: The deceased has been drinking pretty hard lately, and for days past has been collecting and saving up small doses of morphine, until he had accumulated several grains of the deadly drug, which he swallowed yesterday morning about six o'clock. After taking the dose he went into Nanheim's restaurant, where he had been boarding, and said he wished to go to his room and lay down awhile and passed up the stairway without creating any suspicion of what he had done. Shortly afterward he was found in a dying condition and Drs. Smyth and Scott summoned, but he was beyond medical aid and died about nine o'clock. Amaden was one of the best painters in Kansas, and had it not been for his one fatal weakness, would have been a valuable citizen. When not under the influence of liquor he was a generous, gentlemanly man, naturally endowed with many of the nobler qualities of manhood. Whisky, which has been and is continuing to be such a fatal enemy to so many of the race, beat him at last, as it will finally beat the majority of those who tampered with it. Mr. Amaden's death will be regretted by all who knew and respected the many good and noble instincts of his whisky depraved nature. Ed, his son, inherits his father's talents as a fine painter, and if he will avoid the one terrible enemy which was so fatal to his father, may become an ornament to his profession and a valuable member of society.[93]

---

[92]   M. A. Amaden Probate Record, Jackson County estate case #532, District Court, Holton, Kansas.

[93]   "Death of M. A. Amaden," *Holton Weekly Recorder*, 21 May 1885.

As noted above, Edwin assumed the painting business. Two months after his father's death, he married Marie Cubbison, who had relocated with her parents from Pennsylvania the year prior. In April of 1886, Marie gave birth to their son James Paul Amaden in Holton. Edwin was in California at the time of James's birth.[94] In September, Edwin sold the business and his holdings in Ohio, and the family removed to Marie's hometown of Fairview Township, Pennsylvania. Their daughter Addie Axtell Amaden was born there in 1887. By 1900 the family had moved to Pittsburgh, where Edwin was working as a civil engineer.[95] At some point, he was hired as an engineer for Carnegie Steel Works. For several years, the family lived in Newark, New Jersey,[96] but returned to Pittsburgh where Edwin died in 1924. His son, James Paul Amaden, also became an engineer for Carnegie.

Notrum Amaden's birth record indicates a male, yet all future references are as a female. After her parents' divorce, she took the name MacQuilkin – a variation on her mother's first husband's name. Nona, as she was called, excelled in the field of education. She obtained bachelor's, master's and doctoral degrees from the University of Chicago, Columbia University, and the University of California. Beginning as a high school English teacher, she advanced through the positions of high school principal and Professor Emeritus at Superior State College in Superior, Wisconsin, and finally on the Superior city Board of Education. She was recognized throughout the Midwest as an oratory coach whose students won eleven first state prizes and seven interstate first prizes. The Nona MacQuilkin Scholarship was established by Superior State College soon after her death, to recognize her thirty-two years on the faculty.[97] Nona never married.[98]

---

94   "Personal," *Holton Signal*, Holton, Kansas, 21 April 1886, page 8, col. 5.

95   Edwin K. Amadon household, 1900 U.S. census, Allegheny County, Pennsylvania, population schedule, Pittsburgh, Ward 17, SD 18, ED 204, sheet 7B, dwelling 108, family 115; National Archives micropublication T623, roll 1361.

96   Edward A. Amadon household, 1910 U.S. census, Essex County, New Jersey, population schedule, Newark, Ward 4, SD 18, ED 33, sheet 7A, dwelling 116, family 170; National Archives micropublication T624, roll 877.

97   "Nona MacQuilkin Scholarship is Announced Here," *The Evening Telegram* Superior, Wisconsin, 8 February 1952, page 5, column 6.

98   "Nona MacQuilkin, Pioneer Educator In City, Dies at 73", *The Evening Telegram*, Superior, Wisconsin, 10 December 1951, page 1, column 6;

Children of MORTON and NANCY (LUCE) AMADEN:

i. EDWIN AXTELL AMADEN, b. Edgerton, Oh., 28 June 1862;[99] d. Pittsburgh, Penna., 24 Feb. 1924; bur. Millbank Cem., Fredonia, Penna.;[100] m. Holton, Kans., 30 July 1885 MARIE M. HANNAH CUBBISON,[101] b. Fredonia[102] 26 April 1862, dau. of JAMES SAMUEL and ELIZABETH (GAMBLE) CUBBISON.

Children of EDWIN and MARIE (CUBBISON) AMADEN:

a. *James Paul Amaden*, b. Holton 14 April 1886; d. Brookline, Mass., 26 May 1921; bur. Newark, N.J.;[103] m. Newark 15 April 1916 *Helen Engleman Semple*, b. Easton, Pa., 14 May 1891 dau. of *Clarence H. and Mary Ella (Engleman) Semple*,[104] m. 2) *James Edward Gay Jr*. Helen resided E. Hampton, N.Y., 1930.[105]

Children of *James* and *Helen (Semple) Amaden*:

1. James Paul Amaden Jr., b. Boston, Mass., 29 Jan. 1917.[106]

2. Helen S. Amaden, b. Newtonville, Mass., 6 April 1920.[107]

b. *Addie Axtell Amaden*, b. Holton 1 Oct. 1887; d. Fairview Township, Penn., 15 Aug. 1901; bur. Millbank Cem.[108]

ii. FRANKA A. AMADEN, b. probably Edgerton, Oh., 30 April 1864;

Al Miller, University Relations at the University of Wisconsin, Superior, "Former Instructor," email message to Christopher D. Amaden, 2 September 2003.

99 James Paul Amaden death certificate # 321, Massachusetts State Archives, Boston, Massachusaetts. States father's birthplace was Edgerton, Ohio.

100 Edwin A. Amaden death certificate # 11469, State Department of Health, New Castle, Pennsylvania.

101 Amaden-Cubbison Marriage, Jackson County Certificate, County Clerk's Office, Holton, Kansas.

102 James Paul Amaden death certificate # 321, Mass. State Archives. States mother was born at Fredonia.

103 James Paul Amaden death certificate # 321, Mass. State Archives.

104 Amaden-Semple Marriage, Certificate # 397, New Jersey Bureau of Vital Statistics, Trenton, New Jersey.

105 J. Edward Gay Jr. household, 1930 U.S. census, Suffolk County, New York, population schedule, East Hampton, SD 36, ED 52-46, sheet 9A, dwelling 218, family 227; National Archives micropublication T626, roll 1650.

106 Obituary, "J.P. Amaden Jr., Headed Agency," *East Hampton Star*, East Hampton, New York, 21 March 2002, page 2.

107 Obituary, "Helene S. Neff," *East Hampton Star*, 8 May 2003, page 2.

108 Addie E. Amaden death certificate, Mercer County Clerk, Mercer, Pennsylvania.

d. Edgerton 11 Oct. 1865.[109]

iii. HORACE HUGO AMADEN/FRAGER, b. Edgerton 2 Jan. 1868,[110] d. Wetmore, Kans., 22 Dec. 1923; bur. Wetmore Cem., Wetmore;[111] m. March 1883 HANNAH MARGARET THORNBURROW TROUGHTON, b. Memphis, Tenn., dau. of WILLIAM F. and ANNE (DAVYES) TROUGHTON,[112] d. Onaga, Kans., bur. Wetmore Cem.[113]

Children of HORACE and HANNAH (TROUGHTON) AMADEN:

a. *Mildred Anna Frager,* b. Seneca, Kans., 7 May 1894; m. Onaga 9 May 1917 *Lucien Baker Dunn,*[114] b. Onaga 6 Oct. 1894, son of *John William* and *Ella (Grover) Dunn.*[115]

Child of *Lucien* and *Mildred (Frager)Dunn:*

1. Robert Lee Dunn, b. Onaga 22 July 1919; d. Topeka, Kans., 24 July 1925; bur. Onaga Cem.[116]

b. *Edwin Raymond Frager,* b. prob. Gainsville, Tex.,[117] 23 Oct. 1899;[118] m. abt. 1921 *Mabel Mae McKee,*[119] b. Kans., 29 June 1902, dau. of *William Henry* and *Lydia (Dibbern) McKee.*[120]

---

109 Frank A. Amaden obituary, *Bryan Democrat,* Thursday, 9 November 1865, page 3.

110 Williams County, Ohio, guardianship case #1382.

111 "H. H. Frager Passes Away," *The Onaga Herald,* Onaga, Kansas, 27 December 1923.

112 ?, *Genealogical and Biographical Record of North-Eastern Kansas* (Chicago: The Lewis Publishing Company, 1900), 138. Transcribed by Roger Pyle, [online]   <freepages.genealogy.rootsweb.com/~pyle/GBR/WILLIAM_F_ TROUGHTON.html>.

113 Frager obituary, *The Onaga Herald,* 8 March 1934.

114 Mildred F. Dunn obituary, *The Onaga Herald.*

115 Obituary, "Services Were Tuesday for Lucien B. Dunn, 71," *The Onaga Herald,* 5 May 1966.

116 Obituary, "Robert Lee Dunn," *The Onaga Herald,* 30 July 1925.

117 Horace Frager household, 1900 U.S. census, Cooke County, Texas, population schedule, Gainsville, Ward 5, SD 2, ED 30, sheet 13B, dwelling 261, family 266; National Archives publication T623, roll 1623.

118 Edwin Raymond Frager, Ancestry.com, W.W.I. draft registration card #254.

119 Edwin Frager household, 1930 U.S. census, Shawnee County, Kansas, population schedule, Topeka town, 6th ward, SD 1, ED 40, sheet 13B, dwelling 366, family 366; National Archives micropublication T626, roll 723.

120 William H. McKee household, 1920 U.S. census, Shawnee County, Kansas, population schedule, Topeka town, 3rd ward, SD 101, ED 167, sheet 5B, dwelling 136, family 147; National Archives micropublication T625, roll 551.

Child of *Edwin* and *Mabel (McKee) Frager*:
1. Richard Edwin "Dick" Frager, b. Kans. 4 Feb. 1930.[121]
Children of MORTON and NANCY (LUCE) AMADEN:
iv. NOTRUM A. "NONA" AMADEN, b. Batavia, Ill., 29 Sept. 1878.[122]
Never married.

Henry Amaden (1840–1928)

34. HENRY AMADEN *(HORATIO GATES[6], JACOB[5], JACOB[4] AMIDOWN, HENRY[3], PHILIP[2], ROGER[1] AMADOWNE)* was born at Hermon, New York, on 8 May 1840 and died at Hicksville, Ohio, on 3 August 1928.[123] He married at Clarksville, Ohio, on 18 October 1868 HARRIETTE CELESTIA "CELESTIA" (WILCOX) BEVINGTON, widow of WILLIAM BEVINGTON.[124] She was born at Milford, Ohio, on 13 July 1845, the daughter of ALFRED WILLIAM and MARGARET (FEE) WILCOX, and died at Hicksville 20 February 1925.[125]

Henry was born in May 1840 at Hermon, New York, off the northwest corner of the huge Adirondack Preserve. But by 1 June the family was settled in Parishville, thirty-three miles east northeast of Hermon, where Henry was enumerated with his parents and brothers.[126] In 1844 the family struck out for the remote lands of Williams County on the west edge of Ohio. Two years later six-year-old Henry lost his mother. His father placed him in a foster home with a young English immigrant farm family: WILLIAM and BETSEY TRIPHENA (JOHNSON) BABBAGE of Hicksville, Ohio.[127] Betsey Babbage was the daughter of Ebenezer Johnson and may have been an aunt of Henry's. His siblings were scattered in foster homes in various towns of western Ohio. By 1860 Henry's father Horatio had

---

[121] Richard Edwin Frager record, Ancestry.com, *California Death Index, 1940-1997* [database on-line] (Provo, Utah: MyFamily.com, Inc., 2000). Original data: State of California, *California Death Index, 1940-1997* (Sacramento, California: State of California Department of Health Services, Center for Health Statistics).

[122] Notrum Amaden, birth record, Kane County births 1877-1900.

[123] Henry Amaden, Ohio Death Record # 48308, Ohio Dept. of Health.

[124] Henry Amaden, Civil War Pension Application File SO 55554, SC 208469. His obituary indicated her death date as 9 August 1890.

[125] Harriette C. Amaden, Ohio Death Record# 07866, Ohio Dept. of Health.

[126] Horatio G. Ameden household, 1840 U.S. cens., St. Lawrence Co., N.Y., Parishville, p. 267, line 9.

[127] William Babbage household, 1850 U.S. cens., Defiance Co., Oh., pop. sched., Hicksville, p. 90, dw. 1206, fam. 1206.

married Esther ___ and brought Henry and younger son John home to live with him in Milford Township.[128]

Henry, John, and their father Horatio were all carpenters. The Civil War broke out and Henry enlisted at Milford early in the conflict on 29 August 1861. He served in Company E of the 21st Ohio Infantry rising to the rank of corporal. His regiment left Ohio for Kentucky on 2 October. They occupied Nashville on 25 February, captured Huntsville on 11 April, again besieged Nashville during September and October. In 1863 they occupied middle Tennessee until 16 August. They were in the Battle of Chickamauga in September. In 1864, the regiment was part of the Atlanta Campaign, fighting at Resaca, New Hope Church, Kenesaw, and the siege of Atlanta. Just as the siege of Atlanta ended with the fall of the city, Henry's enlistment ended. He reenlisted, but received a disability discharge three months later on 17 November 1864, just as Sherman was starting his "March to the Sea."[129] His discharge paperwork indicated that Henry had been a carpenter, stood five feet six inches, and had light complexion, gray eyes, and brown hair. After the war, he returned to Defiance County, Ohio, and resumed carpentry.

In 1868, Henry married Celestia Wilcox in Clarksville, a village of Milford township. Celestia had been born in Milford in 1845. She was the eldest child of a well-to-do New York farmer, Alfred Wilcox, based on comparing his wealth in 1850 with that of the families around them.[130] By 1860 Alfred Wilcox's wealth had grown substantially and so had the family, to five children.[131] On 24 August 1864, the nineteen-year-old Celestia married at Defiance County, Ohio, WILLIAM H. H. BEVINGTON.[132] That December, she had a

---

    [128]   H. Amadown household, 1860 U.S. cens., Defiance Co., Oh., pop. sched., Milford, p. 391, dwelling 656, family 652.
    [129]   National Park Service, *Civil War Soldiers and Sailors System*, online <www.itd.nps.gov/cwss/regiments.cfm>.
    [130]   Alfred W. Wilcox household, 1850 U.S. cens., Defiance Co., Oh., pop. sched., Melford, p. 85, dw. 1143, fam. 1143.
    [131]   A. Wilcox household, 1860 U.S. cens., Defiance Co., Oh., pop. sched., Milford, p. 99, dw. 693, fam. 689.
    [132]   Bevington-Wilcox marriage. Jordan Dodd, Liahona Research, *Ohio Marriages, 1803-1900* [database on-line] (Provo, Utah: MyFamily.com, Inc., 2001).

daughter, EVA BEVINGTON.[133] But William Bevington died on 20 June 1866.[134]

Henry bought a forty-acre farm in Milford from Desha Patten and his wife in 1867, in the northeast corner of section 20 in Milford.[135] Henry married the widowed Celestia a year later in 1868 and brought her home to this lot. All of their children were born there. The 1870 census shows them living two households from Celestia's birth family. In addition to Eva Bevington, Henry and Celestia had nine-month-old Madora Amaden. Henry was working as a carpenter and joiner.

In 1878, Henry purchased an additional forty acres in corner section 20 from Calvin Casebeer and wife and took up farming.[136] By 1880, the family had grown to five Amaden children (Madora, Guy, Otho, Addie, and John) plus Eva Bevington. Oddly, Eva is listed as a servant, rather than a stepdaughter. We hope that was strictly an error on the census taker's part and not a comment on a Cinderella relationship between Eva and the rest of the family![137] She married in 1883 to VIRGIL KIMPTON MILLER.[138]

George joined the family in 1884; Henry Earl in 1888. Meanwhile, the family continued to expand its farm land. Henry purchased a forty-acre lot from J. D. Patton and wife in 1889, while Celestia purchased a forty-acre lot from her father in 1891 – all in corner section 20.[139] That year tragedy struck when Madora died at age twenty-one. Five months later tragedy struck again when baby Henry died shortly before his third birthday. And eight years later in 1899 George died at age sixteen. Henry purchased another forty-acre lot from Adam Whitman and wife, completing his acquisition of corner section 20.[140]

---

133   Vergil K. Miller household, 1900 U.S. census, Jasper County, Missouri, population schedule, Twin Groves, sheet 12B, SD 13, ED 69, dwelling 264, family 266; National Archives micropublication T623, roll 867.

134   Henry Amaden, Civil War Pension File SO 55554, SC 208469.

135   Defiance County Land Records, Book 18: 601, Defiance County Courthouse, Defiance, Ohio.

136   Defiance County Land Records, Book 29:102.

137   Henry Amaden household, 1880 U.S. cens., Defiance Co., Oh., pop. sched., Milford, SD 1, ED 239, p. 11, dw. 108, fam. 111.

138   Miller-Bevington marriage, Defiance County marriages 2A:535, Defiance County Record Center, Defiance, Ohio.

139   Defiance County Land Records, Book 29:102, 49:15.

140   Defiance County Land Records, Book 61:302.

By 1900, of Celestia's five surviving children, Eva and Guy had married and Otho had left home, but Addie and John were still living with their parents. Henry was still working the farm.[141]

"Let AMADEN Supply Your Dessert!"

— FANCY BRICK ICE CREAM —

Individual Moulds for Special Occasions

PUREST HIGH GRADE MILK — We want to Supply You

AMADEN ICE CREAM & BEVERAGE CO.

16 North Monroe St.   Phone 72

Guy Amaden had moved to Angola, Indiana, where he met and married a local girl, MAUDALENE "MAUDE" WELLS. He attended Tri-State College, from which he graduated, and prepared for the ministry. Guy and Maude eventually settled in Coldwater, Michigan, where he ran a dairy farm and in 1920 bought an ice cream company. By 1928, Amaden & Son expanded into the field of soda water and became Amaden Bottling Company.[142] Guy's children grew up in Coldwater, where they each married and had two children.

Otho left Milford with his half-sister Eva and her husband Virgil Miller. They were living in Twin Grove, Missouri, in 1900 with Virgil working at a zinc mine and Otho working as a day laborer. Eva and Virgil had had two children, Ethel and William.[143] By 1910, Eva's family and Otho had gone their separate ways with Eva's family moving to Seward, Kansas, and Otho moving to Lonoke County, Arkansas. He married GERNSIE DRUCILLA HOWARD there in 1909. He and his wife have not been found in the 1910 census. In his World War I draft registration card, he listed his occupation as an engineer for a construction company in Little Rock, Arkansas. A resident of Lonoke, he stood five foot, six-and-a-half inches tall, was of medium build, and had blue eyes and dark brown hair.[144] In 1920, he was a plumber and the family then had two little boys.[145] Otho's last son was born in 1922. Three years later Otho's mother died, and

---

[141]   Henry Amaden household, 1900 U.S. census, Defiance County, Ohio, population schedule, Milford, sheet 9B, SD 4, ED 15, dwelling 197, family 198; National Archives micropublication T623, roll 1263.

[142]   Guy Amaden obituary, "Dies While At Church," *Coldwater [Mich.] Reporter*, Monday 19 June 1950.

[143]   Vergil K. Miller household, 1900 U.S. cens., Jasper Co., Mo., pop. sched., Twin Groves, sheet 12B, SD 13, ED 69, dw. 264, fam. 266.

[144]   Otho G. Amaden, Ancestry.com, WWI Draft Registration Card.

[145]   O. G. Amadon household, 1920 U.S. census, Lonoke County, Arkansas, population schedule, Lonoke, sheet 2B, SD 6, ED 172, dwelling 40, family 47; National Archives micropublication T625, roll 70.

he was mentioned in her will. The family legend is that Otho left for Florida one day and never came back.[146] He was not mentioned in his father's obituary of 1928, and his wife was listed as a widow in the 1930 census.[147]

By 1910, seventy-year-old Henry was still farming, but now the household consisted only of Henry and Celestia. John had married and was raising a large family next door.[148] Having bought a forty-acre lot from his father,[149] John was a farmer and auctioneer. He and his wife MARY MAY HOOTMAN raised eleven children in Milford, only one dying as a child. Regrettably John died in 1927, just shy of his forty-eighth birthday. Mary sold the farm to her sister-in-law Addie[150] and moved to Hicksville where her older children (who had not yet married) worked to support the family.[151]

In 1917, Henry and Celestia quit farming and moved to Hicksville,[152] where we find the eighty-year-old Henry in the 1920 census at 608 Smith Street. Addie, still single, had moved back home to care for her aging parents. Ida Roe, a twenty-year-old local girl was living with them as a servant, helping Addie.[153]

Addie had taken up nursing, perhaps having been a student at the University of Michigan in Ann Arbor, where she was a roomer in

    [146]   Interview with Kathleen (McCollough) Walter, by Chris Amaden, 15 September 1997.
    [147]   "Old Age Takes Civil War Vet," *Defiance Crescent News*, Saturday 4 August 1928, page 1, column 5.
    Drucie Amaden household, 1930 U.S. census, Lonoke County, Arkansas, population schedule, town of Lonoke, SD 7, ED 26, sheet 10B, dwelling 244, family 257; National Archives micropublication T626, roll 83.
    [148]   Henry Amaden household, 1910 U.S. census, Defiance County, Ohio, population schedule, Milford, sheet 10B, SD 4, ED 17, dwelling 239, family 239; National Archives micropublication T624, roll 1177.
    [149]   Defiance County Land Records, Book 95:40.
    [150]   Defiance County Land Records, Book 105:269.
    [151]   Mary Amaden household, 1930 U.S. census, Defiance County, Ohio, population schedule, town of Hicksville, SD 1, ED 14, sheet 1A, dwelling 17, family 19; National Archives micropublication T626, roll 1789.
    [152]   "Hicksville News (Special Correspondence)", *Fort Wayne [Indiana] News*, 23 January 1917.
    [153]   Henry Aenaden household, 1920 U.S. census, Defiance County, Ohio, population schedule, Milford, sheet 7B, SD 4, ED 13, dwelling 199, family 200; National Archives micropublication T625, roll 1376.

1910.[154] She returned to Ohio and, with Doctor John S. Hull, started the Amaden Hospital in Hicksville.[155] She never married.

Celestia died in 1925 at age seventy-nine of colon cancer. She was buried at Forest Home Cemetery in Hicksville on 23 February 1925.[156] Henry did not survive long without his mate of fifty-six years. He died in 1928 at age eighty-eight. He was buried beside Celestia at Forest Home Cemetery on 5 August 1928.

Children of HENRY and HARRIETTE CELESTIA (WILCOX) AMADEN, all born at Milford, Ohio:[157]

i.   MADORA M. AMADEN, b. 10 Sept. 1869;[158] d. Milford 3 May 1891;[159] bur. Forest Home Cem., Hicksville, Oh.[160]

ii.   GUY WILCOX AMADEN, b. 8 June 1872;[161] m. Angola, Ind., 9 June 1897 MAUDALENE A. WELLS,[162] b. Ind. 23 Aug. 1873, dau. of SYLVANUS W. and ESTELLA (HOWARD) WELLS.[163]

Children of GUY and MAUDALENE "MAUDE" (WELLS) AMADEN:

a.   *Charles Howard Amaden,* b. Angola 23 May 1898; m. Coldwater, Mich., 9 March 1922 *Carmen Ercell Selby,*[164] b. Milroy, Ind., 21 Jan. 1902, dau. of *Harry* and *Rhoda (Peck) Selby.*[165]

Children of *Charles* and *Carmen (Selby) Amaden*:

1.   Kathryn Lorraine Amaden, b. Coldwater 22 Aug.

---

154   Ada Hill household, 1910 U.S. census, Washtenaw County, Michigan, population schedule, Ann Arbor, Ward 6, sheet 7B, SD 2, ED 120, dwelling 227, family 251?; National Archives micropublication T624, roll 677.
155   Interview, Kathleen (McCollough) Walter, 15 September 1997.
156   Harriette C. Amaden, Ohio Death Record, Certificate # 07866.
157   Interview, Kathleen (McCollough) Walter, 15 September 1997.
158   Medora Amaden birth record, Defiance County Birth Records (1866-1908), Defiance County Probate Court, Defiance, Ohio.
159   Madn M Amaden probate, Book 2:4,5, Defiance County Probate Court, Defiance, Ohio,.
160   Forest Home Cemetery Records, Forest Home Cemetery, Hicksville, Ohio.
161   Guy W. Amaden birth record, Defiance County Birth Records (1866-1908), Defiance County Probate Court, Defiance, Ohio.
162   "Dies While At Church, Guy Amaden, 78," *Coldwater [Mich.] Reporter,* Monday, 19 June 1950.
163   Maudalene Amaden obituary, "Plan Funeral Service Here - Amaden Rites To Be Held Thursday," *Coldwater [Mich.]Daily Reporter,* 18 March 1952, page 1.
164   Obituary, "Howard Amaden," *Coldwater [Mich.] Reporter,* 3 Nov. 1977.
165   Obituary, "Carmen Amaden," *Coldwater [Mich.] Reporter,* 2 March 1980.

1923.[166]
    2. Margery Jean Amaden, b. Coldwater 2 May 1926.[167]
b. Estella Harriet Amaden, b. Milford, Oh., 13 May 1905;[168] m. Coldwater 28 June 1924 *George Lester Frost,*[169] b. Camden, Mich., 19 June 1904, son of *George L.* and *Amanda Jane (Lindsay) Frost.*[170]
    Children of *George* and *Estella (Amaden) Frost*:
    1. Robert Lester Frost, b. Coldwater 19 April 1925.[171]
    2. Norma Jane Frost, b. Coldwater 5 Dec. 1926.[172]
iii. OTHO GATES AMADEN, b. 7 Nov. 1874;[173] d. bet. 10 Dec. 1925 and 4 Aug. 1928;[174] m. Lonoke Co., Ark., 23 Dec. 1909 GERNSIE DRUCILLA "DRUCIE" HOWARD,[175] b. Morrilton, Ark., 7 Sept. 1882, dau. of CHARLES ARTHUR and ELLA NANCY (RUSSELL) HOWARD.[176]
    Children of OTHO and DRUCILLA (HOWARD) AMADEN:
a. *Claud Henry Howard "Howard" Amaden,* b. Ark. 24 Sept. 1914.
b. *Otho Ward Amaden,* b. Ark. 3 May 1917.
c. *Russell Charles Amaden,* b. Ark. 18 April 1922.[177]

---

[166]   Kathryn Lorraine Amaden, Michigan birth record, registered 23 August 1926, Department of Health, Lansing, Michigan.
[167]   Margery Jean Amaden, Michigan birth record, registered 5 May 1926.
[168]   Estella H. Amaden birth record, Defiance County Birth Records (1866-1908), Defiance County Probate Court, Defiance, Ohio.
[169]   Frost-Amaden marriage record #9681, Branch County Clerk, Coldwater, Michigan.
[170]   Obituary, "George L. Frost," *Fort Wayne Journal-Gazette,* 21 January 1973, page 12A, col 1; Obituary, "Rites Set for George Frost," *Coldwater [Mich.]Reporter,* 10 May 1963.
[171]   Robert Lester Frost, Michigan birth record, registered 20 April 1925.
[172]   Norma Jane Frost, Michigan birth record, registered 6 December 1925.
[173]   Otho Gates Amaden, Ancestry.com, WWI Draft Registration Card.
[174]   Otho was included in the estate of his mother dated 10 December 1925 (Defiance County Probate # AM-8) and was not included in his father's obituary of 4 August 1928. His wife in 1930 census was listed as widowed.
[175]   Amaden-Howard entry, Lonoke County Marriage Record Book O:82, Lonoke County Clerk, Lonoke, Arkansas.
[176]   Drucilla Amaden, Arkansas death record, Certificate # 4262, Division of Vital Records, Arkansas Department of Health, Little Rock, Arkansas.
[177]   Claud Amaden, Otho Amaden, and Russell C. Amaden – Ancestry.com, *Social Security Death Index* [database on-line] (Provo, Utah: MyFamily.com, Inc., 2006). Original data: Social Security Administration, *Social Security Death Index, Master File,* Social Security Administration.

iv. ADDIE IVES AMADEN, b. 21 May 1877.[178] No issue.
v. JOHN AUGUSTUS AMADEN, b. 1 Nov. 1879; d. Hicksville, Oh., 19 Oct. 1927; bur. Forest Home Cem., Hicksville, Oh.;[179] m. Defiance Co., Oh., 16 June 1902 MARY MAY HOOTMAN, b. Milford 14 April 1884, dau. of JOHN ALLEN and MARY A. (PIERCE) HOOTMAN.[180] Resided Hicksville 1930.[181]

Children of JOHN and MARY (HOOTMAN) AMADEN; all born in Milford, Oh.:

a. *Audrey Therma Amaden*, b. 23 Nov. 1902;[182] m. Defiance, Oh., 16 Feb. 1921 *LaVon Estell McCollough*, b. Hicksville, Oh., 24 Feb. 1900, son of *Charles L.* and *Effie (Stoup) McCollough*.[183]

Children of *LaVon* and *Audrey (Amaden) McCollough*:[184]

1. Kathleen Laverge McCollough, b. Milford 9 Oct. 1921.
2. Margie L. McCollough, b. Hicksville 13 Aug. 1926.

b. *Mark Augustus Amaden*, b. 22 Oct. 1904.[185] Laborer 1930, living with mother.

c. *John Henry Amaden*, b. 22 Feb. 1908;[186] m. 10 June 1929 *Pauline Christiana Fry*,[187] b. Hicksville, Oh., 9 July 1905, dau. of *Frank* and *Matilda (Strabling) Fry*.[188]

d. *Edwin Paul Amaden*, b. 14 Oct. 1909.[189] Truck driver 1930, living with mother.

Drucie Amaden household, 1930 U.S. census, Lonoke County, Arkansas, population schedule, town of Lonoke, SD 7, ED 26, sheet 10B, dwelling 244, family 257; National Archives micropublication T626, roll 83.

178 Addie E. Amaden, Defiance County Birth Records (1866-1908).
179 John A. Amaden, Ohio Death Records, Certificate # 56714.
180 Amaden-Hootman entry, Defiance Co. Marriage Record Book 4:377.
     Mary May Amaden, Ohio Death Records, Certificate # 02197.
181 May Amaden household, 1930 U.S. census, Defiance County, Ohio, population schedule, Hicksville village, SD 1, ED 20-14, sheet 1A, dwelling 17, family 19; National Archives micropublication T626, roll 1789.
182 Audrie Amaden, Defiance County Birth Records (1866-1908).
183 McCullough-Amaden entry, Defiance Co. Marriage Record Book, 8:222.
184 Interview, Kathleen (McCollough) Walter, 15 September 1997.
185 Mark A. Amaden, Defiance County Birth Records (1866-1908).
186 John Henry Amaden, Defiance County Birth Records (1866-1908).
187 Pauline Amaden Divorce Record, Defiance County Probate Records, recorded 26 September 1931.
188 Paulina Christiana Fry, Defiance County Birth Records (1866-1908).
189 Edwin P. Amaden, Ohio Death Record, Certificate # 049584.

    e.   *Mary Celestia Amaden*, b. 31 March 1911; m. Defiance, Oh., 24 Dec. 1928 *Fred Gump*, b. Butler, Ind., 2 Sept. 1905, son of *Tubal Cane* and *Ila E. (Smith) Gump*,[190] d. Hicksville, Oh., 16 Sept. 1929 of suicide.[191] Waitress 1930, living with mother.

    f.   *Valura Bell Amaden*, b. 9 Feb. 1913; d. Fort Wayne, Ind., 22 Oct. 1914; bur. Forest Home Cem., Hicksville, Oh.[192]

    g.   *Alice Pauline Amaden*, b. 25 Feb. 1915.[193]

    h.   *Valona May Amaden*, b. 26 Feb. 1917.[194]

    i.   *Walter Donald Amaden*, b. 21 June 1918.[195]

    j.   *Lee Hugh Amaden*, b. 16 April 1920.[196]

    k.   *Lloyd George Amaden* b. 9 March 1922.[197]

vi.   GEORGE ALFRED AMADEN, b. 30 May 1883; d. Milford, 18 Nov. 1899; bur. Forest Home Cem., Hicksville, Oh.

vii. HENRY EARL AMADEN, b. 4 Nov. 1888; d. Milford, 28 Oct. 1891; bur. Forest Home Cem, Hicksville, Oh.

John Amaden (1842–1911)

35. JOHN AMADEN (*HORATIO*[6], *JACOB AMADEN*[5], *JACOB*[4] *AMIDOWN*, *HENRY*[3], *PHILIP*[2], *ROGER*[1] *AMADOWNE*) was born at Watertown, New York, on 20 January 1842,[198] and died at Toledo, Ohio, on 27 September 1911.[199] He married first at Defiance County, Ohio, on 21 May 1862, HANNAH DORALISKA CRARY.[200] Hannah was born at Ohio, on 24 March 1845, the daughter of NATHANIEL and MERCY MARY (WARTENBEE) CRARY. She died 27 April 1865.[201] He married

---

190   Gump-Amaden entry, Defiance Co. Marriage Record Book, Book 9:187.

191   "Kills Self on Lawn of Mother-in-law. Fred Gump of Hicksville Ends Life Early Monday Morning," *Bryan [Ohio]Democrat*, Thursday 19 September 1929.

192   Velora Bell Amaden death record, Indiana Deaths (1882-1920), Book CH-7:207, Indiana State Department of Health, Indianapolis, Indiana.

       Forest Home Cemetery Records, Forest Home Cemetery, Hicksville, Ohio.

193   John A. Amaden family records, held by Christopher Amaden.

194   Valona M. Myers, Ohio Death Record, Certificate # 089004.

195   Walter D. "Dub" Amaden, Ohio Death Record, Certificate # 089485.

196   Lee H. Amaden, Ancestry.com, *Social Security Death Index*.

197   John A. Amaden family records, held by Christopher Amaden.

198   Birth data from Amaden family records held by Christopher Amaden.

199   John Amaden, death certificate # 49365, Ohio Department of Health.

       Fountain Grove Cemetery Records, pages 66-67, line 225, Bryan, Ohio.

200   Amaden-Crary marriage, Defiance County Marriages, Book 2:7.

201   Charles Judson Crary, *Crary Family Records* (Palo Alto, California: C.J. Crary, 1956), 119-120, 169.

second at Defiance County, Ohio, on 10 September 1865, MARY A. FOUST.[202]   Mary was born at Richland County, Ohio, on 10 September 1844,[203] the daughter of WILLIAM and SUSSANAH (DEARDORFF) FOUST.[204] She died at Bryan, Ohio, on 21 December 1889.[205] He married third at Putnam County, Ohio, on 22 July 1891, MARY ELIZABETH SIMON.[206] Mary was born 6 November 1868 in Dupont, Ohio, the daughter of JOHN J. and JULIA ANN (BROWN) SIMON.[207] John and Mary divorced before 1900.

Figure 2 John Amaden
Courtesy Chris Amaden

In 1840, John's parents, Horatio and Charlotte, were living in Parishville, New York. John was born in 1842; according to family notes he was born in Watertown, about eighty miles southwest of Parishville. It is possible that he was born there, but there are no other records that Horatio lived in Watertown. This may be a merging of facts because Horatio's sister, Aurelia, and brother, John, both lived in Watertown for several years after Horatio had left New York.

Regardless, John's stay in New York was short lived. In 1844, his parents removed to Williams County, Ohio. When John was but four years old, his mother died and was buried in Centre, Ohio. His father sent the children to live with foster families, although John has yet to be found in the 1850 census. By 1860 he had reunited with his father in Milford, Ohio, where he, his brother, Henry, and their father worked as carpenters. As mentioned in Horatio's biography (chapter

---

202   Amaden-Foust marriage, Defiance County Marriages, Book 2:66.

203   Fountain Grove Cemetery Records, pages 16-17, line 293.

204   W. M. Foust, Defiance County Probate Record, book 2:72.

205   Fountain Grove Cemetery Records, pages 16-17, line 293.

206   Amaden-Simon marriage, Putnam County Marriages, 29 July 1891, Putnam County Courthouse, Ottawa, Ohio.

207   DeCamp-Simon marriage, Putnam County Marriages, Volume 6:297.

three), there was another parting of ways in the family, likely due to Horatio's drinking habits.

Although brothers Henry and Morton enlisted for the Civil War, John never served. The family tradition says he was rejected at the recruiting office as too short. His brother, Henry, also short, put silver dollars in his shoes to gain some height and was accepted.

In May of 1862, John was married to Hannah Crary by her father Reverend Nathaniel Crary, most likely in Milford where both families lived. Over several decades and generations, the Crary and Amaden families had both migrated from Rutland County, Vermont, spent several years in St. Lawrence County, New York, and settled in Defiance County, Ohio.

John and Hannah had two daughters: Mary in 1863 and Aurelia "Rilla" in 1865. The year 1865 was a year of joys and tragedies. Hannah died just four months after Rilla's birth. Needing a mother for his children, John married again five months later in September 1865 to Mary Foust. Two months later in November, John's older daughter, Mary, died.

Mary Foust's family had recently removed to Milford from Richland County, Ohio, where Mary had been born. Her father William was a farmer raised in a traditional German family in

Figure 3 Mary Foust Amaden
Photo courtesy Chris Amaden

Perry County, Pennsylvania.[208]

By 1869, John and Mary had taken Rilla and left Defiance County for Edgerton, in Williams County, where John purchased a lot with a little over an acre on Clarkesville Road.[209] Mary's first daughter, Alice, better known as Hazel Della, was born in 1869, likely at that home. The family is seen in the 1870 census living in St.

208　W. M. Foust, Defiance County Probate Record Book 2:72.
　　　Amaden family records maintained by Christopher Amaden.
209　Williams County Land Records, vol. 31:447-448.

Joseph Township, the township containing the village of Edgerton.[210] John continued in carpentry while Mary was keeping house with their two daughters: Rilla from John's first wife and their newborn Hazel Della.

The *1874 Williams County Atlas Patron's Directory* lists John Amaden as a carpenter who arrived in 1844 from New York. The *Business Directory* listed John as a Contractor & Builder.[211] Family legend has it that he "built the N.Y. Central depot at Edgerton, Ohio, and the court house at Bryan."[212] The family was still in Edgerton in 1880, but by now John had taken up a new trade.[213] He was a sewing machine agent. Family legend is that he worked for Singer Sewing Machine Company and made improvements to their machines.

Later in 1880, the family moved eleven miles east to Bryan, the county seat. Here their first son John, better known by his middle name Clyde, was born. It had been eleven years since Mary's earlier child had been born. Four years later another son, Walter, came. In 1885, John's daughter Rilla married Samuel Shaffer in his hometown of Delta, Ohio, about midway by train between Bryan and Toledo, Ohio. Samuel was a barber. To them two children were born, although their young son John died in a drowning accident.

A few days before Christmas in 1889, Mary Amaden died at the family home on West High Street in Bryan leaving John with their twenty-year-old daughter, Hazel Della, and two young boys, Clyde and Walter. Mary was well regarded in Bryan. The First Universalist Church adopted a resolution stating, "that in the death of sister Amaden, this community has lost a most useful and exemplary Christian lady, this church one of its most devoted and beloved members, her intimate acquaintances a faithful friend, and her kindred a most devoted, self-sacrificing and loving wife, mother and sister."[214] She was buried at Fountain Grove Cemetery in Bryan.

---

[210]   John Amaden household, 1870 U.S. cens., Williams Co., Oh., pop. sched., St. Joseph, p. 239, dw. 123, fam. 123.

[211]   ?, *An Illustrated Historical Atlas of Williams County* (Chicago: Andreas & Baskin, 1874), Patron's Directory, Edgerton Village page 26, Business directory, page 31.

[212]   Walter D. Amaden, in family records maintained by Chris Amaden.

[213]   John Amaden household, 1880 U.S. census, Williams County, Ohio, population schedule, St. Joseph, SD 1, ED 9, page 590D, dwelling 109, family 110; National Archives micropublication T9, roll 1078.

[214]   "Resolutions," *Bryan Democrat*, 23 January 1890, Thursday, page 5.

John left Bryan and lived briefly in Granville, Ohio.[215] At the age of forty-nine, John married for a third time in 1891 to twenty-two-year-old Mary Simon. It is not certain where John and his new wife Mary set up their household. In 1898, Hazel Della married in Seneca County to Oscar Shriver. Hazel was a musician and Oscar was an insurance agent. They lived in the Midwest and had no children.

In 1899, John's father-in-law William Foust (father of his deceased second wife Mary) died. He named all three grandchildren in his will – Hazel Della Shriver in Tiffin, Ohio; Clyde Amaden in Hicksville, Ohio; and Walter Amaden in Toledo.[216] It appears that Clyde had taken up residence with his uncle, Henry Amaden. In fact, Clyde and Walter were placed under Henry's guardianship in order to execute the will. It is not certain if John was unable or unwilling to represent his juvenile sons. But of interest is that William allotted money in his will for "a suitable monument at the grave of [his] daughter Mary Amaden." Presumably John had been unable to buy a monument when his second wife died.

Clyde has not been found in the 1900 census. He moved west and settled first in Denver, Colorado. He married twice, the first one ending in divorce and the second with her death during the Influenza Pandemic. He had no children. Clyde worked as an engineer in industrial settings such as The International Smelting and Refining Company's smelter in Tooele,[217] Utah, and a plaster plant for the Pacific Portland Cement Company in California. This industrial life likely contributed to his early death from an asthma and heart attack while climbing El Centro in Boulder Park, California, in 1927.

John and his son Walter are next found living alone in Toledo in 1900, badly indexed on the census as John Emanuelson.[218] John and Mary had already divorced since their 1891 marriage; she was living alone in Fort Wayne, Indiana, under her maiden name, Mary Simon, working as a dressmaker.[219] John was an agent and Walter was at

---

215   Williams County Land Records, Vol 66:366.
216   William M. Foust, Estate # FO-38, Defiance County Probate Court.
217   John C. Amaden, Ancestry.com, WWI Draft Registration Card.
218   John Emanuelson household, 1900 U.S. census, Lucas County, Ohio, population schedule, Toledo, Ward 4, SD -, ED 43, sheet 3A, dwelling -, family 67; National Archives publication T623, roll 1297.
219   Mary V. Simon household, 1900 U.S. census, Allen County, Indiana, population schedule, Wayne, SD 12, ED 27, sheet 2A, dwelling 28, family 33; National Archives publication T623, roll 358.

school — Toledo Public High School, where he graduated in 1903.[220] John's health began to fail. His daughter Rilla came to live with them in Toledo — but she died suddenly of a stroke as recounted in her obituary:

> A few minutes after she had entered the workroom of the Toledo Overall Company, on the fourth floor of the building at 713-717 Jefferson avenue, where she was employed as a machine operator, Mrs. Aurelia Shaffer, 40, who lived with her father John Amedan (sic), at 126 Twelfth street was stricken with a sudden attack of illness, and, falling unconscious to the floor, she gasped once or twice and died before a physician could be summoned. Coroner Charles J. Henzler said death was due to apoplexy.
>
> Mrs. Shaffer arrived at the work shop about three hours late, and was explaining her tardiness to the forewoman ..., when she was stricken with the fatal attack. It is said that she had not complained of feeling ill lately, and that when she started to work she appeared to be as well as usual...[221]

Rilla's daughter Mabel had recently married Robert Burgess. Robert and Mabel were opera singers in the 1910 census in Medford, Oregon, where they were boarding with Robert's father, Henry Burgess.[222] Robert served in World War I.[223] They had no children.

Rilla's death left Walter as John's caretaker. He worked as a manager of the Toledo office of the Phoenix Mutual Life Insurance Company. In the 1910 census, they were still on Twelfth Street in Toledo and John was listed as blind.[224] The following year, John died at the Lucas County Infirmary in Toledo and was buried at Fountain Grove Cemetery in Bryan, Ohio.

---

220 Walter Donald Amaden, *1903 Toledo Central High School Almanac*; Lucas County Public Library, Toledo, Ohio.
221 "Former Delta Woman Dies Suddenly of Apoplexy at Toledo," *Delta Atlas*, Thursday, 9 September 1909, page 1.
222 Henry L. Burgess household, 1910 U.S. census, Jackson County, Oregon, population schedule, Medford, Ward 2, SD 1, ED 114, sheet 16A, dwelling 345, family 382; National Archives publication T624, roll 1281.
223 Robert O. Burgess death certificate #032680 California Vital Records, Sacramento, California.
224 John Amaden household, 1910 U.S. census, Lucas County, Ohio, population schedule, Toledo, Ward 6, SD 8, ED 82, sheet 16A, dwelling 345, family 382; National Archives publication T624, roll 1209.

On 5 June 1901, John's third wife Mary married second at Putnam County, Ohio, WILLIAM H. DECAMP; William was born at Van Wert, Ohio, on 26 August 1872, the son of JOSEPH W. and AMANDA ELLEN (MILLER) DECAMP.[225] Mary and William lived at Fort Wayne, Indiana, for several years before moving to Bryan, Ohio. They had no children and divorced before 1930.[226]

Walter married in 1912 to HERMA DEAN in a triple wedding in Toledo. Her two sisters married at the same time. Walter and Herma had two sons in Toledo and left in 1915 for Chicago where Walter attended law school. He earned an LL.B. from the University of Chicago. Lawyers did not have a steady income at the time, so Walter worked as a postal clerk on the railway for several years before becoming a judge.[227]

Children of JOHN and HANNAH (CRARY) AMADEN:

i.   MARY GENEVA AMADEN, b. 11 March 1863; d. 5 Nov. 1865.[228]
ii.   AURELIA CHARLOTTE "RILLA" AMADEN, b. Farmer, Oh., 18 Jan. 1865;[229] d. Toledo, Oh., 3 Sept. 1909;[230] bur. Greenlawn Cem., Delta, Oh.;[231] m. Delta 19 March 1885[232] SAMUEL THURBER SHAFFER, b. Delta 27 May 1864, son of DAVID and ELIZABETH (HOSTETLER) SHAFFER,[233] he m. 2) Toledo 19 Oct. 1909, LENA (DUSSEAU) BOURDO, widow of SAMUEL BOURDO, b. Toledo 24 April 1874, dau. of JOSEPH and MARY (CLUCKEY) DUSSEAU.[234]

Children of SAMUEL and AURELIA (AMADEN) SHAFFER:

---

225   DeCamp-Amaden marriage, Putnam County Marriages Volume 6:297.
     William DeCamp obituary, *Journal Gazette*, Fort Wayne, Indiana. Friday 5 January 1968.
226   Ellen De Camp household, 1930 U.S. census, Van Wert County, Ohio, population schedule, Van Wert, SD 1, ED 10, page 2A, dwelling 33, family 37; National Archives micropublication T626, roll 1890.
227   Amaden family records maintained by Christopher Amaden.
228   Crary, *Crary Family Records*, 169.
229   Birth date from Amaden family records maintained by Christopher Amaen.
230   Aurelia C Shaffer death certificate 47236, Ohio Department of Health.
231   ?, *Fulton County Grave Transcriptions*, (?:Fulton County Historical Society,1986), Volume 2:147, online <crewfamily.com/tombstones/volume_2_page_147.htm>, downloaded 25 July2006.
232   Crary, *Crary Family Records*, 169.
233   Samuel Thurber Shaffer death certificate #3735, California Office of Vital Records, Sacramento California.
     Harvey Hochstetler, *Descendants of Jacob Hostetler* (Elgin, Ill.: Brethren Publishing House, 1912), 330.
234   Burgess-Shaffer Lucas County Marriage License # 14468.

a. *Mabel Florence Shaffer,* b. Delta 21 July 1886;[235] m. St. Louis, Mo., about 1908 *Robert Otis Burgess,*[236] b. Mankato, Minn., 5 April 1887, son of *Henry Clay* and *Ellen M. (French) Burgess.*[237] No children.

b. *John Archie Shaffer,* b. probably Delta 22 Oct. 1887;[238] d. Delta 8 April 1889; buried Greenlawn Cem., Delta.[239]

Children of JOHN and MARY (FOUST) AMADEN:

iii. ALICE ADELL "HAZEL DELLA" AMADEN, b. Edgerton, Oh., 23 Aug. 1869;[240] m. Seneca Co., Oh., 18 Oct. 1898 OSCAR H. SHRIVER,[241] b. Oh. 18 July 1858, son of JESSE and ANN (SPAYTH) SHRIVER, d. Oskaloosa, Ia., 9 March 1929, bur. Forest Cem, Oskaloosa, Ia.[242] No children.

iv. JOHN CLYDE "CLYDE" AMADEN, b. Bryan, Oh.,[243] 16 Sept. 1880;[244] d. Boulder Park near El Centro, Calif., 20 Sept. 1926; bur. Evergreen Cem., El Centro;[245] m. 1) Golden, Colo., 9

---

235   Birth date of 1886 from Amaden family records maintained by Christopher Amaden, *Crary Family Records,* and 1900 census entry. Conflicting data provided by SS-5, US Social Security Act application, 570-01-9076, and *Descendants of Jacob Hostetler* states 1887. Birth of brother in 1887 gives weight to year of 1886.

236   Robert Burgess obituary, *Medford [Oregon] Mail Tribune,* 21 May 1952.
       Year from Robert O. Burgers household, 1930 U.S. census, Los Angeles County, California, population schedule, town of Los Angeles, SD 16, ED 76, sheet 16A, dwelling 314, family 314; National Archives micropublication T626, roll 134.
       Robert O. Burgess, Death Certificate, California certificate # 032680.
       Robert Otis Burgess, Ancestry.com, WWI Draft Registration Card.

238   Amaden family records maintained by Christopher Amaden: birth date derived from age on cemetery marker is 21 October 1887.

239   ?, *Fulton County Grave Transcriptions,* Volume 2:147.
       John A. Shaffer death record, Fulton County Courthouse, Wauseon, Ohio.

240   Alace A. Amaden birth record, Williams County Ohio.
       Birth location from death certificate: Hazeldell Shriver death certificate #C9153, State Department of Health, Lincoln, Nebraska.
       Shriver obituary, *Daily Herald,* Oskaloosa, Ia., 27 September 1932, p. 5.

241   Shriver-Amaden marriage, book 11:462, Seneca County Courthouse, Tiffin, Ohio.

242   Samuel S. Shriver, *History of the Shriver Family and Their Connections* (Baltimore: Press of Guggenheimer, Weil & Co, 1888), 137.
       "Deaths and Funerals – Shriver", *Oskaloosa Daily Herald,* Oskaloosa, Iowa, Monday, 11 March 1929, page 7.

243   Amaden family records maintained by Chris Amaden.

244   John Clyde Amaden, Ancestry.com, WWI Draft Registration Card.

245   John C. Amaden, California death certificate #41762.

March 1910 ESTHER MARY HULTGREN,[246] b. Sweden abt. 1886, dau. of JOHN P. and ANNA (HULTGREN) JOHNSON,[247] div. Denver 7 June 1916;[248] m. 2) about 1917[249] ANNA MAY SIMPSON, b. Fort Worth, Tex., 16 May 1890, dau. of HARRY H. SIMPSON, d. Tooele, Utah, 17 Dec. 1918, bur. Tooele City Cem., Tooele.[250]

v.   WALTER DONALD AMADEN, b. Bryan, Oh., 18 Sept. 1884; m. Toledo 22 June 1912 HERMA VIOLA DEAN, b. Rudolph, Oh., 12 Dec. 1888, dau. of CHARLES EDWARD and ELIZA ANGELINE (MOMANY) DEAN.[251]

Children of WALTER and HERMA (DEAN) AMADEN:[252]

a.   *Robert Dean Amaden*, b. Toledo 29 Sept. 1914.

b.   *Charles Frederick Amaden*, b. Toledo 3 May 1917.

Aurelia Nancy (Amaden) Leas (1844–1910)

36.   AURELIA NANCY AMADEN *(HORATIO[6], JACOB AMADEN[5], JACOB[4] AMIDOWN, HENRY[3], PHILIP[2], ROGER[1] AMADOWNE)* was born at Ohio in about 1844. She died at Manila, Philippines, on 11 January 1910.[253] She married at Williams County, Ohio, on 7 May 1878 AUGUSTUS SPANGLER "GUS" LEAS.[254] He was born at Stark County, Ohio, on 31 August 1833, son of JOHN and SOPHIA (SPANGLER) LEAS. He died at Waterloo, Indiana, on 25 December 1883.[255]

Aurelia Nancy was probably born at Centre, Ohio, shortly after the

---

[246]   Amaden-Hultgren marriage certificate # 4972, Jefferson County Clerk, Golden, Colorado.

[247]   Esther M. Schlosser death certificate # 03674, Colorado Vital Records Office, Denver, Colorado.

[248]   Denver County Probate Docket # 060839, Denver County Court, Denver, Colorado.

[249]   Marriage date based on divorce date from Esther of 7 June 1916, Denver County Docket # 060839, Denver County Court, Denver, Colorado, and Anna's death in 1918.

[250]   Anna May Amaden death certificate #115, Utah State Department of Health, Salt Lake City, Utah.

[251]   Walter D. Amaden death certificate #71-018266, South Carolina Office of Vital Records, Columbia, South Carolina.

Amaden-Dean Lucas County Marriage Application & License # 18326.

[252]   Amaden family records maintained by Chris Amaden.

[253]   "Mrs. A. T. Leas Dead ," *Waterloo [Indiana] Press*, 20 January 1910.

[254]   Williams Co. Genealogical Society, *Williams County, Ohio Marriage Records* (Bryan, Ohio: Williams Co. Genealogical Society, 1984-), IV:573.

[255]   Fay Willis Leas, *Leas Family* (Waterloo, Indiana: self published, 1950), 92; ?. *Atlas of DeKalb County, Indiana* (Chicago: J. H. Beers & Co., 1880), 16, 49.

family relocated there from New York. As a child, she was called Nancy. Little Nancy lost her mother when she was only two years old. Her father placed all the children in foster care. He was a carpenter, and he likely befriended another newly arriving, childless carpenter by the name of Jacob Teems and his wife Anna. Nancy was raised by JACOB and ANNA (MILLER) TEEMS, in Centre. Jacob later became a photographer.[256] Nancy appears as the only child in their household in 1850, 1860, and 1870.[257] By 1870 she had reverted to using her first name, Aurelia, and was working as a school teacher in Bryan, Ohio. It was probably there she met Gus Leas.

According to the *Leas Genealogy*, Gus's father John Leas came to Starke County, Ohio, in 1839 from Adams County, Pennsylvania. Later the family moved to Salem Township in Steuben County, Indiana, finally settling on a farm in 1868 at Smithfield Township, DeKalb County, near Waterloo, Indiana.[258] Gus left home and settled in neighboring Union Township, Indiana, by 1860,[259] married to his first wife, NANCY FORD.[260] By 1870, still in Union Township, he was married to his second wife, ELECTA FAY, and had three children. Frank, age ten, was Nancy's child; Marion, age two, and Agnes, age three months, were Electa's children.[261] Electa died in 1877 after bearing another child, Fred, leaving Gus with four small children.[262] With four children in the house, Gus needed a mother for them. Perhaps the frontier life of Union Township offered few potential stepmothers. For whatever reason, he traveled east to Williams

---

[256] Jacob Teams household, 1850 U.S. census, Williams County, Ohio, population schedule, Center Township, page 67, dwelling 39, family 39; National Archives micropublication M432, roll 741.

[257] Jacob Seamer household, 1860 U.S. cens., Williams Co., Oh., pop. sched., Center, p. 157, dw. 1236, fam. 1187.

Jacob Fenne household, 1870 U.S. cens., Williams Co., Oh., pop. sched., Bryan, p. 196, dw. 361, fam. 361.

[258] Fay Willis Leas, *Leas Family*, 10.

[259] Augustus Leas household, 1860 U.S. census, DeKalb County, Indiana, population schedule, Union Township, page 31, dwelling 242, family 240; National Archives micropublication M653, roll 254.

[260] Yates Publishing, *U.S. and International Marriage Records, 1560-1900*, database. (Provo, Utah: MyFamily.com, Inc., 2004.)

[261] Augustus Leas household, 1870 U.S. census, DeKalb County, Indiana, population schedule, Union Township, page 19, dwelling 152, family 152; National Archives micropublication M593, roll 309.

[262] Arlene Goodwin, compiler, *Waterloo Cemetery Inscriptions, DeKalb County, Indiana*, II: 105.

County, Ohio, where he married Aurelia Amaden in 1878.

The newlywed couple returned to DeKalb County, Indiana. They appear there in 1880 with the four children of Gus and a local domestic servant, Elizabeth Boyle, age twenty. Through a three cornered election, Gus – a Republican – had been elected the town sheriff, even though his party was the minority.[263] He served four years, and his son Frank served as deputy sheriff.[264] But Aurelia and Gus were not to live long together. He died on Christmas Day, 1883, at age fifty after only five years of marriage to Aurelia. Gus is buried at Waterloo Cemetery in Waterloo, Indiana.

Not much is known about Aurelia's adult relationship with her father and brothers. The family members all lived within about fifteen miles of each other over a span of thirty years. She was never formally adopted by the Teems family, but was often referred to as Nancy or Aurelia Teems. The one person who tied all the siblings together was Aurelia's oldest brother, Morton. Over a twenty-year span, each of his siblings lent him and his wife money through mortgages on lots 365 and 366 in Edgerton: Henry in 1864, John in 1875, and "Aurilla T. Leas and Augustus S. Leas" in 1883.[265]

After Gus's death, Aurelia joined her stepdaughters Agnes and Marion in Ann Arbor, Michigan, where they were students, likely at the University of Michigan.[266] There the girls met Professors Paul Freer and Dean Worcester. Paul was a chemist. Dean was a botanist who made several expeditions to the Philippines. Agnes married Paul in 1891,[267] and Marion married Dean in 1893. In 1891, Dean was appointed U.S. Philippine commissioner by President William McKinley and was part of the delegation that established the Philippine government in 1901, following the Spanish-American War. He was later appointed as Secretary of the Interior in the Philippine

---

263   "Death of Ex-Sheriff Leas," *Waterloo Press,* 27 December 1883, page 4.

264   Augustus Leas household, 1880 U.S. census, DeKalb County, Indiana, population schedule, Auburn Village, SD 6, ED 84, page 44, dwelling 430, family 431; National Archives micropublication T9, roll 273.

265   Williams County [Ohio] Land Records, 25:275, 25:545, 26:134, 41:193, 45:332, 52:171, 172, 636.

266   Ancestry.com, *Ann Arbor, Michigan Directories, 1886, 1888-92* [database on-line] (Provo, Utah: MyFamily.com, Inc., 2000).

267   Paul C. Freer household, 1900 U.S. census, Washtenaw County, Michigan, population schedule, Ypsilanti Ward 7, SD 2, ED 116, sheet 6,B dwelling 103, family 103; National Archives micropublication T623, roll 747.

Islands.[268]

Eventually Agnes, Marion, their brother Fred, and their families removed to the Philippines, where Marion, Fred, and Aurelia may have been during the 1900 census. Agnes and Paul Freer were still living in Ann Arbor.[269] Frank was widowed by 1900 and was boarding with a widow about his age, Theresa Mishler.[270] As conveyed in Aurelia's obituary, she died in 1910. Note that her step-children were identified as her children:

> Word has been received from Fred A. Leas who resides in Oakland, California, that his mother, Aurelia T. Leas, widow of the late Augustus S. Leas, died at Manilla, P. I. Jan. 11, 1910. Death was caused by a second stroke of paralysis. Her two daughters with their husbands live in Manilla and she had only been with them a month. During her residence in Waterloo she made many friends and proved herself to be a woman of more than ordinary ability and culture. Her three children were born here and two girls, Agnes and Nannie [Marion], graduated in the Waterloo High school. They married men of distinguished reputation and they were called by the government to places of great responsibility and trust in the Philippines. Mrs. Leas has one brother who lives in Defiance County, Ohio. It has not yet been learned whether or not her body will be brought to Waterloo for burial.[271]

There are no known children of Aurelia.

Aurelia E. (Amaden) Rounds (1830–1906)

37.   AURELIA E. AMADEN (*JOHN[6], JACOB AMADEN[5], JACOB[4] AMIDOWN, HENRY[3], PHILIP[2], ROGER[1] AMADOWNE*) was born at St. Lawrence County, New York,[272] in August 1830,[273] and died at

---

268   Rossiter Johnson, ed., *The Twentieth Century Biographical Dictionary of Notable Americans*, 10 vols., (Boston: The Biographical Society, 1904), X: W.

269   Paul C. Freer household, 1900 U.S. cens., Washtenaw Co., Mich., pop. sched., Ypsilanti Ward 7, SD 2, ED 116, sheet 6B, dwelling 103, family 103.

270   Theresa Mishler household, 1900 U.S. census, Elkhart County, Indiana, population schedule, Elkhart District 23, SD 13, ED 23, sheet 2A, dwelling 35, family 37; National Archives micropublication T623, roll 369.

271   "Mrs. A. T. Leas Dead ," *Waterloo Press*, 20 January 1910.

272   John Amidon household, 1865 N.Y. state census, Jefferson County, Watertown, page 53, dwelling 388, family 388; New York State Library, Albany,

Watertown, New York, on 13 July 1906.[274]   She married at
Watertown, New York, on 1 November 1860 EDWIN W. ROUNDS,[275]
son of REUBEN and NAOMI (__) ROUNDS.[276]   He was born at
Herkimer County, New York,[277] in August 1832[278] and died at
Watertown, New York, on 28 January 1912.[279]

Aurelia was probably born in Russell, New York, where her
parents were living in 1830. Over the next twelve years, the family
seems to have moved at least four times. They were settled in
Watertown by 1850. Aurelia's mother, Nancy, ran a boarding house
in Watertown until her death in 1872. We can imagine that Aurelia
worked alongside her mother from the early days of the boarding
house. But by 1860 she was working in the paper mills, though still
living in her mother's household.[280]

Edwin Rounds was born in 1832 in Herkimer County in northeast
New York, roughly halfway between the east end of Lake Ontario and
Vermont. By the time he was eighteen, he had left his parents' home
and struck out on his own. He may be the Edwin Rounds in the
household of Samule (sic) Rounds in Farmington, Illinois, who was

---

New York. The 1855 state census gives her birth county as Montgomery, but 1865
and 1875 give it as St. Lawrence County.

[273]   1900 census indicates her birth in August, 1834; however, her ages in the
1850, 1855, 1860 and 1870 censuses indicate a birth year of 1830.

[274]   Aurelia E. Rounds, N.Y. State Death Record, Certificate # 7175; State
Department of Health, Albany New York.

[275]   *Stone St. Presbyterian Church, Watertown, Jefferson Co., New York.*

[276]   Reuben Rounds Probate, Herkimer County, N.Y. Surrogates File # 06382.

Ruben Rounds household, 1860 U.S. census, Herkimer County, New York,
population schedule, Newport, page 67, dwelling 54, family 47; National Archives
micropublication M653, roll 759.

[277]   John Amidon household, 1865 N.Y. state cens., Jefferson Co., Watertown,
p. 53, dwelling 388, family 388.

[278]   Edwin W. Rounds tombstone, Brookside Cemetery, Watertown, N.Y.;
marker indicates birth year of 1832.

Edwin Rounds household, 1900 U.S. census, Jefferson County, New York,
population schedule, Watertown, SD 6, ED 39, sheet 7A, dwelling 102, family 144;
National Archives micropublication T623, roll 1042; census gives birth date as
August 1833. Other census records are not consistent on his birth year.

[279]   Edwin W. Rounds, N.Y. State Death Record, Certificate # 9793.

[280]   Nancy Amidon household, 1860 U.S. census, Jefferson County, New
York, population schedule, Watertown, page 28, dwelling 198, family 195; National
Archives micropublication M653, roll 762.

learning the trade of brick mason from Samule.[281] If so, then Edwin decided masonry wasn't for him. By 1860 he was back home with his parents in Newport, New York, just southwest of the huge Adirondack Mountain Preserve, working as a cabinet maker, as he would for the rest of his life.[282] Edwin must have been on the move that year because he was recorded twice in the 1860 census. He was also listed as a boarder in Nancy Amaden's household in Watertown as a cabinet maker.[283]

Late in 1860 Aurelia married Edwin in Watertown. In May 1862 their home was brightened by the birth of Carrie. By this time the Civil War was fully underway. Edwin was old compared to the average aged twenty-one-year-old soldier. Yet at about thirty years of age, he enlisted at Watertown on 20 August 1862 for three years. Sadly, his new daughter Carrie died soon after he left in September. Edwin first served in Company B, 35th New York Infantry. Edwin saw action at Antietam and Fredericksburg. In May, 1863, he transferred to Company A, 80th New York Infantry. Here he fought at Gettysburg and many lesser battles. He was discharged on 17 June 1865 having attained the rank of corporal.[284]

Edwin returned home to Watertown and rejoined his wife and her family in Watertown. Edwin and his brother-in-law, Edwin Amaden, another Civil War veteran, started a business in Watertown: Rounds

---

281   Samule D. Rounds household, 1850 U.S. census, Fulton County, Illinois, population schedule, Farmington, page 238B/478, dwelling 102, family 113; National Archives micropublication M432, roll 107.
282   Ruben Rounds household, 1860 U.S. cens., Herkimer Co., N.Y., pop. sched., Newport, p. 67, dw. 54, fam. 47.
283   Nancy Amidon household, 1860 U.S. cens., Jefferson Co., N.Y., pop. sched., Watertown, p. 572, dwelling 198, family 195.
284   Edwin W. Rounds, Civil War Pension App. File SO 782654, SC 829630.

& Amaden, Cabinet Makers and Furniture Dealers, located at 16 Public Square near to the family boarding house.[285]

Another positive development occurred in 1868 when their son Frederick Daniel was born. The 1870 census shows the small family living with Aurelia's parents in Watertown. Edwin's personal property of $2000 was surprisingly valuable for such a young couple. Perhaps it reflected inventory for his cabinet-making business.[286] In the early 1870s, Edwin Amaden left for Elgin, Illinois, while Edwin Rounds stayed and continued to run the business. Aurelia's mother died in 1872, so her father John moved in with them by 1875.[287]

By 1880, Edwin and Aurelia had their own house at 9 Holcomb Street in Watertown. Young Fred was now twelve. With Carrie's death, he grew up as an only child. Edwin was still working as a cabinet maker.[288] Edwin and Aurelia lived the rest of their lives at this home.

Son Fred's first position was as a clerk for a Watertown contractor. He was active in the Y.M.C.A. About 1887, he removed to New York City to manage the West Side Branch of the Railroad Y.M.C.A. The national Y.M.C.A., invited by railway companies to establish branch hotels at their expense, was operating 150 of them with 37,000 members by 1900.[289] In 1890, Fred resigned due to ill health and took a position as secretary for the president of the Broadway and Seventh Avenue Railroad Company. In 1897, he married MARIE AGNES HUGHES, a New York City resident and public school teacher. Marie's father, John, was an Irish immigrant and a master painter in the city. Fred and Marie came back to Watertown for the birth of their

---

285   ?, *Polk's Watertown (Jefferson County, N.Y.) city directory, 1867-8* (?: R. L. Polk Publishing Company, 1868); original directory at Flower Memorial Library, Watertown, N.Y.

286   Edwin Rounds household, 1870 U.S. census, Jefferson County, New York, population schedule, Watertown fourth ward, page 71, dwelling 560, family 566; National Archives micropublication M593, roll 258.

287   Edwin W. Rounds household, 1875 N.Y. state census, Jefferson County, Watertown, 3rd ward, lines 374-379; Flower Memorial Library, Watertown, N.Y.

288   Edwin Rounds household, 1880 U.S. census, Jefferson County, New York, population schedule, Watertown, SD 7, ED 149, page 14, dwelling 92, family 102; National Archives micropublication T9, roll 840.

289   Data online, <hotelinteractive.com/index.asp?page_id=5000&article_id =6059>.

daughter, Elizabeth. In 1898, he became the general superintendent of all the New York City Metropolitan lines.[290]

In 1900 Edwin and Aurelia were living alone at 9 Mullin Street in Watertown. By now Edwin was sixty-six years old and retired.[291] Fred and his young family have not been found in the 1900 census; in all likelihood Fred and Marie had separated.

Fred's life fell apart. Marie had filed papers for divorce in June 1900. Fred had been living with a Mrs. Lydia Betts, first at a luxury apartment on Forty-Third Street in New York City and later in a house in Hoboken. He resigned from his position with the railroad on grounds of family problems and then worked in sales of electrical railway supplies for Sterling Meaker Company. His life ended tragically from suicide after a drinking binge. The scandal associated with his death, the accompanying suicide notes, sordid intrigue about his paramour, and the sensational inquest captivated local readers for a week. Fred's remains were collected by his cousin, Charles Snell, and returned for burial in Watertown.[292]

Marie never remarried. She resumed public school teaching and raised her daughter Elizabeth in New York City, although there was a period when Elizabeth lived in Watertown with her grandmother Aurelia and with Aurelia's sister, Mary (Amaden) Palmer.[293] In 1910, Marie was a boarder with the widow Elizabeth Chambers, but without her daughter – Elizabeth was likely in a boarding school based on family history.[294] Marie died in 1915 of pneumonia. A few years later, Elizabeth married DOROTEO PICHEL, a Spanish born importer-exporter. After their four children were born in Queens, the family moved to Spain for several years, where Doroteo died in 1928

---

[290] Obituary, "Disinherits Wife and Kills Himself," *The Evening Journal*, Jersey City, New Jersey, 25 July 1902.

[291] Edwin Rounds household, 1900 U.S. cens., Jefferson Co., N.Y., pop. sched., Watertown, SD 6, ED 39, sheet 7A, dw. 102, fam. 144.

[292] "Disinherits Wife and Kills Himself," *The Evening Journal*.

[293] Aurelia E. and Edwin W. Rounds, Probate Record Boxes R-25, R-44, Jefferson County, New York.

[294] Elizabeth G. Chambers household, 1910 U.S. census, New York County, New York, population schedule, town of Manhattan, Ward 22, SD 1, ED 1305, sheet 2B, dwelling 24, family 35; National Archives micropublication T624, roll 1046.

after only ten years of marriage. The rest of the family eventually returned to New York City.[295]

Aurelia died in 1906 at age seventy-five. She was buried at Brookside Cemetery in Watertown joining her daughter, son, and parents. Edwin carried on another five years before dying in 1912 at age seventy-nine. He was buried beside Aurelia in Brookside Cemetery.[296] In their wills, Aurelia and Edwin remembered several of her relatives including: Mary M. Palmer (sister), Elizabeth B. Rounds (granddaughter), Alma J. Morgan (niece), Adelbert G. Morgan (nephew), Albert Amaden (nephew), and Charles H. Snell (nephew).[297]

Children of EDWIN and AURELIA (AMADEN) ROUNDS:

i.   CARRIE ROUNDS, b. N.Y. abt. May 1862; d. 3 Sept. 1862; bur. Brookside Cem., Watertown, N.Y.[298]

ii.   FREDERICK DANIEL ROUNDS, b. Watertown, N.Y., 16 April 1868; bap. Stone St. Presbyterian Church, Watertown, 1 Oct. 1871;[299] d. Hoboken, N.J., 24 July 1902; bur. Brookside Cemetery, Watertown;[300] m. bef. 1897 MARIE AGNES HUGHES,[301] b. New York, N.Y., Aug. 1859, dau. of JOHN and ELIZABETH (__) HUGHES, d. New York, N.Y., 1915.[302]

Child of FREDERICK and MARIE (HUGHES) ROUNDS:

a.   *Elizabeth Battell Rounds*, b. Watertown 25 May 1897;[303] m. 1917 *Doroteo Gregorio Pichel*, b. Zamaia, Spain, 1886, d. Bilbao, Spain, 26 July 1928.[304]

---

295   Family notes of Rick Carlin of Cincinnati, Ohio, held by Christopher Amaden.

296   Brookside Cemetery Records, Watertown, New York.

297   Aurelia E. Rounds, Jefferson County Probate Record Box R-44.

298   Brookside Cemetery Records, Watertown, New York.

299   *Stone St. Presbyterian Church, Watertown, Jefferson Co., N.Y., 1831-85.*

300   "Disinherits Wife and Kills Himself," *The Evening Journal*, 25 July 1902; Brookside Cemetery Records, Watertown, New York.

301   Daughter's birth record of 1897: Elizabeth Battell Rounds, New York Birth Record, Certificate #22748.

302   Family notes of Rick Carlin of Cincinnati, Ohio, copy held by Christopher Amaden.

John Hughes household, 1860 U.S. census, New York County, New York, population schedule, New York, ward 18-district 2, page 401, dwelling 621, family 779; National Archives micropublication M653, roll 814.

303   Elizabeth Battell Rounds, New York Birth Record, Certificate #22748.

304   Family notes of Rick Carlin, Cincinnati, Ohio, copy with Christopher Amaden.

Children of *Doroteo* and *Elizabeth (Rounds) Pichel* (all born at Hollis, N.Y.):[305]

1. Virginia Elizabeth Pichel, b. 24 April 1918.
2. Dorothy Pichel, b. 24 Dec. 1919.
3. Helena Pichel, b. 10 Sept. 1922.
4. Theodore G. Pichel, b. 10 Nov. 1923.

Ellen Louisa (Amaden) Morgan (1832–1905)

38. ELLEN LOUISA "LOUISA" AMADEN (JOHN[6], JACOB[5], JACOB[4] AMIDOWN, HENRY[3], PHILIP[2], ROGER[1] AMADOWNE) was born at Pierrepont, New York, on 11 May 1832 and died at Dundee, Illinois, on 21 April 1905.[306] She married at Watertown, New York, on 4 April 1855 TRUMAN S. MORGAN.[307] He was born at Pownal, Vermont, on 22 January 1829, son of LEVI and SUSANNAH (FOWLER) MORGAN,[308] and died at Dundee, Illinois, on 20 February 1905.[309]

Louisa was the second child born to John and Nancy Amaden. During the decade of her birth and the subsequent decade, the family was highly mobile, with at least four addresses. By 1850 they had settled in Watertown. John continued to work in a variety of occupations. Nancy began to run a boarding house at 24 Public Square. Probably Louisa helped with the boarding house until her marriage in 1855.

Truman was born in Vermont in 1829. In 1830 he was counted with his family in Pownal, Vermont, the youngest of nine children.[310] In 1850 he was a farmer living in a large boarding house in Bennington, Vermont, run by Anson Petter.[311] He relocated to Watertown soon thereafter and was listed as a tinsmith, boarding at 1 Massey, in the *1855 City Directory*.[312]

---

[305]   Ibid.

[306]   Ellen Louise Amaden Morgan death records, Elgin Death Records Vol 1:2:156, Elgin, Illinois.

[307]   Richard W. Hungerford, Jr., compiler, *Marriages in The New York Reformer, 1850-1861* (?: Hungerford Genealogical Services, 1996), 27.

[308]   Vermont. *General index to vital records of Vermont, early to 1870.*

[309]   Truman S. Morgan, City of Elgin Death Records, Vol 1, Led 2, Page 156.

[310]   Levi Morgan household, 1830 U.S. cens., Bennington Co., Vt., Pownal, p. 50, ln. 15.

[311]   Anson Petter household, 1850 U.S. cens., Bennington Co., Vt., pop. sched., Bennington, p. 199, dw. 214, fam. 288.

[312]   *Watertown, North Watertown and Juhelville Business Directory for 1855.*

That year in Watertown he and Louisa were married. They seem to have gone on a search for the right place to put down roots, while starting their family immediately: Alma was born at Cleveland, Ohio, in 1856; Addie was born at Hannover, Illinois, in 1857. In 1860, Louisa was living in her mother's home in Watertown, where Adelbert was likely born in June of that year.[313] Both Truman and his father-in-law were missing from that census – perhaps working in nearby Canada.

Mary Ella was born in Watertown in 1861. The family was still there for the 1865 New York State census, but soon left for Elgin, Illinois.[314] Also leaving for Elgin was Louisa's brother Edwin, where he married ELIZA BOGUE in 1866. Stella was Louisa's last natural child, born in South Elgin in 1868. Edwin returned to Watertown for a few years, but Elgin became home for the Morgan family. Truman continued his trade as tinsmith, as noted in the 1870 census. That year Addie was only thirteen, but had moved out of the family homestead: she may have been a domestic and not enumerated or perhaps she is the teenager living with Peter Morgan (a relative?) in Farmington, Illinois.[315] The other four children were still living at home.[316] By 1880 Addie had returned home, and the whole family was together.[317] Shortly after the census taker came by, Addie again left home when she married George Washington Snow that October.

George was a recent widower. His first wife, RUTH ELLEN MATTISON, had died on 4 August 1879 in Elgin. It doesn't appear they had any children. George was a house carpenter and veteran of the Civil War. He had served in Company G, 95th Illinois Infantry Regiment, having enrolled at Belvidere, Illinois, on 30 July 1862 as a private for three years. When he joined, he was a twenty-year-old

---

313   Nancy Amidon household, 1860 U.S. cens., Jefferson Co., N.Y., pop. sched., Watertown, p. 572, dw. 198, fam. 195.
314   1865 N.Y. state cens., Jefferson Co., Watertown, 3rd election district, p. 1, dw. 7, fam. 7.
315   Peter Morgan household, 1870 U.S. census, Fulton County, Illinois, population schedule, Farmington, page 14, dwelling 115, family 116; National Archives micropublication M593, roll 223.
316   T. S. Morgan household, 1870 U.S. census, Kane County, Illinois, population schedule, Elgin, page 160, dwelling 1228, family 1228; National Archives micropublication M593, roll 237.
317   Truman Morgan household, 1880 U.S. census, Kane County, Illinois, population schedule, Elgin 1st ward, SD 2, ED 84, page 7, dwelling 1228, family 1228; National Archives micropublication T9, roll 218.

farmer residing at Flora, Illinois, and stood five feet nine inches tall with auburn hair, blue eyes, and a light complexion. He was discharged on 17 August 1865 having fought at Vicksburg and many other minor battles.[318]

Tragedy struck in 1888 when Addie died at her parents' home after suffering a year with consumption, today known as tuberculosis. As Louisa's other children were maturing, Louisa may have felt the need for more children around the house. She and Truman adopted Percy Stanton sometime before 1887, but their joy was short lived because he died of a typhoid-like fever before his second birthday. They also adopted Ralph ___ sometime before 1900.

The next daughter to marry was Stella.   She and CHARLES SINCLAIR were married by his father, a minister, at her parents' home in Elgin in 1890. Charles was a pharmacist for Klock & Sinclair, of Dundee, which later became Sinclair Pharmacy. Dundee is just two miles north of Elgin. Charles's business would become a family affair as his son Ralph, daughter Stella, and her husband Leon Dewey became pharmacists. His last son Merrill became a bookkeeper. The families, except Merrill, were still living in Dundee in 1930.[319]

In 1897, Louisa and Truman's daughter Mary Ella married the widower CHARLES BIGSBY, also at her parents' home. Charles was previously married to CYNTHIA C. BAKER, who had died in Elgin in 1893. He was nearly thirty years Mary's senior. They began their family the next year with the birth of Carl followed by Paul in 1899. Charles's trade was nurseryman. They lived in Elgin until 1912.

The Morgan family's oldest daughter Alma and oldest son Adelbert never married. In 1900 at the age of forty, Adelbert was a grocer living with his elderly parents and adopted brother Ralph in Elgin.[320] By trade, Alma was a dressmaker and milliner, someone who designs and makes hats. In 1900 she and her widowed aunt Mary (Amaden) Palmer were roomers in Robert Moon's home in

---

[318]   George W. Snow, Civil War Pension Application File SO 1324698, SC 1095864, WC 808324.

[319]   Charles Sinclair household, 1930 U.S. census, Kane County, Illinois, population schedule, Dundee, SD 10, ED 49, sheet 17A, dwelling 168, family 195; National Archives micropublication T626, roll 524.

R Thomas Sinclair, Ancestry.com, *Social Security Death Index*.

[320]   Thomas Morgan household, 1900 U.S. census, Kane County, Illinois, population schedule, Elgin, SD 2, ED 95, sheet 7A, dwelling 140, family 155; National Archives micropublication T623, roll 311.

Dundee.[321] When Louisa and Truman's health began to fail, they relocated to Dundee – perhaps to be closer to Mary who was a nurse. Truman died in the winter of 1905 at age seventy-six and was buried in Elgin City Cemetery. Louisa survived him by only two months, age seventy-three, and was buried beside Truman, daughter Addie, and adopted son Ralph.[322]

Soon after Truman and Louisa's death, some of the family left the area. Mary Palmer returned to Watertown, likely to care for another sister, Aurelia (Amaden) Rounds. Alma and her brother Adelbert struck out for Los Angeles, where we find them together in the 1910 census.[323] He was now a photographer while she continued her dressmaking. Interestingly, their cousin Albert Amaden (son of George W. Amaden) had left Watertown and made Los Angeles his new home at this same time. We know that the extended family maintained contact because they were all mentioned in Aurelia Rounds's will of 1906.[324] Charles and Mary Ella moved to Los Angeles in 1912 with their two boys.

In Los Angeles, Adelbert died in 1917. Alma moved in with her sister Mary and the rest of the Bigsby family.[325] Charles Bigsby's death followed in 1921, and Alma in 1922. All were buried or cremated at Forest Lawn Cemetery in Glendale, California. The Bigsby boys stayed in Los Angeles – Carl served in World War I, was a publisher and resident of Compton, California, in 1930.[326] Paul, his location unknown in 1930, became founder and president of Bigsby Electric Guitars.[327]

---

321   Robt. Moon household, 1900 U.S. cens., Kane Co., Ill., pop. sched., Dundee, SD 2, ED 89, sheet 8B, dw. 178, fam. 189.
322   Louisa Morgan, Truman Morgan, Addie Morgan, and Ralph Morgan tombstones, Elgin City Cemetery, Elgin, Illinois; photographs held by Chris Amaden.
323   Adelbert G. Morgan, 1910 U.S. census, Los Angeles County, California, population schedule, Los Angeles, district 74, SD 7, ED 46, sheet 12A, dwelling 358, family 400; National Archives micropublication T624, roll 83.
324   Aurelia E. Rounds, Jefferson County Probate Record Box R-44.
325   Charles L. Bigsby household, 1920 U.S. census, Los Angeles County, California, population schedule, Los Angeles town, District 61, SD 101, ED 118, sheet 6B, dwelling 154, family 160; National Archives micropublication T625, roll 105.
326   Carl M. Bigsby household, 1930 U.S. cens., Los Angeles Co., Calif., pop. sched., Compton, SD 19, ED 877, sheet 10A, dw. 263, fam. 263.
327   History downloaded from Bigsby Electric Guitars at <www.bigsbyguitars.com/history.html>.

Ralph Morgan was with his parents in the 1900 census. Nothing further has been found for him.

Children of TRUMAN and LOUISA (AMADEN) MORGAN:

i.   ALMA J. MORGAN, b. Cleveland, Oh., 28 Feb. 1856; d. Glendale, Calif., 10 Nov. 1922; bur. Forest Lawn Cem., Glendale, Calif.[328]

ii. ADDIE E. MORGAN, b. Hannover, Ill., 15 Sept. 1857; d. Elgin, Ill., 21 June 1888; bur. Elgin City Cem., Elgin;[329] m. Elgin 11 Oct. 1880 GEORGE WASHINGTON SNOW,[330] b. Belmont, N.Y., 3 Oct. 1841,[331] son of JOSIAH and HANNAH (PORTER) SNOW,[332] d. Elgin 20 Feb. 1916, bur. Barrington, Ill., 22 Feb. 1916,[333] m. 2) Elgin 18 July 1889 MARTHA ANN DEVOL, b. Barrington, Ill., April 1845, dau. of WILLIAM and ANNA (GOULD) DEVOL, d. Elgin 31 July 1923, bur. Barrington.[334] No known children.

iii. ADELBERT G. MORGAN, b. probably Watertown, N.Y., 8 June 1860; d. Los Angeles, Calif., 12 Feb. 1917; bur. Forest Lawn Cem.[335]

iv. MARY ELLA MORGAN, b. Watertown, N.Y., 16 Oct. 1861; m. Elgin 7 Oct. 1897 CHARLES LEE BIGSBY, b. Brainards Bridge, N.Y., May 1833,[336] son of WILLIAM and CHRISTIANA (ESSELSTYNE) BIXBY, d. Los Angeles 14 Feb. 1921, cremated Forest Lawn Crematory, Glendale.[337]

Children of CHARLES and MARY (MORGAN) BIGSBY:

a.   *Carl Morgan Bigsby*, b. Elgin 14 Nov. 1898;[338] m. Los Angeles 20 Aug. 1924 *Evelyn Augusta Hoick*, b. Calif. 5

---

328   Alma J. Morgan, California Death Record, Certificate # 47256.

329   Addie E. Snow, Illinois Death Certificate, Record # 5889 of 1888, book 2:208, Illinois State Archives, Springfield, Illinois. Reburial from Channing Cemetery in Elgin to Elgin City (aka Bluff City) Cemetery in 1905 according to phone conversation between Bluff City Cemetery official and Chris Amaden dated 15 March 2005.

330   Kane County, Illinois Marriage Register, Book 1, Page 83, record 1074.

331   George W. Snow, Civil War Pension App. File SO 1324698, SC 1095864.

332   Kane County, Illinois Marriage Register, Book 1, Page 83, record 1074.

333   Geo. W. Snow, Illinois Death Certificate, Certificate # 15980.

334   Kane County, Illinois Marriage Register, Book 2, Page 219, record 6519.
      City of Elgin, Illinois Death Record Vol 1, Led 3, p 83.

335   Adelbert G. Morgan, California Death Record, Certificate # 5472.

336   Charles Bigsby household, 1900 U.S. cens., Kane Co., Ill., pop. sched., Elgin, SD 2, ED 104, sheet 3, dwelling 64, family 71.

337   Kane County, Illinois Marriage Registry, Book 3: 269, Record # 11074.
      Chas. Lee Bigsby, California Death Record, Certificate # 5897.

338   Carl Morgan Bigsby, Illinois Birth Record, recorded 25 November 1898.

March 1899 dau. of *John Edward* and *Grace (Deitz) Hoick*.[339]

    Child of *Carl* and *Evelyn (Hoick) Bigsby*:

    1. Maralyn Ardis Bigsby, b. Los Angeles Co., Calif., 23 April 1929.[340]

  b. *Paul Adelbert Bigsby*, b. Elgin 12 Dec. 1899.[341]

v. STELLA MARYANN MORGAN, b. South Elgin, Ill., 5 Dec. 1868; d. West Dundee Village, Ill., 25 Oct. 1929,; bur. East Dundee Cem., Dundee, Ill.;[342] m. Elgin 2 July 1890 CHARLES STOWE SINCLAIR,[343] b. Saratoga Springs, N.Y., 25 Dec. 1866, son of DANIEL M. and MARY (SWAZEY) SINCLAIR.[344]

    Children of CHARLES and STELLA (MORGAN) SINCLAIR:

a. *Stella Linita Sinclair*, b. Dundee, Ill., Aug. 1892; m. Dundee 2 June 1914 *Leon Henry Dewey*,[345] b. Marshall, Wisc., 2 June 1889, son of *Adelbert* and *Abby J. (Pierce) Dewey*.[346] Stella was a graduate of the University of California and the University of Wisconsin, graduating from the latter as the only woman graduate in a class of 300. Leon was a graduate of the University of Wisconsin in both chemistry and pharmacy and was a member of Stella's graduating class.[347]

    Child of *Leon* and *Stella (Sinclair) Dewey*:

    1. Marjorie Dewey, b. Ill. abt. 1923.[348]

  b. *Ralph Merritt Sinclair*, b. Dundee 22 Feb. 1898;[349] m. abt.

---

339   California Marriage Record, Certificate # 11580.
    Evelyn A. Bigsby, California Death Record, Certificate # 3-90-30-006071.
340   Marilyn Ardis Bigsby, California Birth Index 1905-1995.
341   Paul Bigsby, Illinois Birth Record, recorded 20 December 1899.
342   Stella Morgan Sinclair, Illinois Death Record, Certificate #37848.
343   Kane County, Illinois Marriage Registry, Book 2: 258, Record # 7028.
344   Charles Stowe Sinclair, Illinois Death Certificate, recorded 19 October 1943.
345   Kane County, Illinois Marriage Registry, Book 7:468, Record # 25765.
    Chas. Suchan (sic) household, 1900 U.S. cens., Kane Co., Ill., pop. sched., Dundee, SD 2, ED 89, sheet 7B, dwelling 156, family 166.
346   Leon Henry Dewey, Illinois Death Record, Certificate # 43754.
347   "Dundee Wedding Charming Social Event of Week," *The Elgin Daily Courier*, Wednesday Evening, 3 June 1914, page 9, column 1.
348   Leon Dewey household, 1930 U.S. cens., Kane Co., Ill., pop. sched., West Dundee, SD 10, ED 49, sheet 14A, dwelling 329, family 354.
349   Ralph Merritt Sinclair, Illinois Death Record, Certificate # 1812.

1922 *Catherine Schultz*,[350] b. Shawano, Wisc., 26 May 1895, dau. of *George* and *Margaret (Smith) Schultz.*[351] Ralph served in World War I, was a pharmacist at Sinclair Pharmacy in West Dundee.

Children of *Ralph* and *Catherine (Schultz) Sinclair*:
1. Charles D. Sinclair, b. Elgin 17 June 1923.[352]
2. R. Thomas Sinclair, b. Ill. 15 Dec. 1928.[353]

c. *Merrill Morgan "Rex" Sinclair,* b. Dundee 16 Sept. 1904;[354] m. *Helen Clarissa Bradley.* He was employed as a bookkeeper for Fox Electric Supply Co. and was a graduate of Galesburg College.[355]

vi. RALPH MORGAN, b. Ill. Sept. 1885. Adopted child.[356]
vii. PERCY STANTON MORGAN, b. Minn. 21 Oct. 1885; d. Elgin 21 July 1887; bur. Elgin City Cem. Adopted child.[357]

George W. Amaden (1834–1862)

39. GEORGE W. AMADEN (*JOHN*[6], *JACOB*[5], *JACOB*[4] *AMIDOWN,* *HENRY*[3], *PHILIP*[2], *ROGER*[1] *AMADOWNE*) was born at Oneida County, New York,[358] in 1834[359] and died at Camp Relief on Meridian Hill,

---

350 Charles Sinclair household, 1930 U.S. cens., Kane Co., Ill., pop. sched., Dundee, SD 10, ED 49, sheet 17A, dwelling 168, family 195.

351 "Catherine Sinclair, West Dundee," *Daily Courier News*, Elgin, Illionis, 7 November 1984, page 28, column 3.

352 "Charles Sinclair, West Dundee," *Elgin Daily Courier News*, 19 August 1976, page 29, columns 2,3.

353 Charles Sinclair household, 1930 U.S. cens., Kane Co., Ill., pop. sched., Dundee, SD 10, ED 49, sheet 17A, dwelling 168, family 195.

R Thomas Sinclair, Ancestry.com, *Social Security Death Index.*

354 "Merril (Rex) Morgan Sinclair," *Daily Courier News*, Elgin, Illinois, Wednesday, 27 July 1960.

355 "Merrill E. 'Skip' Sinclair," *The Courier-News*, Elgin, Illinois, 22 January 2003, Section B, Page 6.

356 Thomas Morgan household, 1900 U.S. cens., Kane Co., Ill., pop. sched., Elgin, SD 2, ED 95, sheet 7A, dwelling 140, family 155.

357 Percy Stanton Morgan, Illinois Death Record, Certificate # 5345. Reburial from Channing Cemetery in Elgin to Elgin City (aka Bluff City) Cemetery in 1905 according to phone conversation between Bluff City Cemetery official and Chris Amaden dated 15 March 2005.

358 George Amaden household, 1855 N.Y. State Census, Jefferson County, population schedule, Watertown, ED 3, dwelling 264, family 295; Flower Memorial Library, Watertown, New York.

359 Best, *The Amidon Family*, 137.

Washington D.C., on 30 December 1862.[360] He married first at Watertown, New York, on 30 April 1855 ADELIZA MATILDA BOID BLODGETT.[361] She was born at Russell, New York, on 2 September 1839,[362] daughter of FRANCIS JAMES JACKSON and CLOANTHA (BELL) BLODGETT, and died at Clinton, New York, on 27 January 1858.[363] He married second at Watertown on 4 September 1859, URSULA HASTINGS,[364] daughter of LEMUEL and ABBY (__) HASTINGS. She was born at New York in about 1837,[365] and died at Watertown, New York, on 2 June 1862.[366]

George was born in Oneida County, New York, in 1834. His family was living in Russell, New York, in 1840.[367] Adeliza Blodgett was born there in 1839, which is where we find her family in 1840.[368] George and Adeliza were likely childhood friends. The Blodgett family moved to Watertown in 1846, and the Amaden family followed in 1849. She was barely sixteen when Adeliza married the twenty-one-year-old George Amaden in Watertown. After marrying in 1855, the young couple lived next door to her parents in Watertown. George was an axe maker.[369]

Soon thereafter, they moved seventy miles south to Rome where their son Charles was born in 1857. But Adeliza was not allowed to raise the boy; she died three months after his birth, in 1858 at age eighteen. She was buried in Huntingtonville Rural Cemetery,

---

360   George Amaden, Civil War Pension App. File, Minor Child App. # 11935.
361   Amaden–Blodget marriage record, 1831-1885 registers, Stone St. Presbyterian Church, Watertown, Jefferson County, New York.
362   Personal records of Sandra Coplien, email skcoplien@ameritech.com.
363   George Amaden, Civil War Pension App. File, Minor Child App. # 11935.
364   Hungerford, *Marriages in The New York Reformer, 1850-1861*, 103.
New York Reformer, 15 September 1859.
365   Lemuel Hastings household, 1850 U.S. cens., Jefferson Co., N.Y., pop. sched., Watertown, p. 329, dw. 771, fam. 881.
366   George Amaden, Civil War Pension App. File, Minor Child App. # 11935.
367   John Amaden household, 1840 U.S. cens., St. Lawrence Co., N.Y., Russell, p. 254, line 20.
368   Jackson Blodgit household, 1840 U.S. cens., St. Lawrence Co., N.Y., Russell, p. 262, line 6.
369   George Amaden household, 1855 N.Y. state cens., Jefferson Co, Watertown, ED 3, dw. 264, fam. 295.

Watertown, New York.[370] George returned to his parents' home in Watertown, where he was a painter in 1859.[371]

With an infant in the house, George could not mourn Adeliza for long. After twenty months he married Ursula Hastings in Watertown. This wedding was special for the Amaden family because it was a dual marriage with George's sister, Mary, marrying James Palmer. But 1860 found George living with his mother and siblings, without his wife and children, working as a blacksmith.[372] Ursula was living with her parents enumerated under her maiden name, caring for her newborn infant Albert Amaden.[373] Ursula may have been with her parents as she recovered from childbirth. George's son, Charles, has not been found in the 1860 census.

In May 1862 Ursula delivered a daughter, Hattie. But Ursula, too, was not allowed to raise her children. She died ten days after Hattie was born, at age twenty-five. Hattie was adopted by George's sister, Mary, and her husband, James Palmer.[374]

Losing his second wife in June, perhaps George wanted to make a transition. In August, with the Civil War in full swing, he enlisted as a private at Canton, New York, to be a blacksmith for three years in Company I, 11th Cavalry Regiment New York – known as Scott's 900. It was named "Scott's 900" in honor of Thomas A. Scott of Pennsylvania, the Assistant Secretary of War.[375] Within weeks of enlisting, his daughter Hattie died at age three months. Ursula and Hattie were buried at Huntingtonville Rural Cemetery.[376]

George reported for duty a few days later in Albany and joined his Regiment in Washington D.C. From there he served during a minor battle at Poolesville, Maryland, but fell ill. He returned to

---

[370] Alice Corbett, *Cemetery DAR transcriptions*, copyrighted by Alice Corbett (2006), data downloaded 6 September 2006, <freepages.genealogy.rootsweb.com/~aliecor/Cemeteries/Town_of_Watertown/Huntingtonville.htm>.

[371] *Watertown City Directory for 1859-60*; Flower Memorial Library, Watertown, New York.

[372] Nancy Amidon household, 1860 U.S. cens., Jefferson Co., N.Y., pop. sched., Watertown, p. 28, dw. 198, fam. 195.

[373] Leonard Hastings household, 1860 U.S. cens., Jefferson Co., N.Y., pop. sched., Watertown, p. 186, dw. 1440, fam. 1398.

[374] Corbett, *Cemetery DAR transcriptions*.

[375] Michael McAfee, "11th New York Volunteer Cavalry," *Military Images*, January/February 2002; reprinted by Find Articles, online <www.findarticles.com/p/articles/mi_qa3905/is_200201/ai_n9023607>.

[376] Corbett, *Cemetery DAR transcriptions*.

Washington D.C. at Camp Relief, located on Meridian Hill – the present site of Meridian Hill Park. There George died of typhoid on 30 December 1862.[377] His remains were returned to Watertown and buried alongside his two wives and daughter at Huntingtonville Rural Cemetery.[378]

In 1863, Francis Blodgett – father of George's first wife Adeliza – filed for and received a pension on behalf of George's two sons, Charles and Albert. Francis indicated that he had guardianship of the two boys. In 1865 Charles was living with Francis,[379] and Albert was living with his maternal grandmother, Abby Hastings.[380]

In 1870, young Charles was still with Francis and was a schoolboy.[381] He must have fallen ill, because in January 1878 at age twenty he wrote a will and then died the following month. He left his Uncle James Palmer (husband of Mary Amaden) interest in stock of tobacco and cigars and to his brother, Albert Amaden, his watch.[382] Charles was buried alongside his parents.[383]

Albert's aunt Eliza Hastings married Alonso Dresser. By 1870, they had taken in Eliza's mother Abby and ten-year old Albert.[384] At age twenty-three, he married Harriet "Hattie" Howard in Watertown. Hattie and her sister Adah had moved to Watertown from their immigrant parents' home in Pinckney, New York. Both were servants living with neighboring families in Watertown.[385] Albert became a farmer and lived in East Watertown. Hattie fell ill and was admitted to the St. Lawrence State Hospital in Ogdensburg, New York. By 1900 Albert had returned to live with his aunt and uncle and helped farm their land.[386] Hattie died of anaemia in 1902 at age forty-two and

---

[377]   George Amaden, Civil War Pension App. File, Minor Child App. # 11935.

[378]   Corbett, *Cemetery DAR transcriptions.*

[379]   F. J. J. Blodgett household, 1865 N.Y. state cens., Jefferson Co., pop. sched., Watertown, 3rd election district, p. 28, dw. 181, fam. 180.

[380]   Abba Hastings household, 1865 N.Y. state cens., Jefferson Co., pop. sched., Watertown, 3rd election district, p. 59, dw. 429, fam. 429.

[381]   F. J. J. Blodgett, 1870 U.S. cens., Jefferson Co., N.Y., pop. sched., Watertown, p. 667, dw. 43, fam. 45.

[382]   Charles E. Amaden, Probate Court, Liber 18:253, Jefferson County, N.Y.

[383]   Corbett, *Cemetery DAR transcriptions.*

[384]   Alonson Dresser household, 1870 U.S. cens., Jefferson Co., N.Y., pop. sched., Watertown, p. 1, dw. 3, fam. 3.

[385]   Orville Tolman residence, 1880 U.S. cens., Jefferson Co., N.Y., pop. sched., Watertown, 1st ward, SD 7, ED 146, p. 184C, dw. 109, fam. 115.

[386]   Alonson Dresser household, 1900 U.S. cens., Jefferson Co., N.Y., pop. sched., Watertown, SD 6, ED 46, sheet 7B, dw. 163, fam. 167.

was buried in the Amaden family plot at Huntingtonville Rural Cemetery.

In 1905, Albert was living in Watertown with Frank Farr.[387] Albert was listed as a nephew, but no family relation with Frank or his wife has been established. Albert's aunt Aurelia (Amaden) Rounds died in 1906 and mentioned her nephew, Albert, in the will.[388] Albert left Watertown for California. This was recorded in the *Watertown Herald* in 1910:

> East Watertown, Oct. 7 - Reliable news says that Albert Amaden, an East Watertown boy who went to California as an experiment, liked the country so well that he has taken to himself a wife, and so we have lost him. Amaden was married on Aug. 8.[389]

The 1910 census, taken on 28 April, shows the widowed Albert living with his cousin William Dresser (son of Alonso and Eliza) in Whittier, California. Albert was a carpenter.[390] As stated in the article above, fifty-year old Albert married later that year to thirty-eight-year-old Stella Jackson. Albert died just seven years later of pneumonia and was buried at Mt. Olive Cemetery in Whittier. Nothing more is known about Stella after his death. He was remembered in the local newspaper:

> He came to Whittier about eight years ago. Was married to Miss Stella Jackson in August, 1910, who survives him. Funeral services were held Tuesday afternoon at White's undertaking parlors, conducted by Rev. Day of the Congregational church, after which the services were taken in charge by the I. O. O. F. [International Order of Odd Fellows], of which the deceased was a member. The many beautiful flowers and floral pieces showed the esteem in which he was held. He was an honest, upright man, a loving husband and Brother. More can not be said.[391]

Child of GEORGE and ADELIZA (BLODGETT) AMADEN:

---

[387] Frank D. Farr household, 1905 N.Y. state census, Jefferson County, Watertown, 1st election district, p. 11; Flower Memorial Library, Watertown, N.Y.

[388] Aurelia E. Rounds, Probate Box R-44, Jefferson County, New York.

[389] Article, "Topics of the Week, Likes California!" *Watertown [New York] Herald*, Saturday, 8 October 1910, page 4, column 2.

[390] William L. Dresser, 1910 U.S. cens., Los Angeles Co., Calif., pop. sched., Los Nietos, SD 7, ED 286, sheet 8A, dw. 192, fam. 211.

[391] Obituary, "A. M. Amaden," *Whittier [Calif.] News*, Thurs, 31 May 1917.

i.	CHARLES E. AMADEN, b. Rome, N.Y., 12 Oct. 1857;[392] d. Watertown, N.Y., 16 Feb. 1878;[393] bur. Huntington Rural Cem., Watertown.

Children of GEORGE and URSULA (HASTINGS) AMADEN:

ii.	ALBERT M. AMADEN, b. Eaton, N.Y., 7 March 1860;[394] d. Whittier, Calif., 27 May 1917; bur. Mt. Olive cem., Whittier;[395] m. 1) Watertown 24 Jan. 1883 HARRIET S. HOWARD, b. Rodman, N.Y., 2 Jan. 1860,[396] dau. of BARTHOLOMEW and MARY S. (WOOD) HOWARD, d. Ogdensburg, N.Y., 19 Oct. 1902,[397] bur. Huntingtonville Rural Cem., Watertown; m. 2) Whittier, Calif., 18 Aug. 1910, STELLA M. JACKSON, b. Norwood, Ill., Aug. 1872, dau. of JOSIAH and IMOGENE (PIKE) JACKSON.[398]

iii.	HATTIE U. AMADEN, b. 23 May 1862; d. 27 Aug. 1862; bur. Huntingtonville Rural Cem.[399]

Mary M. (Amaden) Palmer (1836–1907)

40. MARY M. AMADEN (*JOHN⁶, JACOB⁵, JACOB⁴ AMIDOWN, HENRY³, PHILIP², ROGER¹ AMADOWNE*) was born at Saint Lawrence County, New York,[400] in November 1836.[401] She died at Watertown, New York, on 25 November 1907.[402] She married at Watertown on 4 September 1859 JAMES M. PALMER.[403] James was born in Canada in about 1832.[404] He died after 1888.[405]

392	George Amaden, Civil War Pension App. File, Minor Child App. # 11935.

393	Charles E. Amaden, Jefferson County Probate Court, Liber 18, page 253.

394	George Amaden, Civil War Pension App. File, Minor Child App. # 11935.

395	Albert M. Amaden California death record certificate # 732348.

396	Watertown Methodist Church Records; Flower Memorial Library, Watertown, New York.

397	Hattie S. Amaden New York death record #39034.

398	Amaden – Jackson marriage record, Los Angeles County Certificate # 3392, County Clerk, Los Angeles, California.

399	Corbett, *Cemetery DAR transcriptions*.

400	James M. Palmer household, 1875 N.Y. state cens., Jefferson Co., Watertown, 2nd Ward, dw. 291, fam. 322.

401	1900 census gives us month of November, 1839. However 1850 and 1860 censuses point to a birth year of 1836. John Amilton household, 1850 U.S. cens., Jefferson Co., N.Y., pop. sched., Watertown, p. 280, dw. 214, fam. 237.

402	Obituary, "Mrs. Mary Palmer," *Elgin Daily Courier*, 29 November 1907, p. 8, col. 2.

403	Hungerford, "Marriages in The New York Reformer, 1850-1861," *New York Reformer*, 103.

404	James Palmer residence, 1860 U.S. cens., Jefferson Co., N.Y., pop. sched., Watertown, p. 597, dw. 357, fam. 351.

Mary's parents were living in Saint Lawrence County, New York, for her birth in 1836. They were probably in Russell, where they were living for the 1840 census. After several more moves, they settled in Watertown, New York, by 1850. Mary, her brothers, George and Edwin, and sister, Elenor, were in school. In the 1859-60 Watertown directory, Nancy was running a boarding house at 24 Public Square; Mary and her two sisters, Aurelia and Elenor, were listed as paper makers; while her brothers, Edwin and George, were painters.[406]

Mary married James Palmer in 1859. Their wedding was particularly special since it was a double wedding. On that day Mary's brother George married his second wife Ursula Hastings.[407] The minister was Reverend Benjamin S. Wright, a Methodist.

James was a Canadian who probably immigrated to New York after 1850, since he is not found in the 1850 U.S. census. By 1860, he was a cabinet maker in Watertown.[408] Their first home included two other Canadians: Charles Boneslist, a teamster, and Nellie McGee, a tailoress. A New York farmer, Robert Graham, also lived with them.

Mary probably grieved her inability to bear children over the next three years as her brother George and his wife Ursula had two children. Their second child was Hattie U. Amaden, born on 23 May 1862. The following month, Ursula died. Their oldest child, Albert, was taken in by Ursula's parents. Mary and James adopted baby Hattie, probably ecstatic to finally have a child. This new family was short lived. Hattie died at the age of three months and four days. She is buried at Huntington Rural Cemetery in George's family plot.

The 1860s brought a career change for James. He was listed as a "Daguerreian artist" in the 1863-64 Watertown directory and a photographer in the 1865 directory.[409] In 1839, the Frenchman Louis Daguerre was the first to distribute the process for making and developing photographic film – known as Daguerrotypes. This opened up family portraits to the common man, an arena once

---

405   *Watertown, New York Directory 1888-92.*

406   *Watertown City Directory 1859-60.*

407   Hungerford, *Marriages in The New York Reformer, 1850-1861*, p. 103.

408   James Palmer residence, 1860 U.S. cens., Jefferson Co., N.Y., pop. sched., Watertown, p. 597, dw. 357, fam. 351.

409   *Watertown Directory 1863-64, Watertown City Directory 1865.*

exclusively held only by the wealthy with painted portraits.[410] In 1865, James was still a photographer and we learn from the New York State census that he was an Alien Voter – not native born, but still eligible to vote.[411] Mary was accepted in the Stone Street Presbyterian Church in Watertown in 1869. Other members of the church in the family were her mother Nancy, sister Aurelia (Amaden) Rounds, aunt Aurelia (Amaden) Rose, and uncle Ephraim Rose.[412]

The 1870 census shows us that James had returned to cabinet making. He was also listed finally as a U.S. citizen. No children had arrived, and the couple was living alone in the fourth ward of Watertown.[413] In 1880 they were living at 11 State Street in the first ward of Watertown. We learn that James' parents were Canadian born as well. The house must have been very large because along with them were seven boarders and a servant.[414]

The Watertown city directories lead us to believe that James died about 1888. He was listed in that year as being a clerk. In 1889, we find Mrs. James M. Palmer, resident of 40 Stone Street.[415] No record of his death has been found.

Mary removed to the Elgin, Illinois, area, where her sister, Louisa Morgan, and family lived. In 1900, Mary was boarding at Robert Moon's home along with her niece Alma Morgan.[416] A widow, Mary's profession was nursing, which likely helped ease her ailing sister, Louisa, and brother-in-law, Truman Morgan. After their deaths in 1905, she returned to Watertown to take care of her oldest sister, Aurelia (Amaden) Rounds. When Aurelia died in 1906, Mary was listed as a caretaker of Aurelia's grandchild, Elizabeth Rounds.[417]

---

[410]   Nelson, Kenneth E., "A Thumbnail History of the Daguerrotype," *The Daguerreian Society*, <www.daguerre.org/resource/history/history.html>.

[411]   James M. Palmer household, 1865 N.Y. state cens., Jefferson Co., Watertown, 4th election district, p. 19, dw. 122, fam. 127.

[412]   Stone St. Presbyterian Church, Watertown, Jefferson Co., N.Y., 1831-85.

[413]   James Palmer residence, 1870 U.S. cens., Jefferson Co., N.Y., pop. sched., Watertown, 4th ward, p. 779, dw. 538, fam. 542.

[414]   James Parlmer residence, 1880 U.S. cens., Jefferson Co., N.Y., pop. sched., Watertown, 1st ward, SD 7, ED 147, p. 193D, dw. 35, fam. 39.

[415]   *Watertown, New York Directories 1888-92.*

[416]   Robt. Moon household, 1900 U.S. cens., Kane Co., Ill., pop. sched., Dundee, SD 2, ED 89, sheet 8B, dw. 178, fam. 189.

[417]   Aurelia E. Rounds, Probate Box R-44, Jefferson County, New York.

The following year Mary died in Watertown. She was buried in the Amaden-Rounds plot at Brookline Cemetery.[418]
No children.

Edwin C. Amaden (1841–1910)

41. EDWIN C. AMADEN *(JOHN⁶, JACOB⁵, JACOB⁴ AMIDOWN, HENRY³, PHILIP², ROGER¹ AMADOWNE)* was born at Pierrepont, New York, on 10 September 1841[419] and died at Danville, Illinois, on 28 November 1910.[420] He married first at Elgin, Illinois, on 5 September 1866 ELIZA A. WHITWELL BOGUE.[421] She was born at Buffalo Grove, Illinois, on 19 July 1847,[422] daughter of VIRGILIUS and LUCY (WILLIAMS) BOGUE, and died at Sacramento, California, on 25 March 1921.[423] He married second at Chicago, Illinois, on 4 June 1889 CLARA SCHMIDT. She was born at Hingenberg, Düsseldorf, Prussia on 18 November 1864,[424] daughter of ANTON and ANNA (FAHNENESCHMITT) SCHMIDT.

Edwin was born in Pierrepont in 1841. In 1850 he was a schoolboy with the family in Watertown,[425] where he spent most of his youth. By 1859 he and his brother, George, were working as painters, still living at the family home.[426] The next year he left for the Midwest, perhaps alongside his father who also wasn't enumerated at the family home in Watertown.

Edwin went to Fort Wayne, Indiana, where he met Ralph Darrow. Ralph was also a painter. They subsequently moved to Huntington, Indiana, in 1861 and started a paint store.

But the Civil War called the young men to fight. On 3 December 1861 privates Edwin Amaden and Ralph Darrow enlisted in Company

---

⁴¹⁸ Brookline Cemetery Records, Watertown, New York, copies of plat and personal visit by Chris Amaden.

⁴¹⁹ Best, *Amidon Family*, 138.

⁴²⁰ Edwin C. Amaden, Civil War Pension Application File SO 355623, SC 504415, WC 716190.

⁴²¹ Amadin-Bogue Kane County Marriage Record, License #5599.

⁴²² Flora Bogue Deming, *Bogue Genealogy: Descendants of John Bogue of East Haddam, Conn. and wife Rebecca Walkley*, (Rutland, Vermont: The Tuttle Publishing Company, 1944), 169, 170.

⁴²³ Eliza Bogue Amaden, California Death Records, Certificate # 11352.

⁴²⁴ Edwin C. Amaden, Civil War Pension App. File SO 355623, SC 504415.

⁴²⁵ John Amilton household, 1850 U.S. cens., Jefferson Co., N.Y., pop. sched., Watertown, p. 280, dw. 214, fam. 237.

⁴²⁶ *Watertown City Directory 1859-60.*

F, 47th Indiana Volunteers. Ten days after their enlistment, their regiment left Indiana and moved to Bardstown, Kentucky. They supported the siege of New Madrid, Missouri, in March 1862. They supported expeditions around Tennessee for the rest of 1862 and wintered in Helena, Arkansas. The year 1863 saw expeditions in Mississippi, Arkansas, and Louisiana. They fought in battles at Grand Gulf, Port Gibson, and Champion's Hill in Mississippi in April and May. They participated in the siege and assault on Vicksburg in May 1863, which successfully wrested control of the vital Mississippi River from the Confederacy and cut the Confederacy in two.

Watertown Directory, 1867.
Courtesy: Flower Memorial Library, Watertown, New York.

After Vicksburg, the Army of the Mississippi advanced on Jackson, Mississippi, laid siege for a full week in July, and sacked the city. The rest of the year was spent on campaigns in Louisiana. They wintered in New Orleans and Madisonville. In the spring of 1864 they participated in the Red River Campaign, a fruitless effort to cross Louisiana on the Red River and invade Texas, to gather cotton along the way. This frivolous campaign was devised in the belief that Napoleon III would give up his designs on Mexico if the United States held Texas and the Rio Grande. After the Red River Campaign failed, the infantry unit spent the remainder of the war in little known expeditions in Arkansas, Tennessee, and Louisiana. Corporals Edwin Amaden and Ralph Darrow mustered out in December 1864.[427]

After his discharge Edwin returned to Watertown, where we find

---

427　National Parks Service, *Civil War Soldiers & Sailors System*.
　　　Bruce Catton, *The Civil War* (New York: American Heritage / Bonanza Books, 1960), 317-324.

him at the family residence as a painter in 1865.[428] He didn't stay long though. We find him next in Elgin, Illinois. There he married Eliza Bogue in 1866. Eliza was an Illinois girl, just nineteen years old when she married the twenty-five-year-old Edwin Amaden. She grew up in Elgin, the fourth child of a Vermont farmer who left the rocky soil of New England and planted his roots in the fertile soils of the Midwest.[429] The new couple returned to Watertown, New York, almost immediately. By 1870, Eliza had delivered Ralph (named after Edwin's friend Ralph Darrow) and Jessie. Edwin and his brother-in-law, Edwin Rounds (another Civil War veteran), opened a furniture business in Watertown – Rounds & Amaden, Cabinet Makers and Furniture Dealers – located at 16 Public Square.[430][431] Sometime in the early 1870s, the family returned to Elgin.

The Civil War brutalized soldiers, both Union and Confederate. Perhaps it was post-traumatic stress disorder that created a brutal Edwin Amaden. In the spring of 1880 Eliza and Edwin separated. He removed to Chicago, and she and the children stayed in Elgin.[432] She claimed he had been guilty of physical abuse, habitual drunkenness, and child neglect. That summer the census taker found Edwin living alone in Chicago as a saloon keeper, with Frank Scott and Catherine Hawley, bartenders, rooming with him.[433] Eliza and Edwin were granted a divorce on 9 March 1882.

On 28 June 1880, Edwin applied for a disability pension due to rheumatism and hearing loss sustained from cannon fire at the Battle of Vicksburg. Continuing his pension application in 1889, Edwin's old friend and battle veteran Ralph Darrow wrote in an affadavit:

I Am Personally Aquainted (sic) with Edwin C Amaden have known him for 30 years Was in painting

---

[428]   John Amidon household, 1865 N.Y. state cens., Jefferson Co., Watertown, p. 53, dw. 388, fam. 388.

[429]   V. B. Bogue household, 1850 U.S. census, Kane County, Illinois, population schedule, Elgin, page 20, dwelling 340, family 350; National Archives micropublication M432, roll 112.

[430]   Edward Amaden household, 1870 U.S. cens., Jefferson Co., N.Y., pop. sched., Watertown, p. 16, dw. 123, fam. 124.

[431]   *Polk's Watertown (Jefferson County, N.Y.) city directory, 1867-1868.*

[432]   Eliza Amaden household, 1880 U.S. cens., Kane Co., Ill., pop. sched., Elgin, SD 2, ED 86, p. 36, dw. 31, fam. 40.

[433]   Edwin Amaden household, 1880 U.S. census, Cook County, Illinois, population schedule, Chicago, page 7, SD ?, ED 183, dwelling 250, family 662; National Archives micropublication T9, roll 198.

Buisness (sic) with him when the Civil War Broke out in Fall of 1861.

I Further Know he was a Strong Able Bodied young man at that time We Enlisted in Co F. 47 Ind vol Inft & Slept under the Same Blanket, In The Early Part of 1862 we were Marching Throug Kentucky & verry (sic) much Exposed to wet weather Said Amaden got cold which Settled to a cough & he could not get Rid of it.

I was Discharged the Same time he was at Indianapolas (sic) & went home with him to watertown N.Y. & Staid & Slept with him the most of the time until Spring & he Coughed verry (sic) Bad & Complained of Rhumatism in his legs I have been with him a great Deal Since that time was in Business with him again about 6 years ago...[434]

In 1886, Edwin moved to 422 63rd Street in Chicago. A year later his son Ralph came to live with him.[435] They worked together at his paint store of the same address, Edwin in paint and Ralph in wallpaper. Two years later, in 1889, Edwin remarried. This time his bride was a German immigrant, Clara Schmidt, twenty-three years his junior at twenty-five years old. She had arrived in America in May or June, 1886. Her marriage gained her citizenship.

A year later, in 1890, she delivered their son, George. After a barrage of further documentation, Edwin finally received his Civil War Pension. Two years later Clara delivered a girl they called Ruby. Apparently she was no more successful dealing with Edwin's demons than had been Eliza. In 1898 Clara placed her children, George and Ruby, in the Angel Guardian Orphan Asylum in Chicago.[436] By 1900 Clara was working as a servant in the Chicago home of Margaret Fabian, also a German immigrant.[437]

An ailing Edwin entered the National Disabled Volunteer Soldiers Home in Danville, Illinois. In his medical examination in

---

[434]   Edwin C. Amaden, Civil War Pension App. File SO 355623, SC 504415.

[435]   *Poll List of Voters, Town of Lake, District of Illinois*, page 311; <www.ancestry.com>.

[436]   Margaret and George Amaden, Angel Guardian Orphanage Records, Archives and Records Center, Archdiocese of Chicago, Chicago, Illinois.

[437]   Margaret Fabian household, 1900 U.S. census, Cook County, Illinois, population schedule, Chicago, sheet 13B, SD 1, ED 756, dwelling 140, family 231; National Archives micropublication T623, roll 275.

1906 it was noted that at age sixty-six he stood five feet seven inches tall, weighed 160 pounds, and had a dark complexion. Two years later he transferred to the Pacific Branch Veteran's Home in San Francisco, and then back again in 1909 to Danville, where we find him in the 1910 census.[438] At Edwin's request, Clara gave up her room in Chicago, stored her belongings and worked at the Danville Veterans' Home for money, room and board. In 1910 she appealed to the Army for half of Edwin's pension because, she said, he was "a man whose word cannot be believed, who has not supported myself or children, who has frequently threatened my life, kicked and choked me, drove me and my children out into the streets at the muzzle of a revolver." Other affidavits came from Edwin's brothers-in-law, Edwin Rounds and Norman Snell.

Six weeks later Edwin died in 1910 at age sixty-nine and was buried at Danville National Cemetery in Danville, Illinois. Clara applied for a widow's pension as a hardship case, living on a salary of sixteen dollars a month at the veteran's home.

Clara lived out the remainder of her life in Chicago. Her children had left the orphanage in 1905 and rejoined her. George and Clara, along with a lodger named Henry Maas, were together in 1910 in Chicago. George was a machinist.[439] No census records past 1900 for Ruby have been found, but she lived her life in and around Chicago.

From George's World War I registration card in 1917, we learn that George was of medium height and build, had brown hair and eyes, and had suffered an amputated finger and a smashed knee cap. He was a laborer for the railroad, working in Lennox, South Dakota, and was supporting his mother.[440] His injuries didn't sway the army; George served as a private from 24 June 1918 to 13 June 1919 in Company A, 313 Engineer, American Expeditionary Forces in France.[441] Returning from the war, George lived with his mother in

---

[438] Edwin Amaden, 1910 U.S. census, Vermillion County, Illinois, population schedule, Danville – National Home for Disabled Volunteer Soldiers, sheet 19B, SD 9, ED 134, dwelling G; National Archives micropublication T624, roll 329.

[439] Clara Amaden, 1910 U.S. census, Cook County, Illinois, population schedule, Chicago, Ward 32, sheet 14B, SD 9, ED 1377, dwelling 215, family 299; National Archives micropublication T624, roll 278.

[440] George Charles Amaden, Ancestry.com, WWI Registration Cards.

[441] George Amaden, National Personnel Records Center, St. Louis, Missouri, Service # 3309517, response dated 20 February 2004.

Clara Amaden's affidavit in Edwin Amaden's pension record.

Chicago.[442] Clara and George were both living in Chicago in 1930, though separately.[443]

Edwin's son, Ralph, married in Cook County in 1889 to PETRONAILA "LIZZIE" MISKIE, a Polish immigrant. Sometime in the 1890s Ralph returned to Elgin and took in his mother Eliza.[444] Soon thereafter the family removed to California. Ralph and Lizzie, as she was called, welcomed their only child, Ralph Radford Amaden, in Oakland in 1905. Soon the family removed to Sacramento, where the family was recorded in the 1910, 1920, and 1930 censuses, settling at 2530 25th Street.[445] Ralph worked as a manager of a newsstand and finally as a storekeeper for the city of Sacramento. In 1920 Eliza was living with her son Ralph's family and passed away the following year.[446] She was cremated and buried at East Lawn Cemetery in Sacramento.

Edwin and Eliza's daughter Jessie has not been found in the 1900 census or later. She married Frank Davis, a railroad worker, lived in the Western States, and had no children.[447]

Children of EDWIN and ELIZA (BOGUE) AMADEN:

i.   RALPH JAY AMADEN, b. Watertown, N.Y., 20 Sept. 1867;[448] m. Cook Co., Ill., 28 Sept. 1889 PETRONAILA "LIZZIE" MISKIE,[449] b.

---

442   Clara Amaden household, 1920 U.S. census, Cook County, Illinois, population schedule, Chicago, ward 31, SD 1, ED 1918, sheet 9A, dwelling 15, family 15; National Archives micropublication T625, roll 348.

443   George Amakan - employee, 1930 U.S. census, Cook County, Illinois, population schedule, Broadview SD 6, ED 2299, sheet 13B, dwelling Edward Hines Junior Center; National Archives micropublication T626, roll 506.
Clara Amsden household, 1930 U.S. cens., Cook Co., Ill., pop. sched., Chicago, SD 7, ED 16-598, sheet 19A, dw. 157, fam. 392.

444   Raye Amsden household, 1900 U.S. cens., Kane Co., Ill., pop. sched., Elgin, ward 4, SD 2, ED 99, sheet 1A, dw. 4, fam. 6.

445   Ralph J Amaden, 1910 U.S. census, Sacramento County, California, population schedule, Sacramento, ward 7, sheet 10B, SD 2, ED 122, dwelling 220, family 235; National Archives micropublication T624, roll 93.
Joseph Amsden (sic) household, 1930 U.S. census, Sacramento County, California, population schedule, Sacramento, SD 3, ED 90, sheet 8B, dwelling 277, family 277; National Archives micropublication T626, roll 187.

446   Ralph J. Amaden household, 1920 U.S. census, Sacramento County, California, population schedule, Sacramento, SD 3, ED 182, sheet 9A, dwelling 213, family 260; National Archives micropublication T625, roll 127.

447   Correspondence with Joseph Erwin, subject "Hi Chris from Joe," to Chris Amaden, dated 19 July 2004.

448   Ralph J. Amaden, California Death Record, Certificate # 37451.

449   Amaden-Miskie, Illinois Marriage Record, Certificate # 00144415.

Poland 29 June 1870, dau. of JOSEPH and MARY (PRUCKNIAK) MISKIE.[450]

Child of RALPH and PETRONAILA (MISKIE) AMADEN:
a. *Ralph Radford Amaden*, b. Oakland, Calif., 18 Feb. 1905.[451]
ii. JESSIE K. AMADEN, b. probably Watertown 10 April 1870;[452] m. FRANK DAVIS.[453]

Children of EDWIN and CLARA (SCHMIDT) AMADEN:
iii. GEORGE CHARLES AMADEN, b. Chicago, Ill., 6 March 1890;[454] bap. St. Martin Church, Chicago.[455]
iv. RUBY MARGUERITTE AMADEN, b. Chicago 4 Jan. 1892;[456] bap. St. Martin Church, Chicago.[457]

Elenor (Amaden) Snell (1842–1882)

42. ELENOR "NELLIE"AMADEN *(JOHN⁶, JACOB⁵, JACOB⁴ AMIDOWN, HENRY³, PHILIP², ROGER¹ AMADOWNE)* was born probably at Saint Lawrence County, New York, in 1842[458] and died at Watertown, New York, on 25 March 1882.[459] She married at Watertown on 9 May 1861 NORMAN SPENCER SNELL.[460] He was born at Ingham Mills, New York, on 21 August 1837 son of JACOB and MARGARET (HOSE) SNELL and died at Watertown on 19 July 1928.[461]

John and Nancy (Fodder) Amaden's last child, Nellie, was born in New York – likely in Russell as the family was living there in 1840.[462] The family relocated to Watertown in 1849. In the 1850

---

⁴⁵⁰   Petronaila Lizzie Hageman, California Death Record #56 116692.
⁴⁵¹   Obituary, "R. Radford Amaden," *Sacramento Bee*, Saturday 9 June 1956, page 29, column 4.
⁴⁵²   Best, *The Amidon Family*, 138.
     Flora Bogue Deming, *Bogue Genealogy, Descendants of John Bogue*. – Note that 1870 census gives her birth month as May.
⁴⁵³   Joseph Erwin, subject "Hi Chris from Joe," dated 19 July 2004.
⁴⁵⁴   George Charles Amaden, Ancestry.com, World War I Registration Card.
⁴⁵⁵   Georgium Karolim Emmaden, St. Martin's Church Baptismal Record, Archives and Records Center, Archdiocese of Chicago, Chicago, Illinois.
⁴⁵⁶   Ruby Margueritte Amaden, Delayed Birth, Illinois Certificate # 201357.
⁴⁵⁷   Ruby Margareth Amaden, St. Martin's Church Baptismal Record, .
⁴⁵⁸   Larry   Corbett,   *North   Watertown   Cemetery   Records*, <www.geocities.com/lrcorbett/cemeterys.htm>.
⁴⁵⁹   Elenor Snell, Jefferson County, New York Probate, Liber 21: 417-420.
⁴⁶⁰   Snell – Amiden marriage record, Stone St. Presbyterian Church.
⁴⁶¹   Norman Spencer Snell, New York Death Record, recorded 22 July 1928.
⁴⁶²   John Amaden household, 1840 U.S. cens., St. Lawrence Co., N.Y., Russell, p. 254, line 20.

census, Nellie is listed with her family as a school girl.[463] She is not with her parents in the 1855 state census and was likely living as a servant in another household. By 1859, she had returned to the family home and was working with her sisters Mary and Aurelia as paper makers.[464] The 1860 census shows her sister, Aurelia, working at the paper mill, but Elenor was listed without an occupation.[465]

Norman Snell had been born in Ingham Mills, New York, in 1837 and had moved with his family at age six to Three Mile Bay, New York, where he attended school. As a young man, he worked as a clerk and shoe repairman, a trade he had learned from his father. He moved to Watertown in about 1858.[466] There he met Nellie, and the couple was married in 1861 by Reverend Peter Snyder at the Stone Street Presbyterian Church in Watertown.

In January 1864, Norman enlisted at Watertown for three years in Company A, 14th Heavy Artillery Regiment New York. He stood five feet, seven and one-half inches, had light complexion, blue eyes, and brown hair. His stated occupation was artist.

The regiment served in the Provisional Brigade, 1st Division, 9th Corps. As such, Norman saw action at Wilderness and Spotsylvania Courthouse, Virginia, in May 1864. When they fought at Cold Harbor, Virginia, the following month, Norman was injured, receiving a gunshot flesh wound to his left foot. He was transferred to the "three-thousand-bed Harewood Hospital, constructed on a rolling farm northwest of Washington D.C., modeled after an English estate, with landscaped grounds, terraced flower gardens, and a well-tended vegetable plot."[467] He then transferred to the General Hospital in Rochester, New York, at the end of June and was discharged in May 1865.

Norman returned to Watertown and took up the trade of cabinet making, perhaps learning from his two brothers-in-law and fellow veterans, Edwin Amaden and Edwin Rounds.[468] It wasn't until 1879

---

463   John Amilton household, 1850 U.S. cens., Jefferson Co., N.Y., pop. sched., Watertown, p. 280, dw. 214, fam. 237.

464   *Watertown City Directory 1859-60.*

465   Nancy Amidon household, 1860 U.S. cens., Jefferson Co., N.Y., pop. sched., Watertown, p. 28, dw. 198, fam. 195.

466   Norman S. Snell, Civil War Pension App. File SO 71924, SC 349555.

467   The Lincoln Institute, "Campbell General Hospital," *Mr. Lincoln's White House*, online <www.mrlincolnswhitehouse.org/inside.asp?ID =126&subjectID=4>.

468   N. S. Snell household, 1870 U.S. cens., Jefferson Co., N.Y., pop. sched., Watertown, 4th ward, p. 769, dw. 380, fam. 385.

that the family welcomed their son, Charles, to the world. The following year we find the family living at 81 Main Street in Watertown; Norman continued his cabinet making trade.[469]

Elenor bought lot 122 on the island of Wells in Alexandria, New York, from "Mrs. Elizabeth W. Rounds" for $150 in 1881.[470] When the land was originally purchased from the Westminster Park Association of the Thousand Islands in 1879, she was listed as Mrs. E. W. Rounds – one of the witnesses was E. W. Rounds.[471] There may have been a clerical mistake and Mrs. Elizabeth W. Rounds was in fact Aurelia E. (Amaden) Rounds, the wife of Edwin W. Rounds and sister of Elenor. The Westminster Park Association was a group of investors who purchased 500 acres on the northwest point of Wells Island in the St. Lawrence River and developed it into a cottage colony with a hotel, "the object being to furnish a summer resort that would be free from the objectionable features that attach to all fashionable watering-places, and at reasonable charges for entertainment. Although the association was organized under the auspices of the Presbyterians, it is not intended to be sectarian, but contains among its patrons people of various denominations and beliefs."[472]

The month before Charles's birth, Elenor wrote a will. Perhaps she was ill during the pregnancy. She died in 1882, just before Charles's third birthday. Elenor was buried at North Watertown Cemetery, Watertown.[473] In her will, Elenor divided her estate between her husband and child.[474] From this estate, Norman sold the Westminster Park Association lot to her father, John Amaden, for $40.[475] A few years later in 1888, John sold the lot to his daughter, Aurelia (Amaden) Rounds, for $1.[476]

About five months after Elenor's death, forty-five year old Norman married at Watertown, on 1 September 1882, his second wife CORINTHIA "CORA" A. WOOD, age twenty-two. Cora was born at

---

469 Norman Snell household, 1880 U.S. cens., Jefferson Co., N.Y., pop. sched., Watertown, SD 7, ED 140, p. 110C, dw. -, fam. 359.

470 Jefferson County Land Records, Liber 229:347-348.

471 Jefferson County Land Records, Liber 220:62-63.

472 Westminster Park Association of the Thousand Islands (description and bylaws) <cdl.library.cornell.edu/cgi-bin/cul.nys/docviewer?did=nys126>.

473 Corbett, *North Watertown Cemetery Records*.

474 Elenor Snell, Jefferson County, New York Probate, Liber 21: 417-420.

475 Jefferson County Land Records, Liber 229:575.

476 Jefferson County Land Records, Liber 252:429-430.

Picton, Canada, in 1861, daughter of WILLIAM SMITH and ROSE ANNA (MORRISON) WOOD.[477] Norman ran the Depot Restaurant, located on the main floor of the New York Central railway station in Watertown. Even though his bride was less than half his age, Norman would outlive her. Cora died just seven years after their marriage at the age of thirty-nine and was buried at North Watertown Cemetery.[478]

In 1900, Norman, his son Charles, and his mother-in-law Anna Wood were living together in Watertown, still at 81 Main Street.[479] Norman was active in civic affairs. He was a well known amateur astronomer, park policeman for several years, member of several organizations such as the Old Watertown Band, the Joe Spratt post, G. A. R., the Three Mile Bay Baptist church and the Lincoln League.[480]

His son. Charles, married GRACE HURD, a local girl, in 1903. Together the family moved to 939 Franklin Street, where we find them in the 1910, 1920, and 1930 censuses.[481] Charles became a superintendent of the Masonic Temple. His description in the World War I registration cards showed that he had a stout build, black eyes, and gray hair.[482] Charles and Grace had no children.

Norman died in 1927 at the age of ninety and was buried alongside his wives at North Watertown Cemetery.

Child of NORMAN and ELENOR (AMADEN) SNELL:

i.   CHARLES HAWLEY SNELL, b. Watertown, N.Y., 20 July 1879;[483] m. Watertown 17 June 1903 GRACE VIOLA HURD, b. Watertown

---

477   Personal records maintained by Sharon Kominar of Windsor, Canada, posted online at Church of Latter Day Saints – Corintha Wood.

478   Death Notice, "Snell," *Watertown Herald*, Saturday, 1 April 1899, page 1, col 4.

Corbett, *North Watertown Cemetery Records*.

479   Norman Snell household, 1900 U.S. cens., Jefferson Co., N.Y., pop. sched., Watertown, SD 6, ED 43, sheet 8A, dw. 138, fam. 170.

480   Obituary, "Norman S. Snell," *Watertown Daily Times*, 21 July 1928.

481   Charles H. Snell household, 1910 U.S. census, Jefferson County, New York, population schedule, town of Watertown, Ward 7, SD 12, ED 48, sheet 11B, dwelling 404, family 367; National Archives micropublication T624, roll 954.

Charles Snell household, 1920 U.S. census, Jefferson County, New York, population schedule, Watertown town, ward 3, SD 13, ED 46, sheet 10B, dwelling 270, family 296; National Archives micropublication T625, roll 1116.

Charles H. Snell household, 1930 U.S. census, Jefferson County, New York, population schedule, Watertown, SD 2, ED 56, sheet 6A, dwelling 135, family 147; National Archives micropublication T626, roll 1443.

482   Charles Hawley Snell, Ancestry.com, World War I Registration card.

483   Charles Hawley Snell, New York Death Record, Certificate # 446.

18 Sept. 1884,[484] dau. of JAMES W. and FRANCELIA (DEMARSE) HURD.[485] No issue.

Almira J. (Amaden) (Walker) (Roff) Nash (1841–1906)

43. ALMIRA J. AMADEN (*NATHANIEL IVES[6], JACOB[5], JACOB[4] AMIDOWN, HENRY[3], PHILIP[2], ROGER[1] AMADOWNE)* was born probably at Parishville, New York, in April 1841,[486] and died at Williamson Valley, Arizona Territory, on 16 May 1906.[487] She married first between 1856 and 1860[488] GEORGE WASHINGTON WALKER. He was born at Barnard, Vermont, in 2 May 1826,[489] son of ASA and ELIZABETH (MATHEWSON) WALKER,[490] and died at Taylorsville, California, on 6 August 1867.[491] She married second at Sutter County, California, on 14 December 1869 CHARLES PETER MCALVIN ROFF. He was born at Wisconsin about 1835[492] and died at Grand Island, California, on 28 February 1872.[493] She married third at San Buenaventura, California, on 29 December 1873 JAMES HOWARD NASH.[494] He was born at South Bend, Indiana, on 12 November

---

484   Snell – Hurd Marriage Record, Watertown, New York Marriage Registrar, Certificate # 3650.

485   Grace V. Snell, New York Death Record, Certificate # 708.

486   James H. Noah household, 1900 U.S. census, Yavapai County, Arizona Territory, population schedule, Williamson Valley and Walnut Creek, SD -, ED 61, sheet 7A, dwelling 40, family 43; National Archives micropublication T623, roll 47.

487   Yavapai County, Arizona Cemetery Records, <www.sharlot.org/ archives/gene/cemetery/index.html>.

488   In 1856 Iowa State Census, Almira was single living with her parents: N J Amadan household, 1856 Iowa State Census, Fayette County, Westfield, item #137.
        In 1860, she was married: George Walker household, 1860 U.S. cens., Fayette Co., Ia., pop. sched., Westfield, p. 188, dw. 1450, fam. 1243.

489   Family notes of Beverly Luke of Minden, Nevada, great-great-granddaughter of George Walker.

490   Family genealogy papers of Daniel Jerome Mathewson Walker, brother of George Washington Walker, now in possession of great-grandson Matt Porter, Fayette County, Iowa.

491   ?, *Vital records from the Daily Evening Bulletin, San Francisco, California*, volume 88, year 1867 (California : Genealogical Records Committee, California State Society, Daughters of the American Revolution, 1943-1968); California State Library, Sacramento California.

492   Charles Roff entry, *Great Register of Colusa County, California*, Colusa County Clerk, Colusa, California.

493   "Three Men Drowned," *Weekly Sutter Banner*, 16 March 1872.

494   Nash-Roff marriage, Ventura County marriage certificate #243306, Ventura County Recorder, Ventura, California.

1839, son of JAMES and MARY (SCOTT) NASH, and died at Prescott, Arizona, on 4 September 1914.[495]

Almira grew up in St. Lawrence County, New York. We find the family of six in Pierrepont in 1850.[496] Almira's mother, Lucia (Fox) Amaden, had an older brother, Daniel, and at least four younger brothers: Stephen, Lyman, Ezekiel, and John Fox. In the late 1840s, Daniel, Stephen, and Lyman left St. Lawrence County and settled in Franklin, Illinois. In late 1850 or early 1851, Almira's family followed her uncles to Franklin, where her brother, Martin, was likely born. The families must not have found what they were looking for in Illinois. In 1856 they all again moved west to Fayette County, Iowa. There Almira married the widowed George Walker between 1856 and 1860, when she was still a teenager. By 1860, Almira's youngest uncles, Ezekiel and John Fox, as well as her grandparents, Jacob and Susan (Parker) Fox, arrived in Fayette County.[497]

George Walker was born in 1826 in Vermont. He had relocated to Galena, in the northwest corner of Illinois, by the late 1840s. Galena was lead-mining country. The earliest French trappers had found the Indians mining lead in the region before 1700. Galena was organized as a town in 1826. The city name, "Galena," is the technical name for sulphide of lead. The earliest newspaper in Galena was *The Miners Journal*. By 1850 Galena was the busiest port on the Mississippi between St. Paul and St. Louis, with a population of 14,000. Abraham Lincoln and Stephen A Douglas both spoke to crowds in the city during their famous political campaign of 1858. But by then George Walker had already said goodbye to Galena and had moved west.

George married in Galena, on 25 October 1849 MARY F. DOOLEY.[498] Mary was born in New York (or perhaps Ireland) in 1829. It is uncertain who Mary's parents were (George's brother Daniel married the following year, also in Jo Daviess County, BRIDGETT DOOLEY, an Irish immigrant born in 1832. Was she Mary's

---

495   James Howard Nash, Arizona Death Record # 775, Dept. of Health Services, Phoenix, Arizona.
496   Nathan G. Amadan household, 1850 U.S. cens., St. Lawrence Co., N.Y, pop. sched., Pierepont (sic), p. 389, dw. 125, fam. 125.
497   Jacob Fox household, 1860 U.S. cens., Fayette Co., Ia., pop. sched., Center, p. 181, dw. 1397, fam. 1195.
498   Robert Hanson, *Vital Statistics from Galena Newspapers, July 22, 1828 - November 19, 1850: Marriages, Petitions for Divorce, Deaths, Estate Notices, and Sexton Reports*, <www.rootsweb.com/~iljodavi/vitals/VS1b.htm>.

sister?) George and Mary were living in Galena in 1850.[499] George was a plowmaker: presumably he was taking advantage of the lead to improve his plows. In 1852 George and Mary moved one hundred miles west to Fayette County, Iowa,[500] where George was listed with the Iowa militia, and Mary was listed with the new Methodist Episcopal Church.[501] They had three children before Mary died on 26 December 1855 and was buried in Grandview Cemetery.[502] George was both a plowmaker and a farmer in 1856.[503] In that year he bought land in Fayette County from I. and S. Templeton.

Almira, her father, and her brothers arrived in Westfield in 1856 and took the farm next door to the newly widowed George Walker. Before four years had passed, Almira and George had married. The 1860 census taker found the couple with George's three children (Joann, Cornelia and George) living in Westfield Township next door to Almira's parents and brothers.[504] We have to wonder if George's former neighbors in Galena wrote to George about the big debate between Lincoln and Douglas in 1858.

In March and in September, George sold some of his lands in Fayette County. George and Almira welcomed their own child, little Osman, in July 1860, just two weeks after the census taker came. But California called. In February, March, and April 1861 they sold out the remainder of George's properties in Fayette County. On 21 November 1861 they bought 160 acres in Sutter County, California. Fifteen months later they bought and swapped another eighty acres in Sutter County. On 5 February 1866 George attested that he was married, residing with his family on eighty acres in Sutter County and that he intended to use the land and premises as a homestead. Two months later he sold the eighty acre parcel.[505] The next year they welcomed a baby girl, Emma, born in May 1867. But their joy was

---

[499]   George W. Walker household, 1850 U.S. census, Jo Daviess County, Illinois, population schedule, Galena, page 181, dwelling 155, family 143; National Archives micropublication M432, roll 111.

[500]   George Walker household, 1856 Iowa cens., Fayette Co., Ia., #147.

[501]   ?, *The History of Fayette County, Iowa* (Chicago: Western Historical Company, 1878), 510-1.

[502]   *Fayette County Cemetery Index*, <www.angelfire.com/ia/fayette2/fayetteindex.htm >.

[503]   George Walker household, 1856 Iowa cens., Fayette Co., Ia., Westfield.

[504]   George Walker household, 1860 U.S. cens., Fayette Co., Ia., pop. sched., Westfield, p. 188, dw 1450, fam. 1243.

[505]   Sutter County California Deed Books, F:750-751, G:12-14, G:657-658.

short-lived. George died in Taylorsville, California, three months later in August at age forty-two.

The Marysville, California, frontier was no place for a single woman with two small children. Two years later, in 1869, Almira married Charles Roff. Charles had been born in Wisconsin in 1835 and was a painter. Almira and Charles have not been found in the 1870 census (nor were her two brothers). There was a Charles Rouff with his wife Almira in Stockton, California, in 1870, but that Charles Rouff was a German immigrant whose widow was still living in Stockton in 1930, twenty-four years after our Almira died. Our Charles and Almira were soon living at Grand Island, a small village just south of Colusa, California, on the Sacramento River. Charles was listed in the *Great Registration of Colusa County*, a voter registration list, as resident in Colusa County in April 1871, recorded as a musician.

Almira's father, "Amos" Amaden, joined the family. As Almira tried to raise her two young children, tragedy struck once again. When the family was out of provisions, Charles, his father-in-law, Amos, and a neighbor, William C. Smith, constructed a raft for crossing the river to fetch provisions. But the raft broke apart. All three men drowned on 28 February 1872.[506] Only Smith's body was recovered. And so, at age thirty-one, Almira found herself twice widowed and suffered the loss of her father.

Almira's brother, Albert, had married Ordella "Della" Strickland in 1870 in Santa Barbara County. Della's father, George Strickland, was a sheep raiser and had moved his family from Sutter County to Santa Barbara in the 1860s. Albert and his brothers were farm laborers and had likely gone along for the work, and of course the company. Della's mother was Matilda (Nash) Strickland, and through this family tie Almira met Matilda's brother, James Howard Nash. The year following Charles Roff's death in 1873, Almira married James, her third husband. James had grown up in Marshall County, Indiana, just south of South Bend.[507] His family had left Indiana in 1849 and settled in Yuba County, California, where his father died in 1851. His widow, Mary, and her three youngest sons were farming in Yuba

---

506 "Three Men Drowned," *Weekly Sutter Banner,* 16 March 1872.
507 James Nash household, 1840 U.S. census, Marshall County, Indiana, page 3, line 14; National Archives micropublication M704, roll 99.

County in 1860.[508] The Nash family also relocated to Santa Barbara County in the 1860s. By 1870 James had his own farm,[509] next door to his brother Robert, who had a family of his own and was caring for their widowed mother. The Nashes were living in that portion of Santa Barbara County that became Ventura County on 1 January 1873. James and Almira married on 29 December 1873 in San Buenaventura, which was later named Ventura. Almira delivered a baby girl, Grace Della Nash, seven months later in 1874.

Two years later, in 1876, some of these families abandoned California and settled in northern Arizona Territory, thirty-six years before Arizona became a state. The families included James and

Yavapai, Arizona Territory, 1864 Courtesy: Jonathan Sheppard & Co.

Almira Nash, Almira's brother, Albert, and wife, Della Nash, James's brother, Robert Nash, and his family, and James's sister, Matilda Strickland, with her family, including her widowed mother Mary Nash. By 1880, Almira must have been pleased to have her family together. She was keeping house, James was working as a sheep shearer, Osman was twenty-one and working as a cattle tender, and

---

508 Mary Nash household, 1860 U.S. census, Yuba County, California, population schedule, page 112, dwelling 1489, family 1253; National Archives micropublication M653, roll 72.
509 James H. Nash household, 1870 U.S. census, Santa Barbara County, California, population schedule, Township 1, page 13, dwelling 137, family 137; National Archives micropublication M593, roll 87.

the two girls Emma Walker and Grace Nash were attending school.[510]

Figure 5 – Likely Amaden family circa 1885. Rear row: Della (Strickland) Amaden, Ruth (Schooley) Amaden, Albert Amaden, Alice Amaden. Middle row: Albert Amaden (age 4), Minnie Amaden (age 9), Almira (Amaden) Nash, James Nash. Front row: Martin Amaden, Lola Amaden (age 7), Grace Nash, Emma Walker. Courtesy: Betty Farr.

Osman was the first to marry in 1883 to the widow Mary "Mollie" (Gray) Duclin. Her husband William Duclin[511] had died leaving her with a son, Franklin. Osman adopted Franklin, and the family expanded over the next six years to include four more children. Two of the children died young. Their son, Osman Amaden Walker, home from college in California, also died in 1909 at the age of twenty-five from tuberculosis. This left only two children: Franklin and the youngest child, Eugene. Franklin became a bookkeeper and worked for a lumber company, taking him to San Francisco where he

---

510 Howard Nash household, 1880 U.S. census, Yavapai County, Arizona Territory, population schedule, SD [blank], ED 27, page 1, dwelling 1, family 1; National Archives micropublication T9, roll 37.

511 William G. Duclin household, 1880 U.S. cens., Maricopa Co., Ariz. Terr., pop. sched., SD 5, ED 18, p. 87B, dw. 42, fam. 42.

met CHRISTINA SOILAND, a Norwegian immigrant.[512] They had a son, Elbert, and settled in Reno, Nevada.[513] Eugene married in 1913 to BERTHA DENNY, another Arizona Territory native. They raised three sons in Arizona before leaving for California in the 1920s.[514]

Almira's daughter, Emma, married in 1884 to WILLIAM ROBERTS, a native of Australia. To them were born eight children, but their marriage ended in divorce before 1910. In that year Emma was a cook at R. W. Wagner's ranch in Maricopa County, Arizona Territory. Four-year-old Opal was living with her.[515] No further record of Emma has been found. William was living in Yavapai County with four of the children.[516] By 1920, William had remarried MARY B. ERWIN, a widow; however, she died the following year in an automobile accident.[517] In 1930 William was living with his daughter Leonia, her husband Alva Smith and their two boys in Phoenix, Arizona.[518]

As to Emma's other children: eldest daughter Edith married LEON ARTIGUE, who worked in the movie industry. They lived in Los Angeles and had one son, Raymond,[519] but separated in the 1920s. Leon stayed in Los Angeles,[520] and Edith returned to Arizona with

[512] Lace Soeland household, 1900 U.S. census, San Francisco County, California, population schedule, San Francisco, Assembly District 34, SD 1, ED 104, sheet 5A, dwelling 71, family 104; National Archives micropublication T623, roll 102.

[513] Frank Walker household, 1930 U.S. census, Washoe County, Nevada, population schedule, Reno, 1st ward, SD 1, ED 6, sheet 3A, dwelling 60, family 70; National Archives micropublication T626, roll 1297.

[514] Eugene E. Walker household, 1930 U.S. census, Sonoma County, Nevada, population schedule, Santa Rosa, 6th ward, SD 1, ED 50, sheet 1A, dwelling 4, family 4; National Archives micropublication T626, roll 222.

[515] R. W. Wagner household, 1910 U.S. census, Maricopa County, Arizona Territory, population schedule, town of Peoria, SD 2, ED 72, sheet 1A, dwelling 1, family 1; National Archives micropublication T624, roll 40.

[516] Wm Roberts household, 1910 U.S. census, Yavapai County, Arizona Territory, population schedule, town of Simmons, SD 1, ED 99, sheet 1A, dwelling 21, family 21; National Archives micropublication T624, roll 52.

[517] Mrs. Mary B. Roberts, Arizona Death Records, Certificate # 363.

[518] Alva V. Smith household, 1930 U.S. census, Maricopa County, Arizona, population schedule, Phoenix, SD 2, ED 39, sheet 4A, dwelling 81, family 88; National Archives micropublication T626, roll 58.

[519] Leon B. Artigue household, 1920 U.S. cens., Los Angeles Co., Calif., pop. sched., Los Angeles, Assembly Dist. 64, SD 8, ED 231, sh. 1A, dw. 270, fam. 296.

[520] Leon B. Atlige, 1930 U.S. cens., Los Angeles Co., Calif., pop. sched., Los Angeles, SD 17, ED 409, sheet 1B, Elmar Hotel.

her son and was boarding at a rooming house in 1930.[521] Sadly, Emma's eldest son, Osman William Roberts, a single man, killed himself in 1916. Her fourth child, Grace, was living with her father in 1910, but no further record has been found. Emma's fifth child, Martin, served in World War I, had a daughter in California, returned to Arizona and married GLADYS ___.[522] It is unclear what happened to his first wife, but presumably she died. Martin lived in Miami, Arizona. Emma's sixth child Eva married GEORGE MICHAEL, a veteran of World War I. They had a son and a daughter and lived in Prescott, Arizona, in 1930 with his mother, Mary Laswell.[523] Emma's seventh child, LeRoy, died in 1916 from an accidental gunshot wound to his leg. Emma's last child, Opal, was living with her father in 1920, but no further record has been found.

Almira's younger daughter, Grace Nash, married in 1894 to WILLARD ALLEN, a farmer from Iowa. They had one daughter, Hazel, in Arizona Territory. Hazel married another farmer, Arizona Territory native and World War I Navy veteran CHARLES COUGHRAN. The family moved to Monrovia, California, by 1930.[524]

Almira and James were together in Williamson Valley, Arizona Territory, in 1900. James was still farming.[525] Almira died in 1906 at age sixty-five and was buried at Las Vegas Ranch Cemetery, Williamson Valley. James died in 1914 at age seventy-five and was buried beside Almira.[526]

Children of GEORGE and ALMIRA (AMADEN) WALKER:
i. OSMAN E. WALKER, b. prob. Westfield, Ia., 21 July 1860;[527] m. Williamson Valley, Ariz. Terr., 5 July 1883 MARY M. "MOLLIE"

---

521   Bernice Morgan household, 1930 U.S. census, Yavapai County, Arizona, population schedule, Prescott, SD 1, ED 23, sheet 2B dwelling 47, family 48; National Archives micropublication T626, roll 63.
522   Martin Roberts household, 1930 U.S. census, Gila County, Arizona, population schedule, Miami, SD 3, ED 38, sheet 2B dwelling 46, family 45; National Archives micropublication T626, roll 57.
523   Mary Larvesll household, 1930 U.S. cens., Yavapai Co., Ariz., pop. sched., Prescott, SD 1, ED 26, sheet 12A dw. 331, fam. 331.
524   Willard E. Allen household, 1930 U.S. cens., Los Angeles Co., Calif., pop. sched., Monrovia, SD 18, ED 1158, sheet 7A dw. 191, fam. 181.
525   James H. Noah hhd, 1900 U.S. cens., Yavapai Co., Ariz. Terr., pop. sched., Williamson Valley & Walnut Creek, SD -, ED 61, sh. 7A, dw. 40, fam. 43.
526   Yavapai County, Arizona Cemetery Records.
527   Osman E. Walker, Arizona Death Record, Certificate # 355.

GRAY,[528] b. Calif. 26 Nov. 1862, dau. JAMES F. and JULIA A. (___) GRAY, d. Los Angeles, Calif., 31 Aug. 1930.[529]

Children of OSMAN and MARY (GRAY) WALKER:

a. *Franklin E. Walker* b. Ariz. Terr. 24 Sept. 1880; m. 24 Sept. 1907[530] *Christina Soiland*, b. Norway 1 Aug. 1888, dau. of *Lars* and *Malena (Johnson) Soiland*.[531] Adopted child.

Child of *Franklin* and *Christina (Soiland) Walker*:
1. Elbert L. Walker, b. San Francisco Co., Calif., 9 March 1911.[532]

b. *Osman Amaden Walker* b. Ariz. Terr. 11 April 1884; d. Kingman, Ariz. Terr., 29 July 1909; bur. Las Vegas Ranch Cem., Williamson Valley, Ariz. Terr., 30 July 1909.[533]

c. *Julia A. Walker* b. 8 Sept. 1886; d. Big Chino Valley, Ariz. Terr., 15 Aug. 1887; bur. Las Vegas Ranch Cem.[534]

d. *Elmore Flournoy Walker* b. 24 June 1888; d. Williamson Valley, Ariz. Terr., 14 Aug. 1888; bur. Las Vegas Ranch Cem.[535]

e. *Eugene Ensign Walker*, b. Kingman, Ariz. Terr., 2 Aug. 1889;[536] m. Kingman 21 Dec. 1913 *Bertha Emily Denny*, b. Ariz. Terr. 15 July 1889, dau. of *William Henry* and *Anna B. (Martin) Denny*.[537]

---

528 Walker – Duclan Marriage Record, Clerk of Superior Court, Yavapai County, Arizona, 1:162-163.

529 Mary Walker, California Death Record, Certificate # 42557.

530 Walker Family Bible, in possession of Bev Luke of Minden, Nevada.

531 Christina Walker, Ancestry.com, *Social Security Death Index*.
Sister Tomine Soiland entry, Ancestry.com, *California Death Index* indicates mother's maiden name of Johnson.
Lace Soeland hhd, 1900 U.S. cens., San Francisco Co., Calif., pop. sched., San Francisco, Assembly Dist. 34, SD 1, ED 104, sh. 5A, dw. 71, fam. 104.

532 Elbert L. Walker, Ancestry.com, *California Birth Index, 1905-1995* [database on-line] (Provo, Utah: MyFamily.com, Inc., 2005). Original data: State of California. *California Birth Index, 1905-1995* (Sacramento, California: State of California Department of Health Services, Center for Health Statistics).

533 Sharlot Hall Museum, *Cemeteries: Williamson Valley - Pierce and Las Vegas Ranches*, online < sharlot.org/archives/gene/cemetery>.
Middle name provided by Bev Luke, Minden, Nevada, granddaughter of Osman Amaden Walker.

534 Sharlot Hall Museum, *Cemeteries: Williamson Valley*.

535 Sharlot Hall Museum, *Cemeteries: Williamson Valley*.

536 Eugene Ensign Walker, Ancestry.com, World War I Registration Card.

537 Walker family records maintained by Bev Luke of Minden, Nevada.

Children of *Eugene* and *Bertha (Denny) Walker*:[538]
1. Eugene Oswill Walker, b. Kingman 16 Jan. 1916.
2. Robert Franklin Walker, b. Prescott, Ariz., 15 June 1919.
3. Clarence Amaden Walker, b. Kingman 26 Dec. 1920.

ii.   EMMA F. WALKER, b. Calif. May 1867;[539] d. aft. 1910;[540] m. Williamson Valley, Ariz. Terr., 27 Oct. 1884 WILLIAM ROBERTS,[541] b. Meadows, Strathalbyn District, South Australia, Australia, 7 May 1861, son of PHILIP and EUNICE (HARRISON) ROBERTS.[542]

Children of WILLIAM and EMMA (WALKER) ROBERTS:
a.   *Edith Almira Roberts* b. Prescott, Ariz. Terr., 22 July 1885;[543] m. abt. 1905 *Leon Bertrand Artigue*,[544] b. La. 3 March 1875, son of *Louis* and *Leontine (Dazette) Artigue*.[545]

Child of *Leon* and *Edith (Walker) Artigue*:
1. Raymond N. Artigue, b. Calif. 4 June 1911.[546]

b.   *Leonia Roberts*, b. Williamson Valley, Ariz. Terr., June 1886;[547] m. abt. 1908 *Alva Auron Smith*,[548] b. Signal, Ariz. Terr., 12 May 1877, son of *Edward H.* and *Sopha (____) Smith*.[549]

---

538   Ibid.
539   William Roberts household, 1900 U.S. cens., Yavapai Co., Ariz., pop. sched., Williamson Valley, SD 11, ED 61, sheet 2B, dw. 33, fam. 35.
540   R. W. Wagner household, 1910 U.S. cens., Maricopa Co., Ariz. Terr., pop. sched., Peoria, SD 2, ED 72, sheet 1A, dw. 1, fam. 1.
541   Roberts - Walker Marriage Record, Yavapai County, Arizona, A:187.
542   William Roberts birth record 2:447, Strathalbyn District, Australia; Australian Archives, 11-13 Derlanger Avenue, Collinswood South Australia 5081.
543   Edyth Almira Artigue, Arizona Death Record, Certificate # 2842.
544   Geo B. Artigue household, 1910 U.S. cens., Los Angeles Co., Calif., pop. sched., Los Angeles, District 70, SD 7, ED 239, sheet 3B, dw. 87, fam. 89.
545   Leon B. Artigue, Ancestry.com, California Death Index;
Louis Artigue household, 1900 U.S. census, San Diego County, California, population schedule, San Diego, Ward 2, SD 6, ED 191, sheet 10A, dwelling 222, family 236; National Archives micropublication T623, roll 99.
546   Raymond N. Dartigues, Ancestry.com, California Death Index.
547   Birth location from son Lloyd's birth certificate: Lloyd Douglas Smith, Arizona Birth Record, Certificate # 414.
Birth date: William Roberts household, 1900 U.S. cens., Yavapai Co., Ariz., pop. sched., Williamson Valley, SD 11, ED 61, sh. 2B, dw. 33, fam. 35.
548   Albert Smith household, 1910 U.S. cens., Yavapai Co., Ariz. Terr., pop. sched., Prescott, SD Arizona, ED 126, sheet 1A, dw. 8, fam. 8.
549   Birth location from son Lloyd's birth record; Lloyd Douglas Smith, Arizona Birth Record, Certificate # 414.

Children of *Alva* and *Leonia (Walker) Smith*:
1. Clarence Alva Smith, b. Prescott, Ariz. Terr., 24 Aug. 1909.[550]
2. Lloyd Douglas Smith, b. Ray, Ariz., 11 July 1919.[551]

c. *Osman William Roberts* b. Ariz. Terr. 17 Jan. 1890; d. Yavapai Co., Ariz., abt. 5 Dec. 1916; bur. Las Vegas Ranch Cem., Williamson Valley, Ariz.[552]

d. *Grace Roberts* b. Ariz. Terr. Oct. 1892,[553] d. aft. 1910.[554]

e. *Martin Albert Roberts*, b. Williamson Valley, Ariz. Terr., 6 April 1895;[555] m. abt. 1928 *Gladys Naomi ___*,[556] b. W.Va. 16 April 1907.[557]

    Child of *Martin* and *___ (_) Roberts*:
1. Betty Jean Roberts, b. Calif. abt. 1925.[558]

f. *Eva Bernice Roberts* b. Prescott, Ariz. Terr., 29 March 1899; m. 1920 *George Lee Michael*,[559] b. Kingman, Ariz. Terr., 22 Jan. 1895,[560] son of *Mary Josephine Murray*.[561]

    Children of *George* and *Eva (Roberts) Michael*:
1. James Webster Michael, b. Prescott, Ariz., 12 Jan.

Birth date: Alva A. Smith, Arizona Death Record, Certificate # 133.

Mother from census: E. H. Smith household, 1880 U.S. census, Pima County, Arizona Territory, population schedule, Luttrell, SD - , ED 40, page 348A, dwelling 87, family 93; National Archives micropublication T9, roll 36.

[550] Clarence Alva Smith, Arizona Birth Record, Certificate # 254.

[551] Lloyd Douglas Smith, Arizona Birth Record, Certificate # 414.

[552] Sharlot Hall Museum, *Cemeteries: Williamson Valley*.

William Roberts household, 1900 U.S. cens., Yavapai Co., Ariz. Terr., pop. sched., Williamson Valley, SD 11, ED 61, sheet 2B, dw. 33, fam. 35.

[553] William Roberts household, 1900 U.S. cens., Yavapai Co., Ariz. Terr., pop. sched., Williamson Valley, SD 11, ED 61, sheet 2B, dw. 33, fam. 35.

[554] Wm Roberts household, 1910 U.S. cens., Yavapai Co., Ariz. Terr., pop. sched., Simmons, SD 1, ED 99, sheet 1A, dw. 21, fam. 21.

[555] Martin Albert Roberts, Ancestry.com, World War I Registration.

[556] Martin Roberts household, 1930 U.S. cens., Gila Co., Ariz., pop. sched., Miami, SD 3, ED 38, sheet 2B dw. 46, fam. 45.

[557] Gladys Naomi Roberts, Arizona Death Record, Certificate # 2450.

[558] Martin Roberts household, 1930 U.S. cens., Gila Co., Ariz., pop. sched., Miami, SD 3, ED 38, sheet 2B dw. 46, fam. 45.

[559] Mary Larvesll household, 1930 U.S. cens., Yavapai Co., Ariz., pop. sched., Prescott, SD 1, ED 26, sheet 12A dw. 331, fam. 331.

[560] George Lee Michael, Ancestry.com, World War I Registration.

[561] Birth record of his half-brother, Oscar Murray Laswell, Arizona Birth Records, Certificate # 633-524-448.

1923.[562]

2. Loye Michael (female), b. Ariz. abt. 1926.[563]

g. *LeRoy E. Roberts* b. Ariz. Terr. 22 Dec. 1902; d. Prescott, Ariz., 14 Sept. 1924; bur. Mountain View Cem., Prescott, Ariz., 16 Sept. 1924.[564]

h. *Opal A. Roberts* b. Ariz. Terr. abt. 1906; d. aft. 1920.[565]

Child of JAMES and ALMIRA (AMADEN) NASH:

iii. GRACE DELLA NASH, b. Hueneme, Calif.,[566] 25 July 1874;[567] m. Williamson Valley, Ariz. Terr., 25 Dec. 1894 WILLARD ELLSWORTH ALLEN,[568] b. Ia., 18 Feb. 1865,[569] son of JOHN and SARAH (MEAD) ALLEN.[570]

Child of WILLARD and GRACE (NASH) ALLEN:

a. *Hazel Della Allen,* b. Prescott, Ariz. Terr., 15 Aug. 1896;[571] m. abt. 1923 *Charles E. Coughran,*[572] b. Prescott, Ariz. Terr., 19 Feb. 1888, son of *James W.* and *Nancy (Green) Coughran.*[573]

Albert Allen Amaden (1844–1908)

44. ALBERT ALLEN AMADEN *(NATHANIEL IVES[6], JACOB[5], JACOB[4] AMIDOWN, HENRY[3], PHILIP[2], ROGER[1] AMADOWNE)* was born at New York on 7 April 1844.[574] He died at Pennington, California, on 16 June 1908.[575] He married at Santa Barbara County, California, on 28

562　James Webster Michael, Arizona Birth Record, Certificate # 512a.

563　Mary Larvesll household, 1930 U.S. cens., Yavapai Co., Ariz., pop. sched., Prescott, SD 1, ED 26, sheet 12A dw. 331, fam. 331.

564　Sharlot Hall Museum, *Cemeteries: Williamson Valley.*

565　Wm Roberts household, 1920 U.S. census, Yavapai County, Arizona, population schedule, Simmons town, SD 1, ED 99, sheet 1A, dwelling 3, family 3; National Archives micropublication T625, roll 52.

566　Obituary, "Allen," *San Bernardino Daily Sun,* San Bernardino, California, Tuesday, 20 November 1951, p. 13.

567　Grace D. Allen, Ancestry.com. *California Death Index.*

568　Allen-Nash marriage record, Yavapai County Marriages, Book 2:44.

569　Willard E. Allen, Ancestry.com. *California Death Index.*
　　　Middle name from daughter's birth record.

570　Allen family records maintained by Barbara Baker.

571　Grace Della Nash, Arizona Birth Record, Certificate #52767.

572　Willard E. Allen household, 1930 U.S. cens., Los Angeles Co., Calif., pop. sched., Monrovia, SD 18, ED 1158, sheet 7A dw. 191, fam. 181.
　　　Sharlot Hall Museum, *Cemeteries: Williamson Valley.*

574　Amaden family records maintained by Betty Farr of Gridley, California.

575　Obituary, "Death of Al Amaden," *Marysville Appeal,* Marysville, California, 17 June 1908.

October 1870 ORDELLA ALICE "DELLA" STRICKLAND.[576] Della was born at Marysville, California, on 7 March 1855, the daughter of GEORGE ARNOLD and MATILDA (NASH) STRICKLAND.[577]

Albert's childhood was spent in Pierrepont, New York, where he attended school and was listed with his family in 1850.[578] In 1851 the family followed his mother Lucia's brothers and moved west to Franklin, Illinois, where Albert's brother, Martin, was likely born. But Franklin didn't work out. In 1855, the family moved on to Westfield Township, Iowa, with Lucia's brothers and parents. Albert was listed there with his parents in both the 1856 Iowa census[579] and the 1860 federal census.[580] Shortly thereafter, the family followed Albert's sister, Almira, to California. Their mother died just before or after the trip. Albert was inducted as a new member of the Yuba Engine Company #3 of the Marysville [California] Fire Department in September 1863.[581] He and his siblings have not been located in the 1870 census. Their father was in Sutter County.

Della's father, George, had come to California during the Gold Rush and in 1850 was a miner on the South Fork American River in El Dorado County, California, where he earned about seven dollars a day.[582] Mining must not have panned out because George took up farming and raised livestock. Della was born the year following George's marriage to Matilda Nash in Marysville, California. She grew up on a sheep farm in Butte, northeast of San Francisco, where she was enumerated with her family in 1860.[583] But her father must have anticipated greater opportunity in the south part of the young state. By 1870 the family was settled in Santa Barbara County, just up

---

576   Amaden-Strickland marriage record, Santa Barbara County Marriages, Santa Barbara County Clerk, Santa Barbara, California.

577   Ordell Alice Amaden, California Death Record, recorded 24 August 1945.

578   Nathan G. Amadan household, 1850 U.S. cens., St. Lawrence Co., N.Y., pop. sched., Pierepont (sic), p. 389, dw. 125, fam. 125.

579   N. J. Amadan household, 1856 Iowa census, Fayette County, Iowa, Westfield township, #137; FHL microfilm #1021299.

580   N. J. Anderson household, 1860 U.S. cens., Fayette Co., Ia., pop. sched., Westfield, p. 188, dw. 1451, fam. 1244.

581   A. Amaden entry, Marysville [California] City Council Minutes, March 1851-December 1863, page 597; Marysville City Library.

582   George A. Strickland household, 1850 U.S. census, El Dorado County, California, population schedule, town of South Fork of the American River, page 394, dwelling -, family -, line 2; National Archives micropublication M432, roll 34.

583   G. A. Strickland household, 1860 U.S. cens., Sutter Co., Calif., pop. sched., Butte, p. 27, dw. 248, fam. 240.

the coast from Los Angeles.[584]

There Della married Albert Amaden in October 1870. They lived in Hueneme, which was in the part of Santa Barbara that became Ventura County at its formation in 1873. Albert was active in the public arena. He was a delegate from Hueneme on the Democratic Committee on Candidates in February 1873 and sought the office of Constable later that year.[585] In 1875, the family lived on Main Street in Hueneme where Albert was a laborer.[586] Their first three daughters were likely born in this county, the third being born in Ventura in early 1876. Later that year the Amaden, Nash, and Strickland families left Ventura County for Arizona Territory. The covered wagon ride was difficult, and each family suffered losses. Albert and Della's second daughter Nettie died on the trail at age three, kicked in the head by a horse.

Their fourth daughter Lola was born in Prescott, Arizona Territory, in 1878. Arizona Territory must not have suited them. By 1880, the Amaden family had returned to Sutter County, where Albert was farming in Butte Township.[587] This was their home for the rest of their lives. Their only son and last child, Albert Eugene, was born there in 1881.

We learn from the Sutter County Great Registers that Albert stood five feet, eight and three quarters inches tall, had a sandy complexion, hazel eyes, and dark brown hair. He was consistently listed as a laborer from New York.[588]

In 1900, Albert and Della were still farming in a small town in Butte Township named Pennington – just a few miles west of Live Oak. Alice, Lola, and Albert Jr. were still living with them, along with

---

[584]   Geo. E. Strickland household, 1870 U.S. cens., Sutter Co., Calif., pop. sched., Butte, p. 27, dw. 248, fam. 240.

[585]   *Great Register, Ventura, California,* pages 2, 3, 116; Ventura Historical Library, Ventura, California.

[586]   Ventura County Genealogical Society, *Ventura County Directory – 1875,* online < venturacogensoc.org/1875Dir>

[587]   Albert Amaden household, 1880 U.S. census, Sutter County, California, population schedule, Butte, SD 16, ED 134, page 16, dwelling 126, family 134; National Archives micropublication T9, roll 84.

[588]   *Great Register, Sutter County, California, 1880 – 1896*; Community Memorial Museum of Sutter County, Yuba City, California.

Alice's new husband, NELSON BOULWARE.[589] Minnie had married HENRY E. FAIRLEE and moved in with her divorced father-in-law, John E. Fairlee, on his farm in North Butte, just down the road from Pennington.[590]

Albert speculated on 160 acres of land in Redding, California, in 1901. He attempted to purchase it from the Bureau of Land Management, but the Bureau had inadvertently sold the property to both Albert and another buyer on the same day. This created correspondence between Albert and the Bureau, where we learn that Albert came to California as a school boy from Iowa in the 1860s. He had lived in Sutter, Yuba, Santa Barbara, and Ventura Counties. During the last year, he had worked as a laborer and sheep shearer in Sutter County.[591] The land sale was completed in 1905, but Albert died in 1908 at age sixty-four. He was buried the following day at Pennington Cemetery, North Butte, California.[592]

At first, daughter Alice was a school teacher, but soon she and Nelson Boulware began raising a family. They left the farmstead and made their home in Biggs, north of the Sutter County homestead. But after giving birth to six children, Alice died young in 1912, only forty-one years old. Her children were still minors. This must have been too much for Nelson, because their children were not with him in 1920. He died in Sacramento, California, in 1923 and was buried by the hospital at the City Cemetery in Sacramento.[593] Their eldest, Aileen Rose, married at age fifteen to BAYLES WESLEY VANHORN, a man who was thirty years her senior and provided a home for three of her young brothers.[594] Aileen and Bayles also raised three of their

---

589   Albert A. Amadon household, 1900 U.S. census, Sutter County, California, population schedule, Butte, SD 19, ED 118, sheet 10A, dwelling 172, family 172; National Archives micropublication T623, roll 115.

590   John E. Fairlee household, 1900 U.S. cens., Sutter Co., Calif., pop. sched., Butte, SD 4, ED 118, sheet 11B, dw. 200, fam. 202.

591   Albert A. Amaden, land entry file # CACAAA 039360, National Archives, Washington, D.C East half of southwest quarter of section 20 in township 40N of range 4E.

592   Annamae Berry transcriber, Albert A. Amaden cemetery record transcription, *The Digger's Digest*, (Yuba City, California: Sutter-Yuba Genealogical Society, 1980), 10.

593   Nelson Boulware, California Death Record, Certificate # 8254.

594   Bayles W. Van Horn household, 1920 U.S. census, Yuba County, California, population schedule, Marysville ward 1, SD 1, ED 178, sheet 6B, dwelling 104, family 120; National Archives micropublication T625, roll 153.

own children and were living in Humboldt County, California, in 1930.[595]

Albert's daughter Minnie married HENRY E. FAIRLEE. The Fairlee family had been neighbors and long time friends of Albert. Henry and Minnie moved nearby and set up their own farm in Pennington, where they raised five children and lived out their lives. Henry served in World War I.[596]

Albert's daughter Lola stayed with her mother for several years and at about age thirty-five, probably in 1914, married ARTHUR MURLEY CARKEET, a gold miner. In his World War I Registration card, he was described as short, of medium build, having gray eyes, and dark brown hair. They moved east to Grass Valley in the mountains of Nevada County, where they rented at 311 Bennett Street and Arthur worked as a gold miner.[597] Later they removed to Sacramento, where he worked as an auto mechanic and she as a hem stitcher.[598] They had no children.

Albert's only son, Albert, married in 1915 to ELIZABETH HAZEL POWERS, a daughter of Irish and German immigrants. Albert was an almond orchardist and resided in Dunnigan, California. Elizabeth was a school teacher. In his World War I registration card, Albert was described as having medium height, a medium build, blue eyes, and light hair.[599] His mother Della never remarried. By 1920, Albert had taken her in along with his nephew, Norman Boulware.[600] By 1930, Norman had left, but his younger brother, Orlin, had joined Albert,

---

[595]   Baylor W. Vea Hone household, 1930 U.S. census, Humboldt County, California, population schedule, Union,   district 24, SD 1, ED 56, sheet 5B, dwelling 120, family 122; National Archives micropublication T626, roll 120.

[596]   Henry E. Fairlie household, 1930 U.S. census, Sutter County, California, population schedule, Butte, SD 3, ED 1, sheet 3A, dwelling 73, family 73; National Archives micropublication T626, roll 224.

[597]   Arthur Carkeet household, 1920 U.S. census, Nevada County, California, population schedule, Grass Valley district 60, SD 2, ED 60, sheet 6A, dwelling 138, family 146; National Archives micropublication T625, roll 123.

[598]   Arthur M. Carkett household, 1930 U.S. cens., Sacramento Co., Calif., pop. sched., Sacramento, SD 3, ED 47, sheet 6A, dw. 123, fam. 161.

[599]   Albert Eugene Amaden, Ancestry.com, World War I Registration Card.

[600]   Albert Amaden household, 1920 U.S. census, Yolo County, California, population schedule, Dunnigan, SD 3, ED 224, sheet 2B, dwelling 33, family 33; National Archives micropub. T625, roll 128.

Elizabeth, and Albert's mother.[601] Albert and Della had no children. Brother Martin had only a daughter, and so the Amaden surname ended for Nathaniel Amaden's descendants.

Children of ALBERT and ORDELLA ALICE (STRICKLAND) AMADEN:

i.   ALICE LONA AMADEN, b. probably Hueneme, Calif., 11 Feb. 1871; d. Biggs, Calif., 12 Dec. 1912; bur. Pennington Cem., North Butte, Calif.;[602] m. Pennington, Calif., 7 March 1900 NELSON BOULWARE,[603] b. Calif. 16 Nov. 1866, son of CALEB MARION and CAROLINE (HUBBARD) BOULWARE, d. Sacramento, Calif., 7 Feb. 1923, bur. City Cemetery, Sacramento.[604]

   Children of NELSON and ALICE (AMADEN) BOULWARE:

   a.   *Aileen Rose Boulware*, b. Calif. 6 April 1901;[605] m. abt. 1916 *Bayles Wesley Vanhorn*,[606] b. probably Colusa, Calif.,[607] 23 Aug. 1870,[608] son of *John Wesley* and *Sarah Ann (Evans) Vanhorn*.[609]

      Children of *Bayles* and *Aileen (Boulware) Vanhorn*:

      1.   Carol Lorraine Vanhorn, b. Yuba Co., Calif., 14 June 1918.[610] Living with Uncle Darrell Boulware in 1930.[611]

---

601   Albert E. Amaden household, 1930 U.S. census, Yolo County, California, population schedule, Dunnigan, SD 5, ED 7, sheet 1B, dwelling 27, family 29; National Archives micropublication T626, roll 225.

602   Alice Amaden Boulware, California Death Records, Certificate # 448371.

603   Boulware-Amaden marriage, Sutter County Marriage Book D:351.

604   Nelson Boulware, California Death Record, Certificate # 8254.

605   Aileen Rose Rowland, Ancestry.com, *California Death Index*.

606   Baylor W. Vea Hone household, 1930 U.S. cens., Humboldt Co., Calif., pop. sched., Union, district 24, SD 1, ED 56, sheet 5B, dw. 120, fam. 122.

607   John Vanhorne household, 1870 U.S. census, Colusa County, California, population schedule, Colusa, page 282, dwelling 169, family 157; National Archives micropublication M593, roll 71.

608   Bayless Vanhorn entry, Ancestry.com, *California Death Index*.

609   Vanhorn – Evans marriage, Illinois Statewide Marriage Index, online <www.cyberdriveillinois.com/departments/archives/marriage.html>.

   John W. Vanhorn household, 1880 U.S. census, Tehama County, California, population schedule, Cottonwood, SD 1, ED 139, page 432A, dwelling 9, family 9; National Archives micropublication T9, roll 85.

610   Carol L. Vanhorn, Ancestry.com, *California Birth Index*.

   Carol Lorraine Pasinetti, Ancestry.com, *California Death Index*.

611   Darrell Boulware household, 1930 U.S. census, Mendocina County, California, population schedule, Ukiah district 24, SD 1, ED 23-24, sheet 5B, dwelling 120, family 122; National Archives micropublication T626, roll 177.

    2. Wesley E. Vanhorn, b. Yuba Co. 14 Aug. 1920.[612]

    3. Lola A. Vanhorn, b. Sutter Co., Calif., 13 Sept. 1922.[613]

b. *Verne A. Boulware*, b. Calif. 25 April 1903.[614] Living with sister, Aileen Vanhorn, in 1920. Auto mechanic in Homer, Calif., in 1930.[615]

c. *Norman Frederick Boulware*, b. Calif. 4 Feb. 1906;[616] m. abt. 1926 *Inas Joy Brownell*,[617] b. Pagosa Springs, Colo., 19 Feb. 1907, dau. of *Harley* and *Nina Bell (Minium) Brownell*.[618] Lived with Uncle Albert Amaden in 1920. Postal clerk in Sacramento, Calif., 1930.[619]

    Children of *Norman* and *Inas (Brownell) Boulware*:

    1. Robert Lee Boulware, b. Sacramento Co. 16 Nov. 1927.[620]

    2. William Daniel Boulware, b. Sacramento Co. 18 Aug. 1929.[621]

d. *Darrell Eugene Boulware,* b. Calif. 28 Aug. 1907;[622] m. abt. 1929 *Nora Vinton*, b. Calif. 15 May 1908, dau. of *John M.* and *Clara (Shore) Vinton*.[623] Lived with sister, Aileen Vanhorn, in 1920. Farm worker, caring for niece, Carol Vanhorn, in 1930.[624]

e. *Orlin C. Boulware*, b. Butte Co., Calif., 19 July 1909.[625]

---

612   Wesley E. Vanhorn, Ancestry.com, *California Birth Index.*

613   Lola A. Vanhorn, Ancestry.com, *California Birth Index.*

614   Verne A. Boulware, Ancestry.com, *California Death Index.*

615   Verne A. Boulware household, 1930 U.S. census, Mono County, California, population schedule, Homer, SD 12, ED 3, sheet 4A, dwelling 99, family 99; National Archives micropublication T626, roll 178.

616   Norman F. Boulware, California Death Record, Certificate # 44709.

617   Norman F. Boulware household, 1930 U.S. cens., Sacramento Co., Calif., pop. sched., Sacramento, SD 3, ED 56, sheet 13A, dw. 332, fam. 334.

618   Brownell family records maintained by Marvel Hansbraugh.

619   Norman F. Boulware household, 1930 U.S. cens., Sacramento Co., Calif., pop. sched., Sacramento, SD 3, ED 56, sheet 13A, dw. 332, fam. 334.

620   Robert Lee Boulware, Ancestry.com, *California Birth Index.*

621   William Daniel Boulware, Ancestry.com, *California Birth Index.*

622   Darrell Eugene Boulware, Ancestry.com, *California Birth Index.*

623   Nora Boulware, Ancestry.com, *California Death Index.*

John M. Vinton household, 1910 U.S. census, Mendocino County, California, population schedule, town of Round Valley, SD 2, ED 64, sheet 13B, dwelling 187, family 187; National Archives micropublication T624, roll 88.

624   Darrell Boulware household, 1930 U.S. cens., Mendocina Co., Calif., pop. sched., Ukiah district 24, SD 1, ED 23-24, sheet 5B, dw. 120, fam. 122.

625   ____ Boulware, Ancestry.com, *California Birth Index.*

Indexed as female in birth records. Living with sister, Aileen Vanhorn, 1920; uncle Albert Amaden 1930.

ii. NETTIE HEUTA AMADEN, b. prob. Hueneme, Calif., 10 Aug. 1873; d. 29 Sept. 1876, on trail between Calif. and Ariz. from kick to the head by a horse.[626]

iii. MINNIE EMMA AMADEN, b. Ventura, Calif.,[627] 9 March 1876;[628] m. Pennington, Calif., 19 March 1899 HENRY EUGENE FAIRLEE,[629] b. Pennington, Calif.,[630] 25 July 1872, son of JOHN CHRISTOPHER and SARAH E. (GIBSON) FAIRLEE.[631]

Children of HENRY and MINNIE (AMADEN) FAIRLEE, all born Pennington, Calif.:[632]

a. *Vera Fairlee*, b. 14 Sept. 1902;[633] m. abt. 1922 *Ralph Raymond Dennis,*[634] b. prob. Yuba, Calif., 10 April 1900, son of *Jake A.* and *Mary L. (Barnett) Dennis,*[635] separated before 1930. Vera was bookkeeper; lived in Marysville 1930.

b. *Loren E. Fairlee*, b. 16 Oct. 1903;[636] m. abt. 1924 *Margaret I. Harling,*[637] b. Calif. 8 May 1902, dau. of *John D.* and *Katherine (Root) Harling.*[638] Circulation manager at newspaper, Woodland, Calif., 1930.

Child of *Loren* and *Margaret (Harling) Fairlee:*

Orlin Bowlware (sic), Ancestry.com, *Social Security Death Index.*
626 Betty Farr. Gridley, California. Amaden family records,
627 Ibid.
628 Minnie A. Fairlee, Ancestry.com, *California Death Index.*
629 Fairlee-Amaden marriage, Sutter County Marriage Book D:321.
630 Betty Farr. Gridley, California. Amaden family records,
631 Henry Eugene Fairlee, California Death Record, filed 16 November 1954.
632 Betty Farr. Gridley, California. Amaden family records,
633 Vera F. Sears, Ancestry.com, *California Death Index.*
634 Vera O. Dennis household, 1930 U.S. census, Yuba County, California, population schedule, Marysville, SD 3, ED 2, sheet 5A, dwelling 117, family 130; National Archives micropublication T626, roll 228.
635 Ralph Raymond Dennis, Ancestry.com, *California Death Index.*
Jake A. Dennis household, 1900 U.S. cens., Sutter Co., Calif., pop. sched., Yuba, SD 4, ED 122, sheet 5A, dw. 103, fam. 118.
636 Loren E. Fairlee, Ancestry.com, *California Death Index.*
637 Loren E. Fairlee household, 1930 U.S. cens., Yolo Co., Calif., pop. sched., Woodland district 23, SD 5, ED 57-23, sheet 2B, dw. 41, fam. 41.
638 Margaret I. Fairlee, Ancestry.com, *California Death Index.*
John D. Harling household, 1920 U.S. cens., Yolo Co., Calif., pop. sched., Woodland, SD 3, ED 234, sheet 11B, dw. 274, fam. 365.

1. Loren E. Fairlee, b. Yolo Co., Calif., 4 May 1926.[639]

c. *Cecile Mae Fairlee*, b. 16 Dec. 1905;[640] m. Seattle, Wash., 3 Sept. 1924 *Earl Levi Crain*, b. Prineville, Ore., 31 Aug. 1892, son of *Francis Levi* and *Nellie Bramble (Kinder) Crain*.[641] Earl served WWI; mechanic in Klamath Falls, Ore., 1930.[642]

Children of *Earl* and *Cecile (Fairlee) Crain*:[643]

1. Elizabeth Mae Crain, b. Dunnigan, Calif., 9 March 1925.
2. Eston Earl Crain, b. Dunnigan 7 May 1926.
3. Ralph Olin Crain, b. Newcastle, Calif., 16 Aug 1928.

d. *Irma Louise Fairlee*, b. 1 Feb. 1908;[644] m. abt. 1929 *William Moore Metteer*,[645] b. Calif. 10 July 1907, son of *George Baxter* and *Jessie M. (Moore) Metteer*.[646] Both public school teachers Marysville, 1930.

e. *Ivan Louis Fairlee*, b. 13 Oct. 1910.[647]

iv. LOLA MAY AMADEN, b. Prescott, Ariz. Terr., 5 Nov. 1878;[648] m. Nevada Co., Calif., 31 January 1912,[649] ARTHUR MURLEY CARKEET, b. Nevada City, Calif., 7 Sept. 1880, son of RICHARD M. and MARY L. (DOWLING) CARKEET.[650]

v. ALBERT EUGENE AMADEN, b. Live Oak, Calif.,[651] 16 April

---

639   Loren E. Fairlee, Ancestry.com, *California Birth Index.*

640   Cecile Mae Crain, Ancestry.com, *California Death Index.*

641   Crain family records maintained by Don Houk, Tokyo, Japan; Amaden family records maintained by Betty Farr, Gridley, California.

642   Earl A. Crain household, 1930 U.S. census, Klamath County, Oregon, population schedule, Klamath Falls, SD 4, ED 36, sheet 14B, dwelling 312, family 332; National Archives micropub. T626, roll 1945.

643   Amaden family records maintained by Betty Farr, Gridley, California.

644   Irma L. Metter, Ancestry.com, *Social Security Death Index.*

645   William Metteer household, 1930 U.S. cens., Yuba Co., Calif., pop. sched., Marysville, SD 3, ED 11, sheet 11B, dw. 83, fam. 83.

646   William Moore Metteer, Ancestry.com, *California Death Index.*
Amaden family records maintained by Betty Farr, Gridley, California.

647   Ivan Louis Fairlee, Ancestry.com, *California Death Index.*

648   Obituary, "Lola A. Carkeet Dies in Hospital," *Grass Valley Union*, Grass Valley, California, Wednesday, 24 February 1965, page 8, column 4.

649   Carkeet-Amaden marriage, Marriage Records, book 9, page 144, Nevada County Clerk, Nevada City, California.

650   Arthur Murley Carkeet, California Death Record, filed 9 January 1939.

651   Obituary, "A. E. Amaden Rites to be Tuesday, Dunnigan Farmer Dies Suddenly at Home," *Woodland Democrat*, Woodland, California, Monday, 16 February 1942.

1881;[652] m. Marysville, Calif., 29 Dec. 1915 ELIZABETH HAZEL POWERS, b. Dunnigan, Calif.,[653] 1 July 1888, dau. of RICHARD and CHRISTINA KATHERINA (SCHWEIZER) POWERS.[654]

Martin Eugene Amaden (1851–1925)

45. MARTIN EUGENE AMADEN *(NATHANIEL IVES[6], JACOB[5], JACOB[4] AMIDOWN, HENRY[3], PHILIP[2], ROGER[1] AMADOWNE)* was born probably at Franklin, Illinois, on 13 September 1851.[655] He died at Yuba City, California, on 22 November 1925.[656] He married at Live Oak, California, on 14 February 1881 RUTH ANNA "ANNA" SCHOOLEY.[657] She was born at Marysville, California, on 22 December 1863, the daughter of DANIEL A. and ANNA C. SERINA (SCHERMIER) SCHOOLEY.[658]

Martin was born after his family had relocated to Franklin, Illinois, from New York. But the family stayed in Franklin only four years. In 1855 they relocated to Westfield Township, Iowa. Martin was listed there with his parents in both the 1856 Iowa census[659] and the 1860 federal census.[660] Sometime in the next five years, Martin's mother died. In 1865, when he was only fourteen, the family followed Martin's sister, Almira, to California.

Martin and his brother, Albert, have not been found in 1870. But since they were employed as sheep shearers, they may have been missed as they traveled with the flocks. When Martin's father died in 1872, he was likely the son listed in the obituary as living in Sutter

---

652 Albert Eugene Amaden, Ancestry.com, *World War I Draft Registration.*
653 The Learning Company, Hiawatha, Ia. World Family Tree #23, tree 2392.
654 Elizabet H. Franke, Ancestry.com, *California Death Index.*
Richard Powers household, 1900 U.S. census, Yolo County, California, population schedule, Fairview, SD 3, ED 199, sheet 5A, dwelling 68, family 70; National Archives micropub. T623, roll 116.
655 "Martin Amaden of Y.C. is Dead," *Marysville Democrat,* Marysville, California, 23 November 1925.
656 Martin Eugene Amaden death certificate, Sutter County Recorder-Clerk.
657 Amaden – Schooley marriage, Sutter County Calif. Marriage Book C:26.
658 Anna Amaden, California Death Record, filed 16 October 1944.
Pat Lamaster, *Family History of Schermier, Schooley and Amaden Families* (Gold Beach, Oregon: self-published, ?), copy held by Bob Burns, Marysville, California.
659 N. J. Amadan household, 1856 Iowa cens., Fayette Co., Ia., Westfield township, #137.
660 N. J. Anderson household, 1860 U.S. cens., Fayette Co., Ia., pop. sched., Westfield, p. 188, dw. 1451, fam. 1244.

County (see biography of Nathaniel Ives Amaden in chapter 3).[661] His brother and sister, Almira, relocated to the newly formed Ventura County, California, by 1873 and from there to Arizona Territory about 1876. Albert returned to Sutter County by 1880. It is not clear if Martin joined them during any of these travels.

Anna Schooley was born in Marysville in 1863. Her father Daniel owned a trucking business, was a policeman for Marysville in 1862 and 1863, and served as a member of the fire department in 1864. He fell ill and died from pneumonia one year after Anna was born. Her mother, Anna (Schermier) Schooley, became a seamstress and sent her children to live with their grandparents, John and Hannah (Wells) Schermier, on their ranch in Live Oak – about thirty-six miles north of Marysville and Yuba City. After grandfather John died the following year in 1865(?), Anna took her children and her mother to Yuba City.[662] Anna's brother, Henry Clay Schermier, took over the ranch. He hired fourteen-year-old Martin Amaden as a ranch hand, but with Henry's untimely death fourteen years later in 1879 the family persuaded Martin to manage the ranch.

While working at the ranch, Martin was boarding with a local merchant named Henry Armstrong in Yuba City, as recorded in 1880.[663] The next winter when he was twenty-nine, he married Anna at the ranch in Live Oak. Martin and the family returned to the Schermier ranch, where they welcomed their daughter, Hazel, eight years later in 1889. The family sold the ranch in 1895.[664] Martin's and Anna's second daughter Cora was born in 1899.

In the Sutter County Great Register, Martin is described as an Illinois-born farmer.[665] He stood five foot, nine and one-half inches tall. With a mole on his chin, he had a dark complexion, brown eyes, and dark brown hair.

Martin and Anna were still living in Live Oak in 1900. Martin was a farmer. With them were their two daughters, Hazel and Cora,

---

661   *Weekly Sutter (Yuba City, Calif.) Banner,* 16 March 1872.
662   Anna Schooley household, 1880 U.S. cens., Sutter Co., Calif., pop. sched., Yuba, SD 3, ED 138, p. 24, dw. 195, fam. 195.
663   Henry Armstrong household, 1880 U.S. cens., Sutter Co., Calif., pop. sched., Yuba City, SD 3, ED 138, p. 20, dw. 165, fam 165.
664   Lamaster, *Family History of Schermier, Schooley and Amaden Families.*
665   *Great Register, Sutter County, 1880–1896.*

and Anna's mother.[666]

As he aged, Martin retired from farming and the family moved back to Yuba City in 1906. They lived at 726 Cooper Avenue, located at the end of the streetcar line between Yuba City and Marysville. Martin became a self-employed teamster. He died in 1925 at age seventy-four from bronchial pneumonia and was buried at Yuba City Cemetery on 25 November 1925. Anna lived on alone in their house on Cooper Avenue, where she was still living in 1930.[667]

Hazel, their eldest daughter, married first. The groom was Benjamin Kinnicutt, a Massachusetts native. He operated the streetcar that ended in front of Hazel's family home. He was of medium height and build, with blue eyes and dark brown hair.[668] Their marriage in 1909 was followed eleven months later with the birth of Marjorie, probably in Marysville, where the family lived in 1910.[669] They removed to Oakland, California, by 1920,[670] where Benjamin worked as a grocer and in 1930 as a school custodian.[671]

Martin's other daughter, Cora, married in 1919 to Thomas Burns, likely in her parents' home as they were listed as witnesses. Thomas was a tall man with a medium build, blue eyes, and brown hair.[672] They immediately took up residence with Cora's parents, and Thomas worked with her father as a teamster.[673] That same year their son, Robert, was born. They moved to another house in Yuba City by 1930, and Thomas continued the "draying" [dray – to haul on a dray; dray – a strong cart or wagon without sides][674] business.[675]

---

[666]   M.E. Amaden household, 1900 U.S. cens, Sutter Co, Calif, pop sched, Butte district 118, SD 4, ED 118, sheet 6A, dw. 100, fam. 100.

[667]   Ruth A. Amaden household, 1930 U.S. cens., Sutter Co., Calif., pop. sched., Yuba City district 11, SD 3, ED 51-11, sheet 5A, dw. 107, fam. 109.

[668]   Benjamin Russell Kinnicutt, Ancestry.com, *World War I Reg. Card.*

[669]   Benj R Kinnicutt household, 1910 U.S. census, Yuba County, California, population schedule, town of Marysville, 4th ward, SD 2, ED 192, sheet 17A, dwelling 48, family 53; National Archives micropublication T624, roll 111.

[670]   Benjamin R. Kinnicutt household, 1920 U.S. census, Alameda County, California, population schedule, Oakland, SD 5, ED 115, sheet 1A, dwelling 10, family 10; National Archives micropublication T625, roll 90.

[671]   B.R. Kinnicutt household, 1930 U.S. census, Alameda County, California, population schedule, Oakland, SD 8, ED 1-199, sheet 4A, dwelling 69, family 69; National Archives micropub. T626, roll 108.

[672]   Thomas Foster Burns, Ancestry.com, *World War I Registration Card.*

[673]   Benjamin R. Kinnicutt household, 1920 U.S. cens., Alameda Co., Calif., pop. sched., Oakland, SD 5, ED 115, sheet 1A, dw. 10, fam. 10.

[674]   *Merriam-Webster Online*, "dray," 11 October 2006.

Children of MARTIN and ANNA (SCHOOLEY) AMADEN:
i.   HAZEL SERENA AMADEN, b. Live Oak, Calif., 12 July 1889;[676] m.
     Yuba City,   Calif.,   3   June   1909   BENJAMIN   RUSSELL
     KINNICUTT,[677] b. Fairhaven,   Mass.,   5 Aug. 1883,[678] son of
     BENJAMIN TOWNSEND and MARY D. (LINCOLN) KINNICUTT.[679]
         Child of BENJAMIN and HAZEL (AMADEN) KINNICUTT:
     a. *Marjorie Virginia Kinnicutt*, b. probably Marysville, Calif.,
         31 May 1910;[680] m. abt. 1928 *James V. Larkins*, b. Md. abt.
         1905, son of *Charles E.* and *Nora (___) Larkins*.[681]
             Child of *James* and *Marjorie (Kinnicutt) Larkins*:
         1. Patsy J. Larkins, b. probably Oakland, Calif., 19 May
             1929.[682]

ii. CORA ELAINE AMADEN, b. Live Oak 25 July 1899;[683] m. Yuba
     City 22 March 1919 THOMAS FOSTER BURNS,[684] b. Nampa,
     Idaho, 22 March 1919,[685] son of WILLIAM FRANKLIN and
     FANNIE WARE (MORRISON) BURNS.[686]
         Child of THOMAS and CORA (AMADEN) BURNS:
     a. *Robert Lee "Bob" Burns*, b. Marysville, Calif., 30 Oct.

---

675   Thomas H. Burns household, 1930 U.S. cens., Sutter Co., Calif., pop.
sched., Yuba City district 12, SD 3, ED 51-12, sheet 9B, dw. 214, fam. 215.
676   Hazel Serena Amaden, Affidavit of Birth, Sutter County Book 165: 392.
677   Kinnicutt-Amaden marriage, Sutter County Marriages, Book F: 54
678   Obituary, "Kinnicutt," *Walla Walla Union Bulletin*, Walla Walla
Washington, Thursday, 13 December 1973, page 29.
679   Mother's maiden name from brother Minor C. Kinnicutt's entry,
Ancestry.com, *California Birth Index*.
     Parents from Benjamin F. Kinnicutt household, 1900 U.S. census, Tehama
County, California, population schedule, Corning, SD 3, ED 180, sheet 20B,
dwelling 448, family 440; National Archives micropublication T623, roll 115.
680   Marjorie V. Kinnicut, Ancestry.com, *California Birth Index*.
681   B.R. Kinnicutt household, 1930 U.S. cens., Alameda Co., Calif., pop.
sched., Oakland, SD 8, ED 1-199, sheet 4A, dw. 69, fam. 69.
682   Patsy Larkins, Ancestry.com, *California Birth Index*.
683   Cora Elaine Amaden. Affidavit of Birth, Sutter County Book 167: 303.
684   Burns-Amaden marriage, Sutter County Marriages, Book G:87.
685   Thomas Foster Burns, Ancestry.com, *World War I Registration Card*.
686   Burns – Morrison marriage, Ada County Marriages, Volume A:192,
County Clerk, Boise, Idaho.
     William F. Burns household, 1900 U.S. census, Canyon County,
California, population schedule, Nampa, SD 43, ED 136, sheet 7A, dwelling 154,
family 163; National Archives micropublication T623, roll 232.

1919.[687]

Frances C. (Axtell) Chapman (1836–1908)

46. FRANCES C. AXTELL *(ELIZABETH[6] E. AMADEN, JACOB[5], JACOB[4] AMIDOWN, HENRY[3], PHILIP[2], ROGER[1] AMADOWNE)* was born at Saint Lawrence County, New York,[688] on 30 August 1836.[689] She died at Granville, New York, on 11 February 1908.[690] She married at Pierrepont, New York, on 4 September 1854 HUBBARD E. CHAPMAN.[691] Hubbard was born at Moriah, New York, in 1833, the son of ALPHEUS and NANCY (MESSENGER) CHAPMAN.[692] He died at Rensselaer Falls, New York, on 21 September 1885.[693]

The only records of Frances's birth place are her children's death certificates. Her daughter Susan's death certificate indicated Lisbon and daughter May's indicated Pierrepont, both of which are in St. Lawrence County (where both of her parents resided in 1830). By 1840 the young family had moved to Antwerp, in nearby Jefferson County, New York.[694] Then sometime in the 1840s, the family moved 150 miles east and settled in Moriah, New York, just a couple of miles from Lake Champlain and the Vermont border, where we find them in the 1850 census.[695] In the early censuses, a copy of the original census taker's results was made and sent to the Capitol. Perhaps through this process an error was made because Frances was recorded as Thomas. The next year the family moved back west to Lisbon, 140 miles west of Moriah on the Saint Lawrence River, across the river from Canada. Their time in Moriah must have been

---

687   Obituary, "Robert Lee 'Bob' Burns," *Appeal Democrat*, Marysville, California, 2 August 2003, page C2.

688   Daughter Susan Belle (Chapman) Gardner's death certificate, filed 23 May 1916, Bureau of Vital Records, Concord, New Hampshire.

689   Carson A. Axtell, compiler, *Axtell Genealogy*, 78.

690   Frances C. Chapman New York Death Certificate # 07289.

691   Chapman – Asclete marriage record, Walter and Mary Smallman, transcribers, *Marriage Registers kept by the Rev. Wm Whitfield, 1841-1891* (Salt Lake City, Utah: Gen. Society of Utah, 1981); FHL microfilm 1304688 Item 1.

692   Mother's maiden name through brother's biography from: "D. A. Chapman," *Biographical History of Cherokee County, Iowa* (Chicago : W. S. Dunbar, 1889), online <usgennet.org/usa/topic/historical/ cherokee1889idx>.

693   Hubbard E. Chapman, New York Death Certificate # 22201.

694   Edwin Estell household, 1840 U.S. census, Jefferson County, New York, Antwerp, page 552, line 27; National Archives micropub. M704, roll 292.

695   Edwin Hertell household, 1850 U.S. cens., Essex Co., N.Y., pop. sched., Moriah, p. 32, dw. 480, fam. 497.

memorable because a native son, Hubbard Chapman, followed the family west to St. Lawrence County to marry Frances in 1854.

Hubbard was born in 1833, one of at least six children. He was enumerated there with his family in 1840[696] and 1850.[697] He and his bride may have lived in Lisbon, near or with her parents, as their first child, Addie, was born there in 1856. The following month Frances's mother passed away from a stroke. Perhaps with her death, Frances and Hubbard desired to move. Two months later her father, Henry, purchased a farm back in Moriah, which he leased to them.[698] In 1858 Henry sold the farm subject to a two-year lease to Hubbard.[699] Their second child, Susan, was born that year.

According to the deed, the farm was due north from Hubbard's parents' farm. Both Hubbard[700] and his father Alpheus were farmers.[701] In 1861, Alpheus sold his farm to Hubbard[702] and likely left for Iowa, where another son, Danford, was living. Hubbard and Frances returned to Lisbon and from there sold the Moriah farm in 1864.[703] Eva was also born that year. May's birth in Lisbon was celebrated in May 1868, followed by the family's loss of Eva the following month. She was buried in Rensselaer Falls Cemetery, located at Rensselaer Falls, New York.[704]

In 1870 Hubbard was working as a farmer, with a very respectable farm in Lisbon worth $6100.[705] Blanche was born in 1871, Nella in 1876, and their seventh daughter Frances in 1877.

---

[696]   Alpheus Chapman household, 1840 U.S. census, Essex County, New York, Moriah, page 173, line 13; National Archives micropublication M704, roll 282.

[697]   Alpheus Chapman household, 1850 U.S. cens., Essex Co., N.Y., pop. sched., Moriah, p. 23, dw. 328, fam. 344.

[698]   Essex County, New York, Property Records, Bk RR:243-244.

[699]   Essex County, New York, Property Records, Bk UU:327-328.

[700]   Hubbard Chapman household, 1860 U.S. census, Essex County, New York, population schedule, Moriah, page 5, dwelling 103, family 83; National Archives micropublication M653, roll 753.

[701]   Alpheus Chapman household, 1860 U.S. cens., Essex Co., N.Y., pop. sched., Moriah, p. 4, dw. 100, fam. 80.

[702]   Essex County, New York, Property Records, Bk YY:391-2.

[703]   Essex County, New York, Property Records, Bk 55:147-148.

[704]   Anne M. Cady, *Rennselaer Falls Cemetery Inventory*, online <freepages.genealogy.rootsweb.com/~stlawgen/CEMETERY/RenFalls/RenFalls.htm>

[705]   Hubbard Chapman household, 1870 U.S. census, Saint Lawrence County, New York, population schedule, Lisbon, page 1, dwelling 2, family 2; National Archives micropublication M593, roll 1098.

In 1880, Hubbard and Frances were still farming in Lisbon. Addie had married in 1875. The other five children were still living at home.[706] In 1884 the family relocated to Rensselaer Falls, where Hubbard died of typhoid fever the following year at age fifty-two. He was buried at Rensselaer Falls Cemetery. When Frances's father died in 1890, she was still a resident of Rensselaer Falls and his sole surviving biological child.[707]

Frances's daughter Addie married Charles Briggs, a Lisbon native. They moved in with Charles's widowed father in Lisbon and were farmers.[708] They raised four children there. Two of their children, Luna and Alvah, died young and were buried at Rensselaer Falls Cemetery.[709] By 1890 Addie and Charles had moved to Ogdensburg[710] and by 1900 to Potsdam, New York.[711] Their eldest son, Henry, married Harriet Kirkelly of Potsdam, New York, and had a son, Stanley, born in Oswego, New York, in 1900. Following her sister, Susan, and brother-in-law, Leslie Gardner, Addie and Charles removed just after the turn of the century to Enfield, New Hampshire, with their son, Howard, and Henry's young family. Howard died from typhoid fever soon after arriving in 1903. He had been working as a mill hand. Over the next several years, Charles and Addie lived in both Enfield and Canaan, New Hampshire.[712] Addie died of kidney disease in 1924 at age sixty-eight, and Charles took his life in 1927 at age seventy-seven. They are both buried at West Canaan Cemetery in

---

706 Hubbard Chapman household, 1880 U.S. census, Saint Lawrence County, New York, population schedule, Lisbon, SD 7, ED 139, page 11, dwelling 64, family 64; National Archives micropub. T9, roll 839.

707 Henry E. Axtell, St. Lawrence County Probate, Canton, New York, Liber 8:273, case # 1264.

708 William Briggs household, 1880 U.S. cens., St. Lawrence Co., N.Y., pop. sched., Lisbon, SD 7, ED 139, p. 14B, dw. 50, fam. 52.

709 Cady, *Rennselaer Falls Cemetery Inventory* .

710 Charles B. Briggs, *Saint Lawrence County, New York Directory 1890*, ancestry.com.

711 Chas Briggs household, 1900 U.S. census, Saint Lawrence County, New York, population schedule, Potsdam, SD 6, ED 135, sheet 2B, dwelling 50, family 52; Nat'l Archives micropub. T623, roll 1158.

712 Charles Briggs household, 1910 U.S. census, Grafton County, New Hampshire, population schedule, Canaan, SD [], ED 80, sheet 12A, dwelling 238, family 249; National Archives micropublication T624, roll 861.

Charles B. Buggs household, 1920 U.S. census, Grafton County, New Hampshire, population schedule, Enfield, SD 2, ED 40, sheet 14B, dwelling 284, family 328; National Archives micropublication T625, roll 1008.

Canaan with their son, Howard.[713]

Addie's son, Henry, and his family lived in Enfield, Canaan, and Lebanon, New Hampshire. Over the years, he worked as a farmer, railroad worker, and carpenter.[714] He was of medium build and height with gray eyes and brown hair.[715] Henry and Harriet's second son, Charles, was born the month after Henry's brother, Howard, died in 1903. By 1920, both sons had left the family home.[716] Charles married in 1922 Grace Lovering and had two daughters. In 1930 Charles and his family were residing with his parents in Lebanon.[717] Charles was working at the mill. Stanley married Vietta Niles and raised a large family. They lived mostly in Enfield, but in 1930 they were in Wolfeboro, New Hampshire; Stanley was a house painter.[718]

Frances and Hubbard's second daughter, Susan, married Leslie Gardner in 1895 and moved east to Enfield and then Canaan, New Hampshire. They had no children.

May married in 1897 to the widower Charles VanWaters, a local physician fourteen years her senior. They had no children.

Blanche married in 1895 to Benjamin "Frank" Morrison, a native of Rensselaer Falls, New York. They lived in Rensselaer Falls, where their son, Vernon, was born in 1897. Frank was a businessman and at various times he ran a feed store, a grist mill, a cheese box factory, and formed the Morrison and Blair Lighting Company, which "was in operation from dark until midnight and on Tuesday mornings to permit local housewives to iron."[719] Son Vernon married Vida Bradley of Canada, and they had one daughter, Jane. He served in World War I. He was working with his father in the feed business in

---

713　　Charles Barr Briggs New Hampshire Death Certificate # 168.
　　　　Mrs. Addie E. Briggs New Hampshire Death Certificate # 129/494.
714　　Henry Briggs household, 1910 U.S. cens., Grafton Co., N.H., pop. sched., Canaan, SD [], ED 80, sheet 12A, dw. 238, fam. 250.
715　　Henry Axtell Briggs, Ancestry.com, *World War I Draft Registration Card.*
716　　Henry Briggs household, 1920 U.S. cens., Grafton Co., N.H., pop. sched., Canaan, SD 2, ED 35, sheet 3A, dw. 54, fam. 57.
717　　Henry A. Briggs household, 1930 U.S. census, Grafton County, New Hampshire, population schedule, Lebanon, SD 1, ED 27, sheet 17B, dwelling 299, family 346; National Archives micropublication T626, roll 1300.
718　　Stanley H. Briggs household, 1930 U.S. census, Carroll County, New Hampshire, population schedule, Wolfeboro, SD 1, ED 21, sheet 7A, dwelling 127, family 132; National Archives micropublication T626, roll 1298.
719　　Obituary, "Frank Morrison, Rensselaer Falls, Dies in Hospital," *Ogdensburg Journal*, Ogdensburg, New York, page 9, Thursday, 22 June 1944.

1930;[720] both were residents of Rensselaer Falls.[721]

Nella and Frances were enumerated with their mother in 1900 in Potsdam. Frances (the daughter) was enumerated twice, the other being as a lodger in Morristown, which is where she likely taught.[722] Both young ladies were teachers.[723] Nella and Frances married on the same day in 1902:

> At twelve noon Wednesday, Sept. 24th, the strains of Mendelssohn's Wedding march brought a hush upon the joyous company assembled at the home of Mrs. Frances C. Chapman, of Rensselaer Falls. The occasion was the marriage of two daughters, Miss Nella Maude to Mr. Henry Edward Rivenburgh, of Granville, and Miss Frances D. to Mr. James Crawford, of Morristown. The brides-elect in dainty white gowns of mock chiffon and carrying bouquets of pink and white carnations, advanced between lines of white ribbon to the altar where standing in the midst of rich decorations of natural flowers they were joined by the grooms-elect. The march was rendered by Sherwood P. VanWaters. The ring tray was carried by Master Vernon E. Morrison. The ribbon was controlled by Howard C. Briggs, all nephews of the brides-elect. At the instance of Mr. Thomas McKelvey, master of ceremonies, the officiating clergyman, Rev. E. T. Blackmer, in an impressive ring service, heard and declared the sacred vows which changed forever the relations of the contracting parties. Congratulations were tendered the married couples and all sat down to a rich and delicate wedding repast. Soon adieus were spoken and the married cars sped away to begin their wedding trips, leaving on the 2:45 train.

---

[720] Vernon Marrison household, 1930 U.S. census, Saint Lawrence County, New York, population schedule, Rennselaer Falls, SD 1, ED 5, sheet 2B, dwelling 53, family 53; National Archives micropublication T626, roll 1641.

[721] Frank Morrison household, 1930 U.S. cens., St. Lawrence Co., N.Y., pop. sched., Rennselaer Falls, SD 1, ED 5, sheet 2B, dw. 61, fam. 61.

[722] William L. Earing household, 1900 U.S. cens., St. Lawrence Co., N.Y., pop. sched., Morristown, SD 6, ED 113, sheet 5A, dw. 112, fam. 114.

[723] Francis Chapman household, 1900 U.S. cens., St. Lawrence Co., N.Y., pop. sched., Potsdam, SD 6, ED 135, sheet 2B, dw. 50, fam. 52.

Mrs. Chapman is extremely happy in her six daughters, four of whom, Mrs. Dr. C. C. VanWaters, Mrs. Frank Morrison, Mrs. Leslie Gardner and Mrs. Briggs are now enjoying delightful homes. These two are also exceptionally blessed in their husbands, both being prosperous Christian business men in their respective homes. The young brides are ladies of exquisite taste and fine natural bearing with names "rather to be chosen than great riches." Their names both appear among the graduates of Potsdam Normal school, Miss Nella in the class of '96 and Miss Frances in the class of '98. Mr. and Mrs. Rivenburgh will spend several weeks enjoying the beauties of the Catskills and the metropolis, being "at home" after Nov. 8, Granville, N.Y. Mr. and Mrs. Crawford will spend the honeymoon in the east and south, touch W. Canaan, N.H., the bride's sister's home, Boston, New York, Washington and other places of interest, being "at home" after Nov. 1st. Their many friends wish for them years of comfort with heaven's richest blessings.[724]

Neither of them ever had children, though Frances helped raise James's son (who was likely a student of hers in Morristown, thus beginning her relationship with the father). In fact, only Addie and Blanche gave Frances grandchildren.

In 1904, Frances moved in with her daughter, Nella, in Granville and passed away there four years later at the age of seventy-one. She was buried at Rensselaer Falls Cemetery on 14 February 1908.[725]

Children of HUBBARD and FRANCES (AXTELL) CHAPMAN:

i.   ADDIE E. CHAPMAN, b. Lisbon, N.Y.,[726] 3 Jan. 1856; d. Canaan, N.H., 17 Nov. 1924;[727] m. abt. 1875 CHARLES BARR BRIGGS,[728] b. Lisbon 23 Dec. 1849, son of WILLIAM and LUNA (BOSWORTH)

---

[724] Article, "A Double Wedding," *Canton Commercial Advertiser*, Canton, New York, Wednesday, 1 October 1902, vol. 30 #26, page 1, column 6.

[725] Frances C. Chapman, New York Death Certificate # 07289.

[726] Son Howard C. Briggs, New Hampshire Death Record, filed 13 May 1903.

[727] Mrs. Addie E. Briggs, New Hampshire Death Certificate # 129/494.

[728] Chas Briggs household, 1900 U.S. cens., Saint Lawrence Co., N.Y., pop. sched., Potsdam, SD 6, ED 135, sheet 2B, dw. 50, fam. 52.

BRIGGS, d. Canaan 9 June 1927.[729]
Children of CHARLES and ADDIE (CHAPMAN) BRIGGS:
a. *Luna B. Briggs*, b. N.Y. 1 Sept. 1878; d. 2 June 1893; bur. Rensselaer Falls Cem., Rensselaer Falls, N.Y.[730]
b. *Henry Axtell Briggs*, b. Lisbon[731] 10 Sept. 1881;[732] m. abt. 1901[733] *Harriet May Kirkelly*, b. Potsdam, N.Y., 1881.[734]
    Children of *Henry* and *Harriet (Kirkelly) Briggs*:
    1. Stanley Howard Briggs, b. Oswego, N.Y., 1900; m. Enfield, N. H., 26 Oct. 1918 Vietta May Niles, b. Orford, N. H., 29 May 1899, dau. of George D. and Nellie E. (Smith) Niles.[735]
        Children of Stanley and Vietta (Niles) Briggs:
        a. Gordon Walter Briggs, b. Enfield 1 Sept. 1919.[736]
        b. Natalie Mae Briggs, b. Enfield 17 April 1922.[737]
        c. Jeannette Helen Briggs, b. Enfield 30 Jan. 1926.[738]
        d. Arline M. Briggs, b. N. H.[739] 19 June 1927.[740]
        e. Virginia R. Briggs, b. N.H.[741] 27 Oct. 1928.[742]

---

[729] Charles Barr Briggs New Hampshire Death Certificate # 168.
[730] Cady, *Rennslaer Falls Cemetery Inventory*.
    William Briggs household, 1880 U.S. cens., St. Lawrence Co., N.Y., pop. sched., Lisbon, SD 7, ED 139, p. 14B, dw. 50, fam. 52.
[731] Birthplace from son Charles's marriage record: Briggs-Lovering marriage, Enfield, New Hampshire, filed 20 April 1922.
[732] Henry Axtell Briggs, Ancestry.com, World War I Registration Card.
[733] Henry Briggs household, 1910 U.S. census, Grafton County, New Hampshire, population schedule, Canaan, SD [], ED 80, sheet 12A, dwelling 238, family 250.
[734] Birthplace from son Charles's marriage record: Briggs-Lovering Marriage Record, Enfield, New Hampshire, filed 20 April 1922, Bureau of Vital Records, Concord, New Hampshire. Birth year from 1910, 1920, and 1930 census records.
[735] Briggs-Niles marriage, Enfield, New Hampshire, Record #335.
    Vietta Briggs, Ancestry.com, *Social Security Death Index*.
[736] George McKenzie Roberts, compiler, *The Vital and Cemetery Records of the Town of Enfield, Grafton County, New Hampshire* (?:?, 1957), 234, 235.
[737] Ibid.
[738] Ibid.
[739] Stanley H. Briggs household, 1930 U.S. cens., Carroll Co., N.H., pop. sched., Wolfeboro, SD 1, ED 21, sheet 7A, dw. 127, fam. 132.
[740] Arline M. Stieh, Ancestry.com, *Social Security Death Index*.
[741] Stanley H. Briggs household, 1930 U.S. cens., Carroll Co., N.H., pop. sched., Wolfeboro, SD 1, ED 21, sheet 7A, dw. 127, fam. 132.
[742] Virginia R Susee, *U.S. Public Records Index Record*, online <ancestry.com>.

2. Charles Clifton Briggs, b. Enfield 21 June 1903;[743] m. Lebanon, N. H., 25 March 1922 Grace F. Lovering, b. Enfield 3 Feb. 1905, dau. of Ernest D. and Sadie B. (Dennis) Lovering.[744]

Children of Charles and Grace (Lovering) Briggs:
a. Lorraine Harriette Briggs, b. Lebanon, N. H.,[745] 9 Nov. 1922.[746]

b. Pauline Briggs, b. N. H. abt. Feb. 1926.[747]

c. *Howard C. Briggs*, b. Lisbon 13 March 1884; d. Enfield 10 May 1903; bur. W. Canaan Cem., Canaan, N.H.[748]

d. *Alvah E. Briggs*, b. 29 Dec. 1887; d. 10 Dec. 1888; bur. Rensselaer Falls Cem.[749]

ii. SUSAN BELLE CHAPMAN, b. Moriah, N.Y., July 1858; d. Canaan, N.H., 19 May 1916;[750] m. abt. 1895 LESLIE ERNEST GARDNER,[751] b. Canton, N.Y., 18 March 1862, son of HARVEY B. and JANE A. (BENTLEY) GARDNER.[752] Resided on farm in Enfield, N.H., 1900;[753] merchant in Canaan 1910, nine dwellings from sister Addie.[754] No issue.

iii. EVA CHAPMAN, b. abt. 1864; d. 22 June 1868; bur. Rensselaer Falls Cem.[755]

iv. MAY CHAPMAN, b. Lisbon 11 May 1868;[756] m. abt. 1897

---

743 Roberts, *The Vital and Cemetery Records of the Town of Enfield*, 234, 235.
744 Briggs-Lovering New Hampshire Marriage Record.
745 Cantlin - Briggs New Hampshire Marriage Record, Lebanon.
746 Lorraine B. Cantlin, Ancestry.com, *Social Security Death Index*.
747 Henry A. Briggs household, 1930 U.S. cens., Grafton Co., N.H., pop. sched., Lebanon, SD 1, ED 27, sheet 17B, dw. 299, fam. 346.
748 Howard C. Briggs, New Hampshire Death Record.
749 Cady, *Rennslaer Falls Cemetery Inventory*.
750 Susan Belle Gardner, New Hampshire Death Record.
751 Leslie Gardner household, 1900 U.S. census, Grafton County, New Hampshire, population schedule, Enfield, SD [], ED 57, sheet 11B, dwelling 200, family 226; National Archives micropublication T623, roll 946.
752 Leslie Ernest Gardner, New Hampshire Death Record #112 93D.
753 Leslie Gardner household, 1900 U.S. cens., Grafton Co., N.H., pop. sched., Enfield, SD [], ED 57, sheet 11B, dw. 200, fam. 226.
754 Leslie Gardner household, 1910 U.S. cens., Grafton Co., N.H., pop. sched., Canaan, SD [], ED 80, sheet 12A, dw. 238, fam. 249.
755 Cady. *Rennslaer Falls Cemetery Inventory*.
756 May VanWaters, New York Death Record, Certificate #61998 .

CHARLES CORNELIUS VANWATERS,[757] b. Canton, N.Y., 3 Dec. 1854, son of ORIN and SARAH A. (BROWN) VANWATERS, d. Ogdensburg, N.Y., 25 Aug. 1924, bur. Rensselaer Falls Cem.[758] Charles was a physician in Canton, N.Y. 1910;[759] Ogdensburg 1920.[760] No issue.

v.   BLANCHE CHAPMAN, b. Lisbon[761] 26 April 1871;[762] m. 24 April 1895 BENJAMIN FRANKLIN "FRANK" MORRISON, b. Rensselaer Falls, 26 April 1868, son of BENJAMIN FRANK and EMELINE (SPOONER) MORRISON.[763]

Child of FRANK and BLANCHE (CHAPMAN) MORRISON:

a. *Vernon Frank Morrison*, b. Rensselaer Falls   28 April 1897;[764] m. abt. 1918[765] *Vida V. Bradley*, b. Canada 21 April 1894, dau. of *Alva Harry* and *Eva May (Thompson) Bradley*.[766]

Child of *Vernon* and *Vida (Bradley) Morrison*:

1.   Jane Elizabeth Morrison, b. N.Y. 22 June 1924.[767]

vi.   NELLA MAUDE CHAPMAN, b. N.Y. May 1876;[768] m. Rensselaer Falls 24 Sept. 1902 HENRY EDWARD RIVENBURGH,[769] b. N.Y.

---

[757]   Charles Van Waters household, 1900 U.S. cens., St. Lawrence Co., N.Y., pop. sched., Canton, SD 40, ED 78, sheet 12A, dw. 268, fam. 269.

[758]   Charles Cornelius VanWaters, New York Death Record #46417.

[759]   Charles VanWaters household, 1910 U.S. census, St. Lawrence County, New York, population schedule, Canton district 113, SD 10, ED 113, sheet 8B, dwelling 230, family 235; National Archives micropublication T624, roll 1074.

[760]   Charles VanWaters household, 1920 U.S. census, St. Lawrence County, New York, population schedule, Ogdensburg, SD 12, ED 155, sheet 8B, dwelling 116, family 137; National Archives micropublication T625, roll 1260.

[761]   Obituary, "Mrs. Morrison Passes Away At Rensselaer Falls," *Ogdensburg Journal*, Ogdensburg, New York, clipping from Connie Palmer, secretary of Rensselaer Falls Cemetery, Rensselaer Falls, New York.

[762]   Cady, *Rennslaer Falls Cemetery Inventory*.

[763]   "Frank Morrison, Rensselaer Falls, . . .," *Ogdensburg Journal*.

[764]   Vernon Morrison, New York Death Record, Certificate # 48375

[765]   Vernon Morrison household, 1920 U.S. cens., Jefferson Co., N.Y., pop. sched., Theresa, SD 13, ED 40, sheet 4B, dw. 120, fam. 128.

[766]   Vida B. Morrison, Vermont Death Record, Certificate #00930 Division of Vital Statistics, Burlington, Vermont.

[767]   Jane M. Peet, *Vermont Death Index*, Ancestry.com.

[768]   Francis Chapman household, 1900 U.S. cens., St. Lawrence Co., N.Y., pop. sched., Potsdam, SD 6, ED 135, sheet 2B, dw. 50, fam. 52.

[769]   Article, "A Double Wedding," *Canton Commercial Advertiser*.

May 1864,[770] d. bef. 1920. Widowed Nella was living alone in Schodack, N.Y., 1920, not found in 1930.[771] No issue.

vii. FRANCES D. CHAPMAN, b. Lisbon 5 Dec. 1877;[772] m. Rensselaer Falls 24 Sept. 1902 JAMES V. CRAWFORD,[773] b. Morristown 22 Jan. 1858 son of DAVID and MARGARET (MAYBERY) CRAWFORD,[774] d. 30 Sept. 1921, bur. Pine Hill Cem., Morristown, N.Y. James was a retail dry goods merchant.[775] The widowed Frances lived alone in Morristown in 1930, next door to her stepson, JAMES G. CRAWFORD.[776] No issue.

Addie E. (Axtell) Whittlesey (1840–1884)

47. ADDIE E. AXTELL *(ELIZABETH[6] E. AMADEN, JACOB[5], JACOB[4] AMIDOWN, HENRY[3], PHILIP[2], ROGER[1] AMADOWNE)* was born at Antwerp, New York, on 12 July 1840. She died at Lisbon, New York, on 5 March 1884.[777] She married at Lisbon[778] on 20 March 1876 FRANKLIN WHITTLESEY.[779] Franklin was born at Stockbridge, Massachusetts, on 5 April 1818. His parents were ASAPH and CLARINDA (RICHARDS) WHITTLESEY. He died at Geneva, New York, on 5 October 1879.[780]

Addie was born in Antwerp, but grew up in Moriah, New York, near Lake Champlain. In 1851, when Addie was eleven, the family moved across the state to Lisbon, near the St. Lawrence River and the

---

[770] Boarder with Myra Nelson household, 1900 U.S. cens., Washington Co., N.Y., pop. sched., Granville, SD 5, ED 127, sheet 19B, dw. 385, fam. 411.

[771] Nella Rivenburgh household, 1920 U.S. census, Rensselaer County, New York, population schedule, Schodack district 43, SD 11, ED 43, sheet 3B, dwelling 55, family 70; National Archives micropublication T625, roll 1256.

[772] Frances D. Crawford, New York Death Record, Certificate #72204.

[773] Article, "A Double Wedding," *Canton Commercial Advertiser.*

[774] James V Crawford, New York Death Record, Certificate #51568.

Mother's maiden name from: "Margaret Maybery, wife of David Crawford," Anne M. Cady, compiler, *Inventory of Edwardsville Cemetery, Morristown, New York.*

[775] James V Crawford household, 1910 U.S. cens., St. Lawrence Co., N.Y., pop. sched., Morristown, SD 12, ED 147, sheet 1B, dw. 115, fam. 115.

[776] Frances D Crawford household, 1930 U.S. cens., St. Lawrence Co., N.Y., pop. sched., Morristown, SD 1, ED 45-49, sheet 4B, dw. 111, fam. 118.

[777] Addie E. Axtell Wittlesey, New York Death Record, no page #, entry #17.

[778] Charles Barney Whittelsey, *Genealogy of the Whittelsey-Whittlesey Family, 2nd Edition* (New York, London: Whittlesey House, 1941), 274.

[779] Axtell, *Axtell Genealogy,* 78.

[780] Whittelsey, *Whittlesey-Whittlesey Family,* 274.

international border with Canada. The next year her baby brother, Harlon, died. Then Addie's mother, Eliza, died from apoplexy at the family dinner table in 1856, when Addie was sixteen. The next year her older brother, Henry, died. John, the baby of the family died sometime between 1850 and 1856. By the end of the decade the family of seven had dwindled to a family of three. Did these tragedies make Addie hesitant to start a family and not marry until she was thirty-six years old?

By 1860 Addie's father had married again to a woman with two younger children. Addie was working as a domestic.[781] The family was still in Lisbon in 1870. Two young farm laborers were boarding with them.[782] Then in 1876 Addie married the much older widower Franklin Whittlesey. She was thirty-six; he was fifty-eight.

Soon after Franklin's birth, the Whittlesey family had removed from Stockbridge, Massachusetts, to Galen, New York. There Franklin was a successful metal merchant, selling tin and glass in 1860.[783] He and his first wife, Hannah, had four children, one of whom died young. By 1870 the eldest had married leaving them with the two youngest children. They were living in Rochester, New York, on the south shore of Lake Erie.[784] Hannah died the following year, and Franklin found himself single again, but with two children. How he managed to meet Addie, who lived over 200 miles away, is uncertain. However, they married at Lisbon in 1876. Franklin survived only three more years. He died in 1879 at age sixty-one. Franklin was a mason and belonged to an insurance program called the Western N. Y. Masonic Relief Association. They listed his death as being from inflammation of the liver and bowels.[785]

By 1880 Addie was head of the household in Rochester, caring for

---

[781] Henry E. Axtell household, 1860 U.S. census, Saint Lawrence County, New York, population schedule, Lisbon, page 7, dwelling 39, family 36; National Archives micropublication M653, roll 854.

[782] Henry E. Axtell household, 1870 U.S. cens., St. Lawrence Co., N.Y., pop. sched., Lisbon, p. 62, dw. 483, fam. 483.

[783] Franklin Whitley household, 1860 U.S. census, Wayne County, New York, population schedule, Galen, page 117, dwelling 125, family 919; National Archives micropublication M653, roll 876.

[784] Franklin Whittlesey household, 1870 U.S. census, Monroe County, New York, population schedule, Rochester 3rd ward, page 94, dwelling 783, family 768; National Archives micropublication M593, roll 969.

[785] Richard T. Halsey, *Deaths from the Western N.Y. Masonic Relief Association*, online, <rootsweb.com/~nymonroe/vr/relief.htm>.

Franklin's two children, now in their late teens: Frances and Watson.[786] But she did not outlive Franklin by long. She returned home to Lisbon and died in 1884 at age forty-three of "some heart trouble." Her death record indicates that she was buried at "Ogd," which is probably Ogdensburg, New York.[787] She had no children. Interestingly her cousin Morton Amaden named a son Edwin Axtell Amaden, who in turn named his daughter Addie Axtell Amaden, born in 1887.

---

[786]   Addie E. Whittlesey household, 1880 U.S. census, Monroe County, New York, population schedule, Rochester, SD 10, ED 77, page 20, dwelling 783, family 768; National Archives micropub. T9, roll 862.

[787]   Addie E. Axtell Wittlesey, New York Death Record, no page #, entry #17.

Chapter 6 -- Seventh Generation
Grandchildren of John Ameden

Ann Rebecca (Nichols) Dexter (1832-1889)

48. ANN REBECCA NICHOLS[7] (*IRENA[6] AMEDEN, JOHN[5], JACOB[4] AMIDOWN, HENRY[3], PHILIP[2], ROGER[1] AMADOWNE*) was probably born at Lake George, New York, on 21 October 1832.[1] She died on 11 March 1889.[2] She married between 1 June 1849 and 31 May 1850 to JOEL DEXTER.[3] He was born at New York in about 1821,[4] probably the only son of JOEL DEXTER.[5] He died at Glens Falls, New York, on 11 October 1897.[6]

Rebecca grew up in the town of Caldwell. She is likely the young girl in her father's household there in the 1840 census.

Joel probably grew up in Queensbury, just seven houses from Rebecca's grandfather, John Ameden. In the 1830 census for Joel Dexter Sr., there is only one boy, aged five to ten (probably young Joel), along with two teenage girls. The adults, probably the parents, are both aged forty to fifty.[7]

In 1840, Joel Dexter Sr. was still living in Queensbury with his presumed wife, a boy aged fifteen to twenty (Joel Jr.), a young woman aged twenty to thirty, and a girl aged five to ten.[8]

By 1850, young Joel's mother may have died. His father was living with the newlyweds, young Joel and Rebecca, in Queensbury. The census says the newlyweds were married within the previous year. The official date of the 1850 census was June 1, regardless of when the census taker visited the household, so the marriage must have taken place between 1 June 1849 and 31 May 1850. Joel Jr. was listed as a farmer, owning $1200 worth of real estate.[9]

---

1   Ann R. Dexter tombstone, Lake George Cem.; transcribed by John Austin. The tombstone gives her age as 57 yrs, 4 mo, 18 days.

2   Ibid.

3   Joel Dexter household, 1850 U.S. cens., Warren Co., N.Y., pop. sched., Queensbury, p. 112, dw. 450, fam. 467.

4   Ibid.

5   Joel Dexter hhd, 1830 U.S. cens., Warren Co., N.Y., Queensbury, p. 67:12.

6   Austin email to Nancy K. Mullen, 16 July 2005.

7   Joel Dexter hhd, 1830 U.S. cens., Warren Co., N.Y., Queensbury, p. 67:12.

8   Joel Dexter hhd, 1840 U.S. cens., Warren Co., N.Y., Queensbury, p. 66:29.

9   Joel Dexter household, 1850 U.S. cens., Warren Co., N.Y., pop. sched., Queensbury, p. 112, dw. 450, fam. 467.

By 1860 the family had relocated to Rebecca's hometown of Caldwell. Joel's real estate value had declined to $200. But the family had grown. Amelia had been born in about 1851; Sylvester in about 1853; Irena in 1856 but died in 1858; Emma "Anna" in 1858; and Annette in September 1859.[10] Note that Annette's tombstone of 1877 gives her birth as 27 April 1860, but the 1860 census says she was ten-twelfths of a year by July 1860. The 1860 census is more reliable.

By 1880 the children had left home. Joel and Rebecca still lived in Caldwell. By 1880 Joel was done with farming and was working as a charcoal burner, i.e., a worker who made charcoal.[11] Rebecca died in 1889, at age fifty-seven. She is buried in Lake George Cemetery.[12] Joel died in 1897 at age seventy-six at the home of his younger surviving daughter Anna Burnett.[13] He is buried with Rebecca.[14]

Children of JOEL and REBECCA (NICHOLS) DEXTER:[15]

i. AMELIA⁸ F. DEXTER, b. N.Y. March 1851;[16] d. aft. 1930;[17] m. abt 1867 STEPHEN KENYON,[18] b. N.Y. abt. 1835. Amelia was Stephen's second wife; he had a dau. Carrie from his first marriage: Carrie b. abt. 1864, d. 1930, m. abt. 1891 BYRON JACKSON, b. N.Y. Oct. 1853, d. 1901.[19] Amelia lived South Glens Falls 1930.[20]

Child of STEPHEN and AMELIA (DEXTER) KENYON:

a. *Willie Kenyon*, b. N.Y. abt. 1870;[21] d. bef. 1900.[22] No

---

10   Joel Dexter household, 1860 U.S. cens., Warren Co., N.Y., pop. sched., Caldwell, p. 7, dw. 52, fam. [].

11   Joel Dexter household, 1880 U.S. cens., Warren Co., N.Y., pop. sched., Caldwell, SD 6, ED 112, p. 1, dw. 8, fam. 8.

12   Ann R. Dexter tombstone, Lake George Cem.

13   Joel Dexter obituary, *Glens Falls Daily Times*, 11 October 1897, page 8.

14   Joel Dexter tombstone, Lake George Cem.

15   Joel Dexter household, 1860 U.S. cens., Warren Co., N.Y., pop. sched., Caldwell, SD 6, ED 112, p. 1, dw. 8, fam. 8.

16   Steven Kenyon household, 1900 U.S. cens., Washington Co., N.Y., pop. sched., Fort Edward, SD 5, ED 123, p. 5A, dw. 106, fam. 110.

17   Ibid.

18   Ibid.

19   Byron Jackson tombstone, South Side Cemetery, South Glens Falls, Town of Moreau, Saratoga County, New York; <www.rootsweb.com/~nysarato/ssideSGF.htm>.

20   Amelia Kenyon household, 1930 U.S. census, Saratoga County, New York, population schedule, Moreau, SD 5, ED 46-30, sh 24A, dw. 524, fam 619; National Archives micropublication T626, roll 1261.

21   Joel Dexter household, 1880 U.S. cens., Warren Co., N.Y., pop. sched.,

records found of marriage or children.

ii.   SYLVESTER B. DEXTER, b. N.Y. abt. 1853; d. bef. 1897.[23]

iii.   IRENA DEXTER, b. N.Y. 4 May 1856; d. 13 Nov. 1858; bur. Lake George Cem.[24]

iv.   EMMA ANNA DEXTER, b. N.Y. Feb. 1858; m. abt. 1877 ALONZO BURNETT, b. Ashfield, Mass., 7 June 1844, son of LIONEL and MINERVA (RICE) BURNETT,[25] d. bef. 1920.[26] Res. Glens Falls, N.Y., (1900),[27] Ludlow, Mass., (1910),[28] San Francisco with dau. Martha (1920-30).[29]

Child of ALONZO and EMMA (DEXTER) BURNETT:

a.   *Martha Dexter Burnett,* b. N.Y. Sept. 1892;[30] m. abt. 1915 *Charles Wesley Hicks,* b. Pottersville, N.Y., 20 July 1889,[31] son of *Charles H.* and *Amelia E. (___) Hicks.[32]* Resided Ludlow, Mass. (1910),[33] San Francisco (1920-30).

Child of *Charles* and *Martha (Burnett) Hicks:*

Caldwell, SD 6, ED 112, p. 1, dw. 8, fam. 8.

22   Steven Kenyon household, 1900 U.S. cens., Washington Co., N.Y., pop. sched., Fort Edward, SD 5, ED 123, p. 5A, dw. 106, fam. 110.

23   Joel Dexter obituary, *Glens Falls Daily Times,* 11 October 1897, page 8.

24   Irena Dexter tombstone, Lake George Cem, transcribed by John Austin.

25   ?, *Vital Records of Ashfield, Massachusetts, To The Year 1850* (Boston: New England Historic Genealogical Society, 1942), 26, 142.

26   Charles Hicks household, 1920 U.S. census, San Francisco, California, population schedule, San Francisco, SD 4, ED 294, sheet 13B, 451 11th Avenue; National Archives micropublication T625, roll 141.

27   Alonzo Burnett household, 1900 U.S. cens., Warren Co., N.Y., pop. sched., Glens Falls, SD 5, ED 107, sheet 21A, dw. 384, fam. 483.

28   Alonzo Burnett household, 1910 U.S. census, Hampden County, Massachusetts, population schedule, Ludlow, SD 119, ED 550, sheet 12B; National Archives micropublication T624, roll 589.

29   Charles Hicks household, 1930 U.S. census, San Francisco, California, population schedule, San Francisco, SD 7, ED 38-192, sheet 2A, dwelling 12, family 25; National Archives micropublication T626, roll 201.

30   Joel Dexter household, 1880 U.S. cens., Warren Co., N.Y., pop. sched., Caldwell, SD 6, ED 112, p. 1, dw. 8, fam. 8.

31   Charles W. Hicks household, 1930 U.S. cens., San Francisco, Calif., pop. sched., San Francisco, SD 7, ED 38-192, sheet 2A, dwelling 12, family 25.

     Charles Wesley Hicks entry, Ancestry.com, *World War I Registration Cards.*

32   Charles H. Hicks household, 1900 U.S. census, Warren Co., N.Y., pop. sched. Chester, SD 5, ED 94, sheet 10B, dw. 228, fam. 234.

33   Alonzo Burnett household, 1910 U.S. cens., Hampden Co., Mass., pop. sched., Ludlow, SD 119, ED 550, sheet 12B, dw. 8, fam. 8.

1. Virginia D. Hicks, b. San Francisco Co. 17 Nov. 1915.[34]
v. ANNETTE "NETTIE" DEXTER, b. N.Y. 27 Sept. 1859; d. 27 Nov. 1877.[35]

Oscar F. Nichols (1836–1907)

49. OSCAR F. NICHOLS[7] *(IRENA[6] AMEDEN, JOHN[5], JACOB[4] AMIDOWN, HENRY[3], PHILIP[2], ROGER[1] AMADOWNE)* was born at Lake George, New York, in March 1836. He died at Caldwell, New York, on 7 February 1907.[36] He married before 15 August 1870 to EMALINE "EMMA" CADY. She was born at Fort Ann, New York, on 27 June 1846, the daughter of REYNOLDS and MARY (ROBINSON) CADY.[37] She died at Lake George on 28 September 1912.[38]

Oscar was born in the village of Lake George, where he grew up. He was enumerated there with his parents in 1840 and 1850. His father died in 1853 when Oscar was still only sixteen.

Emma grew up in Queensbury,[39] the third of seven children. When she was about eight years old the family relocated to Barnard, Vermont.[40] Perhaps it was there Emma married on 3 October 1860 SARDINE U. COWDREY, son of ISAAC JEROME and LAURA (NEWTON) COWDERY and had a boy, REYNOLDS COWDREY, on 18 December 1863.[41] For whatever reason, the marriage didn't last. By 1869 Sardine remarried to Christina Emerson. The 1870 census shows Sardine and Christina raising the boy, along with eleven-year-old Charles Emerson, probably Christina's son from an earlier marriage.[42] Emma did not even admit she had birthed Reynolds to the census takers over the subsequent decades.

Oscar continued to live with his mother Irena and sister Adelia

---

34   *California Birth Index 1905-1995*, Ancestry.com.
35   Nettie Dexter tombstone, Lake George Cem., transcribed by John Austin.
36   Oscar F. Nichols death certificate #548, Lake George Town Clerk's Office.
37   Hawley-Nichols marriage record, Lake George Town Clerk's Office.
38   Emma Hawley Nichols death cert. #712, Lake George Town Clerk's Ofc.
39   Reynolds Cady household, 1850 U.S. cens., Warren Co., N.Y., pop. sched., Queensbury, p. 65B, dw. 144, fam. 151.
40   Reynolds Cady household, 1860 U.S. cens., Windsor Co., Vt., pop. sched., Barnard, p. 86, dw. 751, fam. 733.
41   Mary Bryant Melling, *Cowdrey-Cowdery-Cowdray Genealogy* (?, Frank Allaben Genealogical Company, 1911), 261.
42   Sardine Condry household, 1870 U.S. census, Windsor county, Vermont, population schedule, Stockbridge, page 16, dwelling 139, household 139; National Archives micropublication M593, roll 1629.

until his mother divided her 100-foot-square lot in half on 3 August 1870, reserving the north half for Oscar at her death.[43] He must have built himself a house there before his mother executed the deed, because the 1870 census, taken on 15 August 1870, shows him living in his own house there with his new bride Emma.[44] By this time he was working as a joiner. A joiner was similar to a cabinetmaker, but made more inexpensive items than did a cabinetmaker.[45]

On 26 May 1873 Oscar seems to have taken steps to protect Emma's future by selling his interest in the lot back to his mother, who promptly sold it to Emma, ensuring that title to the property would pass to Emma at Irena's death. By the 1875 New York state census, Oscar was listed as a builder.[46]

In 1875, after the state census was taken, Emma had a son whom they named Oscar, for his father. A month after Oscar was born, on 2 August, his mother bought an L-shaped lot that adjoined Irena's property on the north and west. The property was about twice as big as Irena's lot. Emma bought it from Eliza and John Gillis of Montreal, Canada, for $300.[47] A week later on 9 August, she sold a slice off the northern end of the lot. The slice was thirty-four feet along the road and 150 feet deep. It lay adjacent to the James H. Carpenter Hotel. James H. Carpenter bought the slice for $100.[48] The net result of the two transactions was an extension of Irena's 100-square foot lot to a combined property of about 150 foot square or about one-half acre. On 20 February 1877, Emma again bought a lot from the Gillises when she paid $300 for a 150-foot square lot on the west side of the Plank Road.[49] It may have adjoined Emma's existing property to the south, though that has not been confirmed. Now the combined properties, including Irena's property, totaled about one acre.

The 1880 census shows Oscar, Emma, and little Oscar living next door to Irena and Oscar's sister, Adelia, now married to Orville

43   Warren County Deeds, Book 22:239-40.
44   Oscar Nichols household, 1870 U.S. cens., Warren Co., NY, pop sched, Caldwell town, page 5, dwelling 25, family 22.
45   Evans, *A to Zax*, 151.
46   Oscar Nichols household, 1875 New York state census, Warren County, population schedule, Caldwell township, household 11; reported in email from John Austin, 16 July 2005.
47   Warren County Deeds, Book 32:268.
48   Warren County Deeds, Book 31:34.
49   Warren County Deeds, Book 33:279-80.

Lockwood. Oscar, now a carpenter, reported that he had been out of work for two months because of a broken arm.[50]

Irena died in 1884. The north half of her lot now belonged to Emma. Oscar's grief did not prevent him from serving his community as one of the town assessors in 1885.[51] In 1900 Oscar and Emma were still living in the same house. They may have expanded the house over the years. In 1912 it was described as a two-story house of thirteen rooms with a mansard roof. Young Oscar was gone. Instead there was twenty-two-year-old Edith who was listed as a daughter, but who was not in the 1880 census when she would have been three years old. Perhaps they adopted her sometime after 1880. Or perhaps she was a servant girl, incorrectly recorded by the census taker. There were also three boarders living in the house in 1900.[52]

Oscar died in 1907 at age seventy of senile debility. He was buried in Lake George Cemetery in Caldwell.[53] In 1910 Emma was living alone, working at a boarding house. She was no longer living next door to her sister-in-law, Adelia Lockwood, but she did own the property. The houses on both sides of Adelia were rented out in 1910, so Emma may have rented out the house where she and Oscar had lived together for so long and moved to a smaller seven-room house in the rear of Canada Street that she also owned.[54]

In Emma's widowhood, she married an old family friend, Charles Hawley, at Lake George on 6 April 1911. Charles's son, Fred Hawley, had been one of Oscar's pallbearers. Their marriage was short-lived. Emma died in September 1912 at age sixty-six from acute nephritis. Her son Oscar served as executor. And finally Emma was able to acknowledge her son, Reynolds Cowdrey. Her will names him as her son and divides her property among her husband, sons, grandchildren from both sons, Cowdrey's wife "Jennie"and Emma's friend, Laura Ameden, wife of Oscar Nichols's first cousin, Eugene Ameden. Oscar's wife, Winnifred, was ignored by the provisions of

---

[50] Oscar Nichols household, 1880 U.S. census, Warren Co., NY, pop. sched., Caldwell town, ED 112, SD 6, page 18, dwelling 214, family 214.

[51] Smith, *History of Warren County*, 569.

[52] Oscar Nichols household, 1900 U.S. cens., Warren Co., N.Y., pop. sched., Caldwell, SD 5, ED 93, sheet 7B, dw. 174, fam. 178.

[53] Oscar Nichols burial notice, *Morning Star*, Glens Falls, N.Y., 11 February 1907; reported in email from John Austin, 16 July 2005.

[54] Emma Nichols household, 1910 U.S. cens., Warren Co., N.Y., pop. sched., Caldwell, SD 190, ED 150, sheet 4B, dw.102, fam.108.

the will. Perhaps Emma did not approve of Winnifred, or perhaps Emma had provided for Winnifred during her lifetime. Jennie Cowdrey received all Emma's silver, furs, and jewelry not specifically allocated. The inventory of Emma's real estate listed three lots, including one with the house on Canada Street, worth $4700. Her personal estate was inventoried as: cash of $79.64, household furniture of $200, clothing of $50, and two diamond rings from her son Oscar worth $70.[55] Emma is buried in Lake George Cemetery.[56]

Children of OSCAR and EMMA (CADY) NICHOLS:

i. OSCAR JAY NICHOLS, b. N.Y. 3 July 1875;[57] m. 1) 1898 MILA J. (___), b. April 1876, d. bef. 1910; m. 2) Sept. 1909 WINNIFRED RICE, b. Westford, Vt., 2 Feb. 1875, dau. of HENRY MARTIN and MARION (MACOMBER) RICE.[58] Resided Plattsburgh, N.Y., 1930.[59]

> Child of OSCAR and WINNIFRED (RICE) NICHOLS:[60]
>
> a. *David Oscar Nichols,* b. N.Y. 28 Dec. 1911.

ii. EDITH O. NICHOLS, b. N.Y. Dec. 1877.[61] Presumed to be adopted. No record found after 1900 census.

Adelia A. (Nichols) Lockwood (1843–1915)

50. ADELIA A. NICHOLS[7] *(IRENA[6] AMEDEN, JOHN[5], JACOB[4] AMIDOWN, HENRY[3], PHILIP[2], ROGER[1] AMADOWNE)* was born in Caldwell, New York, in July 1843.[62] She died 12 October 1915.[63]

---

55   Emma Nichols Hawley estate, Surrogate's Court, Warren County Municipal Center, Route U.S. 9, Lake George, New York.
56   Emma Hawley death notice, *Post-Star,* Glens Falls, N.Y., 28 September 1912; reported in email from John Austin, 18 July 2005.
57   Oscar Jay Nichols. Ancestry.com, *World War I Draft Registration Card.*
58   Warren Forsythe, email to Chris Amaden, RE: Winnifred E. Rice, 8 November 2004.
59   Oscar J. Nichols household, 1930 U.S. census, Clinton Co., New York, population schedule, Plattsburgh – 4th ward, SD 1, ED 10-32, sheet 12B, dwelling 149, family 123; National Archives micropublication T626, roll 1417.
60   Ibid.
61   Oscar Nichols household, 1900 U.S. cens., Warren Co., N.Y., pop. sched., Caldwell town, SD 5, ED 93, sheet 7B, dwelling 174, family 178.
62   Adelia Longwood household, 1900 U.S. cens., Warren Co., N.Y., pop. sched., Caldwell, SD 5, ED 93, sheet 7B, dw. 173, fam. 177.
63   Orville H. Lockwood and Adelia A. Lockwood, widow, Civil War Pension Application File WC 453306.

She married at Bolton on 23 July 1866 ORVILLE H. LOCKWOOD.[64] He was born at Caldwell, New York, on 31 January 1843, the son of LEWIS and MARY ANN (JENKS) LOCKWOOD.[65] He died at Caldwell on 22 July 1897.[66]

Adelia grew up in Caldwell, where she was enumerated with her parents in 1850 and 1860. Orville's boyhood was spent in Glens Falls, where his family lived in 1850.[67] When he grew to manhood, he was five feet nine inches tall, with light complexion, light hair, and brown eyes, working as a farmer.[68]

War came, and Orville enlisted. It was 6 June 1861 when he took himself to Troy, New York, and was mustered in to fight with Company I of the 22nd regiment of New York Volunteers for two years as a private. The unit left New York on 28 June, headed to Washington to bolster the capitol's defenses.

In March 1862 they advanced on Manassas, Virginia. In this campaign, Orville contracted rheumatism, which caused a general debility that never healed. He was treated at Judiciary Square Hospital in Washington for a time. In April his unit advanced on Falmouth, Virginia. They were stationed at Fredericksburg until 25 May when they advanced on Richmond. In June they campaigned against Thomas "Stonewall" Jackson. In July they were at Falmouth and Fredericksburg. They fought in the battles of 2nd Bull Run on 28-30 August, a Southern victory that cost fifteen thousand Federal casualties and nine thousand Southern casualties. They fought at Antietam, Maryland, on 16-17 September, the bloody battle that ended Lee's first effort to invade the north. They fought at Fredericksburg on 12-15 December, in the carnage that cost twelve thousand Federal lives and fifteen hundred Southern.

On 20-24 January 1863 General Ambrose E. Burnside tried to move his men upstream beyond Lee's position at Fredericksburg. Three days of steady, icy rain turned the roads into bottomless mud. The attempted march became forever known as the "Mud March,"

---

64   Ibid.
65   Death certificate, Orville H. Lockwood.
      Orville H. Lockwood, Civil War Pension Application File WC 453306. Birth is calculated from reported age of 54-5-22.
66   Ibid.
67   Lewis Lockwood household, 1850 U.S. cens., Warren Co., N.Y., pop. sched., Queensbury, village of Glens Falls, p. 30, dw. 96, fam. 105.
68   Orville H. Lockwood, Civil War Pension Application File WC 453306.

and the demoralized army had to return to camp. They camped at Belle Plains until 27 April. They fought the battle of Chancellorsville 1-5 May, a brilliant Southern victory by an army half the size of the Federal army, but a devastating loss to the South when General Jackson was accidentally killed by Southern troops. Orville's whole regiment mustered out 19 June 1863 after losing eleven officers and sixty-two men killed, and one officer and twenty-eight men dead from disease.

Orville's enlistment had expired, but the war still raged, so he re-enlisted. He signed up on 9 August 1863 at Schroon, New York, as a private in Company D, 2nd regiment New York Veteran Cavalry. His unit again started out at Washington, defending the capitol. While his first enlistment had been spent in Virginia and Maryland, participating in the major battles of the war, his second enlistment was spent near the Gulf, involved in obscure expeditions. Orville was hospitalized on 6 January 1864 for "gonorrhora." In February 1864 the brigade fought in the Red River Campaign, a fruitless effort to cross Louisiana on the Red River and invade Texas to gather cotton along the way. This frivolous campaign was devised in the belief that Napoleon III would give up his designs on Mexico if the North held Texas and the Rio Grande. After the Red River Campaign failed, the cavalry unit spent the remainder of the war in little known expeditions in Louisiana, Mississippi, Florida, and Alabama. Orville was again hospitalized on 3 January 1865 with conjunctivitis. The regiment mustered out at Talladega, Alabama, on 8 November 1865.[69]

Once the war was over, Orville and Adelia married at Bolton in 1866. Bolton lies eight miles north of Caldwell along the shore of Lake George. Why Bolton? Perhaps Adelia and Orville were both working in Bolton at the time. Two years later in 1867 their first son, Charles, was born. In September 1869 Alvah was born.

By 1870 Adelia's father had died. Orville, Adelia, and the two children were living with her mother in the family homestead in Caldwell. Orville was working as a steam engineer.[70] Little Charlie died in March of 1871, at age three, when his mother was pregnant with her third child. Freddie was born in July but lived only three

---

69   Ibid.

Catton, *Picture History of the Civil War*.

70   Irene Nichols household, 1870 U.S. cens., Warren Co., N.Y., pop. sched., Caldwell, p. 4, dw. 24, fam. 21.

days. Harry was born in 1874. Mary Irene was born in 1877. In 1880, Orville, Adelia, and the three surviving children were still living with Adelia's mother, but now Orville was working as a laborer, still suffering from his wartime debility.[71]

In 1883 Archie was born. Helen was born in 1888. In April 1888 Orville applied to the Department of the Army for an invalid pension. At that time he was working as a painter. His application was approved on 12 May 1888 at twelve dollars per month. Orville applied for an increase in his pension on 23 July 1890, claiming rheumatism and disease of the lungs. In fact, he was completely disabled.[72] This application was approved on 29 July 1893, and Orville received a monthly pension of seventeen dollars until his death.[73]

In July 1897 Orville died of valvular disease of the heart. He was buried in Lake George Cemetery in Caldwell.[74] On 3 August 1897 Adelia applied for a widow's pension, to support her and her three minor children, which was granted at a rate of twelve dollars per month. In about 1895 Harry married and left home. Adelia, with four of her children, Alvah, Irene, Archie, and Helen, was still living in her mother's house in 1900.[75] By 1910 the two girls, Irene and Helen, were gone, probably married. But Alvah and Archie were still living with their mother in the house where Adelia had grown up.[76] Adelia died in 1915.

Children of ORVILLE and ADELIA (NICHOLS) LOCKWOOD:

i.   CHARLES LOCKWOOD, b. N.Y. 26 Oct. 1867; d. 12 March 1871; bur. Lake George Cem.[77]

ii. ALVAH F. LOCKWOOD, b. N.Y. Sept. 1869. Resided with widowed mother 1910.

---

[71]   Orville Lockwood household, 1880 U.S. cens. Warren Co., N.Y., pop. sched., Caldwell, SD 6, ED 112, p. 18, dw. 213, fam. 213.

[72]   Orville Lockwood, 1890 U.S. census, Warren County, New York, veteran's schedule, Caldwell, SD 6, ED 145, page 2; National Archives micropublication M123, roll 51.

[73]   Orville H. Lockwood, Civil War Pension Application File WC 453306.

[74]   Orville H. Lockwood tombstone, Lake George Cemetery.

[75]   Adelia Longwood household, 1900 U.S. cens., Warren Co., N.Y., pop. sched., Caldwell, SD 5, ED 93, sheet 7B, dw. 173, fam. 177.

[76]   Adelia Lockwood household, 1910 U.S. cens., Warren Co., N.Y., pop. sched., Caldwell, SD 190, ED 150, sheet 3B, dw. 69, fam. 71.

[77]   Little Charlie Lockwood tombstone, Lake George Cemetery; transcribed by John Austin.

iii. FREDDIE LOCKWOOD, b. 21 July 1871; d. 24 July 1871; bur. Lake George Cem.[78]

iv. HARRY G. LOCKWOOD, b. N.Y. abt. 1874;[79] m. abt 1895 PHOEBE A. VAN DUSEN, b. N.Y. abt. 1872, dau. of GEORGE W. and MARY (___) VAN DUSEN.[80] Resided Moreau, N.Y., 1910;[81] South Glens Fall, N.Y., 1930.[82]

v. MARY IRENE "IRENE" LOCKWOOD, b. N.Y. Nov. 1877.[83]

vi. ARCHIE E. LOCKWOOD, b. N.Y. 12 May 1883; m. abt. 1913 LAURA B. MURRAY, b. N.Y. July 1895, dau. of JOSEPH and ANNA (___) MURRAY.[84] Archie at home with widowed mother 1910 doing odd jobs. After marriage, lived with in-laws.

Children of ARCHIE and LAURA (MURRAY) LOCKWOOD:[85]

a. *Alfred Lockwood*, b. Glens Falls, N.Y., 4 March 1914.[86]

b. *Helen Lockwood*, b. N.Y. abt. 1916.

c. *Pearl Lockwood*, b. N.Y. abt. 1918.

d. *Harold Joseph Lockwood*, b. N.Y. 10 Nov. 1919.[87]

vii. HELEN M. LOCKWOOD, b. N.Y. 13 Jan. 1888.[88]

Sylvia Jane (Amidon) Baker (1832–1891)

51. SYLVIA JANE AMIDON[7] *(SAMUEL[6], JOHN[5] AMEDEN, JACOB[4] AMIDOWN, HENRY[3], PHILIP[2], ROGER[1] AMADOWNE)* was born at Fort

---

[78]   Little Freedie Lockwood tombstone, Lake George Cemetery; transcribed by John Austin.

[79]   Orville Lockwood household, 1880 U.S. cens. Warren Co., N.Y., pop. sched., Caldwell, SD 6, ED 112, p 18, dw 213, fam 213.

[80]   Geo W. Van Dusen household, 1880 U.S. cens. Warren Co., N.Y., pop. sched., Queensbury, SD 6, ED 123, p. 24, dw. 276, fam. 294.

[81]   Nelson J. Byron household, 1910 U.S. census, Saratoga County, New York, population schedule, town of Moreau, SD 9, ED 119, sheets 1A-1B, dwelling 13, family 15; National Archives micropublication T624, roll 1076.

[82]   Harry C. Lockwood household, 1930 U.S. census Saratoga County, New York, population schedule, town of South Glens Falls, SD 5, ED 46-30, sheet 13B, dwelling 271, family 327; National Archives micropublication T626, roll 1643.

[83]   Adelia Longwood household, 1900 U.S. cens., Warren Co., N.Y., pop. sched., town of Caldwell, SD 5, ED 93, sheet 7B, dw. 173, fam. 177.

[84]   Joseph Murry household, 1900 U.S. cens., Warren Co., N.Y., pop. sched., Queensbury, SD 5, ED 108, sheet 6B, dw. 119, fam. 129.

[85]   Joseph Murray household, 1920 U.S. cens., Warren Co., N.Y., pop. sched., Glens Falls, SD 10, ED 179, sheet 6B, dw. 92, fam. 118.

[86]   Alfred Lockwood entry, Ancestry.com, *Social Security Death Index*.

[87]   Harold J. Lockwood entry, Ancestry.com, *Social Security Death Index*.

[88]   Orville H. Lockwood, Civil War Pension Application File WC 453306.

Ann, New York, on 2 February 1832.[89] She died at Oakdale, Wisconsin, on 28 May 1891.[90] She married at Fort Ann on 25 March 1855 WILLIAM YOUNG BAKER.[91] He was born at Fort Ann on 7 September 1929,[92] the son of ASA GOODWILL and MABEL (YOUNG) BAKER. He died at Oakdale on 27 September 1901.[93]

Sylvia grew up in Fort Ann where she lived with her parents in 1840 and 1850. William also grew up in Fort Ann, the eldest of Asa and Mabel's children. Initially they probably lived in the household of William's grandfather William Baker.[94] By 1840 his parents had established their own farm, but William's father died in 1840,[95] leaving his widow Mabel to run the household of five children.[96] William's mother was still running the farm in 1850 with the help of William, his brother, Alex, and his sisters, Pamelia and Emaline. At $5000, the farm was one of the wealthier farms in the area.[97]

Sylvia and William married in 1855 and immediately moved to the new state of Wisconsin, which had achieved statehood only seven years earlier. They must have traveled down the St. Lawrence River, through the Welland Canal that bypasses Niagara Falls, and through the Great Lakes to Chicago. From there they visited for a few weeks in Illinois.[98] They probably sailed back up the western shore of Lake Michigan to Sheboygan, Wisconsin, where a new military road would have taken them west to Portage. From Portage a rough road followed an old Indian trail to La Crosse. The new settlement of Leroy, which became Oakdale, was opening up on that road. The western part of

---

    89   Sylvia J. Baker obituary, published in E. Carolyn Wildes Habelman, *Genealogical Branches from Monroe County, Wisconsin*, volume 3 (Black River Falls, Wisc.:E. C. W. Habelman, 1973), entry 809.

    90   Sylvia Baker tombstone, center section, Oakdale Township Cemetery, Oakdale, Wisconsin, south of Oakdale off highway 16 on Oakwood Road; transcribed by Nancy K. Mullen July 2003.

    91   William Y. Baker obituary, in Habelman, *Branches fr. Monroe Co.*, 3:31.

    92   Ibid.

    93   Ibid.

    94   William Baker household, 1830 U.S. cens., Washington Co., N.Y., town of Fort Ann, p. 325, line 17.

    95   ?, *Cemetery Records of the Township of Fort Ann, Washington County, New York* (Queensbury, New York: Historical Data Services, 1992), 24.

    96   Mabel Baker household, 1840 U.S. cens., Washington Co., N.Y., town of Fort Ann, p. 238, ln. 11.

    97   Mabel Baker household, 1850 U.S. cens., Washington Co., N.Y., pop. sched., Fort Ann, p. 107B, dw. 614, fam. 614.

    98   William Y. Baker obituary, *Tomah [Wisc.] Journal*, 4 Oct. 1901, p. 4:3.

Wisconsin was being carved into counties. Monroe County had been created just one year earlier, in March 1854. William's older brother, Enoch Baker, his wife, Rachel, and their three children went with them. Together the two families settled in Leroy, arriving on 20 September 1855[99] – barely in time to build shelter against Wisconsin's harsh oncoming winter.

Sylvia's parents, Samuel and Hannah, joined them within a few months. Sylvia's parents had bought federal land in Wisconsin before leaving New York. William and Enoch, along with Ira Slocum, another former resident of Fort Ann, waited until 10 March 1857 to jointly buy a forty-acre parcel of federal land in Byron township, just north of Oakdale township.[100] Their land certificate says all three were of McHenry County, Illinois, which was the residence of Ira Slocum. But local Oakdale records state that William Baker settled in Leroy in 1855. Six months after buying the land, on 30 October 1857, William alone purchased eighty acres of federal land in Leroy.[101] A month later, on 23 November 1857, Leroy was created as a town with independent town government by the county board. Clearly William and Sylvia were some of the earliest settlers of the town, preceding the existence of town government.

The 1860 census shows the two Baker families and the senior Amidons living in consecutive dwellings in Leroy. By 1860 Sylvia had delivered her two children, James and Florence. A teenage boy was living with them, whom the census-taker recorded as George Baker. William did not have any younger brothers, so he may have been a nephew, though probably not a son of Enoch.[102] In 1866, Sylvia's father sold off his lands in Monroe County in preparation for moving fourteen miles east to Juneau County. William Baker bought 480 of those acres on 10 July 1866.[103]

By 1870, Leroy had been renamed Oakdale. William and Sylvia were still living there. Another teenage boy, Samuel Freeman, was

---

99   William Y. Baker obituary, in Habelman, *Branches from Monroe Co*, 3:31.

100   Ira Slocum, William Y. Baker and Enoch Baker patent, #7910, 10 March 1857; online <www.glorecords.blm.gov>.

101   William Y. Baker patent, #10663, 30 October 1857; Bureau of Land Management, General Records Office, Washington, D.C.; online <www. glorecords.blm.gov>.

102   William W. Baker household, 1860 cens., Monroe Co., Wisc., pop. sched., Leroy, p. 148, dw. 1213, fam. 1200.

103   Monroe Co. Deeds, Book 18:512.

living with them, helping William with the farm.[104] When Sylvia's father died, leaving almost 1000 acres of farmland and forest to his three heirs, Sylvia bought out the interests of the other heirs for $1250 and took title to Samuel's lands.[105] In 1878, the prestige with which William was regarded was reflected by his election as Monroe County delegate to the state assembly in the capitol of Madison.[106]

By 1880 son James had found work as a railroad clerk, but the family was still intact.[107] James married in 1887. Sylvia died in 1891 at age fifty-nine. She was buried at Oakdale Township Cemetery.[108] Six months later, daughter Florence married Harry Bostwick, chief accountant for the Wisconsin Valley Railway section between Tomah and Wausau, Wisconsin. They spent the next fifteen years moving about Iowa, Missouri, Kansas and Nebraska as Harry served the railroad as a rod and transit man, surveying for new lines on the expanding railroad.

Alone with only James in the household, William became active in the Old Settlers of the County Club. In 1894 he was elected a vice president when the club had 444 members.[109]

By 1900, James was missing. His wife, Marion, and three children were living with the widowed William on the family farm.[110] All census records for William report he was a farmer, but his early vocation was as a schoolteacher. He was an active Republican. He served one term in the state assembly as a representative from Monroe County. For fourteen years he served the western part of the county as poor commissioner. He was serving Oakdale as a justice of the peace

---

[104]   William Y. Boken household, 1870 census, Monroe County, Wisconsin, population schedule, town of Oakdale, page 4, dwelling 28, family 34; National Archives micropublication M593, roll 1729.

[105]   Monroe Co. Deeds, Books 38:49, 38:50.

[106]   Randolph A. Richards, *History of Monroe County, Wisconsin, Past and Present* (Chicago: C. F. Cooper & Co., 1912), 77.

[107]   William Y. Baker household, 1880 U.S. census, Monroe County, Wisconsin, population schedule, town of Oakdale, SD 3, ED [], page 14, dwelling 134, family 136; National Archives micropublication T9, roll 1439.

[108]   Sylvia Baker tombstone, Oakdale Township Cemetery, Oakdale, Wisconsin.

[109]   Habelman, *Branches from Monroe County*, 1:118.

[110]   Wm. Y. Baker household, 1900 U.S. census, Monroe County, Wisconsin, population schedule, town of Oakdale, SD 7, ED 103, sheet 12, dwelling 214, family 216; National Archives micropublication T623, roll 1808.

at the time of his death.[111] He died in 1901, at age seventy-two, his daughter, Florence, and daughter-in-law, Marion, at his side. His obituary described him as "a generous, warm hearted man, ever ready to do a kind act for one in sickness or trouble, and no task was too great for him to do for his friends." A large procession of carriages carried his body to Oakdale Township Cemetery, where he was laid to rest beside his wife, though today no stone marks his grave.[112]

Children of WILLIAM Y. and SYLVIA (AMIDON) BAKER:

i. JAMES O. BAKER[8], b. prob. Oakdale, Wisc., 23 April 1857;[113] d. Sparta, Wisc., 1 Feb. 1920;[114] m. 1887 MARION ___ b. Wisc. Oct. 1866,[115] living LaCrosse 1930.[116] In 1880 James was a RR clerk. Confined to Monroe Co. insane asylum from 1902 until his death. Wife and daughters living in La Crosse, Wisc., 1930.[117]

Children of JAMES O. and MARION (___) BAKER:

a. *Irene G. Baker*, b. Wisc. Feb. 1890.

b. *Ralph Smythe Baker*, b. Oakdale, Wisc., 2 Aug. 1892.[118] Newsagent for Van Ney Interstate News Co., Kansas City, Mo., 1917; disabled for military service by rupture.[119]

c. *Mabel A. Baker*, b. Wisc. 5 June 1894.[120]

ii. FLORENCE ELLA BAKER, b. Oakdale, Wisc., Oct. 1858;[121] m. Oakdale 23 Sept. 1891 HARRY EDWARD BOSTWICK,[122] b.

111 William Y. Baker obituary, in Habelman, *Branches fr. Monroe Co.*, 3:31.
112 William Y. Baker obituary, *Tomah [Wisc.] Journal*, 4 Oct. 1901, p. 4:3.
113 James A. Baker obituary, in Habelman, *Branches fr. Monroe Co.*, 2:207.
114 Ibid.
115 Wm. Y. Baker household, 1900 U.S. cens., Monroe Co., Wisc., pop. sched., town of Oakdale, SD 7, ED 103, sheet 12, dw. 214, fam. 216.
116 Marion Baker household, 1930 U.S. census, La Crosse County, Wisconsin, population schedule, town of La Crosse, SD 7, ED 16, sheet 16B, dwelling 353, family 433; National Archives micropublication T626, roll 2578.
117 Marion Baker household, 1930 U.S. census, La Crosse Co., Wisc., pop. sched., town of La Crosse, SD 7, ED 16, sheet 16B, dw. 353, fam. 433.
118 Ralph Smythe Baker, Ancestry.com, *World War I Draft Registration Card*.
119 Ibid.
120 Mabel Baker entry, Ancestry.com, *Social Security Death Index*.
121 William W. Baker household, 1860 U.S. cens., Monroe Co., Wisc., pop. sched., Leroy, p. 148, dw. 1213, fam. 1200, which gives her age as 1 year.
     Harry Bostwick household, 1900 U.S. census, Milwaukee County, Wisconsin, population schedule, town of Milwaukee, SD 294, ED 141, sheet 11A, dwelling 176, family 191; National Archives micropublication M653, roll 1424 which gives her birth month as October.
122 Bostwick-Baker marriage, record #2503, *Wisconsin Marriage Records*,

Brighton, N.Y., May 1859, son of EDWIN LEE and FRANCES (BEEBE) BOSTWICK.[123] Moved to Milwaukee 1896, still resident there 1930.[124]

Children of HARRY and FLORENCE (BAKER) BOSTWICK:

a. *Ella B. Bostwick*[9], b. Wauwatosa, Wisc., Oct. 1892; d. Wauwatosa 18 July 1903.[125]

b. *Gertrude Irene Bostwick*, b. Milwaukee, Wisc., 12 Sept. 1898;[126] m. 1916 *Frederick Jackson Pease*, b. Janesville, Wisc., 17 Sept. 1893, son of *Lynn Spencer* and *Emma (Nunns) Pease*. Lived Milwaukee 1930.

   Child of *Frederick* and *Gertrude (Bostwick) Pease*:
   1. Richard Lynn Pease, b. Wisc. 1 June 1919.[127]

c. *Helen Louise Bostwick*, b. Milwaukee 4 May 1900; m. 1) bef. 1920 *Frank Charles Wollinka*, b. Milwaukee 28 Nov. 1897;[128] m. 2) abt. 1920 *Burl Benjamin Webb*, b. Owosso, Mich., 7 June 1891, son of *Lloyd* and *Ida (Whitaker) Pease*. Resided Avon, Mich., 1930.

   Children of *Burl* and *Helen (Bostwick) Webb*:
   1. Howard R. Webb, b. Mich. abt. 1923.
   2. William A. Webb, b. Mich. abt. 1924.
   3. Helen S. Webb, b. Mich. abt 1926.
   4. Marion B. Webb, b. Mich. Feb. 1929.[129]

1823-1907 (Salt Lake City: Genealogical Society of Utah, 1979-80), 3:385.

[123]   E. L. Bostwick, 1880 U.S. cens., Monroe Co., Wisc., pop. sched., La Grange, SD 12, ED 3, p. 26, dw. 131, fam. 134.

[124]   Harry Bestwick household, 1930 U.S. census, Milwaukee County, Wisconsin, population schedule, Milwaukee, SD 10, ED 40-189, sheet 2A, dwelling 24, family 33; National Archives micropublication T626, roll 2591.

[125]   Wisconsin Department of Health and Family Services, *Wisconsin Vital Record Index, pre-1907* (Madison, Wisconsin: Wisconsin Department of Health and Family Services Vital Records Division); Wisconsin Historical Society, Madison, Wisconsin.

[126]   Unnamed Bostwick daughter birth, *Tomah Monitor*, Tomah, Wisconsin, 21 September 1898, page 5, column 1.

[127]   Richard Pease tombstone, Wauwatosa Cemetery, Wauwatosa, Wisc.; online <www.interment.net/data/us/wi/milwaukee/wauwatosa/wauw_pq .htm>.

[128]   Frank Wollinka Ancestry.com, *World War I Draft Registration Card.*

[129]   Bert B. Webb household, U.S. 1930 census, Oakland County, Michigan, population schedule, Avon Township, SD 14, ED 69-5, sheet 22B, dwelling 487, family 486; National Archives micropublication T626, roll 1016.

Llewellyn E. Amidon (1835–1895)

52. LLEWELLYN E. "LEW" AMIDON[7] *(SAMUEL[6], JOHN[5] AMEDEN, JACOB[4] AMIDOWN, HENRY[3], PHILIP[2], ROGER[1] AMADOWNE)* was born at Fort Ann, New York, on 14 August 1835 and died at Oakdale, Wisconsin, on 5 November 1895.[130] He married on 1 January 1861 MARIA "MAY" HILL.[131] She was born at Huntley, Illinois, on 17 May 1840, the daughter of SAMUEL and REBECCA (MASON) HILL.[132]

Lew grew up in Fort Ann where he was recorded with his parents in the 1840 and 1850 censuses. The family moved to Leroy, Wisconsin, in 1856. The 1860 census shows Lew still living with his parents, working on his father's substantial farm. On 10 May 1860 Lew bought eighty acres south of Oakdale from Allan and Adaline Butterfield for $450.[133]

May grew up in Rutland, Illinois, where she was recorded with her family in 1850[134] and 1860.[135] Her obituary says she was born and raised in Huntley, but the census shows that was not true. Probably it was only her birth that was at Huntley.

Lew and May married in early 1861. He served as county surveyor in 1861-62.[136] It may have been that role that gave Llewellyn an informed view of land that became available at tax sales. Later that year, on 18 October, Lew picked up three forty-acre plots at a tax sale for a total of eight dollars. Two years later, on 19 April 1863, he sold one of the parcels to Frederick Geisler for thirty-five dollars, a nice profit on land that was probably relatively undesirable. He picked up yet another forty-acre parcel at a tax sale for $2.03 ten days later. Two months after he bought the land so cheaply, he gave the property to Anne Moulton for one dollar. The next year he sold another of the parcels to Mary Ann Smith for $50, another nice profit.

On 4 February 1864 Lew and Samuel P. Taylor paid $100 for forty

---

130   L. E. Amidon obituary, *Tomah Journal*, 9 November 1895, page 5:4.
131   Mrs. May Amidon obituary, *Tomah Journal*, 17 November 1932.
132   Ibid.
133   The many real estate transactions of L. E. Amidon are found in the Monroe County Deeds, Tax Deeds, and Abstract of State Lands, Monroe County Register of Deeds, Sparta, Wisconsin.
134   Samuel Hill household, 1850 U.S. cens., Kane Co., Ill., pop. sched., Rutland, p. 30, dw. 139, fam. 578.
135   Samuel Hill household, 1860 U.S. census, Kane County, Illinois, population schedule, town of Rutland, page 438-9, dwelling 3574, family 3187; National Archives micropublication M653, roll 191.
136   Richards, *History of Monroe County*, 76.

acres of federal land in Oakdale adjacent to Lew's mother's land. The patent (or title) was issued on 10 January 1865.[137] Taylor had been a neighbor in Fort Ann, who moved to Monroe County at about the same time Lew's family moved. Taylor was a contemporary of Lew's father.

Lew and Mathew Fitzsimmons collaborated to buy 160 acres of land from the state of Wisconsin on 7 August 1866. These were lands that had been deeded to the state by the federal government because the lands were classified as swamplands, and so were not selling successfully as farmland. This new land was in the town of Lincoln, northwest of Oakdale. A month later Lew picked up another forty-acre parcel in Oakdale for back taxes of $2.38. Perhaps Lew tried to sell the lands he acquired so cheaply at tax sales, and was unsuccessful. In 1867 he let the two unsold properties be reclaimed for back taxes. On 1 September 1870 he bought another eighty acres for $3.85 back taxes. On 12 January 1871 he and Mathew Fitzsimmons succeeded in selling the swamplands in Lincoln to Messrs. Dodge and Lowrie for $450. On 13 May 1872 he bought another forty-acre parcel for $1.79.

Lew and May started their family with the birth of Gertrude in 1867. The 1870 census shows the three of them living in Oakdale, operating a very large farm, with the same George Baker who had been living with Lew's married sister, Sylvia Baker, a decade earlier. Lillian was born in 1871 and Arthur in 1873. At some point May had another boy, who died as an infant. His birth and death are not recorded, but the six-year gap between the parents's marriage and Gertrude's birth makes it likely he was the first child.

In 1872 Lew leased a small lot he owned with Asa Lake to the Oakdale school district. On this lot, the school district built Diamond Valley School, a small schoolhouse built for the fifth Oakdale school district. The building was used until 1919 when it was judged too small and the school district auctioned it off to Frank Gabower, who used it as a woodshed as late as 1989.[138]

The family joined Lew's father in New Lisbon, Wisconsin, before

---

[137] Lewellyn Amidon land entry file#16555, National Archives, Washington, D.C. Northeast quarter of the northwest quarter of section 10 in township 17N of range 1E.
[138] Julia E. Middleman, compiler, *History of Monroe County Public Schools* (?: Julia E. Middleman, 1989), 194.

1873 when Arthur was born there. The 1875 state census shows the family living in New Lisbon (two males, three females).[139]

The move to New Lisbon didn't dampen Lew's thirst for real estate deals. On 25 February 1874 he paid $50 for 360 acres of swampland in Lincoln from George and Eliza Runkel. These lands he also allowed to be reclaimed for unpaid taxes. But on 1 April 1876 he converted his 1870 tax purchase into a tidy profit when he sold the parcel to Henry, Ira, and Frank Woods for $300. The next month, on 15 May, Lew bought another eighty acres for back taxes of $3.76. He gave the property to Merit Hodge three days later, for one dollar.

By 1877 the family was back farming in Oakdale. Lew's father had died in 1876. In 1877, Lew sold his interest in the very large land holdings of his father's estate to his sister, Sylvia, for one thousand dollars.

In 1880 Lew himself served as the enumerator for the census, recording his family with his three children on their farm.[140] In 1882 Lew sold the last remaining tax parcel for $100 to Jason Wood.

In 1891, Lillian left the family nest when she married George Eberhart. By late October 1895, Lew knew he was dying. One of his last acts was to give the family homestead to May, on 28 October. He died at home on 5 November and is buried in Camp Douglas cemetery in the Eberhart lot.[141] A county history describes him as "a prominent citizen, civil engineer, and county surveyor of Monroe county and locator of Government and school lands, and in politics a Republican."[142]

Son Arthur had just returned from the west and moved in with his widowed mother on the family homestead. Arthur married in 1899, so May moved to Mauston to live with her elder daughter, Gertrude, and her husband, William Ballantine.[143] On 12 March 1902 she sold the family farm to Henry Gabower, but retained the small lot that

---

139   L. E. Amidon household, 1875 Wisc. state cens., Juneau Co., New Lisbon, p. 1, line 2.

140   Llewellyn E. Amidon household, 1880 U.S. cens., Monroe Co., Wisc., pop. sched., Oakdale, SD 3, ED [blank], sheet 15B, dw. 141, fam. 143.

141   Llewellyne Amidon tombstone, Camp Douglas cemetery, Camp Douglas, Wisconsin, transcribed by Nancy K. Mullen 2004.

142   Richards, *History of Monroe County*, 723.

143   William Ballantine household, 1900 U.S. census, Juneau County, Wisconsin, population schedule, town of Mauston, SD 2, ED 81, sheet 16B; National Archives micropublication T623, roll 1793.

contained the house and farm buildings. By 1904, Arthur was seeking his fortune in Alberta, but his wife, Lillian, moved with May back to the small portion of the family homestead that she had retained.[144] In 1910 May was in the town of Tomah with her widowed brother, Oliver Mason Hill, running his household for him.[145] He died in 1910, and his unmarried son, Cady, took over running the 200-acre farm, adding another 170 acres. May continued looking after the household duties, as she had done for her brother.[146] In 1920 May was back in Mauston with William and Gertrude Ballantine, perhaps because Cady had married.[147] She was still living with William and Gertrude in 1930.[148] By 1930 she was ninety years old, one of the oldest residents in the county, and one of the last of the pioneer settlers of Oakdale.

Children of LLEWELLYN and MAY (HILL) AMIDON:

i.   GERTRUDE WESTCOTT AMIDON, b. Oakdale, Wisc.,[149] Dec. 1867;[150] m. Oakdale 29 June 1898 WILLIAM B. BALLANTINE,[151] b. Wisc. Nov. 1869,[152] son of JAMES and HANNAH (___) BALLANTINE.[153] Resided Mauston, Wisc., 1930.

Child of WILLIAM and GERTRUDE (AMIDON) BALLANTINE:

a.   ___ *Ballantine* b. Mauston, Wisc., 22 Feb. 1902; d. 23 Feb. 1902.[154]

---

144   *Tomah Journal*, 5 August 1904, page 8, column 3.

145   Oliver Hill household, 1910 U.S. census, Monroe County, Wisconsin, population schedule, town of Tomah, SD 6, ED 145, sheet 6A; National Archives micropublication T624, roll 1729.

146   Richards, *History of Monroe County*, 722-3.

147   William B. Ballantine household, 1920 U.S. census, Juneau County, Wisconsin, population schedule, town of Mauston, SD 6, ED 73, sheet 8B; National Archives micropublication T625, roll 1990.

148   William B. Ballentine household, 1930 U.S. census, Juneau County, Wisconsin, population schedule, town of Mauston, SD 7, ED 29-18, sheet 11B; National Archives micropublication T626, roll 2577.

149   Ballantine-Amidon marriage record, Juneau County Recorder, Book 3:277, New Lisbon, Wisconsin.

150   William Ballantine household, 1900 U.S. cens., Juneau Co., Wisc., pop. sched., Mauston, SD 2, ED 81, sheet 16B, dw. 379, fam. 394.

151   Ballantine-Amidon marriage record, Juneau County Recorder, Book 3:277.

152   William Ballantine household, 1900 U.S. cens., Juneau Co., Wisc., pop. sched., Mauston, SD 2, ED 81, sheet 16B, dw. 379, fam. 394.

153   James Ballantine household, 1870 U.S. cens., Juneau Co., Wisc., pop. sched., Lemonweir, p. 9, dw. 58, fam. 57.

154   Baby Ballantine death record, Juneau County Recorder, 1:405.

ii.   LILLIAN R. AMIDON, b. Wisc. Sept. 1871;[155] m. 1891 GEORGE P. EBERHART,[156] b. N.Y. April 1863,[157] son of FRANK and JULIA ANN (___) EBERHART.[158]

Children of GEORGE and LILLIAN (AMIDON) EBERHART:

a. *Fenn A. Eberhart,* b. Wisc. 21 Nov. 1892; d. 17 Sept. 1914; bur. Camp Douglas Cem., Camp Douglas, Wisc.[159]

b. *Harold George Eberhart,* b. Oakdale, Wisc., 6 Sept. 1894;[160] m. bet. 1920-30 *Martha D. Kabelitz,*[161] b. Shanghai, China, 11 Jan. 1902.[162] Officer U.S. Navy, stationed Philadelphia 1920,[163] Oahu 1930.[164]

Child of *Harold* and *Martha (Kabelitz) Eberhart*:

1. Alan Amidon Eberhart, b. Shanghai, China, 9 Nov. 1922.[165]

c. *Llewellyn F. Eberhart,* b. Juneau Co., Wisc., 8 Oct. 1909.[166]

iii. ARTHUR WILLIAM AMIDON, b. New Lisbon, Wisc., 11 July 1873; d. Elroy, Wisc., 22 Feb. 1911, fall from moving train; bur. 25 Feb. 1911 Camp Douglas Cem., Camp Douglas, Wisc.;[167] m. Wonewoc, Wisc., 18 Oct. 1899 LILLIAN MAUD DAKE,[168] b.

---

[155]   George P. Eberhart household, 1900 U.S. cens., Juneau Co., Wisc., pop. sched., Camp Douglas, SD 2, ED 85, sheet 4A, dw. 62, fam. 65.
[156]   Ibid.
[157]   Ibid.
[158]   Frank X. Eberhart household, 1880 U.S. census, Juneau County, Wisconsin, population schedule, Byron, SD 3, ED [], page 382C, dwelling 3, family 3; National Archives micropublication T9, roll 1439.
[159]   Fenn Eberhart tombstone, Camp Douglas Cemetery.
[160]   Harold G. Eberhart birth record, Wisc. DHFS, *Wisc. VR Index, pre-1907.*
[161]   Alan Amidon Eberhart obituary, Madison Newspapers, Inc., <www.madison.com/obits>, 8 June 2004.
[162]   Harold G. Eberhart household, 1930 U.S. census, Oahu County, Hawaii, population schedule, U.S. Naval Station – Pearl Harbor, SD 5, ED 2-113, sheet 2B, dwelling 16, family 18; National Archives micropublication T626, roll 2632.
[163]   U.S.S. Long, 1920 U.S. census, Philadelphia County, Pennsylvania, population schedule, Philadelphia Navy Yard, SD [], ED [], sheet 1A, line 3; National Archives micropublication T625, roll 2040.
[164]   Harold G. Eberhart household, 1930 U.S. cens., Oahu Co., Hi., pop. sched., U.S. Naval Station – Pearl Harbor, SD 5, ED 2-113, sheet 2B, dw. 16, fam. 18.
[165]   Ibid.
[166]   Llewellyn F. Eberhart entry, Wisc. DHFS, *Wisc. VR Index, pre-1907.*
[167]   Arthur W. Amidon obituary, unattributed obituary in obituary file, Sparta Free Library, 124 West Main Street, Sparta, WI 54656.
[168]   Amidon-Dake marriage, Juneau County Marriage Records, 2:337.

prob. Wonewoc, Wisc., Nov. 1878,[169] dau. of ESTES EUGENE and JULIA ETTE (RAY) DAKE.[170]

Children of ARTHUR and LILLIAN (DAKE) AMIDON:

a. *Lillian Maxine Amidon*, b. Monroe Co., Wisc., 11 Feb. 1901.[171]

b. *John Lester Amidon*, b. Camp Douglas, Wisc., 28 June 1902; d. Mauston, Wisc., 6 Oct. 1918; after father's death lived with Aunt Gertrude Ballantine until untimely death while still in high school.[172]

c. *Gertrude Amidon*, b. Wisc. 1905.[173]

Alembert P. Ameden (1839–1900)

53. ALEMBERT P. AMEDEN[7] *(JOHNSON[6], JOHN[5], JACOB[4] AMIDOWN, HENRY[3], PHILIP[2], ROGER[1] AMADOWNE)* was born at Chester, New York, in November 1839,[174] and died at Johnsburg, New York, on 24 October 1900.[175] He married at Sandy Hill, New York, on 5 March 1862 ELIZA JANE "ELSIE" KING.[176] She was born in Vermont on 26 June 1843, the daughter of STEPHEN and ELIZA ANN (GRAY) KING, and died at Johnsburg on 24 December 1916.[177]

Alembert was born in Chester in the north central part of Warren County, but grew up in Sandy Hill, east of the southeast corner of Warren County. His parents moved there when Alembert was about two years old. By 1860 he was still living at home and had become a

---

[169]   Arthur Amidon household, 1900 U.S. cens., Monroe Co., Wisc., pop. sched., Oakdale, SD 7, ED 103, sheet 11B, dw. 204, fam. 206.

[170]   Estes Dake household, 1880 U.S. cens., Juneau Co., Wisc., pop. sched., Wonewoc, SD 2, ED 267, p. 18, dw. 171, fam. 174.

[171]   C. N. Heasty, Index to Birth Registrations in Monroe Co., Wisc., 1860–1945 (Sparta, Wisc.: Angelo Books, 1989), 3.

[172]   John Lester Amidon obituary, obituary file, Sparta Free Library.

[173]   Eugene Dake household, 1910 U.S. census, Juneau County, Wisconsin, population schedule, Wonewoc, SD 3, ED 86, sheet 2A, dwelling 35, family 35; National Archives micropublication T624, roll 1714.

[174]   Alembert Ameden household, 1900 U.S. cens., Warren Co., N.Y., pop. sched., Johnsburg, SD 5, ED 98, sheet 10, dw. 232, fam. 237.

[175]   Alembert Ameden death certificate, register 394, Johnsburg, N.Y.

[176]   Ameden-King marriage, 5 March 1862, in Marriage book, unpaginated, arranged by date, Hudson Falls United Methodist Church, Hudson Falls (formerly Sandy Hill), New York.

[177]   Elsie Ameden death certificate, register 32, Johnsburg, North Creek, N.Y. Her birth date is derived from her age of seventy-three years, five months, twenty-eight days, given on her death certificate.

machinist.

Elsie seems to have acquired the nickname to distinguish her from her mother who was also Eliza. She was probably born in Glover, Vermont, where her mother was born, and where her parents appear in the 1840 census. They have not been found in 1850 or the New York 1855 census, so we don't know when Elsie and her mother moved to New York. By 1860, Elsie's father was dead. On 1 January her mother married a widowed Warren County carpenter, Joseph Baldwin. The marriage was at the same Sandy Hill church where Elsie and Alembert married two years later.[178] Since Sandy Hill is in Washington County, it is likely that Elsie and her mother had settled in Sandy Hill sometime after the 1855 state census.

Joseph Baldwin was born in Vermont but settled in Sandy Hill. He had married another Eliza in 1830, and raised three children. By 1850 the family had become close neighbors to Johnson Ameden, Alembert's father.[179] Joseph's wife died in 1855. Joseph was a carpenter and apparently quite affluent, judging by the size of the tombstone he placed on his wife's grave.[180] In January 1860 he and the widowed Eliza King married at the Methodist Church in Sandy Hill. By July 1860 he had abandoned carpentry and become a lumberman in Glens Falls.

Elsie was not with her mother and Joseph Baldwin in the 1860 census. She was living with the Lewis Chase family in White Creek, in the southeast corner of Washington County.[181] She was probably working for them as a domestic.

Alembert and Elsie were married on 5 March 1862 by the Reverend G. C. Wells in the parsonage of the Sandy Hill Methodist Church. Initially they lived in Sandy Hill. Alembert was a machinist, working in one of Sandy Hills' many mills. The young couple greeted their first child, Ernest, an indiscreet four months later. Eleven months later they welcomed a second son, William, but the baby lived only fourteen months. Elsie bore no more children. After William's death, her focus was entirely on her surviving son, Ernest.

---

178   Baldwin-King marriage, 1 January 1860, Marriage book, Hudson Falls United Methodist Church.

179   Joseph Baldwin household, 1850 U.S. cens., Washington Co., N.Y., pop. sched., Kingsbury, p. 214B, dw. 79, fam. 84.

180   Eliza R. Baldwin tombstone, sect. 1: 71, Union Cem., Ft. Edward, N.Y.

181   Lewis Chase household, 1860 U.S. cens., Washington Co., N.Y., pop. sched., White Creek, p. 6, dw. 43, fam. 43.

The 1865 New York census shows the family of three still living in Sandy Hill.[182] By then Alembert had become a carpenter, perhaps with the help of Eliza's stepfather, Joseph Baldwin. On 22 April 1865 he paid $125 for a small lot on Elm Street in Sandy Hill and built a frame home worth $1800 for his small family. The next year he expanded his property by purchasing eight feet along the east property line from Mary Etter Northrup for $100.[183]

The years following the Civil War fostered an explosion of feminism. This was the beginning of the women's suffrage movement, as well as the development of other "women's causes." During these years, women founded the National Association for the Prevention of Cruelty to Children, the National Association for the Prevention of Cruelty to Animals, the Association for the Advancement of Science, and the National Education Association. Elsie seems to have joined the feminist movement by becoming a dealer in land.

For the next four decades, it was Elsie, assertive and entrepreneurial, who actively bought and sold land, not Alembert. It was she who, in 1867, bought two adjoining parcels of land in Glens Falls for $1100, substantial sums compared to the price Alembert paid for their home lot in 1865. A year later, Elsie sold the smaller lot to her father-in-law, Johnson Ameden. On 1 July 1869 she purchased another lot adjacent to the one she still owned from James and Cornelia Ferguson for $500.

For a brief time, the family lived there in Glens Falls. They were found there in the 1870 census, when Alembert, called Lemuel by the census taker, was listed as a day laborer.[184] However, Elsie lost her two lots in Glens Falls on 18 December 1875 when the Supreme Court of the State of New York ordered Fred E. Ranger to auction off the properties and award the proceeds to the plaintiff, George H. Allen.[185] This probably resulted from defaulting on the mortgages, perhaps triggered by the Panic of 1873. George was an in-law, husband of Alembert's first cousin, Irena Ameden, daughter of Warren Ameden. This debacle sent Alembert and Elsie back to Sandy

---

[182]   Alembert Ameden hhd, 1865 N.Y. state cens., Washington Co., Kingsbury.
[183]   Washington County Deeds.
[184]   Lemual Ameden household, 1870 U.S. cens., Warren Co., N.Y., pop. sched., Queensbury, p. 76, dw. 473, fam. 574.
[185]   Warren County Deeds, 31:448-50 and 31:591-2.

Hill.

In the 1870's, there was an awakening to the natural beauty of the Great Forest that covered the Adirondack region, and the threat to the Great Forest posed by logging. Agitation was rising for legislation to protect the forest. In 1892, that agitation would result in the creation of Adirondack Park, a preserve the size of Massachusetts.

The awakening interest was not lost on the Amedens. A cousin, Eugene Ameden, was the first to invest in land in the northwest part of the county, in the hamlet of North River, in the town of Johnsburg. North River was a tiny community consisting of one hotel and two grocery stores, sitting on a bend in the Hudson River where the rushing, bubbling waters of the spring thaws carried logs down river to market, and the shallow rills and pools among the exposed boulders in summer offered great fishing. The river is only fifty feet wide as it courses past the hamlet of North River, its pounding energy readily audible inside Eugene's grocery. Eugene had bought the store in 1873. However, Eugene didn't stay long in North River.

Alembert and Elsie also heard the call of the Great Forest. In 1879 they began living part of the year in North River while still maintaining a residence back in Sandy Hill. It is quite possible that Alembert was helping Eugene with the store on a part-time basis.

Settled on Cherry Street in Sandy Hill for the 1880 census, Alembert was listed as a carpenter/joiner who had been unemployed for nine months due to kidney stones![186] But the death of Alembert's father in 1880 seems to have given Alembert the cash he needed to give up carpentry and buy a store in North River, apparently in competition with Eugene. Alembert sold his interest in two parcels of his father's lands in Sandy Hill to his sister, Ellen, for $1050.[187] He and Elsie relocated immediately. By 1885 he was recognized as a merchant in North River in the local county history; Simon Towns operated the second store (purchased from Eugene), and Danforth Eldridge operated the hotel.[188] In 1880, the two stores had been operated by Simon Towns and Charles Cheesman,[189] so Alembert

---

186   Alembert Ameden household, 1880 U.S. cens., Washington Co., N.Y., pop. sched., Kingsbury, SD 6, ED 150, p. 2, dw. 14, fam. 15.

187   Washington County Deeds, Book for year 1881, page 187.

188   Smith, *History of Warren County*, 558.

189   Simon Towns household, 1880 U.S. cens., Warren Co., N.Y., pop. sched., Johnsburg, SD 8, ED 118, p. 6, dw. 36, fam. 36.

Charles Cheesman household, 1880 U.S. cens., Warren Co., N.Y., pop.

must have acquired Cheesman's store.

Alembert's property had three buildings on it: a two-story residence, a two-story general store with living quarters upstairs, and an ice barn behind the store. During the winter the family cut blocks of ice from the Hudson River and dragged them to the ice barn, where they were covered deeply in sawdust. The ice provided refrigeration throughout the long summer.

By 1900 Elsie's mother was widowed again, and living with Alembert and Elsie.[190] She died of cancer in June that year.[191] How Elsie must have grieved when Alembert died four months later in a urrina coma at age sixty-one! He had been ill for quite some time – perhaps those kidney stones of 1880 had assailed him for the twenty years in between. The funeral was conducted from their home in North River by the Reverend A. D. Angell of North Creek.[192] Elsie served as administratrix for Alembert's estate. He had left no will, owned no real estate, and owned personal property valued at only $100. Everything else was already in Elsie's name.

Ernest had married shortly after 1880 and was living in nearby Chestertown. He and his family moved to North River, probably into the living quarters over the store, and undertook running the store for Elsie. He became postmaster on 11 May 1901,[193] thereby ensuring a steady flow of customers into the general store as they came to pick up their mail, in those days before postal delivery. He also created a portrait studio over the store from which he developed portraits and postcards of the Adirondack scenic beauty. For a lengthy critique of his photography as art, see Bogdan's *Exposing the Wilderness.*[194]

Elsie continued to deal in land. On 1 July 1902 she sold a quarter acre she owned in North River to George Ordway for $195.56. On 15 June 1906 she sold eighty acres in the town of Johnsburg on the Hudson River to Mary E. Pearce of Nassau County, New York for

---

sched., Johnsburg, SD 8, ED 118, p. 6, dw. 38, fam. 38.
    190   Alembert Ameden household, 1900 U.S. cens., Warren Co., N.Y., pop. sched., Johnsburg, SD 5, ED 98, sheet 10, dw. 232, fam. 237.
    191   Eliza Baldwin death certificate, register 387, Town of Johnsburg.
    192   A. Ameden obituary, *Glens Falls Morning Star*, 26 October 1900.
    193   Records of Appointment of Postmasters 1832-1971, New York, Warren County, North River, National Archives series M841, roll 91.
    194   Robert Bogdan, *Exposing the Wilderness, Early Twentieth-Century Adirondack Postcard Photographers* (Syracuse, N.Y.: Syracuse University Press, 1999), 134-165.

$300. She bought a different forty-acre parcel in Johnsburg from Elbert Stevens on 1 July 1906 for $350, which she sold to Fred Keith for the same price three years later. On 15 May 1913 she bought another acre of land in Johnsburg from Erving Zufelt for $300.[195]

The 1910 census shows Elsie living next door to Ernest's family. By then, Ernest was listed as the merchant, and Elsie was listed as having her own income.[196] She had withdrawn from running the store and left operations to Ernest.

Elsie was seventy-three when she died on Christmas Eve, 1916, from a stroke ("apoplexy"). She left a will leaving everything to her only heir, her son, Ernest, naming him executor.[197] She was a gracious, elegant lady, much admired and respected by younger generations. She and Alembert were buried under a shared tombstone in the same plot as his parents in Union Cemetery, Fort Edward.[198]

Children of ALEMBERT and ELSIE (KING) AMEDEN:

i.   ERNEST JOHNSON AMEDEN, b. Sandy Hill 20 July 1862;[199] m. abt. 1881[200] ELLA CORNELIA BRAGG, b. Ft. Edward, N.Y., 25 Feb. 1864, dau. of LUCIUS and ALMIRA (CONGDON) BRAGG.[201] Worked as photographer, grocer, postmaster in North River.

Children of ERNEST and ELLA (BRAGG) AMEDEN:

a. *Archibald Alembert Ameden,* b. Fort Edward, N.Y., 28 Jan. 1883;[202] d. Dobbs Ferry, N.Y., 9 Dec. 1921 (chronic nephritis);[203] bur. Sleepy Hollow Cem., N. Tarrytown, N.Y., 12 Dec. 1921;[204] m. New York, N.Y., 31 Dec. 1913

---

195   Warren County Deeds.

196   Elsie Ameden household, 1910 U.S. cens., Warren Co., N.Y., pop. sched., Johnsburg, SD 164, ED 164, sheet 224, dw. 154, fam. 170.

197   Elsie Ameden's will, Warren Co. Surrogate Court, 1917 book, pp 349-50.

198   Alembert and Elsie Ameden tombstone, section 1: 116, Union Cemetery.

199   Ernest J. Ameden death record, Johnsburg Town Clerk. The death record states his age at death as seventy-seven years, eight months, sixteen days.

200   Ernest Ameden household, 1900 U.S. cens., Warren Co., N.Y., pop. sched., Chestertown, SD 5, ED 95, sheet 3B, dw. 57, fam. 57.

201   Ella Ameden death record, Johnsburg Town Clerk. The death record states her age at death as ninety years, twenty-two days.

202   Archie Alembert Ameden birth record, Fort Edward Town Clerk.

203   Archibald Alembert Ameden death record, Greensburgh Town Clerk, Dobbs Ferry, New York.

204   Archibald Alembert Ameden interment record, Sleepy Hollow Cemetery, North Tarrytown, New York.

Alvina Paula Mussmann,[205] b. New York, N.Y., 8 Feb. 1884, dau. of German immigrants *Louis* and *Louise (Brommund) Mussmann.*[206] Advertising executive in New York City.

Children of *Archibald* and *Alvina (Mussmann) Ameden*:

1. Alden Alvin Ameden, b. New York, N.Y., 16 Jan. 1915.[207]

2. Kent Alembert Ameden, b. New York, N.Y., 6 Oct. 1917.[208]

b. *John Howard "Howard" Ameden*, b. prob. Fort Edward 17 Sept. 1884;[209] m. 1) Pittsfield, Mass., 10 Oct. 1908 *Evelyn Whittaker*,[210] b. North Creek, N.Y., July 1887, dau. of *John B.* and *Louisa M. (___) Whittaker*,[211] divorced; m. 2) bef. 12 Sept. 1918 *Beulah Brown*,[212] b. N.Y. Jan. 1897,[213] dau. of *John* and *Lillian (___) Brown*, living with parents in 1920 though married.[214]

Child of *Howard* and *Evelyn (Whittaker) Ameden*:

1. Ernest Ameden, b. New York, N.Y., 14 May 1909;[215] adopted by stepfather, Clarence Potter.[216] Resided Warrensburg, N.Y., 1930.[217]

c. *Roswell "Ross" Ameden.* b. Johnsburg, N.Y., 26 Aug. 1890; m. North Creek, N.Y., 6 June 1920 *Minnie Sanders*

---

205   Ameden-Mussman marriage record, New York, N.Y., record 32986-1913.

206   Alvina Mussman birth record, New York, N.Y., record 389382.

207   Alden A. Ameden birth rec., Greensburgh town clerk, Dobbs Ferry, N.Y.

208   Personal testimony of Kent Ameden.

209   John Howard Ameden, Ancestry.com, *World War I Draft Registration.*

210   Ameden-Whittaker marriage announcement, *Warrensburg News*, 15 October 1908.

211   John Whitaker household, 1900 U.S. cens., Warren Co., N.Y., pop. sched., Johnsburg, SD 5, ED 99, sheet 12A, dw. 268, fam. 271.

212   John Howard Ameden, Ancestry.com, *World War I Draft Registration.*

213   John Brown household, 1900 U.S. census, Otsego County, New York, population schedule, Maryland, SD 11, ED 119, sheet 2A, dwelling 31, family 34; National Archives micropublication T623, roll 1145.

214   John Brown household, 1920 U.S. census, Otsego County, New York, population schedule, Otsego, SD 5, ED 223, sheet 4A, dwelling 95, family 108; National Archives micropublication T625, roll 1256.

215   Ernest A. Potter obituary, *The Post-Star*, Glens Falls, New York.

216   Adoption attested by Alden A. Ameden, nephew of Howard Ameden.

217   Clarence Potter household, 1930 U.S. cens., Warren Co., N.Y., pop. sched., Warrensburg, SD 5, ED 57-31, sheet 11A, dw. 327, fam. 3276.

Richardson, b. Johnsburg, N.Y., 13 March 1898, dau. of *Charles* and *Henrietta (Sanders) Richardson.* Minnie and her twin Millie were born one year after five of seven older siblings died in a diphtheria epidemic. Ross suffered infantile paralysis and walked with a severe limp. That did not stop him from being an avid fisherman, scrambling over the rocks and rills of the Hudson River.

Child of *Ross* and *Minnie (Richardson) Ameden*:

1. Preston Ernest Ameden, b. Glens Falls, N.Y., 29 March 1921.[218]

ii. WILLIAM AMEDEN, b. June 1863; d. 19 Aug. 1864; bur. Union Cemetery, Ft. Edward, N.Y.[219]

Ellen A. (Ameden) Hammond (1841–1908)

54. ELLEN A. AMEDEN[7] *(JOHNSON[6], JOHN[5], JACOB[4] AMIDOWN, HENRY[3], PHILIP[2], ROGER[1] AMADOWNE)* was born at Sandy Hill, New York, on 5 July 1841. She died at Sandy Hill on 17 December 1908.[220] She married at Sandy Hill on 14 October 1867 FERNANDO DECOELLA HAMMOND.[221] Fernando was born at Caldwell, New York, on 7 May 1841, the son of PERRY GARDNER and MARY ANN (HAMMOND) HAMMOND. He died at Pawlet, Vermont, on 24 November 1911.[222]

Ellen grew up in Sandy Hill where the census taker recorded her with her parents in 1850, 1855, and 1860.

Fernando grew up in Caldwell, the sixth of thirteen children.[223] Living in the remoteness of Caldwell, it is no surprise to see that his father was a sawyer and carpenter in the early years. As Caldwell

---

218 Attested by Preston's wife, Leona Ameden.

219 William Ameden tombstone, Union Cemetery, Ft. Edward, N.Y.

220 Ellen Hammond death certificate, Kingsbury Town Clerk, 210 Main Street, Hudson Falls, New York 12839.

221 Hammond-Amedon marriage, 14 October 1867, Hudson Falls United Methodist Church, *New York DAR GRC Report,* series 1, volume 55, page 255.

222 Fernando Hammond death record, Pawlet Death Register, Town Clerk, Pawlet, Vermont, volume 4, page 15, number 31.

223 P. G. Hammond household, 1840 U.S. cens., Warren Co., N.Y., Caldwell, p. 362, line 2.

Perry G. Hammond household, 1850 U.S. cens., Warren Co., N.Y., pop. sched., Caldwell, p. 1B-2, dw. 15, fam. 15.

Perry Hammond household, 1860 U.S. cens., Warren Co., N.Y., pop. sched., Caldwell, p. 22, dw. 162, fam. [].

matured and the Great Forest of the Adirondacks was pushed back, he became a farmer. No doubt all thirteen children worked on the farm until they left home. Sometime after 1860 Fernando left home and established himself in Glens Falls as a carpenter.

Did Ellen and Fernando become acquainted because Ellen's brother was also working as a carpenter? Glens Falls and Sandy Hill are adjacent cities on the shore of the Hudson River that now form one continuous metropolitan area, but in the 1860's they were still distinct villages. However it may be that they became acquainted, they were married at the Sandy Hill Methodist Church in 1867 by the Reverend J. Phillips, with Ellen's father, Johnson, present as the witness. Gertrude arrived sometime in 1869. On 12 November 1869 Ellen paid her father $500 for a lot in Glens Falls that Johnson had bought from Ellen's brother Alembert. At that time, Ellen was listed as being "of Glens Falls." But the young couple moved in with Ellen's parents sometime within the next seven months, where the census taker enumerated them in 1870.[224]

Fernando continued working as a carpenter. Antoinette arrived in 1871 while the family was still in Sandy Hill. On 13 January 1877, Ellen bought a lot on Canal Street in Sandy Hill from her father for $1000. But the young family returned to Glens Falls, where they were living at 4 Oak Street in 1880. The house must have been a two-flat, because an unmarried Irish clergyman named James McDermott was also living at 4 Oak Street, but is listed as residing in a different dwelling.[225]

When Ellen's father died in 1880, she bought out her brother's interest in her father's real estate in Sandy Hill. He owned property on Cherry Street that Ellen and the other heirs sold to Cornelia Temple on 12 December 1882 for $1900. Her father's residence lay across Main Street from Zion Episcopal Church. On 1 February 1883 she and her stepmother, Nancy Ameden, sold the property to Zion Church for a manse or rectory for $2700. The church tore down Johnson's house and replaced it with a new structure. Ellen and Fernando continued to reside in Glens Falls for another decade. Fernando

---

224   Johnson Ameden household, 1870 U.S. cens., Washington Co., N.Y., pop. sched., Kingsbury, Sandy Hill post office, p. 423C, dw. 59, fam. 64.

225   F. D. Hammond household, 1880 U.S. cens., Warren Co., N.Y., pop. sched., Queensbury, SD 6, ED 122, p. 11, dw. 77, fam. 104.

continued to work as a carpenter, increasingly becoming a builder.[226]
By 1900 Fernando was almost sixty years old. Perhaps carpentry
had taken its toll. Fernando and Ellen returned to Sandy Hill and
bought a house at 51 Main Street, just a few doors from the house
where Ellen grew up. While still working as a carpenter, Fernando
had been unemployed for six of the twelve months prior to the visit of
the census taker. Antoinette was still single and living at home.
Fernando's nephew, Edward Hammond, was living with them in his
third year of apprenticeship.[227]

Antoinette married in 1902, leaving Fernando and Ellen alone.
Ellen died of heart disease in 1908 and was buried in Union
Cemetery, Fort Edward, just a few lots from her parents and
brothers.[228] In 1910 Fernando was living alone in a rented two-flat at
95 Main Street, in what was now called Hudson Falls, formerly Sandy
Hill. He died of tuberculosis a year later in 1911, at age seventy.
Death was probably at the home of his daughter Antoinette in Pawlet,
Vermont. He was buried beside Ellen in Union Cemetery.[229]

Children of FERNANDO and ELLEN (AMEDEN) HAMMOND:

i.   GERTRUDE HAMMOND, b. prob. Sandy Hill abt. 1869;[230] d. aft.
     1900 when mother reported her two children were still living,
     prob. had married.[231]

ii. ANTOINETTE ADELAIDE HAMMOND, b. Sandy Hill, 29 May
     1871;[232] m. 1901 WILLIAM SMITH HITT,[233] b. Granville,
     N.Y.,[234] March 1870.[235] Dairy farming Pawlet, Vt., 1930.

---

226   Ancestry.com, *Glen Falls, New York Directories, 1888, 1890, 1891-92*,
online (Provo, Utah: Ancestry.com, 2000). Original data: *Glen Falls, NY, 1888*
(Glen Falls, N.Y.: Wm. H. Kirwin., 1888). *Glen Falls, NY, 1890* (Glen Falls, N.Y.:
Wm. H. Kirwin., 1890). *Glen Falls, NY, 1891-92* (Glen Falls, N.Y.: Wm. H.
Kirwin., 1891).
227   Fernando Hammond hhd, 1900 U.S. cens., Washington Co., N.Y., pop.
sched., Kingsbury, Sandy Hill village, SD 5, ED 138, sheet 8A, dw. 144, fam. 159.
228   Ellen Hammond marker, section 1: 121, Union Cem., Ft. Edward, N.Y.
229   Fernando Hammond marker, sect. 1: 121, Union Cem., Ft. Edward, N.Y.
230   Johnson Ameden household, 1870 U.S. cens., Washington Co., N.Y., pop.
sched., Kingsbury, Sandy Hill post office, p. 423C, dw. 59, fam. 64.
231   Fernando Hammond household, 1900 U.S. cens., Washington Co., N.Y.,
pop. sched., Kingsbury, SD 5, ED 138, sheet 8A, dw. 144, fam. 159.
232   Antoinette Hitt death record, Pawlet, Vermont Death Register, vol. 13.
233   William S. Hitt household, 1930 U.S. census, Rutland County, Vermont,
population schedule, Pawlet, SD 2, ED 1-19, sheet 7A, dwelling 140, family 141;
National Archives micropublication T626, roll 2430.
234   Hitt-Pritchard marriage, Pawlet Vermont Marriage License Book 14:31.

Children of WILLIAM and ANTOINETTE (HAMMOND) HITT:[236]

a. *Ellen Hitt*, b. Vt. abt. 1904; living with parents, 1930.
b. *Gertrude Hitt*, b. Vt. abt. 1906; stenographer at Manhattan dept. store, 1930.[237]
c. *Robert Anson Hitt*, b. Vt. abt. 1908; mechanic at bag mill in Hudson Falls, 1930.[238]
d. *Galen Randel Hitt*, b. Vt. abt. 1908; living with parents, 1930.

Archibald Ogden Ameden (1838–1890)

55. ARCHIBALD OGDEN "A.O." AMEDEN[7] (*HAMILTON[6], JOHN[5], JACOB[4] AMIDOWN, HENRY[3], PHILIP[2], ROGER[1] AMADOWNE*) was born at the town of Queensbury, New York, on 21 October 1838.[239] He died at Glens Falls, New York, on 28 November 1890.[240] He married first before 24 November 1868 MARY JANE SEELYE.[241] Mary was born at Queensbury in about 1836, the daughter of DAVID and RHODA (CLEMENTS) SEELYE. She died at Ticonderoga, New York, on 12 September 1876.[242] A.O. married second probably at Glens Falls in 1879 HARRIET CORNELIA "HATTIE" (BACON) DELANO. Hattie was born at Orwell, Vermont, on 17 January 1843, the daughter of JOHN and HARRIET (HUBBARD) BACON.[243]

---

235 Anson Hitt household, 1900 U.S. census, Rutland County, Vermont, population schedule, Pawlet, SD "Vt," ED 199, sheet 9A, dwelling 199, family 216; National Archives micropub. T623, roll 1694.

236 William Hitt household, 1920 U.S. census, Rutland County, Vermont, population schedule, Pawlet, SD 1, ED 122, sheet 14A-B, dwelling 319, family 342; National Archives micropub. T625, roll 1874.

237 Emogene Folger household, 1930 U.S. census, New York County, New York, population schedule, New York, SD 24, ED 31-87, sheet 15A, dwelling 55, family 39; National Archives micropublication T626, roll 1563.

238 Charity Woodrich household, 1930 U.S. cens., Warren Co., N.Y., pop. sched., Hudson Falls, SD 5, ED 58-33, sheet 11A, dw. 304, fam. 281.

239 Smith, *History of Warren County*, 440.

240 A. O. Ameden tombstone, Jenkins Cemetery, Glens Falls, N.Y.

241 Warren County Deed dated 12 September 1876 between Archibald O. Ameden and Mary J. Ameden, his wife, grantors, and Varness Goolah and Angeline Goolah, his wife, grantees.

242 Mary Ameden tombstone, Seelye Cemetery, Warren County, New York, photographed by Nancy Mullen July 1995.

243 Bill Nyland, husband of Hattie's granddaughter, in email to Nancy Mullen 7 June 2000.

A.O. grew up in the Butternut Flats section of Queensbury, where he was counted with his family in 1840, 1850, 1855, and 1860, when he was listed as a laborer. He may have already been working on university studies by 1860. On 14 December 1865 the University of Vermont granted A.O. a medical degree, which was duly recorded by the Warren County clerk. Soon thereafter he must have married Mary Jane Seelye.

Mary also grew up in the town of Queensbury, one of six or more children. Her father owned a typical small farm near Glens Falls. Mary was listed with the family in 1840,[244] 1850,[245] and 1860.[246]

A.O. set up his first practice in Patten's Mills, where he practiced for three years.[247] The first record of A.O. and Mary as husband and wife is a deed dated 24 November 1868, in which A.O. and Mary sold land on the highway leading from Pattens Mills in Washington County to Varness Goolah and his wife Angelina.[248] Perhaps the sale represented A.O.'s decision to move north to Ticonderoga to set up a practice there.

By 1870 A.O. and Mary were settled in Ticonderoga. Their real estate, valued at $500, was the smallest of their neighbors, but they seem to have located in a good neighborhood. The neighbors on either side had large enough households to have live-in domestic servants.[249] Mary did not survive the decade. She died childless in Ticonderoga in 1876 at age forty. A.O. had her body returned to Queensbury and buried in the Seelye Cemetery there.[250]

At the start of 1878 A.O. gave up his practice in Ticonderoga after nine years[251] and returned to Glens Falls, where he lived out the rest of his life. He remarried in 1879; his bride was the widow Harriet Cornelia (Bacon) DeLano. Hattie Bacon grew up in Orwell, Vermont,

---

[244]   David Sela household, 1840 U.S. cens., Warren Co., N.Y., Queensbury, page 285, line 19.

[245]   David Seelye household, 1850 U.S. cens., Warren Co., N.Y., pop. sched., Queensbury, p. 66, dw. 145, fam. 152.

[246]   David Seeley household, 1860 U.S. cens., Warren Co., N.Y., pop. sched., Queensbury, p. 147, dw. 1171.

[247]   Smith, *History of Warren County,* 440.

[248]   Washington County deed, dated 24 November 1868.

[249]   A O Amoden household, 1870 U.S. census, Essex County, New York, population schedule, Town of Ticonderoga, page 1, dwelling 2, family 2; National Archives micropublication M593, roll 936.

[250]   Mary Ameden tombstone, Seelye Cemetery, Warren County, N.Y.

[251]   Smith, *History of Warren County,* 440.

the sixth of seven children. Her father was an affluent farmer of Orwell.[252] In 1868 Hattie married Rollin DeLano, a druggist. They moved west to St. Paul, Minnesota, where young Rollin was born in March 1870 and the family was recorded in the 1870 census.[253] Little Alma was born in 1872, but Rollin Sr. died in the same year, leaving his two infants fatherless. Hattie took her two children and returned to New York. She married A.O. in 1879.

A.O., Hattie, and her children were enumerated at 5 Church Street, Glens Falls, in 1880.[254] A.O. joined the Warren County Medical Society that same year. On 2 December 1880 Hattie bought a small lot at the corner of Church and Main from William and Sarah McEchron for $2700. As A.O. built his medical practice, Hattie grew the family with the addition of Walter, born in 1882. On 27 January 1886, the local newspaper, the *Morning Star*, reported that A.O. and other local physicians were planning to open a "medical and surgical institute" in Glens Falls within a few months. He served as health officer of Glens Falls and Queensbury from 1888 until his death. During his tenure he battled diphtheria and scarlet fever epidemics with energy and efficiency.[255] He was listed in the *Glens Falls City Directory of 1888 and 1890* as physician and surgeon, with his office at 94 Glen Street, and his residence a rental at Central House.[256]

A.O. seems to have been a harsh and critical man. Hattie took her children and fled to Worthfield, Minnesota. From there she sold her property at Church and Main to Melville and Glorianna Sheldon on 4 July 1885, giving them a mortgage for $1144.42. What trauma stalked the family? A.O. filed a criminal indictment against Hattie for kidnapping, claiming that on 13 September 1885 she "unlawfully, willfully and feloniously did steal, take, lead, entice and carry away

---

[252] Wright Bacon household, 1850 U.S. census, Addison County, Vermont, population schedule, Orwell, page 42B, dwelling 153, family 164; National Archives micropublication M432, roll 920.

John W. Bacon household, 1860 U.S. census, Addison County, Vermont, population schedule, Orwell, page 194, dwelling 203, family 204; National Archives micropublication M653, roll 1173.

[253] Rollin DeLano household, 1870 U.S. census, Ramsey County, Minnesota, population schedule, St. Paul, page 59, dwelling 161, family 415; National Archives micropublication T132, roll 10.

[254] A.O. Ameden household, 1880 U.S. cens., Warren Co., N.Y., pop. sched., Queensbury, SD 6, ED 122, p. 16, dw. 128, fam. 157.

[255] John Austin, letter to Nancy K. Mullen, 19 May 1996.

[256] Ancestry.com, *Glens Falls, New York, City Directory*, 1888, 1890.

one Walter Ameden, a child of male sex then and there being under the age of twelve years, with intent then and there to keep and conceal the said Walter Ameden from Archibald O. Ameden, the father and parent of said child, who had then and there the lawful and legal care and control of the said Walter Ameden against the form of the statute in such case made and provided and against the peace of the people of the state of New York and their dignity."[257]

Hattie was still in Worthfield when she sold a second parcel in Glens Falls at Church and Maple, which she must have inherited, to Harriet J. Root on 9 April 1886 for $2900.[258] A.O. followed her in 1886, according to family tradition, and snatched Walter. He seemed to be fascinated by the development of his progeny and kept extensive diaries of everything Walter ate or did.[259] But A.O. was not to see Walter grow to manhood. A.O. suffered a heart attack in 1890. He was buried with his parents and siblings in Jenkins Cemetery, Glens Falls.[260] His obituary described him thus:

> He was faithful and steadfast to his friends, but a strong opponent of everything that met his dislike. He was possessed by an inflexible will which, being fixed upon a goal, nothing could bend or alter. Possessed by a kind heart, those who were experienced in his ways and knew him best, say that people who called him unsympathetic and hard, knew nothing of the tender nature of the man, nor of his devotion to a widowed mother, now left alone almost without a prop in her declining years. Dr. Ameden was without doubt the most efficient and energetic health officer we have ever had here. . .[261]

A.O.'s will named Reuben N. Peck, a local druggist, as guardian for the boy, but he refused to serve, so the court appointed A.O.'s younger brother, Eugene, as guardian for the boy. Eugene apparently decided the best place for Walter was with his mother, and the boy was sent to Minnesota.

When Hattie had returned to Minnesota, she also had returned to

---

257 Warren County Criminal Indictments, book 9:13, Warren County Archives, Lake George, New York.
258 Warren County deeds.
259 Bill Nyland, to Nancy K. Mullen 7 June 2000.
260 A. O. Ameden tombstone, Jenkins Cemetery.
261 *Morning Star*, Glens Falls, New York, 29 November 1890; cited by John Austin in letter to Nancy K. Mullen, 19 May 1996.

the use of the DeLano name. When young Walter joined her, she renamed him Ted DeLano. If A.O. had thought his name would be carried on through his son, he was mistaken!

Tragedy in Hattie's star-crossed life continued when Alma died in San Diego, California, in September 1896, at age twenty-four, from tuberculosis.[262] In 1900 Hattie was living at 897 Dayton Avenue, with her two remaining sons, a German-born teacher who was boarding with her, and an Irish servant.[263] Tragedy struck again just a month after the census taker visited. Rollin drowned in Lake Minnetonka on 1 July 1900.[264] Hattie was devastated, and withdrew into a protective shell, leaving Ted to fend for himself at age seventeen. The 1910 census shows Hattie and Ted living together with a servant in Saint Paul, but gives no hint of the family trauma.[265] No further record has been found for her. A descendant gave her death as occurring in Saint Paul on 19 April 1916, but no death record has been found in Minnesota.[266]

Child of ARCHIBALD and HARRIET (BACON) AMEDEN:

i. WALTER EDWARD AMEDEN aka EDWARD DELANO, b. Glens Falls, N.Y., 30 Sept. 1882; m. Hardisty, Canada, 1 Nov. 1910 MAUDE MYRTLE LAWES, b. Glenco, Ontario, Canada, 21 Nov. 1889, dau. of English immigrants HENRY and EMILY (MOORE) LAWES.[267] Resided Hannah, N.D., 1918; salesman for The Aluminum Cooking Utensil Co.[268]

    Children of WALTER and MAUDE (LAWES) AMEDEN:[269]

    a. *Harriet Alberta Delano*, b. Alberta, Canada, 7 Feb. 1912.
    b. *Frederick L. Delano*, b. St. Paul, Minn., 2 July 1914.
    c. *Mary Delano*, b. St. Paul, Minn., 10 Dec. 1915.

---

262 Alma Delano death certificate, County Clerk, San Diego, California.

263 Harriet DeLano household, 1900 U.S. census, Ramsey County, Minnesota, population schedule, St. Paul, SD 47, ED 120, sheet 14, dwelling 2438, family 264; National Archives micropub. T623, roll 785.

264 John Dalby, *Minnesota Burials*, (Provo, Utah: MyFamily.com, 2003).

265 Darriet B. Delaus household, 1910 U.S. census, Ramsey County, Minnesota, population schedule, Saint Paul ward 7, SD 4, ED 106, sheet 12B, dwelling 254, family 277; National Archives micropublication T624, roll 720.

266 Bill Nyland, in email to Nancy Mullen 7 June 2000.

267 Bill Nyland, in Internet posting at <awtc.ancestry.com/cgi-bin/igm.cgi?op=GET&db=:527708&id=I029>, downloaded 1 July 2006.

268 Walter Edward Delano, Ancestry.com, *World War I Draft Registration*.

269 Ted Delano family genealogy notes, held by his granddaughter, Mrs. Bill Nyland.

d. *June Ogden Delano*, b. Hannah, N.D., 11 June 1917.
e. *Ruth Delano*, b. Hannah, N.D., 11 Feb. 1919.
f. *Robert H. Delano*, b. Grand Forks, N.D., 9 June 1924.

Eugene W. Ameden (1845–1924)

56. EUGENE W. AMEDEN[7] *(HAMILTON[6], JOHN[5], JACOB[4] AMIDOWN, HENRY[3], PHILIP[2], ROGER[1] AMADOWNE)* was born at Warren County, New York,[270] in October 1845.[271] He died at Saratoga Springs, New York, on 15 February 1924.[272] He married at Bolton, New York, on 5 June 1873 LAURA THOMAS.[273] Laura was born in June 1848,[274] probably at Bolton, New York, the daughter of WARREN and REBECCA (___) THOMAS.[275] She died in 1923.[276]

Eugene grew up in the Butternut Flats section of Queensbury, where he was counted with the family in 1850, 1855, 1860, and 1870. By 1870 he was working as a carpenter. On 2 April 1872 he purchased one-and-a-quarter acres in the town of Johnsburg, in the northwest corner of the county, from James and Carrie Kenwill for $500. His land was on Thirteenth Pond Brook, on the road to Indian Lake that runs through the tiny hamlet of North River. Eugene was already resident in Johnsburg when he bought the land. He may have

---

[270] Hamilton Ameden household, 1855 New York state cens., Warren Co., Queensbury, fam. 170.

[271] Eugene Ameden household, 1900 U.S. census, Saratoga County, New York, population schedule, Saratoga Springs, SD 7, ED 128, sheet 13, dwelling 217/213, family 312; National Archives micropublication T623, roll 1159.

[272] Saratoga County Surrogate file 607-4, Surrogate Court, Saratoga, New York; reported by John Austin, in letter to Nancy Mullen 19 May 1996.

[273] *Sandy Hill Herald*, reprinted in: Jackson and Jackson, *Marriage Notices from Washington County*, 101.

[274] The 1900 census gives her birth as June 1849, but the 1850 census reports that she was already two years old. The 1860 census is consistent with 1850, reporting her age as twelve years old. Knowing the censuses closer to her birth are more reliable, it is believed that Laura was born in 1848, not 1849. See subsequent footnotes for census citations.

[275] Warren Thomas was resident at Bolton in 1840 and 1850:
Warren Thomas household, 1840 U. S. census, Warren County, New York, Bolton, page 322/341, line 24.
Warren Thomas household, 1850 U.S. census, Warren County, New York, population schedule, Bolton, page 12, dwelling 35, family 36.

[276] Dave Bixby & Heritage Hunters of Saratoga County, "Greenridge Cemetery, Saratoga Springs," online, <www.rootsweb.com/ ~nysarato/BxbGRC-A.htm>.

been operating one of the two grocery stores in North River, and only now took ownership of the store. Ten weeks later, on 25 June 1872, Eugene sold one-third acre of the land he had just purchased to Simon Towns for $450.[277] It would seem that Eugene and Simon partnered in running the store, with ownership of the store cycling between the two men several times before ending with Simon. North River consisted only of two grocery stores and a hotel. Eugene's first cousin, Alembert Ameden (page 257), ran the other store. One wonders what competitiveness existed between the two cousins!

Laura grew up in Bolton, eighteen miles due north of Glens Falls, on the western shore of Lake George. She was enumerated there with her parents and three siblings in 1850, 1860,[278] and 1870.[279]

Eugene and Laura married in Bolton in 1873, when he was twenty-seven and she was twenty-five. They set up housekeeping in North River.[280] But they may have found the Adirondack hamlet too remote for raising a family. By 17 October 1877 they had relocated to Warrensburgh, down the mountain quite close to Lake George, and only nine miles from Laura's hometown of Bolton. On that day Eugene purchased one-half acre on the highway from North Creek (a larger village than North River) to Indian Lake from Lyman and Amy Robles for $100. He bought back the land in North River he had sold to Simon Towns on 7 January 1878 for $450. He sold the half-acre in North Creek to Henry Smith for $450 on 24 August 1878.

By 1880 two sons had joined them: Albert, age four, and Clarence, age three. Warren was again working as a carpenter.[281] The family did not stay in Warrensburgh. Perhaps it was in anticipation of their departure that, on 7 January 1887, Eugene sold his store and lands to Clara A. Towns, the twelve-year-old daughter of Simon Towns, for $100. By 1888 Eugene and Laura had relocated to Saratoga Springs, New York, thirty-three miles due south of Warrensburgh. They lived

---

277   Warren County deeds.

278   Warren Thomas household, 1860 U.S. cens., Warren Co., N.Y., pop. sched., Bolton, p. 28, dw. 207, fam. 207.

279   Warren Thomas household, 1870 U.S. cens., Warren Co., N.Y., pop. sched., Bolton, p. 15, dw. 132, fam. 133.

280   F. W. Beers, *Atlas of Warren County, New York, 1876*, New York State Library, Albany, New York.

281   Eugene Ameden household, 1880 U.S. cens., Warren Co., N.Y., pop. sched., Warrensburgh, SD 6, ED 126, p. 14, dw. 120, fam. 120.

at 101 Lawrence Street at the corner of Waterbury Street.[282] There they lived out their lives, with Eugene working as a carpenter instead of a merchant.

On 19 November 1889, Laura, along with her mother and sister Betsey Cameron, sold land in Bolton to Conway Sexton for $300. This land sale probably reflected the death of Laura's father, and settlement of his estate.

On 5 March 1894, Eugene was serving as "committee of the person and property of Maria Ogden, lunatic," and was obliged to permit sale of her real estate for payment of her debts.[283] Maria was an aunt, a younger sister of Eugene's mother, Jane. She had never married, and had lived her life on the family farm with her widowed mother and spinster older sister, Electa.

By 1900 both sons, Albert and Clarence, had left Saratoga Springs, and Eugene and Laura were alone. Eugene was still working as a carpenter, and they owned their home at 25 Waterbury Street. It was a two-family dwelling; a shipping clerk named Barney Smith lived in the other half of the building with his wife, Caroline, and their adult son, Clarence.[284] By 1903, younger son Clarence Ameden had returned to Saratoga Springs, where he died at age twenty-six.

Eugene and Laura continued to live at 25 Waterbury Street in 1910[285] and 1920.[286] By 1920, Eugene was no longer able to work as a carpenter and declared that he had no occupation. Laura died in 1923 at age seventy-four or seventy-five. Eugene died in 1924 at age seventy-eight. They are buried together in Greenridge Cemetery, the largest cemetery in the town of Saratoga Springs.

Children of EUGENE and LAURA (THOMAS) AMEDEN:

i.   ALBERT HAMILTON AMEDEN, b. N.Y. 18 July 1875;[287] m. abt. 1901 LUCIA S. COLLINS, b. prob. Saratoga Springs, N.Y., Oct.

---

[282]   Ancestry.com, *Saratoga Springs, New York, Directories, 1888-92,* online (Provo, Utah: Ancestry.com, 2000); Original data: *Saratoga Springs, NY 1888* (Saratoga Springs, N.Y.: William H. Kirwin, 1888).

[283]   Warren County deeds.

[284]   Eugene Ameden household, 1900 U.S. cens., Saratoga Co., N.Y., pop. sched., Saratoga Springs, SD 6, ED 126, p. 14, dw. 120, fam. 120.

[285]   Eugene Ameden household, 1910 U.S. cens., Saratoga Co., N.Y., pop. sched., Saratoga Springs, SD 9, ED 126, p. 1A, dw. 197, fam. 243.

[286]   Eugene Ameden household, 1920 U.S. census, Saratoga County, New York, population schedule, Saratoga Springs, SD 362, ED 136, page 8/83, dwelling 173, family 219; National Archives micropublication T625, roll 1261.

[287]   Albert Hamilton Amidon, Ancestry.com, *World War I Draft Registration.*

1876,[288] daughter of HENRY D. and ELLA S. (___) COLLINS.[289] They lived at 30 Chestnut St., Schenectady, N.Y., on 12 Sept. 1918; an inspector for General Electric Company in Schenectady.[290]

ii.   CLARENCE R. AMEDEN, b. N.Y. 14 Feb. 1877;[291] d. Saratoga Springs, N.Y., 5 June 1903;[292] m. 1899 JULIA F. ___, b. N.Y. July 1879.

Alida A. (Ameden) Worden (1856–1888)

57. ALIDA A. "IDA" AMEDEN[7] *(HAMILTON[6], JOHN[5], JACOB[4] AMIDOWN, HENRY[3], PHILIP[2], ROGER[1] AMADOWNE)* was born in 19 September 1855 probably at Queensbury, New York. She died on 22 August 1888.[293] She married at St. James Episcopal Church, Caldwell, New York, on 28 November 1882 ALLEN H. WORDEN.[294] He was born at Fort Edward, New York, in April 1863, the son of HENRY and ELISABETH (___) WORDEN.[295]

Ida's older siblings were born in Queensbury town, New York. Her parents lived out their lives in the Butternut Flats district of Queensbury. So it is most probable that Ida was also born there. Ida was enumerated with her family in 1860 and 1870. She hasn't been found in the 1880 census.

Allen's boyhood was spent in Fort Edward, but the family moved to Caldwell between 1870[296] and 1880.[297] Allen was still living at home in 1880.

---

288   Henry Collins household, 1900 U.S. cens., Saratoga Co., N.Y., pop. sched., Saratoga Springs, SD 7, ED 133, p. 11A, dw. 231, fam. 259.

289   Henry D. Collins household, 1880 U.S. census, Saratoga County, New York, population schedule, Town of Saratoga Springs, SD 6, ED 87, page 4, dwelling 24, family 52; National Archives micropublication T9, roll 929.

290   Ibid.

291   Greenridge cemetery transcription: <www.rootsweb.com/~nysarato/BxbGRC-A.htm>.

292   Clarence Ameden death certificate, Saratoga Springs death cert. #22483.

293   Alida Worden tombstone, Jenkins Cemetery, Queensbury, New York.

294   Worden-Amedon marriage, register #6, town of Lake George, New York.

295   Henry Worden household, 1880 U.S. cens., Warren Co., N.Y., pop. sched., Caldwell, SD 5, ED 73, sheet 5, dw. 131, fam. 134.

296   Henry Worden household, 1870 U.S. cens., Washington Co., N.Y., pop. sched., Fort Edward, p. 921/208, dw. 555, fam. 708.

297   Henry Worden household, 1880 U.S. cens., Warren Co., N.Y., pop. sched., Caldwell, SD 5, ED 73, sheet 5, dwelling 131, family 134.

Ida and Allen married in 1882. Lawrence was born in 1884. But Lawrence was not to have his mother for long. She died in 1888, age thirty-two, when Lawrence was barely four years old. She is buried in Jenkins Cemetery, along with her parents and most of her siblings.[298]

Allen never remarried. He and his young son returned to the family farm, where his mother helped raise Lawrence.[299] By 1910, Lawrence had married and established his own household, and Allen's father had died. Allen and his mother continued farming the family homestead.[300] By 1920, his mother had probably died, too. He was boarding with Anne Smith in the city of Lake George on Schuyler Heights Street, though still listed as a farmer. Next door was his youngest brother, Fred.[301] By 1930 Allen was seventy-seven years old. He had given up farming and was listed as a carpenter, living in town on Canada Street with a widowed younger brother, Edwin.[302]

Child of ALLEN and ALIDA (AMEDEN) WORDEN:

i.   LAWRENCE EUGENE WORDEN, b. 21 July 1884,[303] prob. Caldwell, N.Y.; m. 1905 NATALIE DARROW, b. N.Y. April, 1886, daughter of FREDERICK A. and EMILY J. (STEVENS) DARROW.[304] Carpenter in Lake George, N.Y., 1930.[305]

    Children of LAWRENCE and NATALIE (DARROW) WORDEN:[306]

    a.   *Ruth T. Worden*, b. prob. Caldwell, N.Y., abt. 1910. Worked as typist/bookkeeper in 1930.

---

298   Alida Ameden tombstone, Jenkins Cemetery.
299   Henry Worden household, 1900 U.S. cens., Warren Co., N.Y., pop. sched., Caldwell, SD 5, ED 93, sheet 19B, dw. 131, fam. 134.
300   Allen Worden household, 1910 U.S. cens., Warren Co., N.Y., pop. sched., Caldwell, SD 7, ED 150, sheet 15A, dw. 370, fam. 385.
301   Anne Smith household, 1920 U.S. cens., Warren Co., N.Y., pop. sched., Caldwell, SD 10, ED 160, sheet 5A, dw. 144, fam. 125.
302   Edwin Worden household, 1930 U.S. cens., Warren Co., N.Y., pop. sched., Caldwell, SD 5, ED 57-2, sheet 1A/1B, dw. 33, fam. 34.
303   Lawrence Worden Ancestry.com, *World War I Draft Registration Card.*
304   Frederick A. Darrow household, 1900 U.S. cens., Warren Co., N.Y., pop. sched., Warrensburg, SD 5, ED 111, sheet 12A, dw. 248, fam. 253.
305   Lawrence Worden household, 1930 U.S. cens., Warren Co., N.Y., pop. sched., Caldwell, SD 5, ED 57-2, sheet 8B, dw. 231, fam. 2326.
306   Lawrence Worden household, 1930 U.S. cens., Warren Co., N.Y., pop. sched., Caldwell, SD 5, ED 57-2, sheet 8B, dw. 231, fam. 232.

    b.   *Arthur C. Worden*, b. prob. Caldwell 13 Feb. 1915.[307]

    c.   *Naomi L. Worden*, b. prob. Caldwell Oct. 1918.[308]

Margarate O. (Ameden) Hawkes (1839–aft 1910)

58. MARGARATE O. AMEDEN[7] *(WARREN[6], JOHN[5], JACOB[4] AMIDOWN, HENRY[3], PHILIP[2], ROGER[1] AMADOWNE)* was born at Queensbury, New York, on 14 August 1838 or 1839,[309] and died at Hudson Falls, New York, on 9 April 1914.[310] She married at Glens Falls, New York, on 7 September 1859 ADOLPHUS F. HAWKES.[311] He was born in New York in about 1835, the son of WILLIAM and SALLY (___) HAWKES.[312] He died after the 1891-92 city directory and before the 1900 census.[313]

Margarate's birth date requires some explanation. Her death certificate implies a birth date of 14 August 1838, but her sister Adela was born in March 1838, making 14 August of the same year unbelievable. The 1900 census says she was born in August 1840. But she must be the infant girl recorded in her father's household as of 1 June 1840, the official date of the 1840 census, making August 1840 unbelievable. The 1850 census, officially recorded as of 1 June that year, lists her as age eleven, which points to the 1838 birth year. But if the census taker erred and recorded her age as of his visit on 27 August 1850, then she was just thirteen days past her eleventh birthday if she was born in 1839. In any event, she grew up in Queensbury.

It is not clear where Adolphus grew up, but his family was in Queensbury by 1850, when young Adolphus was working as a farmer.[314]

Adolphus and Margarate married in 1859 and set up housekeeping in Queensbury. By then Adolphus had started his life work as a

---

307   Arthur Worden entry, Ancestry.com, *Social Security Death Index.*

308   Lawrence Worden household, 1920 U.S. cens., Warren Co., N.Y., pop. sched., Caldwell, SD 7, ED 150, sheet 15A, dw. 370, fam. 385.

    Naomi Lefebvre entry, Ancestry.com, *Social Security Death Index.*

309   Margaret Hawkes death certificate, register number 25, Kingsbury town.

310   Ibid.

311   Austin to Mullen.

312   William Hawks household, 1850 U.S. cens., Warren Co., N.Y., pop. sched., Queensbury, p. 65, dw. 128, fam. 135.

313   The 1900 census lists Margaret Hawkes as widowed.

314   William Hawks household, 1850 U.S. cens., Warren Co., N.Y., pop. sched., Queensbury, p. 65, dw. 128, fam. 135.

machinist. They owned a tiny piece of real estate, valued at $300.[315] The Champlain Canal probably created greater opportunities in Sandy Hill for young machinists. Adolphus and Margarate relocated to Sandy Hill sometime in the next decade. It is not known if that was before or after their children were born. By 1870 they were in Sandy Hill with two children: Willie, born in about 1865, and Nellie, born in 1868.[316] Margarate had a third child who never appeared in a census, but was probably born in the six-year gap between their marriage and Willie's birth. Perhaps he was lost in the Glens Falls smallpox epidemic of 1861.[317] They might have settled directly at 6 Willow Street, which was to be the family homestead for several decades.

By 1880, fifteen-year-old Willie had started clerking. Otherwise the family hadn't changed in the previous decade.[318] Work must have been stable for Adolphus in Sandy Hill. He was recorded there, at 6 Willow Street in Sandy Hill in 1888, 1890, and 1891-2.[319]

Widowhood had overtaken Margarate by 1900. Willie had also died. Nellie had married in 1897, had a daughter Ruth in 1898 and a son Ralph in 1899, but was divorced by 1900. Nellie and her children then lived with Margarate at 6 Willow Street.[320] While Nellie was listed as a music teacher, no occupation was given for Margarate. One wonders how she put food on the table!

The four of them continued together at 6 Willow Street through the next decade.[321] Margarate died in 1914 at age seventy-five from a cerebral hemorrhage. She is buried in Union Cemetery in Fort Edward, New York. [322]

Children of ADOLPHUS and MARGARATE (AMEDEN) HAWKES:

---

315 Alpheus Hawk household, 1860 U.S. cens., Warren Co., N.Y., pop. sched., Queensbury, p. 143, dw. 1139, fam. [].
316 Adolphus F. Hawkes household, 1870 U.S. cens., Washington Co., N.Y., pop. sched., Kingsbury, p. 48, dw. 307, fam. 343.
317 Smith, *History of Warren County*, 426.
318 Adolphus F. Hawks household, 1880 U.S. cens., Washington Co., N.Y., pop. sched., Kingsbury, SD 6, ED 150, p. 7, dw. 64, fam. 66.
319 Ancestry.com, *Glens Falls, New York Directories, 1888, 1890, 1891-92.*
320 Margaret Hawks household, 1900 U.S. cens., Washington Co., N.Y., pop. sched, Kingsbury, SD 5, ED 137, sheet 7B, dw. 136, fam. 164.
321 Margaret Hawks household, 1910 U.S. census, Washington County, New York, population schedule, Kingsbury, SD 6, ED 111, sheet 17B, dwelling 377, family 414; National Archives micropublication T624, roll 1088.
322 Margrate Hawkes tombstone, Union Cemetery, Fort Edward, N.Y.

i.   WILLIE HAWKES, b. N.Y. abt. 1865;[323] d. bef. 1900 (1900 census says only one of his mother's children remained alive, who was Nellie).[324]

ii. NELLIE HAWKES, b. N.Y. March 1868;[325] d. aft. 1920;[326] m. bef. 1898 ___ TANNER, divorced by 1900.[327] Unmarried music teacher in Glens Falls in 1891-2.[328]

Children of __ and NELLIE (HAWKES) TANNER:

a.   *Ruth Tanner*, b. N.Y. April 1898.[329]

b.   *Ralph William Tanner*, b. N.Y. 25 Sept. 1899;[330] m. abt. 1911 *May G. ___*, b. Oh. abt. 1908.[331] Resided with mother in Bridgeport, Conn., 1920.[332] Resident Charlotte, Mich., 1930.[333]

Child of *Ralph W.* and *May G. (__) Tanner*:

1.   Ruth C. Tanner, b. Oh. Jan. 1929.[334]

Irena Adelaide (Ameden) Allen (1842–1874)

59. IRENA ADELAIDE "ADELAIDE" AMEDEN[7] *(WARREN[6], JOHN[5], JACOB[4] AMIDOWN, HENRY[3], PHILIP[2], ROGER[1] AMADOWNE)* was born in Queensbury, New York, in August or September 1842[335] and died on

    [323]   Adolphus F. Hawkes household, 1870 U.S. cens., Washington Co., N.Y., pop. sched., Kingsbury, p. 48, dw. 307, fam. 343.
    [324]   Margaret Hawks household, 1900 U.S. cens., Washington Co., N.Y., pop. sched., Kingsbury, SD 5, ED 137, sheet 7B, dw. 136, fam. 164.
    [325]   Ibid.
    [326]   Nellie Tanner household, 1920 U.S. census, Fairfield County, Connecticut, population schedule, Bridgeport, SD 38, ED 17, sheet 14A, dwelling 294, family 318; National Archives micropub. T625, roll 175.
    [327]   Margaret Hawks household, 1900 U.S. cens., Washington Co., N.Y., pop. sched., Kingsbury, SD 5, ED 137, sheet 7B, dw. 136, fam. 164.
    [328]   Nellie E. Hawkes entry, Ancestry.com, *Glens Fall, New York Directories*.
    [329]   Margaret Hawks household, 1900 U.S. cens., Washington Co., N.Y., pop. sched., Kingsbury, SD 5, ED 137, sheet 7B, dw. 136, fam. 164.
    [330]   Ralph William Tanner, Ancestry.com, *World War I Draft Registration*.
    [331]   Ralph W. Tanner household, 1930 U.S. census, Eaton County, Michigan, population schedule, Charlotte City, SD 13, ED 23-9, sheet 6B, dwelling 160, family 165; National Archives micropublication T626, roll 983.
    [332]   Nellie Tanner household, 1920 U.S. cens., Fairfield Co., Conn., pop. sched., Bridgeport, SD 38, ED 17, sheet 14A, dw. 294, fam. 318.
    [333]   Ralph W. Tanner household, 1930 U.S. cens., Eaton Co., Mich., pop. sched., Charlotte City, SD 13, ED 23-9, sheet 6B, dw. 160, fam. 165.
    [334]   Ibid.
    [335]   Warren Ameden household, 1855 N.Y. cens., Warren Co., Queensbury.

10 September 1874.[336] She married on 10 August 1868 probably in Sandy Hill, New York, to GEORGE HENRY ALLEN.[337] George was born in Cambridge, New York,[338] on 1 January 1834, a son of PELEG and PAMELIA (___) ALLEN.[339] He died at Bolton, New York, on 19 March 1916.[340]

Adelaide's birth is inferred from several records. The 1855 census lists her as age twelve, the 1850 census says seven, and her tombstone says thirty-two. Since the 1850 census was taken in August and she died in September, a birthday of late August or early September 1842 works for all three records. She grew up in Queensbury, where she was recorded with her family in 1850 and 1860.

George's family was in Fort Ann in 1850,[341] but it is not known where they were earlier. George's marriage to Adelaide in 1868 was reported in the *Sandy Hill Herald*, but no location was given. The omission probably means the wedding was in Sandy Hill. Certainly they set up housekeeping in Sandy Hill, next door to George's parents. George worked in a machine shop.[342] A son, Warren, named for his grandfather, was born in 1870.

On 9 August 1873, they were still living in Sandy Hill when they bought Adelaide's family homestead in the village of Jenkinsville, town of Queensbury, from her mother, who was now widowed.[343] Another son, Royal, was born in September 1874. Tragically, Adelaide died on 10 September, probably from complications of childbirth. She was only thirty-two years old. She was buried in Sunnyside Cemetery with her parents and two of her siblings.[344]

George carried on with his two motherless infants for six years,

---

[336]   Irena A. Ameden tombstone, Sunnyside Cemetery, Queensbury, N.Y. "Wife of George H. Allen."

[337]   *Sandy Hill Herald*, reprinted in: Jackson and Jackson, *Marriage Notice,* 70.

[338]   Letter from John Austin to Nancy K. Mullen, 19 July 1996.

[339]   Peleg Allen Household, 1850 U.S. cens., Washington Co., N.Y., pop. sched., Fort Ann, p. 86B, dw. 287, fam. 287.
       George H. Allen household, 1900 U.S. cens., Warren Co., N.Y., pop. sched., Bolton, SD 5, ED 92, sheet 6A, dw. 135, fam. 137.

[340]   George Henry Allen death record, Town Clerk, Bolton, New York.

[341]   Peleg Allen household, 1850 U.S. cens., Washington Co., N.Y., pop. sched., Fort Ann, p. 86B, dw. 287, fam. 287.

[342]   George H. Allen household, 1870 U.S. cens., Washington Co., N.Y., pop. sched., Kingsbury, p. 86B, dw. 287, fam. 287.

[343]   Warren County Deeds, 27:225-6.

[344]   Irena A. Ameden tombstone, Sunnyside Cemetery, Queensbury, N.Y.

with his mother-in-law, Elisabeth, running the household.[345] Elisabeth died in 1880. It was at about that same time that he married CLARISSA _____ and moved the family to a farm in Bolton. Clarissa was born in New York in October 1847. Together they raised George's children, working the farm in Bolton from 1880 through 1910.[346] Bolton lies eighteen miles north of Glens Falls, on the west central shoreline of Lake George. Curiously, the 1888 *Glens Falls Directory* reports that George was working as a mechanic in Sandy Hill.[347] He does not appear in the 1890 directory. Perhaps the crops had failed and he had returned to work in the trades for a time.

Tragedy again struck the household when young Royal died in 1894 before he had yet turned twenty years old.

George died in Bolton in 1916 at age eighty-two.

Children of GEORGE and IRENA (AMEDEN) ALLEN:

i. WARREN P. ALLEN, b. prob. Sandy Hill, N.Y., Jan. 1870.[348] Still single and resident in Bolton in 1930.[349]

ii. ROYAL J. ALLEN, b. Sandy Hill, N.Y., Sept. 1874;[350] d. Bolton 27 May 1894; bur. Warrensburg, N.Y.[351]

Theodore Welch (1843–1895)

60. THEODORE WELCH[7] *(ELIZA ANN[6] AMEDEN, JOHN[5], JACOB[4] AMIDOWN, HENRY[3], PHILIP[2], ROGER[1] AMADOWNE)* was born at Caldwell, New York, on 4 August 1842.[352] He died at Montgomery, Alabama, on 3 January 1895.[353] He married first before 1870

---

345 George Allen household, 1875 New York cens., Warren Co, N.Y., Queensbury, dw. 30, household 34.
346 George H. Allen household, 1880 U.S. cens., Warren Co., N.Y., pop. sched., Queensbury, SD 6, ED 111, sheet 5, dw. 54, fam. 55.
      George H. Allen household, 1900 U.S. cens., Warren Co., N.Y., pop. sched., Bolton, SD 5ED 92, sheet 6A, dw. 135, fam. 137.
      George H. Allen household, 1910 U.S. cens., Warren Co., N.Y., pop. sched., Bolton, SD 1, ED 149, sheet 6A, dw. 89, fam. 94.
347 Ancestry.com, *Glens Falls, New York Directories, 1888, 1890, 1891-92.*
348 George H. Allen household, 1870 U.S. cens., Washington Co., N.Y., pop. sched., Kingsbury, Sandy Hill post office, p. 4, dw. 32, fam. 34.
349 Albert Belden household, 1930 U.S. cens., Warren Co., N.Y., pop. sched., Bolton, SD 5, ED 57-1, sheet 12B, dw. 335, fam. 348.
350 George H. Allen household, 1880 U.S. cens., Warren Co., N.Y., pop. sched., Queensbury, SD 6, ED 111, sheet 5, dw. 54, fam. 55.
351 Royal Allen death record, town clerk, Bolton, New York.
352 Theodore Welch tombstone, Oakwood Cemetery, Montgomery, Alabama.
353 Austin to Mullen, 19 May 1996.

probably in Queensbury, New York, MARY AMANDA SMITH.[354] She was born in New York in about 1843, the daughter of ALONSO and SARAH "SALLY" (___) SMITH. She died at Minneapolis, Minnesota, on 6 March 1873.[355] He married second at Perry County, Alabama, on 17 January 1878 IDA ELIZA WYATT.[356]She was born in Marion, Alabama, on 30 March 1849, the daughter of WILLIAM NEWTON and ELIZA ANN (MILLER) WYATT,[357] and died at Montgomery on 19 June 1911.[358]

Theodore grew up in Caldwell. Despite his blue-collar upbringing, he had become an attorney by the time he was twenty-seven.

Mary Amanda Smith, age seven, was found in Queensbury in 1850 in the household of her widowed mother Sarah, a teacher.[359] The estate of Alonso Smith, who died 20 September 1844, named his widow Sarah as his administrator.[360] It is thus that we derive Mary Amanda's parents. She grew up in Glens Falls in the household of her stepfather Michael Mann, a carpenter.[361]

Theodore and Mary Amanda married shortly before 1870. They were unusually mobile for their time, probably because of his work with various railroads. Theodore was single and resident in Glens Falls in May 1866 when he helped Dennis Cronin transfer title of his half-acre lot to Ellen Cronin: Theodore bought the lot on May 19th and sold it to Ellen on May 21st. Theodore was still resident in Glens Falls on 8 July 1867 when he bought a quarter-acre lot from his future in-laws, Sally and Michael Mann, that lay to the south of the Mann residence, for $150. He and Mary Amanda were resident in Whitehall, twenty-three miles northeast of Glens Falls, when they sold that quarter-acre lot to Alfred Fish for $300 on 29 April 1870.[362] They

---

354   Theodore Welch household, 1870 U.S. cens., Warren Co., N.Y., pop. sched., Queensbury, p. 88, dw. 587, fam. 693.

355   Jackson & Jackson, *Death Notices from Washington County*, 100.

356   Welch-Wyatt marriage record, Perry County Clerk, Alabama, recorded 18 January 1878.

357   Ida Wyatt Welch death record, Alabama Center for Health Statistics, #101-10-00097, Montgomery Alabama.

358   Ibid.

359   Sarah Smith household, 1850 U.S. cens., Warren Co., N.Y., pop. sched., Queensbury, p. 26, dw. 34, fam. 37.

360   Warren County Surrogate Court file 284; Austin to Mullen, 2 Oct. 2004.

361   Michael Mann household, 1860 U.S. cens., Warren Co., N.Y., pop. sched., Queensbury, p. 4, dw. 26, fam. [].

362   Warren County Deeds.

were resident in Sandy Hill, three miles east of Glens Falls, in June 1870 for the Sandy Hill census, sharing a dwelling with John and Sarah Wilber.[363] And they were resident in Glens Falls, living with Mary Amanda's parents, in July 1870 for the Glens Falls census.[364] Mary Amanda died (in childbirth?) in 1873, at age thirty, in Minneapolis, Minnesota.

Theodore left Minneapolis and headed to Montgomery, Alabama. There he was a general freight agent for the Louisville & Nashville Railroad (L&N RR). In 1881 the Railroad extended its track from Montgomery to New Orleans, opening international markets for American produce as well as iron, coal and steel. Theodore was part of that expansion. By 1893 he was responsible for all freight that moved over the L&N RR from Decatur (just south of the Tennessee line) south to Pensacola, Florida, west to New Orleans, and east to River Junction, Florida, near the east of the Florida panhandle.[365]

Theodore married Ida E. Wyatt in Perry County, Alabama, in 1878. She was born at Marion, Alabama, in 1849. She grew up there, the third child of a wealthy farmer.[366] Theodore and Ida settled in Montgomery by 1880, boarding with Mrs. J. C. Lee.[367] They appear in the J. C. Lee boarding house in the 1880 census, although the census taker recorded that Theodore was from Kentucky and Ida was from Tennessee![368] They may have still been living there on 24 April 1881 when Ida delivered a stillborn baby girl. They were living at 312

---

363 John S. Wilber household, 1870 U.S. cens., Washington Co., N.Y., pop. sched., Kingsbury, post office Sandy Hill, p. 25, dw. 175, fam. 186.

364 Wm Wyatt household, 1860 U.S. census, Perry County, Alabama, population schedule, Marion (Eastern Division), pages 741 and 741B, dwelling 766, family 766; National Archives micropublication M653, roll 20.

W. E. Wyatt household, 1870 U.S. census, Perry County, Alabama, population schedule, Marion, page 14, dwelling 96, family 96; National Archives micropublication M593, roll 33.

365 *Travelers' Official Guide of the Railway and Steam Navigation Lines in the United States and Canada* (New York: National Railway Publication Company, 1893), 670-671.

366 [Mrs.] Theodore Welch household, 1900 U.S. census, Montgomery County, Alabama, population schedule, Montgomery, SD 2, ED 96, sheet 4, dwelling 52, family 64; National Archives publication T623, roll 33.

367 Ancestry.com, *Montgomery, Alabama Directories, 1880-95* [database online] (Provo, Utah: MyFamily.com, Inc., 2000).

368 J C Lee household, 1880 U.S. census, Montgomery County, Alabama, population schedule, Montgomery, SD 4, ED 51, page 51, dwelling 437, family 502; National Archives publication T9, roll 26.

Tallapoosa in 1883[369] when little Ida was born.

On 24 August 1886 they were still in Montgomery when Theodore sold his interest in his father's estate back in Caldwell to his brother, William.[370] Theodore and Ida both signed the deed, confirming the name of Theodore's second wife. By 1893 they had settled at 318 Clayton.[371] Theodore died in 1895 at age fifty-two. Ida buried him in Oakwood Cemetery in Montgomery with an epitaph from Psalm 37: *"Mark the perfect man. Behold the upright, for the end of that man is peace."*[372] The *Daily Advertiser*, Montgomery's local paper, remembered him thus:

Yesterday noon, from the First Baptist Church, occurred the funeral of the lamented Mr. Theodore Welch. Rev. Neil Anderson, pastor of the Central Presbyterian Church, opened the services which were beautiful and impressive, and Dr. George B. Eager, in beginning his tribute to the deceased, said that the symbols of love and admiration evidenced in the large outpouring of people, the sweet floral offerings and the sorrow felt in every heart, made it almost out of place for him to recount the virtues of Mr. Welch and the infinite loss which the community sustained in his death.

"And Enoch walked with God: and he was not; for God took him." from Genesis, was the text taken for a review of Mr. Welch's life. Dr. Eager paid special tribute to the simple, faithful Christian character of the deceased; his was a religion free from cant and hypocrisy, and shed its beneficent light on all who came in contact with him. Besides being his pastor, Dr. Eager was a most devoted friend of Mr. Welch, and several times the minister could hardly suppress his deep emotion.

The interment took place at Oakwood Cemetery. The pall-bearers were Hon. Thomas H. Clark, Dr. J. B. Gaston, Messrs. Sterling Wood, Phraes Coleman, Phil Stern, Dr. W. M. Wilkerson, Messrs. L. L. Gilbert and F. G. Browder. A number of intimate friends, including several railroad

---

369   Ancestry.com, *Montgomery, Alabama Directories, 1880-95.*
370   Warren County Deed 52:1.
371   Ancestry.com, *Montgomery, Alabama Directories, 1880-95*
372   Letter from Frank Brown to Nancy K. Mullen, 21 December 2005, with photographs of the grave.

officials from a distance, formed an honorary escort. Among the honorary pall-bearers were ex-Governor [Thomas G.] Jones, Capt. J. M. Falkner, Justice Jon. A. Harralson, F. M. Billing, W. W. Screws, W. A. Gunter and Dr. S. D. Seelye.[373]

The paper continued on with a reprint of an article from *The New Orleans States*:

The railroad circles of New Orleans are and the general public will be, when they are aware of the fact, inexpressibly shocked over the news that Mr. Theodore Welch, general freight agent of the Louisville and Nashville Railroad Company, expired this morning at 4 o'clock. The immediate cause of his death was apoplexy, the stroke being the third that the deceased gentleman had suffered from during his lifetime.

It will be remembered by local newspaper men that in the recent difficulties over the vexed question of differentials Mr. Welch played a prominent part. He was the senior at the meeting that was held in the Grunewald Hotel and served as president pro tem. While a loyal and vigilant conservator of the interests of his company he was a liberal, broad-gauged man, a man who never fought in the bush, but who did all of his fighting in the open, winning the regard and approbation of friends and opponents alike.

In the local railroad world Mr. Welch was a familiar figure. Though his headquarters were located at Montgomery, Ala., much of his time was spent in this city [New Orleans]. With all whom he came in contact he was pleasant and affable, he had a cordial greeting for the reporters and used to say that he always kept "a green spot" in his heart for the press gang. He was not a very accessible man to interview, being generally as close as a clam, but he was never other than the courteous gentleman under any and all circumstances.[374]

Up north, his family installed a memorial stone in the Welch family plot in Lake George Cemetery, beside his parents and five of

---

[373]   "Funeral of Mr. Welch," *The* [Montgomery] *Daily Advertiser*, 5 January 1895.
[374]   Ibid.

his siblings.[375] His will, dated 24 February 1895, left everything to Ida, and named her as executrix.[376]

Ida lived on at Clayton Street with daughter, "Theo," and sister, Willie Wyatt, operating a boarding house. She died there in 1911 at age sixty-two from angina pectoris (chest pain probably brought on by heart disease). She is buried in Oakwood Cemetery beside Theodore with the epitaph *"Entered into rest."*[377] Her death certificate gives a date of death of 19 June 1910, but the death certificate was completed on 20 June 1911 (unbelievable that a full year would have lapsed between the death and the report of the death), and her tombstone says 1911. Also the 1860 and 1870 census records show her as born in 1849. Her death certificate gives her age as sixty-two, which is consistent with a year of death of 1911.

Ida's will, dated 17 August 1904, left everything to her daughter, Ida Theodore Elmore, or her issue if deceased. Otherwise, all her property would go to her sister, Willie Wyatt, or, if she, too, had predeceased Ida, then to her nieces: Mary W. Rushton, Josephine Scott, and Mary W. Lovelace. She named her daughter as her executrix.[378]

Children of THEODORE EUGENE and IDA (WYATT) WELCH:

i.   FEMALE WELCH, b. 24 April 1881, prob. Montgomery, Ala.; d. Montgomery 24 April 1881 (stillborn); bur. Oakwood Cemetery, Montgomery.[379]

ii. IDA THEODORE "THEO" WELCH, b. prob. Montgomery, March 1883;[380] m. 1) Montgomery 6 April 1904 CHARLES GUNTER ELMORE,[381] b. Ala. 30 Jan. 1878, son of FRANKLIN H. and MARY ELLA (GUNTER) ELMORE, d. 7 July 1916; m. 2) abt. 1917 ELWOOD MCLAUGHLIN, b. Md. 18 Sept. 1877,[382] son of ELWOOD and KATE (___) MCLAUGHLIN. Resided Pensacola, Fla.

---

375   "Lake George Cemetery," *Patents.*

376   Theo. Welch will, Book Book 6:321-322, Probate Court, Montgomery, Alabama.

377   Email from Frank Brown to Nancy K. Mullen, 21 December 2005.

378   Ida W. Welch will, Book 8:262, Probate Court, Montgomery, Alabama.

379   Child of Theodore Welch, Record of Interments #912, Oakwood Cem., Montgomery, Ala.

380   [Mrs.] Theodore Welch household, 1900 U.S. cens., Montgomery Co., Ala., pop. sched., Montgomery, SD 2, ED 96, sheet 4, dwelling 52, family 64.

381   Gunter-Welch marriage, Book 11:507, County Clerk, Montgomery, Ala.

382   Elwood McLaughlin record, Ancestry.com, *World War I Draft Regis.*

1930.[383]

Child of CHARLES and IDA (WELCH) ELMORE:

a. *Theo G. (female) Elmore,* b. Fla., abt. 1914.

Child of ELWOOD and IDA (WELCH) MCLAUGHLIN:

b. *Henry Elwood McLaughlin,* b. Fla., Dec. 1918.

Walter Eugene Welch (1849–1931)

61. WALTER EUGENE WELCH[7] *(ELIZA ANN[6] AMEDEN, JOHN[5], JACOB[4] AMIDOWN, HENRY[3], PHILIP[2], ROGER[1] AMADOWNE)* was born at Caldwell, New York, on 9 August 1849.[384] He married at Springfield, Ohio, in 1897 MARY L. BANES.[385] Mary was born probably at Moorefield, Ohio, in March 1860, the daughter of ROBERT M. and LAVINIA (___) BANES.[386] She died at Decatur, Illinois, on 21 October 1917.[387]

Walter grew up in Caldwell. At age fourteen he was baptized at St. James Episcopal Church. At age twenty-one he was still living at home and working as a boatman like his father.[388] He probably worked Lake George on the *Ganouski* or the *Minne-Ha-Ha* with his father.[389] He was working as a teacher when his father died in 1875. Perhaps it was the death of his father that inspired him to go in with his brothers, William and Horace, to buy two lots on the south edge of Caldwell on 24 November 1876.[390]

In 1880 he was still living at home with his widowed mother, Eliza Ann, and two siblings, Horace Jr. and Tillie; Walter was working as a civil engineer.[391] But for the next few years he and his brother, Horace, sold hardware and groceries from the Welch Brothers Stone

---

[383]   Elwood McLauchlin household, 1930 U.S. census, Escambia County, Florida, population schedule, Pensacola, SD 1, ED 17-26, sheet 7A, dwelling 126, family 138; National Archives micropub. T626, roll 315.

[384]   Austin to Mullen, 19 May 1996.

[385]   Austin to Mullen, 19 May 1996.

[386]   Robert M. Banes household, 1860 U.S. census, Clarke County, Ohio, population schedule, Moorefield, Springfield post office, page 31, dwelling 198, family 191; National Archives micropublication M653, roll 943.

[387]   *Illinois Statewide Death Index, 1916-1950.*

[388]   Horace Welch household, 1870 U.S. cens., Warren Co., N.Y., pop. sched., Caldwell, p. 541, dw. 57, fam. 54.

[389]   Ross, *The Steamboats of Lake George, 1817 to 1932*, 55-79.

[390]   Warren County Deeds, Book 32:522.

[391]   Eliza A. Welch household, 1880 U.S. cens., Warren Co., N.Y., pop. sched., Caldwell, SD 6, ED 112, p. 20, dw. 303, fam. 303.

Store beside the family home. On 9 September 1881 he sold his interest in his father's estate to his brother, William.[392] In 1887 he moved to Minnesota and assisted in the construction of the Northern Pacific Railroad. Perhaps it was railroad business that took him to Ohio, where he met Mary Banes.

Mary was born in Moorefield, Ohio, where her parents were working a large farm at the time of the census four months after she was born.[393] She grew up on the farm, the second of five children. Her paternal grandmother, Mary Banes, lived with them in 1870.[394] Perhaps she was her grandmother's namesake. By 1880 her grandmother was gone, but the five children were still all at home.[395]

Walter and Mary married in Ohio in 1897 when he was forty-eight and she was thirty-seven. They returned to New York, settling in Buffalo by May 1899, where Marie was born.[396] Walter was one of the engineers who laid out the grounds for the Pan-American Exposition in Buffalo in 1901.[397] Maybe Mary didn't like Buffalo, or maybe it was engineering work that took them back to Ohio, where Lucile was born in about 1904.

But opportunity beckoned from the West. The Wabash Railroad provided a vital rail artery from Toledo to the "Heart of America," including Indiana, Illinois, Iowa and Missouri. After decades of struggling for funding, it flourished serving Chicago's World's Columbian Exposition in 1892 and St. Louis's Louisiana Purchase Exposition in 1904.[398] Walter and Mary took the two girls and moved west to Decatur, Illinois, where they lived for the rest of their

---

[392]   Warren County Deeds, Book 40:428-30.

[393]   Robert M. Banes household, 1860 U.S. cens., Clarke Co., Ohio, pop. sched., Moorefield, Springfield P.O., p. 31, dw. 198, fam. 191.

[394]   Richard M. Banes household, 1870 U.S. census, Clarke County, Ohio, population schedule, Moorefield, Fremont Station post office, page 7, dwelling 47, family 47; National Archives micropublication M593, roll 1180.

[395]   Robert M. Banes household, 1880 U.S. census, Clarke County, Ohio, population sched, Moorefield, SD 2, ED 40, page 27, dwelling 227, family 232; National Archives micropublication T9, roll 999.

[396]   Walter Welch household, 1900 U.S. census, Erie County, New York, population sched, Buffalo, SD 17, ED 186, sheet 11A, dwelling 215, family 235; National Archives publication T623, roll 1031.

[397]   Austin to Mullen, 19 May 1996.

[398]   Advertising and Public Relations Department of the Wabash Railroad Company, "Wabash Railroad History," August 1959; online <home.comcast.net/~wabashrr/wabhist.html>.

lives. Walter worked as a civil engineer and surveyor for the Wabash. Mary's widowed mother, Lavinia Banes, and Mary's sister, Ella Banes, lived with them in a rented house at 526 Franklin Street that was large enough to accommodate three roomers as well.[399]

Mary died in 1917 at age fifty-seven and was buried in Fairlawn Cemetery in Decatur.[400] Marie had moved to Chicago, and Lavinia probably died. So 1920 found Walter living with his daughter, Lucile, sister-in-law, Ella, and five lodgers. Neither Lucile nor Ella worked outside the home, so they must have operated the boarding house. Walter was now seventy-one years old, working as a factory watchman, a job suited to his advancing age.[401]

Lucile married in 1922, leaving her father in the care of her aunt Ella. By 1930 Walter had given up the large house on Franklin Street for a smaller one at 1103 East Prairie. Ella's elderly sister, Sallie Wilson, had joined them, along with just one roomer, a railroad engineer.[402]

Children of WALTER and MARY (BANES) WELCH:
i.   MARIE WELCH, b. prob. Buffalo, N.Y., May 1899.[403]
ii. LUCILE WELCH, b. Ohio abt. 1904;[404] m. 1922 ROBERT GRAHAM CAPES, b. Penna. 3 Jan. 1900, [405] son of W. G. and EVA (___) CAPES.[406] Robert and Lucile resided Pittsburgh 1930.

---

[399]   Walter Welch household, 1910 U.S. census, Macon County, Illinois, population schedule, Decatur, SD 10, ED 107, sheet 2B, dwelling 45, family 51; National Archives publication T624, roll 307.

[400]   Decatur Genealogical Society, *Macon County, Illinois Cemetery Inscriptions*, volume XI (Decatur, Illinois: Decatur Genealogical Soc., 1975), 91.

[401]   Walter Welch household, 1920 U.S. census, Macon County, Illinois, population schedule, Decatur, SD 11, ED 129, sheet 2A, dwelling 24, family 36; National Archives publication T625, roll 384.

[402]   Ella V. Banes household, 1930 U.S. census, Macon County, Illinois, population schedule, Decatur, SD 22, ED 58-29, sheet 11A, dwelling 234, family 256; National Archives publication T626, roll 538.

[403]   Walter Welch household, 1900 U.S. cens., Erie Co., N.Y., pop. sched., Buffalo, SD 17, ED 186, sheet 11A, dw. 215, fam. 235.

[404]   Walter Welch household, 1910 U.S. cens., Macon Co., Ill., pop. sched., Decatur, SD 10, ED 107, sheet 2B, dw. 45, fam. 51.

[405]   Ancestry.com, *Florida Death Index, 1877-1998*, online (Provo, Utah: MyFamily.com, Inc., 2004). Original data: State of Florida, *Florida Death Index, 1877-1998* (Florida: Fla. Health Department, Office of Vital Records, 1998).

[406]   Robert G. Capes household, 1930 U.S. census, Allegheny County, Pennsylvania, population schedule, Pittsburgh, SD 14, ED 2-81, sheet 15A, dwelling 112, family 241; National Archives publication T626, roll 1971.

Elizabeth (Welch) Cheney (1851–1876)

62. ELIZABETH "LIBBIE" WELCH[7] *(ELIZA ANN[6] AMEDEN, JOHN[5], JACOB[4] AMIDOWN, HENRY[3], PHILIP[2], ROGER[1] AMADOWNE)* was born at Caldwell, New York, on 16 December 1851.[407] She died at Queensbury on 16 December 1876.[408] She married at Caldwell on 4 January 1876 ALBERT LOREN CHENEY.[409] Albert was born at Greenwich, Rhode Island, in July 1851,[410] the son of LOREN BARNEY and AMY (WILLIAMS) CHENEY.[411]

Libbie grew up in Caldwell, where she was found with her parents in the 1855 and 1870 censuses. At age twelve she followed her older brother Horace and was baptized at St. James Episcopal Church, along with her brother, Walter, and her younger sister, Tillie.

Albert grew up in Rhode Island, the youngest of five children of a poor shoemaker. The family was in Greenwich, Rhode Island, in 1850.[412] By 1860 they were in Newport.[413] By 1870 Albert's father had died, and Albert was living alone with his mother in Schenectady, New York, working as a printer.[414]

Libbie and Albert married at St. James Episcopal Church, Caldwell, on 4 January 1876. Baby Elizabeth was born ten months later on 30 November. Libbie may have never recovered from childbirth, because she died two weeks later, on her twenty-fifth birthday. She is buried in Lake George Cemetery, near her parents and siblings.[415]

Libbie's mother, Eliza, took over raising the child. The 1880

---

[407]   "Lake George Cemetery," *Patents.*

[408]   Ibid.

[409]   Jackson & Jackson, *Death Notices from Washington County*, 132.

[410]   Albert Cheney household, 1900 U.S. census, Nassau County, New York, population schedule, town of Oyster Bay, SD 2, ED 723, sheet 14A, dwelling 244, family 255; National Archives micropublication M623, roll 1079.

[411]   John Austin, "Re: Albert Cheney," e-mail message to Nancy K. Mullen, 1 December 2005.

[412]   Loren B. Cheeney household, 1850 U.S. census, Kent County, Rhode Island, population schedule, town of East Greenwich, page 448, dwelling 124, family 144; National Archives micropublication M432, roll 841.

[413]   Loring B. Cheeney household, 1860 U.S. census, Newport county, Rhode Island, population schedule, town of Newport, page 140, dwelling 941, family 1195; National Archives micropublication M653, roll 1204.

[414]   Anna Cheney household, 1870 U.S. census, Schenectady county, New York, population schedule, 3rd ward of City of Schenectady, page 393, dwelling 103, family 127; National Archives micropublication M593, roll 1090.

[415]   "Lake George Cemetery," *Patents.*

census shows little Elizabeth living with her grandmother in Caldwell.[416] But she died before her eighth birthday and is buried beside her mother.[417]

Albert became foreman of the *Glens Falls Republican* in 1874, at age twenty-three. After Libbie's death, he moved about to several newspapers as publisher, including the *Weekly Eagle* at Bridgeport, Connecticut, the *Long Island News Letter* at Port Jefferson, New York, the *Babylon Budget*, the *Suffolk County News*, and the *Brooklyn Record*. [418] In 1879 he married FRANCES E. WILLIAMS of Pittsfield, Massachusetts. Frances was born in about 1855, probably in Pittsfield, Massachusetts, a daughter of HENRY and DELIA (___) WILLIAMS.[419] By 1880 they were settled in Bridgeport, Connecticut, with both of their mothers.[420] By 1900 they were in Oyster Bay, New York, with their daughters Anna and Mabel.[421]

Child of ALBERT and ELIZABETH (WELCH) CHENEY:

i.   ELIZABETH WELCH CHENEY, b. N.Y. 30 Nov. 1876; d. 7 Oct. 1884.[422]

Eliza Matilda (Welch) Ditomasso (1855–1916)

63. ELIZA MATILDA "TILLIE" WELCH[7] *(ELIZA ANN[6] AMEDEN, JOHN[5], JACOB[4] AMIDOWN, HENRY[3], PHILIP[2], ROGER[1] AMADOWNE)* was born in Caldwell in January 1855.[423] She died in 1916.[424] She married first in about July 1880 MR. BENTLEY. She married second after 1899 MR. DITOMASSO.[425]

---

416   Eliza A. Welch household, 1880 U.S. cens., Warren Co., N.Y., pop. sched., Caldwell, SD 6, ED 112, page 20, dwelling 303, family 303.

417   "Lake George Cemetery," *Patents.*

418   Austin, "Re: Albert Cheney," to Mullen, 1 December 2005.

419   Henry Williams household, 1860 U.S. census, Berkshire County, Massachusetts, population schedule, town of Berkshire, page 99, dwelling 756, family 795; National Archives micropublication M653 roll 487.

420   Albert Cheney household, 1880 U.S. census, Fairfield County, Connecticut, population schedule, town of Bridgeport, SD 1, ED 137, page 26, dwelling 186, family 255; National Archives micropublication T9, roll 95.

421   Albert Cheney household, 1900 U.S. cens., Nassau Co., N.Y., pop. sched., Oyster Bay, SD 2, ED 723, sheet 14A, dw. 244, fam. 255.

422   "Lake George Cemetery," *Patents.*

423   Horace Welch household, 1855 N.Y. state cens., Warren Co., Caldwell township, dwelling 24, family 24.

424   "Lake George Cemetery," *Patents.*

425   "Lake George Cemetery," *Patents.* Her tombstone calls her Tillie Welch DiTomasso. She is alone, so there is no hint of who her husband was.

Tillie grew up in Caldwell. She was five months old in the 1855 state census, taken on 1 June 1855. Like Horace and Libbie, she was baptized at St. James Episcopal Church on 27 September 1863, when she was eight years old. She was still in the family homestead with her father in 1870, and her widowed mother on 16 June 1880, when she was working as a telegraph operator.

Six weeks later, Tillie sold her interest in the real estate of her father's estate to her brother, William, on 6 August. In that deed, she is called Eliza Matilda Bentley, and signed as Mrs. E. Matilda Welch Bentley. She was still "of Caldwell."[426] Did she lose her husband in the smallpox epidemic of 1881?[427] No further record of him has been found.

Tillie was active in the temperance movement in Warren County, visiting inmates at the County Jail to convert them. She was an artist and poet. She wrote this unpublished poem, and presented it at a temperance meeting in Caldwell on Christmas day, 1880:

Be Strong
Dear friends of temp'rance, by ye strong,
Though dark the clouds be o'er thee cast,
There never was a cloud so dark,
That long its gloominess could last.
Beyond the shore there is a gleam,
Of golden light, and on its track
A silver lining clear and bright,
Reflects the dawn of daylight back.
Though deep the darkness round us clings,
The light will surely enter in;
And hope will speak with cheering tones,
And peace and joy come after pain.
Aye, after weakness cometh strength,
And gain and triumph follow loss,
And songs of praise shall follow sighs,
Then jeweled crown come after cross.
And after fain the sun will shine,
And after sowing come the sheaves;
Oh! Brother, sister sow ye well;
That gleaning, fruit may come, not leaves.

---

426   Warren County Deed, book 40:331.
427   Smith, *History of Warren County*, 426.

Though victory in the fight seems far,
Work, watch and pray, thy God is near;
Oh! Do not let your ardor flag,
Work in God's strength and never fear.
Go! Bring the wanderer home once more!
And raise thy fallen brother up;
Plead with them gently, tenderly!
Dash from their lips the poison cup!
And sister, while 'tis called today,
Work with thy might, be strong and brave;
Grasp every golden moment now,
And years will be the victor's song.
And brothers, will you join the ranks?
Then in the battle's thickest fight,
With Christ thy leader, strength and hope,
Oh! Win or die! For God and Right! [428]

Tillie died in 1916 at age sixty-one. She is buried in Lake George Cemetery.[429]

Annis S. (Ameden) (Mitchell) (Young) Crandall (1861–aft 1930)

64. ANNIS S. AMEDEN[7] *(WILLIAM[6], JOHN[5], JACOB[4] AMIDOWN, HENRY[3], PHILIP[2], ROGER[1] AMADOWNE)* was born at Dresden, New York, in April 1861. She married first at Wells, Vermont, on 3 July 1881 ISAAC R. MITCHELL.[430] Isaac was born in Wells in June 1828,[431] the son of ALVAH and SYLVIA (GOODSPEED) MITCHELL, and died at Wells 14 May 1911.[432] Annis married second at West Salem, Wisconsin, on 2 April 1884 WILLIAM R. YOUNG.[433] William was born in Wisconsin, the son of WILLIAM R. and MARY A. (PITTENGER)

---

428 Eliza Matilda Welch, "Be Strong," unpublished poem stored at Warren County Historian's Office, Lake George, New York.

429 "Lake George Cemetery," *Patents*.

430 Mitchell-Ameden marriage record, volume 1:14, Town Clerk, Wells, Vt.

431 Jerome Wilcox household, 1900 U.S. cens., Rutland Co., Vt., pop. sched., Wells, SD Vermont, ED 213, sheet 5A, dw. 98, fam. 102. Isaac Mitchell was living alone, boarding with Jerome Wilcox.

432 Isaac Mitchell death record, Town Clerk, Wells, Vermont; Family History Library microfilm 2021324.

433 Young-Amaden marriage, *Wisconsin Marriage Registrations, Pre-1907*, La Crosse, 3: 251.

YOUNG.[434] Annis married third at East Salem in 1888 LEWIS F. CRANDALL.[435] Lewis was born at Columbus, New York, 7 July 1844, son of JOHN and CAROLINE (LOTTRIDGE) CRANDALL[436] and died before 1920.[437]

Annis grew up in Fort Ann, New York, where she was found with her family in 1870. By 1880 the family had moved across the state line to Wells, Vermont. By 1881 she had moved to Poultney, Vermont.

Isaac Mitchell was an established farmer of Wells, born and raised there. In 1881 he was fifty-three and widowed, while Annis was only twenty. He probably seemed like a good catch to a poor girl from a landless family. But when Annis's parents moved west to Wisconsin in 1882, they allowed (or demanded?) Annis to abandon her husband and go with them. Why? Was he mistreating her? Was he incapable of giving her the children she wanted? Was she completely irresponsible? He lived on in Wells without her. He died from pneumonia in Wells in 1911.

For whatever reason, Annis's entire family moved to Bangor, Wisconsin, close to the Mississippi River, fifty miles west of the home of Annis's Uncle Samuel Amidon. In 1884 Annis married a local farmer, William Young, in West Salem, four miles from Bangor. In 1885, Annis's parents moved further west to Huron, South Dakota, leaving Annis behind. What became of William Young is unknown.

Annis married a third time in 1888 to Lewis Crandall while she was still living in La Crosse County, home of Bangor and West Salem. Like Annis, Lewis was born in New York. His family was still in Columbus, New York, in 1850, where his father was a wealthy farmer.[438] The Crandalls were in La Crosse County, Wisconsin, by 1865 when Lewis married CAROLINE "CARRIE" WELDA on 14 July

---

434 Ibid.

435 Louis F. Crandall household, 1900 U.S. census, Trempealeau County, Wisconsin, population schedule, town of Trempealeau, SD 297, ED 137, sheet 15A, dwelling [illeg], family [illeg]; National Archives micropublication T623, roll 1819.

436 John Cortland Crandall, *Elder John Crandall of Rhode Island and His Descendants* (New Woodstock, New York: ?, 1949), 422-3.

437 Clara B. Sward household, U.S. 1920 census, Multnomah County, Oregon, population schedule, town of Portland, SD 3, ED 131, sheet 9A, dwelling 175, family 222; National Archives micropublication T625, roll 1502.

438 John Crandall household, 1850 U.S. census, Chenango County, New York, population schedule, town of Columbus, page 268, dwelling 1930, family 1946; National Archives micropublication M432, roll 487.

1865.[439] Carrie was born in Pennsylvania on 24 June 1844, the daughter of JACOB and ELIZABETH (___) WELDA.[440] By 1870 he and Carrie had two children: Mary and Charles, and lived on their own farm in La Crosse County.[441] By 1880 they had moved to Jackson County. Lewis was working as an insurance agent, and Carrie had borne two more children, Herma and Homer.[442] In 1887, typhoid hit the area. Carrie died on 25 November at age forty-three;[443] young Charles died a week later on 3 December 1887. Lewis married Annis the next year.

Annis and Lewis were in Minnesota in late 1888 when she delivered a boy they named Charles, namesake of the son that had been lost to typhoid the year before. They were back in Wisconsin by 1893 when Blanche was born in Columbia County. Annis's parents returned from living in the Dakotas and settled in Columbia County at about the same time. Annis's father William died there in 1891; perhaps Annis and Lewis moved to Columbia County to be near her widowed mother. Annis and Lewis remained in Columbia County for the births of Rupert in 1895 and Clara in 1898. Carrie's children were probably with them, because her surviving son Homer was of Columbia County when he married ELSIE JAMES of Portage, Wisconsin, daughter of HENRY and MARY ANN (HALL) JAMES at Portage on 9 November 1898.

By 1900 when Bertha was born, Annis and Lewis had relocated to Trempealeau County, on the Mississippi River, just north of La Crosse County where they had married. Lewis owned a farm in the town of Trempealeau, twenty-five miles north of La Crosse. Annis's five children were all still at home, the eldest being twelve years old.[444] Mary was gone. Herma had married GRANT MCCLINTOCK in 1891 but was childless, living on a rented farm in nearby

---

439 Crandall-Welda marriage, county clerk, La Crosse County, Wisconsin.

440 Caroline Crandall death record, La Crosse County death register 1:258, La Crosse county clerk; Wisconsin Historical Society microfiche.

441 Lewis F. Crandall household, 1870 U.S. census, La Crosse County, Wisconsin, population schedule, town of Farmington, page 10, dwelling 70, family 73; National Archives micropublication M593, roll 1721.

442 Louis Crandall household, 1880 U.S. census, Jackson County, Wisconsin, population schedule, town of Melrose, SD 3, ED 78, page 24D, dwelling 15, family 15; National Archives micropub. T9, roll 1429.

443 Caroline Crandall death record, La Crosse County death register 1:258.

444 Louis F. Crandall household, 1900 U.S. cens., Trempealeau Co., Wisc., pop. sched., Trempealeau, SD 297, ED 137, sheet 15A, dw. [illeg], fam. [illeg].

Hamilton.[445] Homer was living on his own farm in Trempealeau.[446]

By 1910 Lewis and Annis had relocated to Langley, Washington, where Lewis was a farmer. Annis's five children were still living at home. The 1910 census says Annis had two additional children who were deceased.[447] Since the 1900 census says she had had five children at that time, who were the same as the five children in the household in 1910, the two deceased children must have been born after 1900.

In the next decade, the children came of age, married, and moved out of Annis's home. Blanche married Lytle Oscar Jones in 1914 probably in Washington or Oregon. Charles married Viola Jones in 1916 in Oregon. Bertha married C. E. Nichols in Oregon in the same year. Rupert married Myrtle Scarbury in 1920. Clara married first a Mr. Sward, then a Mr. Ryan but was twice widowed by 1920.

Also by 1920 Lewis Crandall had died. Annis was living with the widowed Clara Sward in Portland, Oregon, at 426 Ross Street.[448] Annis and Clara were still living together at 3648 San Pedro Street in Los Angeles in 1930, where Clara was now Widow Clara Ryan.[449]

Children of LEWIS and ANNIS (AMEDEN) CRANDALL:

i.   CHARLES HERBERT CRANDALL, b. Pipestone Co., Minn., 24 Nov. 1888;[450] m. Multnomah, Ore., 26 March 1916 VIOLA JONES,[451] b. Nebr. 21 June 1900, dau. of ___ and ___ (YOTTY) JONES.[452] Lived in Boise, Idaho, in 1918, when he was reported to be blind

445   Grant McClintock household, 1900 U.S. census, La Crosse County, Wisconsin, population schedule, Hamilton, SD 7, ED 65, sheet 3A, dwelling 46, family 46; National Archives micropublication T623, roll 1795.

446   Homer L. Crandall household, 1900 U.S. cens., Trempealeau Co., Wisc., pop. sched., Trempealeau, SD 297, ED 137, sheet 16A, dw. [illeg], fam. [illeg].

447   Lewis F. Crandall household, U.S. 1910 census, Island County, Washington, population schedule, town of Langley, SD 1, ED 5, sheet 4A, dwelling 76, family 78; National Archives micropublication T624, roll 1656.

448   Clara B. Sward household, U.S. 1920 cens., Multnomah Co., Ore., pop. sched., Portland, SD 3, ED 131, sheet 9A, dw. 175, fam. 222. The census missed Annis when listing Clara's household, and entered her later on the same page.

449   Clara Ryan household, U.S. 1930 cens., Los Angeles Co., Calif., pop. sched., Los Angeles, SD 17, ED 19-237, sheet 13A, dw. 195, fam. 268.

450   Charles Herbert Crandall Ancestry.com, *World War I Draft Registration.*

451   Crandall-Jones marriage record, Ancestry.com, *Oregon Marriages, 1906-20* [database on-line] (Provo, Utah: MyFamily.com, Inc., 2000). Original data: State of Oregon, *Oregon Marriage Index, 1906-1920* (Portland, Oregon: Oregon Health Division, Center for Health Statistics).

452   Viola Crandall entry, Ancestry.com, *California Death Index, 1940-1997.*

in one eye.[453] Lived with widowed sister, Clara, and worked as salesman in 1920[454] while his wife and infant son, Lewis, lived elsewhere in Portland as servants to Ernest John;[455] Charles and Viola shared a residence with Clara in 1930.[456]

Child of CHARLES and VIOLA (YOTTY) CRANDALL:

a. *Lewis B. Crandall,* b. Ore. 1 Aug. 1919.[457]

ii. BLANCHE A. CRANDALL, b. Cambria, Wisc., 25 April 1893;[458] m. 1914 LYTLE OSCAR JONES, b. W. Va. 23 July 1880.[459] Resided Portland, Ore., 1920;[460] Port Angeles, Wash., 1930.[461]

Children of LYTLE and BLANCHE (CRANDALL) JONES:[462]

a. *Howard Jones,* b. Wash. abt. 1915.

b. *Melvin Jones,* b. Wash. May 1917.

c. *Alice Jones,* b. Ore. Sept. 1919; d. bef. 1930.

d. *Annis Jones,* b. Ore. abt. 1921.

e. *Esther Jones,* b. Ore. abt. 1922.

f. *Helen Jones,* b. Wash. abt. 1923.

iii. RUPERT FLOYD CRANDALL, b. Cambria, Wisc., 10 May 1895;[463]

---

453 Charles Herbert Crandall Ancestry.com, *World War I Draft Registration.*

454 Clara B. Sward household, U.S. 1920 cens., Multnomah Co., Ore., pop. sched., Portland, SD 3, ED 131, sheet 9A, dw. 175, fam. 222.

455 Ernest John household, U.S. 1920 cens., Multnomah Co., Ore., pop. sched., Portland, SD 3, ED 192, sheet 5B, dw. 114, fam. 131.

456 Charles Chandall household, U.S. 1930 cens., Los Angeles Co., Calif., pop. sched., Los Angeles, SD 17, ED 19-237, sheet 13A, dw. 195, fam. 267.

457 Lewis B. Crandall entry, Ancestry.com, *California Death Index.*

458 Crandall birth record, *Wisconsin Births, 1820-1907,* Columbia County, 34:1704; Wisconsin Historical Society. Confirmed by the 1900 census for Louis F. Crandall (see above), which gives her birthday as April 1893.

459 Lytle Oscar Jones, Ancestry.com, *World War I Draft Registration Card.*

460 Lytle O. Jones household, 1920 U.S. cens., Multnomah Co., Ore., pop. sched., Portland Precinct 317-1/2, SD 3, ED 192, sheet 6B, dw. 138, fam. 155.

461 Lytle O. Jones household, 1930 U.S. census, Clallam County, Washington, population schedule, Port Angeles, SD 1, ED 5-24, sheet 3A, dwelling 43, family 73; National Archives micropublication T626, roll 2486.

462 Lytle O. Jones household, 1920 U.S. cens., Multnomah Co., Ore., pop. sched., Portland Precinct 317-1/2, SD 3, ED 192, sh 6B, dw. 138, fam. 155.

Lytle O. Jones household, 1930 U.S. cens., Clallam Co., Wash., pop. sched., Port Angeles, SD 1, ED 5-24, sheet 3A, dw. 43, fam. 73.

463 Crandall birth record, Wisc. DHHS, *Wisconsin Births, 1820-1907,* Columbia County, 34:002283. Confirmed by the 1900 cens. for Louis F. Crandall (above), which gives his birthday as May 1895.

Rupert Crandall entry, Ancestry.com, *World War I Registration Card.*

m. 1920 MYRTLE R. SCARBURY,[464] b. Ky. 1903, dau. of SHERMAN and MINNIE (___) SCARBURY.[465] Resided Portland, Ore., 1930.

   Children   of   RUPERT   and   MYRTLE   (SCARBURY) CRANDALL:[466]

   a. *Glenn L. Crandall*, b. Ore. 16 May 1920.[467]

   b. *June O. Crandall*, b. Ore. abt. 1922.

   c. *Royal F. Crandall*, b. Ore. abt. 1924.

   d. *Violet R. Crandall*, b. Ore. abt. 1926.

   e. *Lola M. Crandall*, b. Ore. abt. 1928.

iv. CLARA B. CRANDALL, b. Cambria, Wisc., 6 Feb. 1898; m. 1) bef. Oct. 1918 ____ SWARD, b. Sweden, d. bef. 1920;[468] m. 2) bef. 1923 ____ RYAN,[469] d. bef. 1930. Worked as saleswoman 1930.[470]

   Child of ___ and CLARA (CRANDALL) SWARD:[471]

   a. *Ruth H. Sward*, b. Ore. abt. 1919.

   Child of ___ and CLARA (CRANDALL) RYAN:[472]

   b. *William Ryan*, b. Los Angeles Co., Calif., 20 May 1923.[473]

v. BERTHA A. CRANDALL, b. Trempealeau Co., Wisc., 13 May 1900;[474] m. Multnomah Co., Ore., 24 Aug. 1916 C. E. NICHOLS

---

   464   Rupert F. Crandall household, U.S. 1930 census, Multnomah County, Oregon, population schedule, city of Portland, SD 3, ED 26-474, sheet 1B, dwelling 29, family 29; National Archives micropublication T626, roll 1953.

   465   U. S. Scarburg household, U.S. 1910 census, Skagit County, Washington, population schedule, town of Sedro-Wooley, SD 1, ED 259, sheet 12B, dwelling 228, family 240; National Archives micropublication T624, roll 1667.

   466   Rupert F. Crandall household, U.S. 1930 cens., Multnomah Co., Ore., pop. sched., city of Portland, SD 3, ED 26-474, sheet 1B, dw. 29, fam. 29.

   467   Glenn Crandall entry, Ancestry.com, *California Death Index.*

   468   Clara B. Sward household, U.S. 1920 cens., Multnomah Co., Ore., pop. sched., Portland, SD 3, ED 131, sheet 9A, dw. 175, fam. 222. Assumes that they married before the birth of their daughter in October 1918.

   469   Based on birth of son William Ryan in May 1923: William Ryan birth, Ancestry.com, *California Birth Index, 1905-1995*, 20 May 1923.

   470   Clara Ryan household, U.S. 1930 cens., Los Angeles Co., Calif., pop. sched., Los Angeles, SD 17, ED 19-237, sheet 13A, dw. 195, fam. 268.

   471   Ibid.

   472   Ibid.

   473   William Ryan entry, Ancestry.com, *California Birth Index.*

   474   Bertha Crandall birth record, Wisc. DHHS, *Wisconsin Births, 1820-1907*, Columbia County, 285:00286.

(this might be a different Bertha Crandall).[475]

vi. INFANT CRANDALL, b. aft. 1900, d. bef. 1910.[476]

vii. INFANT CRANDALL, b. aft. 1900, d. bef. 1910.[477]

Mary Melissa (Ameden) (Archer) Kohler
(1863–1930)

65. MARY MELISSA "MINNIE" AMEDEN[7] *(WILLIAM[6], JOHN[5], JACOB[4] AMIDOWN, HENRY[3], PHILIP[2], ROGER[1] AMADOWNE)* was born at Dresden, New York,[478] on 30 October 1863.[479] She died at Pardeeville, Wisconsin, on 19 May 1930.[480] She married first probably at Huron, South Dakota, in June 1887 FRED ARCHER.[481] She married second in Waupun, Wisconsin, on 21 February 1894 JAMES JACKSON KOHLER.[482] He was born at Seneca County, Ohio, in January 1846, son of REUBEN and ANNA BARBARA (NILL) KOHLER[483] and died probably at Columbia County, Wisconsin, in 1928.[484]

Minnie spent her young girlhood in Fort Ann, New York, where she was listed with her family in 1870. Her teen years were spent in Vermont, where she was found in Wells in 1880. In 1882 she moved with her parents to Bangor in western Wisconsin, close to the Mississippi River.

In 1887 the family moved four hundred miles west to Huron, South Dakota. In that year, Minnie married Fred Archer there. They had a son who lived only six months. Pioneer life in South Dakota was harsh. We have not found what became of Fred Archer. Minnie returned to Wisconsin, probably before 1891, with her parents when

---

[475] Letter from Greg Wibe, Multnomah County Library to Nancy K. Mullen, 6 Jan. 2006.

[476] Lewis F. Crandall household, U.S. 1910 cens., Island Co., Wash., pop. sched., Langley, SD 1, ED 5, sheet 4A, dwelling 76, family 78.

[477] Ibid.

[478] Kohler-Archer marriage record, Wisc. DHHS, *Wisconsin Marriages, Pre-1907*, Dodge County, 8:230.

Minnie Kohler obituary, *The Pardeeville-Wyocena Times*, 22 May 1930, 4.

[479] Minnie Kohler obituary, *The Pardeeville-Wyocena Times*, 22 May 1930, 4.

[480] Ibid.

[481] Ibid,

[482] Kohler-Archer marriage record, Wisc. DHHS, *Wisconsin Marriages, Pre-1907*, Dodge County, 8:230.

[483] Ibid.

[484] James J. Kohler tombstone, Marcellon Cemetery, Pardeeville, Wisconsin, *Wisconsin State Genealogical Soc. Newsletter*, volume 33, number 3, Jan. 1987, 57.

they returned to Pardeeville.

In 1894 Minnie married James Jackson Kohler in Waupun, Wisconsin. The Kohler family has a distinguished history in Wisconsin. In 1873 Austrian immigrant John Michael Kohler founded the prestigious Kohler Company, known for its innovations in plumbing design and manufacture. He created a planned village outside the factory gates, today called Kohler, and he built housing for immigrant employee families, which today is the prestigious five-star American Club. The family has provided a state governor. But Minnie's link to the prestigious side of the family is unknown. What is known is that the Kohlers that married into the Ameden family had been in America for at least a generation by 1894. James was a poor farmer who married CATHERINE MOORE, daughter of JAMES and MARY (___) MOORE, at Columbia County, Wisconsin, on 31 May 1868[485] and had at least five children: Mary, born December 1869,[486] William E. born 1872, John W. born 1874, Reuben born 1875, and Agnes born December 1878.[487] Catherine and her children appear with "John" Kohler in the 1880 census, but are not found after that. For whatever reason, James was single by 1894.

Minnie and James married at the Congregational Church in Waupun in 1894. Waupun is thirty miles east of Pardeeville, where Minnie's parents were living. Minnie may have been living and working in Waupun, rather than Pardeeville. They returned to the area of Pardeeville soon after their marriage. Minnie wasted no time having children. Grace was born in 1896, Izma in 1898, Minnie in 1900 and Hannah in 1903. The first two children appear with their parents in 1900, living next door to James's father and stepmother. James was working as a carpenter, and they owned their home.[488]

---

485 Kohler-Moore marriage record, Wisc. DHHS, *Wisconsin Marriages, Pre-1907*, Columbia County, Wisconsin, 1:441.

486 James Kohler household, 1870 U.S. census, Columbia County, Wisconsin, population schedule, town of Wyocena, page 2, dwelling 14, family 14; National Archives micropublication M593, roll 1706.

487 John Kohler household, 1880 U.S. census, Waupaca County, Wisconsin, population schedule, town of Dayton, SD 4, ED 164 Suppl, page 10, dwelling 87, family 89; National Archives micropublication T9, roll 1451.

488 James J Kohler household, 1900 U.S. cens., Columbia Co., Wisc., pop. sched., Wyocena, SD 1, ED 19, sheet 8A, dw. 170, fam. 172.

Columbia County, Wisconsin, 1873. Courtesy: Jonathan Sheppard Books.

Little Hannah died before her third birthday. The other three girls were still living with their parents in 1910 in Wyocena township, on Marcellon Road.[489]

By 1920, Grace had married a farmer, Edwin Rundle, and was living next door to her parents, still on Marcellon Road. Izma had married Edwin's brother, Warren Rundle, a farm laborer, and was living thirty-five miles east of her parents in Beaver Dam. Youngest daughter Minnie was still at home with her parents. James was still a carpenter; Minnie was working as a weaver; young Minnie was a domestic.[490]

James died in 1928 at age eighty-two. He was buried in Marcellon Cemetery, down the road from their home.[491] Minnie moved in with her daughter, Grace, son-in-law, Edwin, and six grandchildren, where

---

[489] James J Kohler household, 1910 U.S. census, Columbia County, Wisconsin, population schedule, town of Wyocena, SD 2, ED 25, sheet 21A, dwelling 429, family 435; National Archives micropublication T624, roll 1705.

[490] James J Kohles household, 1920 U.S. census, Columbia County, Wisconsin, population schedule, town of Wyocena, SD 2, ED 18, sheet 14B-15A, dwelling 356, family 362; National Archives micropublication T625, roll 1980.

[491] Kohler tombstone, Marcellon Cemetery, Pardeeville, Wisc., *WSGS Newsletter*, vol. 33:3, Jan. 1987, 57.

she was living in 1930.[492]

Children of JAMES and MINNIE (AMEDEN) KOHLER:

i. GRACE ELIZABETH KOHLER, b. Wyocena, Wisc., 22 June 1896;[493] m. Pardeeville, Wisc., 24 Sept. 1913 EDWIN C. RUNDLE, b. Aurora, Ill., 15 Oct. 1887,[494] son of ORLANDO and ALICE (WHITFORD) RUNDLE.[495] Lived Pardeeville 1930.[496]

Children of EDWIN and GRACE E. (KOHLER) RUNDLE:

a. *James O. Rundle,* b. Wyocena, Wisc., 22 Jun 1915.[497]

b. *Durward E. Rundle,* b. Wyocena 1 Dec. 1917.[498]

c. *Harold E. Rundle,* b. Wyocena 26 April 1921.[499]

d. *Esther Barbara Rundle,* b. Wyocena 22 Jan. 1923.

e. *Alice M. Rundle,* b. Wyocena abt. 1925.

f. *Naomi Jean Rundle,* b. Wyocena 5 Mar 1929.

ii. IZMA NAOMI KOHLER, b. Pardeeville 16 Aug. 1898; m. 1) abt. 1916 WARREN RUNDLE, b. Aurora, Ill., 4 Sept. 1890,[500] son of ORLANDO and ALICE (WHITFORD) RUNDLE, brother of Edwin Rundle who married sister Grace Kohler,[501] d. bet. 1917-20;[502] m. 2) 12 Sept. 1923 ALVIN GEORGE KELLOM, b. Trenton, Wisc., 29 Oct. 1884,[503] son of BION and EFFIE MAE (WIGGINS) KELLOM. Resided Trenton, Wisc., 1930.[504]

---

[492] Edwin E. Rundle household, 1930 U.S. census, Columbia County, Wisconsin, population schedule, Pardeeville, SD 9, ED 11-23, sheet 1A, dwelling 8, family 8; National Archives micropublication T626, roll 2565.

[493] James J Kohler household, 1900 U.S. cens., Columbia Co., Wisc., pop. sched., Wyocena, SD 1, ED 19, sheet 8A, dw. 170, fam. 172.

[494] Edwin Rundle entry, Ancestry.com, *World War I Draft Registration Card.*

[495] Orlando Rundel household, 1900 U.S. census, Kendall County, Illinois, population schedule, Oswego township, SD 2, ED 125, sheet 8A, dwelling 139, family 140; National Archives micropublication T623, roll 313.

[496] Edwin E. Rundle household, 1930 U.S. cens., Columbia Co., Wisc., pop. sched., Pardeeville, SD 9, ED 11-23, sheet 1A, dw. 8, fam. 8.

[497] James O. Rundle entry, Ancestry.com, *Social Security Death Index.*

[498] Durward E. Rundle entry, Ancestry.com, *Social Security Death Index.*

[499] Harry E. Rundle entry, Ancestry.com, *World War I Draft Registration.*

[500] Warren Rundle entry, Ancestry.com, *World War I Draft Registration.*

[501] Orlando Rundel household, 1900 U.S. cens., Kendall Co., Ill., pop. sched., Oswego, SD 2, ED 125, sheet 8A, dw. 139, fam. 140.

[502] Warren Rundle card, Ancestry.com, *World War I Draft Registration.*

[503] Alvin Kellom entry, Ancestry.com, *World War I Draft Registration.*

[504] Alvin A. Kellom household, 1930 U.S. census, Dodge County, Wisconsin, population schedule, Trenton Township, SD 9, ED 14-47, sheet 7B, dwelling 144, family 147; National Archives micropublication T626, roll 2568.

Children of WARREN and IZMA (KOHLER) RUNDLE:
a. *Viola M. Rundle*, b. prob. Trenton, Wisc., June 1919.[505]
iii. MINNIE BARBARA KOHLER, b. Wyocena 10 Sep. 1900; m. aft.
1920 JOHN B. WOLFE,[506] b. Wisc. abt. 1891.[507] Resided Beaver
Dam, Wisc., 1930.[508] John Wolfe served in WWI.
iv. HANNAH A. KOHLER, b. 9 June 1903; d. 31 March 1906; bur.
Marcellon Cemetery, Marcellon, Wisconsin.[509]

Hannah E. (Ameden) (Whittingham) Price
(1866–aft 1930)

66. HANNAH E. AMEDEN[7] *(WILLIAM[6], JOHN[5], JACOB[4] AMIDOWN,
HENRY[3], PHILIP[2], ROGER[1] AMADOWNE)* was born at Whitehall, New
York, in November 1866. She married first at Portage, Wisconsin, on
25 May 1895 JAMES B. WHITTINGHAM.[510] James was born in
Springvale, Wisconsin, in 1872, the son of WILLIAM and MIRIAM
( ) WHITTINGHAM. They separated before 1900. She married
second at Pardeeville, Wisconsin, on 21 July 1907 JOHN ELMER
PRICE.[511] John was born at West Sparta, New York,[512] on 2 March
1862, the son of GEORGE SMITH and AMANDA MELISSA (VAN
STEENBERG) PRICE.[513]

Hannah spent her early girlhood in Fort Ann, New York, and her
teen years in Wells, Vermont. In 1882 she moved with her parents to
Bangor in western Wisconsin; in 1887 she moved four hundred miles
further west to Huron, South Dakota. By 1891 the family had returned
to Wisconsin, and was living in Pardeeville, in the central part of the
state.

In 1895 Hannah married a painter, James Whittingham. We can

---

505   Ibid.
506   John B. Wolf household, 1930 U.S. cens., Dodge Co., Wisc., pop. sched.,
Beaver Dam, SD 9, ED 14-7, sheet 6A, dw. 115, fam. 133.
507   Ibid.
508   Ibid.
509   Marcellon Cemetery, *WSGS Newsletter*, vol. 33:3, Jan. 1987, 57.
510   Whittingham-Ameden marriage record, Wisc. DHHS, *Wisconsin
Marriages, Pre-1907*, Columbia County, Wisconsin, 4:269.
511   Price-Whittingham marriage record, Wisc. DHHS, *Wisconsin Marriages*,
Pre-1907, Columbia County, Wisconsin, 5:214.
512   Price-Hodges marriage record, Wisc. DHHS, *Wisconsin Marriages, Pre-
1907*, Columbia County, Wisconsin, 4:18.
513   Price-Whittingham marriage record, Wisc. DHHS, *Wisconsin Marriages*,
Pre-1907, Columbia County, Wisconsin, 5:214.

only imagine the festivities as Hannah's brother Adonijah married at the same time, and they were witnesses to each other's marriages. Hannah settled into James's home in Portage, ten miles west of Pardeeville.[514] The marriage went badly. By 1900 James had disappeared, and the abandoned Hannah was living with her brother, Adonijah, in Pardeeville.[515]

Seven years later Hannah married a widowed public school teacher of Pardeeville, John Price. John had moved to Pardeeville in 1867 at age five. He had married in Wyocena, the township of Pardeeville, on 25 August 1888 to ALICE MAUDE "MAUDE" HODGES, with both of their mothers serving as witnesses.[516] Maude delivered a daughter, Bernice, the next year, but the little girl lived only two months.[517] Did cancer doom the infant? Her mother died of cancer of the uterus six years later in Pardeeville on 17 January 1895 at age twenty-seven.[518] She and Bernice are buried together in Pardeeville Cemetery.[519]

In 1897-8, John married a local girl, ANNA C. GEYMANN, daughter of German and Swiss immigrants, HENRY and JULIA (___) GEYMANN.[520] John and Anna were living in Pardeeville in 1900. Anna suffered from debilitating rheumatism, from which she died in 1906 at age forty-one.[521] She is buried with Maude and Bernice in Pardeeville Cemetery.[522]

Now John was twice widowed. Eleven months later, in August 1907, he and Hannah married in Pardeeville. They were still in Pardeeville when the census taker came by in April 1910.[523] But

---

514   James Whittingham household, Wisconsin 1895 census, Columbia County, Pardeeville.

515   C. Andrew B. Amedeo household, U.S. 1900 cens., Columbia Co., Wisc., pop. sched., Pardeeville, SD 1, ED 2, sheet 3A, dw. 63, fam. 64.

516   Price-Hodges marriage record, Wisc. DHHS, *Wisconsin Marriages, Pre-1907*, Columbia County, 4:18.

517   Pardeeville Cemetery, *WSGS Newsletter*, Vol. 35:4, April 1989, 77.

518   Alice Maude Price death record, Wisc. DHHS, *Wisconsin Deaths, Pre-1907*, Columbia County, 1:323.

519   Pardeeville Cemetery, *WSGS Newsletter*, Vol. 35:4, April 1989, 77.

520   John E. Price household, U.S. 1900 cens., Columbia Co., Wisc., pop. sched., Pardeeville, SD 1, ED 20, sheet 7B, dw. 167, fam. 175.

521   Anna Price death record, Wisc. DHHS, *Wisconsin Deaths, Pre-1907*, Columbia County, 2:379.

522   Pardeeville Cemetery, *WSGS Newsletter*, Vol. 35:4, April 1989, 77.

523   James E Price household, 1910 U.S. cens., Columbia Co., Wisc., pop.

John's health was failing. Hannah's sister, Annis, was living in Langley, Washington, and must have encouraged them to abandon Wisconsin's harsh winters and move to the balmy climate of the northwest. John and Hannah moved to Langley in the fall of 1910 and bought a poultry farm.[524] They were still living in Langley in 1930.[525] John's health had continued to decline. Probably Hannah's health had also declined, so John's brother Frank moved his family to Langley to help care for John. No children.

Adonijah Burton Ameden (1869–1923)

67. ADONIJAH BURTON "ADAM" AMEDEN[7] *(WILLIAM[6], JOHN[5], JACOB[4] AMIDOWN, HENRY[3], PHILIP[2], ROGER[1] AMADOWNE)* was born at Fort Ann, New York, on 14 August 1869.[526] He died at Everett, Washington, on 22 July 1923.[527] He married at Portage, Wisconsin, on 25 May 1895 AGNES CHRISTINA KOHLER.[528] Agnes was born at Marcellon, Wisconsin, in December 1878,[529] the daughter of JAMES and CATHERINE (MOORE) KOHLER.[530]

Adam's infancy was spent in Fort Ann, New York, and his pre-adolescence in Wells, Vermont. In 1882 at age thirteen he moved with his family to Bangor, Wisconsin. In 1885 the family moved on to Huron, South Dakota. In 1892 his parents were already relocated to Pardeeville, Wisconsin, when Adam returned to Wisconsin. He first settled in Cambria, ten miles east of his parents in Pardeeville. Then he moved on to Waupun, twenty miles east of Cambria. In 1894 he

---

sched., Pardeeville, SD 4, ED 35, sheet 13A, dw. 243, fam. 246.

524   John E. Price household, U.S. 1920 census, Island County, Washington, population schedule, Langley, SD 2, ED 26, sheet 1B, dwelling 31, family 32; National Archives micropublication T625, roll 1923.

525   John E. Price household, U.S. 1930 census, Island County, Washington, population schedule, Langley, SD 1, ED 15-9, sheet 3A, dwelling 76, family 76; National Archives micropublication T626, roll 2489.

526   Ameden-Kohler marriage, Wisc. DHHS, *Wisconsin Marriages, Pre-1907*, Columbia County, Wisconsin, 4:269.

527   "Old Pardee Resident Passes in West," *Pardeeville-Wyocena Times*, 27 July 1923, page 1.

528   Ameden-Kohler marriage, Wisc. DHHS, *Wisconsin Marriages, Pre-1907*, Columbia County, Wisconsin, 4:269.

529   C Andrew B. Amedeo household, 1900 U.S. cens., Columbia Co., Wisc., pop. sched., Pardeeville, SD 1, ED 2, sheet 3A, dw. 63, fam. 64.

530   Ameden-Kohler marriage, Wisc. DHHS, *Wisconsin Marriages, Pre-1907*, Columbia County, Wisconsin, 4:269.

joined his widowed mother in Pardeeville. There, in 1895, he married a local girl, Agnes Christina Kohler.[531]

Agnes grew up on a farm in Dupont, Wisconsin, seventy miles north of Pardeeville. She was the fourth child, and the first girl.[532] We have to wonder if ministers were hard to come by in Pardeeville, or if Adam and Agnes were especially close to Adam's sister Hannah. Whatever the reason, Hannah married James Whittingham on the same day in 1895, and they served as witnesses for each other, under the eye of J. A. Prescott, a justice of the peace in Portage.

Adam and Agnes settled in nearby Portage.[533] Portage didn't suit them, and they moved back to Pardeeville by 1897. There they lost no time producing a family: James (1897), Adonijah Jr. (1898), and Stephen (1901). But there must have been economic hard times. In March, 1898, Adam and his brother-in-law, Will Kohler, left their young families behind and traveled twenty-six miles west to Baraboo, hoping to get a job with the Northwestern Railroad.[534] The extensive historical files of the Northwestern Railroad do not show Adam or Will as employees, so the trip may have been in vain.

By 1900 Adam was back in Pardeeville as a day laborer, living with his wife, first two children, widowed mother, and abandoned sister, Hannah.[535]

Between 1901 and 1904 Adam and Agnes moved north to Wood County where Amos was born in 1904. Although Amos was born in Grand Rapids (today called Wisconsin Rapids), the family lived in the mill town of Nekoosa. Nekoosa had been built by the Nekoosa Paper Company in March 1893 when the company had built the paper mill, the dam on the Wisconsin River, and the town.[536] Three railroads served Nekoosa, carrying away the product of the paper mill. Adam was a machinist, probably at the paper mill. In 1907 the Wisconsin legislature authorized the Wisconsin Valley Improvement Company

---

[531]   "Old Pardee Resident ...," *Pardeeville-Wyocena Times*, 27 July 1923, p. 1.

[532]   John Kohler household, 1880 U.S. cens., Waupaca Co., Wisc., pop. sched., Dupont, SD 4, ED 164, p. 10, dw. 87, fam. 89.

[533]   Adonijah Ameden hhd, 1895 Wisc. state cens., Columbia Co., Portage.

[534]   "Correspondence - Wyocena," *The Crank* [Pardeeville, Wisc.], 30 March 1898, vol. 1, no. 1.

[535]   C. Andrew B. Amedeo household, 1900 U.S. cens., Columbia Co., Wisc., pop. sched., Pardeeville, SD 1, ED 2, sheet 3A, dw. 63, fam. 64.

[536]   George O. Jones, *History of Wood County, Wisconsin* (La Crosse, Wisconsin.; Brookhaven Press, 2001), 250.

to own all dams and reservoirs on the river, for the purpose of producing an even flow on the river, to prevent floods and improve navigation.[537] This bill may have secured steady work for Adam.

In 1910 Adam was renting a home, so he hadn't yet established himself financially.[538] In November 1913 young Amos received a perfect attendance award for the third grade in the Nekoosa schools. He was eight years old that fall, right on track by modern standards.[539]

In 1917 the family took advantage of the burgeoning lumber industry in the northwest and moved to Everett, Washington. But we have to wonder why. In November 1916 a confrontation between the industrialists who built the town and the Industrial Workers of the World, a socialist union representing most of the workers in the mills, led to the "Everett Massacre."[540] Why would Adam have been led to take his family to a town where such violence had recently occurred?

By 1917 the heyday of Wisconsin lumbering was over. The heart of the lumber industry had moved to the Pacific Northwest. Fortunes had been made and lost and made again in the rough capitalism of the forest. Socialism was a growing worldwide phenomenon, nowhere more active than in the timber camps of the Northwest.

Everett, which had begun as just a clearing in the dense wilderness, had become the fourth largest city in the state of Washington. Industrialists who had built the town of Everett on Port Gardner Bay, an extension of Puget Sound, proclaimed it would be the New York of the West Coast. John D. Rockefeller was led to invest heavily. In a wave of enthusiasm, a railroad, paper mill, nail factory, shipyards, hotels, mines, barge works and a smelter had been built. The Panic of 1893 wreaked disaster, bankrupting the Northern Pacific Railroad and halting construction on the Great Northern. Wages fell sixty percent. Everett became an armed camp beset by violence and class hatred. Rockefeller pulled out and Frederick Weyerhaeuser moved in.

---

537   Jones, *History of Wood County*, 42.

538   A. B. Amadon household, 1910 U.S. census, Wood County, Wisconsin, population schedule, Nekoosa, SD 9, ED 201, sheet 14B, dwelling 255, family 288; National Archives micropublication T624, roll 1742.

539   "Nekoosa 1913 Perfect School Attendance Report," Wood County, Wisconsin; online (Provo, Utah: Rootsweb.com, 2004). Original data: *Wood County Times,* 4 December 1913.

540   Norman H. Clark, *Mill Town: A Social History of Everett, Washington* (Seattle: University of Washington Press, 1970).

Weyerhaeuser was followed by several industrialists who lacked Weyerhaeuser's vision but excelled at turning raw material and cheap labor into personal fortunes. At the same time, the laborers who worked in the mills ten hours a day suffered grotesque irregularities of torn and broken hands and arms for low wages that rarely rose when industrialist wealth soared.

Starting in 1905 the Industrial Workers of the World (IWW), known as "Wobblies," worked to organize all wood workers for class revolution. The American Federation of Labor (AFL) also worked passionately to organize workers to achieve shared prosperity with the mill owners. But the mill owners' conviction that unions spelled the destruction of America worked against the moderation of the AFL.

The year 1913 brought another major depression, when the cost of producing lumber exceeded the market value of the product. By 1915 only 389 mills existed in Washington of the 1,143 that had existed in 1909. The industrial work year was only 129 days. The depression fostered increasing militarism.

The depression ended abruptly in late 1915. Prosperity returned for the industrialists. Wages rose in towns across the Northwest, except in Everett. Everett mill owners were determined they alone would share in the renewed prosperity. On 1 May 1916 union stewards requested restoration of the 1914 wage scale. When the owners refused, the workers went on strike and shut down every mill in Everett. On 19 August, guards and strikebreakers beat ten pickets mercilessly with fists and clubs while city police looked on. That evening a crowd of 150 furious union men approached the strikebreakers with clubs of their own. This time the police intervened, shots were fired and one striker was wounded. The sheriff organized a semiprivate army of several hundred men from the Commercial Club. On 30 October the IWW decided it was time to provoke a confrontation. Forty-one union members from Spokane sailed into Everett. The sheriff and his "deputies" met the ship, hustled the "Wobblies" to Beverley Park and forced them through a gauntlet of two hundred vigilantes with clubs, ax handles, rifle butts, and boots. Their screams alarmed farmers a quarter mile away.

Five days later, four hundred naïve Wobblies returned to Everett to continue the class war – cocky men from the logging camps, willing to be bloodied for the chance to fight an idealistic battle for workers rights, to battle for bread, happiness, and liberty. Their ship was met at the dock by the sheriff and his vigilantes, who forbade them to disembark. In the subsequent verbal exchange, someone fired three shots. More shooting erupted. Men on the ship rushed to the far side, causing the ship to lurch, throwing both living and dead into the water. Only the mooring lines prevented the ship from capsizing. At least six were dead and three dozen wounded on both sides. The number of drowned was never determined. The incident became forever known as the Everett Massacre.

It may be that the World War prevented civil war in Everett. The demands for lumber fueled by the war effort finally forced the Everett mills to pay union wages in early summer 1917. Over the course of 1917-8, seventy-five percent of workers in the lumber industry abandoned the AFL and joined the radical IWW. It invented a new kind of strike to demand an eight-hour workday – feigning the stupidity and ignorance expected of them by capitalists, they stretched eight hours of work across ten hours and followed orders with an infuriating literal-mindedness. Mill owners soon despaired of ever meeting a production schedule. The federal government intervened, jailed the most articulate IWW leaders, created the Loyal League of Loggers and Lumbermen to replace both the IWW and the AFL, and demanded the mills accept the eight-hour day. Wartime prosperity screeched to a halt with the depression of 1921-2. The old mills never recovered. They were already in the process of being replaced by mills with new technology and unprecedented efficiency, whose managers were engineers and whose employees were more technicians than laborers.[541]

Perhaps it was early demand for these skilled technicians that took Adam, a machinist, to Everett in 1917, despite the industrial unrest that must have frightened his family.

On 15 August 1918, James and Adonijah Jr. enlisted in the Coast Artillery. They were already members of Company M, 3rd Washington Infantry, National Guard, before enlisting in the artillery. For training, they were sent to Fort Worden at Port Townsend at the mouth of Puget Sound. On 2 November Adonijah contracted influenza and died on 11 November. More men died from the influenza pandemic than from all the savagery of the world war. James's unit was transferred to New York, ready to sail to France, when the war ended. His unit returned to Washington where he was

---

[541]   Ibid.

discharged on 27 December 1918.[542]

By 1920 Adam and Agnes were living in a home at 2525 Virginia Avenue in Everett. With them were their two unmarried sons, Stephen and Amos, and married James and his family. Adam owned this home, an accomplishment his father had never achieved. Adam and James worked as laborers in a saw mill. James had married Helen in about 1918 and had a son James in November 1919.[543]

This was a time when fraternal orders were extremely popular. In both the woods of Wisconsin and the remote northwest, the societies would have provided companionship and mutual support in many ways. Adam belonged to several societies in Everett: Pilgrim Lodge of the International Order of Odd Fellows (IOOF), the Grand Encampment of Knights Templar, Canton Lodge, Plymouth Rebekah, the Modern Woodmen, and the Royal Neighbors.[544] Adam died in 1923 from peritonitis and is buried in Evergreen Cemetery in Everett.[545]

Agnes married FRANK FLYNN, the proprietor of a service station in Union township, rural Snohomish County. It must have been a second marriage for both of them. Agnes's son, Amos, and his wife Charlotte were living with them in 1930.[546]

Children of ADONIJAH and AGNES (KOHLER) AMEDEN:

i. JAMES M. AMEDEN, b. Wyocena 16 Aug. 1897; m. abt. 1918 HELEN MAY O'HEIL, b. Wash. 1902 dau. of an Irish immigrant.[547] Resided 2009 Pacific Ave., Everett, Wash., 1930, laborer in paper mill.[548]

---

[542] William H. Mason, *Snohomish County in the War: The Part Played in the Great War by the Soldiers, Sailors, Marines and Patriotic Civilians of Snohomish County, Washington, U.S.A.* (Everett, Wash.: The Mason Publishing Co., 1920); extraction published at <www.rootsweb.com/~waskagit/snohmill.html>.

[543] Adonijah B. Amaden household, 1920 U.S. census, Snohomish County, Washington, population schedule, Everett, SD 2, ED 150, sheet 2A, dwelling 38, family 39; National Archives micropublication T625, roll 1938.

[544] "Old Pardee Resident ...," *Pardeeville-Wyocena Times*, 27 July 1923, p. 1.

[545] Ibid.

[546] Frank Flynn household, 1930 U.S. census, Snohomish County, Washington, population schedule, Everett, SD 3, ED 31-133, sheet 7A, dwelling 166, family 167; National Archives micropublication T626, roll 2520.

[547] Adonijah B. Amaden household, 1920 U.S. cens., Snohomish Co., Wash., pop. sched., Everett, SD 2, ED 150, sheet 2A, dw. 38, fam. 39.

[548] James Ameden household, 1930 U.S census., Snohomish Co., Wash., pop. sched., Everett, SD 3, ED 31-46, sheet 5B, dw. 98, fam. 134.

Children of JAMES and HELEN (O'HEIL) AMEDEN:[549]
a. *James B. Ameden,* b. Everett, Wash., 18 Oct. 1919.[550]
b. *William Arthur Ameden,* b. Wash. 4 Oct. 1921.
c. *Richard M. Ameden,* b. Snohomish Co., Wash.,[551] 18 May 1923.
d. *Patricia Ameden,* b. Wash. abt. 1926.

ii. ADONIJAH BURTON AMEDEN JR., b. Wyocena, Wisc., 6 Sept. 1898;[552] d. Fort Worden, Wash., 11 Nov. 1918 from influenza.[553]

iii. STEPHEN E. AMEDEN, b. Pardeeville, Wisc., 13 April 1901;[554] m. abt. 1921 DOROTHY ___. Boarding alone with Eunice Buttery, 3125 Hoyt St., Everett, 1930, though listed as married. Occupation: lumber mill laborer.[555]

iv. AMOS W. AMEDEN, b. Grand Rapids, Wisc., 24 Oct. 1904;[556] m. abt. 1924 CHARLOTTE "LOTTIE" B. ____, b. Ky. 28 Aug. 1903.[557]

William H. Ameden (1872–aft 1930)

68. WILLIAM H. AMEDEN[7] *(WILLIAM[6], JOHN[5], JACOB[4] AMIDOWN, HENRY[3], PHILIP[2], ROGER[1] AMADOWNE)* was born at New York (probably Fort Ann) on August 1872.[558] He married first in about

---

549   James Ameden household, 1930 U.S cens., Snohomish Co., Wash., pop. sched., Everett, SD 3, ED 31-46, sheet 5B, dw. 98, fam. 134.
550   James B. Amedon, Ancestry.com, *Wash. State Birth Index 1907-1919.*
551   Richard M. Ameden record, National Archives and Records Administration, *U.S. World War II Army Enlistment Records, 1938-1946* [database on-line] (Provo, Utah: MyFamily.com, Inc., 2005). Original data: Electronic Army Serial Number Merged File, 1938-1946 [Archival Database]; World War II Army Enlistment Records; Records of the National Archives and Records Administration, Record Group 64; National Archives at College Park, College Park, MD.
552   Adonijah B. Ameden birth registration, Wisc. DHHS, *Wisconsin Births, 1820-1907,* Columbia County, Wisconsin, 36:2049.
553   Mason, *Snohomish County in the War.*
554   Baby Ameden birth Regis., Wisc. DHHS, *Wisconsin Births, 1820-1907,* Columbia Co., Wisc., 35:1614.
555   Eunice Buttery household, 1930 U.S cens., Snohomish Co., Wash., pop. sched., Everett, SD 3, ED 31-41, sheet 1A, dw. 4, fam. 28.
556   Baby Ameden birth registration, Wisc. DHHS, *Wisconsin Births, 1820-1907,* Wood Co., Wisc., 1:143.
557   Charlotte Ameden entry, Ancestry.com, *Social Security Death Index..*
558   William H. Amsden household, 1900 U.S. cens., Columbia Co., Wisc., pop. sched., Pardeeville, SD 1, ED 20, sheet 6B, dw. 145, fam. 153.

1896 ELIZABETH "LIZZIE" KIEHL.[559] She was born in Wisconsin in September, 1879,[560] the daughter of Columbia County farmers TAGDORE and TILDA (___) KEEL.[561] William and Lizzie probably divorced. He married second about 1904 MARY A. (FRANCIS) ANDERSON.[562] Mary was born in Canada in September 1870.[563]

William's infancy was spent in Fort Ann and his early childhood in Wells, Vermont. He moved with his parents to Wisconsin in about 1882 at age seven. In 1885 the family moved on to Huron, South Dakota. By 1892 his parents were relocated to Pardeeville, Wisconsin. Probably eighteen-year-old William was with them.

In 1896 William married a local girl, Elizabeth "Lizzie" Kiehl. She grew up in nearby Springvale. Her farmer father was the child of German immigrants; her mother was herself a German immigrant.[564] William and Lizzie started their family the next year: Irene was born 1897 and Theodore in 1899. They were living in a rented house in Pardeeville on 9 June 1900.[565]

More children arrived: Howard was born in 1901 and Clarence in 1903. By 1908, William and Lizzie were divorced and William had married a Canadian immigrant, Mrs. MARY (FRANCIS) ANDERSON,[566] the widow of THEODORE A. ANDERSON of Clark County, Wisconsin, a son of Norwegian immigrants.[567] Mary had been living in the United States since 1889. The 1910 census says William and Mary had been married for ten years, but the census of a decade earlier shows

---

[559] Ibid.

[560] Ibid.

[561] Tagdore Keel household, 1880 U.S. census, Columbia County, Wisconsin, population schedule, Springvale, SD 2, ED 38, page 3, dwelling 24, family 24; National Archives micropublication T9, roll 1420.

[562] William H. Ameden household, 1910 U.S. census, Santa Cruz County, California, population schedule, Santa Cruz 2nd ward, SD 5, ED 127, sheet 12B, dwelling 326, family 334; National Archives micropublication T624, roll 1353.

[563] Theodore A. Anderson household, 1900 U.S. census, Clark County, Wisconsin, population schedule, Eaton, SD 8, ED 18, sheet 3A, dwelling 53, family 56; National Archives micropublication T623, roll 1781.

[564] Tagdore Keel household, 1880 U.S. cens., Columbia Co., Wisc., pop. sched., Springvale, SD 2, ED 38, p. 3, dw. 24, fam. 24.

[565] William H. Amsden household, 1900 U.S. cens., Columbia Co., Wisc., pop. sched., Pardeeville, SD 1, ED 20, sheet 6B, dw. 145, fam. 153.

[566] ___ Ameden birth record, *California Birth Index, 1905-10*, 31 May 1908; online, Ancestry.com.

[567] Theodore A. Anderson household, 1900 U.S. cens., Clark Co., Wisc., pop. sched., Eaton, SD 8, ED 18, sheet 3A, dw. 53, fam. 56.

William still living with Lizzie. Considering the birth of Lizzie's children in 1901 and 1903, and Mary's child in 1904, it is likely that William and Lizzie separated in about 1903. Mary Anderson had two children from her first marriage: George, born in March 1887, and Flossie, born in September 1892.[568] Mary and William had a boy, Morton, in Minnesota in 1904 and a girl, Lucile, in California in 1908. They were living in Santa Cruz, California, in 1910.[569] In 1905 Lizzie was living alone in Springvale, Wisconsin, with Elmore West, as his housekeeper.[570] In 1910 her three older children were living with her younger brother, Leadro, her widowed mother, and her younger sister, Jessie, in Lizzie's hometown of Springvale, Wisconsin.[571]

William and Mary resettled by 1920 in Tacoma, Washington, with Morton and Lucile, where the census-taker mis-recorded the family surname as "Valentine" or perhaps William changed his name.[572] No further record for the family has been found. Lizzie appears with Howard and the youngest son, Clarence, renting a house in 1920 in Beaver Dam.[573] Clarence doesn't appear in the 1910 census, when he would have been seven years old, so he must have been living with another family in 1910.

Children of WILLIAM and ELIZABETH (KEIHL) AMEDEN:

i.   IRENE E. AMEDEN, b. Cambria, Wisc., 25 April 1897.[574]

ii. THEODORE WILLIAM AMEDEN, b. Wyocena, Wisc., 14 Jan. 1899;[575] m. 1918 LILLIAN EMMA PIERCE, b. Wis. abt. 1902 dau.

---

568   Ibid.

569   William H. Ameden household, 1910 U.S. cens., Santa Cruz Co., Calif., pop. sched., Santa Cruz, SD 5, ED 127, sheet 12B, dw. 326, fam. 334.

570   Elmore West household, 1905 Wisconsin census, Columbia County, Springvale, page 655; Wisconsin Historical Society.

571   Leadro Keel household, 1910 U.S. cens., Columbia Co., Wisc., pop. sched., Springvale, SD 2, ED 33, sheet 7B, dw. 143, fam. 144.

572   William Valentine household, 1920 U.S. cens., Pierce Co., Wash., pop. sched., Tacoma, SD 3, ED 266, sheet 1B, dw. 13, fam. 19.

573   Elizabeth Ameden household, 1920 U.S. census, Dodge County, Wisconsin, population schedule, Beaver Dam, SD 2, ED 32, sheet 13A, dwelling 306, family 319; National Archives micropublication T625, roll 1982.

574   Ameden birth registration, Wisc. DHHS, *Wisconsin Births, 1820-1907*, Columbia Co., Wisc., 34:2962.

575   Ameden birth registration, Wisc. DHHS, *Wisconsin Births, 1820-1907*, Columbia Co., Wisc., 35:759.

of BERTIE DEWITT and NELLIE (GUILES) PIERCE.[576] Resided Beaver Dam, Wisc., 1918,[577] Milwaukee 1930. Mechanic.

     Children of THEODORE and LILLIAN (PIERCE) AMEDEN:[578]

     a. *Kenneth Lyle Ameden*, b. Wisc. 18 Oct. 1921.

     b. *Romana Carol Ameden*. b. Wisc. abt. 1922.

iii. HOWARD HAROLD AMEDEN, b. Marcellon, Wisc., 12 Jan. 1901;[579] m. abt. 1925 MABEL G. WOHT, dau. of SCHUYLER C. and ANNIE S. (____) WOHT. Resided Hudson, Wisc., 1930. Worked as a shoemaker.[580]

     Children of HOWARD and MABEL (WOHT) AMEDEN:[581]

     a. *Ammryliss M. Ameden* b. Wisc. Nov. 1929.

     b. *William H. Ameden* b. Wisc. Nov. 1929.

iv. CLARENCE AMEDEN, b. Wisc. 1903; resided Beaver Dam 1920.[582]

     Children of William and Mary (Francis) (Anderson) Ameden:[583]

i.   MORTON AMEDEN, b. Minn. 1904.

ii.   LUCILE AMEDEN, b. Santa Cruz Co., Calif., 31 May 1908.[584]

---

576   Theodore Ameden household, 1930 U.S. cens., Milwaukee Co., Wisc., pop. sched., Milwaukee, SD 10, ED 40-327, sheet 8B, dw. 36, fam. 45.

577   Theodore Wm. Ameden Ancestry.com, *World War I Draft Registration*.

578   Theodore Ameden household, 1930 U.S. cens., Milwaukee Co., Wisc., pop. sched., Milwaukee, SD 10, ED 40-327, sheet 8B, dw. 36, fam. 45.

579   Howard Ameden birth registration, Wisc. DHHS, *Wisconsin Births, 1820-1907*, Columbia County, Wisconsin, 35:1558.

580   Howard Ameden household, 1930 U.S. census, St. Croix County, Wisconsin, population schedule, Hudson, SD 3, ED 55-16, sheet 9B, dwelling 36, family 45; National Archives micropublication T626, roll 2598.

581   Ibid.

582   Elizabeth Ameden household, 1920 U.S. cens., Dodge Co., Wisc., pop. sched., Beaver Dam, SD 2, ED 32, sheet 13A, dw. 306, fam. 319.

583   William H. Ameden household, 1910 U.S. cens., Santa Cruz Co., Calif., pop. sched., Santa Cruz, SD 5, ED 127, sheet 12B, dw. 326, fam. 334.

584   ____ Ameden birth record, *California Birth Index, 1905-10*, 31 May 1908.

Chapter 7 -- Seventh Generation
Grandchildren of Horatio Gates Ameden

Crawford Ameden (1830–1910)

69. CRAWFORD AMEDEN[7] *(ELIAKIM[6], HORATIO GATES[5], JACOB[4] AMIDOWN, HENRY[3], PHILIP[2], ROGER[1] AMADOWNE)* was born at Dorset, Vermont, on 26 August 1830[1] and died at Winhall, Vermont, on 5 January 1910.[2] He married first in about 1852 ELIZABETH H. BURBANK. She was born about 1833 and died at Dorset on 16 September 1857.[3] He married second after 1857 NANCY GORDON. Nancy was born at Winhall in about 1843,[4] the daughter of ANDREW and MARIA (HILL) GORDON.[5] She died at Greenfield, Massachusetts, on 3 December 1914.[6]

Crawford grew up in Sandgate, Vermont, where his parents had moved when Crawford was a young boy. It may be there that he met and married Elizabeth Burbank. No marriage record has been found for them. They settled in Dorset, where their daughter Mary was born in 1854. Elizabeth died there in 1857.

Crawford and little Mary relocated to the adjoining town of Winhall where they lived with Crawford's parents, and Crawford supported his family working as a farmer.[7] It is not clear if Crawford's parents, Eliakim and Permelia, had lived in Dorset with Crawford and they all went to Winhall together, or if Crawford had gone to Winhall alone. Farming in Winhall had to be a struggle for Crawford, as the rough hilly terrain is not well suited to farming. But in Winhall, Crawford married Nancy Gordon in the next year or two.

Nancy was still a teenager herself, the daughter of an Irish immigrant farmer and his American wife. Her birth raises many questions. Winhall vital records record the death of Nancy Gordon,

---

1   Crawford Amidon death record, Winhall Deaths, Book 11:27.
2   Ibid.
3   Elizabeth Ameden death entry, Vermont Secretary of State, *General Index to Vital Records of Vermont, Early to 1870.*
4   Nancy Amidon, death record #1914-00169, Town Clerk, Greenfield, Mass.
5   Ibid.
6   Ibid.
7   Eliakim Amedon household, 1860 U.S. cens., Bennington Co., Vt., pop. sched., Winhall, p. 230, dw. 1824, fam. 1859.

West central Vermont, 1864. Courtesy: Jonathan Sheppard & Co.

daughter of Andrew and Maria Gordon on 11 December 1842, age one year, three months.[8] Crawford's wife's death certificate at age seventy implies she was born on 11 October 1844.[9] Age is not very reliable on the death certificate of one so elderly. Age on the 1850 census is more reliable. It says she was seven on 1 June 1850.[10] If her birthday were actually in October, then she was born in 1842, before the death of the first Nancy. It is unlikely that she would have been given the same name as the first child if the first child were still alive. Since there is no birth record for her, it is possible that she was adopted by Andrew and Maria shortly after the death of the older girl, and given the same name. She was raised in Winhall among at least ten Gordon children.[11]

Nancy's first child, Flora, was born in Winhall in 1860. Silas, Cola Viola, Pamelia, Eli, and Burton followed in rapid succession.[12] At

---

8   Nancy Gordon death record, Winhall town clerk.

9   Nancy Amidon, Greenfield town death certificate #1914-00169.

10   Andrew Gordon household, 1850 U.S. cens., Bennington Co., Vt., pop. sched., Winhall, page 70, dwelling 481, family 529.

11   Ibid.

12   Crawford Ameden household, 1870 U.S. cens., Bennington Co., Vt., pop. sched., Winhall, p. 10, dw. 85, fam. 90.

some point between 1860 and 1870, the name of the post office changed to Bondville, which became better known than the town of Winhall.

The family was saddened by the death of little Eli in 1871, at age two. In 1872 Crawford and Nancy embarked on an aggressive land acquisition campaign.[13] On 25 January 1872 Crawford bought an equal half interest in land in Peru, Vermont, from W. R. Dean and R. B. Taylor for fifty dollars. On 13 November he bought seventy-one acres in Winhall from Leonard Foster for $500. On 11 December he bought four more parcels in Winhall from Mason Briggs for $100. On 17 January 1873 he bought another thirty acres from Paul Bedor for $100. On 5 February Nancy bought 120 acres from John S. Parsons for $200. On 31 March Crawford bought thirty-five acres from David C. Hosley for $200. On 23 April he bought thirty-five acres from James Douglass for $250. On 20 May he loaned $140 to Daniel Taft, taking a mortgage on Taft's seventy acre parcel. On 28 July Nancy bought the Woodcock mill lot with a distilling house and barn and another forty acres. On 15 November Nancy paid $700 to Zeno H. Capen for an undivided half of 105 acres.

At some point Crawford became the owner of a mortgage by Paul Bedor for $200. When the due date passed and $155.05 was still unpaid, Crawford sought foreclosure through the Chancery Court of Manchester. On 13 June 1874 the Court gave Bedor one year to pay the balance due, plus court costs of $23.90. On 1 January 1875 Crawford and Nancy mortgaged ten of the fourteen parcels they had purchased in order to borrow $800 from the Jamaica Savings Bank. Two months later Crawford sold to his father three of the parcels he had purchased from Mason Briggs. He purchased them for fifty dollars, but sold them to his father for $500. This looks like Crawford needed more money than he had been able to borrow from the bank, so Eliakim gave it to him. Later that same year, on 2 November 1875, Nancy acquired the other undivided half of Zeno Capen's 105 acres from James H. Capen by assuming his $1000 mortgage and agreeing to pay all back taxes on the property. A year later, on 23 September 1876 Crawford took full advantage of Nathaniel Brown's inability to pay his taxes when he bought Brown's twenty-five acres for $5.39 at auction.

At this point, Crawford's finances seem to have been overwhelmed

---

13   Winhall Land Records, books 9-10, Town Clerk.

and the buying spree came to an end. On 21 December 1876 Crawford sold his interest in the land in Peru to the Barnum Richardson Company of Sims Rock, Connecticut, for fifty dollars. By 11 April 1877 Crawford had not repaid the mortgage from Jamaica Savings Bank but he again mortgaged his properties. This time he mortgaged five of them to Harrison Hubbard, again for $800. This mortgage also included Crawford's interest in his father's estate, Eliakim having died in November 1876. On the same day he mortgaged the land he had bought for back taxes and the Corn Barn that stood on land owned by his father's estate to C. B. Williams for $200. Late the same year, on 28 December 1877, Jamaica Savings Bank sued in Bennington Chancery Court seeking foreclosure on the mortgage, which remained unpaid. The court gave Crawford one year to pay the mortgage or he would be foreclosed. He was unable to pay the mortgage and lost all ten properties through foreclosure.

In the midst of the land-buying spree, the family must have rejoiced with the addition of Cecil Gladys in 1875. But even as Nancy was still bearing children, the older children were starting to leave home. Mary had married in 1871. Flora married in 1878. Viola moved out of the household. By 1880 only four of the eight children, Silas, Pamelia, Burton, and Gladys, were still living at home. Crawford had given up farming and was running an inn.[14]

By 1884, Crawford and Nancy's remaining land holdings consisted of two properties totaling sixty acres. On 18 August 1884 they sold the twenty-five acres they had bought at auction to Paul Bedor for twenty dollars. The land they had acquired from Paul Bedor through foreclosure had been lost to Jamaica Savings Bank. This property was in the same geographical area, restoring Bedor in part to his earlier position.

They sold the last property to C. B. Williams on 12 February 1886 for $150. He already held the mortgage on this property, so the $150 was probably the balance remaining on the mortgage.

Crawford and Nancy divorced sometime after 1880. It is likely that the financial stresses were too much for the marriage. It may be that the final land sales reflected the breakup of the marriage. On 26 June 1886 Crawford gave his son, Silas, a bond for his support and maintenance for his natural life, plus $100, in exchange for all

---

[14]   Crawford Ameden household, 1880 U.S. cens., Bennington Co., Vt., pop. sched., Winhall, p. 11, dw. 113, fam. 107.

Crawford's interest in father Eliakim's remaining estate.[15] Since the bond makes no mention of Nancy, it is reasonable to assume they were already separated.

Viola and Pamelia both married in 1887. Silas married in 1890. Burton died in 1897, killed by a railroad car. Gladys married in 1900.

By 1900 Crawford was boarding with George and Clara Barnard, and working as a laborer on their Winhall farm.[16] Nancy was living with her married daughter, Gladys, and her husband, William Kennon, in Springfield, Vermont, on the east border by New Hampshire.[17] Nancy and her surviving son, Silas, changed the spelling of the family name to Amidon, probably in response to the anguish caused by the divorce. Crawford died in 1910 at age eighty and is buried in Bondville Cemetery. Nancy moved with William and Gladys to Greenfield, Massachusetts,[18] where she died in 1914 at age seventy-three. She is buried in Green River Cemetery in Greenfield, beside her son Burton.[19]

Child of CRAWFORD and ELIZABETH (BURBANK) AMEDEN:

i.   MARY E. AMEDEN, b. Dorset, Vt., 1854;[20] d. Winhall 9 Sept. 1879 (childbirth);[21] m. Winhall 29 Nov. 1871 LORENZO KIDDER BURBANK,[22] b. Winhall April 1849,[23] son of ABEL K. and SILVIA (SPRAGUE) BURBANK, d. Winhall 24 Oct. 1918.[24]

Children of LORENZO and MARY (AMEDEN) BURBANK:

---

15   Winhall Land Records, book 11:461, Town Clerk, Winhall, Vermont.

16   George Barnard household, 1900 U.S. cens., Bennington Co., Vt., pop. sched., Winhall, SD 274, ED 40, sheet 4A, dw. 81, fam. 82.

17   William Kennon household, 1900 U.S. census, Windsor County, Vermont, population schedule, town of Springfield, SD 99-01, ED 286, sheets 1A-1B, dwelling 11, family 11; National Archives micropublication T623, roll 1696.

18   William Cannon household, 1910 U.S. census, Franklin County, Massachusetts, population schedule, town of Greenfield, SD 119, ED 500, sheet 71A, dwelling 118, family 155; National Archives micropublication T624, roll 588.

19   Nancy Ameden, Greenfield town death certificate #1914-00169.

20   Her death record cites her age as twenty-five and place of birth as Dorset.

21   Winhall Vermont Town Clerk, *Records of births, ... 1857-1896*, 2:174.

22   Winhall Vermont Town Clerk, *Records of births, ... 1857-1896*, 2:4.

23   Lorenzo K. Burbank household, 1900 U.S. cens., Bennington Co., Vt., pop. sched., Winhall, SD 274, ED 40, sheet 4A, dw. 92, fam. 93.

24   Winhall Vermont Town Clerk, *Indexes to births, deaths, and marriages, 1857-1976* (Montpelier, Vt.: Public Records Division, 197?). Microfilm 1844447, FHL, Salt Lake City, Utah.

   a. *Gilbert L. Burbank,* b. Winhall, Vt., 17 April 1873;[25] m. Winhall 25 Oct. 1898 *Lora J. Williams,*[26] b. Oct. 1860, dau. of *Chester B.* and *Emma J. (__) Williams,*[27] d. Winhall 21 Feb. 1927.[28] No children. Gilbert res. Winhall 1930.[29]

   b. *Sprague Burbank,* b. Winhall 29 April 1875; d. New York, N.Y., 27 Dec. 1909;[30] m. bef. 1904 *Nellie ___,* b. N.J. abt. 1875.

       Children of *Sprague* and *Nellie (__) Burbank:*[31]

     1. Dorothy I. Burbank, b. N.Y. 26 Sept. 1904;[32] m. abt. 1925 Henry R. Stadler, b. Penna 11 Oct. 1895,[33] son of Jacob and Katharina (__) Stadler.[34]

       Child: Jean E. Stadler, b. N.J. abt. March 1929.[35]

     2. Marion C. Burbank, b. Vt. abt. 1907.

   c. *Mary D. Burbank,* b. Winhall 16 May 1877;[36] d. Winhall 15 Oct. 1877.[37]

Children of CRAWFORD and NANCY (GORDON) AMEDEN:

ii. FLORA P. AMEDEN, b. Winhall, Vt., 31 March 1860;[38] d. Greenfield, Mass., 21 May 1917; m. 1) Londonderry, Vt., 21 Dec. 1878 FRANK H. NEWTON, b. Orwell, Vt., 15 Sept. 1856, son of ADNA and SARAH C. (WHITCOMB) NEWTON,[39] d. Winhall 15

---

25   Winhall Vermont Town Clerk, *Records of births, ... 1857-1896* , 2:90.

26   Winhall Vermont Town Clerk, *Indexes to births, ..., 1857-1976.*

27   Chester Williams household, 1900 U.S. cens., Bennington Co., Vt., pop. sched., Winhall, SD 274, ED 40, sheet 3A, dw. 53, fam. 54.

28   Winhall Vermont Town Clerk, *Indexes to births, ..., 1857-1976.*

29   Gilbert L. Burbank household, 1930 U.S. cens., Bennington Co., Vt., pop. sched., Winhall, SD 2, ED 2-27, sheet 1A, dw. 6, fam. 6.

30   Ibid.

31   Allison Benson household, 1920 U.S. cens., Bennington Co., Vt., pop. sched., Winhall, SD 1, ED 40, sheet 2B, dw. 30, fam. 30.

32   Dorothy I. Stadler, Ancestry.com, *Social Security Death Index.*

33   Henry Stadler, Ancestry.com, *Social Security Death Index.*

34   Jacob Stadler household, 1930 U.S. census, Blair County, Pennsylvania, population schedule, Logan, SD 131, ED 84, sheet 18A, dwelling 226, family 232; National Archives micropublication T623, roll 1831.

35   Henry Stadler household, 1930 U.S. cens., Bennington Co., Vt., pop. sched., Winhall, SD 25, ED 3-288, sheet 4A, dw. 7, fam. 101.

36   Winhall Town Clerk, *Records of births, ... 1857-1896,* 2:94.

37   Winhall Town Clerk, *Records of births, ... 1857-1896,* 2:174.

38   Winhall Town Clerk, *Records of births, ... 1857-1896,* 1:14.

39   Adna Newton household, U.S. 1860 census, Windsor County, Vermont, population schedule, Springfield, page 8, dwelling 63, family 63; National Archives micropublication M653, roll 1329.

July 1879 (fell from flooded bridge and lived twelve days);[40] m.
2) Winhall 21 June 1881 WILLIAM CHAUNCEY WHEELER,[41] b.
Vt. April 1849 son of CHANCEY C. and PHILADELPHIA (BENSON)
WHEELER.

Child of FRANK and FLORA (AMEDEN) NEWTON:
a.　*Florence B. Newton*, b. Winhall 22 Oct. 1879.[42]

Children of WILLIAM and FLORA (AMEDEN) WHEELER:
b.　*Harry Chauncey Wheeler*, b. Winhall 6 Nov. 1881.[43]
c.　*Frank Hoyt Wheeler*, b. Winhall 22 Aug. 1883.[44]
d.　*Cola Delpha Wheeler*, b. Winhall 10 Feb. 1893.[45]
e.　*Gladys Davenport Wheeler*, b. Vt. June 1897.[46]

iii.　SILAS H. AMIDON, b. Winhall 12 March 1862; d. Springfield, Vt.,
15 Dec. 1901, ruptured appendix; m. Springfield 3 July 1890
SARAH JANE CORBETT, b. Springfield 4 July 1859, dau. of
MICHAEL and MARGARET (TORPEY) CORBETT.[47]

Children of SILAS and SARAH (CORBETT) AMIDON:[48]
a.　*Zoa Margaret Amidon*, b. Chester, Vt., 23 March 1891; m.
1921 *Thomas Edward Spain*, b. Brockton, Mass., 18 Jan.
1879, son of *Daniel* and *Mary (___) Spain*.

Child of *Thomas* and *Zoa (Amidon) Spain:*
1.　Dorothy Mary Spain, b. Springfield, Vt., 28 March
1921.
b.　*Harrison Eli Amidon*, b. Grafton, Vt., 19 Nov. 1892;[49] m.

40　Winhall Vermont Town Clerk, *Records of births, ... 1857-1896*, 2:174.
41　Winhall Vermont Town Clerk, *Records of births, ... 1857-1896*, 2:12.
42　Female Newton birth record, Winhall Vermont Town Clerk, *Records of births, ... 1857-1896*, 2:96.
43　Harry C. Wheeler birth record, Winhall Vermont Town Clerk, *Records of births, ... 1857-1896*, 2:98.
44　Frank Hoyt Wheeler birth record, Winhall Vermont Town Clerk, *Records of births, ... 1857-1896*, 2:100.
45　Cola Delpha Wheeler birth record, Winhall Vermont Town Clerk, *Records of births, ... 1857-1896*, 2:110.
46　Winhall Vermont Town Clerk, *Indexes to births, ..., 1857-1976*.
47　Michael Corbett household, 1850 U.S. census, Windsor County, Vermont, population schedule, Springfield, page 71, dwelling 578, family 598; National Archives micropublication M432, roll 931.
48　Sarah Amadon household, 1920 U.S. census, Windsor County, Vermont, population schedule, town of Springfield, SD 2, ED 155, sheet 13A, dwelling 237, family 298; National Archives micropublication T625, roll 1873.
49　Harrison Amidon, Ancestry.com, *World War I Draft Registration Cards, 1917-1918*.

Springfield, Vt., 22 Oct. 1928 *Florence Gertrude Vincent,* b. Vt. 19 June 1898, dau. of *Rufus E.* and *Rose G. (Derosia) Vincent.*

   c. *Foster Burton Amidon,* b. Chester 6 Sept. 1895;[50] m. 1919 *Hazel M. Lawrence,* b. Hardwick, Vt., 20 Nov. 1897, dau. of *George H.* and *Margaret M. (___) Lawrence.*

iv. COLA VIOLA AMEDEN, b. Vt. Oct. 1864;[51] d. aft. 1920;[52] m. bef. 1884 BENJAMIN SMITH, b. N.Y. abt. 1849,[53] d. bef. 1900. In 1880, age sixteen, Cola was working as domestic for Daniel Taft in Palmer, Mass.[54] Widow in New Britain, Conn., 1900.[55] In Hartford, Conn. 1910[56] and 1920.[57]

     Children of BENJAMIN and VIOLA (AMEDEN) SMITH:

   a. *George Smith,* b. Vt. Nov. 1884; d. bef. 1910.[58]

   b. *Hattie Maria Smith,* b. Winhall 4 Sept. 1887;[59] m. ___ *McLeod* bef. 1909, divorced bef. 1910.[60]

     Child of ___ and *Hattie (Smith) McLeod*:

---

[50] Foster Burton Amidon, Ancestry.com, *World War I Draft Registration Cards, 1917-1918.*

[51] Viola Smith household, 1900 U.S. census, Hartford County, Connecticut, population schedule, town of New Britain, SD 26, ED 202, sheet 12B, dwelling 202, family 209; National Archives micropublication T623, roll 138.

[52] John Strunk household, 1920 U.S. census, Hartford County, Connecticut, population schedule, town of Hartford, SD 1, ED 87, sheet 16A, dwelling 145, family 232; National Archives micropublication T625, roll 183.

[53] Kenny Haskell household, 1870 U.S. census, Franklin County, Massachusetts, population schedule, town of Deerfield, page 67/146; National Archives micropublication M593, roll 615.

[54] Daniel Taft household, 1880 U.S. cens., Hampden Co., Mass., pop. sched., Palmer, SD 6, ED 60, p. 293, dw. 57, fam. 70.

[55] Viola Smith household, 1900 U.S. cens., Hartford Co., Conn., pop. sched., New Britain, SD 26, ED 202, sheet 12B, dw. 202, fam. 209.

[56] Viola Smith household, 1910 U.S. census, Hartford County, Conn., pop. sched., Hartford – 2nd ward, SD 29, ED 160, sheet 9A, dwelling 70, family 171; National Archives micropublication T624, roll 132.

[57] John Strunk household, 1920 U.S. cens., Hartford Co., Conn., pop. sched., Hartford – 8th ward, SD 1, ED 86, sheet 16A, dw. 145, fam. 232.

[58] Viola Smith household, 1910 U.S. cens., Hartford Co., Conn., pop. sched., Hartford, SD 29, ED 160, sheet 9A, dwelling 70, family 171.

[59] Hattie Maria Smith birth record, Winhall Vermont Town Clerk, *Records of births, marriages, and deaths, v. 1-2, 1857-1896* (Montpelier, Vt.: Public Records Division, 197?), 2:104. Microfilm 1844447, FHL, Salt Lake City, Utah.

[60] Viola Smith household, 1910 U.S. cens., Hartford Co., Conn., pop. sched., Hartford, SD 29, ED 160, sheet 9A, dw. 70, fam. 171.

1. Burton C. McLeod, b. Conn. 20 Dec. 1908.[61]

v.   PAMELIA M. AMEDEN, b. Winhall April 1866; m. Greenfield, Mass., 14 Dec. 1887, JOHN HAWKS SAXTON, b. Deerfield, Mass., Aug. 1865, son of JAMES HAWKS and KATHERINE R. (TRASK) SAXTON. Divorced bef. 1920. Res. Hartford, Conn., 1930.[62]

Children of JOHN and PAMELIA (AMEDEN) SAXTON:

a.   *Katherine V. Saxton*, b. Mass. April 1889; m. __ *McGregor*, bef. 1900.

Child of __ and *Katherine (Saxton) McGregor*:
1. Gertrude E. McGregor, b. Mass. abt. 1906.

b.   *Henry Hoyt Saxton*, b. Greenfield, Mass., 14 March 1891; d. Greenfield 4 Sept. 1891, hydrocephalus.

c.   *Lyman John Saxton*, b. Greenfield 7 Aug. 1895; m. abt. 1916 *Catherine D. Mahon*, b. Conn. Jan. 1893., dau. of *Thomas F. and Margaret ( ) Mahon*. Resident with *Uncle William Cannon*, Greenfield 1910; head of household in Hartford, Conn., 1920 and 1930.

Children of *Lyman* and *Catherine (Mahon) Saxton*:[63]
1. Lyman John Saxton Jr., b. Hartford 16 Feb. 1919.
2. Catherine D. Saxton, b. Conn. abt. 1922.
3. Gertrude Saxton, b. Conn. abt. 1924.
4. Margaret T. Saxton, b. Conn. abt. Aug. 1925.

d.   *Marjorie Gordon Saxton*, b. Greenfield 2 Aug. 1899; m. 1920, *John Francis Coyne*, b. Holyoke, Mass., 27 Feb. 1897, son of *Peter* and *Mary ( ) Coyne*. Resident with mother 1930.

Child of *John* and *Marjorie (Saxton) Coyne:*
1. John Francis Coyne Jr., b. Conn. abt. 1922.[64]

vi.   ELI SEYMOUR AMEDEN, b. Winhall 12 Nov. 1868;[65] d. Winhall 6

---

   61   Burton C. McLeod entry, *California Death Index*.

   62   Permelia Saxton household, 1930 U.S. census, Hartford County, Connecticut, population. schedule., Hartford, SD 2, ED 2-84, sheet 31A, dwelling ?, family 405; National Archives micropublication T626, roll 265.

   63   Lyman Saxton household, 1930 U.S. census, Hartford County, Connecticut, pop. schedule., Hartford, 7th ward, SD 2, ED 2-47, sheet 12B, dwelling 108, family 266.

   64   Permelia Saxton household, 1930 U.S. cens., Hartford Co., Conn., pop. sched.., Hartford, 7th ward, SD 2, ED 2-84, sheet 31A, dwelling ?, family 405.

   65   Eli Seymour Ameden birth record, Winhall Vermont Town Clerk, *Records of births, marriages, and deaths, v. 1-2, 1857-1896*, 2:82.

Sept. 1871 of "dropsy on the brain."[66]

vii. BURTON C. AMEDEN, b. Winhall, Vt., Feb 1870;[67] d. 1 March 1897 killed by railroad car; bur. Green River Cem., Greenfield, Mass.[68]

viii. CECIL GLADYS AMEDEN, b. Winhall 21 Feb. 1875;[69] m. 1900 WILLIAM C. KENNON, b. West Dover, Vt., 16 May 1871, son of NELSON AKEN and ALMIRA WILSON (ELWELL) KENNON. Resident Greenfield 1910.[70]

Child of WILLIAM and GLADYS (AMEDEN) KENNON:

    a. *Gordon E. Kennon*, b. Mass. Sept. 1909.[71]

Mary Eliza (Baldwin) Chapman (1842–)

70. MARY ELIZA BALDWIN[7] *(ELIZA[6] AMEDEN, HORATIO GATES[5], JACOB[4] AMIDOWN, HENRY[3], PHILIP[2], ROGER[1] AMADOWNE)* was probably born in Dorset, Vermont, in about 1842. She married at Dorset on 22 June 1866 ALBERT WASHINGTON CHAPMAN. He was born at Greenwich, New York, in about 1846 and died after 1880.

Mary was born and raised in Dorset. She was a teacher in 1860, though still living at home.[72]

Albert was a private in Company C and Company G, 1st Vermont Heavy Artillery Regiment, in the Civil War.[73] After the war, Mary and Albert married at Dorset in 1866. They must have still been living there in 1870, since daughter May was born there in 1871. But Mary probably died. Albert was living with his mother, Caroline Chapman,

---

    66 Eli Seymour Ameden death record, Winhall Vermont Town Clerk, *Records of births, marriages, and deaths, v. 1-2, 1857-1896,* 2:166.
    67 Crawford Ameden household, 1870 U.S. cens., Bennington Co., Vt., pop. sched., Winhall, p. 10, dw. 85, fam. 90.
    68 Burton Amedon tombstone, Green River Cemetery, Greenfield, Massachusetts; letter from cemetery to Chris Amaden, July 2005.
    69 Cecil G. Ameden birth record, Winhall Vermont Town Clerk, *Records of births, marriages, and deaths, v. 1-2, 1857-1896,* 2:92. The birth register says Cecil G. Ameden, a female. Subsequent census records show that this was Gladys. See especially William Kennon household, 1900 U.S. cens., Windsor Co., Vt., pop. sched., Springfield, SD 99-01, ED 286, sheets 1A-1B, dw. 11, fam. 11.
    70 William Cannon household, 1910 U.S. cens., Franklin Co., Mass., pop. sched., Greenfield, SD 119, ED 500, sheet 71A, dwelling 118, family 155.
    71 Ibid.
    72 George Baldwin household, 1860 U.S. cens., Bennington Co., Vt., pop. sched., Dorset, p. 46, dw. 343, fam. 359.
    73 United States National Archives. *Civil War Service Records* [database online] (Provo, UT, USA: The Generations Network, Inc., 1999).

in Dorset in 1880, where he was listed as single.[74] He was ill with consumption. No further records for them have been found. It is possible that the orphaned May Chapman, age eight, living at the Church Home for Children (Episcopal) in Philadelphia in 1880[75] is their daughter, but no confirmation has been found.

Child of ALBERT and MARY (AMEDEN) CHAPMAN:

i.   MAY CHAPMAN, b. Dorset, Vt., 29 Dec. 1871.[76]

Daniel W. Baldwin (1847–aft 1920)

71. DANIEL W. BALDWIN[7] *(ELIZA[6] AMEDEN, HORATIO GATES[5], JACOB[4] AMIDOWN, HENRY[3], PHILIP[2], ROGER[1] AMADOWNE)* was probably born in Dorset, Vermont, in about 1847.[77] He married at Dorset 31 May 1868 HARRIET "CAROLINE" REED.[78] She was born in Vermont in about 1852, the daughter of SIMEON and MARTHA ( ) REED,[79] and probably died before 1904. Daniel married second about 1904 MARY ( ) MCKENZIE.[80] She was born in England in October 1849.[81]

Daniel grew up in Dorset where he was enumerated with his parents in 1850 and 1860. Caroline also grew up in Dorset. While their marriage record calls her Harriet, all the census records throughout her life call her Caroline. She was enumerated in Dorset with her parents in 1860.[82]

---

74   Caroline Chapman household, 1880 U.S. census, Bennington Co., Vt., pop. sched., Dorset, district 27, SD [], ED 27, page 9, dw. 88, fam. 92.
75   Church Home for Children, 1880 U.S. census, Philadelphia County, Pennsylvania, population schedule, Philadelphia, SD 1, ED 578, page 27, dwelling ? (follows 40), family ? (follows 42); Micropublication T9, roll 1186.
76   May Chapman birth entry, Dorset Vt., *Indexes to births, ..., 1734-1994.*
77   George Baldwin household, 1850 U.S. cens., Bennington Co., Vt., pop. sched., Dorset, p. 77, dw. 254, fam. 267.
78   Daniel Baldwin marriage rec., Dorset Vt., *Indexes to births, ..., 1734-1994.*
79   Simeon Reed household, 1860 U.S. cens., Bennington Co., Vt., pop. sched., town of Dorset, page 65, dwelling 504?, family 522.
80   Dan W. Baldwin household, 1910 U.S. census, Kossuth County, Iowa, population schedule, Whittemore, SD 10, ED 172, sheet 3A, dwelling 49, family 49; National Archives micropublication T624, roll 409.
81   Mary McKenzie household, 1900 U.S. census, Kossuth County, Iowa, population schedule, Whittemore, SD 10, ED 146, sheet 1A, dwelling 9, family 9; National Archives micropublication T623, roll 442.
82   Simeon Reed household, 1860 U.S. cens., Bennington Co., Vt., pop. sched., town of Dorset, p. 65, dw. 504?, fam. 522.

After Daniel and Caroline married in 1868, they set up housekeeping in Dorset, where Daniel worked as a laborer. Their only child, Joseph B. Baldwin, was born in September 1869.[83]

By 1880, Caroline's father had died. She, her husband, and her son moved in with her mother and sisters.[84] No record has been found for Daniel and Caroline in 1900.

By 1910, Daniel had married Mary (___) McKenzie, an English immigrant twice-widowed. Son Joseph Baldwin was widowed with three children in 1900, living in Whittemore, Iowa, boarding with the widowed Mary McKenzie.[85] There's no sign of Daniel in 1900, so the imagination plays with questions of how Joseph's father from Vermont became acquainted with Joseph's landlady from Iowa! Daniel and Mary married in about 1904 and moved into a rented house next door to Joseph in Whittemore. Mary had immigrated in 1853 at age four, borne eleven children, lost two husbands and five children. The 1910 census says this was also a third marriage for Daniel, though who he had earlier married in addition to Caroline has not been identified.[86]

The 1920 census shows father and son still living next door to each other in Whittemore. Daniel and Mary now had an empty nest; all the stepchildren had grown and moved away.[87]

Daniel and Mary have not been found in the 1930 census, nor have cemetery records been found.

Child of DANIEL and CAROLINE (REED) BALDWIN:

i.   JOSEPH B. BALDWIN, b. Dorset 26 Sept. 1869;[88] d. 1922, prob. Whittemore, Ia.; bur. Plainview Cemetery, Whittemore, Ia.;[89] m.

---

83   Daniel Baldwin household, 1870 U.S. cens., Bennington Co., Vt., pop. sched., town of Dorset, p. 14, dw. 116, fam. 114.
84   Martha Reed household, 1880 U.S. cens., Bennington Co., Vt., pop. sched., town of Dorset, p. 1, dw. 2, fam. 2.
85   Mary McKenzie household, 1900 U.S. cens., Kossuth Co., Ia., pop. sched., Whittemore, SD 10, ED 146, sheet 1A, dw. 9, fam. 9.
86   Dan W. Baldwin household, 1910 U.S. cens., Kossuth Co., Ia., pop. sched., Whittemore, SD 10, ED 172, sheet 3A, dw. 49, fam. 49.
87   Daniel Baldwin household, 1920 U.S. census, Kossuth County, Iowa, population schedule, Whittemore, SD 10, ED 187, sheet 4A, dwelling 77, family 77; National Archives micropublication T625, roll 498.
88   Joseph B. Baldwin entry, *Index to births, ... 1734-1994.*
89   Joe Baldwin cemetery record, Ancestry.com. *Iowa Cemetery Records* (Provo, Utah: Ancestry.com, 2000). Original Data: Works Project Administration, Graves Registration Project, Washington, D.C.

1) bef. 1889 ___ FOX; m. 2) 1901 prob. Whittemore MARY G. ___, b. Ia. abt. 1886. Resided Ill. 1889-97, Whittemore 1900,[90] 1910,[91] 1920.[92] By 1930 Mary was remarried to Charles Ninnmen, living in Charles City, Ia.[93]

Children of JOSEPH B. and ___ (FOX) BALDWIN:[94]

a. *Caroline Baldwin*, b. Ill. Oct. 1889.
b. *Lee Edward Baldwin*, b. Ill. 26 Jan. 1896;[95] m. Liverpool, England, 30 Aug. 1919 Doris Catherine ___, b. 16 Nov. 1899.[96] Res. Concord, Calif. Machinist.
c. *Lennel Webster Baldwin*, b. Ill. 29 Sept. 1897;[97] m. Mallard, Ia., 8 Sept. 1919[98] *Agnes S.* ___, b. Ia. abt. 1900.[99]

Children of *Lennel* and *Agnes ( ) Baldwin*: [100]

1. Virginia W., b. Ia. abt. 1923.
2. Roland E., b. Ia. 1923.
3. Marion M., b. Ia. abt. July 1926.

Children of JOSEPH and MARY (___) BALDWIN:[101]

d. *Bert B. Baldwin*, b. Bancroft, Ia., 10 Feb. 1904;[102] m. abt.

---

[90]   Mary McKenzie household, 1900 U.S. cens., Kossuth Co., Ia., pop. sched., Whittemore, SD 10, ED 146, sheet 1A, dw. 9, fam. 9.

[91]   Joseph B. Baldwin household, 1910 U.S. cens., Kossuth Co., Ia., pop. sched., Whittemore, SD 10, ED 172, sheet 3A, dw. 50, fam. 50.

[92]   Joseph Baldwin household, 1920 U.S. cens., Kossuth Co., Ia., pop. sched., Whittemore, SD 10, ED 187, sheet 4A, dw. 76, fam. 76.

[93]   Charles Ninnmen household, 1930 U.S. census, Floyd Co., Iowa, population schedule, St. Charles, SD 3, ED 34-2, sheet 8B, dwelling 209, family 235; National Archives micropublication T626, 655.

[94]   Mary McKenzie household, 1900 U.S. cens., Kossuth Co., Ia., pop. sched., Whittemore, SD 10, ED 146, sheet 1A, dw. 9, fam. 9.

[95]   Lee Edward Baldwin, Ancestry.com, *World War I Draft Registration Cards, 1917-1918.*

[96]   Al Starr, "Street Scene," *Waterloo Daily Courier*, Waterloo, Indiana. 15 October 1950, section 2, page 13, column 1.

[97]   Lennel Webster Baldwin. Ancestry.com, *World War I Draft Registration Cards, 1917-1918.*

[98]   Al Starr, "Street Scene," *Waterloo Daily Courier*, 15 October 1950.

[99]   Lennel W. Baldwin household, 1930 U.S. census, Black Hawk County, Iowa, population schedule, Waterloo, SD 6, ED 7-16, sheet 5A, dwelling 108, family 109; National Archives micropublication T626, roll 643.

[100]   Ibid.

[101]   Joseph B. Baldwin household, 1910 U.S. cens., Kossuth Co., Ia., pop. sched., Whittemore, SD 10, ED 172, sheet 3A, dw. 50, fam. 50.

[102]   Bert Baldwin entry, Ancestry.com, *Social Security Death Index.*

1921 *Beatrice Dixon*, b. Ia. 20 Oct. 1904, dau. of *William Archibald*[103] and *Lillian Estella (Minus) Dixon*.[104]

Children of *Bert* and *Beatrice (Dixon) Baldwin*: [105]

1. Arlene, b. Ia. abt. 1922.
2. Alma, b. Ia. abt. 1927.
3. Ruth, b. Ia. abt. 1928.

e. *Bertha M. Baldwin*, b. Ia. abt. 1906.[106]
f. *Richard H. Baldwin*, b. Ia. abt. 1908,[107] prob. d. bef. 1920.
g. *Carl W. Baldwin*, b. Ia. 29 April 1910.[108]
h. *Harvey Baldwin*, b. Ia., 23 June 1912.[109]
i. *Ruth V. Baldwin*, b. Ia. abt. 1914.[110]
j. *Jay J. Baldwin*, b. Ia., abt. 1921.[111]

Pamelia (Baldwin) Allin (1849 – aft 1900)

72. PAMELIA BALDWIN[7] *(ELIZA[6] AMEDEN, HORATIO GATES[5], JACOB[4] AMIDOWN, HENRY[3], PHILIP[2], ROGER[1] AMADOWNE)* was probably born in Dorset, Vermont, in March 1849.[112] She married in about 1885 A. N. ALLIN.[113] He was born in New York in August 1848.[114]

Pamelia grew up in Dorset. She lived with her parents through 1870. On 18 October 1876, while still resident in Dorset, she bought

---

103   William Dixon draft registration 811:A2623, Ancestry.com, *World War I Draft Registration Cards.*

104   W. A. Dixon household, 1920 U.S. census, Kossuth Co., Ia., pop. sched., Union, SD 10, ED 187, sheet 4A, dw. 76, fam. 76.

105   Bert Baldwin household, 1930 U.S. census, Kossuth County, Iowa, population schedule, Algona city, SD 2, ED 55-3, sheet 7A, dwelling 179, family 183; National Archives micropublication T626, roll 663.

106   Joseph B. Baldwin household, 1910 U.S. cens., Kossuth Co., Ia., pop. sched., Whittemore, SD 10, ED 172, sheet 3A, dw. 50, fam. 50.

107   Ibid.

108   Joseph B. Baldwin household, 1920 U.S. cens., Kossuth Co., Ia., pop. sched., Whittemore, SD 10, ED 187, sheet 4A, dw. 76, fam. 76.

109   Ibid.

110   Ibid.

111   Charles Ninnmen household, 1930 U.S. cens., Floyd Co., Iowa, pop. sched., St. Charles, SD 3, ED 34-2, sheet 8B, dwelling 209, family 235.

112   A. N. Allin household, 1900 U.S. census, McCook County, South Dakota, population schedule, Richland township, supervisor district 2, ED 359, sheet 1A, dwelling 5, family 5; National Archives micropublication T623, roll 1551.

113   Ibid.

114   Ibid.

160 acres in Nobles County, Minnesota, from Philip T. Reynolds[115] and moved west. But the southwest corner of Minnesota wasn't for her. She retreated to Kane County, Illinois, and sold her land to her brother Joseph C. Baldwin on 11 April 1879.[116] By the 1880 census, she was back in Dorset with her parents, working as a school teacher. She married in about 1885. By 1886 she was in Richland Township, McCook County, in the southeast corner of South Dakota, when her daughter Maud was born. They were still there in 1889 when a son Ray was born and at the turn of the century for the census. But no subsequent record has been found for any member of the family.

Children of A. N. and PAMELIA (BALDWIN) ALLIN:

i.   MAUD ALLIN, b. S.D. July 1886.[117]
ii.   RAY ALLIN, b. S.D. April 1889.[118]

Joseph C. Baldwin (1851–aft 1930)

73. JOSEPH C. BALDWIN[7] *(ELIZA[6] AMEDEN, HORATIO GATES[5], JACOB[4] AMIDOWN, HENRY[3], PHILIP[2], ROGER[1] AMADOWNE)* was probably born in Dorset, Vermont, in about 1851. He married first before 1880 ELLA E. ___. She was born in Vermont in about 1855. He married second in about 1908 LETTIE (___) MCWAYNE.[119] Lettie was born in Vermont in April 1874.

Joseph grew up in Dorset, where he was enumerated with his parents in 1860 and 1870. By 1879 he had married Ella, bought 160 acres of farmland from his sister Pamelia in Nobles County, Minnesota,[120] and was farming the land in Bigelow Township where his first son, Hiram, was born.[121] Perhaps it was the harsh conditions of a Minnesota winter that cost him his son when the boy was only fifteen months old.

The frontier that had offered so much hope in 1880 no longer

---

[115]   Nobles County [Minnesota] Land Records, Book C:298, Register of Deeds, Worthington, Minnesota; microfilm 1403175, FHL, Salt Lake City, Utah.

[116]   Nobles County Land Records, Book D:402-403.

[117]   A. N. Allin household, 1900 U.S. cens., McCook Co., S.D., Richland township, SD 2, ED 359, sheet 1A, dw. 5, fam. 5.

[118]   Ibid.

[119]   Joseph C. Baldwin household, 1910 U.S. cens., Bennington Co., Vt., pop. sched., Dorset, SD ?, ED 27, sheet 3A, dw. 63, fam. 64.

[120]   Nobles Co. Land Records, Book D:402-403.

[121]   Joseph C. Baldwin household, 1880 U.S. census, Nobles County, Minnesota, population schedule, Bigelow township, SD 1, ED 193, page 11, dwelling 91, family 93; National Archives micropublication T9, roll 627.

looked so promising. Prairie fires and drought turned promising Minnesota harvests into dust. Prices for corn and wheat fell. Many homesteaders gave up and moved back East. By 1910 Joseph had abandoned the pioneer life of Minnesota and was back in Dorset, running his own dairy farm on Danby Mountain Road. By then he had been married to Lettie for two years, and they were raising her five McWayne children from her previous marriage, all born in Vermont: Elizabeth, born about 1894; John about 1898, Veda about 1901, Erma about 1905, and Beatrice about 1906.[122]

Over the next decade, Lettie bore three Baldwin children: Joseph Jr. born 1912, Bernice C. born 1915, and Ruth H. born November 1917. The two youngest stepdaughters, Erma and Beatrice, were still living at home. Joseph was continuing to work the same farm as a decade earlier.[123]

In 1930, Joseph was still working the farm. His younger brother, George, now sixty-six years old, was living with Joseph and Lettie, along with their three children: Joseph Jr., Bernice, and Ruth.[124]

Child of JOSEPH and ELLA (___) BALDWIN:

i. HIRAM CLINTON BALDWIN, b. Bigelow, Minn., 14 Oct. 1879;[125] d. Bigelow 28 Jan. 1881 of lung fever.[126]

Children of JOSEPH and LETTIE (___) BALDWIN:[127]

ii. JOSEPH C. BALDWIN, b. Dorset, Vt., 5 Sept. 1912.[128]

iii. BERNICE C. BALDWIN, b. Dorset abt. 1915.

iv. RUTH H. BALDWIN, b. Dorset abt. Nov. 1917.

Mary Frances (Ameden) Taylor (1851–1909)

74. MARY FRANCES AMEDEN[7] (LARNARD[6], HORATIO GATES[5], JACOB[4] AMIDOWN, HENRY[3], PHILIP[2], ROGER[1] AMADOWNE) was born probably at

---

122   Joseph C. Baldwin household, 1910 U.S. cens., Bennington Co., Vt., pop. sched., Dorset, SD ?, ED 27, sheet 3A, dw. 63, fam. 64.

123   Joseph C. Baldwin household, 1920 U.S. cens., Bennington Co., Vt., pop. sched., Dorset, SD 1, ED 29, sheet 7A, dw. 148, fam. 154.

124   Joseph C. Baldwin household, 1930 U.S. cens., Bennington Co., Vt., pop. sched., Dorset, SD 2-Vt, ED 2-12, sheet 1A, dw. 5, fam. 5.

125   Hiram Baldwin, birth record, Book A:43, Nobles County, Minnesota: microfilm no. 1403234, FHL, Salt Lake City, Utah.

126   Hiram Baldwin, death record, Book A:19, Nobles County, Minnesota: microfilm no. 1403233, FHL, Salt Lake City, Utah.

127   Joseph C. Baldwin household, 1920 U.S. cens., Bennington Co., Vt., pop. sched., Dorset, SD 1, ED 29, sheet 7A, dw. 148, fam. 154.

128   Joseph C. Baldwin entry, Ancestry.com, *Social Security Death Index*.

Hebron, New York, in April 1851.[129] She died at Manchester, Vermont, 19 November 1909.[130] She married at Manchester on 19 August 1874 DEXTER PAINE TAYLOR.[131] Dexter was born in Vermont in November 1849, the son of JONATHAN G. and MARY (___) TAYLOR.[132] He died at Manchester 17 February 1911.[133]

Mary Frances grew up in Hebron, where she was enumerated with her father in 1855, 1860, 1865, and 1870. In mid-1873 the family moved across the state line to Manchester. She married Dexter Taylor a year later.

Dexter's boyhood was spent in the household of his grandparents, SAMUEL and LUCY (___) TAYLOR, in Manchester. He was the second of four children in the family. The 1850 census for his grandfather's household names his presumed father as Jonathan G. Taylor. By 1860 his grandfather had died, and his father, J. G. Taylor, had become head of household, caring for Dexter's widowed grandmother as well as his own growing family.[134] Dexter was still working on the family farm in 1870, when his assumed father was named as James G. Taylor.[135] So what was the name of Dexter's father? It was probably Jonathan G. Taylor. A Manchester deed dated 18 March 1875 names Jonathan G. Taylor and Dexter P. Taylor as grantees for 110 acres adjoining Jonathan's existing property.[136] The 1880 census names Dexter's father as "J.G." This is the only J.G. Taylor in Manchester in the period 1850–1880. The fact that there are three deeds in the Manchester deed books for 1864–1914 for Jonathan G. Taylor, and none for James G. Taylor suggests that it was an error by the census taker that named Dexter's father as James. We believe it was Jonathan.

Dexter and Mary Frances married in 1874 and returned to his

---

129   Dexter P. Taylor household, 1900 U.S. cens., Bennington Co., Vt., pop. sched., Manchester, SD [], ED 30, sheet 12B, dw. 280, fam. 284.

130   *Index to Births and Deaths 1857-1932*, town clerk, Manchester, Vermont; FHL microfilm 1844445.

131   Taylor-Ameden marriage, Manchester Marriage Book 2:7, Town Hall, Manchester, Vermont; microfilm 1844445, FHL, Salt Lake City, Utah.

132   Samuel Taylor household, 1850 U.S. cens., Bennington Co., Vt., pop. sched., Manchester, p. 116B, dw. 838, fam. 857.

133   *Index to Births and Deaths 1857-1932*, Manchester, Vt.

134   J. G. Taylor household, 1880 U.S. cens., Bennington Co., Vt., pop. sched., Manchester, SD [], ED 30, p. 27, dw. 281, fam. 294.

135   Ibid.

136   Manchester Deeds, 18:613.

father's farm.[137] Their only child, Earl, was born in 1878.

Earl married in 1900 and brought his bride home to the family farm.[138] Keeping the family tradition, Earl raised his family on the farm, caring for his parents until they died.[139]

Dexter and Mary Frances stayed on the farm for the rest of their lives. Mary Frances died there in 1909 at age fifty-eight. Dexter died there two years later at age sixty-one.

Child of DEXTER and MARY FRANCES (AMEDEN) TAYLOR:

i.   EARL MERRITT TAYLOR, b. Manchester 8 March 1878;[140] m. Manchester 13 Dec. 1899 AGNES ANNA TOWNSEND,[141] b. Woodford, Vt., Nov. 1875, daughter of HUGH M. AND ELLEN (__) TOWNSEND. Lived in Manchester on the family dairy farm. Served as first president of county cooperative.[142]

Children of EARL and AGNES (__) TAYLOR:

a.   *Charles Earl Taylor* b. Manchester 16 Sept. 1900;[143] m. prob. Manchester 1926 *Elizabeth Mary Gilmore*, b. Manchester 8 Oct. 1900, dau. of *Fred Bucklin* and *Katherine (Hurd) Gilmore*.[144] Resided with parents in Manchester 1920;[145] with widowed mother-in-law in Manchester 1930.[146] Worked in ice delivery business with father.

Child of *Charles* and *Elizabeth (Gilmore) Taylor*:
1.   Katherine Hurd Taylor b. Manchester 10 Nov. 1929.[147]

b.   *Mildred Ellen Taylor* b. Manchester 20 Jan. 1902.[148] Living with parents 1930.[149]

---

137   James G. Taylor household, 1870 U.S. cens., Bennington Co., Vt., pop. sched., Manchester, p. 2, dw. 12, fam. 12.

138   Dexter P. Taylor household, 1900 U.S. cens., Bennington Co., Vt., pop. sched., Manchester, SD [], ED 30, sheet 12B, dw. 280, fam. 284.

139   Dexter P. Taylor household, 1910 U.S. cens., Bennington Co., Vt., pop. sched., Manchester, SD 2, ED 30, sheet 20B, dw. 355, fam. 400.

140   Earl Merritt Taylor, Ancestry.com, *World War I Draft Registration Cards, 1917-1918*.

141   Manchester Marriage Book, 4:22.

142   "220 Attend County Coop Annual Meeting," *Bennington Evening Banner*, Bennington, Vermont, 2 February 1955, 5.

143   Manchester Births 3:19.

144   Manchester Births 3:24.

145   Earl Taylor household, 1920 U.S. cens., Bennington Co., Vt., pop. sched., Manchester, SD 1, ED 32, sheet 21A, dw. 492, fam. 525.

146   Katherine Gilmore household, 1930 U.S. cens., Bennington Co., Vt., pop. sched., Manchester Center, SD 2, ED 2-16, sheet 1A, dw. 5, fam. 6.

147   *Index to Births and Deaths 1857-1932*, town clerk, Manchester, Vt.

James Edwin Amedon (1854– aft 1910)

75. JAMES EDWIN AMEDON[7] *(LARNARD[6], HORATIO GATES[5], JACOB[4] AMIDOWN, HENRY[3], PHILIP[2], ROGER[1] AMADOWNE)* was born at Hebron, New York, in August 1854.[150] He married at Manchester, Vermont, on 24 November 1874 MARIA "MINNIE" WILSON.[151] Minnie was born at Manchester[152] on 15 September 1855, the daughter of BAKER and MAHALA (STANNARD) WILSON.[153] She died at Manchester on 28 December 1893 of consumption.[154]

James grew up in Hebron, New York, where he was found with his family in the censuses of 1855, 1860, 1865, and 1870. The family moved across the state line to Manchester in 1873. There he met Minnie Wilson.

Minnie grew up on the Dorset farm of her grandfather, where she and her parents were found in the 1860 census.[155] Her mother is believed to be Mahala Stannard, because Mahala Stannard was the only female named Mahala who appeared in the 1850 Dorset census. Her age and birthplace match that of Minnie's mother in the 1860 census. By 1870 Minnie's birth family had grown to four children. Her father had taken a job as agent for a coal company, and the young family had moved to Manchester. In that census, Minnie was recorded by her given name of Maria.[156]

James and Minnie married at Manchester in 1874. Six years later James was established as a mason, like his father before him. Little Henry was born in April 1878, but died less than six months later from pneumonia. If any other children were born before 1880, they did not survive the high infant mortality of those times. The

---

[148] Manchester Births 3:24.

[149] Earl Taylor household, 1930 U.S. cens., Bennington Co., Vt., pop. sched., Manchester Center, SD 2, ED 0-16, sheet 14A, dw. 345, fam. 370.

[150] James E. Arneson household, 1900 U.S. cens., Bennington Co., Vt., pop. cens., Manchester, SD 279, ED 32, sheet 8B, dw. 183, fam. 186.

[151] Ameden-Wilson marriage, Manchester Marriage Book 2:7.

[152] Ibid.

[153] Minnie J. Amedon death record, *Manchester Deaths 1857-1896,* 2:26.

[154] Ibid.

[155] J. T. Wilson household, 1860 U.S. cens., Bennington Co., Vt., pop. sched., Dorset, p. 72, dw. 549, fam. 570.

[156] Baker Willson household, 1870 U.S. cens., Bennington Co., Vt., pop. sched., Manchester, p. 17, dw. 148, fam. 143.

household remained childless.[157]

But Minnie was pregnant. A few months after the census taker visited in 1880, she delivered a healthy baby girl that they named Jessie. She was to be their only hope for grandchildren. Three years later, Robert was born. But Robert was to die without issue before his twenty-second birthday.

Minnie was not to know the sadness of her son's life snuffed out so early. She died of consumption in 1893, at age thirty-six. James did not marry again. In 1900 he was still living with his two surviving children, working as a mason, and living in a rented homestead.[158]

By 1910, death had taken James's wife and both sons. Only Jessie was left to him. Jessie married Charles Brewster, and James moved in with the young couple. He continued to run his own business, contracting for mason work. He was listed as an employer, rather than working on his own account, so he may have operated a good-sized business.[159] No record has been found for James after 1910.

Children of JAMES and MINNIE (WILSON) AMEDON:

i.   HENRY E. AMEDON, b. Manchester, Vt., 12 Apr 1878;[160] d. Manchester 5 Oct. 1878, pneumonia.[161]

ii. JESSIE E. AMEDON, b. Manchester 2 Aug. 1880;[162] d. 1925;[163] m. 28 June 1900 CHARLES ORSON BREWSTER,[164] b. Manchester 1 May 1879,[165] son of WILLIAM FAYETTE[166] and CARRIE AMELIA (HASTINGS)[167] BREWSTER.

───────────────

   157   James H. Amedon household, 1880 U.S. cens., Bennington Co., Vt., pop. sched., Manchester, SD [none], ED 30, p. 34, dw. 359, fam. 372.
   158   James E. Arneson (sic) household, 1900 U.S. cens., Bennington Co., Vt., pop. sched., Manchester, SD [blank], ED 32, p. 2, de. 183, fam. 186.
   159   James E. Amedon household, 1910 U.S. cens., Bennington Co., Vt., pop. sched., Manchester, SD [blank], ED 30, sheet 17A, dw. 297, fam. 338.
   160   Henry Ameden entry, Manchester Births, book 2:13.
   161   Henry Ameden entry, Manchester Deaths, book 2:11.
   162   Jessie Ameden entry, Manchester Births, book 2:15.
   163   Moore, Charles B., *Cemetery Records, the Town of Greenwich, Washington County, New York* (Glens Falls, N.Y.: Historical Data Services, 2001), 46.
   164   Brewster-Ameden marriage, *Manchester Marriages*, book 3:99.
   165   Charles Orson Brewster, Ancestry.com, *World War I Draft Registration Cards, 1917-1918*.
   166   W. F. Brewster household, 1880 U.S. cens., Bennington Co., Vt., pop. sched., Manchester, p. 20, dw. 206, fam. 216.
   167   Carrie Amelia Brewster death record, *Vermont index to births, deaths, marriages 1909-42, Brearet-Brink*, FHL microfilm 1983856.

Children of CHARLES and JESSIE (AMEDEN) BREWSTER:
a.   *Robert   Clayton   Brewster*,   b.   Manchester   25   June   1901, named for Uncle Robert Ameden; m. Manchester 28 Jun 1928 *Cecile Tetreault*, b. Vt. 2 Feb. 1908, dau. of *Eugene* and *Georgiana C. (__) Tetreault*.[168]
Child of *Robert* and *Cecile (Tetreault) Brewster*:
1. Cecilla Brewster, b. Vt. abt. 1929.
b.   *Helen Wilson Brewster*, b. Manchester 26 October 1904.[169]
iii.   ROBERT L. AMEDON, b. Manchester 28 Sept. 1883; d. 4 Kendall Place, Brookline, Massachusetts, 29 Nov. 1904. He worked as a typesetter and never married. Cause of death: peritonsellar abscess.[170]

Harriet Elizabeth (Ameden) (Ameden) Whedon (1861-1916)

76. HARRIET ELIZABETH "HATTIE" AMEDEN[7] *(LARNARD[6], HORATIO GATES[5], JACOB[4] AMIDOWN, HENRY[3], PHILIP[2], ROGER[1] AMADOWNE)* was born at Hebron, New York,[171] on 30 September 1861.[172] She died probably at Manchester, Vermont, on 7 May 1916.[173] She married first at Rupert, Vermont, on 14 January 1891 WILLIAM FRANKLIN "FRANK" AMEDEN, her first cousin. Frank was born at Hebron, New York, on 12 September 1848, the son of NATHANIEL and PHEBE (MUNSON) AMEDEN (see subsequent biography in this chapter for Frank). She married second about 1900 HERBERT P. WHEDON. Herbert was born in Rupert, Vermont, in October 1859,[174] the son of JOHN N. and HARRIET F. (EVANS) WHEDON.[175]

Hattie's girlhood was spent in Hebron, New York, where the family lived out the Civil War and doubtless waited with bated breath for news of their father who fought at Fredericksburg,

---

168   Brewster-Tetreault marriage, *Index to Vermont births, ..., 1909-42*.
169   Helen Wilson Brewster birth record, *Manchester Births, book 3:38*.
170   Robert L. Amidon entry, *Manchester Deaths*, book 3:40. He died at age twenty-one years, two months, one day.
171   Birth record for daughter Minnie Frances, *Manchester Births*, Book 3:2.
172   Hattie Ameden tombstone, East Hebron Cemetery, Hebron, New York; transcribed by Nancy Mullen, July 1995.
173   Hattie Ameden tombstone, East Hebron Cemetery, Hebron, N.Y..
174   Hattie E. Ameden household, 1900 U.S. cens., Bennington co., Vt., pop. sched., Manchester, SD [blank], ED 32, sheet 6A, dw. 112, fam. 113.
175   John W. Whedon household, 1880 U.S. cens., Bennington Co., Vt., pop. sched., Rupert, p. 2, dw. 18, fam. 20.

Chancellorsville, Gettysburg, and the opening fight of the Atlanta Campaign: Resaca. Meanwhile, Hattie's mother was acquiring a little land and putting it into crops. We wonder if only the boys worked the fields, or if Hattie worked in the fields alongside her brothers. Her father returned in May 1865, blind in one eye and lame in one arm, and resumed his life's work as a mason. The family moved across the state line to Manchester, Vermont, in 1873.

Between 1885 and 1889, Hattie's first cousin, Frank Ameden, also moved from Hebron to Bennington County. Frank was married and still creating his family. In 1887, Hattie became involved with someone unknown, became pregnant, and delivered a son, Wesley Larnard, in 1888. The birth record is silent about the father. Frank's wife delivered a child at about the same time, so there is no particular reason to believe Frank was the father, although Wesley always called Frank his father. Frank's wife, Gusta, died in 1890, leaving Frank a widower with six children in the house, from age nineteen to age one.

See biography on page 336 for details of Frank's boyhood.

For Frank, a household of six children, including a toddler, meant a second marriage was vital. Perhaps it was the shared need to give his children a mother, and Hattie's need to give her son a father. For whatever reason, they married at Rupert in the winter of 1891. Hattie wasted no time bearing two children: Libbie in 1892 and Minnie Frances in 1897. Minnie lived only four days. But that was not to be the full extent of Hattie's heartbreak. After just eight years of marriage, Frank developed a fatal case of pneumonia in 1899, and Hattie was alone again. The 1900 census shows her with her two surviving children and a widowed boarder named Herbert Whedon, who had a ten-year-old daughter named Elizabeth.[176] Frank's children were either on their own or boarding with others.

Herbert Whedon grew up in Rupert, Vermont, just over the state line from Hebron and fifteen miles northwest of Manchester. He was there with his parents in the 1870[177] and 1880[178] censuses. He became a harness maker. He married an unnamed woman and had a daughter in 1889 they named Elizabeth.

[176] Hattie E. Ameden household, 1900 U.S. cens., Bennington Co., Vt., pop. sched., Manchester, SD [blank], ED 32, sheet 6A, dw. 112, fam. 113..
[177] John N. Whedon household, 1870 U.S. cens., Bennington Co., Vt., pop. sched., Rupert, p. 4, dw. 28, fam. 28.
[178] John W. Whedon household, 1880 U.S. cens., Bennington Co., Vt., pop. sched., Rupert, p. 2, dw. 18, fam. 20.

By 1900 Herbert was widowed and running his own harness making business. He was caring for his daughter by himself, and boarding with the widowed Hattie Ameden, whose children were much the same age as Elizabeth. When the census taker came by in June 1900, Hattie and Herbert were landlady and boarder. But it was probably that same year they married. Their daughter Hazel was born in January 1901.

In 1910, Herbert was still running his own harness shop in Manchester. Libbie had left the household and was probably planning her wedding to Jesse Mattison, which occurred a month after the census was taken. Wesley was still living at home, working as a store clerk. Hazel was just nine years old. Ann Adams was an elderly widow who was boarding with Herbert and Hattie.[179]

Hattie died six years later at age fifty-four. Herbert buried her with her brothers and sisters in Hebron Cemetery.[180] Their only child, Hazel, married the next year, and Herbert was alone. Herbert relocated to Arlington, eight miles southwest of Manchester. In 1920 he was living there alone, operating his cobbler shop.[181]

By 1930, Herbert had moved to Massachusetts and remarried. His third wife, Katherine, was a Scottish immigrant, eleven years his junior. He was then working as a baggage handler for the railroad in Arlington, Massachusetts.[182]

Child of ___ ___ and HARRIET AMEDEN:

i.   WESLEY LARNARD AMEDEN, b. Salem, N.Y., 18 June 1888;[183] m. Manchester Center 27 May 1911 HAZEL ADELLE BOLSTER,[184] b. Manchester 13 July 1893, dau. of EUGENE L. and FLORA ADELLE (HUGHS/HEWES) BOLSTER.[185] Worked as a

---

[179]   Herbert P. Whedon household, U.S. 1910 U.S. cens., Bennington Co., Vt., pop. sched., Manchester, SD [blank], ED 30, sheet 17B, dw. 307, fam. 351.

[180]   Hattie Ameden tombstone, Hebron Cemetery, Hebron, New York, transcribed by Nancy Mullen in July 1995.

[181]   Herbert P. Whedon household, U.S. 1920 U.S. cens., Bennington Co., Vt., pop. sched., Arlington, SD 1, ED 24, sheet 8A, dw. 132, fam. 159.

[182]   Herbert P. Whedon household, 1930 U.S. census, Middlesex county, Massachusetts, population schedule, Arlington, SD 10, ED 9-192, sheet 8B, dwelling 125, family 184; National Archives micropublication T626, roll 914.

[183]   Wesley Ameden birth record, Manchester Births.

[184]   Ameden-Bolster marriage, Manchester Marriages.

[185]   Hazel Adelle Bolster birth record, Manchester Births.

farmer in Jamaica, Vt., in 1930.[186]

Children of WESLEY and HAZEL (BOLSTER) AMEDEN:

a. *Eugene Larnod Ameden*, b. Manchester, Vt., 16 Sept. 1912.
b. *Robert Keith Ameden*, b. Jamaica, Vt., 30 July 1917.
c. *Richard Earl Ameden*, b. Jamaica 23 Sept. 1919.
d. *Dennis Guy Ameden*, b. Jamaica 10 April 1921.
e. *Elizabeth Adele Ameden*, b. Jamaica 3 Nov. 1922.
f. *Alwin Wesley Ameden*, b. Jamaica 15 April 1925.
g. *Jesse Charles Ameden*, b. Manchester 14 Sept. 1929.

Children of WILLIAM and HARRIET (AMEDEN) AMEDEN:

ii. MARY ELIZABETH "LIBBIE" AMEDEN, b. Manchester 3 Aug. 1892; m. Manchester 15 June 1910 JESSE PEABODY MATTISON, b. Manchester 11 March 1870, son of EDWIN D. and JANE M. (ELLIOTT) MATTISON. Libbie resided as a boarder with Jesse Mattison and his widowed mother in 1910.[187] Resided Manchester with husband and two sons 1920[188] and 1930.[189] Known for independent thinking. Married a man aged forty when she was seventeen. When family barn burned and neighbors took up a collection to rebuild the barn, Libbie used the money to buy one of the first cars in Manchester. Enjoyed taking her grandchildren fishing.[190]

Children of JESSE and MARY (AMEDEN) MATTISON:

a. *Clyde Edwin Mattison*, b. Vt. 29 July 1911.
b. *Leo James Mattison*, b. Manchester 10 Nov. 1914.

iii. MINNIE FRANCES AMEDEN, b. Manchester 14 May 1897;[191] d. Manchester 18 May 1897.[192]

Child of HERBERT and HARRIET (AMEDEN) WHEDON:

iv. HAZEL MARGUERITE WHEDON, b. Manchester 25 Jan. 1901; m.

---

[186] Wesley Ameden draft registration, 864:65, Ancestry.com, *World War I Draft Registration Cards* .
[187] Jesse Mattison household, 1910 U.S. cens., Bennington Co., Vt., pop. sched., Manchester, SD [blank], ED 30, sheet 26B, dw. 445, fam. 423.
[188] Jessie Mattison household, 1920 U.S. cens., Bennington Co., Vt., pop. sched., Manchester, SD 1, ED 32, sheet 8A, dw. 178, fam. 187.
[189] Jessie Mattison household, 1930 U.S. cens., Bennington Co., Vt., pop. sched., Manchester, SD 2, ED 2-16, sheet 11A, dw. 271, fam. 294.
[190] Mary Sallisky email to Nancy Mullen, 7 October 1999.
[191] Minnie Frances Ameden entry, Manchester Births, Book 3:2.
[192] Minnie Frances Ameden entry, Manchester Deaths.

abt. 1917 CLYDE HERBERT RAWSON,[193] b. Prob. Jamaica, Vt., 15 May 1896, son of JUDSON L. and EVA A. (___) RAWSON. Clyde sold Fuller brushes door-to-door in 1930. Rented half a duplex in Brattleboro, Vt., 1920.[194] Rented a single-family home in Newfane, Vt., 1930.[195]

Child of CLYDE and HAZEL (WHEDON) RAWSON:

a. *Sharon P. Rawson* (male), b. Vt. 16 Feb. 1919.[196]

William Franklin Ameden (1848–1899)

77. WILLIAM FRANKLIN "FRANK" AMEDEN[7] *(NATHANIEL[6], HORATIO GATES[5], JACOB[4] AMIDOWN, HENRY[3], PHILIP[2], ROGER[1] AMADOWNE)* was born at Hebron, New York,[197] on 12 September 1848.[198] He died at Manchester, Vermont, on 5 September 1899.[199] He married first at Salem, New York, on 9 May 1871, MARY AUGUSTA "GUSTA" ROBBINS.[200] She was born at Peru, Vermont, on 31 December 1848, the daughter of DAVID and ELIZA (DAVIS) ROBBINS, and died at Rupert, Vermont, on 17 March 1890.[201] He married second HARRIET ELIZABETH "HATTIE" AMEDEN.[202] See her biography earlier in this chapter.

Frank grew up at Hebron, the second of nine children, where he was listed with his parents in 1850, 1860, 1865, and 1870. In 1871, he married the lovely Gusta Robbins.

---

[193]   Clyde H. Rawson household, 1930 U.S. census, Windham County, Vermont, population schedule, Newfane, SD 3, ED 13-17, sheet 1B, dwelling 24, family 27; National Archives micropublication T626, roll 2432.

[194]   Clyde H. Rawson household, 1920 U.S. census, Windham County, Vermont, population schedule, Brattleboro, SD 2, ED 108, sheet 12B, dwelling 247, family 281; National Archives micropublication T625, roll 1876.

[195]   Clyde H. Rawson household, 1930 U.S. cens., Windham Co., Vt., pop. sched., Newfane, SD 3, ED 13-17, sheet 1B, dw. 24, fam. 27.

[196]   Clyde H. Rawson household, 1920 U.S. cens., Windham Co., Vt., pop. sched., Brattleboro, SD 2, ED 108, sheet 12B, dw. 247, fam. 281. SS Death Index.

[197]   Birth record for daughter Minnie Frances, Manchester Births, Book 3:2.

[198]   Wm. F. Ameden entry, *Washington County School Birth Records, 1847-49*; Town Historian, Fort Edward, New York.

[199]   Wm. F. Ameden entry, Manchester Deaths, book 3:14.

[200]   Jackson & Jackson, *Marriage Notices from Washington County*, 76.

[201]   Augusta Ameden entry, *Death Register*, Rupert, Vermont town clerk, p. 5.

[202]   Ameden-Ameden entry, *Marriage Register*, Rupert, Vermont town clerk.

Gusta grew up in Peru. Oddly, the 1850 census calls her Betsy[203] but the 1860 calls her Mary A.[204] The 1860 shows the elderly Betsy Davis living in the household; she is presumed to be the widowed mother of Eliza: the source of the belief that Eliza Robbins's maiden name was Davis. By 1870 the family had moved to Manchester.[205] Since Frank seems to have always lived in New York before his marriage, and Gusta seems always to have lived in Vermont, it's not clear how these two got together!

Figure 1 Gusta Ameden Courtesy: Stacy Niedzweicki

Frank and Gusta set up housekeeping in his hometown of Hebron, living with his parents. He was listed as a farmer, probably working on his father's farm. Gusta did her part to preserve the Ameden name. In the course of eighteen years, she bore four sons and two daughters. Her youngest, Mary Augusta, was born at Rupert, Vermont, suggesting that Frank moved his family across the state line sometime after George was born in Hebron in 1885. Gusta was not to live to see her children grow up. In 1890, when baby Mary was just five months old, Gusta died of heart failure at the premature age of forty-one.

With six children in the household, Frank needed a wife. Ten months after Gusta's death, Frank married his first cousin, Hattie Ameden. She delivered two girls, Libbie in 1892 and Minnie in 1897. Minnie lived only four days.

Frank was working as a butcher when Minnie was born. Perhaps his health was already failing so he could no longer do farming. Pneumonia took him in 1899 just before his fifty-third birthday.

Children of WILLIAM F. and AUGUSTA (ROBBINS) AMEDEN:

---

[203] David Robins household, U.S. 1850 cens., Bennington Co., Vt., pop. sched., Peru, p. 98B, dw. 575, fam. 590.

[204] David Robins household, U.S. 1860 cens., Bennington Co., Vt., pop. sched., Peru, p. 208, dw. 1637, fam. 1672.

[205] David Robins household, U.S. 1870 cens., Bennington Co., Vt., pop. sched., Manchester, p. 51, dw. 10, fam. 7.

i.   DAVID NATHANIEL "NATE" AMEDEN, b. Salem, N.Y., 1871;[206] m. Bennington, Vt., 4 May 1897 FANNIE BRIGGS,[207] b. Searsburg, Vt., 4 Jan 1874, dau. of ELI and MARTHA (MALLORY) BRIGGS,[208] d. Bennington, Vt., 16 Jan 1915.[209] Resident New Castle, Nebraska, 1920.[210]

Children of NATE and FANNIE (BRIGGS) AMEDEN:

a.   *Infant Ameden*, b. Bennington, Vt., 13 March 1898;[211] d. Bennington 13 March 1898 stillborn.[212]

b.   *Harry Briggs Amidon*, b. Bennington 28 March 1899;[213] m. 1) Bennington 3 March 1921 *Edith Evalina Baker*,[214] b. Vt. July 1890, dau. of *B. Allen* and *Roll G. (Emory) Baker*, divorced 1926;[215] m. 2) Bennington 16 Nov. 1929 *Marguerite Merle Dow*, b. Vt. 1910.[216] Resided with maternal grandparents in Bennington, 1920.[217] Lived down the street from grandparents in 1930 after marriage.[218]

c.   *Francis Carl Amidon*, b. Bennington 25 July 1902.[219]

---

[206]   Ameden-Briggs marriage record, *General index to vital records of Vermont, 1871-1908.*

[207]   Ibid.

[208]   Fannie Briggs birth record, *Record of births, marriages, and deaths, 1829-1952,* Searsburg (Vermont) Town Clerk, 54; FHL, Salt Lake City, Utah. Microfilm 28921.

[209]   Lynne M. Cassano, comp., *Gravestone Inscriptions from the Village Cemetery, Bennington, Vermont,* (Bennington, Vermont: Bennington Museum, 1987), 121.

[210]   Albert Chase household, 1920 U.S. census, Dixon County, Nebraska, population schedule, New Castle, SD 3, ED 91, sheet 7A, dwelling 6, family 6; National Archives micropublication T625, roll 985.

[211]   Clyde H. Rawson household, 1920 U.S. cens., Windham Co., Vt., pop. sched., Brattleboro, SD 2, ED 108, sheet 12B, dw. 247, fam. 281.

[212]   Ibid.

[213]   Harry Ameden birth record, *General index to vital records of Vermont, 1871-1902.*

[214]   Amidon-Baker marriage record, *General index to vital records of Vermont, 1909-1942.*

[215]   Amidon-Dow marriage record, *General index to vital records of Vermont, 1909-1942.*

[216]   Ibid.

[217]   Ely Briggs household, 1920 U.S. cens., Bennington Co., Vt., pop. sched., Bennington, SD [], ED 28, sheet 31B, dw. 758, fam. 815.

[218]   Harry B. Amadon household, 1930 U.S. cens., Bennington Co., Vt., pop. sched., Bennington, SD 2, ED 2-8, sheet 10B, dw. 236, fam. 259.

[219]   Francis Ameden birth record, *General index to vital records of Vermont, 1871-1902.*

Resided with maternal grandparents in Bennington, 1920[220] and 1930.[221]

ii. CHARLES O. AMEDEN, b. Peru, Vt., 8 April 1875. Resided in Manchester with second cousin, Earl Taylor, 1920: still single, working as teamster.[222]

iii. SYLVESTER ELIJAH AMEDEN, b. Hebron 4 February 1877;[223] m. bef. 1905 MINNIE K. STRATTMAN,[224] b. Conn. 2 Dec. 1885,[225] dau. of German immigrants AUGUST and ELIZABETH (___) STRATTMAN.[226] Resided 74 Prospect, Torrington, Conn., in 1918; worked as teamster. Resided Torrington 1930.

Child of SYLVESTER and MINNIE (STRATTMAN) AMEDEN:

a. *Franklin William Ameden*, b. Torrington, Conn., 22 Nov. 1905. Resided Torrington 1920.[227]

iv. INEZ J. AMEDEN, b. Hebron, N.Y., May 1880; m. Manchester 15 July 1909 JOHN J. PROVAN,[228] b. Sandgate, Vt., 2 Jan. 1878, son of JAMES M. and ADELINE M. (BENTLEY) PROVAN.[229]

Child of JOHN and INEZ (AMEDEN) PROVAN:

a. *Robert A. Provan*, b. Vt. abt. Jan. 1910.

v. GEORGE HERMON AMEDEN, b. Hebron, N.Y., 17 June 1885;[230] m. 1) abt 1910 MARY DEWEY, b. N.Y. abt. 1888, dau. of ROBERT and

---

[220] Ely Briggs household, 1920 U.S. cens., Bennington Co., Vt., pop. sched., Bennington, SD [], ED 28, sheet 31B, dw. 758, fam. 815.
[221] Martha Briggs household, 1930 U.S. cens., Bennington Co., Vt., pop. sched., Bennington, SD 2, ED 2-8, sheet 10B, dw. 227, fam. 251.
[222] Earl Taylor household, 1920 U.S. cens., Bennington Co., Vt., pop. sched., Manchester, SD 1, ED 32, sheet 21A, dw. 492, fam. 325.
[223] Sylvester Ameden, Ancestry.com, *World War I Draft Registration Card.*
[224] Based on birth of son in 1905.
[225] Minnie Ameden entry, Ancestry.com, *Social Security Death Index.*
[226] August Strattman household, 1900 U.S. census, Litchfield County, Connecticut, population schedule, Torrington, SD 26, ED 256, sheet 7A, dwelling 106, family 122; National Archives micropublication T625, roll 2426.
[227] Sylvester C. Ameden household, 1920 U.S. census, Litchfield County, Connecticut, population schedule, Torrington, SD 2, ED 216, sheet 2B, dwelling 32, family 33; National Archives micropublication T625, roll 186.
[228] Provan-Ameden marriage record, *General index to vital records of Vermont, 1909-42.*
[229] James M. Provan household, 1900 U.S. cens., Bennington Co., Vt., pop. sched., Sandgate, SD 274, ED 36, sheet 3B, dw. 67, fam. 69.
[230] George Hermon Ameden entry, Ancestry.com, *World War I Draft Registration Card.*

AMANDA (___) DEWEY;[231] m. 2) Rupert 10 Nov. 1923 VIOLA SMITH,[232] b. Rupert 25 Feb. 1898,[233] dau. of FLOYD and MARY (CASSIDY) SMITH.[234]

vi. MARY AUGUSTA AMEDEN, b. Rupert, Vt., 26 Oct. 1889; m. Arlington, Vt., 16 June 1912 JAMES MITCHELL PROVAN, b. Salem, N.Y., 5 April 1892,[235] son of PAUL PROVAN. Paul Provan was the brother of John Provan, who married Mary's sister, Inez Ameden; Paul died prematurely, leaving the young James to be raised by his grandparents, James and Adeline Provan.[236] James and Mary Augusta resided Manchester 1920[237] and New Windsor, N.Y., 1930.[238] No issue.

Children of WILLIAM and HARRIET (AMEDEN) AMEDEN:
See family 76 Harriet Elizabeth Ameden.

Ashell Sheldon Ameden (1854– aft 1920)

78. ASHELL SHELDON AMEDEN[7] (NATHANIEL[6], HORATIO GATES[5], JACOB[4] AMIDOWN, HENRY[3], PHILIP[2], ROGER[1] AMADOWNE) was born at Hebron, New York, on Christmas Day, 1854.[239] He died after 1920.[240] He married at Hebron, New York, on 1 January 1879 EMILY TAYLOR.[241] Emily was born at Jamaica, Vermont, in November 1853,[242] the daughter of JOSEPH and ELLEN M. (___) TAYLOR.[243]

231   Robert Dewey household, 1910 U.S. cens., Washington Co., N.Y., pop. sched., Hebron, SD 6, ED 105, sheet 2B, dw. 35, fam. 35.
232   Ameden-Smith record, *General index to vital records of Vt., 1909-42.*
233   Viola Ameden record, Ancestry.com, *Social Security Death Index.*
234   Floyd Smith household, 1900 U.S. cens., Washington Co., N.Y., pop. sched., Salem, SD 5, ED 140, sheet 8A, dw. 176, fam. 176.
235   James Mitchell Provan entry, Ancestry.com, *World Wat I Draft Registration Card.*
236   James M. Provan household, 1900 U.S. cens., Bennington Co., Vt., pop. sched., Sandgate, SD 274, ED 36, sheet 3B, dw. 67, fam. 69.
237   James M. Provan household, 1920 U.S. cens., Bennington Co., Vt., pop. sched., Manchester, SD 1, ED 32, sheet 9A, dw. 198, fam. 212.
238   James M. Provan household, 1930 U.S. census, Orange County, New York, population schedule, New Windsor, SD 19, ED 36-86, sheet 8A, dwelling 127, family 144; National Archives micropublication T626, roll 1633.
239   Best, 121.
240   Herman Ameden household, 1920 U.S. cens., Washington Co., N.Y., pop. sched., Greenwich, SD 384, ED 201, sheet 8A, dw. 76, fam. 90.
241   Jackson & Jackson, *Marriage Notices from Washington County*, 39.
242   Ashell Amsden household, 1900 U.S. cens., Bennington Co., Vt., pop. sched., Manchester, SD [], ED 32, sheet 14A, dw. 330, fam. 336.

She died after 1910.[244]

Ashell grew up in Hebron, New York, where he was listed with his family in the 1860, 1870, and 1875 censuses. He married Emily Taylor in Hebron in 1879, and settled down in Manchester, Vermont.

Emily grew up in Manchester, the younger of two girls, daughter of a subsistence farmer. The 1860 census shows a very poor family, with no real estate and only thirty dollars worth of personal property.[245]

Sheldon and Emily wasted no time starting their family. Caroline was born a year after they married, in 1880. An unnamed infant was born a year later, who probably died before being named. A year later a son was born who died of fever after a month. Five more children followed in rapid succession.

The naming of the daughters is peculiar. The daughter born in 1889 was named Eva according to the Manchester vital records, and the subsequent censuses in 1900,[246] 1910,[247] 1920,[248] and 1930.[249] A daughter born in 1891 was also named Eva in the vital records, but called Ruth in the censuses of 1900 and 1910. The daughter born in 1894 was named Ruth in the birth record, but called Shirley in the censuses of 1900, 1910 and 1920.

The 1900 census shows Ashell and Emily with their six surviving children living in a rented house in Manchester, where Sheldon worked as a mason, like his father before him.

By 1910 Sheldon and Emily seem to have lost another child, Harrison. Herman, Eva and Shirley were still living at home.[250] Herman was working as a stone mason like his father. Caroline was

---

243   Joseph Taylor household, 1860 U.S. cens., Bennington Co., Vt., pop. sched., Winhall, p. 226, dw. 1793, fam. 1830.
244   Sheldon Ameden household, 1910 U.S. cens., Bennington Co., Vt., pop. sched., Manchester, SD [], ED 20, sheet 88, dw. 306, fam. 348.
245   Joseph Taylor household, 1860 U.S. cens., Bennington Co., Vt., pop. sched., Winhall, page 226, dw. 1793, fam. 1830.
246   Ashell S Ameden household, 1900 U.S. cens., Bennington Co., Vt., pop. sched., Manchester, SD [], ED 32, sheet 14A, dw. 330, fam. 336.
247   Sheldon Ameden household, 1910 U.S. cens., Bennington Co., Vt., pop. sched., Manchester, SD [], ED 30, sheet 17A, dw. 306, fam. 348.
248   Sherman Ameden household, 1920 U.S. cens., Washington Co., N.Y., pop. sched., Greenwich, SD 384 ED 201, sheet 8A, dw. 76, fam. 90.
249   Herman Ameden household, 1930 U.S. cens., Washington Co., N.Y., pop. sched., Greenwich, SD 5 ED 58-24, sheet 19A, dw. 487, fam. 574.
250   Sheldon Ameden household, 1910 U.S. cens., Bennington Co., Vt., pop. sched., Manchester, SD [], ED 30, sheet 17A, dw. 306, fam. 348.

working as a private nurse for the Herbert Shaw family in Manchester.[251] Ruth was working as a domestic for the Frederick S. Reed family in Manchester.[252]

By 1920, Emily had died. The widowed Sheldon, along with Eva and Shirley, moved in with Hermon in Greenwich, New York. Hermon and Eva were listed as married, though there is no sign of spouses in the household. Shirley was listed as single, but had a four-year-old son Keith.[253] Caroline had married, but was already widowed, living with her in-laws, the Nathanael Towsley family in Manchester.[254]

Children of ASHELL SHELDON and EMILY (TAYLOR) AMEDEN:[255]

i.   CAROLINE E. AMEDEN, b. Manchester 11 Nov. 1880; m. Rutland 3 July 1913 LEWIS L. TOWSLEY,[256] b. Manchester June 1888, son of NATHANAEL and MARY A. (___) TOWSLEY, d. bef. 1920.[257]

ii.   INFANT AMEDEN, b. Manchester 3 Nov. 1881.

iii. INFANT AMEDEN (dau.), b. Manchester 11 Nov. 1882; d. Manchester 16 Dec. 1882.

iv.   HERMON JOSEPH AMEDON, b. Manchester 11 June 1884; m. bef. 1918 OLA MAY CORP,[258] b. N.Y. 10 May 1897, d. 7 Oct. 1918, bur. Greenwich Cem., Greenwich, N.Y.[259]

v.   HARRISON W. AMEDEN, b. Manchester 18 Oct. 1886; d. bef. 1910.

vi.   EVA V. AMEDEN, b. Manchester 8 Sept. 1889; m. 1) bef. 1920 ___ MILLETT,[260] m. 2) aft. 1920 ___ CONNERS, d. bef. 1930.[261]

---

[251] Herbert Shaw household, 1910 U.S. cens., Bennington Co., Vt., pop. sched., Manchester, SD [], ED 30, sheet 10A. dw. 154, fam. 177.

[252] Frederick S. Reed household, 1910 U.S. cens., Bennington Co., Vt., pop. sched., Manchester, SD [], ED 30, sheet 17A, dw. 293, fam. 334.

[253] Herman Ameden household, 1920 U.S. census, Washington County, New York, population schedule, Greenwich, SD 384, ED 201, sheet 8A, dwelling 76, family 90; National Archives micropublication T625, roll 1272.

[254] Nathanael Towsley household, 1920 U.S. cens,, Bennington Co,, Vt. pop. sched., Manchester, SD 1, ED 32, sheet 2A, dw. 43, fam. 45.

[255] Manchester birth records.

[256] Manchester Marriages, 5:87.

[257] Nathanael Towsley household, 1920 U.S. cens., Bennington Co., Vt., pop. sched., Manchester, SD 1, ED 32, sheet 2A, dw. 43, fam. 45.

[258] Hermon Joseph Amedon record, Ancestry.com, *World War I Draft Registration Cards, 1917-1918.*

[259] Charles B. Moore, *Cemetery Records, the Town of Greenwich*, 33.

[260] Herman Ameden household, 1920 U.S. cens., Washington Co., N.Y., pop. sched., Greenwich, SD 384, ED 201, sheet 8A, dw. 76, fam. 90.

Resided with brother Hermon and widowed father in Greenwich, N.Y., 1920; census says husband was living, though absent. Resided with brother, Hermon, in 1930.

Child of EDWARD DONAHUE and EVA (AMEDEN) CONNERS:

a. *Ronald Conners*, b. Vt. abt. 1929.[262]

vii. RUTH E. AMEDEN, b. Manchester 3 Nov. 1891.

viii. SHIRLEY A. AMEDEN, b. Manchester 18 Dec. 1894; d. aft. 1920.

Child of EDWARD DONAHUE and SHIRLEY AMEDEN:

a. *Keith D. Ameden*, b. Manchester 16 March 1915;[263] res. N.Y. State School for the Blind, 1930.[264]

Jennie (Burke) Daniels (1849–1907)

79. JENNIE BURKE[7] *(JANE[6], HORATIO GATES AMEDEN[5], JACOB[4] AMIDOWN, HENRY[3], PHILIP[2], ROGER[1] AMADOWNE)* was born at New York on 5 September 1849.[265] She died at Dubuque, Iowa, 7 September 1907.[266] She married at Oswego County, New York, in 1870[267] JOHN L. DANIELS. John was born at Oswego County, New York, 15 February 1844,[268] probably a son of EZRA and HARRIET (___) DANIELS.[269] John died at Dubuque, Iowa, on 26 May 1926.[270]

Jennie probably grew up in her mother's household, though the family has not been found during Jennie's childhood.

John grew up in Oswego on the eastern shores of Lake Ontario,

---

[261]   Herman Ameden household, 1930 U.S. census, Washington County, New York, population schedule, Greenwich, SD 5, ED 58-24, sheet 19A, dwelling 487, family 574; Washington: National Archives micropublication T626, roll 1657.

[262]   Ibid.

[263]   Keith Ameden entry, *Index to Vermont Vital Records, 1909–42.*.

[264]   N.Y. State School for the Blind, 1930 U.S. census, Genesee County, New York, population schedule, Batavia, SD 8, ED 19-9, sheet 1B, dwelling 1, family 1, line 72; National Archives micropublication T626, roll 1440.

[265]   John Daniels household, 1900 U.S. census, Dubuque County, Iowa, population schedule, Dubuque 5th ward, SD 3, ED 118, sheet 3, dwelling 180, family 183; National archives T623, roll 430. This census taker recorded full birth dates, although he was only supposed to record month and year.

[266]   Jennie Daniels obituary, *Telegraph-Herald*, Dubuque, Iowa, 7 Sept. 1907.

[267]   John Daniels household, 1900 U.S. cens., Dubuque Co., Ia., pop. sched., Dubuque 5th ward, SD 3, ED 118, sheet 3, dw. 180, fam. 183.

[268]   John Daniels obituary, *Telegraph-Herald*, Dubuque, Iowa, 26 May 1926.

[269]   Ezra Daniels household, 1850 U.S. census, Oswego County, New York, Oswego, page 124, dwelling 943, family 955; National Archives micropublication M432, roll 577.

[270]   John Daniels obituary, *Telegraph-Herald*, Dubuque, Iowa, 26 May 1926.

where he is found in the household of his father, Ezra, in 1850.[271] By 1860, it may be that his father was widowed, had married Catherine ___, and relocated to Berlin, Ohio.[272]

If Jennie Burke's obituary is correct, she moved to Dubuque, Iowa, in 1868. There she may have met John Daniels, who had settled in Dubuque in 1866. They returned to Oswego County, New York, for their wedding in 1869, but immediately returned to Dubuque where they were settled by 1870. John was working as a teamster.[273] Jennie's parents followed the young couple to Dubuque by 1873, and lived with them.

In 1870 John and Jennie started their family with little Eunice. Five years later they added Fred. And in 1884 they added Mabel. All three children were born in Dubuque.[274]

In 1894 eldest Eunice married an English immigrant, Harry Proctor. Harry had immigrated as a ten-year-old child in 1881. The young couple moved in with John and Jennie. Once little John was born, there were three generations sharing the home at 2815 Pine Street. But ten months after the arrival of little John, Fred married Emily Marshall and moved out of the house. By 1900, the household consisted of John and Jennie, her parents, their elder daughter with husband and child, and their younger daughter. John had given up the physically demanding work of a teamster and was a traveling salesman.[275]

In 1901 youngest child Mabel married William H. Thompson and moved out of the family household. Jennie died from cancer in 1907, and was buried at Linwood Cemetery in Dubuque.[276] Two years later, in 1909, John married the younger Lottie ___. It was a second marriage for both of them; he was fifty-eight; she was forty-one. They

---

[271]   Ezra Daniels household, 1850 U.S. census, Oswego County, New York, Oswego, page 124, dwelling 943, family 955; National Archives micropublication M432, roll 577.

[272]   E. Daniels household, 1860 U.S. census, Erie County, Ohio, population schedule, Berlin, page 10,   dwelling 74, family 74; National Archives micropublication M653, roll 958.

[273]   John Daniels household, 1870 U.S. cens., Dubuque Co., Ia., pop. sched., Dubuque 3rd ward, p. 54, dwelling 455, family 430.

[274]   John Daniels household, 1885 Iowa census, Dubuque County, Dubuque, page 444.

[275]   John Daniels household, 1900 U.S. cens., Dubuque Co., Ia., pop. sched., Dubuque 5th ward, SD 3, ED 118, sheet 3, dw. 180, fam. 183.

[276]   Mrs. John Daniels death certificate, Dubuque, Iowa.

settled into a home outside the city in Dubuque township and John worked in real estate.

By 1920, John was seventy-six years old, working as a popcorn vendor, and Lottie was a helper in a Victrola factory. John died from stomach cancer in 1926 at age eighty-two at the home of his younger daughter Mabel, and is buried in Linwood Cemetery.[277] No mention is made of Lottie, John's second wife, in his obituary. But John is buried beside her in Linwood Cemetery.

Children of JOHN and JENNIE (BURKE) DANIELS:[278]

i.   EUNICE DANIELS, b. Dubuque, Ia., 5 Feb. 1870;[279] m. Dubuque 4 Oct. 1894 HARRY PROCTOR, b. Ilkley, England, 4 Oct. 1871.[280] Lived Dubuque 1930.[281]

Child of HARRY and EUNICE (DANIELS) PROCTOR:

a. *John Proctor*, b. Ia. Jan. 1897;[282] d. 13 April 1930.

ii.   FRED JOWEL DANIELS, b. Dubuque 15 March 1875;[283] m. 1) Dubuque 10 Nov. 1897 EMILY MARSHALL, b. Dubuque 23 May 1878, dau. of GEORGE and BARBARA (SCHUSTER) MARSHALL, div.; m. 2) Lincoln, Ill., abt. 1909[284] CLARA HENKE,[285] b. Lincoln, Ill.,[286] 8 Dec. 1886,[287] dau. of AUGUST and GERTRUDE

---

277   John Daniels obituary, *c* 26 May 1926.

278   John Daniels household, 1900 U.S. cens., Dubuque Co., Ia., pop. sched., Dubuque 5th ward, SD 3, ED 118, sheet 3, dw. 180, fam. 183.b. Ia. 15 Nov. 1900, son of William Wiedner

279   John Daniels household, 1900 U.S. cens., Dubuque Co., Ia., pop. sched., Dubuque 5th ward, SD 3, ED 118, sheet 3, dw. 180, fam. 183. This census taker recorded full birth dates, although he was only supposed to record month and year.

280   John Daniels household, 1900 U.S. cens., Dubuque Co., Ia., pop. sched., Dubuque 5th ward, SD 3, ED 118, sheet 3, dw. 180, fam. 183. This census taker recorded full birth dates, although he was only supposed to record month and year.

281   Harry Prosth household, 1930 U.S. census, Dubuque County, Iowa, population schedule, Dubuque-Julien, SD 7, ED 31-37, sheet 4B, dwelling 90, family 91; National Archives micropublication T626, roll 654.

282   John Daniels household, 1900 U.S. cens., Dubuque Co., Ia., pop. sched., Dubuque 5th ward, SD 3, ED 118, sheet 3, dw. 180, fam. 183.

283   John Daniels household, 1900 U.S. cens., Dubuque Co., Ia., pop. sched., Dubuque 5th ward, SD 3, ED 118, sheet 3, dw. 180, fam. 183. This census taker recorded full birth dates, although he was only supposed to record month and year.

284   Fred Daniels household, 1930 U.S. census, Dubuque County, Iowa, population schedule, Dubuque-Julien, SD 7, ED 31-37, sheet 5A, dwelling 105, family 106.

285   Fred Daniels obituary, *Telegraph-Herald*, Dubuque, Iowa, 25 Feb. 1948.

286   Clara Daniels obituary, *Telegraph-Herald*, Dubuque, Iowa, 10 Nov. 1972.

287   Clara Daniels entry, Ancestry.com, *Social Security Death Index*.

(BIRNBAUM) HENKE. Steamfitter in Dubuque 1930.[288]
   Child of FRED and EMILY (MARSHALL) DANIELS:
   a. *Hazel Eunice Daniels*, b. Ia. Oct. 1898;[289] m. 1) 18 Nov.
      1916 *Leslie James Rapp*, b. East Dubuque, Ill., 7 July 1894,
      son of *Fred* and *Bridget (Kinslow) Rapp*; m. 2) abt. 1927
      William Wiedner, b. Ia. 15 Nov. 1900, son of *William H.* and
      Mary (__) Wiedner.
         Children of *Leslie* and *Hazel (Daniels) Rapp*:
         1. Robert M. Rapp, b. Ia. 1917.
         2. Dorance J. Rapp, b. Ia. abt. 1919.
      Children of FRED and CLARA (HENKE) DANIELS:[290]
   b. *Harold D. Daniels*, b. Chicago, Ill., 20 Sept. 1913.
   c. *Esther E. Daniels*, b. Webster, Wisc., Feb. 1916.
   d. *Jane Daniels*, b. Iowa, abt. Feb. 1918; d. bef. 1930.
   e. *Jennie L. Daniels*, b. Sioux City, Ia., 24 Dec. 1919.
iii. MABEL A. DANIELS, b. Dubuque 7 May 1884;[291] m. Dubuque 10
     Oct. 1901 WILLIAM HENRY THOMPSON, b. Ia. 26 July 1880.[292]
        Children of WILLIAM and MABEL (DANIELS) THOMPSON:[293]
     a. *Frederick W. Thompson*, b. Ia. 1903.
     b. *Bernice J. Thompson*, b. Ia. abt. 1907.
     c. *Elmer L. Thompson*, b. Dubuque Co., Ia, 1915.

---

   [288]   Fred Daniels household, 1930 U.S. census, Dubuque County, Iowa,
population schedule, Dubuque-Julien, SD 7, ED 31-37, sheet 5A, dwelling 105,
family 106.
   [289]   Fred Daniels household, 1900 U.S. census, Dubuque County, Iowa,
population schedule, Dubuque 5th ward Julien, SD 3, ED 117, sheet 16A, dwelling
303, family 329.
   [290]   Fred Daniels household, 1920 U.S. census, Woodbury County, Iowa,
population schedule, Sioux City, SD -, ED 206, sheet 27A, dwelling 610, family
659; micropublication T625, roll 520.
   [291]   John Daniels household, 1900 U.S. cens., Dubuque Co., Ia., pop. sched.,
Dubuque 5th ward, SD 3, ED 118, sheet 3, dw. 180, fam. 183. This census taker
recorded full birth dates, although he was only supposed to record month and year.
   [292]   William Thompson household, 1910 U.S. census, Dubuque County, Iowa,
population schedule, Dubuque, SD 3, ED 130, sheet 11B, dwelling 122, family 124;
National Archives micropublication T624, roll 401.
   [293]   William Thompson household, 1920 U.S. census, Dubuque County, Iowa,
population schedule, Dubuque, SD 3, ED 148, sheet 9B, dwelling 154, family 158;
National Archives micropublication T625, roll 488.
      William Thompson household, 1930 U.S. census, Dubuque County, Iowa,
population schedule, Dubuque-Julien, SD 7, ED 31-38, sheet 10B, dwelling 200,
family 249.

Jane A. (Parkerson) King (1848–1904)

80. JANE A. "JENNIE" PARKERSON[7] *(FRANCES ANN[6], HORATIO GATES AMEDEN[5], JACOB[4] AMIDOWN, HENRY[3], PHILIP[2], ROGER[1] AMADOWNE)* was born at New York in April 1848.[294] She died 8 April 1904, probably at Washington County, New York.[295] She married before 1874 ANDREW J. KING.[296] Andrew was born at New York in about 1840, the son of __ and LENORA (__) KING.[297] He died before 1900.[298]

Jennie grew up in Hebron where she was found with her family in 1850 and 1860. Sometime in her late teens the family moved a few miles southwest to Greenwich.

Andrew King grew up in Hartford, twenty miles north of Greenwich. His mother, Lenora King, was head of household in 1850, with three children.[299] By 1860 she had married Lewis Burton, a local farmer, and had two more children.[300] The elder of the two Burton children, Willard, later married Jane's younger sister, Ida.

By 1874 Andrew had established himself as a stone mason, and married Jennie. Their only child, Ada, was born in late 1874. They continued to live in Hartford until Andrew died in 1894 at age fifty-four. That was about the same time that Ada married Sigismund Morris. Jennie moved in with the young couple, and remained with them until she died in 1904 at age fifty-six. Jennie and Andrew are buried side-by-side in New Hebron Cemetery.

Child of ANDREW and JENNIE (PARKERSON) KING:

i.   ADA F. KING, b. N.Y. 22 Dec. 1874; d. 16 Nov. 1927; bur. New Hebron Cemetery; m. abt. 1894 SIGISMUND E. MORRIS, b. 20 Nov.

---

[294]   Sigismund Morris household, 1900 U.S. census, Washington County, New York, population schedule, Greenwich, SD 5, ED 129, sheet 6A, dwelling 121, family 129.

[295]   Jennie A. Parkerson King tombstone, New Hebron Cem., Hebron, N.Y.

[296]   Andrew J. King household, 1880 U.S. census, Washington County, New York, population schedule, Hartford, SD 6, ED 145, page 13, dwelling 141, family 153. The marriage date is estimated from the age of their child in the 1880 census.

[297]   Lenora King household, 1850 U.S. census, Washington County, New York, population schedule, Hartford, page 260B, dwelling 740, family 741.

[298]   Sigismund Morris household, 1900 U.S. census, Washington County, New York, population schedule, Greenwich, SD 5, ED 129, sheet 6A, dwelling 121, family 129. Andrew's wife is listed as widowed.

[299]   Lenora King household, 1850 U.S. census, Washington County, New York, population schedule, Hartford, page 260B, dwelling 740, family 741.

[300]   Lewis Burton household, 1860 U.S. census, Washington County, New York, population schedule, Hartford, page 116, dwelling 8, family 7.

1870 prob. in Hebron, son of GEORGE and SUSETUYER (__) MORRIS.

Children of SIGISMUND and ADA (KING) MORRIS:[301]

a. *W. Clinton Morris*, b. prob. 1894; d. 4 Sept. 1894; bur. New Hebron Cem.

b. *Harrold Eugene Morris,* b. N.Y. 8 August 1898;[302] m. *Alma A. __,* b. N.Y. 14 Feb. 1903.[303]

   Child of *Harrold* and *Alma (__) Morris*:

   1. Shirley M. Morris, b. N.Y. abt. 1921.

c. *Arietta Morris*, b. N.Y. abt. 1910.

---

[301] William Thompson household, 1920 U.S. census, Dubuque County, Iowa, population schedule, Dubuque, SD 3, ED 148, sheet 9B, dwelling 154, family 158; National Archives micropublication T625, roll 488.

   William Thompson household, 1930 U.S. census, Dubuque County, Iowa, population schedule, Dubuque-Julien, SD 7, ED 31-38, sheet 10B, dwelling 200, family 249.

[302] Harold Morris entry, Ancestry.com, *Social Security Death Index*.

[303] Alma Morris entry, Ancestry.com, *Social Security Death Index*.

Appendixes

Appendix I

The Inventory of Roger Annadowne[1]

The Inventory of the Goods and Chattles of Roger Annadowne
deceased apprised by Phillip Walker and Anthony Perrey of Rehoboth
the 20th of Nouember 1673
Impr: his wearing apparrell
Item 1 paire of serge Brieches 01 02 00
Item a paire of Cloth breiches 00 12 00
Item a short Coate 001 02 00
    Item a Coate att 1li 14s a doublett 14s 02 08 00
Item his euery day apparrell 000 18 00
Item an old paire of boots [.. ..] 00
Item 2 paire of stockens 000 04 06
Item a Caster hatt 001 05 00
Item 4 neckclothes 2 bands 1 Capp 000 07 00
Item a shirt 000 05 00
Item a Great old Coate 000 12 00
Item 3 paire of sheets 001 12 00
Item 4 pillowebeers 000 10 00
Item 3 Napkins 000 [.2] 00
Item 4 old pillowes 000 08 00
Item a Green blankett [.. ..] 00
Item an old Rugg and an old blankett 000 10 00
a white blankett 00 [1.] 00
Item a feather bolster 00 12 00
Item a feather bed and 2 old blanketts 1 15 00
Item a bedsted C[...]d and bed matt [..] 10 00
Item a little Childrens bed and bed stead 00 07 00
Item a Table 00 09 00
Item a Chest 000 11 00
Item a broad axe and a narrow axe 000 07 06
Item an adds 5s a paire of Chissells 2s 000 07 00
Item 2 hamers 1s 6d a paire of Compasses 8d 000 02 02
Item a Gimbled and a kniffe fyle 000 03 08
betle Ringes & 3 [.......] 000 05 00
Item a paire of pincers and an holdfast 000 02 00
Item a hand saw 3s 2 springe lockes 2s 6d 000 05 06
Item a Ioynter a fore plaine a Cressing

---

[1] Bowman, "Plymouth Colony Wills," III: 110–111.

p[.....] 000 05 00

Item an auger and a wimble tree 000 02 06

Item a share and coulter 000 07 00

Item 2 pound of sheepes woole 3 pound of Cotten woole 000 05 06

Item an old broad hoe 000 01 06

Item an old sickle 000 00 06

Item a Calkeing mallett 000 00 08

Item a drawing knife 000 02 00

Item a brasse skillett 00 06 06

Item a pewter platter 5s 2 old basons 1 porrenger 1s 000 12 00

Item a Glasse bottle and a stone Iugg 00 02 00

Item a pewter pott one shilling 4d 4 trayes & wooden ware 000 02 04

Item 3 smale Indian trayes 000 01 06

Item 3 earthen potts 000 [.4] 00

Item an Iron pott 000 14 00

Item an Iron kettle 000 12 00

Item an Iron pott and pott hookes 000 14 00

item ann old brasse kettle 000 06 00

Item a warming pan 000 08 00

Item a little brasse kettle 000 03 00

Item a narrow hoe nad a spade 000 02 06

Item a muskett and sword and lead 02 [.0] 08

Item 2 pound of wollen yearne 4s [*sic*] of Cotten yearne 000 09 00

Item Tobacco and a tubb 1s 6d a new Tubb 3s 000 04 06

[111]

Item 2 Chaires 2s 6d a wheel and spindle 1s 6d 000 04 0

Item 2 pothanger 6s a [.....] 8d 00 06 08

Item meale trough and seiues 00 02 00

Item salt 1s 6d Cheese 2s frying pan and tonges 00 07 06

Item 13 bushells of Indian Corne 01 19 00

Item a linnine wheele 00 04 0

Item a horese Cheines 15s Cart haines 3s 00 18 00

Item barrells and 1 hayshed 00 15 00

Item a Grindston 00 05 00

Item Syder beer 9s syder 14 01 03 0

Item 2 meat tubbs 3s 6d an apple trough 2s 00 05 6

Item a bushell of Rye 2 Bushells of pease 00 10 00

Item 2 hoges 16s 5 piggs 1li 01 16 00

Item 1 Cow 4li 1 Cow 3li a heiffer 2li 09 00 00

Item a horse 03 00 0

Item the houssing and homlott 45 00 00
Item 13 acrees of vpland and a peece of salt Marsh att the end of it 14 00 0
Item 3 acrees of land lying neare shapstree 01 16 0
Item 100 pound Comonage 08 00 00

The totall 113 02 8
[116 05 08
Phillip Walker
Anthony Perrey
The debts of Roger Annadowne deceased
Item owing to mr Steuen Paine senir: as appeers by his booke 15 17 10
To Thomas Olney of Prouidence 01 06 02
To Leift: peter hunt 02 06 05
To Gorge Kenicke 00 07 06
To Abraham Peren 00 15 00
To Thomas Wilmouth 01 03 06
To Ieremiah Wheaton 00 14 00
To Phillip Walker 01 19 00
To Anthony Perrey a bushell and an halfe of Corne 00 05 00
There is as wee vnderstand more debts owing by Roger Annadowne
that are not yett demaunded 24 14 02

---

debts owing to the estate of Roger Annadowne
From Iohn Cobley for a barrell of Syder 00 12 00
To Nathaniel dickens for a barrelll of syder
This is alsoe to giue the honored Court to vnderstand that the widdow
of Roger Annadowne did not bringe out to vs that were the Aprissors
of the estate of the said Annadowne;
any of the Moueables that shee brought with her att her Marriage;
The honored Court may be pleased to take Notice that there is an Iron
pott prised att 14s shillings and makes vp the sume which is since that
time Challenged by Ieremiah Wheaton as Giuen him by his father in
law Roger Annadowne;
As alsoe there was 9 acrees & an halfe of vpland and an acree of
Fresh meddow prised att 8 pound which is not put into the sume
which since that time, Testimony both shew it was Giuen to Ebenezer
Annadowne by his father; of these particulars our honored Majestrate
Mr Iames Browne Can further enforme the honored Court;

To preuent further agitation that probably might be, there was an old Gret Coate which att the first prising was not put downe but since that the widdow was willing it should be prised;

This Inventory of the estate of Roger Annadowne was exhibited to the Court held att Plymouth the 29th of October 1673 on the oath of Ionnah Annadowne widdow and ordered to be heer Recorded;

Appendix II

Will of Philip Amidown:
Will allowed May 12, 1747.

In the name of God, Amen, this sixteenth day of December in the year of our Lord one thousand seven hundred and forty three, I, Philip Amidown of Oxford in the County of Worcester, in the province of the Massachusetts Bay in New England, yeoman, being advanced in years and in a weak and low condition, Do make this my last will and testament, as follows, viz:— First and principally, I commit my soul into the hands of the Almighty God, my creator, hoping in his mercy thro the merits Death and Passion and prevailing intercession of Jesus Christ my Lord and Saviour and my body I desire may be decently interred at the discretion of my executor hereinafter named in faith of the resurrection of it at the last day and as touching such temporal estate as God has betrusted me with (after my just debts and funeral charges are are paid) I will and bequeath the same as follows:— That is to say

Impr. I give and bequeath unto my beloved wife Ithamar Amidown the improvement use profit and incomes of one quarter part of my farm whereon now I dwell in quantity and quality, as also my house which we now occupy, and the equal half of my barn together with all my moveables of the within doors as well as without to be possessed and enjoyed by her during her natural life, and at her decease the said quarter part of my farm house and barn to be to my son Ephraim Amidown his heirs and assigns forever as his and their proper estate and inheritance, and my moveables estate and goods to be distributed as herafter expressed in this my last will and testament. Item, I give and bequeath unto my sons Henry Amidown, Roger Amidown, Ichabod Amidown, Philip Amidown, and John Amidown, to each of them three pounds in Good public bills of credit or good current lawful money of New England, each and every pound equal to six shillings and eight pence in bills of credit of the new tenor of the said province to be paid to each of them for their respective heirs and assigns before or at the expiration of one year of my decease. Also my carpenter's tools to be divided equally among them, my said sons and their respective heirs and assigns having already given unto my said sons their full part and portion of all my estate real and personal.

Item. I give and bequeath unto the heirs of my son Ithamar Amidon three pounds of money as above specified to be paid to them after their heirs and assigns at the expiration of one year of my decease.

The said Ithamar Amidown having in his life time received his part & portion of my estate real and personal.

Item. I give and bequeath unto my daughter Mary Chamberlain three pounds in money as above specified to be paid to her and the heirs begotten of her body at the expiration of one year after my decease and one moiety of my household goods after the decease of my said wife to be possessed and enjoyed by her and her aforesaid as above expressed.

Item. I give and bequeath unto my daughter Hannah Wheelock three pounds to be paid unto her heirs and assigns at the expiration of one year after my decease in money as above specified and also the other moiety of my household goods after the decease of my said wife, having already given to my said daughters their part & portion of my estate.

Item. I give, grant and devise unto my son Ephraim Amidown his heirs and assigns all my real and personal estate whatsoever together with all my buildings, profits, incomes of my said real estate after the decease of my said wife Ithamar Amidown appointing and ordaining the said Ephraim Amidown sole executor of this my last will & testament and to pay all my just debts and legacies in manner as is above expressed.

In witness whereof I, the said Philip Amidown have hereunto put my hand and seal the day and year first hereinbefore written.

Philip Amidown (Seal)

Signed, sealed and delivered in the presence of us by the said Philip Amidown and by him declared to be his last will and testament.

Benj. Davis,
Duncan Campbell
John Campbell,
Worcester, ss, Probate Office

April 20, 1747. The Revd. Mr.

John Campbell and Duncan Campbell two other witnesses to this within instrument personally appearing made oath that they saw Philip Amidown the testator sign and seal and heard him publish pronounce and declare the same instrument to be and contain his last will and testament and that when he did so he was of sound disposing mind according to those deponants best deeming & that then with Benjamin Davis the other witness set to their names as witness thereof at the same time in said testators presence.

Sworn before me John Chandler, Judg. Prob.

Oxford, May 12, 1745

These lines may notify you that I am satisfied with the will of my husband.

to witness my hand.

her

ITHAMAR X AMIDOWN

Mark[2]

---

[2] Best, *Amidon Family*, 6.

Glossary

(All definitions from Merriam-Webster Online, unless otherwise
noted.)

Apoplexy. Stroke

Bark(e). A sailing ship of three or more masts with the aftmost
mast fore-and-aft rigged and the others square-rigged

Boatman. A man who works on, deals in, or operates boats

Consumption. 1) A progressive wasting away of the body
especially from pulmonary tuberculosis **2)** Tuberculosis

Cooper. One that makes or repairs wooden casks or tubs

Cordwainer. 1) A worker in cordovan leather **2)** A shoemaker

Coroner's jury. Citizens who officially inquire into a death
thought to be not of natural causes. The coroner presides
over the inquest(Evans)

Draying. Hauling on a cart

Dropsy. Edema. An abnormal infiltration and excess
accumulation of serous fluid in connective tissue or in a
serous cavity

Dyer. One who imparts a color by dyeing

Executrix. A woman who is an executor

Goodman. Used in Colonial days to denote a male head of a
household (Evans)

Grist mill. A mill for grinding grain

Hayward. 1) The man whose duty it was to catch stray cattle
and fine their owners for allowing them to stray **2)** The
official whose duty it was to see all the hogs had nose rings
and yokes. They were to be warded off the highway **3)** At a
later time, all newly married men were appointed haywards.
It was said that young men were adept at putting rings on
young ladies' fingers (Evans)

Hog reeve. See hayward

Homelot. The plot of land upon which a home is built. This
distinction is used in Colonial documents to denote land
used for homes rather than farms. It also referred to the
area surrounding the house, enclosed with a high protective
fence. Inside it were rail fences used to separate garden,
pigpen, cow yard, barnyard, etc. (Evans)

Hostler. One who takes care of horses or mules

Husbandman. A farmer. (Evans) One who farms for a living,
rather than someone who keeps a small farm but has
another occupation

Indentured servant. A person who signs and is bound by indentures to work for another for a specified time especially in return for payment of travel expenses and maintenance

Intestate. Having made no valid will

Joiner. A person whose occupation is to construct articles by joining pieces of wood

Julian calendar. A calendar introduced in Rome in 46 B.C. establishing the twelve-month year of 365 days with each fourth year having 366 days and the months each having 31 or 30 days except for February, which has 28 or in leap years 29 days

Machinist. 1) A worker who fabricates, assembles, or repairs machinery **2)** A craftsman skilled in the use of machine tools **3)** One who operates a machine

Mansard. A roof having two slopes on all sides with the lower slope steeper than the upper one

Messuage. Premises. A tract of land with the buildings thereon

Milliner. A person who designs, makes, trims, or sells women's hats

Millwright. 1) A person whose occupation is planning and building mills or setting up their machinery **2)** A person who maintains and cares for mechanical equipment (as of a mill or factory)

Nephritis. Acute or chronic inflammation of the kidney caused by infection, degenerative process, or vascular disease

Ordnance. Military supplies including weapons, ammunition, combat vehicles, and maintenance tools and equipment

Proprietor. One granted ownership of a colony (as one of the original American colonies) and full prerogatives of establishing a government and distributing land

Sawyer. One that saws

Selectman. A New England town board member elected annually (Evans)

Shipwright. A carpenter skilled in ship construction and repair

Spiritualism. A movement comprising religious organizations emphasizing spiritualism: a belief that spirits of the dead communicate with the living usually through a medium

Teamster. One who drives a team or motortruck especially as an occupation

Tinsmith. A worker who makes or repairs things of sheet metal

Tythingman/Tithingman. 1) A person who gave one-tenth of his income to the church 2) A person whose official job was to wake those worshipers who nodded, keep order and make certain that persons attended church in Colonial New England. He also made certain there were no loafers in taverns who should have attended church 3) Men appointed by a jury of the court to represent their towns, to appear in court two times each year to report those who had violated a by-law of the court, e.g., a boundary post in poor condition. One term was as long as a man would care to serve (Evans)

Bibliography

"123rd Regiment, New York Infantry." *Civil War Soldiers and Sailors System.* Online <"http://www.itd.nps.gov/cwss/">, downloaded 7 March 2005.

1903 Toledo Central High School Almanac. Lucas County Public Library, Toledo, Ohio.

Adams, J. W. *Supplement to the Warrensburgh News: Souvenir Edition.* Warrensburgh, N.Y.: Warrensburgh News, 1898.

Advertising and Public Relations Department of the Wabash Railroad Company, "Wabash Railroad History," August 1959; condensed and published online at <home.comcast.net / ~wabashrr / wabhist.html>.

Alabama. Montgomery.
- Alabama Center for Health Statistics. Deaths. Marriages.
- Oakwood Cemetery. Tombstone data.

Alabama. Montgomery County.
- Probate Court.
- U.S. census, 1880-1900, population schedule. Washington : National Archives.

Alabama. Perry County.
- County Clerk. Marriages.
- U.S. census, 1860-1870, population schedules. Washington: National Archives.

Aldrich, Alvin James. *George Aldrich Genealogy.* Decorah, Iowa: Anundsen Publishing Company, 1971-88.

Amaden family records, held by Christopher Amaden, San Diego, California.

Ameden, Alden. Personal testimony to Nancy K. Mullen.

Ameden, Kent. Personal testimony to Nancy K. Mullen.

Ameden, Leona. Personal testimony to Nancy K. Mullen.

American Antiquarian Society. *Index of Obituaries in Massachusetts Centinel and Columbian Centinel, 1784 to 184.,* 5 volumes. Boston: G. K. Hall Co., 1961.

"The Amidon Family." Online < http://www.rootsweb.com/ ~nyononda / AMIDON.HTM>.

Ammidown, Holmes. *Genealogical Memorial, Family Record, The Ammidown Family, Southbridge, Mass.* New York: Holmes Ammidown, 1877.

Ammidown, Lucius E. *The Ammidown Family,* Quinabaug Historical Society Leaflets, delivered 26 March 1906, Volume 3, No. 8.

Ancestry.com. Ann Arbor, Michigan Directories, 1886, 1888-92 Online. Provo, Utah: MyFamily.com, Inc., 2000.

Ancestry.com. *California Birth Index, 1905-1995.* Online. Provo, Utah: MyFamily.com, 2005. Original data: State of California,

California Birth Index, 1905-1995. Sacramento, California: State of California Department of Health Services, Center for Health Statistics.

Ancestry.com. *California Death Index, 1940-1997*. Online. Provo, Utah: MyFamily.com, 2000. Original data: State of California, *California Death Index, 1940-1997*. Sacramento, California: State of California Department of Health Services, Center for Health Statistics.

Ancestry.com. *Chicago Voter Registration, 1888*. Online. Provo, Utah: Ancestry.com, 2001. Original data: Illinois State Archives microfilm (25 rolls).

Ancestry.com. *Florida Death Index, 1877-1998*. Online. Provo, Utah: MyFamily.com, Inc., 2004. Original data: State of Florida. *Florida Death Index, 1877-1998*. Florida: Florida Health Department, Office of Vital Records, 1998.

Ancestry.com. *Glens Falls, New York Directories, 1888, 1890, 1891-92*. Online. Provo, Utah: Ancestry.com, 2000. Original data: *Glens Falls, NY, 1888*. Glens Falls, N.Y.: Wm. H. Kirwin, 1888. *Glens Falls, NY, 1890*. Glens Falls, N.Y.: Wm. H. Kirwin, 1890. *Glens Falls, NY, 1891-2*. Glens Falls, N.Y.: Wm. H. Kirwin, 1891.

Ancestry.com. *Indiana Marriage Collection 1800-1941*.Provo, UT, USA: The Generations Network, Inc., 2005.

Ancestry.com. *Iowa Cemetery Records*. Online. Provo, Utah: Ancestry.com, 2000). Original data: Works Project Administration, Graves Registration Project, Washington, D.C.

Ancestry.com. *Montgomery, Alabama Directories, 1880-95* Online. Provo, Utah: My Family.com, Inc., 2000.

Ancestry.com. *New York Births and Baptisms, Schoharie and Mohawk Valleys, 1694-1906* Online. Provo, Utah: Ancestry.com, 2002. Original data: Arthur, Kelly, and Nancy. Original data extracted by Arthur and Nancy Kelly.

Ancestry.com. *Oregon Marriages, 1906-20*. Online. Provo, Utah: MyFamily.com, Inc., 2000. Original data: State of Oregon, *Oregon Marriage Index, 1906-1920*. Portland, Oregon: Oregon Health Division, Center for Health Statistics.

Ancestry.com. *Saratoga Springs, New York Directories, 1888-92*. Online. Provo, Utah: Ancestry.com, 2000. Original data: *Saratoga Springs, NY, 1888*. Glens Falls, N.Y.: Wm. H. Kirwin, 1888.

Ancestry.com. *Social Security Death Index*. Online. Provo, Utah: MyFamily.com, Inc., 2006. Original data: Social Security Administration. *Social Security Death Index, Master File*.

Ancestry.com. *Washington State Birth Index 1907-1919* Online. Provo, UT, USA: MyFamily.com, Inc., 2002. Original data: Washington Department of Health. *Washington State Births 1907-1919*. Washington, USA: Department of Health.

Ancestry.com. *World War I Draft Registration Cards, 1917-1918* Online. . Provo, UT, USA: MyFamily.com, Inc., 2005. Original data: United States, Selective Service System. *World War I Selective Service System Draft Registration Cards, 1917-1918.* Washington, D.C.: National Archives and Records Administration. M1509, 4,582 rolls.

Appeal Democrat, Marysville, California. 2 August 2003.

Appleton, William S., ed. *Boston Births, Baptisms, Marriages, and Deaths 1630–1699.* Boston: Rockwell & Churchill, 1888.

Arizona. Gila County. U.S. census, 1930, population schedule. Washington: National Archives.

Arizona. Maricopa County. U.S. census, 1910 & 1930, population schedules. Washington: National Archives.

Arizona. Phoenix. Dept. of Health Services. Births. Deaths.

Arizona. Pima County. U.S. census, 1880, population schedule. Washington: National Archives.

Arizona. Yavapai County.
- Clerk Superior Court. Marriages.
- U.S. census, 1880-1930, population schedules. Washington: National Archives.
- Yavapai County Cemetery Records. Online. <www. sharlot.org/archives/gene/ cemetery/index/html>.

Arkansas. Little Rock. Department of Health. Death records.

Arkansas. Lonoke County.
- Marriage records.
- U.S. census, 1920-1930, population schedules. Washington: National Archives.

Army and Navy Journal, 18 December 1886, 15 January 1887.

Arnold, James N. *Vital Record of Rehoboth, 1642–1896. Marriages, Intentions, Births, Deaths, with Supplement containing the Record of 1896, Colonial Returns, Lists of the Early Settlers, Purchasers, Freemen, Inhabitants, the Soldiers serving in Philip's War and the Revolution.* Providence: Narragansett Historical Publ., 1897.

Arnold, James N. *Vital Record of Rhode Island 1636-1850.* Providence: Narragansett Historical Publishing Co., 1894.

Atlas of DeKalb County, Indiana. Chicago: J. H. Beers & Co., 1880.

Austin, James M, transcriber. *St. Lawrence Republican and General Advertiser,* Ogdensburg, New York.
- 1 October 1844. Online <www.rootsweb.com/~nystlawr/ 1850_VR_NewsItems.htm>.
- 26 February 1856. Online <www.rootsweb.com/ ~nystlawr / 1860_VR_ViTALS.htm>.

Austin, John, letter. 19 May 1996 to Nancy K. Mullen.

Austin, John. "Re: Albert Cheney." Email message to Nancy K. Mullen, 1 December 2005.

Austin, John. "Re: Ameden genealogy." Email message to Nancy K. Mullen, 16 July 2005.

Austin, John Osborne. *Genealogical Dictionary of Rhode Island Families Comprising three Generations of Settlers Who Came Before 1690.* Baltimore, Genealogical Publishing Company, 1995.

Australia. South Australia. Australian Archives. 11-13 Derlanger Avenue, Collinswood 5081.

Axtell, Carson A., compiler. *Axtell Genealogy.* Fairhaven, Mass.: The Darwin Press, 1945.

Bailey, Sally, letter. Undated, from Wallingford Town Historian, Wallingford, VT 05773 to Grace Ameden; copy held in 2005 by Nancy K. Mullen.

Baker, Barbara. Allen family records.

Baldwin, Thomas W., compiler. *Vital Records of Mendon, Massachusetts, To The Year 1850.* Boston, Wright & Potter Printing Company, 1920.

Baldwin, Thomas W., ed., *Vital Records of Uxbridge, Massachusetts, To The Year 1850.* Boston: Wright & Potter Printing Co., 1916.

Beach, Joseph P. *History of Cheshire, Connecticut from 1694 to 1840.* Cheshire, Conn.: Lady Fenwick Chapter, D.A.R., 1877.

Beaman, Alden Gamaliel, comp. Washington County, Rhode Island births from probate records, 1685-1860: comprising the towns of North Kingstown, South Kingstown, Exeter, Westerly, Charleston, Richmond, Hopkinton. Princeton, Mass.: Alden Gamaliel Beaman, 1978.

Beers, F. W., *CountyAtlas of Warren County, New York, 1876.* New York State Library, Albany, New York.

Bennington Evening Banner, Bennington, Vermont, 2 February 1955.

Berry, Annamae, transcriber. Albert A. Amaden cemetery record, *The Digger's Digest.* Yuba City, California: Sutter-Yuba Genealogical Society, 1980.

Bessey's Springfield Directory 1855-.6. Springfield: M. Bessey, 1855.

Best, Frank E. *The Amidon Story.* Chicago: Frank E. Best, 1904.

Bigsby Electric Guitars. Online <www.bigsbyguitars.com/history. html>

Biographical History of Cherokee County, Iowa. Chicago: W. S. Dunbar, 1889. Transcribed online <usgennet.org/usa/topic/ historical / cherokee1889idx>.

Bixby, Dave, and Heritage Hunters of Saratoga County. "Greenridge Cemetery, City of Saratoga Springs. Online <www.rootsweb.com /~nysarato/BxbGRC-A.htm.>

Bogdan, Robert. *Exposing the Wilderness, Early Twentieth-Century Adirondack Postcard Photographers.* Syracuse, N.Y.: Syracuse University Press, 1999.

Boston Registry Department. *Boston Births from A.D. 1700 to A.D. 1800.* Boston: Rockwell & Churchill, 1894.

Bowen, Clarence Winthrop. *The History of Woodstock, Conn.* 8 volumes. Norwood, Mass.: The Plimpton Press, 1930.

Bowen, Richard LeBaron. *Early Rehoboth, Documented Historical Studies of Families and Events in This Plymouth Colony Township.* 4 volumes. Rehoboth: Concord, N.H.: Privately printed, 1945–1950.

Bowman, George Ernest. "Plymouth Colony Wills and Inventories." *Mayflower Descendant,* volume XXV (1916).

Briggs, Charles B. *Saint Lawrence County, New York Directory 1890.* Online <ancestry.com>.

Brookside Cemetery, Watertown, New York.

Brown family records maintained by Gil Murray, Cheney, Washington.

Brown, Frank letter to Nancy K. Mullen, 21 December 2005.

Bryan Democrat, Bryan, Ohio, 9 November 1865, 23 January 1890.

Bryan Press, Bryan, Ohio, 18 March 1875.

Bureau of Labor Statistics. U.S. Department of Labor. *Occupational Outlook Handbook, 2004-05 Ed. Millwrights.* Online < http://www.bls.gov/oco/ ocos190.htm>.

Cady, Anne M., compiler. *Inventory of Edwardsville Cemetery, Morristown, New York.* Online <freepages.genealogy.rootsweb. com/~stlawgen/ CEMETERY/ Edwardsville/Edwardsville.htm>.

Cady, Anne M., comp. *Rennselaer Falls Cemetery Inventory.* Online <freepages. genealogy.rootsweb.com/~stlawgen/CEMETERY/ RenFalls/RenFalls.htm>.

California. Alameda County. U.S. census, 1880, 1920-1930 population schedules. Washington: National Archives.

California. Canyon County. U.S. census, 1900, population schedule. Washington: National Archives.

California. Colusa County.
- Recorder's Office, Colusa. Great Register of Colusa County. Marriage Registers.
- U.S. census, 1870, population schedule. Washington: National Archives.

California. El Dorado County. U.S. census, 1850, population schedule. Washington: National Archives.

California. Humboldt County. U.S. census, 1930, population schedule. Washington: National Archives.

California. Los Angeles County.
- County Clerk, Los Angeles. Marriage records.
- U.S. census, 1910-1930, population schedules. Washington: National Archives.

California. Marysville. Marysville City Council Minutes, March 1851-December 1863, page 597; Marysville City Library.

California. Mendocino County. U.S. census, 1910, 1930, population schedules. Washington: National Archives.

California. Mono County. U.S. census, 1930, population schedule. Washington: National Archives.

California. Nevada County.
- County Clerk, Nevada City. Marriage records.
- U.S. census, 1920, population schedule. Washington: National Archives.

California. Sacramento. California Vital Records. Births. Deaths. Marriages.

California. Sacramento County. U.S. census, 1910-1930, population schedules. Washington: National Archives.

California. San Diego County.
- County Clerk, San Diego. Death certificates.
- U.S. census, 1900, population schedule. Washington: National Archives.

California. San Francisco County.
- Recorder's Office, San Francisco. Deeds.
- U.S. census, 1870-1930, population schedules. Washington: National Archives.

California. Santa Barbara County. Santa Barbara. County Clerk. Marriages.

California. Santa Clara County. U.S. census, 1870, population schedule. Washington: National Archives.

California. Santa Cruz County. U.S. census, 1910, population schedule. Washington: National Archives.

California. Sutter County.
- Recorder, Yuba City. Births. Death Registers. Deeds. Marriages.
- U.S. census, 1860-1900, 1930, population schedules. Washington: National Archives.

California. Tehama county. U.S. census, 1880-1900, population schedules. Washington: National Archives.

California. Ventura County. Recorder's Office. Marriages.

California. Yolo County. U.S. census, 1900, 1920-1930, population schedules. Washington: National Archives.

California. Yuba County. U.S. census, 1860, 1910-1930, population schedules. Washington: National Archives.

Canal Society of New York State., *Champlain Canal: Watervliet to Whitehall.* ?: Canal Society of New York State, 1985.

Canton Commercial Advertiser. Canton, New York. 1 October 1902.

Carlin, Rick, Cincinnati, Ohio.

Cassano, Lynne M., compiler. *Gravestone Inscriptions from the Village Cemetery, Bennington, Vermont.* Bennington, Vermont: Bennington Museum, 1987.

Catton, Bruce. *The Civil War.* New York: American Heritage / Bonanza Books, 1960.

Cemetery Records of the Township of Fort Ann, Washington County, New York. Queensbury, New York: Historical Data Services, 1992.

Center Township Williams County, Ohio Cemetery Records (Inclusive to January 1992). ?: Williams County Genealogical Soc., 1992.

Chaffee, William H. *The Chaffee Genealogy (embracing the Chafe, Chafy, Chafie, Chafee, Chaphe, Chaffy, Chaffie, Chaffey, Chaffe, Chaffee Descendants of Thomas Chaffe, of Hingham, Hull, Rehoboth and Swansea, Massachusetts also certain Lineages from Families in the United States, Canada, England, not descended from Thomas Chaffe) 1635-1909*. The Grafton Press, New York, 1909.

Chamberlain, George Walter. *History of Weymouth, Massachusetts, Genealogy of Weymouth Families*. 4 volumes. Weymouth: Weymouth Historical Society, 1923.

Cheshire - Connecticut: Town History, 1694-1840. Provo, UT: Ancestry.com, 2001. Original data: Joseph P. Beach. *History of Cheshire, Connecticut from 1694 to 1840*, Including Prospect which, as Columbia Parish, was a part of Cheshire until 1829. Cheshire, Conn.: Lady Fenwick Chapter, D.A.R., 1877.

Child, Hamilton. *Gazetteer and Business Directory of Bennington County, Vermont 1880-1*. Syracuse, N.Y.: Journal Office, 1880.

Clark, Norman H. *Mill Town: A Social History of Everett, Washington*. Seattle: University of Washington Press, 1970.

Coles, Harry L. *The War of 1812*. Chicago: University of Chicago Press, 1965.

Coldwater Reporter, Coldwater, Michigan, 19 June 1950.

Colorado. Denver.
- Colorado Vital Records Office. Death records.
- Denver County Court. Divorce. Probate.

Colorado. Jefferson County. County Clerk, Golden, Colorado. Marriages.

Congregational Church of Christ (Tinmouth, Vermont), 1780–1868. Salt Lake City, Utah: Genealogical Society of Utah, 1956.

Connecticut. Ashford.
- Ashford Town Clerk. Ashford Vital Records.
- Ashford Town Register of Deeds. Ashford Deeds.

Connecticut (Colony). *The Public Records of the Colony of Connecticut, from April 1636 to October 1776 ... transcribed and published*, [in accordance with a resolution of the General assembly]. 15 volumes. Hartford: Brown & Parsons. 1850–1890.

Connecticut. Fairfield County. U.S. census, 1880, 1920, population schedules. Washington: National Archives.

Connecticut. Hartford County. U.S. census, 1900-1930, population schedule. Washington: National Archives.

Connecticut. Jefferson County. U.S. census, 1850, population schedule. Washington: National Archives.

Connecticut. Killingly. Killingly Town Clerk. Deeds. Vital Records.

Connecticut. Litchfield County. U.S. census, 1920-1930, population schedules. Washington: National Archives.

Connecticut. North Woodstock. Congregational Church. Baptisms.

Connecticut. Pomfret. Pomfret District Probate Court, Probate records, 1814-1824.

Connecticut. Stafford District. Register of Probate Records. Henry Amidon estate: Microfilm no. 5744, Family History Library, Salt Lake City, Utah.

Connecticut. Wallingford. Town Clerk.
- Marriage Records of Wallingford, Vermont.
- Town Records of Wallingford, Vermont.

Connecticut. Willington Registrar. Vital Records.

Connecticut. Windham County. U.S. census, 1820-1840; 1850, population schedule. Washington: National Archives.

Connecticut. Woodstock. Woodstock Town Hall, Woodstock, Connecticut Vital Records; Land Records; Town Records.

Copeland, Alfred Minot. *A History of Hampden County, Massachusetts.* ?: The Century Publishing Company, 1902. Online <http://www.rootsweb.com/~mahampde/sp_offic.htm>, downloaded 11 January 2005.

Coplien, Sandra. Personal records.

Corbett, Alice. *Cemetery DAR Transcriptions.* Online <freepages.genealogy.rootsweb.com/~aliecor/Cemeteries/Town_of_Watertown/Huntingtonville.htm>.

Corbett, Larry. *North Watertown Cemetery Records.* Online <www.geocities.com/lrcorbett/cemeterys.htm>.

Courier-News, Elgin, Illinois, 22 January 2003.

Crandall, John Cortland. *Elder John Crandall of Rhode Island and His Descendants.* New Woodstock, New York: ?, 1949.

The Crank. Pardeeville, Wisconsin. 30 March 1898.

Crary, Charles Judson. *Crary Family Records.* Palo Alto, California: C. J. Crary, 1956.

Cutter, William Richard. *New England Families Genealogical and Memorial: Third Series.* 4 volumes. Publication: 1913. Reprint Baltimore Genealogical Publishing Co., Inc., 1996.

Daily Advertiser. Montgomery, Alabama. 5 January 1895.

Daily Courier News. Elgin, Illinois. 27 July 1960, 7 November 1984.

Daily Herald. Oskaloosa, Iowa. 27 September 1932.

Dalby, John. *Minnesota Burials.* Provo, Utah: MyFamily.com, 2003.

Daniels, George F. *History of the Town of Oxford, Massachusetts with Genealogies and notes on persons and estates.* Oxford, Mass.: By the author, with the co-operation of the town, 1892.

Daughters of the American Revolution, National Society, Washington, D.C. Application of Antoinette Hammond Hitt, national no. 94146.

Death Records for Russell, NY. Online: <http://freepages.genealogy.rootsweb.com/~stlawgen/MISC/Vital%20Records/1848_russell_death.HTM.>

Decatur Genealogical Society, *Macon County, Illinois Cemetery Inscriptions.* Decatur. Illinois: Decatur Genealogical Soc., 1975.

Defiance County, Ohio, Newspaper Obituaries, undated collection, Defiance Public Library, Defiance, Ohio.

Delano, Walter Edward, family records. Described in email from Bill Nyland to Nancy K. Mullen, 10 June 2000, held in 2004 by Nancy K. Mullen.

Deming, Flora Bogue. *Bogue Genealogy: Descendants of John Bogue of East Haddam, Conn. and Rebecca Walkley.* Rutland, Vermont: The Tuttle Publishing Company, 1944.

Dodd, Jordan, Liahona Research. *Ohio Marriages, 1803-1900.* Online. Provo, Utah: MyFamily.com, Inc., 2001.

East Hampton Star, East Hampton, New York, 21 March 2002, 8 May 2003.

Elgin Daily Courier, Elgin, Illinois, 29 November 1907, 3 June 1914, 19 August 1976.

Erhardt, John G. *Rehoboth, Plymouth Colony, 1645–1692.* 3 volumes. Greenwich, R.I.: Greenwich Public Library, 1983–1990.

Erwin, Joseph. email correspondence with Christopher Amaden. 19 July 2004.

Evans, Barbara Jean. *A to Zax, A Comprehensive Dictionary for Genealogists & Historians,* 3rd edition. Alexandria, Va.: Hearthside Press, 1995.

Evening Journal, Jersey City, New Jersey, 25 July 1902.

Evening Telegram, Superior, Wisconsin. 10 December 1951, 8 February 1952.

Farr, Betty. Gridley, California. Amaden family records.

Fayette County Cemetery Index. Online <www.angelfire.com/ia/fayette2/fayetteindex.htm>.

Filion, Ron S. *San Francisco History: Masonic Cemetery.* Online <http://www.sfgenealogy.com/sf/history/ hcmmas.htm>.

Florida. Escambia County. U.S. census, 1930, population schedule. Washington: National Archives.

Foot, Rev. John. *Congregational Church of Cheshire, Connecticut.* 12 volumes. Hartford: Connecticut State Library, 1939.

Forest Home Cemetery Records. Hicksville, Ohio.

Forsyth, Warren. Email to Christopher Amaden. Re: Winnifred E. Rice, 8 November 2004.

Fountain Grove Cemetery records, Bryan, Ohio.

French, J.H. *Gazetteer of New York State, Embracing a Comprehensive View of the Geography, Geology, and General History of the State, and a Complete History and Description of Every County, City, Town, Village and Locality, with Full Tables of Statistics.* Online <www.rootsweb.com/~nywarren/history/1860french2.html#Top>, 8 September 2004. Previously published in hard copy: Syracuse: R.P. Smith, 1860.

"French nobility." Online <http://www.baronage.co.uk/2001/french-1.html>. Data downloaded 7 November 2004.

Fulton County Grave Transcriptions. Fulton County Historical Society, 1986.

Genealogical and Biographical Record of North-Eastern Kansas. Chicago: The Lewis Publishing Company, 1900.

Glens Falls Daily Times, Glens Falls, New York. 11 October 1897.

Glens Falls Morning Star. Glens Falls, New York. 26 October 1900.

Goodwin, Arlene, compiler. *Waterloo Cemetery Inscriptions, DeKalb County, Indiana.*

Grass Valley Union. Grass Valley, California. 24 February 1965.

Great Register, Sutter County, California, 1880-1896. Community Memorial Museum of Sutter County, Yuba City, California.

Great Register, Ventura, California. Ventura Historical Society, Ventura, California.

Green, Mason A. *Springfield Memories.* Springfield, Massachusetts: Whitney and Adams, 1876.

Habelman, E. Carolyn Wildes. *Genealogical Branches from Monroe County.* 3 volumes. Black River Falls, Wisconsin: E. C. W. Habelman, 1973.

Hale, Edward Everett, Jr., ed. Notebook Kept by Thomas Lechford, Esquire: Lawyer in Boston, Massachusetts Bay 1638–1641. Camden: Picton Press, 1988.

Halsey, Richard T., *Deaths from the Western N.Y. Masonic Relief Association.* Online <rootsweb.com/~nymonroe/vr/relief.htm>.

Hance, Dawn D. Extracts from the Rutland Herald 1816-1820. Rutland, Vt.: D. D. Hance, 2001?

Hansbraugh, Marvel. Brownell family records.

Hanson, Robert. *Vital Statistics from Galena Newspapers, July 22, 1828 – November 19, 1850: Marriages, Petitions for Divorce, Deaths, Estate Notices, and Sexton Reports.* Online <www.rootsweb.com/~iljodavi/vitals/VS1b.htm>.

Hanson, Robert Brand, ed. *Vital Records of Dedham, Massachusetts 1635-1845.* Camden, Maine: Picton Press, 1997.

Hanson, Robert Brand, ed. *Vital Records of Needham, Massachusetts 1711-1845.* Camden, Maine: Picton Press, 1997.

Hawaii. Oahu County. U.S. census, 1930, population schedule. Washington: National Archives.

Heasty, C. N. *Index to Birth Registrations in Monroe Co., WI, 1860-1945.* Sparta, Wisc.: Angelo Books, 1989.

Hemenway, Abby Maria. *Vermont Historical Gazetteer, A Local History of All the Towns in the State.* 5 volumes. Brandon, Vermont: Mrs. Carrie H. Page, 1891.

Historical Data Services. *Cemetery Records of the Township of Fort Ann, Washington County, N.Y.* Queensbury, N.Y.: Historical Data Services, 1995.

Historical Data Services. *Military Records of Individual Civil War Soldiers.* Online <www.ancestry.com>.

Histories of Wood County, WI Communities. Wisconsin Rapids, Wisc.: Heart O' Wisconsin Genealogical Society, 1993.

History and Biography of Washington County and the Town of Queensbury, New York. New York: Gresham Publishing Company, 1894.

History of Fayette County, Iowa. Chicago, Western Historical Company, 1878.

History of Washington Co., New York. Philadelphia: Everts & Ensign, 1878.

Hochstetler, Harvey. *Descendants of Jacob Hochstetler.* Elgin, Illinois: Brethren Publishing House, 1912.

Holbrook, Jay Mack. *Massachusetts Vital Records: Springfield, 1640-1894.* Oxford, Mass.: Holbrook Research Institute, 1987.

Holbrook, Jay Mack. *Massachusetts Vital Records: Sturbridge 1723–1891.* Oxford, Mass., Holbrook Research Institute, 1986.

Holton Weekly Recorder, Holton, Kansas, 21 May 1885.

Home, Daniel Douglass. "Incidents in My Life." NY: Carleton, 1863. Online <www.harvestfields.ca/ebook/01/068/ 02.htm>, downloaded 12 January 2005.

Houk, Don. Tokyo, Japan. Crain family records.

Howes, Martha O. and Sidney Perley, eds. *Town Records of Salem, 1634-1659 Essex Institute Historical Collections.* 9 volumes, Second Series. Salem: Essex Institute Press, 1869.

Humphrey, Zephine. *The Story of Dorset, Vermont.* Rutland, Vt.: Charles E. Tuttle Company, 1971.

Hungerford, Richard W. *Marriages in the New York Reformer, 1850-1861.* ?: Hungerford Genealogical Services, 1996.

Idaho. Ada County. County Clerk, Boise, Idaho. Marriages.

Illinois. Chicago. Archdiocese of Chicago. Archives and Record Center.
  • Angel Guardian Orphanage Records.
  • St. Martin's Church Baptismal Records.

Illinois. Cook County.
  • Clerk's Office, Chicago. Death Registrations.
  • U.S. census, 1880-1930, population schedules. Washington: National Archives.

Illinois. Elgin. City Cemetery. Tombstone data.

Illinois. Elgin. County Clerk. Death Records.

Illinois. Fulton County. U.S. census, 1850, 1870, population schedules. Washington: National Archives.

Illinois. Jo Daviess County. U.S. census, 1850, population schedule. Washington: National Archives.

Illinois. Kane County.
  • Kane County Admin. Bldg. Geneva, Illinois. Births. Deaths. Marriages.

Illinois. Kane County (continued).
- U.S. census, 1850-1900, 1930, population schedules. Washington: National Archives.

Illinois. Kendall County. U.S. census, 1900, population schedule. Washington: National Archives.

Illinois. Macon County. U.S. census, 1910-1930, population schedules. Washington: National Archives.

Illinois. McHenry County. U.S. census, 1850-1860, population schedules. Washington: National Archives.

Illinois. Springfield. Illinois State Archives. Births. Delayed Births. Deaths. Marriages.

Illinois Statewide Death Index. Springfield, Illinois: Illinois State Archives. Online <www.cyberdriveillinois.com/departments/archives/deathsrch.html>.

Illinois Statewide Marriage Index. Springfield, Illinois: Illinois State Archives. Online <www.cyberdriveillinois.com/departments/archives/marriage.html>.

Illinois. Vermillion County. U.S. census, 1910, population schedule. Washington: National Archives.

Illustrated Historical Atlaws of Williams County. Chicago: Andreas & Baskin, 1874.

Indiana. Allen County. U.S. census, 1900, population schedule. Washington: National Archives.

Indiana. Boone County. U.S. census, 1870, population schedule. Washington: National Archives.

Indiana. Dekalb County. U.S. census, 1860-1880, population schedules. Washington: National Archives.

Indiana. Elkhart County. U.S. census, 1900, population schedule. Washington: National Archives.

Indiana. Indianapolis. Indiana State Department of Health. Death records.

Indiana. Marshall County. U.S. census, 1840. Washington: National Archives.

Indiana Works Progress Administration, compiler, *Index to Marriage Record 1850 - 1920 Volume I Letters A – L.* White County, Indiana: WPA, 1938.

Iowa. Black Hawk County. U.S. census, 1930, population schedule. Washington: National Archives.

Iowa. Dubuque County. U.S. census, 1870-1900, population schedules. Washington: National Archives.

Iowa. Fayette County.
- 1856 Iowa state census. Fayette County Genealogical Society, West Union, IA; Family History Library. FHL microfilm #1021299.
- U.S. census, 1860, population schedule. Washington: National Archives.

Iowa. Kossuth County. U.S. census, 1900-1930, population schedules. Washington: National Archives.

Jackson, Mary S. and Edward F. Jackson. *Death Notices from Washington County, New York Newspapers, 1799-1880.* Bowie, Maryland: Heritage Books, Inc, 1995.

Jackson, Mary S. and Edward F. Jackson, *Marriage Notices from Washington County, New York Newspapers, 1799-1880.* Bowie, Md.: Heritage Books, Inc., 1995.

Jackson, Ronald V., Accelerated Indexing Systems, comp. *Vermont Census, 1790-1860.* Online. Provo, UT: Ancestry.com, 1999. Compiled and digitized by Mr. Jackson and AIS from microfilmed schedules of the U.S. Federal Decennial Census, territorial/state censuses, and/or census substitutes

Jenks, Margaret R. *Granville Cemetery Inscriptions, Washington County, New York.* ?: Privately published, 1993. Washington County Historian's Office, Fort Edward, N.Y.

Johnson, Paul Franklin, ed. *Captain John Johnson of Roxbury, Massachusetts, Generations I to XIV including the Generations I to IX from the 1932 and 1935 Manuscript of Frank Leonard Johnson, Completed with Additions and Corrections by Ada Johnson Modern, 1948.* Los Angeles: privately printed, 1951.

Johnson, Rossiter, ed. *The Twentieth-Century Biographical Dictionary of Notable Americans.* 10 volumes. Boston: The Biographical Society, 1904.

Johnston, Henry P., edit. *The Record of Connecticut Men in the Military and Naval Service During the War of the Revolution 1775-1783.* Volumes I-II. Hartford, CT: 1889-92. Republished in "Connecticut Men in the Revolutionary War, 1775-1783" Online. Provo, Utah: MyFamily.com, Inc., 2003.

Jones, George O. *History of Wood County, Wisconsin.* La Crosse, Wisconsin: Brookhaven Press, 2001.

Journal Gazette. Fort Wayne, Indiana. 5 January 1968.

Kansas. Jackson County. Holton Kansas. Probate record #532. Amaden-Cubbison marriage record.

Kansas. Jackson County. U.S. census, 1880, population schedule. Washington: National Archives.

Kansas. Shawnee County. U.S. census, 1920-1930, population schedules. Washington: National Archives.

Kominar, Sharon. Posted online at Church of Latter Day Saints.

Konig, Michael F. and Martin Kaufman. *Springfield 1636-1986.* ?: Springfield Library and Museums Association, 1987.

Labbe, Marilyn, comp. *First Congregational Church Thompson, Conn., 1730-1930.* Danielson, Conn.: Killingly Historical Society, 2000.

"Lake George Cemetery." *Patents*, South Glens Falls, N.Y., volume 9, number 5, September 1990.

The Lakeside Annual Directory of the City of Chicago, 1874-5., 1879, 1884, 1892. Chicago: The Chicago Directory Company, 1874, 1879, 1884, 1892.

Lamaster, Pat. *Family History of Schermier, Schooley and Amaden Families.* Gold Beach, California: self-published, ?. Copy held by Bob Burns, Marysville, California.

Langley's San Francisco Directory, 1868-9, 1888, 1889. San Francisco: Francis, Valentine & Co., 1868, 1888, 1889.

The Learning Company, Hiawatha, Iowa. World Family Tree #23, tree 2392.

Leas, Fay Willis, *Leas Family.* Waterloo, Indiana: self published, 1950.

Librarian of the Rhode Island Historical Society, ed. *The Early Records of the Town of Warwick.* Providence: E. A. Johnson & Co. Publishers, 1926.

Lincoln Institute, "Campbell General Hospital, *Mr. Lincoln's White House.* Online <www.mrlincolnswhitehouse.org/ inside.asp?ID= 126&subjectID=4>.

Luke, Beverly family notes, Minden, Nevada.

Madison Newspapers, Inc. Online <www.madison.com/obits>, 8 June 2004.

Marysville Appeal, Marysville, California. 17 June 1908.

Marysville Democrat, Marysville, California. 23 November 1925.

Mason, William H. *Snohomish County in the War: The Part Played in the Great War by the Soldiers, Sailors, Marines and Patriotic Civilians of Snohomish County, Washington, U.S.A.* (Everett, Washington: The Mason Publishing Company, 1920. Online <www.rootsweb.com/~waskagit/ snohmil1.html>.

Massachusetts. Berkshire County. U.S. census, 1860, population schedule. Washington: National Archives.

Massachusetts. Boston.
- Massachusetts Judicial Archives, Henery Annadown probate, Bristol County probate docket # 4217.
- Massachusetts State Archives, James Paul Amaden death certificate #321.

Massachusetts, Bristol County. County Clerk's Office, Taunton, Massachusetts. Samuel Perry will.

Massachusetts. Dudley.
- Congregational Church. Baptisms; Marriages.
- Town Clerk. *Town Records of Dudley, Masachusetts, 1754–1794.* Pawtucket, R.I.: The Adam Sutliffe Co., 1894.
- *Town proceedings, births, deaths, and miscellaneous records, 1713-1752,* Oxford, Massachusetts.

Massachusetts. Franklin County. U.S. census, 1870, 1910-1920, population schedule. Washington: National Archives.

Massachusetts. Greenfield.
- Green River Cemetery. Letter from cemetery to Christopher Amaden, July 2005.
- Town Clerk. Deaths.

Massachusetts. Hampden County.
- Probate Court, Springfield. Mass. Probate file no. 3949, Rufus Elmer.
- U.S. census, 1840; 1850-1860, 1880, 1910 population schedules. Washington: National Archives.

Massachusetts. Middlesex County. U.S. census, 1930, population schedule. Washington: National Archives.

Massachusetts. Rehoboth. Rehoboth Town Meetings, 1636-1966, Town Clerk's office, Rehoboth.

Massachusetts. Worcester County.
- Register of Deeds. Worcester County Deeds.
- U.S. census, 1790. Micropublication M637, roll 4. Washington: National Archives.

The Mauston Star. Mauston, Wisconsin, 22 June 1876.

McAfee, Michael. "11th New York Volunteer Cavalry," *Military Images*, January/February 2002.

McGowan, John J. Toledo, Ohio. Fahlbusch family records.

McTeer, Francis Davis and Frederick C. Warner. "The Millards of Rehoboth, Massachusetts." *The Detroit Society for Genealogical Research Magazine*, volume 23, no. 2 (Winter 1959).

Medford Mail Tribune. Medford, Oregon. 21 May 1952.

Melling, Mary Bryant. *Cowdrey-Cowdery-Cowdray Genealogy.* ?: Frank Allaben Genealogical Company, 1911.

Merriam-Webster Online. Online <www.m-w.com/dictionary>.

Michigan. Eaton County. U.S. census, 1930, population schedule. Washington: National Archives

Michigan. Oakland County. U.S. census, 1930, population schedule. Washington: National Archives

Michigan. Washtenaw County. U.S. census, 1900, population schedule. Washington: National Archives

Middleman, Julia E., compiler. *History of Monroe County Public Schools.* ?: Julia E. Middleman, 1989.

Miller, Al, University Relations, Univ. of Wisconsin Superior, email to Christopher Amaden, 2 September 2003.

Minnesota. Minneapolis. Minnesota Department of Health, Section of Vital Statistics.

Minnesota. Nobles County.
- Births and deaths; FHL, Salt Lake City, Utah, microfilm 1403233, 1403234.
- Register of Deeds, Worthington, Minnesota. Land Records; FHL, Salt Lake City, Utah, microfilm 1403175.
- U.S. census, 1880 population schedule. Washington: National Archives.

Minnesota. Ramsey County. U.S. census, 1870, 1900-1910 population schedule. Washington: National Archives.

Missouri. Jasper County. U.S. census, 1900, population schedule. Washington: National Archives.

Missouri. Jefferson City. Missouri State Archives.

Missouri. Saint Louis. National Personnel Records Center, Service #3309517.

Moore, Charles B. *Cemetery Records, the Town of Greenwich, Washington County, New York.* Glens Falls, New York: Historical Data Services, 2001.

Morning Star. Glens Falls, N.Y., 11 June 1885, 29 November 1890, 21 January 1903, 11 February 1907.

Munson, Myron A. *The Munson Record,* 2 volumes. New Haven, Conn.: The Munson Association, 1895.

Murray, Gil. Cheney, Washington. Brown family records.

"My 3rd Great-Grandmother, Eunice Southwick Spoor Amedon." Online <artisticdesigns.home.att.net/Genealogy/peoplefiles/ EuniceSouthwickSpoorAmedon.html>, downloaded 21 September 2004.

Nadaud, Abby Joseph. *Nobiliaire du diocèse et de la généralité de Limoges.* 4 volumes. Limoge, 1863-1882.

National Archives and Records Administration. *U.S. World War II Army Enlistment Records, 1938-1946* Online. Provo, Utah: MyFamily.com, Inc., 2005. Original data: Electronic Army Serial Number Merged File, 1938-1946 [Archival Database]: World War II Army Enlistment Records. Records of the National Archives and Record Administration Record Group 64; National Archives at College Park, College Park, Maryland.

National Park Service, *Civil War Soldiers and Sailors System.* Online. <www.itd.nps.gov/cwss/regiments.cfm>.

Nebraska. Dixon County. U.S. census, 1920, population schedule. Washington: National Archives.

Nebraska. Lincoln. State Department of Health. Death certificates.

Nelson, Kenneth E., "A Thumbnail History of the Daguerreotype," *The Daguerreian Society.* Online . <www.daguerre.org/resource/ history/history.html>.

Nevada. Sonoma County. U.S. census, 1930, population schedule. Washington: National Archives.

Nevada. Washoe County. U.S. census, 1930, population schedule. Washington: National Archives.

New Hampshire. Carroll County. U.S. census, 1930, population schedule. Washington: National Archives.

New Hampshire. Concord. Bureau of Vital Records. Deaths. Marriages.

New Hampshire. Grafton County. U.S. census, 1900-1930, population schedule. Washington: National Archives.

New Jersey. Bureau of Vital Statistics, Trenton. Amaden-Semple marriage certificate #397.

New Jersey. Essex County. U.S. census, 1910, population schedule. Washington: National Archives.

New Jersey. Union County. U.S. census, 1930, population schedule. Washington: National Archives.

New York. Albany. State Department of Health, Vital Records Section. Birth Registers. Death Registers.

New York Army Register Book, Washington: National Archives.

New York. Bolton. Town Clerk. Deaths.

New York. Chenango County. U.S. census, 1850, population schedule. Washington: National Archives.

New York. Clinton County. U.S. census, 1930, population schedule. Washington: National Archives.

New York. Erie County. U.S. census, 1900, population schedule. Washington: National Archives.

New York. Essex County.
- County Clerk's Office, Elizabethtown. Deeds.
- U.S. census, 1810, 1840; 1850-1870 population schedules. Washington: National Archives.

New York. Genesee County. U.S. census, 1930, population schedule. Washington: National Archives.

New York. Greensburgh. Town Clerk. Dobbs Ferry, N.Y.

New York. Hebron.
- East Hebron Cemetery. Tombstone data.
- Hebron Cemetery. Tombstone data.
- Hebron Cemetery Burial Book, in possession of Stacy Niedzwiecki, great-granddaughter of Eunice (Southwick) (Spoor) Ameden.
- Town Clerk. Death records.

New York. Herkimer County.
- Surrogate Court, Herkimer, New York. Surrogate files.
- U.S. census, 1860, population schedule. Washington: National Archives.

New York. Hudson Falls. Hudson Falls Methodist Church.
- *New York DAR Cemetery Church & Town Records,* 653 volumes. DAR Library Washington, D.C.
- Marriage book.

New York. Jefferson County.
- County Clerk. Land Records. Probate Records.
- State census, 1855, 1865, 1875, 1905. New York State Library, Albany, New York.
- U.S. census, 1840; 1850-1930, population schedules. Washington: National Archives.

New York. Johnsburg. Town Clerk, North Creek. Death Registers.

New York. Kingsbury. Town Clerk, Hudson Falls. Death registers.

New York. Lake George.
- Lake George Cemetery. Tombstone data.
- St. James Episcopal Church, baptism records. Reported in letter from John Austin to Nancy K. Mullen, 19 May 1996.
- Town Clerk. Death records. Marriage records.

New York. Monroe County. U.S. census, 1870-1880, population schedules. Washington: National Archives.

New York. Nassau County. U.S. census, 1900, population schedule. Washington: National Archives.

New York. New York County.
- City Clerk. Marriage records.
- U.S. census, 1860, 1900-1930, population schedules. Washington: National Archives.

New York. North Tarrytown. Sleepy Hollow Cemetery. Interment records.

New York. Orange County. U.S. census, 1930, population schedule. Washington: National Archives.

New York. Otsego County. U.S. census, 1900, 1920, population schedules. Washington: National Archives.

New York. Queensbury. Town Clerk. Death records. Marriage records.

New York. Rensselaer County. U.S. census, 1920, population schedule. Washington: National Archives.

New York. Saint Lawrence County.
- Surrogate Court, Canton, New York. Probate.
- U.S. census, 1820-1849; 1850-1930, population schedules. Washington: National Archives.

New York. Saratoga County.
- Surrogate Court. Saratoga. Court files.
- U.S. census, 1820; 1880-1920, population schedules. Washington, National Archives.

New York. Schenectady County. U.S. census, 1870, population schedule. Washington, National Archives.

New York. South Glens Falls. South Side Cemetery, Moreau, New York. Online <www.rootsweb.com/~nysarato/ssideSGF.htm>. Tombstone data.

New York. Suffolk County. U.S. census, 1930, population schedule. Washington: National Archives.

New York. Warren County.
- Archives, Lake George. Criminal Indictments.
- Cemeteries. Tombstone data.
- Friends Cemetery.
- Jenkins Cemetery.
- Lake George Cemetery, Lake George.
- Seelye Cemetery.

378   *Bibliography*

New York. Warren County (continued).
- Sunnyside Cemetery.
- County Clerk's Office. Minutes of Common Pleas. Mortgages. Probate. Wills.
- State census, 1845, 1855, 1875. New York State Archives. New York State Library, Albany.
- Surrogate's Court. Emma Hawley estate.
- U.S. census, 1820-1840; 1850-1930, population schedules; 1890, veteran's schedule. Washington: National Archives.

New York. Washington County.
- Cemeteries. Tombstone data.
  - East Hebron Cemetery, Hebron.
  - Hebron Cemetery, Hebron.
  - Tipladys Rd. Cemetery, Hebron.
  - Union Cemetery, Fort Edward.
- Municipal Center, Fort Edward. Court Records. Deeds. Minutes of Common Pleas 1831-44, Vital Records.
- State census, 1855, 1865. New York State Archives. New York State Library, Albany.
- U.S. census, 1790, 1810-1840; 1850-1930, population schedule. Washington: National Archives.

New York. Watertown.
- Brookline Cemetery Records.
- Marriages.

New York. Wayne County. U S. census, 1860, population schedule. Washington: National Archives.

Nyland, Bill. Correspondence with Nancy K. Mullen, 7 June 2000.

Ogdensburg Journal. Ogdensburg, New York. 22 June 1944.

Ohio. Clarke County. U.S. census, 1860-1880, population schedule. Washington: National Archives.

Ohio. Columbus. Ohio Department of Health . Birth Registrations. Death Registrations.

Ohio. Defiance County.
- Defiance Courthouse. Birth records. Land records. Marriage records. Probate files.
- U.S. census, 1850-1900, 1930, population schedule. Washington: National Archives.

Ohio. Fayette County. U.S. census, 1860, population schedule. Washington: National Archives.

Ohio. Fulton County. Fulton County Courthouse, Wauseon, Ohio. Death records.

Ohio. Lucas County.
- Calvary Cemetery. Toledo.
- Toledo. Probate Judge. Birth records. Marriage records.

Ohio. Lucas County (continued).
- U.S. census, 1900-1910, population schedule. Washington: National Archives.

Ohio. Putnam County.
- Ottawa. Marriage records.
- U.S. census, 1850, population schedule. Washington: National Archives.

Ohio. Seneca County. County Courthouse, Tiffin, Ohio. Marriage records.

Ohio. Van Wert County. U.S. census, 1930, population schedule. Washington: National Archives.

Ohio. Williams County.
- U.S. census, 1850-1880, population schedule. Washington: National Archives.
- Williams County Courthouse, Bryan, Ohio. Birth records. Guardianship files. Land records. Court cases roll 15 #153, roll 16 #82. Probate cases #1623, #1713.

Onaga Herald, Onaga, Kansas, 27 December 1923.

Oregon. Jackson County. U.S. census, 1910, population schedule. Washington: National Archives.

Oregon. Klamath County. U.S. census, 1930, population schedule. Washington: National Archives.

Oregon. Multnomah County. U.S. census, 1920-1930, population schedule. Washington: National Archives.

Oskaloosa Daily Herald, Oskaloosa, Iowa, 11 March 1929.

The Pardeeville-Wyocena Times, Pardeeville, Wisconsin, 27 July 1923, 22 May 1930.

Pearson, Jonathan, IV. transcriber, *Marriages at St. George's Church (Episcopal), Schenectady, NY - 1771-1850*. Cliff Lamere website. Online <http://freepages.genealogy.rootsweb.com/~clifflamere/Mg/MG-StGeorge-Schen-Br.htm>. Text, downloaded February 2001.

Pennsylvania. Allegheny County. U.S. census, 1900, 1930, population schedule. Washington National Archives.

Pennsylvania. Mercer County. County Clerk, Mercer. Death certificates.

Pennsylvania. New Castle. State Department of Health. Edwin Amaden death certificate #11469.

Pennsylvania. Philadelphia County. U.S. census, 1880, 1920, population schedules. Washington National Archives.

Perley, Sidney. *A History of Salem Massachusetts*. 3 volumes. Salem: Sidney Perley, 1924.

Polk's Watertown (Jefferson County, N.Y.) city directory, 1867-8. ?: R. L. Polk Publishing Company, 1868.

Pope, Charles Henry, *The Pioneers of Massachusetts, A Descriptive List*. Baltimore: Genealogy Publishing Co., 1965.

Portrait and Biographical Album for Fayette County. Chicago: Lake City Publishing Co.; 1891.

Post-Star. Glens Falls, New York. 28 September 1912.

Proprietor's Records of the Town of Mendon, Massachusetts. Boston: Rockwell & Churchill Press, 1899.

Radford, Dwight A. "From Seances to Ouija Boards." *NGS News Magazine*, volume 30, number 2, 2004.

Recruiting Book of Lt K. Bradley, 2nd Regt, Infr, Recruiting Officer, Washington: National Archives, ?.

Rhode Island. Kent County. U.S. census, 1850, population schedule. Washington: National Archives.

Rhode Island. Newport County. U.S. census, 1860, population schedule. Washington: National Archives.

Rhode Island. Warwick. *Records of Warwick, Rhode Island*.

Rice, Franklin P., publisher. *Vital Records of Dudley, Massachusetts, To the End of the Year 1849*. Boston: Stanhope Press, 1908.

Rice, Franklin P., publisher. *Vital Records of Oxford, Massachusetts, To the End of the Year 1849*. Boston: Stanhope Press, 1905.

Richards, Randolph A. *History of Monroe County, Wisconsin, Past and Present*. Chicago: C. F. Cooper & Co., 1912.

Roberts, George McKenzie, compiler. *The Vital and Cemetery Records of the Town of Enfield, New Hampshire*. ?: ?, 1957.

Rogers, Horatio, ed. *Early Records of the Town of Providence*. Providence: Rhode Island Historical Society, 1892–1915.

Rollins, Alden M. *Vermont Warnings Out*, 2 volumes. Camden Maine: Picton Press, 1997.

Rose, Christine. *Ancestors and Descendants of Robert Rose of Wethersfield and Branford, Connecticut, Who Came on the Ship "Francis" in 1634 from Ipswich, England*. San Jose, California: Rose Family Association, 1983.

Ross, Ogden J. *The Steamboats of Lake George, 1817 to 1932*. Albany: The Lake George Steamboat Company, c1932.

Sacramento Bee, Sacramento, California. 9 June 1956.

St. Francis de Sales Catholic Church, Toledo, Ohio. Marriage records.

St. Joseph Township, Ohio Cemetery Records. Bryan, Ohio: Williams County Genealogical Society, 1993.

St. Lawrence County Historical Association. *Lisbon, New York Cemeteries*. Typescript, St. Lawrence. County Historical Association. Microfilm 1451080, FHL, Salt Lake City, Utah.

St. Lawrence Republican, Ogdensburg, New York, 1 October 1844, 1856.

Sallisky, Mary. Email to Nancy K. Mullen, 7 October 1999.

San Bernardino Daily Sun. San Bernardino, California, 20 November 1951.

San Francisco Call. San Francisco, California, 12 January 1870, 17 November 1880, 10 July 1883.

San Francisco Chronicle, Sanfrancisco, California, 5 February 1916.

Sandy Hill [NY] Herald, Hudson Falls, N.Y., 10 June 1880.

Savage, James. *Genealogical Dictionary of the First Settlers of New England, Before 1692.* 4 volumes. Boston: 1860–1862. Reprint. Baltimore: Genealogical Publishing Co., 1990.

Sharlot Hall Museum, *Cemeteries: Williamson Valley – Pierce and Las Vegas Ranches..* Online. <sharlot.org/archives/gene/cemetery>.

Sharples, Stephen Paschall, ed. *Records of the Church of Christ at Cambridge in New England 1632-1830.* Boston: Eben Putnam, 1906.

Shriver, Samuel S. *History of the Shriver Family and Their Connections.* Baltimore: Press of Guggenheimer, Weil & Co., 1888.

Shurtleff, Nathaniel B. and David Pulsifer, eds. *Records of the Colony of New Plymouth in New England.* 12 volumes. New York: AMS Press, 1968.

Slott, Clifford L. *Vital Records of Springfield, Massachusetts to 1850.* USA: New England Historic and Genealogical Society, 2002.

Smallman, Mary, transcriber. *Parishville Land Office Book,* File #25. St. Lawrence County Historical Society, Canton, N.Y.

Smallman, Walter and Mary, transcribers. *Marriage Registers Kept by the Rev. Wm Whitfield, 1841-1891.* Salt Lake City, Utah: Genealogical Society of Utah, 1981.

Smith, Dean Crawford. *The Ancestry of Emily Jane Angell, 1844–1910.* Boston: New England Historic Genealogical Society, 1992. Online <inman. surnameweb.org/documents/angell.htm>. Printout dated 12 November 2003.

Smith, H. P., ed. *History of Warren County.* Syracuse: D. Mason & Co., 1885.

Snell, Nellie. *North Watertown Cemetery Records.*

South Carolina. Columbia. Office of Vital Records. Deaths.

South Dakota. McCook County. U.S. census, 1900, population schedule. Washington: National Archives.

Spiritual Telegraph. New York, New York, 24 June 1854. Online <http://www.spirithistory.com/54mass.html>, downloaded 27 October 2004.

Springfield, Massachusetts City Directory Listing. Springfield: Samuel Bowles and Company. 1859, 1864-5, 1870.

Springfield (Massachusetts) Republican. Springfield, Massachusetts, 7-9 April 1853. Online <http://www.spirithistory.com /53spring.html>, downloaded 27 October 2004.

Stevens, Ken. *Vital Records of Putney, Vermont.* Pittsford, Vt.: Genealogical Society of Vermont, 1992.

Stone St. Presbyterian Church, Watertown, Jefferson Co., N.Y., 1831-1885. Flower Memorial Library, Genealogy Dept., Watertown, New York.

Stratton, Eugene Aubrey. *Plymouth Colony: Its History & People 1620 – 1691.* Salt Lake City: Ancestry Publishing, 1986.

Susee, Virginia R. *U.S. Public Records Index Record.*.Online <ancestry.com>.

Texas. Cooke County. U.S. census, 1900, population schedule. Washington: National Archives.

Thorpe, Walter. *History of Wallingford, Vermont.* Rutland, Vermont: The Tuttle Co., 1911.

"Three Men Drowned," *Weekly Sutter (Yuba City, California) Banner,* 16 March 1872.

Toledo Birth Records Index. Toledo, Ohio, 1868-1910.

Torrey, Clarence Almon. *New England Marriages Prior to 1700.* Baltimore: Genealogical Publishing Co., Inc, 1997.

Toledo Blade, Toledo, Ohio, 17 April 1918, 20 September 1928, 11 April 1986, 21 January 1993, 28 August 2005.

Tomah Journal. Tomah, Wisconsin, 9 November 1895. 4 October 1901. 5 August 1904. 5 July 1907. 17 November 1932.

Tomah Monitor. Tomah, Wisconsin, 21 September 1898.

Town of Ashford, Conn. *Supplement to Commemorative Issue Two Hundred Fiftieth Anniversary.* ?:Ashford, Conn., ?.

Travelers' Official Guide of the Railway and Steam Navigation Lines in the United States and Canada. New York: National Railway Publication Company, 1893.

Trim, Robert S., letter. 14 April 1979 to Miss Buckland. Held by the Blanding Public Library, Rehoboth, Massachusetts.

United States. National Archives, Washington.

- Land Entry Files. Albert A. Amaden land entry #CACAAA 039360.
- Land Entry Files. Hannah Amidon land entry #10657.
- Land Entry Files. Lewellyn Amidon land entry #16555.
- Land Entry Files. Samuel Amidon land entry #9685.
- Land Entry Files. Ephraim Rose land bounty file #50-160, WT 16898.
- Records of Appointment of Postmasters 1832-1971, series M841, roll 91.
- Records of the Veterans Administration, Record Group 15. Civil War Pension Application Files.
- Edwin C. Amaden, SO 355623, SC 504415, WC 716190.
- George Amaden, Minor Child Application #11935.
- Henry Amaden, SO 55554, SC 208469.
- Larned Ameden, SC 85709.
- Horace T. Brown and Mary Brown, widow, SO 1038031, SC 830151, WC 526734
- Orville Lockwood and Adelia A. Lockwood, widow, WC 453306.
- Flora McQuilkin, widow: SC 302395, WC 400376.

United States. National Archives, Washington (continued).
- Ephraim Rose; Aurelia Rose, widow: SO 3245, SC 11607, WC 17677.
- George W. Rose, SO 1132010, SC 843677.
- Justus O. Rose, SO 571498, SC 803967.
- Edwin W. Rounds, SO 782654, SC 829630.
- Norman S. Snell, SO 71924, SC 349555.
- Harvey Smith, SC 717953.
- George W. Snow, SO 1324698, SC 1095864, WC 808324.

Utah. Salt Lake City. Utah State Department of Health. Deaths.

VanAntwerp, Lee D. compiler. *Vital Records of Plymouth, Massachusetts to the year 1850.* Camden, Maine: Picton Press, 1993.

Ventura County Genealogical Society. *Ventura County Directory – 1875.* Online <venturacogensoc/1875Dir>.

Vermont. Addison County. U.S. census, 1850-1860, population schedules. Washington: National Archives.

Vermont. Bennington County.
- Probate Court. Probate files volume 33, page 159. Larned S. Ameden.
- U.S. census, 1810, 1830-1840; 1850-1930, population schedules. Washington: National Archives.

Vermont. Burlington. Bureau of Vital Statistics. Deaths.

Vermont, Dorset.
- *Indexes to births, marriages, deaths, 1734-1994.* Salt Lake City: Genealogical Society of Utah, 1995. Microfilm 1985937, FHL, Salt Lake city, Utah.
- Town Clerk. Land Records. Microfilm 28142, 28143, and 28144, FHL, Salt Lake City, Utah.

Vermont. *General index to vital records of Vermont, early to 1870.* Salt Lake City: Genealogical Society of Utah, 1951; Microfilm 27460, FHL, Salt Lake City, Utah.

Vermont. *General index to vital records of Vermont, 1871-1908.* Salt Lake City: Genealogical Society of Utah, 1967; Microfilm 540053, FHL, Salt Lake City, Utah.

Vermont. *General index to vital records of Vermont, 1909-42.* Salt Lake City: Genealogical Society of Utah, 1967; Microfilm 1983856, FHL, Salt Lake City, Utah.

Vermont. Manchester. Town clerk. *Index to Births and Deaths, 1857-1932.* Marriages. Microfilm 1844445. FHL, Salt Lake City, Utah.

Vermont. Pawlet. Town Clerk. Death Registers.

Vermont. Rupert. Town Clerk. Death Registers. Marriage Registers.

Vermont. Rutland County. Probate Office, Rutland. Probate Book 10:483, Horatio Gates Amaden.

Vermont. Rutland County. U.S. census, 1800-1830; 1880-1930, population schedules. Washington: National Archives.

Vermont. Searsburg. Town Clerk. *Record of births, marriages, and deaths, 1829-1952.* Microfilm 28921. FHL, Salt Lake City, Utah.

Vermont. Tinmouth. Congregational Church. Baptisms.

Vermont. Vernon. *Records 1763-1901*, Rufus Elmer entry. Microfilm 29030, FHL, Salt Lake City, Utah.

Vermont. Wallingford. Marriage Records. Town Records. Land Records. Town Miscellaneous Records.

- *Wallingford Town miscellaneous records 1772-1890*, Wallingford, Vermont. Microfilm 29216, item 1, FHL, Salt Lake City, Utah.

Vermont. Wells. *Records of marriages, births, and deaths.* Microfilms 2021324, 2025060, FHL, Salt Lake City, Utah.

Vermont. Windham County. U.S. census, 1800-1820; 1920-30, population schedules. Washington: National Archives.

Vermont. Windsor County. U.S. census, 1850-1870, 1900, 1920, population schedules. Washington: National Archives.

Vermont. Winhall. Town Clerk. Land records.

- *Records of births, marriages, and deaths, v. 1-2, 1857-1896.* Montpelier Vt.: Public Records Division, 197?. FHL, Salt Lake City, Utah. Microfilm 1844447.
- *Indexes to births, marriages, and deaths.* FHL, Salt Lake City, Utah. Microfilm 1844447.

Vital Records of Ashfield, Massachusetts, to the year 1850. Boston: New England Historic and Genealogical Society, 1942.

Vital Records of Attleborough, Massachusetts, to the End of the Year 1849, Births-Marriages-Deaths. Salem: Essex Institute, 1934.

Vital Records from the Daily Evening Bulletin, San Francisco, California. California: Genealogical Records Committee, California State Society, Daughters of the American Revolution, 1943-1968.

Vital Records of Douglas, Massachusetts, to the end of the year 1849. Worcester, Massachusetts: Franklin P. Rice, 1906.

Vital Records of Dudley, Massachusetts, to the end of the year 1849. Boston: Franklin P. Rice, 1908.

Vital Records of Medfield, Massachusetts, to the end of the year 1850. Boston: Stanhope Press, 1903.

Vital Records of Oxford, Massachusetts, to the end of the year 1849. Worcester, Massachusetts: Franklin P. Rice, 1905.

Vital Records of Plympton, Massachusetts, to the year 1850. Boston: Wright & Potter Printing Company, 1923.

Vital Records of Springfield, Massachusetts, 1638-1887. Salt Lake City: Genealogical Society of Utah, 1958, Microfilm 185417. FHL, Salt Lake City, Utah.

Vital Records of Sturbridge, Massachusetts, to the year 1850. Boston: New England Historic Genealogical Society, 1906.

Vital Records of Sutton, Massachusetts, to the year 1850. Boston: Franklin P. Rice, 1907.

Vital Records of Woodstock 1686-1854. Hartford: The Case, Lockwood and Brainard Co., 1914.

Walker, Daniel Jerome Mathewson papers, held by Matt Porter, Fayette County, Iowa.

Walker Family Bible, in possession of Bev Luke, Minden, Nevada.

Walker family records, maintained by Bev Luke, Minden, Nevada.

Walla Walla Union Bulletin, Walla Walla, Washington, 13 December 1973.

Walter, Kathleen McCullough, interview. 15 September 1997 with Christopher Amaden.

Warren County, A History and Guide. Glens Falls, N.Y.: Warren County Board of Supervisors, 1942.

Warrensburgh News. Warrensburgh, New York. 15 October 1908.

Washington. Clallam County. U.S. census, 1930, population schedule. Washington: National Archives.

Washington. Island County. U.S. census, 1910-1930, population schedules. Washington: National Archives.

Washington. Olympia. State Department of Health. Vital records.

Washington. Skagit County. U.S. census, 1910, population schedule. Washington: National Archives.

Washington. Snohomish County. U.S. census, 1920-1930, population schedules. Washington: National Archives.

Washington. Spokane County. U.S. census, 1900-1910, 1930, population schedules. Washington: National Archives.

Washington. Spokane County. Walla Walla. County Auditor. Birth records.

Waterloo Daily Courier, Waterloo, Indiana. 15 October 1950.

Waterloo Press, Waterloo, Indiana. 20 January 1910.

Watertown City Directory for 1859-60, 1863-4, 1865, 1888-89, 1892. Flower Memorial Library, Watertown, New York.

WatertownDaily Times, 21 July 1928.

Watertown Herald, Watertown, N.Y., 1 April 1899. 8 October 1910.

Watertown Methodist Church Records, Flower Memorial Library, Watertown, New York.

Watertown, North Watertown and Juhelville Business and Residence Directory for 1855. Transcribed by GenWeb Volunteers. Online <www.rootsweb.com/~nyjeffer/1855wcd.htm>.

Weekly Sutter (Yuba City, California) Banner. Three Men Drowned. 16 March 1872.

Welch, Alexander McMillan. *Philip Welch of Ipswich, Mass., 1654 and His Descendants.* Richmond, Va.: W. Byrd Press, 1947.

Welch, Eliza Matilda. "Be Strong." Unpublished poem stored at Historian's Office, Lake George, New York.

Westminster Park Association of the Thousand Islands. Online <cdl.library.cornell.edu / cgi-bin / cul.nys / docviewer?did= nys126>.

White, Lorraine Cook. *The Barbour Collection of Connecticut town vital records – Pomfret.* 55 volumes. Baltimore: Genealogical Publishing Co., 1994.

Whittelsey, Charles, Barney. *Genealogy of the Whittlesey-Whittelsey Family.* 2nd edition. New York, London: Whittlesey House, 1941.

Whittier News, Whittier, California, 31 May 1917.

Wibe, Greg, Multnomah County Library, in letter to Nancy K. Mullen, 6 January 2006.

Williams County Chapter of the Ohio Genealogical Society, *Williams County, Ohio, Marriage Records, December 2, 1824-May 12, 1868.* Bryan, Ohio: Williams County Chapter of the Ohio Genealogical Society, 1984.

Winthrop Papers, 1498–1654. 5 volumes. Boston: The Massachusetts Historical Society, 1925–1947.

Wilson, Donna. "Re: Marietta Sheldon." Email to Christopher D. Amaden. 12 September 2005.

Wisconsin. Camp Douglas. Camp Douglas Cem. Tombstone data.

Wisconsin Cartographers' Guild. *Wisconsin's Past and Present: A Historical Atlas.* Madison, Wisc.: The University of Wisconsin Press, 1998.

Wisconsin. Clark County.
- U.S. census, 1900, population schedule. Washington: National Archives.

Wisconsin. Columbia County.
- Deaths. Microfilm, Wisconsin Historical Society.
- Pardeeville Cemetery. Tombstone Data.
- State census, 1895, 1905. Wisconsin State Historical Society.
- U.S. census, 1870-1930, population schedules. Washington: National Archives.

Wisconsin Department of Health and Human Services. Madison, Wisconsin: Wisconsin Department of Health and Human Services. Wisconsin Historical Society, Madison, Wisconsin.
- *Wisconsin Births, 1820-1907.*
- *Wisconsin Deaths, Pre-1907.*
- *Wisconsin Marriages, 1823-1907.*
- *Wisconsin Vital Record Index, pre-1907.*

Wisconsin. Dodge County. U.S. census, 1920-1930, population schedules. Washington. National Archives.

Wisconsin. Douglas County. Birth records, Douglas County Recorder, Superior, Wisconsin.

Wisconsin. Jackson County. U.S. census, 1880, population schedule. Washington. National Archives.

Wisconsin. Juneau County.
- Juneau County Deeds. Marriages. Clerk's Office, Mauston, Wisconsin.

Wisconsin. Juneau County (continued).
- New Lisbon City Cemetery, New Lisbon. Tombstone Data.
- State census, 1875. Wisconsin State Historical Society.
- U.S. census, 1870-1930, population schedules. U.S. census, 1870, population schedule. Washington. National Archives.

Wisconsin. La Crosse County.
- County Clerk, La Crosse, Wisconsin. Deaths. Marriages.
- U.S. census, 1870, 1900, population schedules. Washington. National Archives.

Wisconsin. Milwaukee County. U.S. census, 1900, 1930, population schedules. Washington. National Archives.

Wisconsin. Monroe County.
- Monroe County Deeds, Clerk's Office, Sparta, Wisconsin.
- U.S. census, 1860-1910, 1930, population schedule. Washington: National Archives.

Wisconsin. Oakdale. Oakdale Township Cemetery. Tombstone data.

Wisconsin. Pardeeville. *Wisconsin State Genealogical So. Newsletter.*
- Marcellon Cemetery. Tombstone data. Volume 33:3, January 1987.
- Pardeeville Cemetery. Tombstone data. Volume 35:4, April 1989.

Wisconsin. Saint Croix County. U.S. census, 1930, population schedule. Washington: National Archives.

Wisconsin. Sparta. Sparta Free Library. Obituary file.

Wisconsin. Trempealeau County. U.S. census, 1900, population schedule. Washington: National Archives.

Wisconsin. Waupaca County. U.S. census, 1880, population schedule. Washington: National Archives.

Wisconsin. Wauwatosa. Wauwatosa Cemetery. Tombstone data.

Wisconsin. Wood County.
- "Nekoosa 1913 Perfect School Attendance Report." Online. Provo, Utah: Rootsweb.com, 2004. Original data: Wood County Times, 4 December 1913.
- U.S. census, 1910, population schedule. Washington: National Archives.
- Wood County Deeds, Register of Deeds, Wisconsin Rapids, Wisconsin.

Woodland Democrat. Woodland, California. 16 February 1942.

Yates Publishing. *U.S. and International Marriage Records, 1560-1900.* Online. Provo, Utah: MyFamily.com, Inc., 2004.

AMADEN – all variants
  Mariette (1816-1879),
    80,83,85
  Mark Augustus (1904-), 155
  Martin Eugene (1851-1925),
    71,73,198,209,213, 217-
    221
  Mary (-1703), 14-15
  Mary (1706-), 20
  Mary A. (1844-1889), 157-
    164
  Mary A. (FRANCIS) (1870-),
    309-311
  Mary Ann (1815-1850), 85-88
  Mary Ann (1860-), 90,92
  Mary Augusta "Gusta" (1848-
    1890), 123,333,336-340
  Mary Augusta (1889-),
    337,340
  Mary Celestia (1911-), 156
  Mary DEWEY (1888-), 339
  Mary E. (1854-1879), 112,
    312, 315,316
  Mary E. (1868-), 157-164
  Mary Elizabeth "Libbie"
    (1892-), 333-335,337
  Mary Frances (1851-1909),
    117,120,121,327-329
  Mary Geneva (1863-1865),
    158,162
  Mary M. (1836-1907),
    68,69,171,172,175,
    176,181,182, 184-187,194
  Mary May (1884-), 152,155
  Mary Melissa (1864-1930),
    106-107,296-300
  Mary, dau. of Ithamar, 19
  Maudalene "Maude" (1873-),
    151,153
  Maude Myrtle (1889-), 268
  Mehitable (1680-1699), 16-
    17, 19
  Mehitable (1722/3-), 23,25
  Meltiah (1690-1780), 21-23
  Minnie Emma (1876-),
    211,212,215

AMADEN – all variants
  Minnie Frances (1897-1897),
    333,335,337
  Minnie K. (1885-), 339
  Minnie Sanders
    RICHARDSON (1898-),
    260-261
  Morton (1836-1885), 60,65-
    67,135,136,141-
    148,158,166,232
  Morton (1904-aft 1920),
    310,311
  Nancy -- see Aurelia Nancy
  Nancy (1808-1872), 67-
    69,168,169,173, 186
  Nancy (1841-1869), 141-148
  Nancy H. (1843-1914), 312-
    321
  Nancy S. (1817-1895), 86,262
  Nathaniel Ives (1810-1872),
    36,38,63,68-73,199,200
  Nathaniel John (1865-1866),
    123,125
  Nathaniel William (1825-
    1890), 48,50-51,116,120-
    125,332
  Nettie Heuta (1873-1876),
    210,215
  Notrum "Nona" (1878-),
    143,145,148
  Ola May (1897-1918), 342
  Ordella "Della" Alice (1855-),
    200,202,209-217
  Orlen (1834-1839), 81,85
  Otho Gates (1874-192?), 150-
    152,154
  Otho Ward (1917-), 154
  Pamelia M. (1866-), 313,
    315, 316,320
  Patience (1742/3-1816), 23-
    24
  Patricia (1926-), 308
  Pauline Christiana (1905-),
    155
  Permelia (1805-1880), 107-
    113,312

Index

occupation
  bookkeeper, 175,179,202,
    215,273
  boot and shoe manuf, 53
  boot maker (shop), 52
  botanist, 166
  builder, 237,262
  businessman, 224
  butcher, 337
  cabinet maker, 66,169,170,
    185,186, 194,195
  carpenter, 19,36,62,66,71,
    78,93,94,135,141,149,150,
    157,159,165,174,183,224,
    238,255-257,261-263,269-
    271,273,279,297,298
  cattle tender, 202
  census enumerator, 251
  charcoal burner, 234
  chemist, 166
  circulation manager, 215
  civil engineer, 145,284
  clerk, 128,170,186,194
  clothier, 60
  cobbler, 334
  collector of taxes, 111,112,
    119
  constable, 18,210
  cook, 203
  cooper, 18,19
  cordwainer, 26
  county surveyor, 249
  craftsmen, 40
  custodian, 219
  Daguerreian artist, 185
  dairy, 151,263,327
  day laborer, 151
  deacon, 17
  deputy sheriff, 166
  domestic, 231,255,298
  draying, 219
  dressmaker, 160,175,176
  druggist, 265,267
  dyer, 69
  education, 145
  engineer, 145,151,160,241,
    251,285,286

occupation
  English teacher, 145
  factory watchman, 286
  farm laborer, 123,200,
    214,298
  farmer, 19,82,97,105,106,
    110,123,150-152,158,185,
    199, 204,209,218,222-
    224,233,240,246,251,261,
    265,274,285,291,293,297,
    312,327,329,335,337
  farmhand, 142
  feed business, 224
  fireman, 218
  foreman, 130
  freight agent, 280,282
  Fuller Brush sales, 336
  garnet mining, 91
  gold miner, 212
  grocer, 129,175,219,257,
    259,284
  harness maker, 333,334
  haward, hayward, 46
  health officer, 266
  hem stitcher, 212
  high school principal, 145
  hog reeve, 22
  hostler, 69
  hotelkeeper, 110
  house builder, 135
  husbandman, 22,25
  ice delivery, 329
  inn keeper, 315
  inspector, 272
  insurance agent, 133,160,
    292
  joiner, 63,66,150,237,257
  judge, 162
  justice of the peace, 111,246,
    303
  laborer, 155,210,211,242,
    256,264,303,307,316, 323
    lumber mill, 308
    railroad, 191
  landlady / landlord, 69, 334
  lieutenant, U.S. Navy, 102
  lumberman, 255

ABOUT THE AUTHORS

Christopher D. Amaden

A native of Tampa, Florida, Chris has been an amateur genealogist since he inherited the family notes from his great-grandmother over twenty years ago. Most recently a graduate of *Le Collège Interarmées de Défense* in Paris, France, he is a navy commander currently stationed in San Diego, California. He is married to the former Sara Linda Robinson and has a daughter Chloé and a son Jonathan.

Nancy K. Mullen

Nancy K. Mullen is a retired management consultant who is making a second career as a genealogist. In addition to this genealogy on her maiden name, Ameden, she is currently working on a genealogy of one of her husband's lines. She has published *Record of the Proceedings of the Town of Cottage Grove, Wisconsin, 1847-1870*. Happily settled in Sun Prairie, Wisconsin, she and her husband John have been married for forty-two years.

www.ingramcontent.com/pod-product-compliance
Lightning Source LLC
Chambersburg PA
CBHW071826270326
41929CB00013B/1912